Contents

Maps

Foreword

We would like to express our gratitude to Barbara Walsh Angelillo and Rob Andrews for their patience, enthusiasm, and hard work in preparing this new edition.

While every care has been taken to ensure the accuracy of the information in this guide, the passage of time will always bring change, and consequently, the publisher cannot accept responsibility for errors that may occur.

All prices and opening times quoted here are based on information supplied to us at press time. Hours and admission fees may change, however, and the prudent traveler will avoid inconvenience by calling ahead.

Fodor's wants to hear about your travel experiences, both pleasant and unpleasant. When a hotel or restaurant fails to live up to its billing, let us know and we will investigate the complaint and revise our entries where the facts warrant it.

Send your letters to the editors of Fodor's Travel Publications, 201 E. 50th St., New York, NY 10022.

Highlights'93 and Fodor's Choice

Highlights '93

With the removal of practically all trade barriers in the European Community as of January 1993, Italy will be angling to keep up with the competition. A new tide of efficiency is expected, some of which may make life easier for the tourist; for example, competition from other European banks has motivated Italian banks to offer streamlined services, including such departments as currency exchange and traveler's checks. It's possible, though, that austerity measures designed to keep Italy's economy in line with the rest of the EC may mean even higher costs. Italy is now the most expensive country in Europe to visit, according to surveys conducted by CTS, a Rome-based student and youth travel agency. Since tourism is one of the country's major sources of income, travel authorities are busily promoting special ways to save, including discount packages offered by local tourist boards and hotel associations. It's wise to inquire about these offers when you are planning your trip.

Italy is participating in the program to provide Europe with a network of very fast international trains (such as the TGV in France and the ETR in Italy). The **FS,** Italy's state-run railway system, is implementing a modernization program that should make travel within Italy faster and easier, though fare hikes are likely.

Deregulation of European airline fares in 1993 will no doubt affect **Alitalia,** Italy's national airline. In 1992, Alitalia was the first European airline to introduce a frequent flier program. The airline recently also introduced a train service that should make Rome's **Leonardo da Vinci International Airport** in Fiumicino even more attractive to international travelers. The new Airport Train can speed passengers directly between the airport and either Florence or Naples, allowing visitors to these two popular destinations to bypass Rome entirely. Da Vinci airport has been designated by the EC as an airport hub for southern Europe and the Mediterranean area, and as a result, it is busy modernizing and expanding. Similar expansion is under way at Milan's **Malpensa airport.**

Restoration is afoot all over the country. In **Rome,** more and more churches and palaces have been cleaned and restored, including Santa Maria Maggiore. The marble of the Spanish Steps also is being cleaned and missing pieces replaced, but the most important work on this Roman landmark is belowstairs, as its underpinnings are being reinforced. Sometime in 1993, the Museo Nazionale should open its new annex in Palazzo Massimo, where at least part of the museum's stunning archeological collections will finally be on view.

Restoration work is nearly complete on Leonardo da Vinci's famous fresco, *The Last Supper*, in **Milan.** Two major restorations are in progress in **Genoa:** the Palazzo Ducale and the Palazzo Doria. Genoa has also gained two permanent new attractions from 1992's Columbus exposition—the Bigo, a panoramic elevator on the harbor, and the Aquarium, the most modern of its kind in Europe. In **Florence,** the gorgeously frescoed chapel on Palazzo Medici Riccardi has been restored; Florence's famous enclosed bridge over the Arno, the Ponte Vecchio, may still be undergoing reinforcement in 1993, to repair the dismaying damage caused by traffic on adjacent streets. Sadly, one of Italy's most famous landmarks—the **Tower of Pisa**—will remain closed this year while engineers try to reinforce it to prevent further fatal toppling.

On Italy's **northern Adriatic coast,** the slick of algae that outraged bathers in 1988 and 1989 has become less visible, though the pollution that caused it—industrial effluents poured into the Po River and the Venetian lagoon—will have to be stringently controlled for many more years before the danger really fades. Bathers in the resorts around Rimini should continue to bear in mind the possible hazards of immersion in this stretch of the sea. Keep track of factors such as winds, tides and currents, which affect the water condition from day to day.

Among the Italian hotel groups that are expanding is the **Cogeta Palace Hotels** chain, associated with the Royal Monceau Group of Paris. Cogeta Palace hotels include the refurbished Luna Hotel Baglioni in Venice and the renovated Bristol Palace in Genoa. The prestigious **CIGA Hotels** groups is reportedly for sale by its owner, the Aga Khan; CIGA recently renovated its three stellar Milan properties, the Principe, the Palace, and the Duca. **RestHotel Primavere,** A European chain with properties mostly in France, is expanding into north and central Italy in a big way, with two hotels already opened and twelve more on the boards.

Fodor's Choice

No two people will agree on what makes a perfect vacation, but it's fun and helpful to know what others think. We hope you'll have a chance to experience some of Fodor's Choices yourself while visiting Italy. For detailed information about each entry, refer to the appropriate chapters (given in parentheses) within this guidebook.

Picturesque Villages and Towns

Alberobello (Apulia)

Asolo (The Venetian Arc)

Cinque Terre (Liguria)

Dobbiaco/Toblach (The Dolomites)

Orta San Giulio (Milan, Lombardy, and the Lakes)

San Gimignano (Tuscany)

Positano (Campania)

Taormina (Sicily)

Classical Sites

Agrigento (Sicily)

Aosta (Piedmont/Valle d'Aosta)

Fiesole (Florence)

Herculaneum (Campania)

Nora (Sardinia)

Ostia Antica (Excursions from Rome)

Paestum (Campania)

Pompeii (Campania)

Roman Forum (Rome)

Siracusa (Sicily)

Works of Art

Byzantine mosaics in Ravenna (Emilia-Romagna)

Donatello's *Judith and Holofernes* (Florence)

Duccio di Boninsegna's *Maestà* in Siena (Tuscany)

Giotto's paintings in the Cappella Scrovegni, Padua (The Venetian Arc)

Leonardo's *Last Supper*, Milan (Milan, Lombardy, and the Lakes)

Michelangelo's *David* and *Slaves* (Florence)

Michelangelo's Sistine Chapel ceiling (Rome)

Raphael's Vatican *Stanze* (Rome)

Titian's *Martyrdom of St. Lawrence* (Venice)

Veronese's *Feast at the House of Levi* (Venice)

Churches

Basilica di Santa Croce, Lecce (Apulia)

Basilica di San Salvatore, Spoleto (Umbria and the Marches)

Basilica San Marcs (Venice)

Duomo, Milan (Milan, Lombardy, and the Lakes)

Frari (Venice)

Il Gesù (Rome)

Basilica of San Francesco, Assisi (Umbria)

San Miniato al Monte (Florence)

San Vitale, Ravenna (Emilia-Romagna)

Santa Maria Maggiore (Rome)

Museums

Accademia (Venice)

Galleria degli Uffizi (Florence)

Museo Archeologico, Cagliari (Sardinia)

Museo Archeologico, Naples (Campania)

Museo Egizio, Turin (Piedmont/Valle d'Aosta)

Museo Etrusco Guarnacci, Volterra (Tuscany)

Museo Nazionale, Taranto (Apulia)

Museo Nazionale, Urbino (Umbria and the Marches)

Vatican Museums (Rome)

Villa Giulia (Rome)

Architectural Gems

Baptistry (Florence)

Capodimonte, Naples (Campania)

Castel del Monte (Apulia)

Castello di Buonconsiglio, Trento (The Dolomites)

Castello Sforzesco, Milan (Milan, Lombardy, and the Lakes)

Duomo, Siena (Tuscany)

Palazzo Barberini (Rome)

Palazzo Ducale (Venice)

Villa Rotonda, Vicenza (The Venetian Arc)

Hotels

Hassler (Rome) *Very Expensive*

Villa d'Este, Cernobbio (Milan, Lombardy, and the Lakes) *Very Expensive*

Villa Igiea, Palermo (Sicily) *Very Expensive*

Santa Caterina, Amalfi (Campania) *Expensive–Very Expensive*

Baglioni (Florence) *Very Expensive*

Accademia (Venice) *Moderate*

Internazionale (Rome) *Moderate*

Alpino Monte Rota/Alpengasthof Ratsberg, Dobbiaco (The Dolomites) *Inexpensive–Moderate*

Agnello d'Oro, Bergamo (Milan, Lombardy, and the Lakes) *Inexpensive*

Stella Maris, Levanto (Liguria) *Inexpensive*

Restaurants

El Toulà (Rome) *Very Expensive*

Marchesi Milan (Milan, Lombardy, and the Lakes) *Very Expensive*

Alberto, Messina (Sicily) *Expensive*

Fiaschetteria Toscana (Venice) *Expensive*

La Smarrita, Turin (Piedmont/Valle d'Aosta) *Expensive*

Tiffany Grill/Schloss Maur, Merano (The Dolomites) *Expensive*

Tre Frecce, Bologna (Emilia-Romagna) *Expensive*

Al Marsili, Siena (Tuscany) *Moderate*

Beccherie, Treviso (The Venetian Arc) *Moderate*

Ristorante Tornasacco, Ascoli Piceno (Umbria and the Marches) *Inexpensive–Moderate*

Angiolino (Florence) *Inexpensive*

Cafés

Baratti e Milano, Turin (Piedmont)

Cafrisch, Naples (Campania)

Florian (Venice)

Pedrocchi, Padua (The Venetian Arc)

Tre Scalini (Rome)

Taste Treats

Biscottini di Prato (Tuscany)

Bistecca alla Fiorentina (Florence)

Canederli (The Dolomites)

Cardi in Bagna Cauda (Piedmont/Valle d'Aosta)

Cotoletta alla Bolognese (Emilia-Romagna)

Orecchiette (Apulia)

Porcheddu (Sardinia)

Risotto milanese (Milan, Lombardy, and the Lakes)

Tiramesù (Venice)

Zuppa di Datteri (Liguria)

Off the Beaten Track

Catacombs of San Gennaro, Naples (Campania)

Earth Pyramids, Renon (The Dolomites)

Elba (Tuscany)

Island of Torcello (Venice)

Museo Spaghetti, Pontedassio (Liguria)

Santa Maria in Organo, Verona (The Venetian Arc)

Tremiti Islands (Apulia)

Valnerina (Umbria and the Marches)

Times to Treasure

Attending the open-air opera performances in Verona's Roman Arena (The Venetian Arc)

Cheering for the boats in Venice's Historic Regatta (Venice)

Experiencing the pageantry and excitement of Siena's Palio (Tuscany)

Following the four-day folklore procession of Sant'Efisio (Sardinia)

Looking down on the Bay of Naples from Villa Jovis, Capri (Campania)

Monte Cervino (the Matterhorn) seen from Breuil-Cervinia (Piedmont/Valle d'Aosta)

Peeping through the Knights of Malta keyhole to see St. Peter's dome (Rome)

Rose-colored walls in Assisi catching the autumn sun (Umbria and the Marches)

The pink peaks of the Catinaccio in the Dolomites at dusk (The Dolomites)

The sleepy view of Florence and the Arno valley from Via San Francesco, Fiesole (Florence)

Italy

xviii

SWITZERLAND

AUSTRIA

SLOVENIA

CROATIA

BOSNIA
AND
HERZEGOVINA

MONTENEGRO

FRANCE

Mt. Blanc

Aosta

Lugano

Lago di Lugano

Lago Maggiore

Novara

Turin

Asti

Po

San Remo

Como

Lago di Como

Bergamo

Milan

Pavia

Po

Ligurian Sea

Genoa

Rapallo

La Spezia

THE DOLOMITES

ALPI

Bolzano

Trento

Lago di Garda

Brescia

Cortina d'Ampezzo

Belluno

Udine

Trieste

Treviso

Vicenza

Verona

Mantua

Adige

Po

Ferrara

Padua

Venice

Golfo di Venezia

Adriatic Sea

Parma

Modena

Bologna

Ravenna

Rimini

SAN MARINO

Ancona

Macerata

Pescara

A P P E N

Lucca

Pistoia

Florence

Arno

Pisa

Livorno

Siena

Arezzo

Assisi

Perugia

Tiber

Orvieto

Terni

Grosseto

Viterbo

Elba

Civitavecchia

Corsica

N

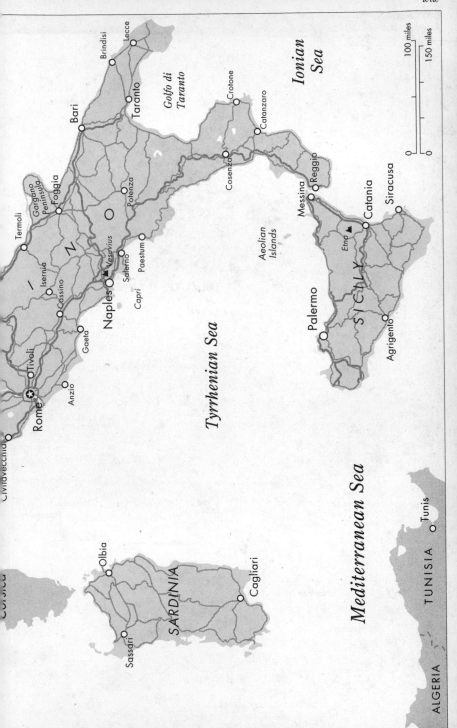

Civitavecchia

Rome

Tivoli

Anzio

Gaeta

Cassino

Isernia

I

Termoli

N

Foggia

Gargano
Peninsula

O

Naples

Vesuvius

Salerno

Capri

Paestum

Potenza

Bari

Brindisi

Lecce

Taranto

Golfo di
Taranto

Crotone

Catanzaro

Cosenza

Ionian
Sea

Reggio

Messina

Aeolian
Islands

Palermo

Etna

SICILY

Catania

Siracusa

Agrigento

Tyrrhenian Sea

Olbia

SARDINIA

Sassari

Cagliari

Mediterranean Sea

Tunis

TUNISIA

ALGERIA

100 miles

150 miles

World Time Zones

Numbers below vertical bands relate each zone to Greenwich Mean Time (0 hrs.).
Local times frequently differ from these general indications,
as indicated by light-face numbers on map.

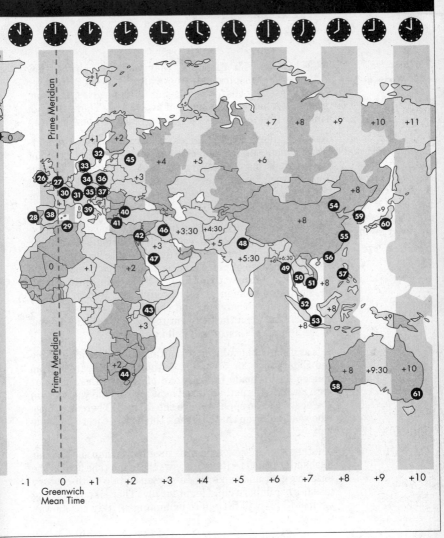

Introduction

By Barbara
Lazear Ascher

*A frequent writer
about Italy for
the* New York
Times *and*
European Travel
and Life,
*Barbara Lazear
Ascher is also the
author of a
collection of
essays,* Playing
After Dark.

They went for the light, they went for culture, they went for inspiration. Above all, they went to discover something that was missing in themselves. Passion, perhaps. A heightened sense of awareness. They came not simply to find themselves but to become their best selves.

Keats, Shelley, Byron, James, Goethe, Wagner, Prendergast, Renoir, Monet, and centuries of tourists who did not record their inspiration for the ages, but who, like Miss Lavish in E. M. Forster's *Room with a View*, knew that "one doesn't come to Italy for niceness . . . one comes for life."

And how is this life delivered unto one? If you ask the traveler of this decade, the answers will be various. For some it is the layers of history, physically present to walk upon, the reassuring sense of place and continuity that comes from a casual coexistence with antiquity. Twentieth-century businessmen and women stroll through the Roman Forum, swinging their briefcases and chatting of today's deals as they pass between the 5th-century-BC Corinthian columns of the Temple of Castor and Pollux.

It is as if one could hold out a hand and feel the touch of Pliny the Elder, Livy, or Catullus. A young woman, fresh from college Latin, made the mistake of visiting the Forum at high noon in August, suffered heat stroke, and was certain she heard Cicero speak before she fainted. There are those who would tell you that it wasn't the heat—Cicero *had* spoken.

Another woman, seven months pregnant when she and her husband traveled to Ravenna, swears that as she beheld the dazzling gold and lapis lazuli of San Vitale's 5th-century mosaics her unborn child leapt for joy. There is no guarding against it; life will fill you to brimming as Italy has its way with you.

For the sybarite, the palate is awakened by the clear, true flavors of wine and food that taste faintly of the earth and sea from which they came. Buckwheat pasta in Bormio; polenta, black with squid ink, in Venice; creamy gelato at Giolitti in Rome; or the perfectly comforting bowl of risotto in Siena, served by a family in their nameless restaurant. You will hear, on the other side of the Atlantic, the longings of travelers returned home, who, as the light begins to change in early September, yearn for *gamberetti*, Venetian shrimps the size of a baby's fingertip. Summer causes them to recall the simple delight of sitting beneath large shade trees on the banks of Lake Como, drinking cool wine from earthenware pitchers. Winter's winds bring memories of Alpine chills chased by a fiery draft of grappa.

It is the dream that takes you back, just as it was the dream that enveloped you while you were there. You will notice that those who travel in Italy seem to do so in a state of reverie. Perhaps it is the diaphanous gauze of light that softens physical outlines and blurs the distinction between past and present. A light conducive to daydreams. A light that both intensifies life and makes it gentler to the touch.

Of course, there are those who have been rudely awakened from the dream by a revved-up 1990s state-of-the-art motorcycle outside their 19th-century Roman hotel. They will grumpily tell of the shocking presence of 20th-century blight in a land that seemed impervious to such intrusion. In the heat of disillusion, they will complain of the "real" Italy, of Roman traffic jams, thefts in Naples, Venice as Disneyland, a highway system around Milan as attractive as the New Jersey Turnpike. They will warn that you, a woman, must not be persuaded by the charms of an Italian gentleman who commits his heart and future within a three-minute walk across a piazza.

There is truth in what they say, but the generosity of the Italians and the striking physical beauty of their land make it possible to live in the dream alongside the blight. You cannot arrive in Venice without driving through the gray air of Mestre, polluted by oil refineries. But once your water taxi is negotiating the Grand Canal, you lose yourself in time and space. And that is what Italy is about . . . losing and finding yourself in time and space. By morning, as the rudely awakened dreamer stands on the Palatine Hill and smells the wild fennel just as Horace did, all is forgiven.

It is the natural as well as the man-made wonders that entrance. In the Valtellina Valley you will sit in grottoes where the caesars sat to soak in hot mineral springs, and you will feel the curing effects of waters that were said to ease the pain of gout, arthritis, and politics. You can indulge in the mindless delights of the Amalfi Coast exactly as 19th-century English travelers did when they came to rest their minds, weary from the obligatory acquisition of culture in the north. Here, where rocky cliffs are caught in a perpetual dive to the sea, nothing seems more important than tonight's dinner or lovemaking.

Italy may be the most sensual of countries. Perhaps it is the basic simplicity that returns one to the simplest human emotions: the organic nature of all that surrounds you, each century seeming to grow from the land. Or perhaps it is the heightened sense of romance that comes from the constant reminders of the very best of which people are capable; the serenity of Bellini's altarpiece in San Zaccaria, the compassion of Michelangelo's Pietà in St. Peter's, the symmetry of a Palladian villa rising from the earth of the Veneto. Or it could be living among people for whom life's pleasures are celebrated rather than guiltily indulged.

Whatever it is, to experience Italy one needs time, not necessarily in days but in solitude. It is in the silent times that Italy will be revealed to you. Early morning, watching the light shine on the Pantheon, while strong Italian coffee wakens your senses. Dawn on the Grand Canal as dark green water is sprayed with gold and the only sound is a gondolier's oar breaking the silent surface. Midnight in the Forum, Daisy Miller's undoing and Byron's inspiration. Sunrise in Stelvio National Park, where eagles soar overhead and you are knee-deep in wildflowers.

And one must believe in that elusive commodity, happiness. This is a country that, through the ages, in fact and fiction, has promised that possibility. Goethe, having fled the restrictive court life of Weimar, wrote from Rome in September 1788: "I can honestly say I have never been so happy in my life as now." And in *Room with a View*, Forster observed that when his young provincial heroine, Lucy, finally dared forfeit her Baedeker for experience, "then the pernicious charm of Italy worked on her, and, instead of acquiring information, she began to be happy."

You, too, should relinquish this book from time to time and observe with an uninstructed eye, drift into the dream, and allow yourself to be charmed.

1 Essential Information

Before You Go

Government Tourist Offices

In the U.S. Contact the Italian National Tourist Offices at 630 5th Ave., Suite 1565, New York, NY 10111, tel. 212/245–4822; 500 N. Michigan Ave., Chicago, IL 60611, tel. 312/644–0990; 360 Post St., Suite 801, San Francisco, CA 94108, tel. 415/392–6206.

In Canada 1 Place Ville Marie, Montreal, Quebec H3B 3M9, tel. 514/866–7667.

In the U.K. 1 Princes St., London W1R 8AY England, tel. 071/408–1254.

Tour Groups

Tour groups are not just for beginners anymore. While the whistle-stop express tour of all the most famous sights is still around—and still a good introduction for those making a first visit—there are a growing number of more focused and more sophisticated packages. In fact, considering the wealth of options available, the toughest part of your vacation may well be to find the tour that best fits your personal style. Listed below is a sampling of programs to give you an idea of what is available. For more information, contact your travel agent and/or the Italian National Tourist Office.

When considering a tour, be sure to find out exactly what expenses are included (particularly tips, taxes, side trips, additional meals, and entertainment); government ratings of all hotels on the itinerary and the facilities they offer; and, if you are traveling alone, what the single supplement is. Note whether the tour operator reserves the right to change hotels, routes, or even prices after you've booked, and ask about its policy regarding cancellations, complaints, and trip-interruption insurance. Most tour operators request that bookings be made through a travel agent—there is no additional charge for doing so.

General-Interest Tours **CIT Tours** (342 Madison Ave., Room 207, New York, NY 10173, tel. 212/697–2100 or 800/248–8687) offers several popular packages that benefit from the operator's extensive support network of 47 offices throughout Italy. **Central Holiday** (206 Central Ave., Jersey City, NJ 07307, tel. 201/798–5777 or 800/526–6045) offers reasonably priced tours. **Maupintour** (Box 807, Lawrence, KS 66044, tel. 913/843–1211 or 800/255–4266) runs 12-day "Italy's Famous Places" tours that visit Milan, Venice, Florence, and Rome; and 19-day "Italy Grand and Leisurely" tours that include Venice, Florence, Rome, Assisi, and Capri. Both **Olson-Travelworld** (Box 10066, Manhattan Beach, CA 90226, tel. 310/546–8400, 800/421–5785 in CA or 800/421–2255) and **Trafalgar Tours** (11 E. 26th St., New York, NY 10010, tel. 212/689–8977 or 800/854–0103) offer 14-day panoramic tours of Italy. **American Express Vacations** (300 Pinnacle Way, Norcross, GA 30093, tel. 800/241–1700 or 800/421–5785 in GA) is a veritable supermarket of tours—you name it, they've either got it packaged or will customize a package for you.

Other major operators to Italy include **Globus-Gateway/Cosmos** (95–25 Queens Blvd., Rego Park, NY 11374, tel. 718/268–7000 or 800/221–0090), **Donna Franca Tours** (470 Commonwealth

Ave., Boston, MA 02215, tel. 617/227–3111 or 800/225–2690), **Perillo Tours** (577 Chestnut Ridge Rd., Woodcliff Lake, NJ 07675, tel. 201/307–1234 or 800/431–1515) and **Italiatour** (666 5th Ave., New York, NY 10103, tel. 212/765–2183 or 800/237–0517).

Special-Interest　**Travel Concepts** (373 Commonwealth Ave., Suite 601, Boston,
Tours　MA 02115–1815, tel. 617/266–8450) serves up such specialties
Wine/Cuisine　as "Tuscan Cuisine with Lorenza de Medici," featuring a one-week cooking course at the Badia a Coltibuono wine estate. **Connaissance & Cie** (790 Madison Ave., New York, NY 10021, tel. 212/472–5772) offers a wine tour of Italy with Melissa Sere, noted wine educator.

Art/Architecture　There is a staggering wealth of both in Italy, and **Esplanade Tours** (581 Boylston St., Boston, MA 02116, tel. 617/266–7465) delves into much of it. Tours include "Renaissance Italy" and "Hilltowns of Italy."

Culture　"Just Sicily," from **Amelia Tours** (280 Old Country Rd., Hicks-ville, NY 11801, tel. 516/433–0696 or 800/SICILY–1), explores the art, mythology, and history of a colorful region.

Skiing　**CIT Tours**' ski package takes you to the challenging slopes of the Dolomites.

Ballooning　**Buddy Bombard Balloon Adventures** (6727 Curran St., Mc-Lean, VA 22101–3804, tel. 703/448–9407 or 800/862–8537), takes groups of a dozen or fewer for gentle floats above Siena, San Gimignano, and the rolling hills of the Tuscan countryside. Fine dining back on the ground complements the program. A special package featuring the famed Il Palio race is also available.

Singles and　**Trafalgar Tours** (11 E. 26th St., New York, NY 10010, tel. 212/
Young Couples　689–8977 or 800/854–0103) offers "Club 21–35," faster-paced tours for travelers unafraid of a little physical activity—whether it's bike riding or discoing the night away.

Music　**Dailey-Thorp Travel** (315 W. 57th St., New York, NY 10019, tel. 212/307–1555) offers deluxe opera and music tours, including "Opera Capitals of Italy" (Rome, Naples, Florence, Bologna, Milan). Itineraries vary, according to available performances.

Package Deals for Independent Travelers

Custom design your own package with **Italiatour**. (*See* General-Interest Tours, *above*.) Air transportation, transfers, car rental, and accommodations ranging from five-star hotels to private residences are available, as well as a broad selection of sightseeing options. **TWA Getaway Vacations** (tel. 800/GET-AWAY) has a reasonably priced eight-day "Roman Holiday." **TourCrafters** (30 S. Michigan Ave., Chicago, IL 60603, tel. 312/726–3886 or 800/621–2259) offers city tours and self-drive tours of the countryside. **American Airlines Fly AAway Vacations** (tel. 800/433–7300 or 817/355–1234) lets you design your own fly/drive itinerary from a selection of hotels, rental cars, and rail passes.

When to Go

The main tourist season runs from mid-April to the end of September. The best months for sightseeing are April, May, June,

September, and October, when the weather is generally pleasant and not too hot. In general, the northern half of the peninsula and the entire Adriatic Coast, with the exception of Apulia, are rainier than the rest of Italy. Foreign tourists crowd the major art cities at Easter, when Italians flock to resorts and to the country. From March through May, bus loads of eager schoolchildren on excursions take cities of artistic and historical interest by storm.

If you can avoid it, don't travel at all in Italy in August, when much of the population is on the move. The heat can be oppressive, and vacationing Italians cram roads, trains, and planes on their way to shore and mountain resorts. All this is especially true around the August 15 national holiday, when cities such as Rome and Milan are deserted and many restaurants and shops are closed. Except for a few year-round resorts, such as Taormina and some towns on the Italian Riviera, coastal resorts usually close up tight from October or November to April; they're at their best in June and September, when everything is open but uncrowded.

The hottest months are July and August, when brief afternoon thunderstorms are common in inland areas. Winters are relatively mild in most places on the main tourist circuit but always include some rainy spells.

Major cities, such as Rome, Florence, and Milan, have no off-season as far as hotel rates go, though some hotels will reduce rates during the slack season upon request. You can save considerably on hotel rooms in Venice and in such resorts as Sorrento and Capri during their off-seasons.

You may want to plan your trip to take in some spectacular *festas* (local festivals) or satisfy special interests, such as opera festivals or wine tours. From May through September the calendar is dotted with festas. Outdoor music and opera festivals are held mainly in July and August (*see* Festivals and Seasonal Events, *below*).

Climate The following are average daily maximum and minimum temperatures for Italy.

Milan								
Jan.	40F	5C	May	74F	23C	Sept.	75F	24C
	32	0		57	14		61	16
Feb.	46F	8C	June	80F	27C	Oct.	63F	17C
	35	2		63	17		52	11
Mar.	56F	13C	July	84F	29C	Nov.	51F	10C
	43	6		67	20		43	6
Apr.	65F	18C	Aug.	82F	28C	Dec.	43F	6C
	49	10		66	19		35	2

Rome								
Jan.	52F	11C	May	74F	23C	Sept.	79F	26C
	40	5		56	13		62	17
Feb.	55F	13C	June	82F	28C	Oct.	71F	22C
	42	6		63	17		55	13
Mar.	59F	15C	July	87F	30C	Nov.	61F	16C
	45	7		67	20		49	10
Apr.	66F	19C	Aug.	86F	30C	Dec.	55F	13C
	50	10		67	20		44	6

Venice	**Jan.**	42F	6C	**May**	70F	21C	**Sept.**	75F	24C
		33	1		56	13		61	16
	Feb.	46F	8C	**June**	76F	25C	**Oct.**	65F	19C
		35	2		63	17		53	12
	Mar.	53F	12C	**July**	81F	27C	**Nov.**	53F	12C
		41	5		66	19		44	7
	Apr.	62F	17C	**Aug.**	80F	27C	**Dec.**	46F	8C
		49	10		65	19		37	3

Current weather information for foreign and domestic cities may be obtained by calling **The Weather Channel Connection** at 900/WEATHER from a touch-tone phone. In addition to the weather report, The Weather Channel Connection offers local time and travel tips as well as hurricane, foliage, and ski reports. The call costs 95¢ per minute.

Festivals and Seasonal Events

Top seasonal events in Italy include carnival celebrations in January and February; Epiphany celebrations in January; Easter celebrations in Rome and Florence; the Florence May Music Festival; Siena's Palio horse race in July and August; The Maritime Republics Regatta in June, alternatively in Venice, Genoa, Amalfi, or Pisa; and the Venice Film Festival in late August. Contact the **Italian National Tourist Office** for exact dates and further information.

January 5–6   **Epiphany Celebrations.** Roman Catholic Epiphany celebrations and decorations are evident throughout Italy. Notable is the Epiphany Fair at Piazza Navona in Rome.

Late January   **Festival of Italian Popular Song.** A three-day festival in San Remo is actually a competition, with the latest Italian songs being performed by leading artists.

February   **Carnival in Viareggio.** Masked pageants, fireworks, a flower show, and parades are among the festivities along the Tuscan Riviera.
Carnival in Venice includes plays, masked balls, fireworks, and more in Venice's squares and in sites throughout the city.

April 9   The **Good Friday Procession** in Rome is led by the Pope, from the Colosseum past the Forum and up the Palatine Hill. This nighttime parade is torchlit.

Easter Sunday (April 11)   The **Scoppio del Carro,** or "Explosion of the Cart," in Florence, is a pyramid of fireworks in the Cathedral Square, set off by a mechanical dove released from the altar during High Mass.

Late April– Early July   The **Florence May Music Festival** is the oldest and most prestigious Italian festival of the performing arts.

May 1   The **Feast of Sant'Efisio** in Cagliari sees a procession of marchers and others in splendid Sardinian costume.

Mid-May   **Race of the Candles.** This procession, in local costume, leads to the top of Mount Ingino in Gubbio.

May 20   **Sardinian Cavalcade.** A traditional procession of more than 3,000 people in Sardinian costumes makes its way through Sassari.

Late May	The **Palio of the Archers** is a medieval crossbow contest in Gubbio.
Early June	The **Battle of the Bridge,** in Pisa, is a medieval parade and contest.
	The **Flower Festival,** in Genzano (Rome), is a religious procession along streets carpeted with flowers in magnificent designs.
	The **Regatta of the Great Maritime Republics** sees keen competition among the four former maritime republics—Amalfi, Genoa, Pisa, and Venice.
Late June	**Soccer Games in 16th-Century Costume,** in Florence, commemorate a match played in 1530. Festivities include fireworks displays.
Late June–Early July	The **Festival of Two Worlds,** in Spoleto, is a famous performing-arts festival.
July and August	The **Summer Operetta Festival** is held in Trieste.
Early July and Mid-August	The **Palio Horse Race,** in Siena, is a colorful bareback horse race with participants competing for the *Palio* (Banner).
Early July–Late August	The **Arena of Verona Outdoor Opera Season** heralds spectacular productions in the 20,000-seat Roman amphitheater of Verona.
Mid-July	The **Feast of the Redeemer** is a procession of gondolas and other craft, commemorating the end of the epidemic of 1575 in Venice. The fireworks over the lagoon are spectacular.
Early August	The **Joust of the Quintana** is a historical pageant in Ascoli Piceno.
Late August–Early September	The **Siena Music Week** features opera, concerts, and chamber music.
	The **Venice Film Festival,** oldest of the international film festivals, takes place mostly on the Lido.
Late August–Mid-September	The **Stresa Musical Weeks** comprise a series of concerts and recitals in Stresa.
Early September	The **Historic Regatta** includes a traditional competition between two-oar gondolas in Venice.
	The **Joust of the Saracen** is a tilting contest with knights in 13th-century armor in Arezzo.
Mid-September	The **Joust of the Quintana** is a 17th-century-style joust and historical procession in Foligno.
Early October	Alba's **Truffle Fair** is a series of events and a food fair centered on the white truffle.
October 4	The **Feast of St. Francis** is celebrated in Assisi, his birthplace.
Early December	The **Feast of St. Ambrose,** in Milan, officially opens La Scala Opera House.
December–June	The **Opera Season** is in full swing at the Teatro alla Scala, Italy's premier opera and ballet house in Milan.

What to Pack

The weather is considerably milder in Italy all year round than it is in the north and central United States or Great Britain. In summer, stick with clothing that's as light as possible; women should carry a scarf, light stole, or jacket to cover bare arms and shoulders when visiting churches or the Vatican Museums.

Shorts or otherwise revealing clothes—on women or men—are
taboo in churches; Italians are very strict about this in St. Peter's in Rome and St. Mark's in Venice and in other churches in
general. A sweater or woolen stole is a must for the cool of the
evening, even during the hot months. In summer, brief afternoon thunderstorms are common in Rome and inland cities, so
carry a folding plastic raincoat. And if you go into the mountains, you will find the evenings there quite chilly. During the
winter a medium-weight coat and a raincoat will stand you in
good stead in Rome and farther south; Northern Italy calls for
heavier clothes, gloves, hats, and boots. You'll probably need
an umbrella, too, but you can pick it up on the spot (or invest in
a good folding one). Pack comfortable, sturdy shoes. Cobblestones are murder on the feet; crepe soles are a help.

In general, Italians dress well and are not sloppy. They usually
don't wear shorts in the city, unless longish bermudas happen
to be in fashion at the time. Even when dressed casually or in-
formally, they are careful about the way they look; that's why
so few restaurants establish dress codes. Men aren't required
to wear ties or jackets anywhere, except in some of the grander
hotel dining rooms and top-level restaurants. Formal wear is
the exception rather than the rule at the opera nowadays,
though people in expensive seats usually do get dressed up. For
the huge general papal audiences, no rules of dress apply other
than those of common sense. For other types of audience, the
Vatican Information Office will give requirements.

To protect yourself against purse snatchers and pickpockets,
take a handbag with long straps that you can sling across your
body bandolier-style and with a zippered compartment for
your money and other valuables. Better yet, wear a money belt.

Pack light—luggage restrictions on international flights are
tight. Airlines generally allow two pieces of check-in luggage
and one carry-on piece per passenger. No piece of check-in luggage can exceed 62 inches (length + width + height) or weigh
more than 70 pounds. The carry-on luggage cannot exceed 45
inches (length + width + height) and must fit under the seat or
in the overhead luggage compartment. Passengers in first and
business classes are also allowed to carry on one garment bag.
It's always best, however, to check with your airline ahead of
time to find out about its luggage restrictions.

You'll need an electrical adapter for hair dryers and other small
appliances. The current is 220 volts and 50 cycles. If you stay in
budget hotels, take your own soap. Many do not provide soap or
else give guests only one tiny bar per room.

Taking Money Abroad

Traveler's checks and major U.S. credit cards, particularly
Visa and American Express, are accepted in larger cities and
resorts. In smaller towns and rural areas, you'll need cash.
Small restaurants and shops in the cities also tend to operate on
a cash basis. You won't get as good an exchange rate at home as
abroad, but it's wise to change a small amount of money into
Italian lire before you go, to avoid long lines at airport curren-
cy-exchange booths. Most U.S. banks will change U.S. money
into lire. If your local bank can't provide this service, you can
exchange money through **Thomas Cook Currency Service.** To

find the office nearest you, contact them at 630 Fifth Ave., New York, NY 10111, tel. 212/757–6915.

For safety and convenience, it's always best to take traveler's checks. The most recognized traveler's checks are **American Express, Barclay's, Thomas Cook,** and those issued through major commercial banks such as **Citibank** and **Bank of America.** American Express now offers the extra convenience of joint traveler's checks, which can be used by either person in a couple traveling together. Some banks will issue checks free to established customers, but most charge a 1% commission fee. Buy part of the traveler's checks in small denominations to cash toward the end of your trip. This will save you from having to cash a large check and ending up with more foreign money than you need. You can also buy traveler's checks in lire—a good idea if the dollar is falling and you want to lock in the current rate. Remember to take the address of offices where you can get refunds for lost or stolen traveler's checks.

Banks and bank-operated exchange booths at airports and railroad stations are the best places to change money. Hotels and privately run exchange firms will give you a significantly lower rate.

American Express allows cardholders to withdraw up to $1,000 in a seven-day period from their personal checking accounts at Express Cash machines at American Express offices in Florence, Milan, Rome, and Venice. (Gold cardmembers can receive up to $2,500 in a seven-day period.) Express Cash is not a cash advance service; only money already in the linked checking account can be withdrawn. Every transaction carries a 2% fee, with a minimum charge of $2 and a maximum of $6. Apply for a PIN (Personal Identification number) and to link your accounts at least two to three weeks before departure. Call 800/227–4669 to receive an application or a list locating the nearest Express Cash machine.

Getting Money From Home

There are at least three ways to get money from home:

(1) Have it sent through a large commercial bank with a branch in the town where you're staying. The only drawback is that you must have an account with the bank; if not, you'll have to go through your own bank and the process will be slower and more expensive.

(2) Have it sent through American Express. If you are a cardholder, you can cash a personal check or a counter check at an American Express office for up to $1,000 ($5,000 for gold cardholders; $10,000 for platinum) in cash and traveler's checks. There is a 1% commission on traveler's checks. American Express also provides another service which you don't have to be a cardholder to use: The American Express MoneyGram. You will have to call home and have someone go to an American Express office or MoneyGram agent and fill out the necessary form. The amount sent must be in increments of $50, and must be paid for with cash, MasterCard or Visa, Discover, or the Optima card. The American Express MoneyGram agent authorizes the transfer of funds to an American Express office in the town where you're staying. You'll need to show identification when picking up the money. Depending on where you are, the

money will be available in 15 minutes to 48 hours. Fees vary according to the amount of money sent. For sending $500, the fee is $45; for $1,000, $70. For the American Express MoneyGram location nearest your home and the locations of offices in Italy, call 800/543–4080.

(3) Have it sent through Western Union (tel. 800/325–6000). If you have a MasterCard or Visa, you can have money sent for any amount up to your credit limit. If not, have someone take cash or a certified cashier's check to a Western Union office. The money will be available in one to two days. Fees vary with the amount of money being sent. For $1,000 the standard fee is $64, for $500, $54.

Italian Currency

The unit of currency in Italy is the lira. There are bills of 500,000, 100,000, 10,000, 5,000, 2,000 and 1,000 lire. Coins are 1,000, 500, 100, 50, 20, and 10 (the last two are hardly ever used because cashiers often round out sums). At press time (mid-May 1992) the exchange rate was about 1,070 lire to the U.S. dollar, 1,935 to the Canadian dollar, and 2,260 to the pound sterling.

What It Will Cost

Italy's prices are in line with the rest of Europe, with costs comparable to those in other major capitals, such as Paris and London. Its days as a country with a low Mediterranean price tag are over. With the cost of labor and social benefits rising and in the face of a persistently weak dollar, Italy is no longer a bargain. Travelers are finding hotels and restaurants much more expensive than they used to be, and many are opting for lower-category hotels and giving up such luxuries as cars with drivers. Package tours, group or individual, remain the best way to beat increasing costs. Among major cities, Venice and Milan are the most expensive; resorts such as the Costa Smeralda, Portofino, and Cortina d'Ampezzo cater to the rich and famous and charge top prices. Though Capri is generally considered a millionaire's playground, it can accommodate the less affluent also. Everywhere in Italy, if you want the luxury of a five-star hotel, be prepared to pay top rates—and likewise with many four-star first-class hotels.

As in most countries, prices vary from region to region and are a bit lower in the countryside than in the cities. You can get good value for your money in the scenic region of Trentino–Alto Adige and in the Dolomites, in Umbria and the Marches, and on the Amalfi Coast. With a few exceptions, southern Italy, Sicily, and Sardinia offer good values, but hotels are not always up to par.

When you make hotel reservations, ask explicitly whether breakfast is included in the rate. By law, breakfast is optional, but some hotels pressure guests to eat breakfast on premises—and then charge a whopping amount for it. Find out what you're being charged for breakast, and if it seems high, clearly state that you want a room without breakfast, at the time you book or at least when you check in, to avoid misunderstanding.

Taxes are usually included in hotel bills, but some five-star hotels quote rates not inclusive of the whopping 19% IVA (VAT) for that category. There are several direct taxes in Italy that affect the tourist, such as the 19% IVA on car rentals.

Passports and Visas

Americans A visa is not required of U.S. citizens for stays up to three months. Check with the Italian Embassy, 1601 Fuller St., N.W., Washington, DC 20009, tel. 202/328–5500, or with the nearest consulate for longer stays. Passports are required for all U.S. citizens. To obtain a new passport, apply in person; renewals can be obtained in person or by mail. First-time applicants should apply to one of the 13 U.S. Passport Agency offices at least five weeks in advance of their departure date. In addition, local county courthouses, many state and probate courts, and some post offices accept passport applications. Necessary documents include: (1) a completed passport application (Form DSP-11); (2) proof of citizenship (certified birth certificate issued by the Hall of Records of your state of birth, or naturalization papers); (3) proof of identity (valid driver's license or state, military, or student ID card with your photograph and signature); (4) two recent, identical, two-inch-square photographs (black-and-white or color head shot with white or off-white background); and (5) a $65 application fee for a 10-year passport (those under 18 pay $40 for a five-year passport). You may pay with a check, money order, or exact cash amount; no change is given. Passports are mailed to you in about 10–15 working days. To renew your passport by mail, you'll need to send a completed Form DSP-82, two recent, identical passport photographs, your current passport (if less than 12 years old and issued after your 16th birthday), and a check or money order for $55.

Canadians Visas are not required of Canadian citizens for stays of up to three months in Italy. Check with the nearest Italian consulate for longer stays. Passports are required for all Canadian citizens. To acquire a passport, send a completed application (available at any post office or passport office) to the Bureau of Passports (Suite 215, West Tower, Guy Favreau Complex, 200 René Lévesque Blvd. W., Montreal, Quebec H2Z 1X4). Include $25, two photographs, a guarantor, and proof of Canadian citizenship. Applications can be made in person at regional passport offices in many locations, including Edmonton, Halifax, Montreal, Toronto, Vancouver, and Winnipeg. Passports are valid for five years and are nonrenewable.

Britons Visas are not required of British citizens staying in Italy for up to three months. Passports are required of all British citizens traveling to Italy; applications are available from travel agencies or a main post office. Send the completed form to your nearest regional passport office or to the Passport Office, Clive House, 70–78 Petty France, London SW1H 9HD (tel. 071/279–3434). The application must be countersigned by your bank manager or by a solicitor, barrister, doctor, clergyman, or justice of the peace who knows you personally. In addition, you'll need two photographs and the £15 fee. The occasional tourist may opt for a British Visitor's Passport. It is valid for one year and allows entry into other European Community (EC) countries only. It costs £7.50 and is nonrenewable. You'll need two passport photographs and identification. Apply at your local post office.

Customs and Duties

On Arrival   There are two levels of duty-free allowances for visitors to Italy.

For goods obtained anywhere outside the EC or for goods purchased in a duty-free shop within an EC country, the allowances are: (1) 200 cigarettes or 100 cigarillos or 50 cigars or 250 grams of tobacco (these allowances are doubled if you live outside of Europe); (2) 2 liters of still table wine plus (3) 1 liter of spirits over 22% volume or 2 liters of spirits under 22% volume (fortified and sparkling wines) or 2 more liters of table wine; and (4) 60 milliliters of perfume and 250 milliliters of toilet water.

For goods obtained (duty and tax paid) within another EC country, the allowances are: (1) 300 cigarettes or 150 cigarillos or 75 cigars or 400 grams of tobacco; (2) 5 liters of still table wine plus (3) 1.5 liters of spirits over 22% volume or 3 liters of spirits under 22% volume (fortified or sparkling wines) or 3 more liters of table wine; and (4) 90 milliliters of perfume and 375 milliliters of toilet water.

Officially, 10 rolls of still camera film and 10 reels of movie film may be brought in duty-free. Other items intended for personal use are generally admitted, as long as the quantities are reasonable.

On Departure   **U.S. Customs.** If you are bringing any foreign-made equipment from home, such as a camera, it's wise to carry the original receipt with you or register it with U.S. Customs before you leave (Form 4457). Otherwise, you may end up paying duty upon your return. For each 30-day period, U.S. residents may bring home duty-free up to $400 worth of foreign goods, as long as they have been out of the country for at least 48 hours. Each member of the family is entitled to the same exemption, regardless of age, and exemptions can be pooled. For the next $1,000 worth of goods, a flat 10% rate is assessed; above $1,400, duties vary with the merchandise. Included for travelers 21 or older are one liter of alcohol, 100 cigars (non-Cuban), and 200 cigarettes. Only one bottle of perfume trademarked in the United States may be brought in. However, there is no duty on antiques and art more than 100 years old. Anything exceeding these limits will be taxed at the port of entry and may be taxed additionally in the traveler's home state. Gifts valued at under $50 may be mailed to friends or relatives at home duty-free, but not more than one package per day to any one addressee, and packages may not include perfumes costing more than $5, tobacco, or liquor. "Know Before You Go," a free brochure outlining what U.S. customs policies are for U.S. residents, can be quite useful; to obtain a copy, write to the U.S. Customs Service (1301 Constitution Ave., Washington, DC 20229).

Canadian Customs. Exemptions for returning Canadians range from $20 to $300, depending on length of stay out of the country. For the $300 exemption, you must have been out of the country for one week. For any given year, one $300 exemption is allowed. You may bring in duty-free up to 50 cigars, 200 cigarettes, 2.2 pounds of tobacco, and 40 ounces of liquor, provided these are declared in writing to customs on arrival and accompany the traveler in hand or in checked baggage. Personal gifts should be mailed as "Unsolicited Gift—Value under $40." For further details, request the Canadian customs brochure "I Declare."

British Customs. Returning to the United Kingdom, there are two levels of duty-free allowances; tobacco and alcohol allowances are for travelers aged 17 and over.

For goods obtained anywhere outside the EC or for goods purchased in a duty-free shop within Italy, the allowances are: (1) 200 cigarettes or 100 cigarillos or 50 cigars or 250 grams of tobacco (these allowances are doubled if you live outside of Europe); (2) 2 liters of still table wine plus (3) 1 liter of spirits over 22% volume or 2 liters of spirits under 22% volume (fortified and sparkling wines) or 2 more liters of table wine; (4) 60 milliliters of perfume and 250 milliliters of toilet water; (5) other goods to the value of £32.

For goods obtained (duty and tax paid) within Italy, the allowances are: (1) 300 cigarettes or 150 cigarillos or 75 cigars or 400 grams of tobacco; (2) 5 liters of still table wine plus (3) 1.5 liters of spirits over 22% volume or 3 liters of spirits under 22% volume (fortified or sparkling wines) or 3 more liters of table wine; (4) 90 milliliters of perfume and 375 milliliters of toilet water; (5) other goods to the value of £420.

No animals or pets of any kind can be brought into the United Kingdom without a lengthy quarantine. The penalties are severe and strictly enforced.

Traveling with Film

If your camera is new, shoot and develop a few rolls of film before you leave home. Pack some lens tissue and an extra battery for your built-in light meter. Invest about $10 in a skylight filter and screw it onto the front of your lens. It will protect the lens and also reduce haze.

Film doesn't like hot weather. If you're driving in summer, don't store film in the glove compartment or on the shelf under the rear window. Put it behind the front seat on the floor, on the side opposite the exhaust pipe.

On a plane trip, never pack unprocessed film in check-in luggage; if your bags get X-rayed, you can say good-bye to your pictures. Always carry undeveloped film with you through security, and ask to have it inspected by hand. (It helps to isolate your film in a plastic bag, ready for quick inspection.) Inspectors at American airports are required by law to honor requests for hand inspection; abroad, you'll have to depend on the kindness of strangers.

The old airport scanning machines—still in use in some countries—use heavy doses of radiation that can turn a family portrait into an early morning fog. The newer models—used in all U.S. airports—are safe for many more scans, depending on the speed of your film. The effects are cumulative; you can put the same roll of film through several scans without worry. After five scans, though, you're asking for trouble.

If your film gets fogged and you want an explanation, send it to the **National Association of Photographic Manufacturers** (550 Mamaroneck Ave., Harrison, NY 10528). They will try to determine what went wrong. The service is free.

Language

In the main tourist cities, language is no problem. You can always find someone who speaks at least a little English, albeit with a heavy accent; remember that the Italian language is pronounced exactly as it is written (many Italians try to speak English as it is written, with disconcerting results). You may run into a language barrier in the countryside, but a phrase book and close attention to the Italians' astonishing use of pantomime and expressive gestures will go a long way.

Try to master a few phrases for daily use, and familiarize yourself with the terms you'll need to decipher signs and museum labels. You will find the basics in the Vocabulary and Menu Guide in the back of this book.

The exhortation, "Va via!" (Go away!) is useful in warding off beggars.

Staying Healthy

There are no serious health risks associated with travel to Italy. However, the Centers for Disease Control (CDC) in Atlanta caution that most of Southern Europe is in the "intermediate" range for risk of contacting traveler's diarrhea. Part of this risk may be attributed to an increased consumption of olive oil and wine, which can have a laxative effect on stomachs used to a different diet. The CDC also advises all international travelers to swim only in chlorinated swimming pools, unless they are absolutely certain the local beaches and fresh-water lakes are not contaminated.

If you have a health problem that might require purchasing prescription drugs while in Italy, have your doctor write a prescription using the drug's generic name or bring a supply with you. Brand names vary widely from country to country.

If you wear glasses or contact lenses, take along a spare pair or the prescription.

The **International Association for Medical Assistance to Travelers (IAMAT)** is a worldwide association offering a list of approved English-speaking doctors whose training meets British and American standards. For a list of Italian physicians and clinics that are part of this network, contact IAMAT (417 Center St., Lewiston, NY 14092, tel. 716/754–4883; in **Canada:** 40 Regal Rd., Guelph, Ontario N1K 1B5; in **Europe:** 57 Voirets, 1212 Grands–Lancy, Geneva, Switzerland). Membership is free.

Shots and Medications Inoculations are not needed for entering Italy. The American Medical Association (AMA) recommends Pepto Bismol for minor cases of traveler's diarrhea.

Insurance

Travelers may seek insurance coverage in four areas: health and accident, loss of luggage, flight and trip cancellation. Your first step is to review your existing health and home-owner policies; some health insurance plans cover health expenses incurred while traveling, some major medical plans cover emergency transportation, and some home-owner policies cover the theft of luggage.

Health and Accident Several companies offer coverage designed to supplement existing health insurance for travelers:

Carefree Travel Insurance (Box 310, 120 Mineola Blvd., Mineola, NY 11501, tel. 516/294–0220 or 800/323–3149) provides coverage for emergency medical evacuation and accidental death and dismemberment. It also offers 24-hour medical phone advice.

International SOS Assistance (Box 11568, Philadelphia, PA 19116, tel. 215/244–1500 or 800/523–8930), a medical assistance company, provides emergency evacuation services, worldwide medical referrals, and optional medical insurance.

Travel Guard International, underwritten by Transamerica Occidental Life Companies (1145 Clark St., Stevens Point, WI 54481, tel. 715/345–0505 or 800/782–5151), offers reimbursement for medical expenses with no deductibles or daily limits, as well as emergency evacuation services.

Wallach and Company, Inc. (Box 480, Middleburg, VA 22117-0480, tel. 703/687–3166 or 800/237–6615) offers comprehensive medical coverage, including emergency evacuation services worldwide.

Lost Luggage Loss of luggage is usually covered as part of a comprehensive travel insurance package that includes personal accident, trip cancellation, and sometimes default and bankruptcy insurance. Several companies offer comprehensive policies: **Access America, Inc.,** a subsidiary of Blue Cross–Blue Shield (Box 11188, Richmond, VA 23230, tel. 800/334–7525 or 800/284–8300); **Near Services** (450 Prairie Ave., Suite 101, Calumet City, IL 60409, tel. 708/868–6700 or 800/654–6700); and **Travel Guard International** (*see above*).

On international flights, airlines are responsible for lost or damaged property up to $9.07 per pound (or $20 per kilo) for checked baggage and up to $400 per passenger for unchecked baggage. If you're carrying any valuables, either take them with you on the airplane or purchase additional lost-luggage insurance. Not all airlines sell you this added insurance. Those that do will sell it to you at the counter when you check in, but you have to ask for it. Others will refer you to the insurance booths located throughout airports, which are operated by **Tele-Trip** (tel. 800/228–9792), a subsidiary of Mutual of Omaha. They will insure your luggage for up to 180 days. Rates vary according to the length of the trip. **The Traveler** (Ticket and Travel Dept., 1 Tower Square, Hartford, CT 06183–5040, tel. 203/277–0111 or 800/243–3174) will insure checked or hand baggage for $500–$2,000 valuation per person, up to 180 days. Rates for 1–5 days for $500 valuation are $10; for 180 days, $85. Check with your travel agent or the travel section of your Sunday newspaper for the names of other insurance companies. Itemize the contents of each bag in case you need to file a claim. If your lost luggage is recovered, the airline will deliver it to you at your home. There will be no charge to you.

Trip-Cancellation and Flight Insurance Consider purchasing trip-cancellation insurance if you are traveling on a promotional or discounted ticket that does not allow changes or cancellations. You are then covered if an emergency causes you to cancel or postpone your trip. Trip-cancellation insurance is usually included in combination travel insurance packages available from most tour operators, travel agents, and insurance agents.

Flight insurance, which covers passengers in the case of death or dismemberment, is often included in the price of a ticket when paid for with American Express, MasterCard, or other major credit cards.

Renting Cars

If you're flying into a major Italian city and planning to spend some time there, save money by arranging to pick up your car in the city the day you depart; otherwise, arrange to pick up and return your car at the airport. You'll have to weigh the added expense of renting a car from a major company with an airport office against the savings on a car from a budget company with offices in town. If you're arriving and departing from different airports, look for a one-way car rental with no return fees. If you're traveling to more than one country, make sure your rental contract permits you to take the car across borders and that the insurance policy covers you in every country you visit. Be prepared to pay more for a car with an automatic transmission, and reserve them in advance. Rental rates vary widely, but in most cases, rates quoted include unlimited free mileage and standard liability protection. Not included are a collision damage waiver (CDW), which eliminates your deductible payment should you have an accident; personal accident insurance; gasoline; and European value-added taxes (IVA). Again, the IVA in Italy is 19%.

Driver's licenses issued in the United States, Canada, and Britain are valid in Italy. You might also take out an International Driving Permit before you leave, to smooth out difficulties if you have an accident, or as additional identification. Permits are available for a small fee through local offices of the American Automobile Association (AAA) and the Canadian Automobile Association (CAA), or from their main offices: **AAA,** 1000 AAA Dr., Heathrow, FL 32746, tel. 800/336–4357; **CAA,** 2 Carlton St., Toronto, Ontario M5B 1K4, tel. 416/964–3002).

It's best to arrange a car rental before you leave. Rental companies usually charge according to the exchange rate of the dollar at the time the car is returned or when the credit card payment is processed. Two companies with special programs to help you hedge against the falling dollar, by guaranteeing advertised rates if you pay in advance, are **Budget Rent-a-Car** (3350 Boyington St., Carrollton, TX 75006, tel. 800/527–0700) and **Connex Travel International** (23 N. Division St., Peekskill, NY 10566, tel. 800/333–3949). Other budget rental companies serving Italy include **Europe by Car** (1 Rockefeller Plaza, New York, NY 10020, tel. 800/223–1516 or, in New York, 212/245–1713 or 212/581–3040, in California, 800/252–9401); **Auto Europe** (Box 1097, Sharps Wharf, Camden, ME 04843, tel. 800/223–5555); **Foremost Euro-Car** (5430 Van Nuys Blvd., Suite 306 Van Nuys, CA 91401-5680, tel. 800/272–3299, in Canada 800/253–3876); and **Kemwel** (106 Calvert St., Harrison, NY 10528, tel. 800/678–0678).

Other companies include **Avis** (tel. 800/331–1212); **Hertz** (tel. 800/654–3131 or, in New York, 800/654–3001); and **National Interrent** (tel. 800/227–3876).

Rail Passes

For those planning on doing a lot of traveling by train, the **Italian RailPass** is an excellent value because it covers the entire system, including Sicily. The pass is available in first class for periods of 8 days ($226), 15 days ($284), 21 days ($330), and 30 days ($396). In second-class the prices for the same periods are $152, $190, $220, and $264. There is also a $10 processing fee.

Also available is the **Italy Flexi Railcard,** which entitles purchasers to four days of travel within 9 days; eight days of travel within 21 days; and 12 days of travel within one month. Rates for first-class travel are $170, $250, and $314; for second-class travel, rates are $116, $164, and $210. To all rates you must add a $10 processing fee.

Although you can buy the passes at major train stations in Italy, you'll save about 30% by buying them before you leave. They can be bought through travel agents or through CIT, representative for **Italian State Railways** (342 Madison Ave., Room 207, New York, NY 10173, tel. 212/697–2100 or 800/248–8687 for orders).

A good bet for families is the **Italian Kilometric Ticket,** good for 20 train trips or 300 km (1,875 miles) of train travel, which can be used for two months by up to five people. Children under 12 are counted for only half the distance, those under 4 travel free. A second-class Kilometric Ticket costs about 160,000 lire, plus a 12,000 lire per person fee. When purchasing the ticket, make sure the agent stamps the date on it to validate it; the pass must be stamped at the station ticket office each time you use it. The Kilometric Ticket can be bought in the U.S. from the Italian State Railways office, but it is slightly cheaper in Italy, where it is sold at main train stations and CIT offices.

The **EurailPass,** valid for unlimited first-class train travel through 20 countries, including Italy, is an excellent value if you plan on traveling around the Continent. The ticket is available for periods of 15 days ($430), 21 days ($550), one month ($680), two months ($920), and three months ($1,150). For two or more people traveling together, a 15-day rail pass costs $340. Between April 1 and September 30, you need a minimum of three in your group to get this discount. For those under 26 (on the first day of travel), there is the **Eurail Youthpass,** for one or two months' unlimited second-class train travel at $470 and $640.

For travelers who like to spread out their train journeys, there is the **Eurail Flexipass.** With the 15-day Flexipass ($280), travelers get 5 days of unlimited first-class train travel, but they can spread that travel out over 15 days; a 21-day pass gives you 9 days of travel ($450), and a one-month pass gives you 14 days ($610). The **Eurail Youth Flexipass** permits 15 days of second-class travel within a two-month period ($420).

The EurailPass is available only if you live outside Europe or North Africa. The pass must be bought from an authorized agent before you leave for Europe. Apply through your travel agent or **Italian State Railways** (*see above*).

Ask also about the **EurailDrive** Pass, which lets you combine four days of train travel with three days of car rental (through Hertz) at any time within a 21-day period. Charges vary according to size of car, but two people traveling together can get the basic package for $269 per person. Contact **Rail Europe, Inc.** (230 Westchester Ave., White Plains, NY 10604, tel. 800/ 4–EURAIL; or 2087 Dundas East, Suite 105, Mississauga, Ontario L4X 1M2, tel. 416/602–4195).

Once in Italy, travelers under 26 can buy the **Cartaverde** (10,000 lire), which is valid for a year and entitles the holder to a 30% discount (20% June 26–August 14) on all trains in the state railway system.

Travelers under 26 who have not invested in a **Eurail Youthpass,** or any of the other rail passes, should inquire about discount travel fares under the Billet International Jeune (BIJ) scheme. The special one-trip tickets are sold by **EuroTrain International** (no connection with Eurailpass), at its offices in London, Dublin, Paris, Madrid, Lisbon, Rome, Zurich, Athens, Brussels, Budapest, Hanover, Leiden, Vienna, and Tangier, and at travel agents, mainline rail stations, and by youth-travel specialists.

Student and Youth Travel

The **International Student Identity Card** (ISIC) entitles students to youth rail passes, special fares on local transportation, intra-European Student Charter flights, and discounts at museums, theaters, sports events, and many other attractions. If purchased in the United States, the $14 ISIC also includes $3,000 in emergency medical insurance, plus $100 a day for up to 60 days of hospital coverage and a collect phone number to call in case of emergency. Apply to the **Council on International Student Exchange** (CIEE), 205 E. 42nd Street, 16th Floor, New York, NY 10017, tel. 212/661–1414. In Canada, the ISIC is available for CN$13 from **Travel Cuts** (187 College St., Toronto, Ont. M5T 1P7, tel. 416/979–2406).

The **Youth International Educational Exchange Card** (YIEE), issued by the Federation of International Youth Travel Organizations (FIYTO), 81 Islands Brugge, DK-2300 Copenhagen S, Denmark, provides similar services to nonstudents under age 26. In the United States, the card is available from CIEE (*see* above). In Canada, the YIEE is available from the Canadian Hostelling Association (CHA), 1600 James Naismith Drive, Suite 608, Gloucester, Ont. K1B 5N4, tel. 613/748–5638.

An **International Youth Hostel Federation** (IYHF) membership card is the key to inexpensive dormitory-style accommodations at thousands of youth hostels around the world. Hostels provide separate sleeping quarters for men and women at rates ranging from $7 to $20 a night per person and are situated in a variety of facilities, including converted farmhouses, villas, and restored castles, as well as specially constructed modern buildings. There are more than 5,000 hostel locations in 70 countries around the world. IYHF memberships, which are valid for 12 months from the time of purchase, are available in the United States through American Youth Hostels (AYH, Box 37613, Washington, DC 20013, tel. 202/783–6161). The cost for a first-year membership is $25 for adults 18 to 54. Renewal thereafter is $20. For youths (17 and under) the rate is $10 and for seniors (55 and older) the rate is $15. Family membership is available for $35. Every national hostel association arranges special reductions for members visiting their country, such as discounted rail fare or free bus travel, so be sure to ask for an international concessions list when you buy your membership.

Economical **bicycle tours** for small groups of adventurous, energetic students are another popular AYH student travel service. The AYH 16-day tour of England is a typical offering. For information on these and other AYH services and publications, contact AYH at the above address.

Council Travel, a CIEE subsidiary, is the foremost U.S. student travel agency, specializing in low-cost charters and serving as the exclusive U.S. agent for many student airfare bargains and student tours. (CIEE's 72-page *Student Travel Catalog* and "Council Charter" brochure are available free from any Council Travel office in the United States (enclose $1 postage if ordering by mail). In addition to CIEE headquarters at 205 E. 42nd St. and a branch office at 35 W. 8th St. in New York City, there are Council Travel offices in Berkeley, La Jolla, Long Beach, Los Angeles, San Diego, and San Francisco, California; Chicago, Illinois; Amherst, Boston, and Cambridge, Massachusetts; Portland, Oregon; Providence, Rhode Island; Austin and Dallas, Texas; and Seattle, Washington, to name a few.

Students who would like to work abroad should contact CIEE's Work Abroad Department (at 205 E. 42nd St. in New York City; *see above*). The Council arranges various types of paid and volunteer work experiences overseas for up to six months. CIEE also sponsors study programs in Europe, Latin America, and Asia and publishes many books of interest to the student traveler; these include *Work, Study, Travel Abroad: The Whole World Handbook* ($12.95 plus $1.50 book-rate postage or $3 first-class postage) and *Volunteer! The Comprehensive Guide to Voluntary Service in the U.S. and Abroad* ($8.95 plus $1.50 book-rate postage or $3 first-class postage).

The Information Center at the **Institute of International Education** has reference books, foreign university catalogues, study-abroad brochures, and other materials that may be consulted by students and nonstudents alike, free of charge. The Information Center (809 UN Plaza, New York, NY 10017, tel. 212/883–8200) is open weekdays 10–4. It is not open on weekends or holidays.

IIE administers a variety of grant and study programs offered by U.S. and foreign organizations and publishes a well-known annual series of study-abroad guides, including *Academic Year Abroad, Vacation Study Abroad,* and *Study in the United Kingdom and Ireland*. The institute also publishes *Teaching Abroad*, a book of employment and study opportunities overseas for U.S. teachers. For a current list of IIE publications with prices and ordering information, write Publications Service, Institute of International Education, 809 UN Plaza, New York, NY 10017. Books must be purchased by mail or in person; telephone orders are not accepted.

General information on IIE programs and services is available from its regional offices in Atlanta, Chicago, Denver, Houston, San Francisco, and Washington, DC.

For information on the Eurail Youthpass, *see* Rail Passes, *above.*

Traveling with Children

Publications *Family Travel Times* is a newsletter published 10 times a year by **TWYCH** (Travel with Your Children, 45 W. 18th St., 7th Floor Tower, New York, NY 10011, tel. 212/206–0688). A subscription includes access to back issues and twice-weekly opportunities to call in for specific advice. The book *Traveling with Children—and Enjoying It* (Globe Pequot Press, $11.95) suggests successful techniques for packing, eating out, fighting jet lag, and keeping kids entertained on lengthy trips.

Hotels **CIGA** Hotels (reservations: tel. 800/221–2340) have 22 properties in Italy, all of which welcome families. Notable are the two on the Lido in Venice: They are right on the beach and have a parklike area for children to enjoy. **Club Med** (40 W. 57th St., New York, NY 10019, tel. 800/CLUB–MED) has a "Mini Club" (for ages 4–6) and "Kids Club" (for ages 8 and up during school holidays) at its resort village in Sestriere.

Villa Rentals Contact **At Home Abroad, Inc.** (405 E. 56th St., Suite 6H, New York, NY 10022, tel. 212/421–9165); **Villas International** (605 Market St., Suite 510, San Francisco, CA 94105, tel. 415/281–0910 or 800/221–2260); **Hideaways Int'l** (Box 1270, Littleton, MA 01460, tel. 508/486–8955); **Vacanze in Italia** (Box 297, Falls Village, CT 06031; tel. 203/824–5155 or 800/533–5405); or **Italian Villa Rentals** (Box 1145, Bellevue, WA 98009, tel. 206/827–3694).

Home Exchange Exchanging homes is a surprisingly low-cost way to enjoy a vacation abroad, especially a long one. The largest home-exchange service, **Intervac U.S./International Home Exchange** (Box 590504, San Francisco, CA 94159, tel. 415/435–3497) publishes three directories a year. Membership costs $45 and entitles you to one listing and all three directories. **Loan-a-Home** (2 Park Lane, Apt. 6E Mount Vernon, NY 10552, tel. 914/664–7640) is popular with the academic community on sabbatical and businesspeople on temporary assignment. There's no annual membership fee or charge for listing your home; however, one directory and a supplement costs $45.

Getting There On international flights, children under two not occupying a seat pay 10% of adult fare. Various discounts apply to children two to 12 years of age. Regulations about traveling with infants on airplanes are in the process of changing. Until they do, however, if you want to be sure your infant is secure and traveling in his or her own safety seat, you must buy your baby a separate ticket and bring your own infant car seat. (Check with the airline in advance; certain seats aren't allowed.) Some airlines allow babies to travel in their own car seats at no charge if there's a spare seat available; otherwise safety seats will be stored, and the child will have to be held by a parent. (For the booklet *Child/Infant Safety Seats Acceptable for Use in Aircraft*, write to the Federal Aviation Administration, APA–200, 800 Independence Ave., SW, Washington DC 20591 tel. 202/267–3479.) If you opt to hold your baby on your lap, do so with the infant outside the seatbelt so he or she won't be crushed in case of a sudden stop.

Also inquire about special children's meals or snacks. The February 1990 and 1992 issues of *Family Travel Times* include TWYCH's Airline Guide, which contains a rundown of the children's services offered by 46 airlines.

Tour Operators	**Grandtravel** (600 Wisconsin Ave., Suite 706, Chevy Chase, MD 20815, tel. 301/986–0790 or 800/247–7651) specializes in package tours for grandparents and grandchildren.
Baby-sitting Services	Check with the hotel concierge or maid for recommended childcare arrangements. Rome agency: **La Lampada di Aladino** (42 Via Isonzo, Rome, tel. 06/841–2312). Milan agency: **Baby's Club** (5 Via Cusani, Milan, tel. 02/805–6039). Bologna agency: **Baby Sitters** (10 Via Battisti, Bologna, tel. 051/261223).

Hints for Disabled Travelers

Italy has only recently begun to provide for handicapped travelers, and facilities such as ramps, telephones, and toilets for the disabled are still the exception, not the rule. ENIT (Italian government travel bureau) offices can provide disabled travelers with a list of hotels accessible to the disabled and with the addresses of Italian associations for the disabled. Travelers' wheelchairs must be transported free of charge, according to Italian law, but the logistics of getting a wheelchair on and off trains and buses can make this requirement irrelevant. Seats are reserved for the disabled on public transportation, but buses have no lifts for wheelchairs. High, narrow steps for boarding trains create additional problems. In many monuments and museums, even in some hotels and restaurants, architectural barriers make it difficult, if not impossible, for the handicapped to gain access. In Rome, however, St. Peter's, the Sistine Chapel, and the Vatican Museums are all accessible by wheelchair. To bring a Seeing Eye dog into the country with you, you must have an import license, a current certificate of your dog's inoculations, and a letter from your veterinarian certifying your dog's health. Also, contact the nearest Italian consulate before you depart to make sure all the dog's documents are in order before departing.

The **Information Center for Individuals with Disabilities** (Fort Point Pl., 27–43 Wormwood St., Boston, MA 02210, tel. 617/727–5540) offers useful problem-solving assistance, including lists of travel agents that specialize in tours for the disabled.

Moss Rehabilitation Hospital Travel Information Service (1200 West Tabor Rd., Philadelphia, PA 19141–3099, tel. 215/456–9600; TDD 215/456–9602) provides information on tourist sights, transportation, and accommodations in destinations around the world for a small fee.

Mobility International USA (Box 3551, Eugene, OR 97403, tel. 503/343–1284) coordinates exchange programs for disabled people and offers information on accommodations and organized study programs around the world.

The **Society for the Advancement of Travel for the Handicapped** (347 5th Ave., Suite 610, New York, NY 10016, tel. 212/447–7288) offers access information. Annual membership costs $45, or $25 for senior travelers and students. Send a stamped, self-addressed envelope.

The Itinerary (Box 2012, Bayonne, NJ 07002, tel. 201/858–3400) is a bimonthly travel magazine for the disabled.

Nautilus Tours (5435 Donna Ave., Tarzana, CA 91356, tel. 818/343–6339) has for nine years operated international trips and cruises for the disabled. **Travel Industry and Disabled Ex-**

change (TIDE, at the same address, tel. 818/368–5648), an industry-based organization with a $15 annual membership fee, provides a quarterly newsletter and information on travel agencies and tours.

Hints for Older Travelers

In Italy, travelers over 60 can purchase the **Carta Argento,** a rail pass good for a 30% discount on the Italian State railway system. It is valid for one year, except for June 26–August 14 and December 18–28. Travelers over 60 are also entitled to free admission to state museums. Older travelers planning to visit Italy during the hottest months should be aware that few public buildings, restaurants, and shops are air-conditioned. Public toilets are few and far between, other than those in coffee bars, restaurants, and hotels. Older travelers may find it difficult to board trains and some buses and trams with very high steps and narrow treads.

The **American Association of Retired Persons** (AARP, 601 E. St. NW, Washington, DC 20049, tel. 202/434–2277) has two programs for independent travelers: (1) The Purchase Privilege Program, which offers discounts on hotels, airfare, car rentals, and sightseeing, and (2) the AARP Motoring Plan, provided by Amoco, which offers emergency aid and trip routing information for an annual fee of $33.95 per couple. The AARP also arranges group tours, including apartment living in Europe, through **AARP Travel Experience from American Express** (400 Pinnacle Way, Suite 450, Norcross, GA 30071, tel. 800/927–0111). AARP members must be 50 or older. Annual dues are $5 per person or per couple.

When using an AARP or other identification card, ask for a reduced hotel rate at the time you make your reservation, not when you check out. At participating restaurants, show your card to the maitre d' before you're seated, since discounts may be limited to certain set menus, days, or hours. When renting a car, be sure to ask about special promotional rates which might offer greater savings than the available discount.

Elderhostel (75 Federal St., Boston, MA 02210–1941, tel. 617/426–7788) is an innovative, low-cost educational program for people 60 and older. Participants live in dorms on some 1,600 campuses around the world. Mornings are devoted to lectures and seminars; afternoons, to sightseeing and field trips. The all-inclusive fee for two- to three-week international trips, including room, board, tuition, and round-trip transportation, ranges from $1,800 to $4,500.

Saga International Holidays (120 Boylston St., Boston, MA 02116, tel. 800/343–0273) specializes in group travel for people over age 60. A selection of variously priced tours allows you to choose the package that meets your needs.

National Council of Senior Citizens (1331 F St. NW, Washington, DC 20004, tel. 202/347–8800) is a nonprofit advocacy group with some 5,000 local clubs across the country. Annual membership is $2 per couple. Members receive a monthly newspaper with travel information and an ID card for reduced-rate hotels and car rentals.

Mature Outlook (6001 N. Clark St., Chicago, IL 60660, tel. 800/336–6330), a subsidiary of Sears Roebuck & Co., is a travel club for people over 50 that offers hotel and motel discounts and a bimonthly newsletter. Annual membership is $9.95 per couple. Instant membership is available at participating Holiday Inns.

Further Reading

To read about other American tourists in Italy, look for *The Enchanted Ground: Americans in Italy, 1760–1980*, by Erik Amfitheatrof. *The Italians*, by Luigi Barzini, is a comprehensive and lively analysis of the Italian national character.

For some good historical fiction set in Italy, pick up Samuel Shellabarger's *Prince of Foxes*, about Renaissance Venice. Irving Stone's *Agony and the Ecstasy* is based on the life of Michelangelo. *The Leopard*, by Giuseppe di Lampedusa, is a compelling portrait of Sicily during the political upheavals of the 1860s. For World War II historical fiction, look for *History: A Novel* by Elsa Morante; *Two Women* by Alberto Moravia; Walter F. Murphy's *The Roman Enigma;* John Hersey's *A Bell for Adano;* or *Bread and Wine* by Ignazio Silone, a novel about Italian peasants under the control of the Fascists. Also, *Century*, by Fred M. Stewart, spans several generations of an Italian family.

Adventure novels set in Italy include *Any Four Women Could Rob the Bank of Italy* by Ann Cornelisen, Helen MacInnes's *North From Rome* and *The Venetian Affair*, Ngaio Marsh's *When in Rome*, Evelyn Anthony's *The Company of Saints*, Daphne DuMaurier's *The Flight of the Falcon* and *Don't Look Now*, and *Peter's Pence*, by Jon Cleary. Magdalen Nabb's entertaining thrillers, such as *Death in Autumn* and *Death of a Dutchman* are set in Florence.

Other recommended titles include *Death in Venice* by Thomas Mann, *A Room with a View* by E. M. Forster, Joseph Heller's *Catch-22*, *A Farewell to Arms* by Ernest Hemingway, *The Stories of Elizabeth Spencer*, *Venice Observed* by Mary McCarthy, and *Italian Days* by Barbara Grizzuti Harrison.

Arriving and Departing

From North America by Plane

Since the air routes between North America and Italy are heavily traveled, the passenger has many airlines and fares from which to choose. Fares change with stunning rapidity, so consult your travel agent on which bargains are currently available.

Be certain to distinguish among nonstop flights (no changes, no stops); direct flights (no changes but one or more stops); and connecting flights (two or more planes, one or more stops).

Airlines The airlines that serve Italy from the United States are **TWA** (tel. 800/892–4141), **Delta** (tel. 800/221–1212), and **Alitalia** (tel. 800/223–5730). All fly to Rome and Milan.

Flying Time The flying time to Rome from New York is 8½ hours; from Chicago, 10–11 hours; from Los Angeles, 12–13 hours.

Discount Flights The major airlines offer a range of tickets that can increase the price of any given seat by more than 300%, depending on the day of purchase. As a rule, the further in advance you buy the ticket, the less expensive it is and the greater the penalty (up to 100%) for canceling. Check with airlines for details.

The best buy is not necessarily an APEX (advance purchase) ticket on one of the major airlines. APEX tickets carry certain restrictions: They must be bought in advance (usually 21 days); they restrict your travel, usually with a minimum stay of seven days and a maximum of 90; and they penalize you for changes— voluntary or not—in your travel plans. But if you can work around these drawbacks (and most travelers can), they are among the best-value fares available.

Travelers willing to put up with some restrictions and inconveniences in exchange for a substantially reduced airfare may be interested in flying as air couriers, to accompany shipments between designated points. For a telephone directory listing courier companies by the cities to which they fly, send $5 and a self-addressed, stamped, business-size envelope to Pacific Data Sales Publishing (2554 Lincoln Blvd., Suite 275-F, Marina Del Rey, CA 90291). For "A Simple Guide to Courier Travel," send $15.95 (postpaid) to Box 2394, Lake Oswego, OR 97035. For more information, call 800/344–9375.

Charter flights offer the lowest fares but often depart only on certain days, and seldom on time. Though you may be able to arrive at one city and return from another, you may lose all or most of your money if you cancel your ticket. Don't sign up for a charter flight unless you've checked with a travel agency about the reputation of the packager. It's particularly important to know the packager's policy concerning refunds. One of the most popular charter operators to Europe is **Council Charter** (tel. 212/661–0311 or 800/800–8222), a division of CIEE (Council on International Educational Exchange). Other companies advertise in the Sunday travel section of newspapers.

Somewhat more expensive—but up to 50% below the cost of APEX fares—are tickets purchased through companies known as consolidators that buy blocks of tickets on scheduled airlines and sell them at wholesale prices. Here again, you may lose all or most of your money if you change plans, but at least you will be on a regularly scheduled flight with less risk of cancellation than on a charter. Once you've made your reservation, call the airline to make sure you're confirmed. Among the best-known consolidators are **UniTravel** (Box 12485, St. Louis, MO 63132, tel. 314/569–2501 or 800/325–2222) and **Access International** (101 W. 31st St., Suite 1104, New York, NY 10001, tel. 212/465–0707 or 800/825–3633). Others advertise in the Sunday travel section of newspapers as well.

Yet another option is to join a travel club that offers special discounts to its members. Three such organizations are **Moment's Notice** (425 Madison Ave., New York, NY 10017, tel. 212/486–0500); **Discount Travel International** (114 Forrest Ave., Suite 203, Narberth, PA 19072, tel. 215/668–7184 or 800/334–9294); **Travelers Advantage** (CUC Travel Svce., 49 Music Sq. W, Nashville, TN 37203, tel. 800/548–1116); and **Worldwide Discount Travel Club** (1674 Meridian Ave., Suite 300, Miami Beach, FL 33139, tel. 305/534–2082). These cut-rate tickets should be compared with APEX tickets on the major airlines.

Enjoying the Flight If you're lucky enough to be able to sleep on a plane, it makes sense to fly at night. Many experienced travelers, however, prefer to take a morning flight to Europe and arrive in the evening, just in time for a good night's sleep. Since the air on a plane is dry, it helps, while flying, to drink a lot of nonalcoholic liquids; drinking alcohol contributes to jet lag, as does eating heavy meals on board. Feet swell at high altitudes, so it's a good idea to remove your shoes while in flight. Sleepers usually prefer window seats to curl up in; those who like to move about the cabin should ask for aisle seats. Bulkhead seats (located in the front row of each cabin) have more legroom, but seat trays are attached to the arms of your seat rather than to the back of the seat in front.

From the U.K. by Plane, Car, Train, and Bus

By Plane **Alitalia** (tel. 01/081/745–8200) and **British Airways** (tel. 01/897–4000) operate direct flights from London (Heathrow) to Rome, Milan, Venice, Pisa, and Naples. Flying time is 2½ to three hours. There's also one direct flight a day from Manchester to Rome. Standard fares are extremely high. Several less expensive tickets are available. Both airlines offer APEX tickets (usual booking restrictions apply) and PEX tickets (which don't have to be bought in advance). The Eurobudget ticket (no length-of-stay or advance-purchase restrictions) is another option. Air Europe offers low fares.

Less expensive flights are available: It pays to look around in the classified advertisements of reputable newspapers and magazines such as *Time Out*. But remember to check the *full* price, inclusive of airport taxes, fuel, and surcharges. Some of the bargains are not as inexpensive as they seem at first glance.

By Car The distance from London to Rome is 1,810 kilometers (1,124 miles) via Calais/Boulogne/Dunkirk and 1,745 kilometers (1,084 miles) via Oostende/Zeebrugge (excluding sea crossings). Milan is about 644 kilometers (400 miles) closer. The drive from the Continental ports takes about 24 hours; the trip in total takes about three days. The shortest and quickest channel crossings are via Dover or Folkestone to one of the French ports (Calais or Boulogne); the ferry takes around 75 minutes and the Hovercraft just 35 minutes. Crossings from Dover to the Belgian ports take about four hours, but Oostende and Zeebrugge have good road connections. The longer crossing from Hull to Zeebrugge is useful for travelers from the north of England. The Sheerness-Vlissingen (Holland) route makes a comfortable overnight crossing; it takes about nine hours.

Fares on the cross-channel ferries vary considerably from season to season. Until the end of June and from early September onward, savings can be made by traveling midweek. Don't forget to budget for the cost of gas and road tolls, plus a couple of nights' accommodations, especially if crossing in daytime.

Roads from the channel ports to Italy are mostly toll-free. The exceptions are the road crossing the Ardennes, the Swiss superhighway network (for which a special tax sticker must be bought at the frontier or in advance), the St. Gotthard Tunnel, and the road between the tunnel and the Italian superhighway system. Remember that the Italian government offers special packages of reduced-price petrol coupons (15%–20% off) and highway toll vouchers. They must be bought in advance from the **AA, RAC,** or **CIT** (50 Conduit St., London W1R 9FB, tel. 071/434–3844). These are available to personal callers only; the driver must produce his or her passport and vehicle registration document when applying.

If these distances seem too great to drive, there's always the Motorail from the channel ports. However, no car/sleeper expresses run beyond Milan, 628 kilometers (390 miles) north of the capital.

By Train Visitors traveling to Italy by train have several options. You can leave London's Victoria train station at 11:30 AM for Folkestone and Boulogne; from Boulogne Maritime, you take the train to Gare du Nord in Paris and then a taxi or metro across town to Gare de Lyons. From there, you pick up the "Napoli Express" for Rome. There are first- and second-class sleeping cars and second-class couchettes for the overnight run into Italy. From Paris to Dijon there's a refreshment service, and a buffet car is attached in the morning. The train reaches Turin at 5:46 AM and Rome about 1:35 PM the next day.

Alternatively, the 10 AM train from Victoria meets the Hovercraft in time for a crossing to Paris via Boulogne. It arrives at 4:30 PM, which gives you plenty of time to cross Paris by metro or taxi to catch the 6:47 PM Paris–Rome "Palatino" service. If you don't like the Hovercraft, the 9:15 AM Victoria service catches the Dover–Calais ferry crossing; arrival time in Paris is 5:20 PM. The "Palatino" leaves Paris at Gare de Lyons and travels via Chambéry and the Mont Cenis tunnel to Turin, arriving about 2:50 . You reach Rome by 9:35 AM. The train has first- and second-class sleepers and second-class couchettes, but no ordinary day cars for sitting up overnight. There's a buffet car from Paris to Chambéry and from Genoa to Rome.

A year-round service leaves Victoria at 1:30, catching the Jetfoil for Oostende in plenty of time to take the 8:53 PM train to Basel. Change there and take the 7:22 AM train, which gets you to Rome by 6:05 PM.

Train, ferry, and hovercraft schedules are subject to change, so consult with **French Railways** (tel. 071/493–9731) and **British Rail** (tel. 071/928–5151) before you leave.

By Bus **Eurolines** (13 Lower Regent St., London SW1Y 4LR, tel. 071/730–0202, or any National Express agent) runs a weekly bus service to Rome that increases to three times a week between June and September. Buses leave on Sunday, Wednesday, and Friday over the summer, and on Sunday the rest of the year. The trip takes about 2½ days. Buses travel via Dover, Calais, Paris, and Lyon. Have a few French francs for spending en route. Fares are quite high, especially when you consider the long and tiring overnight journey and compare the price with that of a charter flight. Further details are available from National Express, at the Eurolines address (*see above*).

Staying in Italy

Getting Around

By Plane **Alitalia** and its domestic affiliate **ATI**, in addition to smaller, privately run companies such as **Meridiana**, complete an extensive network of internal flights in Italy. Apart from the major international airports, you can find frequent flights between airports serving smaller cities, such as Bologna, Genoa, Naples, Palermo, Turin, and Verona. Flight times are never much more than an hour (long flights usually are those going from the extreme north to Naples or Sicily), and most of these smaller airports are close to the cities and linked by good bus services. Italian travel agents will inform you of the discounts available, some of which include a 50% family reduction for a spouse and/ or children traveling with you, or up to 30% for certain night flights.

By Train The fastest trains on the **FS,** the state-owned railroad, are *Intercity* and *Rapido* trains, for which you pay a supplement and for which seat reservations may be required and are always advisable. *Espresso* trains usually make more stops and are a little slower. *Diretto* and *Locale* are the slowest.

To avoid long lines at station windows, buy tickets and make seat reservations at least a day in advance at travel agencies displaying the FS emblem. If you have to reserve at the last minute, reservation offices at the station accept reservations up to three hours before departure. You can also get a seat assignment just before boarding the train; look for the conductor on the platform near the train. Trains can be very crowded on weekends and during holiday and vacation seasons; we strongly advise reserving seats in advance or, if the train originates where you get on, getting to the station early to find a seat. A card over the seat or just outside the compartment indicates whether that seat has been reserved. Carry compact bags for easy overhead storage. You can buy train tickets for destinations close to main cities at tobacconists.

Note that in some Italian cities (including Milan, Turin, Genoa, Naples, and Rome) there are two or more main-line stations, although one is usually the principal terminus or through-station. Be sure of the name of the station at which your train will arrive, or from which it will depart.

There is refreshment service on all long-distance trains, with mobile carts and a cafeteria or dining car. Tap water on trains is not drinkable.

Rail Passes For those planning on doing a lot of traveling by train, the **Italian RailPass** is an excellent value. (*See* Rail Passes in Before You Go, *above*.)

By Bus Italy's bus network is extensive, although not as attractive as those in other European countries, partly because of the low cost of train travel. Buses operated by members of **ANAC** travel the length of the country, and most are air-conditioned and comfortable. An up-to-date timetable, published by ANAC, is available from most tourist information offices within Italy. **SITA** (Viale Cadorna 105, Florence, tel. 055/278611) operates a similar service, and its schedule is available at tourist offices or at its office at the address above.

Local bus companies operate in many regions (*see* Getting Around By Bus in most chapters). In the hillier parts of Italy, particularly in the Alpine north, they take over when the gradients become too steep for train travel. A village shop or café will sometimes double as the ticket office and bus stop for these services. You should have your ticket before you board.

Most of the major cities have urban bus services, usually operating on a system involving the prepurchase of tickets (from a machine, a newsstand, or a tobacco store). These services are

Golf Relatively new to Italy, golf is catching on, and more courses are being laid out near major cities. For information, contact **Federazione Italiana Golf** (Via Flaminia 388, 00196 Rome, tel. 06/323–1825).

Canoeing The swift rivers rushing down the slopes of the Alps and Apennines make for exciting canoeing. Kayak races are held in the Dolomites and on the Aniene River near Subiaco in Lazio. For information, get in touch with the **Federazione Italiana Canoa e Kayak** (Viale Tiziano 70, 00196 Rome, tel. 06/368–58215).

Skiing One of the country's most popular participant sports, skiing, is practiced along the Alpine Arc and in the Apennines, as well. (*See* regional chapters for recommended resorts and package deals.)

Horseback Riding An excursion on horseback is a pleasant way to see the countryside, and many types of tours are offered. Some of these tours include overnight stays in country estates in Lazio, Tuscany, and other regions. For information, contact **Associazione Nazionale per il Turismo Equestre** (Via A. Borelli 5, 00161 Rome, tel. 06/444–1179).

Tennis Tennis is one of Italy's most popular sports, and most towns and villages have public courts available for a booking fee. Many hotels have courts that are open to the public, and some private clubs offer temporary visitors' memberships to those traveling through the country. Contact local tourist information offices for information.

Spectator Sports

Soccer *Calcio* (soccer) is the most popular spectator sport in Italy. All major cities, and most smaller ones, have teams playing in one league or another. Big-league games are played on Sunday afternoons from September to May. Inquire locally or write to **Federazione Italiana Giuoco Calcio** (Via G. Allegri 14, 00198 Rome, tel. 06/84911).

Horse Racing There are tracks in Milan, Rome, Palermo, and many other cities. Inquire locally for the best racing days.

Basketball Many Americans play on Italian pro teams, and basketball is gaining a big following around the country. For information, contact **Federazione Italiana Pallacanestro** (Via Fogliano 15 00199 Rome, tel. 06/886–3071).

Tennis A major international Grand Prix tennis tournament is held in Rome in May.

Beaches

Italy isn't the place for an exclusively "beach" holiday. With the exception of Sardinia, you'll find cleaner water and better beaches at lower prices in other parts of the world. The waters that are least polluted and best for swimming are in Sardinia (except around Cagliari, Arbatax, and Porto Torres); off portions of the coasts of Calabria and Apulia; and off the islands of Elba, Capri, Ischia, Ustica, the Aeolians, and western Sicily. Topless bathing is widespread, except for a few staid family-type beaches near large cities. Nudism is discreetly practiced on out-of-the-way beaches, mainly on the islands and on deserted stretches of the mainland coast. Singles will find the liveliest resorts on the Adriatic Coast and on the coasts of Tuscany and Calabria.

Dining

Dining in Italy is a pleasant aspect of the total Italian experience, a chance to enjoy authentic Italian specialties and ingredients. Visitors have a choice of eating places, ranging from a *ristorante* (restaurant) to a *trattoria, tavola calda,* or *rosticceria.* A trattoria is usually a family-run place, simpler in decor, menu, and service than a ristorante, and slightly less expensive. Some rustic-looking spots call themselves *osteria* but are really restaurants. (A true osteria is a wineshop, a very basic and down-to-earth tavern.) The countless fast-food places opening up everywhere are variations of the older Italian institutions of the tavola calda or rosticceria, which offer a selection of hot and cold dishes that you may take out or eat on the premises. A tavola calda is more likely to have seating. At a tavola calda or rosticceria, some items are priced by the portion, others by weight. You usually select your food, find out how much it costs, then pay the cashier and get a stub that you must give to the counterman when you pick up the food.

None of the above serves breakfast; in the morning you go to a coffee bar, which is where, later in the day, you will also find sandwiches and pastry and other snacks. In a bar you tell the cashier what you want, pay for it, and then take the stub to the counter, where you order. Remember that table service is extra, and you are expected not to occupy tables unless you are being served; on the other hand, you can linger as long as you like at a table without being pressed to move on.

In eating places of all kinds, the menu is always posted in the window or just inside the door so you can see what you're getting into (in a snack bar or tavola calda the price list is usually displayed near the cashier). In all but the simplest places there's a *coperto* (cover charge) and usually also a *servizio* (service charge) of 10%–15%, only part of which goes to the waiter. These extra charges will increase your check by 15%–20%. A *menu turistico* (tourist menu) includes taxes and service, but beverages are usually extra.

Beware of items on à la carte menus marked "SQ" (according to quantity), which means you will be charged according to the weight of the item you have ordered, or "L. 4,000 hg," which means the charge will be 4,000 lire per hectogram (3½ ounces). This type of price generally refers to items such as fresh fish or Florentine steaks and fillets.

Mealtimes Lunch is served in Rome from 1 to 3, dinner from 8 to 10, or later in some restaurants. Service begins and ends a half-hour earlier in Florence and Venice, an hour earlier in smaller towns in the north, a half-hour to one hour later in the south. Almost all eating places close one day a week and for vacations in summer and/or winter.

Precautions Tap water is safe almost everywhere unless labeled "*Non Potabile.*" Most people order bottled *acqua minerale* (mineral water), either *gassata* (bubbles) or *naturale,* or *non gassata* (without). In a restaurant you order it by the *litro* (liter) or *mezzo litro* (half-liter); often the waiter will bring it without being asked, so if you don't like it, or want to keep your check down, make a point of ordering *acqua semplice* (tap water). You can also order *un bicchiere di acqua minerale* (a glass of mineral water) at any bar. If you are on a low-sodium diet, ask for everything (within reason) *senza sale* (without salt).

Ratings Restaurants in our listings are divided by price into four categories: Very Expensive, Expensive, Moderate, and Inexpensive. (*See* Dining in individual chapters for specific prices, which vary from region to region.) Prices quoted are for a three-course meal with house wine, including all service and taxes; particularly recommended establishments are indicated by a star ★.

Lodging

Italy offers a good choice of accommodations, especially in the main tourist capitals of Rome, Florence, and Venice. However, it's becoming more difficult to find satisfactory accommodations in the lower categories in these cities, where many hotels are being refurbished and upgraded. Throughout Italy you will find everything from deluxe five-star hotels to charming country inns, villas for rent, camping grounds, and hostels, in addition to well-equipped vacation villages in resort areas. In the major cities, room rates are on a par with other European capitals: Deluxe and superior first-class rates can be downright extravagant. In those categories, ask for one of the better rooms, since less desirable rooms—and there usually are some—don't give you what you're paying for. Otherwise, consider booking the better rooms in hotels that are one category lower than what you would ordinarily ask for. Hotels are justifying higher rates by refurbishing rooms and bathrooms and installing such accessories as hair dryers and personal safes. Such amenities as porters, room service, and in-house cleaning and laundering are disappearing in Moderate and Inexpensive hotels.

Taxes and service are included in the room rate, although a 19% IVA tax may be a separate item in deluxe hotels. Breakfast is an extra, optional, charge, but most hotels quote rates inclusive of breakfast. When you book a room, ask specifically whether the rate includes breakfast (*colazione*). You are under no obligation to take breakfast at your hotel, but in practice most hotels expect you to do so.

Moderate and Inexpensive hotels may charge extra for optional air-conditioning. In older hotels the quality of rooms may be very uneven; if you don't like the room you're given, ask for another. This applies to noise, too. Front rooms may be larger and have a view, but they also may get a lot of noise. Specify if you care about having either a bath or shower, since not all rooms have both. In the Moderate and Inexpensive categories, showers may be the drain-in-the-floor type, guaranteed to flood the bathroom. Major cities have hotel-reservation service booths in train stations.

Hotels Italian hotels are officially classified from five-star (deluxe) to one-star (guest houses and small inns). Prices are established by local authorities and are listed in the *Annuari Alberghi* (hotel yearbooks), available at tourist information offices but rarely up to date. The rate quoted is for the room, unless otherwise stated. A rate card on the door of your room or inside the closet door tells you exactly what you will pay for that particular room. Any unforeseen variations are cause for complaint and should be reported to the local tourist office. **CIGA, Jolly, Space, Atahotels,** and **Italhotels** are among the reliable chains or groups operating in Italy. **Relais et Chateaux** hotels are small, quiet, and posh. Jolly hotels and the **AGIP** motels on main highways offer functional but anonymous accommodations that are the best choice in many out-of-the-way places. **Family Hotels** (Via Faenza 77, 50123 Florence, tel. 055/217975, fax 055/210101) is a group of independently owned family-run hotels that give good value.

Rentals Ideal for families and for extended vacations, rented villas offer fully equipped accommodations, often with maid service included. Make sure you see a photograph of the place you're intending to rent before you commit yourself. Also, make plans early because rentals are increasingly popular.

In the United States, **At Home Abroad, Inc.** (405 E. 56th St., New York, NY 10022, tel. 212/421–9165) and **Hometours International, Inc.** (1170 Broadway, New York, NY 10001, tel. 212/689–0851 or 800/367–4668, fax 212/689–0679) have properties all over Europe, including a good selection in Italy.

Two London-based companies have a good selection of rentals on their books. **Villas Italia Ltd** (227 Shepherds Bush Rd., London W6, tel. 081/748–8668) has villas in Tuscany, Rome, and Positano. **CV Travel** (43 Cadogan St., London SW3 2PR, tel. 071/581–0851) has properties to rent in Tuscany and Umbria: Choices include a palazzo in southern Italy and luxurious apartments on the sea.

Camping Camping is becoming a popular choice for Italians themselves, who take to the hills and lakes, where there are many campgrounds and bungalows. Apart from cost considerations, camping is a good way to find accommodations in otherwise overcrowded resorts. Make sure you stay only on authorized campsites (camping on private land is frowned upon). You must also have an international camping *carnet* (permit), which you can obtain from your local camping association before you leave home. Alternatively, you can apply for a carnet by writing to the **Federazione Italiana del Campeggio** (Casella postale 23,50041 Calenzano, Florence). Send several passport-style photos with your application. The federation publishes a multilingual *Guida Camping Italiana* (campsite directory), which costs about 8,000 lire. Camp rates for two persons, with tent, average about 15,000 lire a day.

Camper rental agencies operate throughout Italy: Contact your travel agency for details. One package, for example, allows you to fly to Sardinia or Sicily, pick up a fully equipped camper on arrival, and explore the island as you please.

Youth Hostels There are about 155 hostels in Italy, some in such beautiful settings as the 14th-century Castle of Rocca degli Alberi at Montagnana, near Padua; the Castle of Murat, at Pizzo, in Calabria; and the Castle of Scilla, on the Straits of Messina. Hostel rates are about 18,000 lire per person per night, including breakfast, but it's not easy to find accommodations, especially in tourist centers, unless you have reservations. Contact the **Associazione Italiana Alberghi per la Gioventù** (Via Cavour 44, Rome, tel. 06/487–1152), a member of the International Youth Hostel Federation.

In the United States, contact **American Youth Hostels, Inc.** (Box 37613, Washington, DC 20013–7613, tel. 202/783–6161). In Canada contact the **Canadian Hostelling Association's** national office (1600 James Naismith Dr., Suite 608, Gloucester, Ontario K1B 5N4, tel. 613/748–5638). In the United Kingdom, contact the **Youth Hostel Association of England and Wales** (Trevelyan House, 8 St. Stephen's Hill, St. Albans, Hertfordshire AL1 2DY, tel. 0727/55215).

Ratings Hotels in our listings are divided by price into four categories: Very Expensive, Expensive, Moderate, and Inexpensive. (*See* Lodging sections in individual chapters for specific prices, which differ according to region.) Hotels in some regions, particularly the northern mountainous areas, offer attractive half- and full-board packages (in which some or all meals are included in the price) and usually require that you stay a number of days. These deals can often "lower" an establishment into a less expensive classification in real terms because the inclusive deal is a bargain. Particularly recommended places are indicated by a star ★.

Credit Cards

The following credit card abbreviations are used: AE, American Express; DC, Diners Club; MC, MasterCard; V, Visa.

Great Itineraries

Rome to Florence

This itinerary offers you the chance to experience a wide range of scenery and historical influences in a relatively short distance. The route and terrain would be equally familiar to an Etruscan nobleman, Roman centurion, or medieval cardinal because the main lines of communication in central Italy have always run along, or parallel to, the Apennines.

Heading north from Rome along the coast, you pass the Etruscan city of Tarquinia before reaching Viterbo, which still features its medieval walls and crafts shops. The next stop is Orvieto, perched on the top of a rocky peak and living up to its reputation as a romantic medieval city. The area boasts one of Italy's most famous white wines, and the surrounding countryside, made up of jagged outcrops of volcanic rock, is as dramatic as Orvieto itself.

A few miles north and you're in Tuscany, with its rolling countryside of olive groves and cypresses that captivated the Renaissance painters. The next stop is welcoming Siena, the beautiful art city famous for its motto on the city gates: *Cor Magis tibi Sena pandit* (Siena opens its heart to you). Siena's medieval past comes alive twice a year when the colorful riders in the Palio horse race charge round the fan-shaped Piazza del Campo. North of Siena lies Chianti country, a hilly district producing Italy's most famous wines. There are plenty of chances to stop and sample a glass in one of many medieval stone villages.

The last stop is Florence, the cradle of the Renaissance and the highlight of many trips to Italy. Birthplace of artistic and literary giants, Renaissance Florence nurtured its native talents and attracted others from all over Italy and Europe. The result is one of the world's greatest concentrations of art and architecture, crammed into what is really a compact city along the banks of the river Arno. Just northeast of Florence is Fiesole, the hilltop village that dates as far back as the Etruscans and provides some of the best views of the Arno Valley and Florence itself.

Length of Trip Seven days.

Getting Around The most direct route from Rome to Florence is 277 kilometers
By Car (160 miles), but to appreciate the scenery you should add to that figure by keeping off the direct superhighway (A1). Instead, take S2 almost all the way, leaving it only to head east to Orvieto along S71.

By Public Take an express bus to Viterbo and then another bus from
Transportation Viterbo to Orte, where you can get a fast train to Orvieto. A slower train makes the scenic trip to Siena, passing through Montepulciano. Take the local train north from Siena, changing at Empoli for Florence.

The Main Route **One Night: Viterbo.** Either stop en route (taking S1 from Rome to Tarquinia) or make a side trip to the Etruscan settlement of Tarquinia from Viterbo. In Viterbo explore the Piazza San Lorenzo, and the bustling heart of the medieval city, the San Pellegrini quarter.

One Night: Orvieto. Stop a few miles west of Orvieto, on S71, to appreciate the best view of the cliff-top city. In Orvieto, visit the Duomo, one of Italy's most dramatically sited cathedrals, noted for its intricate facade. Walk to St. Patrick's Well. Make sure to sample some of the local white wine.

Two Nights: Siena. You could spend a whole day relaxing in the beguiling Piazza del Campo, which is bathed in a warm and ever-changing light. Visit the Palazzo Pubblico, the Pinacoteca Gallery, and the Duomo (Cathedral). Try to be on hand for one of the two runnings of the Palio.

Three Nights: Florence. This is the minimum stay in one of the world's great cities. If you do nothing else, visit the Duomo, Baptistry, Piazza della Signoria, Uffizi Gallery, Palazzo Pitti, Galleria dell'Accademia, and the charming church of San Miniato al Monte. If all the art is overwhelming, make a side trip to Fiesole and relax while overlooking the entire valley of the Arno.

Information See Chapters 3, 4, 5, and 13.

From the Ligurian Sea to the Adriatic

Italy's sea trade in the Middle Ages was dominated by two maritime republics—Genoa, on the Ligurian Sea, and Venice, on the Adriatic. It was inevitable that these two powers would eventually clash over supremacy in the eastern Mediterranean: The Venetian victory at the Battle of Chioggia, in 1381, settled more than 100 years of conflict.

The development of the two cities since the decisive battle in the 14th century would have been hard to predict at the time. Genoa, defeated militarily, developed economically into one of the world's great ports. Powerful Venice remained in ascendancy for more than a century, amassing colonies along the eastern

Adriatic Coast and as far east as Cyprus before sinking into a languid decline.

This west-to-east itinerary offers you the chance to explore these contrasting cities—busy, modern port and caretaker of a gilded past. In between you'll pass the spectacular scenery of the Ligurian Coast, which culminates in the remote fishing villages of the Cinque Terre. After turning inland (and out of the medieval domain of Genoa), you'll reach Parma, known for its harmonious medieval cathedral and majestic baptistry as much for its famous ham and cheese. Farther east, along the banks of the fast-flowing Adige River, is Verona, with its Roman arena and attractive medieval quarter—the setting for Shakespeare's *Romeo and Juliet.* Between Verona and Venice is Padua, noted for its famous university and the Scrovegni Chapel, decorated with magnificent wall paintings by Giotto. Finally there is glorious Venice, a city that has learned to cope with the tides of visitors and of the waters of its lagoon in equal measure.

Length of Trip Eight to 11 days.

Getting Around The total distance is about 450 kilometers (270 miles). The
By Car coastal S1 route is the most scenic way to get to La Spezia from Genoa, although you'll need to hike or take a train if you want to visit the Cinque Terre. From there to Parma, Verona, Padua, and Venice, you have the choice of fast superhighways or good secondary roads the entire way.

By Public Good trains connect all the destinations on the tour. The slow-
Transportation est, but most scenic, are from Genoa to La Spezia (the route follows the coast, winding along cliffs and through mountains); between La Spezia and Parma the train crosses some dramatic Apennine passes.

The Main Route **Two Nights: Genoa.** Visit the port, with its 16th-century lighthouse (La Lanterna), and admire the view from above the city at Monte Righi. Visit Genoa's well-preserved medieval quarter around Piazza San Matteo; see Via Garibaldi and the Palazzo Bianco.

Two Nights: La Spezia. Leave your city concerns behind as you hike along Italy's most imposing coastline, with the fishing villages of the Cinque Terre as your aim. Visit the coastal towns of Lerici and Portovenere.

One Night: Parma. Sample the excellent Parma ham and cheeses and meander through the old streets around Piazza del Duomo. Satisfy your artistic yearnings with visits to the Galleria Nazionale and the medieval baptistry. See Correggio's frescoes in the cathedral and the church of San Giovanni Evangelista.

Two Nights: Verona. Visit the Roman Arena and the spacious Piazza Brà that abuts it. Wander through the medieval quarter and see the Castelvecchio and the church of San Zeno.

One Night: Padua. See the famous university and Giotto's masterpiece, the Cappella Scrovegni. Join the pilgrimage to the Basilica di San Antonio, patron saint of Padua, and stop for coffee at the grand Caffè Pedrocchi.

Three Nights: Venice. This is the minimum stay for the world's most romantic city. Not-to-be-missed sights include St.

Mark's, Piazza San Marco, the Doge's Palace, the church of the Frari, the Accademia, and the Grand Canal.

Information See Chapters 6, 7, 8, and 12.

Lake Route to the Dolomites

This itinerary takes you into the lakes and mountains north of Milan, the busy financial and fashion capital of northern Italy. Starting on the Lombard plain, you begin to climb as you head north toward Bergamo in the foothills of the Alps. From there it's an off-the-beaten-track circuit around Lake Iseo and then a breathtaking drive along the western shore of Lake Garda, Italy's largest lake, on your way to Riva del Garda on the northern shore.

A direct and attractive road takes you from there to Trento, an important trading post on the north-south trade route to Germany and Austria and famous for the Council of Trent, which formulated the Catholic response to the Reformation. The road from Trento (either main highway or equally direct S road) goes almost due north to Bolzano, also known as Bozen because of the large German-speaking population in this region. Bolzano has some intriguing medieval architectural gems, but its main attraction is its handy location, on the doorstep of the dramatic Dolomite mountain range.

Length of Trip Five days.

Getting Around The total distance to Bolzano is 380 kilometers (210 miles).
By Car Take Autostrada A4 to Bergamo. From there, S42 runs up the west coast of Lake Iseo, and S510 goes down the east to Brescia. Join S45bis along Lake Garda and continue into Trento. From there you can take either S12 or A22 north to Bolzano.

By Public Good train service takes you as far as Brescia (east of Berga-
Transportation mo), where you can take the bus to Riva del Garda and Trento. From Trento to Bolzano you can either continue on the bus or go by train.

The Main Route **One Night: Bergamo.** Visit the Colleoni chapel and the Piazza Vecchio in the Città Alta (Upper Town) and the Carrara Academy in the lower. Make an early start the next day to wind your way past Lake Iseo. Stop at Gardone Riviera along Lake Garda to see Il Vittoriale, the imaginatively designed mansion built by the poet Gabriele D'Annunzio.

One Night: Riva del Garda. Relax in this attractive town, which is one of Europe's best windsurfing centers. Visit the Torre Apponale, in the town center overlooking the lake.

One Night: Trento. Wander through the medieval quarter of town before climbing one of the narrow streets to the Castello del Buonconsiglio, which commands an excellent view of the city and surrounding valley.

Two Nights: Bolzano (Bozen). Savor the German-Italian atmosphere of the capital of the Alto-Adige region. Make the best of the dramatic scenery and the hiking and skiing options of the nearby Dolomites. Savor the view from the plateau of the Renon.

Information See Chapters 10 and 11.

Classical Highlights

Well colonized by the ancient Greeks, then epicenter of the Roman Empire, Italy has a wealth of classical sites, many of them quite well-preserved, thanks in part to the Italian appreciation for history and heritage. Rome was, of course, the glorious capital of the Roman Empire, and a number of ancient sites remain there today, seemingly plunked down in the middle of the bustling modern metropolis. It is quite an experience to turn a corner and see a famous building, such as the Colosseum, across the street, with Fiats and Vespas buzzing blithely past its crumbling arches. Campania, too, has a number of important classical landmarks, from both the Roman and the Greek eras. Below the volcanic cone of Mount Vesuvius, the buried ruins of Pompeii are the most famous, but even better-preserved relics are still being unearthed from the lava at nearby Herculaneum. Farther down the coast is Paestum, the remains of an ancient town with both Greek and Roman buildings; some classicists enjoy uncrowded Paestum more than either Pompeii or Herculaneum.

Those with more time or a more intense interest in ancient times will want to follow this itinerary all the way to Sicily, the large island just off the toe of Italy's boot. Heavily colonized by the Greeks, Sicily was a center of trade and culture in the Hellenic world, and it still is richly endowed with remarkable sites, most notably Agrigento and Siracusa.

Length of Trip Seven to 17 days.

Getting Around On the A2 autostrada, it takes about three hours to drive from
By Car Rome to Naples. Most of the classical sites in Campania can be seen on day trips from Naples; the farthest away is Paestum, 99 kilometers (60 miles) down the coast on S18. If you choose to continue on to Sicily, take either the overnight car ferry from Naples to Palermo, Sicily, or drive down the A3 autostrada (488 kilometers/302 miles) to Villa San Giovanni in Calabria, where frequent ferry service crosses the strait in a half hour to Messina, Sicily, 235 kilometers (145 miles) east of Palermo. Sicily's main sites are spread out to every corner of the large island, so you will have to stop overnight near each site. It's a 128-kilometer (80-mile) drive south from Palermo to Agrigento, on the island's southwest coast; Seliunte is up the coast from Agrigento, along Route E931 about 90 kilometers (56 miles). Agrigento is 212 kilometers (132 miles) from Siracusa.

By Public Train service between Rome and Naples is fast and frequent,
Transportation taking less than two hours on express trains. The Circumvesuviana train line can take you conveniently from Naples to Pompeii and Herculaneum, and there is a train station right in Paestum. You can get to Palermo, Sicily, by ferry from Naples, and there is a main train line from Palermo to Siracusa. Other sites on Sicily are better reached by bus than by the unreliable local train service.

The Main Route **Two–Three Nights: Rome.** Spend at least a day exploring Ancient Rome—the Capitoline Hill, the Roman Forum, the Circus Maximus, the Colosseum, the Pantheon—and on subsequent days, venture out to the Catacombs and the Appian Way, or study classical sculptures in the Vatican museums and antiquities in the Museo Nazionale.

Three–Five Nights: Naples. After arriving from Rome, spend the afternoon at the Museo Archeologico Nazionale. Herculaneum and Pompeii can be visited in one day from Naples, though it is a full day—some travelers may want to break it into two separate excursions. On another day, enjoy an excursion down the Amalfi coast to Paestum, with its well-preserved Greek temples. An optional day can be spent touring the area just south and west of Naples, taking in the Roman amphitheater at Pozzuoli, spooky Lake Avernus, the Roman resort town at Baia with its excavated baths, and the Sibyl's Cave at Cumae, perhaps the oldest Greek colony in Italy.

One Night: Ferry to Sicily.

One Night: Palermo. Visit the National Archeological Museum and nearby Segesta, with its fine Doric Greek temple.

One–Two Nights: Agrigento. Explore the Valley of the Temples, an extensive Greek site, and if you have time, make your way up the coast to see the Greek temple complex at Seliunte.

One–Two Nights: Siracusa: Visit the Archaelogical Park in town, the splendid Archeological Museum, and, if there's time, take an excursion to the Imperial Roman Villa at Casale, just north of Piazza Amerina.

One Night (Optional): Taormina. Get a fine view of Mount Etna and see the town's Greek theater, still used for the summer arts festival.

One Night: Ferry to Naples.

One Night: Return to Rome.

Information   See Chapters 3, 14, and 16.

2 Portraits of Italy

Italy at a Glance: A Chronology

c. 1000 BC Etruscans arrive in central Italy.

c. 800 Rise of Etruscan city-states.

753 Traditional date for the founding of Rome.

750 Greek city-states begin to colonize Sicily and southern Italy.

600 Latin language becomes dominant in Etruscan League; Rome becomes established urban center.

510 Foundation of the Roman republic; expulsion of Etruscans from Roman territory.

410 Rome adopts the 12 Tables of Law, based on Greek models.

343 Roman conquest of Greek colonies in Campania.

312 Completion of Appian Way to the south of Rome; an extensive Roman road system begins to develop.

264–241 First Punic War (with Carthage): Increased naval power helps Rome gain control of southern Italy and then, Sicily.

218–200 Second Punic War: Hannibal's attempted conquest of Italy, using elephants, is eventually crushed.

176 Roman Forum begins to take shape as the principal civic center in Italy.

146 Third Punic War: Rome razes city of Carthage and emerges as the dominant Mediterranean force.

133 Rome rules entire Mediterranean Basin except Egypt.

49 Julius Caesar conquers Gaul.

45 Civil War leaves Julius Caesar as sole ruler (dictator); Caesar's Forum is established.

44 Julius Caesar is assassinated.

31 The Battle of Actium resolves the power struggle that continued after Caesar's death; Octavian becomes sole ruler.

27 Rome's Imperial Age begins; Octavian (now named Augustus) becomes the first emperor and is later deified. The Augustan Age is celebrated in the works of Virgil (70 BC–AD 19), Ovid (43 BC–AD 17), Livy (59 BC–AD 17), and Horace (65 BC–AD 27).

AD 14 Augustus dies.

29 Jesus Christ crucified in the Roman colony of Judea.

43 Rome invades Britain.

50 Rome is now the largest city in the world, with a population of a million.

65 Emperor Nero begins the persecution of Christians in the empire; saints Peter and Paul are executed.

70–80 Vespasian builds the Colosseum.

98–117   Trajan's Imperial military successes are celebrated with his Baths (98), Forum (110), and Column (113); The Roman Empire reaches its apogee.

165   A smallpox epidemic ravages the Empire.

c 200–150   Christianity gains a foothold within the Empire, with the theological writings of Clement, Tertullian, and Origen.

212   Roman citizenship is conferred on all nonslaves in the Empire.

238   The first wave of Germanic invasions penetrates Italy.

293   Diocletian reorganizes the Empire into West and East.

313   The Edict of Milan grants toleration of Christianity within the empire.

330   Constantine founds a new Imperial capital in the East (Constantinople).

410   Rome is sacked by Visigoths.

476   The last Roman Emperor, Romulus Augustus, is deposed.

552   Eastern Emperor Justinian (527–565) recovers control of Italy.

570   Lombards gain control of much of Italy, including Rome.

590   Papal power expands under Gregory the Great.

610   Heraldius revives the Eastern Empire, thereafter known as the Byzantine Empire.

774   Frankish ruler Charlemagne invades Italy under papal authority and is crowned Holy Roman Emperor by Pope Leo III (800).

c 800–900   The breakup of Charlemagne's (Carolingian) realm leads to the rise of Italian city-states.

811   Venice founded by mainlanders escaping Barbarian invasions.

1054   The Schism develops between Greek (Orthodox) and Latin churches.

c 1060   Europe's first university founded in Bologna.

1077   Pope Gregory VII leads the Holy See into conflict with the Germanic Holy Roman Empire.

1152–1190   Frederick I (Barbarossa) is crowned Holy Roman Emperor (1155); punitive expeditions by his forces (Ghibellines) are countered by the Guelphs, creators of the powerful Papal States in central Italy. Guelph-Ghibelline conflict becomes a feature of medieval life.

1204   Crusaders, led by Venetian Doge Dandolo, capture Constantinople.

1257   The first of four wars is declared between Genoa and Venice; at stake is the maritime control of the eastern Mediterranean.

1262   Florentine bankers issue Europe's first bills of exchange.

1264   Charles I of Anjou invades Italy, intervening in the continuing Guelph-Ghibelline conflict.

1275   Marco Polo reaches the Orient.

1290–1375   Tuscan literary giants Dante Alighieri (1265–1321), Francesco Petrarch (1304–74), and Giovanni Boccaccio (1313–75) form the basis of literature in the modern Italian language.

1309 The pope moves to Avignon in France, under the protection of French kings.

1355 Venetian Doge Marino Falier is executed for treason.

1376 The pope returns to Rome, but rival Avignonese popes stand in opposition, creating the Great Schism until 1417.

1380 Venice finally disposes of the Genoese threat in the Battle of Chioggia.

1402 The last German intervention into Italy is repulsed by the Lombards.

1443 Brunelleschi's dome is completed on Florence's Duomo (Cathedral).

1447 Nicholas V founds the Vatican Library. This begins an era of nepotistic popes who devalue the status of the papacy but greatly enrich the artistic and architectural patronage of the Holy City.

1469–92 Lorenzo "Il Magnifico," the Medici patron of the arts, rules in Florence.

1498 Girolamo Savonarola, the austere Dominican friar, is executed for heresy after leading Florence into a drive for moral purification, typified by his burning of books and decorations in the "Bonfire of Vanities."

1499 Leonardo da Vinci's *Last Supper* is completed in Milan.

1508 Michelangelo begins work on the Sistine Chapel.

1509 Raphael begins work on his *Stanze* in the Vatican.

1513 Machiavelli's *The Prince* is published.

1521 The Pope excommunicates Martin Luther of Germany, precipitating the Protestant Reformation.

1545–63 The Council of Trent formulates the Catholic response to the Reformation.

1546 Andrea del Palladio, architectural genius, wins his first commission in Vicenza.

1571 The combined navies of Venice, Spain, and the Papacy defeat the Turks in the Battle of Lepanto.

1626 St. Peter's is completed in Rome.

1633 Galileo Galilei faces the Inquisition.

1652 The church of Sant'Agnese, Borromini's Baroque masterpiece, is completed in Rome.

1667 St. Peter's Square, designed by Bernini, is completed.

c 1700 Opera develops as an art form in Italy.

1720–90 The Great Age of the Grand Tour. Northern Europeans visit Italy and start the vogue for classical studies. Among the famous visitors are Edward Gibbon (1758), Jacques-Louis David (1775), and Johann Wolfgang von Goethe (1786).

1778 Teatro Alla Scala is completed in Milan.

1796 Napoleon begins his Italian campaigns, annexing Rome and imprisoning Pope Pius VI four years later.

1809 Napoleon annexes papal states to France.

1815 Austria controls much of Italy after Napoleon's downfall.

1848 Revolutionary troops under Risorgimento (Unification) leaders Giuseppe Mazzini (1805–72) and Giuseppe Garibaldi (1807–82) establish a republic in Rome.

1849 French troops crush rebellion and restore Pope Pius IX.

1860 Garibaldi and his "Thousand" defeat the Bourbon rulers in Sicily and Naples.

1870 Rome finally captured by Risorgimento troops and declared capital of Italy by King Victor Emmanuel II.

1900 King Umberto I is assassinated by an anarchist; he is succeeded by King Victor Emmanuel III.

1915 Italy enters World War I on the side of the Allies.

1922 Fascist "black shirts" under Benito Mussolini march on Rome; Mussolini becomes prime minister and later "Duce" (head of Italy).

1929 The Lateran Treaty: Mussolini recognizes Vatican City as a sovereign state, and the Church recognizes Rome as the capital of Italy.

1940–44 In World War II Italy fights with the Axis powers until its capitulation (1943), when Mussolini flees Rome. Italian partisans and Allied troops from the landings at Anzio (January 1944) win victory at Cassino (March 1944) and force the eventual withdrawal of German troops from Italy.

1957 The Treaty of Rome is signed, and Italy becomes a founding member of the European Economic Community.

1966 November flood damages much of Florence's artistic treasure.

1968–1979 The growth of left-wing activities leads to the formation of the Red Brigade and provokes right-wing reactions. Bombings and kidnappings culminate in the abduction and murder of Prime Minister Aldo Moro in 1980.

1980 Southern Italy is hit by a severe earthquake.

1991 Waves of refugees from neighboring Albania flood southern ports on the Adriatic. Mont Etna erupts, spewing forth a stream of lava that eventually threatens the Sicilian town of Zafferana.

1992 The Christian Democrat Party loses its hold on a relative majority in Parliament in elections that underscore voters desire for institutional reforms.

Italian Art Through the Ages

By Sheila Brownlee

A long-time contributor to Fodor's Guides, Sheila Brownlee is an art historian who writes regularly on the arts for many publications.

Italy is the nursery of Western art. The discoveries that Italian artists made in the 14th and 15th centuries about how to render a realistic image of a person or an object determined the course of art in the Western world right up until the late 19th century, when, with the introduction of photography, representational art went out of fashion.

Art in the Middle Ages

The eastern half of the Roman Empire, based in Constantinople (Byzantium) remained powerful long after the fall of Rome in AD 476: Italy remained influenced—and at times ruled—by the Byzantines. The artistic revolution began when artists started to rebel against the Byzantine ethic, which dictated that art be exclusively Christian and that its aim be to arouse a sensation of mystical awe and reverence in the onlooker. This ethic forbade frivolous pagan portraits, bacchanalian orgy scenes, or delicate landscapes with maidens gathering flowers, as painted and sculpted by the Romans. Instead, biblical stories were depicted in richly colored mosaics—rows of figures against a gold background. (You can see some of the finest examples of this art at Ravenna, once the Western capital of the Empire, on the Adriatic coast.) Even altarpieces, painted on wood, followed the same model—stiff figures surrounded by gold, with no attempt made at an illusion of reality.

In the 13th century, the era of St. Francis and of a new humanitarian approach to Christianity, artists in Tuscany began to make an effort to portray real people in real settings. Cimabue was the first to feel his way in this direction, but it was Giotto who broke decisively with the Byzantine style. Even if his sense of perspective was nowhere near correct and his figures still had typically Byzantine slanting eyes, he was painting palpably solid people who you could tell were subject to real emotions.

By the end of the 14th century the International Gothic Style (which had arrived in Italy from France) had made further progress toward realism, but more with depictions of plants, animals, and clothes than with the human figure. And, as you can see from Gentile da Fabriano's *Adoration of the Magi*, in the Uffizi Gallery, in Florence, it was mainly a decorative art, still very much like a Byzantine mosaic.

Italian architecture during the Middle Ages followed a number of different trends. In the south, the solid Norman Romanesque style was predominant; towns such as Siena or

Pisa in central Italy had their own individual Romanesque style, more graceful than its northern European counterparts. Like northern Romanesque, it was dominated by simple geometrical forms, but buildings were covered with decorative toylike patterns done in multicolored marble. In northern Italy building was in a more solemn red brick.

In Tuscany, the region around Florence, the 13th century was a time of great political and economic growth, and there was a desire to reflect the new wealth and power in the region's buildings. This is why civic centers such as the Palazzo Vecchio in Florence are so big and fortresslike. Florence's cathedral, the Duomo, was built on a colossal scale mainly in order to outdo the Pisans and the Sienese, Florence's rivals. All these Tuscan cathedrals are in the Italian version of Gothic, a style that originated in France and found its expression there in tall, soaring, light-and-airy verticality, intended to elevate the soul. The spiritual aspect of Gothic never really caught on in Italy, where the top priority for a church (as representative of a city) was to be grander and more imposing than the neighboring cities' churches.

Art in the Renaissance

The Renaissance, or "rebirth," did not evolve simply from a set of new-found artistic skills; the movement comprised a revolution in attitudes, in which each individual was thought to have a specific role to play in the divine scheme of things. By fulfilling this role, it was believed, the individual gained a new dignity. It was no coincidence that this revolution should have taken place in Florence, which in the 15th century was an influential, wealthy, highly evolved city-state. Artists here had the leisure, the prestige, and the self-confidence to develop their talent and produce works that would reflect this new dignity and strength, as well as their own prowess.

The sculptor Donatello, for instance, wanted to astound, rather than please, the spectator with his defiant warts-and-all likenesses and their intense, heroic gazes. In painting, Masaccio's figures have a similarly assured air.

Art had changed gears in the early Renaissance: The Classical Age was now the model for a noble, moving, and realistic art. Artists studied ancient Roman ruins for what they could learn about proportion and balance. They evolved the new science of perspective and took it to its limits with sometimes bizarre results, as in Uccello's dizzily receding *Deluge* (in Florence's church of Santa Maria Novella), or his carousellike *Battle of San Romano* (in the Uffizi in Florence). One of the most frequently used perspective techniques was that of foreshortening or making an object seem smaller and more contracted, to create the illusion of distance. From this technique emerged the *Sotto in Su* effect—literally, "from below upwards," meaning that the action in the picture takes place above you, with figures, buildings, and landscapes correspondingly foreshortened. It's a clever visual trick that must have delighted the visitors who walked into, for example, Mantegna's Camero degli Sposi, in Mantua, and saw what appeared to be people looking curiously down at them through a gap in the ceiling.

The concept of the universal man was epitomized by the artist who was at home with an array of disciplines, including the science of perspective, Greek, Latin, anatomy, sculpture, poetry, architecture, philosophy—even engineering, as in the case of Leonardo da Vinci, the universal man par excellence. Not surprisingly, there was a change in attitude toward artists: Whereas previously they had been considered merely anonymous workmen trained to carry out commissions, now they were seen as giant personalities, immensely skillful, with highly individual styles.

The new skills and realistic effects of Florentine painting rapidly found a sympathetic response among Venetian painters. Gentile Bellini and Antonio Carpaccio, just two of the many whose work fills the Accademia, took to covering their canvases with crowd scenes, buildings, canals, processions, dogs, ships, parrots, chimneys. These were generally narrative paintings, telling the story of a saint's life or simply everyday scenes recording a particular event.

It was its emphasis on color, though, that made Venetian art Venetian, and it was the 15th-century masters of color, preeminently Giovanni Bellini and Giorgione, who began to use it no longer as decoration but as a means to create a particular atmosphere. Imagine how different the effect of Giorgione's *Tempest* (in the Accademia) would be with a sunny blue sky instead of the ominous grays and dark greens that fill the background. For the first time, the atmosphere, not the figures, became the central focus of the painting.

In architecture the Gothic excesses of the 13th century were toned down in the 14th, while the 15th ushered in a completely new approach. The humanist ideal was expressed through classical Roman design. In Florence, Brunelleschi used Roman columns for the Basilica of San Lorenzo; Roman-style rustication (massive rough-surfaced blocks on the exteriors) for the Pitti Palace; and Roman round arches—as opposed to pointed Gothic ones—for his Spedale degli Innocenti (Foundling Hospital), which is generally considered the first truly classical building of the Renaissance. Leon Battista Alberti's treatise on ideal proportion was even more influential as a manifesto of the Renaissance movement. Suddenly, architects had become erudite scholars, and architecture correspondingly far more earnest.

High Renaissance and Mannerism

Florence in the late 15th century, and Rome in the early 16th, (following its sack in 1527) underwent a traumatic political and religious upheaval that naturally came to be reflected in art. Classical proportion and realism no longer seemed enough. Heroism suddenly looked hollow and out of date. Tuscan artists such as Pontormo and Rosso found expression for their unease in discordant colors, elongated forms, tortured looks in staring eyes. Giambologna carved his *Hercules and the Centaur* (in Florence's Museo del Bargello) at the most agonizing moment of their battle, when Hercules bends the Centaur's back to the point where it is about to snap. This is Mannerism, a style in which optimism and self-confidence are gone. What remains is a self-conscious, stylized show of virtuosity, the effect of which is neither to please (like Gothic) nor to impress (like Renaissance art), but to disquiet. Even Bronzino's portraits are cold and unsmiling and far removed from the relaxed mood of the Renaissance portrait. By the 1530s an artistic exodus from Florence had taken place; Michelangelo had left for Rome, and Florence's golden age was over.

Venice meanwhile was following its own path. Titian's painting was a more virtuoso version of Bellini's and Giorgione's poetic style, but Titian later shifted the emphasis back to the figures, rather than the atmosphere, as the central focus of his paintings. Titian's younger contemporaries in Venice—Veronese, Tintoretto, and Bassano—wanted to make names for themselves independently of Titian. They started working on huge canvases—which gave them more freedom of movement—playing all sorts of visual games, juggling with viewpoints and perspective and using dazzlingly bright colors. This visual trickery suggests a natural parallel with the self-conscious artifice of Florentine painting of the same period, but the exuberance of these Venetian painters, and the increasingly emotional quality of their work, chiefly their mysterious and subtle use of color, always remained significantly more vital than the arid and ever more sterile products of central Italy toward the end of the 16th century.

Mannerism found a fairly precise equivalent in architecture. In Florence the rebellious younger generation (Michelangelo, Ammanati, Vasari) used the same architectural vocabulary as the Renaissance architects, but distorted it deliberately and bizarrely in a way that would have made Alberti's hair stand on end. Michelangelo's staircase at the Biblioteca Laurenziana, in Florence, for instance, spreads out like a stone fan, filling almost the entire floor space of the vestibule. Likewise, the inside walls are treated as if they were facades, though with columns and niches disproportionately large for the size of the room.

Andrea del Palladio was one of the greatest architects of the period, whose theories and elegant palaces were to be immensely influential on architecture elsewhere in Europe and as far north as England.

The 17th and 18th Centuries

In the second half of the 16th century, Italy was caught up in the Counter-Reformation. This movement was a reaction against the Protestant Reformation of the Christian church that was sweeping through Europe. The Counter-Reformation enlisted art as a weapon: an instrument for the diffusion of the Catholic faith. Artists were discouraged from expressing themselves as freely as they had before and from creating anything that was not of a religious nature. But within this religious framework, they were able to evolve a style that appealed to the senses.

The Baroque—an emotional and heroic style that lasted through most of the 17th century—was propaganda art, designed to overwhelm the masses through its visual illusion, dramatic lighting, strong colors, and violent movement. There was an element of seduction in this propaganda: The repressive religiosity of the Counter-Reformation went hand in hand with a barely disguised eroticism. The best-known example of this ambiguity is Bernini's sculpture of the *Ecstasy of Santa Teresa*, in Rome, in which the saint sinks back in what could be a swoon, of either pain or pleasure, while a smiling angel stands over her, holding an arrow in his hand. Both the painting and architecture of this period make extensive use of sensuous curves.

The cradle of the Baroque was Rome, where Pietro da Cortona and Bernini channeled their genius into spectacular, theatrical frescoes; sculptures; palaces; and churches. Rome had become the artistic center of Italy. Florence was politically and artistically dead by this time, and Venice was producing only hack imitations of Titian's and Tintoretto's paintings.

In the 18th century Venice came back into its own, and Rome was practically finished as an artistic center. Venetian artists adopted the new Rococo style, which had originated in France and was a softer, overripe version of the Baroque—a style that celebrated sensuality for its own sake, without the strength of Baroque. Although Venice was nearing the last stages of its political decline, there was still immense wealth in the city, mostly in the hands of families who wished to make the world know about it—and what better way than through vast, dazzling Rococo canvases, reassuringly stylized and removed from reality? The revival began with Sebastiano Ricci and was expertly elaborated on by Tiepolo. But it could never have taken place had there not been a return to the city's great artistic traditions. Late-16th-century color technique and expertise were drawn on and fused with what had been learned from the Baroque to create the breathtaking, magical, decadent world of the Venetian Rococo.

This was the final flowering of Venetian painting. The death of Francesco Guardi in 1793, compounded by the fall of the Republic of Venice in 1797, marked the effective end of the city's artistic life. Neoclassicism found no champion here, except for the sculptor Canova, who, in any case, did his finest work once he had left Venice. Italy had made its contribution to the world of art, and went into an inexorable decline.

The Wines of Italy

By Harry Eyres

A freelance journalist and wine writer, Harry Eyres is a regular contributor to the Time of London and the Spectator. He is a frequent visitor to Italy's wine-producing regions.

The Roman poets liked to speak of Italy as *"oenotria tellus,"* the land of wine (the phrase fits well at the end of a hexameter); Oenotria, in fact, was the old Greek name for southeast Italy. Long before those poets' time the Greeks (who colonized southern Italy from around 800 BC) and the Etruscans had established viticulture in this land, which offers, throughout its 800-mile length, so many favorable sites to the vine. In terms of quantity Italy still is the land of wine, heading the list of wine-producing countries in four years out of five; but in terms of quality, few people would think of comparing it with the world's second-largest wine producer, France.

There is a tendency to regard Italian wines as cheap and cheerful, Chianti in a wicker *fiasco* (tasting not much better than a fiasco either); sweet, frothy Lambrusco, and little more, and Italian wine exporters, who have concentrated on the bulk, cut-price end of the market, have only themselves to blame. But just as those who explore Italian cuisine find that is is far, far more than pasta in *bolognese* sauce, so those prepared to go beyond the liter bottle of cheap Valpolicella into the lesser-known names will be rewarded by some of the most exciting and varied taste experiences in the whole world of wine. They will also discover that the Italian wine industry, for so long introverted and stagnant, has been galvanized by a new, dynamically progressive, spirit.

If Italian wines have lagged far behind the French in terms of international repute, that is partly because Italy itself is such a recent creation. The regionalism of Italy is reflected in its wines: Just as a Florentine may consider him or herself a Tuscan first, an Italian very much second, so the wine of the region is considered a Chianti first, then a Tuscan wine—with the concept of Italian wine probably seeming excessively abstract and incomprehensible. The wines of each region have developed more or less independently of others. And whereas a gastronomic visit to Bordeaux, for instance, can be a severe disappointment, the wines of Italy have developed, to a greater extent than in other countries, in close association with the regional cuisine. The tough, austere red wines of Piedmont, Barolo and Barbaresco, come into their own in combination with the rich game and beef dishes of the region; Piedmont's more lowly Barbera, often harsh and rough seeming, is the perfect match for *fasoeil al furn*, the sturdy country staple of red haricot beans. The pale white Verdicchio dei Castelli de Jesi, which often seems dull and neutral, can suddenly taste deliciously fresh and crisp when drunk with seafood in an Adriatic resort like Riccione or Ancona. In Tuscany, you might progress from a simple, early-drinking Chianti Putto with a starter of *funghi porcini* (porcini mushrooms) to a more subtle aged Riserva with the main course of, say, *bistecca* (steak) *alla fiorentina*. The Romans, it seems, drink Frascati with everything, but the soft, deep yellow wine that can be such a disappointment in SoHo is perfect with, say, fettuccine Alfredo.

Given Italy's regional diversity and the legendary individualism of the Italians, it is hardly surprising that wine legislation in Italy was slow to be developed and that, to some leading producers, it still seems more of a hindrance than a help. It was only in 1963 that the system of *denominazioni di origine controllata* (DOC) was instituted, specifying more than 200 delimited areas and laying down rules about approved grape varieties, yields, and periods of aging. Even today, though, only 10%–12% of Italian wine production qualifies for DOC. A growing feeling that these rules were not sufficiently stringent led to the establishment in 1979 of another category, DOCG, standing for the same as DOC but with the addition of the word *garantita* (guaranteed). The first denominations to achieve the DOCG standard include Barolo, Barbaresco, Chianti Classico, and Brunello di Montalcino. Some of Italy's very finest wines, however, stand outside both systems of classification, which their makers—artists and individualists—consider impossibly restrictive: The 100% Cabernet Sauvignon Tuscan Sassicaia, marketed by Antinori; the fine Trentino Muller-Thurgau of Pojer i Sandri; and Volpaia's blend of Sangioveto and Mammolo, Coltassala, are all incongruously called *vini da tavola* (table wine), the lowest category of Italian wine. This does not stop them from fetching twice the price of a DOCG. The old maxim about wine, that the only true guarantee of quality is the name of a trustworthy producer, is particularly valid in Italy. In 1986 a small group of Italian wine producers committed a murderous breach of trust by boosting the alcoholic degree of certain wines with poisonous methanol; they claim that these wines were intended for distillation into industrial alcohol and not to be sold as wine. The fact was that the wines got onto the market, and 20 people lost their lives. Horrific though this incident was, two points should be made: First, that the wine concerned was of the lowest quality and, second, that none of the contaminated wine ever left Italy.

The methanol scandal has certainly had an effect on the market for Italian wine both at home and overseas. Italians are now drinking substantially less wine than previously, but they are also becoming more discriminating. Higher-quality Italian wines are also gaining ground in most of the export markets, such as the United States, Germany, and Holland; in Britain, the cheap and cheerful image is proving harder to shake off. But in the better Italian restaurants, both in Italy itself and overseas, the sight of a bottle of Chianti Classico Riserva, Barolo, or high-class white from

Friuli or Alto Adige, rather than the standard carafe of house wine, is becoming increasingly common.

This development reflects the enormous changes, the great majority of them—despite the methanol scandal—changes for the better, which have been taking place in Italian cellars and vineyards over the past 10 or 15 years. The most far-reaching change has certainly been the widespread introduction of temperature-controlled fermentation, enabling producers to make consistently clean, healthy, lively red, and especially white, wines in place of the dull, flat oxidized stuff of yesteryear. Furthermore, attention has turned to the vineyards, and to the awesome task of sorting out the myriad varieties of vine that old Oenotria had allowed to flourish, often with little control or even knowledge. A few years ago there was a rush to plant the fashionable French varieties, like Chardonnay and Cabernet Sauvignon: That has now abated somewhat, and there are encouraging signs of a return to old native varieties capable of bearing high-quality, but distinctively Italian, fruit. Arneis and Grecchetto are notable among the whites, and Sangiovese is notable among the reds. Italy's wine makers are rediscovering a pride in themselves and the potential of the old heartland of the vine.

The Wine Regions of Italy

The Northwest **Piedmont.** Together with Tuscany, Piedmont forms Italy's premier-quality wine-producing region. Its most famous wine is probably the semisweet sparkling Asti Spumante. This, as well as its slightly less fizzy brother, Moscato d'Asti, is a deliciously fresh grapey wine, which no one should feel ashamed of enjoying. Piedmont is proudest, though, of the stern tannic reds made from the Nebbiolo grape near the town of Alba: Barolo and Barbaresco. These are something of an acquired taste: First-timers might be advised to try the less austere Nebbiolo-based wines called Gattinara, Ghemme, and Spanna. They are also considerably cheaper. The two other red wines worth looking for are Barera, often rough, but delicious in the hands of a good producer, and the deep purple, softly fruity Dolcetto. Piedmont's only DOC white wine of note is the clean but somewhat neutral (and overpriced) Gavi, sometimes called Cortese di Gavi. Watch, though, for the subtle, rich Arneis (still only *vino da tavola*). Fine producers include Gaja, Pio Cesare, Ceretto, and the Conterno family.
Lombardy. Lombardy has never made much fuss about its wines, which are some of Italy's most underrated. Try the vigorious, almost Bordeaux-style, reds from Franciacorta and the fruity white Lugana from the southern shore of Lake Garda.

The Northeast **Trentino-Alto Adige.** The Alto Adige is also known as the Südtirol, a German-speaking former province of Austria consisting of high Alpine valleys. The wine-making tradition is more Germanic than Latin: Aromatic white varieties like Riesling, Gewürztraminer, and Muller-Thurgau flourish and make crisp perfumed dry whites unlike any others in Italy. Notable Chardonnays are made by producers like Lageder and Tiefenbrunner. The light red from the local Lagrein grape is worth a try. Trentino, the southern half of the area, makes similar wines, with more emphasis on red (Cabernet and an attractive Beaujolais-style local variety called Teroldego Rotaliano), a little softer and fuller in style. *Veneto*'s three most famous wines are the light reds Valpolicella and Bardolino and the crisp dry white Soave—all names tarnished by industrial mass production. Good examples can still be found: The Bardolino of Fraterna Portalupi is deliciously fresh and cherry scented; Masi's Valpolicella has a distinctive bitter tang; and the Soaves of Anselmi and Pieropan are fine and fruity. Veneto's *vino di meditazione* (to be drunk reflectively on its own) is the strong, deep, bitter Recioto Amarone della Valpolicella made from selected half-dried bunches.

Friuli-Venezia Giulia. Italy's most highly prized whites, not much seen on the export markets, are made in this eastern province bordering Yugoslavia. Pinot Bianco and Pinot Grigio give wines with great depth of fruit and richness of texture. The native Tocai makes a full dry white with an intriguingly herbaceous character. Among the reds, grassy Cabernet Franc and supple Merlot can be excellent. Jermann, Collavini, Schiopetto, and EnoFriulia are good producers.

Central Italy **Emilia-Romagna.** This is a better region for food than for wine, though Lambrusco can be dry and delicious, not just sweet and frothy.

Tuscany. This region produced the Italian red wines closest in structure to great red Bordeaux: These are the top wines of Chianti Classico, from the hill country between Florence and Siena and Brunello di Montalcino, a little farther south. It must be said that the name of Chianti was besmirched in the '60s and '70s by a lot of very dull, astringent wine sold under its appellation: The region is now going through a dynamic phase of self-regeneration. Lighter, less serious Chianti makes delicious quaffing wine; the Riservas can age for at least 10 years and acquire a fascinating complexity of flavor. Recently arrived on the scene are the so-called super-Tuscans, premium wines often made from a blend of Sangiovese and Cabernet (and therefore qualifying only as *vini da tavola*) and aged in small oak barrique. Some of the best are Sassicaia (100% Cabernet Sauvignon), Tignanello, and Coltassala. Brunello di Montalcino (DOCG) is one of Italy's most powerful (and expensive) reds: The most famous producer is Biondi-Santi, but an excellent lighter and cheaper version is made by Altesino. Another Tuscan specialty is *vin santo*, an extraordinary sweet, liquorous white made from grapes dried on straw mats and fermented over many years.

Wine Regions

HUNGARY

AUSTRIA

SWITZERLAND

FRANCE

SLOVENIA

CROATIA

BOSNIA AND HERZEGOVINA

Adriatic Sea

Ligurian Sea

Corsica

Elba

TRENTINO-ALTO ADIGE/ SOUTH TIROL

FRIULI VENEZIA GIULIA
Pinot Grigio
Pinot Bianco
Grave del Friuli
Tocai

Trieste

VENETO
Venice
Bardolino
Valpolicella
Soave
Lake Garda
Lugana
Lugana

Adige
Po

VALLE D'AOSTA
PIEDMONT
Turin
Gattinara
Spanna
Ghemme
Asti
Spumante
Alba
Asti
Gavi
Barbaresco
Barolo
Barbera
Milan
Pavia
LOMBARDY
LIGURIA
Genoa
La Spezia
Parma

EMILIA-ROMAGNA
Bologna
Ravenna
Lambrusco
Albana di Romagna
Sangiovese di Romagna
Trebbiano di Romagna
SAN MARINO

MARCHE
Verdicchio
Ancona

ABRUZZO
Pescara
Montepulciano d'Abruzzo

UMBRIA
Orvieto
Orvieto
Perugia
Tiber

TUSCANY
Florence
Chianti Classico
Vernaccia
Siena
Brunello di Montalcino
Pisa
Arno
Civitavecchia

N

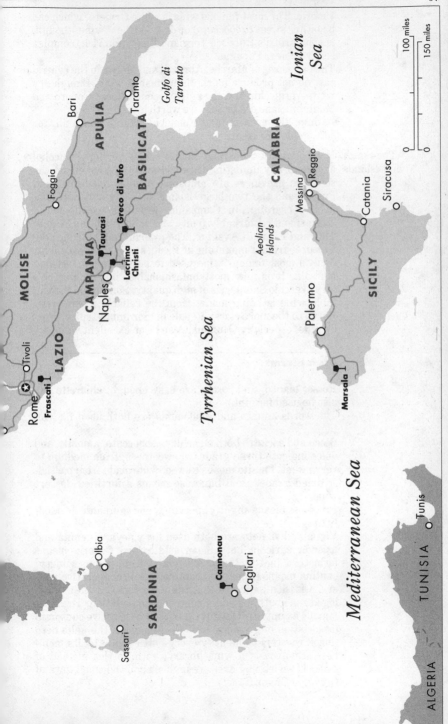

Umbria. The most famous wine is white Orvieto, which can be either sweet (*abboccato*) or dry. The best wine, though, is Lungarotti's Rubesco Torgiano Riserva: a rich, complex red from near Perugia.

The provinces of **Marche, Abruzzi,** and **Molise** in the central east do not produce much distinguished wine, though dry white Verdicchio and the sturdy reds of Rosso Conero and Montepulciano d'Abruzzo are worth investigating.

Latium, the area around Rome, is notable above all, for soft, golden Frascati.

The South and Islands Huge quantities of strong, mainly red, wine, high in alcohol and generally undistinguished in quality, pour out of the southern provinces of Campania, Apulia, Basilicata, and Puglia, and the two large islands of Sicily and Sardinia. Mastroberardini, in Campania, produces excellent red Taurasi and remarkably fruity and refined white Greco di Tufo and Fiano di Avellino. The pwerful red Aglianico del Vulture, from a mountain in Basilicata, can be excellent. Sicily's most famous wine used to be the tangy fortified Marsala. It is now most unfashionable, but de Bartoli's (dry) Vecchio Samperi is of high quality. Some good Sicilian table wine is being made, from the reliable, commercial Corvo to the more classy Regaleali. Sardinia's fruity, sturdy reds, especially Cannonau, can be an excellent value.

Useful Terms

Rosso, bianco, and **rosato** are easy enough; **chiaretto** can also be used for pink.

The words **annata** and **vendemmia** are both used for vintage.

Secco and **asciutto** both mean dry. **Abboccato, amabile,** and **dolce** indicate three grades of sweetness, from medium to very sweet. **Passito** means a sweet wine made from partially dried grapes, and **liquoroso** means a fortified dessert wine.

Frizzante means slightly sparkling, and **spumante** decidedly fizzy.

Vigna and **vigneto** are both used for vineyard; **tenuta** and **azienda agricola** both mean estate; and **fattoria** means farmstead (not factory). **Azienda vinicola** means winery, **cantina** means cellar, and **cantina sociale** cooperative winery. **Classico** indicates that the wine comes from a privileged zone within a wider controlled appellation. The most famous example is Chianti Classico, whose active **consorzio** (association of growers) uses the symbol of the **gallo nero** (black rooster) to identify every bottle made by its members. **Enoteca** is a wine library, with bottles instead of books: Two leading ones are in Siena and the small town of Greve, in Chianti.

3 Rome

From ancient times, Romans have been piling the present on top of the past, blithely building, layering, and overlapping their more than 2,500 years of history to create the haphazard fabric of modern Rome. The result is a city where antiquity is taken for granted, where you can have coffee in a square designed by Bernini and go home to a Renaissance palace. Normal life in Rome is carried on in the most extraordinary setting.

Don't be self-conscious in your wanderings about the city. Poke and pry under the surface of things. Walk boldly through gates that are just ajar to peek into the hidden world of Roman courtyards. But do it with a smile, to show the people you meet that you're truly interested in them. Warm and straightforward, the Romans are pleased to show you the nooks and crannies of their hometown.

The good-humored Romans have their problems, of course. The city is noisy, polluted, afflicted with hellish traffic, and exasperatingly inefficient. But at least the traffic problem is being tackled. Sizable areas of the city center have been designated for pedestrians only. The pollution problem is less easy to cure, and far too many of the monuments you will want to see are shielded in fine green netting, while work proceeds on cleaning and repairing them.

Keep your sightseeing flexible. You'll have to plan your day to take into account the wide diversity of opening times—which will mean mixing classical sites with Baroque, museums with parks, the center with the environs. However you do it, be sure to take plenty of time off for simply sitting and observing the passing pageant of the city's teeming streets.

Inevitably, the environs of Rome are overshadowed by the five-star attractions of the Eternal City. However, the surrounding region, known as Lazio (Latium), has plenty to offer in its own right—ancient art and archaeology, medieval hill towns and abbeys, Renaissance pleasure gardens, lake and mountain scenery, and an easygoing pace, not to mention great local wines and homemade pasta. Intersperse city sightseeing with jaunts into the countryside. A breath of country air and a change of scenery can enhance your enjoyment of Rome and give you a new perspective on its many delights.

Essential Information

Arriving and Departing by Plane

Airports and Airlines Most international (there are nonstop flights from the United States with Alitalia, Delta, and TWA), and all domestic flights arrive at **Leonardo da Vinci** airport, also known as **Fiumicino,** 30 kilometers (18 miles) outside the city. Some international charter flights land at **Ciampino,** a military airport on the Via Appia Nuova, 15 kilometers (9 miles) from the center of Rome.

Between Leonardo da Vinci Airport and Downtown
By Train An express train (FS) service connects Fiumicino airport and the Air Terminal at Ostiense Station in Rome, with departures every 20 minutes 6:30 AM–12:45 AM. The trip takes 30 minutes. At Fiumicino, tickets can be purchased (6,000 lire) from ticket machines on the arrivals level or at a ticket window near the track. After intermediate stops (Muratella, Trastevere), the train arrives at the Ostiense Air Terminal. From here you can take a

taxi (often easier to find at the Piazza Partigiani exit), a bus (there is a shuttle bus to Termini station), or walk the considerable distance (only partly served by moving sidewalks) to the Piramide Metro station, where you can take the metro (Line B) to the center of town. Centrally located hotels are a fairly short taxi ride from Ostiense air terminal.

By Taxi A taxi from the airport to the center of town costs about 60,000 lire, including supplements for airport service and luggage, and the ride takes 30–40 minutes, depending on traffic. Private limousines can be hired at booths in the arrivals hall; they charge a little more than taxis but can take more passengers. Ignore gypsy drivers; stick to yellow cabs. A booth inside the arrivals hall provides taxi information.

By Car Follow the signs for Rome on the expressway, which links with the Grande Raccordo Anulare (GRA), the beltway around Rome. The direction you take on the GRA depends on where your hotel is located, so get directions from the car-rental people at the airport.

Arriving and Departing by Car, Train, and Bus

By Car The main access routes from the north are A1 (Autostrada del Sole) from Milan and Florence or the A12/E80 highway from Genoa. The principal route to or from points south, including Naples, is the A2. All highways connect with the GRA (Grande Raccordo Anulare beltway), which channels traffic into the center. Markings on the GRA are confusing: Take time to study the route you need.

By Train Termini Station is Rome's main train terminal; the Tiburtina and Ostiense stations serve a few long-distance trains. Some trains for Pisa and Genoa leave Rome from, or pass through, the Trastevere Station. For train information, call tel. 06/4775, 7 AM–10:40 PM. You can find English-speaking staff at the information office at Termini Station, or ask for information at travel agencies. If you purchase tickets and book seat reservations in advance either at the main stations or at travel agencies bearing the FS (Ferrovie dello Stato) emblem, you'll avoid long lines at ticket windows. Tickets for train rides within a radius of 100 kilometers of Rome can also be purchased at tobacco shops.

By Bus There is no central bus terminal in Rome. Long-distance and suburban buses terminate either near Termini Station or near Metro stops. For ACOTRAL bus information, call tel. 06/591–5551, Mon.–Fri. 7 AM–6 , Sat. 7 AM–2 PM.

Getting Around

Although most of Rome's sights are in a relatively circumscribed area, the city is too large for you to be able to get around solely on foot. Take the Metro (subway), a bus, or a taxi to the area you plan to visit, and expect to do a lot of walking once you're there. Wear a pair of comfortable, sturdy shoes, preferably with rubber or crepe soles to cushion the impact of the cobblestones. Heed our advice on security and get away from the noise and polluted air of heavily trafficked streets by taking parallel streets whenever possible. You can buy transportation-route maps at newsstands and at ATAC (Rome's public transit authority) information and ticket booths. The free city map distributed by Rome EPT offices is good; it also shows

Rome Metro

Metro and bus routes, although bus routes are not always marked clearly.

By Metro This is the easiest and fastest way to get around, but it's limited in extent. The Metro opens at 5:30 AM, and the last trains leave the farthest station at 11:30 PM. The A line runs from the eastern part of the city to the Ottaviano stop, near the Vatican Museums. The fare is presently 1,000 lire. There are ticket booths at major stations, but elsewhere you must use ticket machines. It's best to buy single tickets or books of five or 10 at newsstands and tobacconists. The "BIG" daily tourist ticket, good on buses as well, costs 4,000 lire and is sold at Metro and ATAC ticket booths.

By Bus Orange ATAC city buses and two tram lines run from about 6 AM to midnight, with skeleton (*notturno*) services on main lines through the night. Remember to board at the back and exit at the middle. The fare is 1,000 lire and is valid on all ATAC bus lines for a total of 90 minutes. You must buy your ticket before boarding, and time-stamp it in the machine on the first bus you board. Tickets are sold singly at tobacconists and newsstands. A weekly tourist ticket costs 10,000 lire and is sold at ATAC booths. The BIG tourist ticket is also valid on the Metro for one day (*see above*).

By Taxi Taxis wait at stands and can also be called by phone, in which case you're charged a small supplement. The meter starts at 6,400 lire, a fixed rate for the first 3 kilometers (1.8 miles); there are supplements for service after 10 PM and on Sundays or holidays, as well as for each piece of baggage. Use only metered yellow cabs. To call a cab, dial tel. 3875, 3570, 4994, or 8433. **Radio**

Taxi (tel. 06/3875) accepts American Express and Diners Club credit cards, but you must specify when calling that you will pay that way.

By Bicycle Pedaling through Villa Borghese, along the Tiber, and through the center of the city when traffic is light is a pleasant way to see the sights, but remember: Rome is hilly. (For bicycle rentals, *see* Sports and Fitness in Exploring Rome, below.)

By Scooter You can rent a moped or scooter and mandatory helmet at **Scoot-a-Long** (Via Cavour 302, tel. 06/678–0206) or **St. Peter's Moto** (Via di Porta Castello 43, tel. 06/687–5714).

Important Addresses and Numbers

Tourist Information The main **EPT** (Rome Provincial Tourist Office) is at Via Parigi 5, tel. 06/488–3748. Open Mon.–Sat. 9–1:30, 2–7. There are also EPT booths at Termini Station and Leonardo da Vinci airport.

For information on places other than Rome, there is a booth at the **ENIT** (National Tourist Board), Via Marghera 2, tel. 06/497–1222.

Consulates **U.S. Consulate** (Via Veneto 121, tel. 06/46741). **Canadian Consulate** (Via Zara 30, tel. 06/440–3028). **U.K. Consulate** (Via Venti Settembre 80A, tel. 06/482–5441).

Emergencies **Police,** tel. 06/4686.

Ambulance (Red Cross), tel. 06/5100.

Doctors and Dentists: Call your consulate or the private Rome American Hospital (tel. 06/22551), which has English-speaking staff, for recommendations.

Late-Night Pharmacies You will find American and British products—or their equivalents—and English-speaking staff at **Farmacia Internazionale Capranica** (Piazza Capranica 96, tel. 056/679–4680), **Farmacia Internazionale Barberini** (Piazza Barberini 49, tel. 06/482–5456), and **Farmacia Doricchi** (Via Venti Settembre 47, tel. 06/487–3880), among others. Most are open 8:30–1, 4–8; some are open all night. Pharmacies take turns opening on Sundays. A schedule is posted in each pharmacy.

English-Language Bookstores English-language paperback books and magazines are available at newsstands in the center of Rome, especially on Via Veneto. For all types of books in English, you should visit the **Economy Book and Video Center** (Via Torino 136, tel. 06/474–6877), the **Anglo-American Bookstore** (Via della Vite 27, tel. 06/679–5222), or the **Lion Bookshop** (Via del Babuino 181, tel. 06/322–5837).

Travel Agencies **American Express** (Piazza di Spagna 38, tel. 06/67641), **CIT** (Piazza della Repubblica 64, tel. 06/47941), **Wagons Lits** (Via Boncompagni 25, tel. 06/481–7655).

Opening and Closing Times

Rome's churches have erratic and unpredictable opening times; they are *not* open all the time. Most are open from about 7 to 12 and 3 to 7, but don't be surprised if the church you were especially keen on seeing is closed even during these times. Many churches that are shut during the week can, however, be visited on Sundays. Appropriate dress—no shorts—is required when visiting any church.

Banks are open weekdays from 8:30 to 1:30 and 3 or 3:30 to 4 or 4:30. Shops are open Monday to Saturday, 9:30 to 1 and 3:30 or 4 to 7 or 7:30. Many are closed Monday mornings from September to June and Saturday afternoons from July to August.

Guided Tours

Orientation **American Express** (tel. 06/67641), **CIT** (tel. 06/47941), **Appian Line** (tel. 06/488–4151), and other operators offer three-hour tours in air-conditioned 60-passenger buses with English-speaking guides. There are four itineraries: "Ancient Rome" (including the Roman Forum and Colosseum), "Classic Rome" (including St. Peter's Basilica, Trevi Fountain, and the Janiculum Hill), "Christian Rome" (some major churches and the Catacombs), and "The Vatican Museums and Sistine Chapel." Most cost about 35,000 lire, but the Vatican Museums tour costs about 45,000 lire. American Express tours depart from Piazza di Spagna, and CIT from Piazza della Repubblica; Appian Line picks you up at your hotel.

American Express and other operators can provide a luxury car for up to three people, a limousine for up to seven, and a minibus for up to nine—all with English-speaking driver—but guide service is extra. A minibus costs about 360,000 lire for three hours. Almost all operators offer "Rome by Night" tours, with or without pizza or dinner and entertainment. You can book tours through travel agents.

The least-expensive organized sightseeing tour of Rome is that run by **ATAC,** the municipal bus company. Tours leave from Piazza dei Cinquecento, in front of Termini Station, last about two hours, and cost about 6,000 lire. There's no running commentary, but you're given an illustrated guide with which you can easily identify the sights. Buy tickets at the ATAC information booth in front of Termini Station. The least expensive sightseeing tours are the routes of bus no. 119 downtown, bus no. 56 across Rome to Trastevere, or the circle route of the No. 19 tram. For each, the cost is 800 lire one way.

Special-Interest You can attend a public papal audience in the Vatican or at the Pope's summer residence at Castel Gandolfo through **CIT** (tel. 06/47941), **Appian Line** (Via Barberini 109, tel. 06/488–4151), or **Carrani** Tours (Via V. E. Orlando 95, tel. 06/482–4194). A bus tour of the sights, including a stop at the Vatican for a papal audience and returning you to or near your hotel, costs about 35,000 lire. An excursion to Castel Gandolfo costs about 40,000 lire.

Tourvisa Italia (Via Marghera 32, tel. 06/445–3224) organizes boat trips on the Tiber, leaving from Ripa Grande, at Ponte Sublicio. There are spring and September excursions to Ostia Antica, with a guided visit of the excavations, that return by bus. During the summer, boats equipped with telescopes head upstream on stargazing expeditions in the late evenings, with astronomers on hand to point out the planets.

Excursions Most operators offer half-day excursions to Tivoli to see the fountains and gardens of Villa d'Este. **Appian Line's** (tel. 06/488–4151) morning tour to Tivoli includes a visit to Hadrian's Villa, with its impressive Roman ruins. Most operators also have full-day excursions to Assisi, to Pompeii, to Capri, and to Florence. **CIT** (tel. 06/47941) also offers excursions to Anzio and Nettuno; its "Etruscan Tour" takes you to some interesting old towns in the countryside northwest of Rome.

Personal Guides You can arrange for a personal guide through **American Express** (tel. 06/67641); **CIT** (tel. 06/47941); or the main **EPT Tourist Information Office** (tel. 06/488-3748).

Walking If you have a reasonable knowledge of Italian, you can take advantage of the free guided visits and walking tours organized by Rome's cultural associations and the city council for museums and monuments. These usually take place on Sunday mornings. Programs are announced in the daily newspapers.

Exploring Rome

Our exploration of Rome is divided into 10 small tours that highlight the city's major areas and attractions. We begin where Rome itself began, amid the ancient ruins, and follow with a look at the Vatican and its museums. From here, the next six tours explore the sights and places of interest to be found in various sections of central Rome, while Tour 10 takes you on a short trip outside the city walls. With the exception of Tours 2 and 3, which concentrate on the Vatican, and Tour 9, which crosses the Tiber to the Trastevere district, the nine central-Rome tours begin in or around Piazza Venezia.

At the end of the chapter are three excursions into the surrounding countryside. Although all the places we suggest visiting could be seen on a day's trip from Rome, some itineraries combine several destinations and could be broken by an overnight stop somewhere along the way, to maintain the easy pace that makes rambling through the region a pleasure. If you're driving, you'll find good roads, but you may run into pockets of local traffic in the suburbs. Try not to schedule your excursions for Sundays, when the Romans make their weekly exodus and create traffic jams on their return.

Highlights for First-time Visitors

Campidoglio (Tour 1: Ancient Rome).

Castel Sant'Angelo (Tour 2: The Vatican).

Colosseum (Tour 1: Ancient Rome).

Fountain of Trevi (Tour 5: The Spanish Steps and the Trevi Fountain).

Piazza Navona (Tour 4: Old Rome).

Roman Forum (Tour 1: Ancient Rome).

Saint Peter's (Tour 2: The Vatican).

Santa Maria Maggiore (Tour 6: Historic Churches).

Spanish Steps (Tour 5: The Spanish Steps and the Trevi Fountain).

Sistine Chapel (Tour 3: The Vatican Museums).

Tour 1: Ancient Rome

Numbers in the margin correspond to points of interest on the Rome map.

Rome, as is common knowledge, was built on seven hills. Its legendary founders, the twins Romulus and Remus, were abandoned as infants but were suckled by a she-wolf on the banks of the Tiber and adopted by a shepherd. Encouraged by the gods to build a city, the twins chose a site in 735 BC, fortifying it with a wall that has been identified by archaeologists digging on the Palatine, the first hill of Rome to be inhabited. During the building of the city, the brothers quarreled and in a fit of anger Romulus killed Remus. Excavations on the Palatine and in the Forum area have revealed hard evidence of at least some aspects of the city's legendary beginnings.

The monuments and ruins of the two most historic hills—the Capitoline and the Palatine—mark the center of ancient Rome, capital of the classical world and seat of a vast empire. The former hill held the seat of government, the Capitol, whose name is commemorated in every "capital" city in the world, as well as in government buildings, such as the Capitol in Washington, DC.

If you stand on the Capitoline and gaze out over the ruins of the Forum to the Palatine, with the Colosseum looming in the background, you can picture how Rome looked when it was the center of the known world. Imagine the Forum filled with immense, brightly painted temples. Picture the faint glow from the temple of Vesta, where the Vestal Virgins tended their sacred fire, and the glistening marble palace complex on the Palatine, its roof studded with statues, where the emperors and their retinues lived in incredible luxury. Then think of how the area looked in the Dark Ages, when Rome had sunk into malaria-ridden squalor.

The **Capitoline hill** is a good place to begin when exploring the city. Rome's first and most sacred temples stood here. The city's archives were kept in the Tabularium (hall of records), the tall, gray stone structure that forms the foundations of today's city hall, the **Palazzo Senatorio.** By the Middle Ages, the Campidoglio, as the hill was then known, had fallen into ruin. In 1537, Pope Paul III called on Michelangelo to restore it to grandeur, and the artist designed the ramp, the buildings on three sides of the **Campidoglio** Square, the slightly convex pavement and its decoration, and the pedestal for the bronze equestrian statue of Marcus Aurelius. A copy of the statue is due to go back on the pedestal; meanwhile the restored original is on view indoors in the Palazzo dei Conservatori (*see below*).

The palaces flanking Palazzo Senatorio contain two museums, the **Museo Capitolino** and the **Palazzo dei Conservatori,** whose collections were assembled in the 15th century by Pope Sixtus V, one of the earliest of the great papal patrons of the arts. Those with a taste for Roman and Greek sculpture will appreciate both museums; others may find the collections dull but the setting impressive. Many of the statues were restored by overconscientious 18th- and 19th-century collectors who added heads and limbs with considerable abandon. Originally, almost all these works were brilliantly colored and gilded. Remember that many of the works here and in Rome's other museums are copies of Greek originals. For hundreds of years, craftsmen of ancient Rome prospered by producing copies of Greek statues on order; they used a process called "pointing," by which exact copies could be made.

Portraiture, however, was one area in which the Romans outstripped the Greeks. The hundreds of Roman portrait busts in the **Museo Capitolino** are the highlight of a visit here. In the courtyard, the reclining river god is one of the "talking statues" to which citizens of ancient Rome affixed anonymous political protests and satirical barbs. The most interesting pieces, on display upstairs, include the poignant *Dying Gaul* and the delicate *Marble Faun*, which inspired novelist Nathaniel Hawthorne's tale of the same name. Then you'll come upon the rows of portrait busts, a kind of ancient *Who's Who*, though rather haphazardly labeled. Look for cruel Caracalla, vicious Nero, and haughty Marcus Aurelius.

Across the square is **Palazzo dei Conservatori** (Palace of Preserved Treasures), which contains similar treasures. The huge head and hand in the courtyard are fragments of a colossal statue of the emperor Constantine; these immense effigies were much in vogue in the later days of the Roman empire. The resplendent Salone dei Orazi e Curiazi upstairs is a ceremonial hall with a magnificent gilt ceiling, carved wooden doors, and 16th-century frescoes. Farther on, you'll see the famous *Capitoline Wolf*, a 6th-century BC Etruscan bronze; the twins were added during the Renaissance to adapt the statue to the legend of Romulus and Remus. *Museo Capitolino and Palazzo dei Conservatori, Piazza del Campidoglio, tel. 06/671–02071. Admission: 8,000 lire. Open May–Sept., Tues. 9–1:30 and 5–8, Wed.–Fri. 9–1:30, Sat. 9–1:30 and 7:30–11:30, Sun. 9–1; Oct.–Mar., Tues. and Sat. 9–1:30 and 5–8, Wed.–Fri. 9–1:30, Sun. 9–1.*

The Capitoline's church of **Aracoeli** was one of the first in the city built by the emerging Christians. It's known for Pinturicchio's 16th-century frescoes in the first chapel on the right and for a much-revered wooden figure of the Christ Child, kept in a small chapel in the sacristy.

The Campidoglio gardens offer the best view of the sprawling ruins of ancient Rome. **Caesar's Forum** lies below the garden, to the left of Palazzo Senatorio. It is the oldest of the Imperial Fora, those built by the emperors, as opposed to those built during the earlier, Republican period (6th–1st centuries BC), as part of the original Roman Forum.

Across Via dei Fori Imperiali, the broad avenue created by Premier Benito Mussolini for his triumphal parades, are, from the left, **Trajan's Column,** under which the emperor Trajan was buried, **Trajan's Forum,** with its huge semicircular market building, and the ruins of the **Forum of Augustus.**

Now turn your attention to the Roman Forum, in what was once a marshy valley between the Capitoline and Palatine hills. The shortest way down is Via San Pietro in Carcere—actually a flight of stairs descending to the church that stands over the **Mamertine Prison,** a series of gloomy, subterranean cells where Rome's vanquished enemies were finished off. Legend has it that St. Peter was held prisoner here and that he miraculously brought forth a spring of water in order to baptize his jailers. *Donation requested. Open daily 9–12:30 and 2–7:30.*

Rome

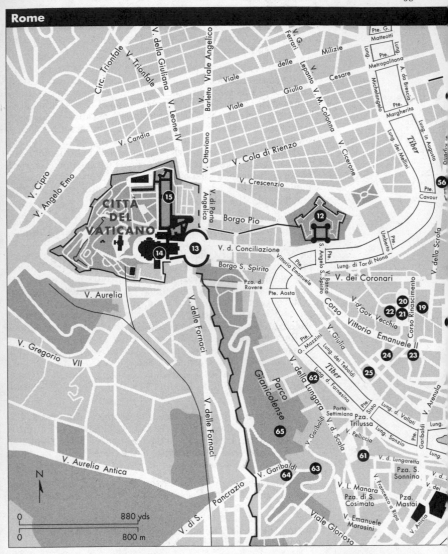

From the main entrance on Via dei Fori Imperiali, descend into
❼ the extraordinary archaeological complex that is the **Roman
Forum.** This was the civic heart of Republican Rome, the austere Rome that preceded the hedonistic society that grew up
under the emperors in the 1st to the 4th century AD. Today it
seems no more than a baffling series of ruins, marble fragments, isolated columns, a few worn arches, and occasional
paving stones. Yet it once was filled with stately and extravagant buildings—temples, palaces, shops—and crowded with
people from all corners of the world. What you see are the ruins
not of one period, but of almost 900 years, from about 500 BC to
AD 400. As the original buildings became too small or old-fashioned, they were pulled down and replaced by more lavish
structures. Making sense of these scarred and pitted stones is
not easy; you may want just to wander along, letting your imagination dwell on Julius Caesar, Cicero, and Mark Antony, who
delivered the funeral address in Caesar's honor from the rostrum just left of the Arch of Septimius Severus. *Entrances on
Via dei Fori Imperiali, Piazza Santa Maria Nova, and Via di
San Gregorio, tel. 06/699–0110. Admission: 10,000 lire. Open
Apr.–Sept., Mon., Wed.–Sat. 9–6, Tues. and Sun. 9–1; Oct.–
Mar., Mon., Wed.–Sat, 9–4, Sun. 9–1.*

Leave the Forum by the exit at Arco Tito (Arch of Titus), which
is at the end of the Forum away from the Capitoline. From
here, the Clivus Palatinus walkway leads up the Palatine hill,
where the emperors built their palaces. From the belvedere
❽ you can see the **Circus Maximus,** where more than 300,000 spectators could watch chariot and horse races while the emperors
looked on from this very spot. The Italian garden on the Palatine was laid out during the Renaissance. Leaving the Palatine
by way of the Via di San Gregorio exit, you'll pass the imposing
❾ **Arch of Constantine,** erected in AD 315 to commemorate
Constantine's victory over Maxentius at the Milvian bridge.

❿ Just beyond is the **Colosseum,** the most famous monument of
ancient Rome. Begun by the Flavian emperor Vespasian in AD
72, it was inaugurated by Titus eight years later with a program of games and shows lasting 100 days. On the opening day
alone, 5,000 wild beasts perished in the arena. Its 573-yard circumference could contain more than 50,000 spectators. It was
faced with marble and boasted an ingenious system of awnings
to shade spectators from the sun. Originally known as the
Flavian Amphitheater, in later centuries it came to be called
the Colosseum, after a colossal gilded bronze statue of Nero
that stood nearby. It served as a fortress during the 13th century and then as a quarry from which materials were filched to
build sumptuous Renaissance churches and palaces. Finally it
was declared sacred by the popes, in memory of the many
Christians believed martyred there. If you pay admission to
the upper levels, you can see a scale model of the Colosseum as
it was in its heyday. *Piazza del Colosseo, tel. 06/700–4261. Admission free; admission to upper levels: 6,000 lire. Open Mon.,
Tues., Thurs.–Sat. 9–one hour before sunset, Wed. and Sun.
9–1.*

Behind the Colosseum at the Colle Oppio (Oppian Hill) on the
Esquiline Hill, you can see what's left of Nero's fabulous
⓫ **Domus Aurea,** a sumptuous palace later buried under Trajan's
Baths.

Time Out Facing the Colosseum, the appropriately named **Il Gladiatore** is a handy place for a moderately priced lunch. *Piazza del Colosseo. Closed Wed.*

If you head back toward Piazza Venezia on Via dei Fori Imperiale, you can get a good look at the Imperial Fora and Trajan's Market.

Tour 2: The Vatican

While the ancient Roman emperors presided over the decline of their empire, a vibrant new force emerged. Christianity came to Rome, the seat of the popes was established over the tomb of St. Peter, and the Vatican became the spiritual focus of the Roman Catholic Church. There are two principal reasons for seeing the Vatican. One is to visit St. Peter's, the largest church in the world and the most overwhelming architectural achievement of the Renaissance. The other is to visit the Vatican Museums—which contain collections of staggering richness and diversity—including, of course, the Sistine Chapel. There's little point in trying to take it all in on just one visit. See St. Peter's first, and come back later to see the Vatican Museums.

⑫ Start at **Castel Sant'Angelo,** the fortress that guarded the Vatican for hundreds of years. One of Rome's most beautiful bridges, **Ponte Sant'Angelo,** spans the Tiber in front of the fortress and is studded with graceful angels designed by Giovanni Lorenzo Bernini (1598–1680). The distinctive silhouette of Castel Sant'Angelo is a throwback to its original function; it was built as a mausoleum, or tomb, for the Emperor Hadrian in AD 135. By the 6th century, it had been transformed into a fortress, and it remained the military stronghold of Rome and a refuge for the popes for almost 1,000 years.

According to legend, the castle got its name during the plague of 590, when Pope Gregory the Great, passing by in a religious procession, had a vision of an angel sheathing its sword atop the stone ramparts. He interpreted this as a sign that the plague would end immediately, and, after it did, he had a chapel built on the highest level of the fortress, where he had seen the angel. Visit the lower levels, the base of Hadrian's mausoleum, and then climb ancient ramps and narrow staircases, to explore the castle's courtyards and frescoed halls; the collection of antique arms and armor; and the open loggia, where there's a café. Climb to the upper terraces for views of the city's rooftops and the lower bastions of the castle, as well as the Passetto, the fortified corridor connecting Castel Sant'Angelo with the Vatican. *Lungotevere Castello 50, tel. 06/687–5036. Admission: 8,000 lire. Open Apr.–Sept., usually Mon.–Sat. 9–7, though hours vary from year to year; Oct.–Mar., Mon. 2–7, Tues.–Sat. 9–1, Sun. 9–noon.*

From Castel Sant'Angelo, turn right onto Via della Conciliazione, a broad, rather soulless avenue conceived by Mussolini in the 1930s to celebrate the "conciliation" between the Vatican and the Italian government under the Lateran Pact of 1929. The pact ended 60 years of papal protest against the state. (After Italian troops wrested control of Rome from the pope in 1870 to make it the capital of a newly united Italy, the popes refused to leave the Vatican or recognize the new state.)

The Via della Conciliazione approach to St. Peter's gives your eye time to adjust to the enormous dimensions of the square and the church, although the intent of Baroque artist Bernini, who designed the square, was to surprise the visitor emerging suddenly from shadowy alleys into the square's immense space and full light. The **Piazza di San Pietro** (St. Peter's Square) is one of Bernini's masterpieces, completed after 11 years' work—a relatively short time in those days, considering the vastness of the job. The square can hold as many as 400,000 people and is surrounded by a pair of quadruple colonnades, topped by a balustrade and 140 statues of saints. Look for the two stone disks set into the pavement on each side of the obelisk, between the obelisk and the fountains. If you stand on one disk, a trick of perspective makes the colonnades seem to consist of a single row of columns.

The history of **St. Peter's** goes back to the year AD 319, when the Emperor Constantine built a basilica here over the site of the tomb of St. Peter. The original church stood for more than 1,000 years, undergoing a number of restorations, until it threatened to collapse. Reconstruction began in 1452 but was soon abandoned due to a lack of funds. In 1506 Pope Julius II instructed the architect Donato Bramante (1444–1514) to raze the existing structure and build a new and greater basilica, but it wasn't until 1626 that the new church was completed and dedicated. Five of Italy's greatest Renaissance artists died while working on it—Bramante, Raphael, Peruzzi, Antonio Sangallo the Younger, and Michelangelo. Bramante outlined a basic plan for the church and built the massive pillars that were to support the dome. After his death in 1514, his successors made little progress with the work and altered his master plan. In 1546 Pope Paul III more or less forced the aging Michelangelo to take on the job of completing the building. Michelangelo returned to Bramante's ground plan and designed the dome to cover the crossing, but his plans, too, were modified after his death. The result is nevertheless breathtaking. As you approach the church, look at the people going in and out of the portico, and note the contrast between their size and the immense scale of the building. Persons wearing shorts, miniskirts, sleeveless T-shirts, or other revealing clothing are not allowed entrance to St. Peter's or the Vatican Museums. Women should carry scarves to cover their bare upper arms.

Now climb the broad steps yourself and enter the portico. Notice Filarete's 15th-century bronze doors, salvaged from the old basilica. Once inside, pause a moment to consider the size of this immense temple. Look at the massive pillars, the holy-water stoups borne by colossal cherubs, the distance to the main altar. Look for the brass inscriptions in the marble pavement along the center of the nave (the long central section), indicating the approximate length of the world's principal Christian churches, all of which fall far short of St. Peter's. The chapel immediately to your right holds Michelangelo's *Pietà*, one of the world's most famous statues. It is now screened behind shatterproof glass, after a serious incident of vandalism; it was masterfully restored in the Vatican's workshops. This is the only sculpture ever signed by Michelangelo. (Look for the signature on one of the left-arm folds of the Virgin's clothing.) The story goes that he completed the work unsigned but stole back to sign it when he was told that others might take credit for it.

Four massive piers support the dome at the crossing, where the mighty Bernini *baldacchino* (canopy), made of bronze stripped from the Pantheon by order of the Barberini Pope Urban VIII, rises high above the papal altar. The pope celebrates mass here, over the crypt holding the tombs of many of his predecessors. Deep in the earth under the foundations of the original basilica is what is believed to be the tomb of St. Peter. A very old bronze statue of the saint stands at the last pillar on the right before the crossing, its foot worn and burnished by the kisses of the faithful over the centuries. Beautiful bronze vigil lights flicker around the ceremonial entrance to the crypt in front of the papal altar. In the niche below is an antique casket containing the *pallia* (bands of white wool conferred by the pope on archbishops as a sign of authority). The splendid gilt-bronze throne above the altar in the apse was designed by Bernini and contains a wooden-and-ivory chair that St. Peter was supposed to have used, though in fact it dates back no further than the Middle Ages. You can see a copy of the chair in the Treasury. Stroll up and down the aisles and transepts, noting the wealth of art works in mosaic, marble, bronze, and stucco.

Stop in to see the small collection of Vatican treasures in the little **museum** in the sacristy, among them priceless antique chalices and the massive 15th-century bronze tomb of Pope Sixtus V by Antonio Pollaiuolo (1429–98). *Admission: 3,000 lire. Open Apr.–Sept., daily 9–6:30; Oct.–Mar., daily 9–5:30.*

Take the elevator or climb the stairs from the entrance near the right crossing to the **roof** of the church, an interesting landscape of domes and towers. From here, climb a short interior staircase to the base of the dome for a dove's-eye view of the interior of the church. It's a taxing climb to the lantern—the architectural term for the delicate structure crowning the dome; the stairs are steep and narrow and one-way only, so there's no turning back. Those who make it are rewarded with views embracing the Vatican gardens and all Rome. *Entrance to roof and dome between Gregorian Chapel and right crossing. Admission: 5,000 lire if you use the elevator to the roof, 4,000 if you use the stairs. Open Apr.–Sept., daily 8–6; Oct.–Mar., daily 8–5.*

Finally, go from the heights to the depths and visit the **crypt** to see the tombs of the popes. The only exit from the crypt leads outside St. Peter's, so leave this for last. *Entrance at St. Longinus Pier but alternatively at one of the other piers. Admission free. Open Apr.–Sept., daily 7–6; Oct.–Mar., daily 7–5.*

For many, a **papal audience** is a highlight of a trip to Rome. The pope holds mass audiences on Wednesday mornings at about 11, and at 10 in the hottest months. During winter and summer, audiences take place in a modern audience hall. In spring and fall they may be held in St. Peter's Square and in summer sometimes at the papal residence at Castel Gandolfo. You must apply for tickets in advance; you may find it easier to arrange for them through a travel agency. Of course, you can avoid the formalities by seeing the pope when he makes his weekly appearance at the window of the Vatican Palace, every Sunday at noon when he is in Rome. He addresses the crowd and gives a blessing. *For audience tickets, apply in writing well in advance, or go to the Papal* (Prefettura) *Prefecture through the bronze door in the right-hand colonnade, tel. 06/6982. Open Mon., Tues., and Thurs.–Sat. 9–1, Wed. 9 until shortly before* *the audience commences, though last-minute tickets may not be available. You can also pick up free tickets at the office of the North American College, Via dell'Umiltà 30, tel. 06/678–9184, or through Santa Susanna American Church, Piazza San Bernardo, tel. 06/482–7510. For a fee, travel agencies make arrangements* (see *Guided Tours in Essential Information,* above).

Tour 3: The Vatican Museums

The Vatican Palace, which has been the residence of the popes on and off since 1377, is made up of several interlocking buildings containing 1,400 rooms, chapels, and galleries. The pope and his household occupy only a small part of the palace, most of which is given over to the Vatican Library and Museums. There is bus service between Piazza San Pietro and a secondary entrance to the museums; it takes a route through the Vatican gardens and costs 2,000 lire. The main entrance is a long walk from the Piazza. The bus service takes you to a side entrance and saves a lot of walking, while giving you the chance to see some of Vatican City that would be off-limits otherwise. *Service 8:45–12:45 on the half-hour, except Sun. and Wed.*

Time Out The street of Borgo Pio, a block or two from St. Peter's Square, has several trattorias offering tourist menus for about 15,000 lire. For about 18,000 lire you can have a simple à la carte meal at **La Casareccia,** which also serves pizza for lunch. *Borgo Pio 40. Closed Thurs.*

⑮ The collections of the **Vatican Museums** are immense, covering about 4½ miles of displays. Special posters at the entrance and throughout the museum plot a choice of four color-coded itineraries, the shortest taking approximately 90 minutes and the longest five hours. You can rent a taped commentary in English, explaining the Sistine Chapel and the Raphael Rooms. You're free to photograph what you like, although if you want to use a flash, tripod, or other special equipment, you have to get permission. The main entrance is on Viale Vaticano and can be reached by the No. 49 bus from Piazza Cavour, which stops right in front; on foot from the No. 81 bus or No. 19 tram, which stop at Piazza Risorgimento; or from the Ottaviano metro line A stop. Pick up a leaflet at the main entrance to the museums in order to see the overall layout. The Sistine Chapel, the main attraction for most visitors, is at the far end of the complex, and the leaflet charts two abbreviated itineraries through other collections to reach it. It would be a shame to miss the collections en route to the Sistine Chapel, and below we give some of the highlights, whether or not you follow the itineraries suggested by the curators. *Viale Vaticano, tel. 06/698–3333. Admission: 10,000 lire; free on last Sun. of month. Open Easter week and July–Sept., weekdays 8:45–5 (no admission after 4), Sat. 8:45–2; Oct.–June (except Easter) Mon.–Sat. 9–2 (no admission after 1). Closed Sun. year-round, except last Sun. of month (open 9–2, admission free), and on religious holidays: Jan. 1, Jan. 6, Feb. 11, Mar. 19, Easter Sun. and Mon., May 1, Ascension Thurs., Corpus Christi, June 29, Aug. 15–16, Nov. 1, Dec. 8, Dec. 25–26.*

Among Vatican City's many riches, probably the single most important is the Sistine Chapel. However, unless you're following one of the two abbreviated itineraries, you'll begin your visit at the **Egyptian Museum** and go on to the **Chiaramonti** and **Pio Clementino Museums,** which are given over to classical sculptures (among them some of the best-known statues in the world—the *Laocoön*, the *Belvedere Torso*, and the *Apollo Belvedere*—works that, with their vibrant humanism, had a tremendous impact on Renaissance art). Next come the **Etruscan Museum** and three other sections of limited interest. All itineraries merge in the **Candelabra Gallery** and proceed through the **Tapestry Gallery,** which is hung with magnificent tapestries executed from Raphael's designs.

The **Gallery of Maps** is intriguing; the **Apartment of Pius V,** a little less so. After them you'll enter the **Raphael Rooms,** second only to the Sistine Chapel in artistic interest. In 1508, Pope Julius II employed Raffaelo Sanzio, on the recommendation of Bramante, to decorate the rooms with biblical scenes. The result was a Renaissance masterpiece. Of the four rooms, the second and third were decorated mainly by Raphael; the others, by Giulio Romano and other assistants of Raphael. The lovely Loggia (covered balcony) was designed and frescoed by the master himself. Next you pass through the Chiaroscuro Room to the tiny **Chapel of Nicholas V,** aglow with frescoes by Fra Angelico (1387–1455), the Florentine monk whose sensitive paintings were guiding lights for the Renaissance. If your itinerary takes you to the **Borgia Apartments,** you'll see their elaborately painted ceilings, designed and partially executed by Pinturicchio (1454–1513). The Borgia Apartments have been given over to the Vatican's large, but not particularly interesting, collection of modern religious art, which continues at a lower level. Once you've seen the Borgia Rooms, you can skip the rest in good conscience and get on to the Sistine Chapel.

In 1508, while Raphael was put to work on his series of rooms, Pope Julius II commissioned Michelangelo to fresco the more than 10,000 square feet of the **Sistine Chapel** ceiling singlehandedly. The task took four years of mental and physical anguish. It's said that for years afterward Michelangelo couldn't read anything without holding it up over his head. The result, however, was the masterpiece that you can now see, its colors cool and brilliant after recent restoration. Bring a pair of binoculars to get a better look at this incredible work, and if you want to have some leisure to study it, try to beat the tour groups by getting there early in the day. Some 20 years after completing the ceiling, Michelangelo was commissioned to paint the *Last Judgment* on the wall over the altar. The aged and embittered artist painted his own face on the wrinkled human skin in the hand of St. Bartholomew, below and to the right of the figure of Christ, which he clearly modeled on the *Apollo Belvedere*. The restoration of the fresco should be completed sometime in 1993.

After this experience, which can be marred by the crowds of tourists, you pass through some of the exhibition halls of the **Vatican Library.** Look in on Room X, Room of the Aldobrandini Marriage, to see its beautiful Roman frescoes of a nuptial rite. You can see more classical statues in the new wing and then, perhaps after taking a break at the cafeteria, go on to the **Pinacoteca** (Picture Gallery). It displays mainly religious paintings by such artists as Giotto, Fra Angelico, and Filippo Lippi. The **Raphael Room** holds his exceptional *Transfiguration*, *Coronation*, and *Foligno Madonna*.

In the **Pagan Antiquities Museum,** modern display techniques enhance another collection of Greek and Roman sculptures. The **Christian Antiquities Museum** has early-Christian and medieval art, while the **Ethnological Museum** shows art and artifacts from exotic places throughout the world. The complete itinerary ends with the **Historical Museum**'s collection of carriages, uniforms, and arms.

In all, the Vatican Museums offer a staggering excursion into the realms of art and history. It's foolhardy to try to see all the collections in one day, and it's doubtful that anyone could be fervidly interested in everything on display. Simply aim for an overall impression of the artistic riches and cultural significance of the Vatican collections. If you want to delve deeper, you can come back another day.

Time Out Try the good neighborhood trattorias that are far better and far less popular with tourists than those opposite the Vatican Museum entrance. At **Hostaria Tonino** (Via Leone IV 60, closed Sun.), you can dine on typical Roman fare at moderate, even inexpensive, prices. On Piazza Risorgimento, look for the simple trattoria with the long name: **La Mejo Pastasciutta der Monno** for great inexpensive pasta dishes (Piazza Risorgimento 5, closed Mon.).

Tour 4: Old Rome

A district of narrow streets with curious names, airy Baroque piazzas, and picturesque courtyards, Old Rome *(Vecchia Roma)* occupies the horn of land that pushes the Tiber westward toward the Vatican. It has been an integral part of the city since ancient times, and its position between the Vatican and the Lateran palaces, both seats of papal rule, put it in the mainstream of Rome's development from the Middle Ages onward. Today it's full of old artisans' workshops, trendy cafés and eating places, and offbeat boutiques. On weekends and summer evenings Old Rome is a magnet for crowds of young people.

🔟 Start at Piazza Venezia and take Via del Plebiscito to the huge Baroque **Il Gesù,** comparable only with St. Peter's for sheer grandeur. Inside it's encrusted with gold and precious marbles and topped by a fantastically painted ceiling that flows down over the pillars to become three-dimensional, merging with painted stucco figures in a swirling composition glorifying the Jesuit order. Then head for nearby Piazza della Minerva to see

🔟 the church of **Santa Maria Sopra Minerva,** a Gothic church with some beautiful frescoes, in a side chapel, by Filippo Lippi (1406–69), the monk who taught Botticelli. The tomb of another great artist-monk, Fra Angelico (c.1400–1455), stands to the left of the altar. Bernini's charming elephant bearing an obelisk stands in the center of the piazza.

🔟 The huge brick building opposite is the **Pantheon,** one of the most harmonious and best-preserved monuments of antiquity. It was first erected in 27 BC by Augustus's general Agrippa and completely redesigned and rebuilt by Hadrian, who deserves the credit for this fantastic feat of construction. At its apex, the dome is exactly as tall as the walls, so that you could imagine it as the upper half of a sphere resting on the floor; this balance gives the building a serene majesty. The bronze doors are the original ones; most of the other decorations of gilt bronze and marble that covered the dome and walls were plundered by later Roman emperors and by the popes. The Pantheon gets light and air from the apex of the dome—another impressive feature of this remarkable edifice. *Piazza della Rotonda. Admission free. Open Oct.–June, Mon.–Sat. 9–5, Sun. 9–1; July–Sept., daily 9–6.*

Time Out The café scene in the square in front of the Pantheon rivals that of nearby Piazza Navona. The area is ice-cream heaven, with some of Rome's best *gelaterie* (ice-cream parlors) within a few steps of one another. Romans consider **Giolitti** superlative and take the counter by storm. Remember to pay the cashier first and hand the stub to the man at the counter when you order your cone. Giolitti has a good snack counter, too. *Via Uffizi del Vicario 40. Closed Mon.*

From Piazza della Rotonda in front of the Pantheon, take Via ⑲ Giustiniani onto Via della Dogana Vecchia to the church of **San Luigi dei Francesi.** In the last chapel on the left are three stunning works by Caravaggio (1571–1610), the master of the heightened approach to light and dark. A light machine (operated with a couple of 100-lire coins) provides illumination to view the paintings. *Open Fri.–Wed. 7:30–12:30 and 3:30–7, Thurs. 7:30–12:30.*

In the church of **Sant'Agostino,** close by (Piazza di Sant'Agostino), there is another Caravaggio over the first altar on the ⑳ left. Just beyond these churches is **Piazza Navona,** a beautiful Baroque piazza that stands over the oval of Emperor Domitian's stadium. It still has the carefree air of the days when it was the scene of Roman circus games, medieval jousts, and 17th-century carnivals. Bernini's splashing **Fountain of the** ㉑ **Four Rivers,** with an enormous rock squared off by statues representing the four corners of the world, makes a fitting center- ㉒ piece. Behind it stands the church of **Sant' Agnese in Agone.** Its Baroque facade is by Francesco Borromini (1599–1667), a contemporary and sometime rival of Bernini. One story has it that the Bernini statue nearest the church is hiding its head because it can't bear to look upon the inferior Borromini facade; in fact, the facade was built after the fountain, and the statue hides its head because it represents the Nile River, whose source was unknown until fairly recently.

Time Out The sidewalk tables of the **Tre Scalini** café offer a grandstand view of the piazza. This is the place that invented the *tartufo,* a luscious chocolate ice-cream specialty. *Piazza Navona 30. Closed Wed.*

If you leave Piazza Navona by way of the Corsia Agonalis, midway along you'll see the 17th-century **Palazzo Madama,** now the Senate, on Corso Rinascimento. To the right, at the end of ㉓ the street, the huge church of **Sant' Andrea della Valle** looms mightily over a busy intersection. Puccini set the first act of his opera *Tosca* here.

㉔ Now make your way through side streets to **Campo dei Fiori.** Once the scene of public executions (including that of philosopher-monk Giordano Bruno, whose statue broods in the center), it now holds one of Rome's busiest, most colorful morning markets.

Continue on to Piazza Farnese, where Michelangelo had a hand
㉕ in building **Palazzo Farnese,** now the French Embassy and perhaps the most beautiful of the Renaissance palaces in Rome.
The twin fountains in the piazza are made with basins of Egyptian granite from the Baths of Caracalla. Behind Palazzo Farnese, turn onto Via Giulia, where you'll see some elegant
palaces (step inside the portals to take a look at the courtyards), old churches, and a number of antiques shops.

Tour 5: The Spanish Steps and the Trevi Fountain

The walk up the Corso from Piazza Venezia takes you to Rome's
classiest shopping streets and to two visual extravaganzas: the
Spanish Steps and the Fountain of Trevi.

㉖ Start at the **Vittorio Emanuele Monument** in Piazza Venezia.
Rome's most flamboyant landmark, it was erected in the late
19th century to honor Italy's first king, Vittorio Emanuele II,
and the unification of Italy. This vast marble monument, said to
resemble a wedding cake or a Victorian typewriter, houses the
Tomb of the Unknown Soldier, with its eternal flame. Although
the monument has been closed to the public for many years,
plans are in the works to reopen it; the views from the top of the
steps are among Rome's best.

㉗ On the left, as you look up Via del Corso, is **Palazzo Venezia,** a
blend of medieval solidity and Renaissance grace. It contains a
good collection of paintings, sculptures, and *objets d'art* in
handsome salons, some of which Mussolini used as his offices.
Notice the balcony over the main portal, from which Il Duce ad-
dressed huge crowds in the square below. *Via del Plebiscito
118, tel. 06/679–8865. Admission: 8,000 lire. Open Mon.–Sat.
9–2, Sun. 9–1.*

Along the Corso you'll pass some fine old palaces and a church
㉘ or two. Make a detour to the left to see the church of **Sant'
Ignazio,** where what seems to be the dome is really an illusion-
ist canvas. Put some coins in the light machine to illuminate the
dazzling frescoes on the vault of the nave. Next you'll come to
㉙ Piazza Colonna, named for the ancient **Column of Marcus Aurelius,** with its extraordinarily detailed reliefs spiraling up to the
top.

Time Out **Alfio,** on the corner of Via Bergamaschi, is popular for a stand-
up lunch of sandwiches at the counter or a more relaxing meal
in the upstairs dining room. *Via Della Colonna Antonina 33.
Closed Sun.*

From Largo Goldoni, on Via del Corso, you get a head-on view
of the Spanish Steps and the church of Trinità dei Monti as you
start up Via Condotti, an elegant and expensive shopping
street. Look for the historic **Caffè Greco** on the left. More than
200 years old, it was the haunt of Goethe, Byron, and Liszt; now
it's a hangout for well-dressed ladies carrying Gucci shopping
bags.

㉚ Piazza di Spagna and the **Spanish Steps** get their names from
the Spanish Embassy to the Holy See (the Vatican), opposite
the American Express office, though they were built with
French funds. This was once the core of Rome's bohemian quarter, especially favored by American and British artists and
writers in the 18th and 19th centuries. At the center of the

③① square is Bernini's **Fountain of the Barcaccia** (the Old Boat), and just to the right of the steps is the house where Keats and Shelley lived. Sloping upward in broad curves, the Spanish Steps are perfect for socializing, and they draw huge crowds on weekend and holiday afternoons. From mid-April to early May, the steps are blanketed with azaleas in bloom.

Time Out **La Rampa,** in a corner of Piazza Mignanelli, behind the American Express office, is a picturesque place for lunch, with an extensive menu of moderately priced dishes. *Piazza Mignanelli 18. Closed Sun.*

From the narrow end of the piazza, take Via Propaganda Fide to Sant'Andrea delle Fratte, swerving left on Via del Nazareno, then crossing busy Via del Tritone to Via della ③② Stamperia. This street leads to the **Fountain of Trevi,** one of Rome's most spectacular fountains when it's gushing. It was featured in the 1954 film *Three Coins in the Fountain.* And legend has it that you can ensure your return to Rome by tossing a coin in the fountain. Unfortunately, legend doesn't tell you how to cope with the souvenir vendors and aggressive beggars who are looking for a share of your change.

Tour 6: Historic Churches

Three churches are the highlights of this walk, two of them major basilicas with roots in the early centuries of Christianity. Not far from Piazza Venezia and the Roman Forum off Via Ca-
③③ vour is the church of **San Pietro in Vincoli.** Look for Via San Francesco da Paola, a street staircase that passes under the old Borgia palace and leads to the square in front of the church. Inside the church are St. Peter's chains (under the altar) and Michelangelo's *Moses,* a powerful statue almost as famed as his frescoes in the Sistine Chapel. The *Moses* was destined for the tomb of Julius II, but Michelangelo was driven to distraction by the interference of Pope Julius and his successors, and the tomb was never finished. The statue of Moses, intended as part of the tomb, is a remarkable sculpture and a big tourist attraction. Crass commercialism has ruined the starkly majestic effect of this memorial: The church is usually jammed with tour groups, and the monument itself is a front for a large and ugly souvenir shop.

③④ Continue along Via Cavour to **Santa Maria Maggiore,** one of the oldest and most beautiful churches in Rome. Built on the spot where a 3rd-century pope witnessed a miraculous midsummer snowfall, it is resplendent with gleaming mosaics—those on the arch in front of the main altar date back to the 5th century; the apse mosaic dates to the 13th century—and an opulent carved wood ceiling supposed to have been gilded with the first gold brought from the New World. Urgently needed restoration may continue into 1993, hiding some of the interior from view.

③⑤ Via Merulana runs straight as an arrow from Santa Maria Maggiore to the immense cathedral of Rome, **San Giovanni in Laterano,** where the early popes once lived and where the present pope still officiates in his capacity as Rome's bishop. The towering facade and Borromini's cool Baroque interior emphasize the majesty of its proportions.

The adjoining **Lateran Palace,** once the popes' official residence and still technically part of the Vatican, now houses the offices of the Rome Diocese and the **Vatican Historical Museum** (admission 6,000 lire; open first Sun. of each month, 8:45–1). Across the street, opposite the Lateran Palace, a small build-

36 ing houses the **Scala Santa** (Holy Stairs), claimed to be the staircase from Pilate's palace in Jerusalem. Circle the palace to see the 6th-century octagonal **Baptistery of San Giovanni,** forerunner of many similar buildings throughout Italy, and Rome's oldest and tallest obelisk, brought from Thebes and dating to the 15th century BC.

37 One more church awaits you just down Via Carlo Felice. **Santa Croce in Gerusalemme,** with a pretty Rococo facade and Baroque interior, shelters what are believed to be relics of the True Cross found by St. Helena, mother of the Emperor Constantine and a tireless collector of holy objects.

Tour 7: The Quirinale and Piazza della Repubblica

Although this tour takes you from ancient Roman sculptures to Early Christian churches, it's mainly an excursion into the 16th and 17th centuries, when Baroque art—and Bernini—triumphed in Rome. The **Quirinale** is the highest of Rome's seven original hills (the others are the Capitoline, Palatine, Esquiline, Viminal, Celian, and Aventine) and the one where ancient Romans and later the popes built their residences in order to escape the deadly miasmas and the malaria of the low-lying

38 area around the Forum. **Palazzo del Quirinale,** the largest on the square, belonged first to the popes, then to Italy's kings, and is now the official residence of the nation's president. The fountain in the square boasts ancient statues of Castor and Pollux reining in their unruly steeds and a basin salvaged from the Roman Forum.

Along Via del Quirinale (which soon becomes Via XX Settembre) are two interesting little churches, each an archi-

39 tectural gem. The first you'll come upon is **Sant' Andrea,** a small but imposing Baroque church designed and decorated by Bernini, who considered it one of his finest works and liked to come here occasionally just to sit and enjoy it. The second is the

40 church of **San Carlo alle Quattro Fontane** (Four Fountains) at the intersection. It was designed by Bernini's rival, Borromini, who created a building that is an intricate exercise in geometric perfection, all curves and movement.

Turn left down Via delle Quattro Fontane to a splendid 17th-

41 century palace, **Palazzo Barberini.** Inside, the **Galleria Nazionale** offers some fine works by Raphael (the *Fornarina*) and Caravaggio and a salon with gorgeous ceiling frescoes by Pietro da Cortona. Upstairs, don't miss the charming suite of rooms decorated in 18th-century fashion. *Via delle Quattro Fontane 13, tel. 06/481–4591. Admission: 6,000 lire. Open Mon.–Sat. 9–2, Sun. 9–1.*

42 Down the hill, Piazza Barberini has Bernini's graceful **Tritone Fountain,** designed in 1637 for the sculptor's munificent patron, Pope Urban VIII, whose Barberini coat of arms, featuring bees, is at the base of the large shell.

Time Out Located on Via Barberini, next to a movie house, **Italy Italy** offers the Italian version of fast food, tasty and inexpensive. *Via Barberini 19. Closed Sun.*

Via Veneto winds its way upward from Piazza Barberini past
43 **Santa Maria della Concezione,** a Capuchin church famous for its crypt, where the skeletons and assorted bones of 4,000 dead monks are artistically arranged in four macabre chapels. *Via Veneto 27, tel. 06/462850. Donations requested. Open daily 9–noon, 3–6.*

The avenue curves past the American Embassy and Consulate; the luxurious Excelsior Hotel; and Doney's and the Café de Paris, famous from the days of *la dolce vita* in the 1950s. At the U.S. Embassy, take Via Bissolati to Piazza San Bernardo. The
44 church of **Santa Maria della Vittoria,** on the corner, is known for Bernini's sumptuous Baroque decoration of the Cornaro Chapel, an exceptional fusion of architecture, painting, and sculpture, in which the *Ecstasy of St. Theresa* is the focal point. The statue represents a mystical experience in what some regard as very earthly terms. This could be a good point at which to interrupt this tour and pick it up again after a rest.

An interesting side trip from Piazza San Bernardo takes you to
45 the Early Christian churches of **Sant'Agnese** and **Santa Costanza,** about a mile beyond the old city walls. Take bus No. 36, 37, 60, or 136 (lines to be unified by 1993) along Via Nomentana to get there. Santa Costanza, a church-in-the-round, has vaults decorated with bright 4th-century mosaics. The custodian of the catacomb of Sant'Agnese accompanies you up the hill to see it. Art buffs should make this side trip; others may find it unrewarding. *Via di Sant'Agnese, tel. 06/832–0743. Admission to Sant'Agnese catacombs: 4,000 lire. Admission to Santa Costanza is free, but a tip is in order if you do not buy a ticket to Sant'Agnese. Open Mon., Tues., Thurs.–Sat. 9–noon and 4–6, Wed. 9–noon, Sun. 4–6.*

From Piazza San Bernardo, it's not far to Piazza della Repub-
46 blica, where the pretty **Fountain of the Naiadi** (nymphs), a turn-of-the-century addition, features voluptuous bronze ladies wrestling happily with marine monsters. On one side of the square is an ancient Roman brick facade, which marks the
47 church of **Santa Maria degli Angeli,** adapted by Michelangelo from the vast central chamber of the colossal Baths of Diocletian, built in the 4th century AD, the largest and most impressive of the ancient baths. The baths were on such a grandiose scale that the church and the former monastery, which now houses the Museo Nazionale around the corner to the right, account for only part of the area occupied by them. Inside the church, take a good look at the eight enormous columns of red granite that support the beams; these are the original columns of the baths' central chamber and are 45 feet high and more than 5 feet in diameter.

48 After years of delay and restorations, the **Museo Nazionale,** home of the famous Ludovisi collection of ancient sculptures is expected to open its new annex in 1993 in Palazzo Massimo, across the square on the other side of the gardens. Meanwhile it has opened a smaller annex in the Octagonal Hall off Piazza della Repubblica. In an upstairs gallery of the former monastery, frescoes from Empress Livia's villa outside Rome are delightful depictions of a garden in bloom. *Via delle Terme di*

Diocleziano, tel. 06/488–0530. Admission: 4,000 lire. Open Tues.–Sat. 9–2, Sun. 9–1.

Tour 8: The Villa Borghese to the Ara Pacis

㊾ A half-mile walk northwest from Piazza della Repubblica up Via Orlando and Via Vittorio Veneto leads you to **Porta Pinciana** (Pincian Gate), one of the historic city gates in the Aurelian Walls surrounding Rome. The Porta itself was built in the 6th century AD, about three centuries after the walls were built to keep out the Barbarians. These days it is one of the entrances to the **Villa Borghese,** which is in fact the name of Rome's large 17th-century park, built as the pleasure gardens of the powerful Borghese family.

㊿ Once inside the park, turn right up Viale del Museo Borghese and make for the **Galleria Borghese,** in what was once the summer house and casino. Despite its size, the building was never lived in. At the time of this writing, it was undergoing extensive renovations, so parts of the gallery may be closed. The second floor contains the picture collection. There is a sculpture collection on the first floor, where you can see Canova's famous statue of Pauline Borghese, wife of Camillo Borghese and sister of Napoleon. Officially known as *Venus Vincitrix,* it is really a depiction of a haughty (and very seductive) Pauline, lying provocatively on a Roman sofa. The next two rooms hold two important Baroque sculptures by Bernini: *David* and *Apollo and Daphne.* In each you can see the vibrant attention to movement that marked the first departure from the Renaissance preoccupation with the idealized human form. Daphne is being transformed into a laurel tree while fleeing from a lecherous Apollo: Twigs sprout from her fingertips while her pursuer recoils in amazement. *Piazzale Museo Borghese, tel. 06/858577. Admission free for duration of renovation. Open Mon.–Sat. 9–1:30, Sun. 9–1.*

(51) A right, then a left turn from the museum lead across the park to the **Galleria Nazionale d'Arte Moderna** (the National Gallery of Modern Art), a large white building boasting the leading collection of 20th-century works in Italy. A large new wing was opened in 1988. *Via delle Belle Arti 131, tel. 06/322–4151. Admission: 8,000 lire. Open Tues.–Sat. 9–2, Sun. 9–1.*

(52) Close by is the **Museo di Villa Giulia,** housing one of the world's great Etruscan collections. The villa is a former papal summer palace set in lovely gardens. This is the place to study the strange, half-understood Etruscan civilization, for here are magnificent terra-cotta statues, figurines, jewelry, household implements, sarcophagi—a whole way of life on display. Among the most precious gems are the *Apollo of Veio* and the *Sarcophagus of the Sposi.* When you have had your fill of these treasures, step out into the nymphaeum (the architectural term for this place of cool recesses and fern-softened fountains) and take a close look at the full-scale reconstruction of an Etruscan temple in the garden. *Piazza di Villa Giulia 9, tel. 06/320–1951. Admission: 8,000 lire. Open Wed. 9–7:30, Tues. and Thurs.–Sat. 9–2, Sun. 9–1.*

(53) The **Pincio** is an extension of Villa Borghese, with gardens on a terrace overlooking much of Rome. It was laid out by the early-19th-century architect Valadier as part of his overall plan for Piazza del Popolo. The Pincio offers a superb view, absolutely

spectacular when there is a fine sunset, and it's also a vantage
⑤④ point from which you can study Valadier's arrangement of **Piazza del Popolo.**

This is one of Rome's largest squares and a traditional place for
mass meetings and rallies. At the center, four dignified stone
lions guard an obelisk relating the life and times of Ramses II in
the 13th century BC. Next to the 400-year-old **Porta del Popolo,**
⑤⑤ Rome's northern city gate, stop in at the church of **Santa Maria
del Popolo** to see a pair of Caravaggios and some Bernini sculptures in a rich Baroque setting.

From here, it's a short walk down Via Ripetta to the large
Augusteum, the mausoleum built by Augustus for himself and
his family. It gives you an idea of what Hadrian's Mausoleum
must have looked like before it became Castel Sant'Angelo.

Next to it is an unattractive modern edifice that shelters the
⑤⑥ **Ara Pacis** (Altar of Augustan Peace), erected in 13 BC to celebrate the era of peace ushered in by Augustus's military victories. The reliefs on the marble enclosure are magnificent. *Via
Ripetta, tel. 06/671–0271. Admission: 3,750 lire. Open Wed.–
Fri. 9–1:30, Tues. and Sat. 9–1:30 and 3:30–7:30, Sun. 9–1.*

Tour 9: The Jewish Ghetto and Trastevere

For the authentic atmosphere of Old Rome, explore the old
Jewish ghetto and the narrow streets of Trastevere, two tight-
ly knit communities whose inhabitants proudly claim descent—whether real or imagined—from the ancient Romans.
Then climb the Janiculum, a hill with views over the whole city,
a vantage point beloved of all Romans.

The shadowy area bounded by Piazza Campitelli and Lungotevere Cenci constituted Rome's ancient Jewish ghetto. Within
this cramped quarter, until 1847, all Rome's Jews (and they
were many, tracing their presence in the city to ancient Roman
times) were confined under a rigid all-night curfew. At the little church opposite Quattro Capi bridge, they were forced to attend sermons that aimed to convert them to Catholicism, and to
pay for the privilege.

Many Jews have remained here, close to the bronze-roofed
⑤⑦ **synagogue** on Lungotevere Cenci and to the roots of their community. Among the most interesting sights in the ghetto are
⑤⑧ the pretty **Fontana delle Tartarughe** (Turtle Fountain) on Piazza Mattei; the old houses on Via Portico d'Ottavia, where medieval inscriptions and ancient friezes testify to the venerable
⑤⑨ age of these buildings; and the **Teatro di Marcello,** hardly recognizable as a theater now, but built at the end of the 1st century
BC by Julius Caesar to hold 20,000 spectators.

Time Out Stop to indulge in American and Austrian baked goods at
Dolceroma. *Via Portico d'Ottavia 20/b. Closed Sun. afternoon
and Mon.*

⑥⓪ Cross the Tiber over the ancient Ponte Fabricio to the **Tiberina
Island,** where a city hospital stands on a site that has been dedicated to healing ever since a temple to Aesculapius was erected
here in 291 BC. If you have time, and if the river's not too high,
go down the stairs for a different perspective on the island and
the Tiber.

Then continue across Ponte Cestio into **Trastevere,** a maze of narrow streets that, despite creeping gentrification, is still one of the city's most authentically Roman neighborhoods (for another, explore the jumble of streets between the Roman Forum, Santa Maria Maggiore, and the Colosseum). Among self-consciously picturesque trattorias and trendy tearooms, you'll also find old shops in alleys festooned with washing hung
61 out to dry and dusty artisans' workshops. Be sure to see **Piazza Santa Maria in Trastevere,** the heart of the quarter, with one of Rome's oldest churches, decorated inside and out with 12th- and 13th-century mosaics.

Follow Via della Scala to Via della Lungara, where Raphael
62 decorated the garden loggia of **Villa Farnesina** for extravagant host Agostino Chigi, who delighted in impressing guests by having his servants clear the table by casting precious gold and silver dinnerware into the Tiber. Naturally, the guests did not know of the nets he had stretched under the water line to catch everything. *Via della Lungara 230, tel. 06/654–0565. Admission free. Open Mon.–Sat. 9–1.*

Trastevere's population has become increasingly diverse, and it has acquired a reputation for purse-snatching and petty thievery, much to the chagrin of the authentic Trasteverini, so keep a close eye on your belongings as you stroll these byways.

From Porta Settimiana you can follow Via Garibaldi as it curves
63 up to the Janiculum, past the church of **San Pietro in Montorio,** known for its views and for the Tempietto, Bramante's little
64 temple in the cloister. Beyond the impressive **Acqua Paola**
65 **Fountain,** you'll come upon the **Janiculum Park,** which offers splendid views of Rome.

Tour 10: The Catacombs and the Appian Way

This tour gives you a respite from museums, though it's no easier on the feet. Do it on a sunny day and either take along a picnic or plan to have lunch at one of the pleasant restaurants near the catacombs. Take the No. 118 bus from San Giovanni in
66 Laterano to the **Via Appia Antica** ("the Queen of Roads"), completed in 312 BC by Appius Claudius, who also built Rome's first aqueduct. You pass Porta San Sebastiano, which gives you a good idea of what the city's 5th-century fortifications looked like, and farther along you'll see the little church of **Domine Quo Vadis,** where tradition says that Christ appeared to St. Peter, inspiring him to return to Rome to face martyrdom.

There are two important **catacombs** on the Via Appia Antica. The first you come upon is that of **San Callisto,** one of the best preserved of these underground cemeteries. A friar will guide you through its crypts and galleries. *Via Appia Antica 110, tel. 06/513–6725. Admission: 6,000 lire. Open Apr.–Sept., Thurs.– Tues. 8:30–noon and 2:30–6; Oct.–Mar., Thurs.–Tues. 8:30– noon and 2:30–5.*

The 4th-century catacomb of **San Sebastiano,** a little farther on, which was named for the saint who was buried here, burrows underground on four levels. The only one of the catacombs to remain accessible during the Middle Ages, it is the origin of the term "catacomb," for it was located in a spot where the road dips into a hollow, a place the Romans called *catacumbas* (near the hollow). Eventually, the Christian cemetery that had existed here since the 2nd century came to be known by the same name, which was applied to all underground cemeteries discovered in Rome in later centuries. *Via Appia Antica 136, tel. 06/ 788–7035. Admission: 6,000 lire. Open Fri.–Wed. 8:30–noon and 2:30–5.*

On the other side of Via Appia Antica are the ruins of the **Circus of Maxentius,** where the obelisk now in Piazza Navona once stood. Farther along the ancient road is the circular **Tomb of Cecilia Metella,** mausoleum of a Roman noblewoman who lived at the time of Julius Caesar. It was transformed into a fortress in the 14th century.

Time Out There are several trattorias along the Via Appia Antica, most of which are moderately priced (*see* Dining, *below*). For a sandwich or a snack, the bar on the corner of Via Appia Antica and Via Cecilia Metella, just beyond the tomb, can provide sustenance and a relaxing pause in the adjoining garden.

The Tomb of Cecilia Metella marks the beginning of the most interesting and evocative stretch of the Via Appia Antica, lined with tombs and fragments of statuary. Cypresses and umbrella pines stand guard over the ruined sepulchers, and the occasional tracts of ancient paving stones are the same ones trod by triumphant Roman legions.

Rome for Free

Sightseeing in many capital cities can often lead to a steady draining of your resources, leaving your budget blown by day one. Rome is an exception because most of its sights are either inexpensive or, more commonly, free of charge. You could construct several memorable itineraries devoted exclusively to architecture and religious art—taking in dozens of piazzas, churches, streets, and fountains—and not part with a single lira. Museums and galleries, of course, usually do charge admission, but it's rarely steep, and there are some surprising exceptions, such as the following:

The Colosseum—Lower Level (Tour 1: Ancient Rome).
The Tombs of the Popes (Tour 2: The Vatican).
The Vatican Museums on the Last Sunday of the Month (Tour 3: The Vatican Museums).
The Pantheon (Tour 4: Old Rome).
Galleria Borghese (Tour 8: The Villa Borghese to the Ara Pacis).
Villa Farnesina (Tour 9: The Jewish Ghetto and Trastevere).

What to See and Do with Children

There's a lot to do in Rome that children—and their parents—will enjoy. Take the children to a **pizzeria** with a wood-burning oven, where they can see the chef work with the dough. Take a ride in a **horse and carriage**—it's fun and feels a lot less silly than it looks. Visit the **Zoo** in Villa Borghese, or climb to **the top of St. Peter's**—arduous but worth it for the incomparable views inside and outside the church. Spend some time in the **Villa Borghese,** perhaps taking in a **Punch and Judy show** on the Pincio. There's another Punch and Judy show on the **Janiculum** hill, where there is also a colorful stand selling puppets.

In December and early January, visit the big **Christmas bazaar** at Piazza Navona, then stop at the huge toy store at the north end of the square. For an almost comical display of orchestration, pause awhile to watch the policeman directing traffic from his little podium in the middle of **Piazza Venezia.** A small-scale spectacle, but completely serious, is the daily **changing of the guard** at the Quirinale Palace, the residence of the president of Italy. Every day at 4 PM there's a military band and parade as the guards change shifts.

Rome's residential suburb EUR is the home of the well-run **Luna Park** amusement center. The park's big Ferris wheel is an attraction, as are the roller coaster and other rides and games. It can be reached by bus No. 707 from San Paolo fuori le Mura. *Via delle Tre Fontane, tel. 06/592–5933. Admission free, but you pay for each ride. Closed Tues.*

There's usually a **circus** somewhere in town: Check billboards and newspaper listings. Also check listings for cartoon films at the movies and for puppet shows and other children's programs at theaters.

Explore **Castel Sant'Angelo** (*see* Tour 2: The Vatican, *above*). It's got dungeons, battlements, cannons, and cannonballs, and a collection of antique weapons and armor.

Rent **bicycles** and ride around Villa Borghese and the center of town on Sunday, when the traffic is lighter.

In spring or summer, take a boat ride to **Ostia Antica** (*see* Excursion 1: Ostia Antica, below).

Off the Beaten Track

Stroll through the quiet, green neighborhood of the **Aventine Hill,** one of the seven hills of ancient Rome that most tourists don't see. It has several of the city's oldest and least-visited churches, as well as a delightful surprise: the view from the keyhole in the gate to the garden of the Knights of Malta (Piazza Cavalieri di Malta).

Visit the excavations under St. Peter's for a fascinating glimpse of the underpinnings of the great basilica, which was built over the cemetery where archaeologists say they have found **St. Peter's tomb.** *Apply several days in advance to the Ufficio Scavi (Excavations Office), to the right beyond the Arco delle Campane entrance to the Vatican, which is left of the basilica. Just tell the Swiss guard you want the Ufficio Scavi, and he will let you enter the confines of the Vatican City. Tel. 06/698–5318. Admission: 8,000 lire with guide, 5,000 lire with taped guide.*

See the **Protestant Cemetery** behind the Piramide, a stone pyramid built in 12 BC at the order of the Roman praetor (senior magistrate) who was buried there. The cemetery is reminiscent of a country churchyard. Among the headstones you'll find Keats's tomb and the place where Shelley's heart was buried. *Via Caio Cestio 6, tel. 06/574–1141. Ring for the custodian. An offering of 500–1,000 lire is customary. Open daily 8–11:30 and 3:20–5:30.*

Explore the subterranean dwellings under the church of **San Clemente.** *Via San Giovanni in Laterano, tel. 06/704–51018. Donation requested. Open Mon.–Sat. 9–noon and 3:30–6, Sun. 10–noon.*

Have an inexpensive lunch at **L'Eau Vive,** run by lay Catholic missionary workers, whose mission in this case is running a restaurant. Though it's elegant and fairly expensive for an evening meal, the good fixed-price lunch is a bargain. *Via Monterone 85 (off Piazza Sant'Eustachio), tel. 06/654–1095. AE, DC, V. Closed Sun.*

Shopping

Shopping in Rome is part of the fun, no matter what your budget. You're sure to find something that suits your fancy *and* your pocketbook, but don't expect to get bargains on Italian brands, such as Benetton, that are exported to the United States; prices are about the same on both sides of the Atlantic.

Shops are open from 9 or 9:30 to 1 and from 3:30 or 4 to 7 or 7:30. There's a tendency in Rome for shops in central districts to stay open all day, but for many this is still in the experimental stage. Department stores and centrally located UPIM and Standa stores are open all day. Remember that most stores are closed Sunday and, with the exception of food and technical-supply stores, are also closed Monday mornings from September to June and Saturday afternoons in July and August. Most Italian sizes are not uniform, so always try on clothing before you buy or measure gift items. Glove sizes are universal. In any case, remember that Italian stores generally will *not* refund your purchases and that they often cannot exchange goods because of limited stock. *Always* take your purchases with you; having them shipped home from the shop can cause hassles. If circumstances are such that you can't take your goods with you and if the shop seems reliable about shipping, get a firm statement of *when* and *how* your purchase will be sent.

Prezzi fissi means that prices are fixed and it's a waste of time bargaining unless you're buying a sizable quantity of goods or a particularly costly object. Most stores have a fixed-price policy, and most honor a variety of credit cards. They will also accept foreign money at the current exchange rate, give or take a few lire. Ask for a receipt for your purchases; you may need it at customs on your return home. Bargaining is still an art at Porta Portese flea market and is routine when purchasing anything from a street vendor.

It's theoretically possible to obtain a refund on the VAT tax, which is included in the selling price. In practice, however, the mechanism is so complex that it is hardly worthwhile worrying about it. To be eligible for a refund, you must spend more than 605,000 lire on one item in a store and then endure considerable rigmarole at the airport when you leave. The Europe Tax-free Shopping system streamlines the process somewhat. Look for the "Tax-free for Tourists" sign in shops if you plan to purchase anything for that amount.

Shopping Districts The most elegant and expensive shops are concentrated in the **Piazza di Spagna** area especially along **Via Condotti. Via Margutta** is known for art galleries and **Via del Babuino** for antiques. There are several high-fashion outlets on **Via Gregoriana** and **Via Sistina.** Bordering this top-price shopping district is **Via del Corso,** which—along with **Via Frattina** and **Via del Gambero**—is lined with shops and boutiques of all kinds where prices and goods are competitive.

Rome Shopping

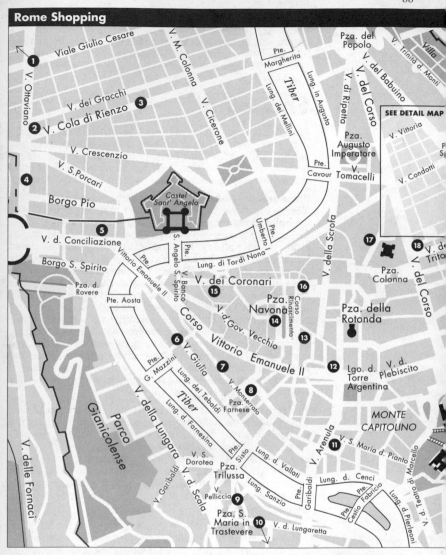

SEE DETAIL MAP

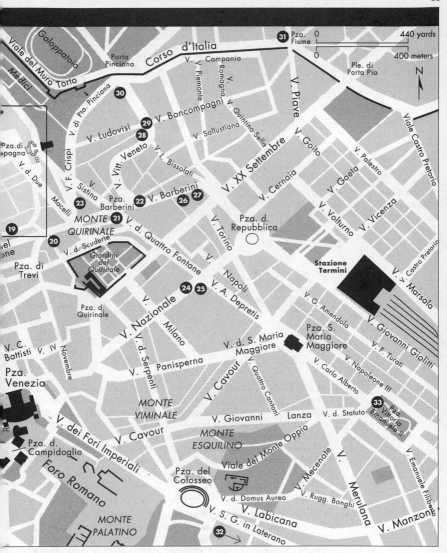

Galoppatoio

Viale del Muro Torto

Medici

Porta Pinciana

Corso d'Italia

V. Campania

V. Piemonte

V. Romagna

V. Quintino Sella

31 Pza. Fiume

Ple. di Porta Pia

0 ___ 440 yards

0 ___ 400 meters

N

V. Piave

Viale Castro Pretorio

30

V. di Pta. Pinciana

V. Boncompagni

V. Ludovisi

29

28

Vitt. Veneto

V. L. Bissolati

V. Sallustiana

V. XX Settembre

V. Goito

V. Goito

V. Palestro

Pza. di pagna

V. d. Due

V. F. Crispi

Sistina

Macelli

23

Pza. Barberini

22

V. Barberini

26 27

V. Cernaia

V. Gaeta

V. Volturno

V. Vicenza

19

21

MONTE QUIRINALE

20

V. d. Scuderie

V. d. Quattro Fontane

V. Torino

Pza. d. Repubblica

Castro Pretorio

one

Pza. di Trevi

Giardini del Quirinale

Napoli

Stazione Termini

V. Castro Pretorio

V. Marsala

Pza. d. Quirinale

24 25

V. A. Depretis

V. G. Amendola

V. Nazionale

Milano

V. d. Serpeni

V. d. S. Maria Maggiore

Pza. S. Maria Maggiore

V. Giovanni Giolitti

V. F. Turati

V. C. Battisti

V. IV

Novembre

Panisperna

V. Cavour

V. Quattro Cantoni

V. Carlo Alberto

V. Napoleone III

Pza. Venezia

MONTE VIMINALE

V. Giovanni Lanza

V. d. Statuto

33

Pza. Vittorio Emanuele II

V. dei Fori Imperiali

V. Cavour

MONTE ESQUILINO

V. Emanuele Filiberto

Pza. d. Campidoglio

Foro Romano

Pza. del Colosseo

Viale del Monte Oppio

V. Mecenate

V. Ruggero Bonghi

Merulana

V. Manzoni

MONTE PALATINO

V. d. Domus Aurea

V. S. G. in Laterano

V. Labicana

32

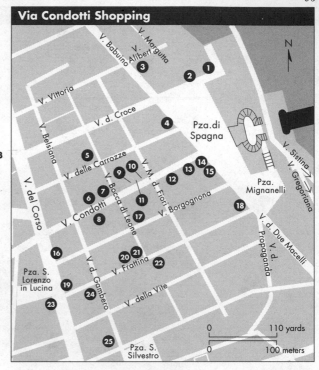

Via Condotti Shopping

Via del Tritone, leading up from Piazza Colonna off Via del Corso, has some medium-priced, and a few expensive, shops selling everything from fashion fabrics to trendy furniture. Still farther up, on **Via Veneto,** you'll find more high-priced boutiques and shoe stores, as well as newsstands selling English-language newspapers, magazines, and paperback books. **Via Nazionale** features shoe stores, moderately priced boutiques, and shops selling men's and women's fashions. **Via Cola di Rienzo** offers high-quality goods of all types; it's a good alternative to the Piazza di Spagna area.

In Old Rome, **Via dei Coronari** is lined with antique shops and some new stores selling designer home accessories. **Via Giulia** and **Via Monserrato** also feature antiques dealers galore, plus a few art galleries. In the **Pantheon** area there are many shops selling liturgical objects and vestments. But the place to go for religious souvenirs is, obviously, the area around St. Peter's, especially **Via della Conciliazione** and **Via di Porta Angelica.**

Department Stores Rome has only a handful of department stores. **Rinascente,** at Piazza Colonna, sells clothing and accessories only. Another Rinascente, at Piazza Fiume, has the same stock. **Coin,** on Piazzale Appio, near San Giovanni in Laterano, has fashions for men and women. There is another Coin store in the U.S.-style shopping mall at Cinecittà Due (Subaugusta Metro stop). The **UPIM** and **Standa** chains offer low to moderately priced medium-quality goods. They're the place to go if you need a pair of slippers, a sweater, a bathing suit, or such to see you through until you get home. In addition, they carry all kinds of toiletries and first-aid needs. Most Standa and UPIM stores have invaluable while-you-wait shoe-repair service counters.

Food and Flea Markets Rome's biggest and most colorful outdoor food markets are at **Campo dei Fiori** (just south of Piazza Navona), **Via Andrea Doria** (Trionfale, about a quarter mile north of the entrance to the Vatican museums), and **Piazza Vittorio** (just down Via Carlo Alberto from the church of Santa Maria Maggiore). There's a flea market on Sunday morning at **Porta Portese;** it now offers mainly new or secondhand clothing, but there are still a few dealers in old furniture and sundry objects, much of it intriguing junk. Bargaining is the rule here, as are pickpockets; beware. To reach Porta Portese, take Via Ippolito Nievo, off Viale Trastevere. All outdoor markets are open from early morning to about 2, except Saturdays, when they may stay open all day.

Clothing Boutiques All the big names in Italian fashion—Versace, Ferre, Valentino, Armani, Missoni—are represented in the Piazza di Spagna area. **Sorelle Fontane** (Salita San Sebastianello 6), one of the first houses to put Italy on the fashion map, has a large boutique with an extensive line of ready-to-wear clothing and accessories. **Carlo Palazzi** (Via Borgognona 7) has elegant men's fashions and accessories. **Mariselaine** (Via Condotti 70) is a top-quality women's fashion boutique. **Camomilla** (Piazza di Spagna 85) has trendy styles for women.

Specialty Stores
Antiques and Prints For old prints and antiques, the **Tanca** shop (Salita dei Crescenzi 10, near the Pantheon) is a good hunting ground. Early photographs of Rome and views of Italy from the archives of **Alinari** (Via Aliberti 16/a) make interesting souvenirs. **Nardecchia** (Piazza Navona 25) is reliable for prints. **Le Bateleur** (71 Via S. Simone, tel. 06/654–4676), in a tiny 11th-century sacristy under a flight of stone steps, shows changing exhibits and a bit of everything from the 17th to the 20th century.

Handicrafts For pottery, handwoven textiles, and other handicrafts, **Myricae** (Via Frattina 36, with another store at Piazza del Parlamento 38) has a good selection. **Galleria del Batik** (Via della Pelliccia 29) in Trastevere is off the beaten track but well worth a visit; it has a wealth of handicrafts, beautifully displayed in a rustic setting. A bottle of liqueur, jar of marmalade, or bar of chocolate handmade by Cistercian monks in several monasteries in Italy makes an unusual gift to take home; they are all on sale at **Ai Monasteri** (Piazza Cinque Luna 2).

Household Linens and Embroidery **Frette** (Piazza di Spagna 10) is a Roman institution for fabulous trousseaux. **Cesari** (Via Barberini 1) is another; it also has less-expensive gift items, such as aprons, beach towels, and place mats. **Lavori Artigianali Femminili** (Via Capo le Case 6) offers exquisitely embroidered household linens, infants' and children's clothing, and blouses.

Jewelry **Bulgari** (Via Condotti 10) is to Rome what Cartier is to Paris; the shop's elegant display windows hint at what's beyond the guard at the door. **Buccellati** (Via Condotti 31) is a tradition-rich Florentine jewelry house famous for its silverwork; it ranks with Bulgari for quality and reliability. **Fornari** (Via Frattina 71) and **Frugoni** (Via Arenula 83) have tempting selections of small silver objects. **Bozart** (Via Bocca di Leone 4) features dazzling costume jewelry geared to the latest fashions.

Knitwear   **Luisa Spagnoli** (Via del Corso 382, with other shops at Via
              Frattina 116 and Via Veneto 130) is always reliable for good
              quality at the right price and styles to suit American tastes.
              Miranda (Via Bocca di Leone 28) is a treasure trove of warm
              jackets, skirts, and shawls, handwoven in gorgeous colors of
              wool or mohair, or in lighter yarns for summer.

Leather Goods **Gucci** (Via Condotti 8 and 77) is the most famous of Rome's
              leather shops. It has a full assortment of accessories on the first
              floor; a fashion boutique for men and women and a scarf depart-
              ment on the second floor; and a full complement of Japanese
              customers, who line up to get in on busy days. **Roland's** (Piazza
              di Spagna 74) has an extensive stock of good-quality leather
              fashions and accessories, as well as stylish casual wear in wool
              and silk. **Ceresa** (Via del Tritone 118) has more reasonably
              priced fine-leather goods, including many handbags and leath-
              er fashions. **Volterra** (Via Barberini 102) is well stocked and
              offers a wide selection of handbags at moderate prices.
              Sermoneta (Piazza di Spagna 61) shows a varied range of gloves
              in its windows, and there are many more inside. **Di Cori**, a few
              steps away, also has a good selection of gloves; there's another
              Di Cori store at Via Nazionale 183. **Merola** (Via del Corso 143)
              carries a line of expensive top-quality gloves and scarves.

              Nichol's (Via Barberini 94) is in the moderate price range and is
              one of the few stores in Rome that stocks shoes in American
              widths. **Ferragamo** (Via Condotti 73) is one of Rome's best
              stores for fine shoes and leather accessories, and its silk
              scarves are splendid; you pay for quality here, but you can get
              great buys during the periodic sales. **Mario Valentino** (Via
              Frattina 58) is a top name for stylish shoes and leather fashions.
              Magli (Via del Gambero 1 and Via Veneto 70) is known for well-
              made shoes and matching handbags at high to moderate prices.
              Campanile (Via Condotti 58) has four floors of shoes in the lat-
              est, as well as classic styles, and other leather goods.

Silks and Fabrics **Galtrucco** (Via del Tritone 18), **Bises** (Via del Gesù 56), and
              Meconi (Via Cola di Rienzo 305) have the best selections of
              world-famous Italian silks and fashion fabrics. You can find
              some real bargains when remnants *(scampoli)* are on sale.

Sports

Biking   You can rent a bike at Via di Porta Castello 43, (tel. 06/687–
              5714) and at Piazza Navona 69. There are rental concessions at
              metro stops at Piazza di Spagna, Piazza del Popolo, Largo San
              Silvestro, Largo Argentina, Viale della Pineta in Villa Borghe-
              se, and at Viale del Bambino on the Pincio.

Bowling   There's a large American-style bowling center, **Bowling Bruns-
              wick** (Lungotevere Acqua Acetosa, tel. 06/808–6147) and a
              smaller one, **Bowling Roma** (Viale Regina Margherita 181, tel.
              06/855–1184).

Fitness Facilities **The Cavalieri Hilton** (Via Cadlolo 101, tel. 06/35091) offers a
              600-meter jogging path on the hotel grounds as well as an out-
              door pool, two clay tennis courts, an exercise area, a sauna, and
              a steam room. **The Sheraton Roma** (Viale del Pattinaggio, tel.
              06/5453) has a heated outdoor pool, a tennis court, two squash
              courts, and a sauna, but no gym. **The Sheraton Golf** (Viale
              Parco de'Medici 22, tel. 06/65977) has a fitness center and golf
              course. **The St. Peter's Holiday Inn** (Via Aurelia Antica 415, tel.

06/6642) has two tennis courts on the hotel grounds. It also has a 25-meter outdoor pool.

The **Roman Sport Center** (Via del Galoppatoio 33, tel. 06/320–1667) is a full-fledged sports center occupying vast premises next to the underground parking lot in Villa Borghese; it has two swimming pools, a gym, aerobic workout areas, squash courts, and saunas. It is affiliated with the **American Health Club** (Largo Somalia 60, tel. 06/839–4488).

Golf The oldest and most prestigious golf club in Rome is the **Circolo del Golf Roma** (Via Acqua Santa 3, tel. 06/780–3407). The newest are the **Sheraton Golf** course (Viale Parco de' Medici 22, tel. 06/65977, or 06/655–3477 for clubhouse) and the **Country Club Castel Gandolfo** (Via Santo Spirito 13, Castel Gandolfo, tel. 06/931–2301). The **Golf Club Fioranello** (Viale della Repubblica, tel. 06/713–8291) is at Santa Maria delle Mole, off the Via Appia Antica. There is a 18-hole course at the **Olgiata Golf Club** (Largo Olgiata 15, on the Via Cassia, tel. 06/378–9141). Nonmembers are welcome in these clubs but must show membership cards of their home golf or country clubs.

Horseback Riding There are several riding clubs in Rome. The most central is the **Associazione Sportiva Villa Borghese** (Via del Galoppatoio 23, tel. 06/360–6797). You can also ride at the **Società Ippica Romana** (Via Monti della Farnesina 18, tel. 06/396–6214) and at the **Circolo Ippico Olgiata** (Largo Olgiata 15, tel. 06/378–8792), outside the city on the Via Cassia.

Jogging The best bet for jogging in the inner city is at the **Villa Borghese.** A circuit of the Pincio, among the marble statuary, measures half a mile. A longer run in the park of Villa Borghese itself might include a loop around **Piazza di Siena,** a grass horse track measuring a quarter of a mile. Although most traffic is barred from Villa Borghese, government and police cars sometimes speed through. Be careful to stick to the sides of the roads. For a long run away from all traffic, try **Villa Ada** and **Villa Doria Pamphili** on the Janiculum. On the other hand, if you really love history, you can jog at the old **Circus Maximus,** or along Via delle Terme di Caracalla, which is flanked by a park. (Also, *see* **The Cavalieri Hilton** in Fitness Facilities, above.)

Swimming The outdoor pools of the **Cavalieri Hilton** (Via Cadlolo 101, tel. 06/35091) and the **Hotel Aldovrandi** (Via Ulisse Aldovrandi 15, tel. 06/322–3993) are lush summer oases open to nonguests. The **Roman Sport Center** (Via del Galoppatoio 33, tel. 06/320–1667) has two swimming pools, and there's another one at the **American Health Club** (Largo Somalia 60, tel. 06/839–4488).

Tennis Increasingly popular with Italians, tennis is played in private clubs and on many public courts that can be rented by the hour. Your hotel *portiere* will direct you to the nearest courts and can book for you. A prestigious Roman club is the **Tennis Club Parioli** (Largo de Morpurgo 2, Via Salaria, tel. 06/862–00882).

Spectator Sports

Basketball Basketball continues to grow in popularity (in Italy) with many American pros now playing on Italian teams. In Rome, games are played at the **Palazzo dello Sport** in the EUR district (Piazzale dello Sport, tel. 06/592–5107).

Horseback Riding The **International Riding Show,** held the last few days of April and the first week in May, draws a stylish crowd to the amphitheater of Piazza di Siena in Villa Borghese. The competition is stiff, and the program features a cavalry charge staged by the dashing mounted corps of the *carabinieri.* For information, call the **Italian Federation of Equestrian Sports** (Viale Tiziano 70, tel. 06/323–3806).

Horse Racing There's flat racing at the lovely century-old **Capanelle** track (Via Appia Nuova 1255, tel. 06/718–3143), frequented by a chic crowd on big race days. The trotters meet at the **Tor di Valle** track (Via del Mare, tel. 06/529–0269).

Soccer Italy's favorite spectator sport stirs passionate enthusiasm among partisans. Games are usually held on Sunday afternoons throughout the fall–spring season. Two teams—Roma and Lazio—play their home games in the Olympic Stadium at **Foro Italico.** Tickets are on sale at the box office before the games; your hotel *portiere* may be able to help you get tickets in advance. The Olympic Stadium is on Viale dei Gladiatori, in the extensive Foro Italico sports complex built by Mussolini on the banks of the Tiber (tel. 06/333–6316).

Tennis A top-level international tournament is held at the Tennis Stadium at **Foro Italico** in May. For information, call the **Italian Tennis Federation** (Viale Tiziano 70, tel. 06/368–58510).

Beaches

The beaches nearest Rome are at **Ostia,** a busy urban center in its own right; **Castelfusano,** nearby; **Fregene,** a villa colony; and **Castelporziano,** a public beach area maintained by the city. At Ostia and Fregene, you pay for changing cabins, cabanas, umbrellas, and such, and for the fact that the sand is kept clean and combed. Some establishments, such as **Kursaal** (Lungomare Catullo 36 at Castelfusano, tel. 06/562–1303) have swimming pools, strongly recommended as alternatives to the murky waters of the Mediterranean, which are notoriously polluted. You can reach Ostia by train from Ostiense Station, Castelfusano and Castelporziano by bus from Ostia, and Fregene by ACOTRAL bus from the Via Lepanto stop of Metro Line A in Rome. All beaches are crowded during July and August.

For cleaner water and more of a resort atmosphere, you have to go farther afield. To the north of Rome, **Santa Marinella** and **Santa Severa** offer shoals, sand, and attractive surroundings. To the south, **Sabaudia** is known for miles of sandy beaches, **San Felice Circeo** is a classy resort, and **Sperlonga** is a picturesque old town flanked by beaches and pretty coves.

Dining

Our restaurant recommendations have been compiled under the direction of Eliana Cosimini, noted Italian food and travel writer.

There was a time when you could predict the clientele and prices of a Roman eating establishment by whether it was called a *ristorante,* a *trattoria,* or an *osteria* (tavern). Now these names are interchangeable. A rustic-looking spot that calls itself an osteria or hostaria may turn out to be chic and expensive. Generally speaking, however, a trattoria is a family-run place, simpler in decor, menu, and service—and slightly less expensive—than a ristorante. A true osteria is a wine shop, very basic and down to earth, where the only function of the food is to keep the customers sober.

As the pace of Roman life quickens, more fast-food outlets are opening, offering tourists a wider choice of light meals. They are variations on the older Italian institutions of *tavola calda* (literally, "hot table") and *rosticceria* (roast meats), both of which offer a selection of hot and cold dishes to be taken out or eaten on the premises. A tavola calda is more likely to have seating. At both, some dishes are priced by portion; others by weight. You usually select your food, find out how much it costs, and pay the cashier, who'll give you a stub to give to the counter person when you pick up the food. Snack bars cater to the new demand for fast food with cold or toasted sandwiches. If you want to picnic, buy your provisions in any *alimentari* (grocery) store. *Pizza Rustica* outlets sell slices of various kinds of pizza; there's one on every other block in Rome, or so it seems.

Despite these changes, many Romans stick to the tradition of having their main meal at lunch, from 1 to 3, although you won't be turned away if hunger strikes shortly after noon. Dinner is served from 8 or 8:30 until about 10:30 or 11. Some restaurants stay open much later, especially in summer, when patrons linger at sidewalk tables to enjoy the cool breeze *(ponentino)*. Almost all restaurants close one day a week (it's usually safest to call ahead to reserve) and for at least two weeks in August, when it can sometimes seem impossible to find sustenance in the deserted city.

Tap water is safe everywhere in Rome. Most Romans order bottled mineral water *(acqua minerale)*, either with bubbles *(gassata)* or without *(naturale* or *non gassata)*. It comes by the liter *(litro)* or the half-liter *(mezzo litro)*. If you're on a budget, keep your check down by ordering tap water *(acqua semplice)*. If you are on a low-sodium diet, ask for everything *senza sale* (without salt).

Always check the menu that's on display in the window of a restaurant or just inside the door. In all but the simplest places, there will be a cover charge *(pane e coperto)* and usually a service charge *(servizio)* of 10%–15%. A *menu turistico* (fixed-price tourist menu) includes taxes and service, but usually not drinks. Beware dishes on à la carte menus, such as fish, Florentine steaks, or fillets: For those marked "SQ," you will be charged according to the weight of the item; for those marked "L. 4,000 hg," you'll be charged 4,000 lire for a hectogram (about 3½ ounces).

Highly recommended restaurants are indicated by a star ★.

Category	Cost*
Very Expensive	over 110,000 lire
Expensive	65,000–110,000 lire
Moderate	30,000–65,000 lire
Inexpensive	under 30,000 lire

*per person, for a three-course meal, including house wine and taxes

Central Rome

Very Expensive **La Cupola.** The elegant restaurant of the Hotel Excelsior serves classic regional Italian and international cuisine with flair. The empire decor is luxurious; service is courteous and highly professional. Perfect pasta dishes, such as *bucatini all'amatriciana* (an earthy Roman specialty) and *gnocchetti di ricotta all' Excelsior* (small ricotta dumplings with tomato-and-basil sauce), are reason enough to eat here. *Hotel Excelsior, Via Veneto 125, tel. 06/4708. Reservations not required. Jacket and tie preferred. AE, DC, MC, V.*

Le Jardin. Located in the Parioli residential district, this restaurant is one of Rome's classiest establishments. It's in the exclusive Lord Byron Hotel, itself a triumph of studied interior decoration. The imaginative menu is a tempting compendium of seasonal specialties served with style. If they are on the menu, try the risotto with seafood and vegetable sauce or the fillet of beef with morels. *Hotel Lord Byron, Via Giuseppe De Notaris 5, tel. 06/322-0404. Reservations required. Jacket and tie preferred. AE, DC, MC, V. Closed Sun.*

★ **Le Restaurant.** The restaurant of the luxurious Grand hotel (*see* Lodging, below) is the ultimate in elegance and the discreet haunt of Rome's most chic crowd. The resplendent dining room is a model of 19th-century opulence, lavished with crystal chandeliers, fine oil paintings, and damasks and velvets in pale golden tones. The menu varies with the season; there are always daily recommendations. Among the specialties are *carpaccio tiepido di pescatrice* (brill—a flatfish—with thin slices of raw beef) and *medaglioni di vitello al marsala con tartufo* (veal medallions with marsala wine and truffles). The wine list offers some choice vintages. *Via Vittorio Emanuele Orlando 3, tel. 06/482931. Reservations advised. Jacket and tie required. AE, DC, MC, V.*

★ **El Toulà.** Take a byway off Piazza Nicosia in Old Rome to find this prestigious restaurant, one of a number in Italy of the same name; all are spin-offs of a renowned restaurant in Treviso in northern Italy (*see* Dining and Lodging in Chapter 7). Rome's El Toulà has the warm, welcoming atmosphere of a 19th-century country house, with white walls, antique furniture in dark wood, heavy silver serving dishes, and spectacular arrangements of fruits and flowers. There's a cozy bar off the entrance, where you can sip a *prosecco* (Venetian semi-sparkling white wine), the aperitif best suited to the chef's Venetian specialties, which include the classic *pasta e fagioli* (pasta and bean soup), risotto with artichokes, and *fegato alla veneziana* (liver with onions). *Via della Lupa 29/b, tel. 06/687-3750. Reservations required. Jacket and tie required. AE, DC, MC, V. Closed Sat. lunch, Sun., Aug., Dec. 24-26.*

Expensive **Alberto Ciarla.** Located on a large square in Trastevere, scene
★ of a busy morning food market, Alberto Ciarla is thought by many to be the best seafood restaurant in Rome. In contrast with its workaday location, the interior is polished with red-and-black decor. Bubbling aquariums—a sure sign that the food is superfresh—are set along the wall. Seafood salads are a specialty. Meat eaters will find succor in the house pâté and the lamb. Order carefully, or the check will soar. *Piazza San Cosimato 40, tel. 06/581-8668. Reservations required. Jacket and tie suggested. AE, DC, MC, V. Dinner only. Closed Sun., Aug. 5-25, Christmas.*

★ **Andrea.** Ernest Hemingway and King Farouk used to eat here; Nowadays, you're more likely to hear the murmured conversation of Italian powerbrokers. Half a block from Via Veneto, this restaurant offers classic Italian cooking in an intimate, clubby setting, in which snowy table linens gleam against a discreet background of dark-green paneling. The menu features delicacies such as homemade *tagliolini* (thin noodles) with shrimp and spinach sauce, spaghetti with seafood and truffles, and mouth-watering *carciofi all'Andrea* (artichokes simmered in olive oil). *Via Sardegna 26, tel. 06/482–1891. Reservations advised. Dress: casual but neat. AE, DC, MC, V. Closed Sun. and most of Aug.*

Coriolano. The only tourists who find their way to this classic restaurant near Porta Pia are likely to be gourmets looking for quintessential Italian food, and that means light homemade pastas, choice olive oil, and market-fresh ingredients, especially seafood. The small dining room is decorated with antiques, and tables are set with immaculate white linen, sparkling crystal, and silver. Although seafood dishes vary, *tagliolini all'aragosta* (thin noodles with lobster sauce) is usually on the menu, as are *porcini* mushrooms in season (cooked to a secret recipe). The wine list is predominantly Italian, but includes some French and California wines, too. *Via Ancona 14, tel. 06/ 855–1122. Jacket and tie preferred. Reservations advised. AE, DC, MC, V. Closed Sun. and Aug. 1–25.*

Passetto. Benefiting from a choice location near Piazza Navona, Passetto has been a favorite with Italians and tourists for many years: It's a place you can rely on for classic Italian food and courteous service. If you can, eat on the terrace—it's especially memorable at night; the mirrored dining room is more staid. Roman specialties, such as *cannelloni* (stuffed pasta tubes) and *abbacchio* (baby lamb), are featured. *Via Zanardelli 14, tel. 06/ 654–0569. Reservations advised. Jacket and tie preferred. AE, DC, MC, V. Closed Sun., Mon. lunch.*

Piperno. A favorite, located in the old Jewish Ghetto next to historic Palazzo Cenci, Piperno has been in business for more than a century. It is *the* place to go for Rome's extraordinary *carciofi alla giudia* (crispy-fried artichokes, Jewish-style). You eat in three small wood-paneled dining rooms or at one of a handful of tables outdoors. Try *filetti di baccalà* (cod fillet fried in batter), *pasta e ceci* (a thick soup of pasta tubes and chickpeas), *fiori di zucca* (stuffed zucchini flowers), and *carciofi* (artichokes). *Monte dei Cenci 9, tel. 06/654–2772. Reservations advised. Dress: casual. AE, DC, MC, V. Closed Sun. dinner, Mon., Christmas, Easter, Aug.*

★ **Ranieri.** Walk down a quiet street off fashionable Via Condotti, near the Spanish Steps, to find this historic restaurant, founded by a one-time chef of Queen Victoria. Ranieri remains a favorite with tourists for its traditional atmosphere and decor, with damask-covered walls, velvet banquettes, crystal chandeliers, and old paintings. The Italian-French cuisine is excellent: Portions are abundant and checks remain comfortably within the lower range in this category. Among the many specialties on the vast menu are *gnocchetti alla parigina* (feather-light dumplings with cheese sauce) and *mignonettes alla Regina Vittoria* (veal with pâté and an eight-cheese sauce). *Via Mario de' Fiori 26, tel. 06/679–1592. Reservations advised. Dress: casual but neat. AE, DC, MC, V. Closed Sun.*

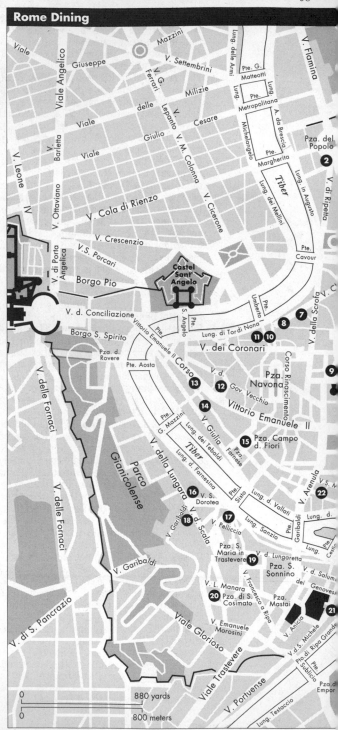

Moderate   **Dal Bolognese.** Long a favorite with the art crowd, this classic
restaurant on Piazza del Popolo is a handy place for a leisurely
lunch between sightseeing and shopping. While dining, feast
your eyes on an extensive array of contemporary paintings,
many of them by customers, both illustrious and unknown. As
the name of the restaurant promises, the cooking here adheres
to the hearty tradition of Bologna, with homemade pastas in
creamy sauces and steaming trays of boiled meats. For dessert,
there's *dolce della mamma*, a concoction of ice cream, zabaglione, and chocolate sauce. *Piazza del Popolo 1, tel. 06/361-1426.
Reservations advised. Dress: casual. DC, V. Closed Mon. and
Aug. 7-22.*

La Campana. This inconspicuous trattoria off Via della Scrofa
has a centuries-old tradition: There has been an inn on this spot
since the 15th century, and the two plain dining rooms occupy
what were once stables. It's a homey place, with friendly waiters, a vigil light in front of a painted Madonna over the kitchen
entrance, and good Roman food at reasonable prices. The menu
offers specialties like *vignarola* (sautéed fava beans, peas, and
artichokes), rigatoni with *prosciutto* (ham) and tomato sauce,
and *olivette di vitello con puré* (tiny veal rolls with mashed potatoes). *Vicolo della Campana 18, tel. 06/686-7820. Reservations advised for dinner. Dress: casual. AE, V. Closed Mon.
and Aug.*

Cannavota. Located on the square next to San Giovanni
Laterano, Cannavota has a large and faithful following and has
fed generations of neighborhood families over the years. Seafood dominates, but carnivores are catered to, also. Try one of
the pastas with seafood sauce—fettuccine with shrimp and
scampi is a good choice—and then go on to grilled fish or meat.
The cheerful atmosphere and rustic decor make for an authentically Roman experience. *Piazza San Giovanni in Laterano
20, tel. 06/775007. Reservations advised. Dress: casual. AE,
DC, MC, V. Closed Wed. and Aug. 1-20.*

Da Checcho er Carrettiere. You'll find Da Checcho tucked away
behind Piazza Trilussa in Trastevere. It has the look of a country inn, with braids of garlic hung from the roof and an antipasto table that features some unusual specialties, such as a
well-seasoned mashed potato-and-tomato mixture. Among the
hearty pasta offerings are *spaghetti alla carrettiera*, with
black pepper, sharp cheese, and olive oil, and linguine with
scampi. Seafood (which can be expensive) is the main feature on
the menu, but traditional Roman meat dishes are offered, too.
This is a great place to soak up genuine Trastevere color and
hospitality. *Via Benedetta 10, tel. 06/581-7018. Reservations
advised. Dress: casual. AE, DC, V. Closed Sun. evening and
Mon.*

Colline Emiliane. Not far from Piazza Barberini, this unassuming trattoria offers exceptionally good food. Behind an opaque
glass facade are a couple of plain dining rooms, where you are
served light homemade pastas, a special chicken broth, and
meats ranging from boiled beef to *giambonetto di vitella* (roast
veal) and *cotoletta alla bolognese* (veal cutlet with cheese and
tomato sauce). Family run, it's quiet and soothing, a good place
to rest after a sightseeing stint. Service is cordial and discreet.
*Via degli Avignonesi 22, tel. 06/481-7538. Reservations ad-
vised. Dress: casual. No credit cards. Closed Fri.*

Fortunato al Pantheon. Just a block away from the House of
Representatives, Fortunato is a favorite of politicos. (It's also a
couple of paces from Piazza della Rotonda by the Pantheon.)

With politicians around, there is, of course, a back room, but you can happily settle for the largest of the three dining rooms or even a table outside in good weather. For his faithful and demanding clientele, Fortunato varies his specialties, offering several pastas—such as *penne all'arrabbiata*, with piquant tomato sauce—and *risotto alla milanese*, with saffron or with *porcini* mushrooms. He also serves many types of fish and meat dishes, some with expensive truffles. *Via del Pantheon 55, tel. 06/679-2788. Reservations advised. Dress: casual but neat. AE. Closed Sun.*

★ **Mario.** Mario has been running this restaurant in the heart of Rome's shopping district for 30 years. Even when crowded, the restaurant has an intimate and relaxed feeling. The walls are full of paintings and photographs of celebrity customers who come for hearty Tuscan food. *Papardelle alla lepre* (noodles with hare sauce) and *coniglio* (rabbit) are specialties, but be sure to try *panzanella* (Tuscan bread salad), perhaps as an antipasto. The house Chianti can be recommended. *Via della Vite 55, tel. 06/678-3818. Dress: casual. Dinner reservations advised. AE, DC, MC, V. Closed Sun. and Aug.*

Da Meo Patacca. A picturesque square in Trastevere is the setting for an entertaining evening of live music in an endearingly bogus Old Rome atmosphere. Strolling musicians in folk costumes sing and play your requests, and everybody joins in. The food is surprisingly good, and you can't go wrong with the pasta and meat specialties "alla Meo." The ground-floor and downstairs dining rooms are strewn with an array of garlic, peppers, and antique junk. In the summer, you can dine outside. *Piazza del Mercanti, in Trastevere, tel. 06/581-6198. Reservations advised. Dress: casual. AE, DC, V. Dinner only.*

Orso 80. This bright and bustling trattoria is located in Old Rome, on a street famed for artisans' workshops. It has both a Roman and an international following, and is known, above all, for a fabulous antipasto table. If you have room for more, try the homemade egg pasta or the *bucatini all'amatriciana* (thin, hollow pasta with a tomato, bacon, and pecorino cheese sauce); there's plenty of seafood on the menu, too. For dessert, the ricotta cake, a genuine Roman specialty, is always good. *Via dell'Orso 33, tel. 06/686-4904. Reservations advised. Dress: casual. AE, DC, MC, V. Closed Mon. and Aug. 10-20.*

Osteria da Nerone. Between the Colosseum and the church of San Pietro in Vincoli, this family-run trattoria features a tempting antipasto table and fresh-made pastas. The specialty is *fettuccine al Nerone* (noodles with peas, salami, and mushrooms), but homemade ravioli are good, too. In fair weather you eat outdoors with a view of the Colosseum. *Via Terme di Tito 96, tel. 06/474-5207. Dinner reservations advised. Dress: casual. No credit cards. Closed Sun. and mid-Aug.*

Otello alla Concordia. The clientele in this popular spot—it's located off a shopping street near Piazza di Spagna—is about evenly divided between tourists and workers from shops and offices in the area. The former like to sit outdoors in the courtyard in any weather; the latter have their regular tables in one of the inside dining rooms. The menu offers classic Roman and Italian dishes, and service is friendly and efficient. Since every tourist in Rome knows about it and since the regulars won't relinquish their niches, you may have to wait for a table; go early. *Via della Croce 81, tel. 06/678-1454. No reservations. Dress: casual. AE, DC. Closed Sun. and Christmas.*

Paris. On a small square just off Piazza Santa Maria in

Trastevere, Paris (named after a former owner, not the city) has a reassuring, understated ambience, without the hoky, folky flamboyance of so many eating places in this gentrified neighborhood. It also has a menu featuring the best of classic Roman cuisine: homemade *fettuccine*, delicate *fritto misto* (zucchini flowers and artichokes, among other things, fried in batter) and, of course, *baccalà* (fried cod fillets). In fair weather you eat at tables on the little piazza. *Piazza San Callisto 7/a, tel. 06/585378. Reservations advised for dinner. Dress: casual. AE, DC, MC, V. Closed Sun. eve. and Mon., and 3 weeks in Aug.*

Pierluigi. Pierluigi, in the heart of Old Rome, is a longtime favorite with foreign residents of Rome and Italians in the entertainment field. On busy evenings it's almost impossible to find a table, so make sure you reserve well in advance. Seafood dominates (if you're in the mood to splurge, try the lobster), but traditional Roman dishes are offered, too, including *orecchiette con broccoli* (ear-shaped pasta with greens) and simple spaghetti. Eat in the pretty piazza in summer. *Piazza dei Ricci 144, tel. 06/686–8717. Reservations advised. Dress: casual. AE, V. Closed Mon. and 2 weeks in Aug.*

★ **La Rampa.** A haven for exhausted shoppers and sightseers, La Rampa is right behind the American Express office on Piazza Mignanelli, off Piazza di Spagna. The attractive decor evokes a colorful old Roman marketplace, and there are a few tables for outdoor dining on the piazza. The specialties of the house are a lavish antipasto, *gnocchetti al gorgonzola* (small pasta dumplings with cheese), fillet of beef with speck (smoked prosciutto), and *frittura alla Rampa* (deep-fried vegetables and mozzarella). La Rampa is popular and busy, and you may have to wait for a table. Get there early (or late). *Piazza Mignanelli 18, tel. 06/678–2621. No reservations. Dress: casual. No credit cards. Closed Sun., Mon. lunch, and Aug.*

★ **Romolo.** Generations of Romans and tourists have enjoyed the romantic garden courtyard and historic dining room of this charming Trastevere haunt, reputedly the one-time home of Raphael's lady love, the Fornarina. In the evening, strolling musicians serenade diners. The cuisine is appropriately Roman; specialties include *mozzarella alla fornarina* (deep-fried mozzarella with ham and anchovies) and *braciolette d'abbacchio scottadito* (grilled baby lamb chops). Alternatively, try one of the new vegetarian pastas featuring *carciofi* (artichokes) or radicchio. Meats are charcoal-grilled; there's also a wood-burning oven. *Via di Porta Settimiana 8, tel. 06/581–8284. Reservations advised. Dress: casual. AE, DC, V. Closed Mon. and Aug. 2–23.*

Tullio. This Tuscan trattoria opened in the 1950s between Via Veneto and Piazza Barberini, in the Dolce Vita days when this area was the center of Roman chic and bohème. It soon acquired a faithful clientele of politicians, journalists, and creative people, and it has changed little over the years. Decor and menu are simple. The latter offers typically Tuscan *pasta e fagioli*, grilled steaks and chops, and *fagioli all 'uccelletto* (beans with tomato and sage). *Via San Nicolò da Tolentino 26, tel. 06/481–8564. Reservations advised. Dress: casual but neat. AE, DC, MC, V. Closed Sun. and Aug.*

Inexpensive **Baffetto.** The emphasis here is on good old-fashioned value: The food is much more important than the surroundings. Baffetto is Rome's best-known inexpensive pizza restaurant, plainly decorated and very popular. You'll probably have to wait in line outside on the *sampietrini* (cobblestones) and then share your table once inside. The interior is mostly given over to the ovens, the tiny cash desk, and the simple, paper-covered tables. *Bruschetta* (toast) and *crostini* (mozzarella toast) are the only variations on the pizza theme. Turnover is fast: This is not the place to linger over your meal. *Via del Governo Vecchio 114, tel. 06/686–1617. No reservations. Dress: casual. No credit cards. Open evenings only. Closed Sun. and Aug.*

Birreria della Scala. This restaurant and music club in Trastevere is often crowded in the evening; it's a favorite among young Americans and Romans. Everything on the menu, which features salads and pasta, is reasonably priced; best bets are the *tagliatelle all'amatriciana* (noodles with tomato and bacon sauce) and *penne al gorgonzola* (tube pasta with creamy blue cheese sauce). There is no additional charge for the live music from 8 to 10 PM. *Piazza della Scala 58, tel. 06/580–3763. Reservations advised. Dress: casual. AE, DC, V. Closed Wed.*

★ **Birreria Tempera.** This old-fashioned beer hall is very busy at lunchtime, when it's invaded by businesspeople and students from the Piazza Venezia area. There's a good selection of salads and cold cuts, as well as pasta and daily specials. Bavarian-style specialties such as goulash and wurst and sauerkraut prevail in the evening, when light or dark Italian beer flows freely. *Via San Marcello 19, tel. 06/678–6203. No reservations. Dress: casual. No credit cards. Closed Sun. and Aug.*

Fiammetta. For an inexpensive meal at the Fiammetta, you have to order pizza and, perhaps, a vegetable dish or a salad; other dishes will send your check into the Moderate range. Pizza is available at lunch except in July and August. Near Piazza Navona, Fiammetta betrays its Tuscan origins in the frescoed views of Florence. In fair weather you sit outdoors under an arbor. *Piazza Fiammetta 8, tel. 06/687–5777. Dinner reservations advised. Dress: casual. AE, DC. Closed Tues.*

Hostaria Farnese. This is a tiny trattoria between Campo dei Fiori and Piazza Farnese, in the heart of Old Rome. Mamma cooks; Papa serves; and, depending on what they've picked up at the Campo dei Fiori market, you may find rigatoni with tuna and basil, spaghetti with vegetable sauce, *spezzatino* (stew), and other homey specialties. *Via dei Baullari 109, tel. 06/654–1595. Reservations advised. Dress: casual. AE, V. Closed Thurs.*

Polese. It's best to come here in good weather, when you can sit outdoors under trees and look out on the charming square off Corso Vittorio Emanuele in Old Rome. Like most centrally located, inexpensive eateries in Rome, it is crowded on weekends and weekday evenings in the summer. Straightforward Roman dishes are featured; specialties include *fettuccine alla Polese* (with cream and mushrooms) and *vitello alla fornara* (roast brisket of veal with potatoes). *Piazza Sforza Cesarini 40, tel. 06/686–1709. Reservations advised on weekends. Dress: casual. AE, DC, MC, V. Closed Tues., 15 days in Aug., 15 days in Dec.*

Tavernetta. The central location—between the Trevi Fountain and the Spanish Steps—and the good-value tourist menu make this a reliable bet for a simple but filling meal. The menu features Sicilian and Abruzzi specialties; try the pasta with eggplant or the *porchetta* (roast suckling pig). Both the red and the white house wines are good. *Via del Nazareno 3, tel. 06/679–*

*3124. Reservations required for dinner. Dress: casual. AE,
DC, MC, V. Closed Mon. and Aug.*

Along Via Appia Antica

Moderate **L'Archeologia.** In this farmhouse just beyond the catacombs,
you dine indoors beside the fireplace in cool weather or in the
garden under age-old vines in the summer. The atmosphere is
friendly and intimate, and specialties include homemade pastas, *abbacchio scottadito* (grilled baby lamb chops), and seafood. *Via Appia Antica 139, tel. 06/788-0494. Reservations
advised for dinner and weekends. Dress: casual. No credit
cards. Closed Thurs.*

Cecilia Metella. From the entrance on the Via Appia Antica,
practically opposite the catacombs, you walk uphill to a low-lying but sprawling construction designed for weddings feasts
and banquets. There's a large terrace shaded by vines for outdoor dining. Although obviously geared to larger groups, Cecilia Metella also gives couples and small groups full attention,
good service, and fine Roman-style cuisine. The specialties are
the searing-hot *crespelle* (crepes), served in individual casseroles, and *pollo alla Nerone* (chicken à la Nero; *flambéed*, of
course). *Via Appia Antica 125, tel. 06/513-6743. Reservations
advised on weekends. Dress: casual. AE. Closed Mon.*

Lodging

The wide range of Roman accommodations are graded officially
from five stars down to one. You can be sure of palatial comfort
and service in a five-star establishment, but some of the three-
star hotels are, in reality, more modest affairs, superficially
spruced up to capitalize on a central location. You'll find less
charm, perhaps, but more standard facilities in newer hotels in
the moderate or expensive category. The old-fashioned Roman
pension no longer exists as an official governmental category,
but, while now graded as inexpensive hotels, some preserve the
homey atmosphere that makes visitors prefer them, especially
for longer stays.

There are distinct advantages to staying in a hotel within easy
walking distance of the main sights, particularly now that so
much of downtown Rome is closed to daytime traffic. You can
leave your car at a garage and explore by foot. One disadvan-
tage, however, can be noise, because the Romans are a voluble
people—with or without cars to add to the racket. Ask for an
inside room if you are a light sleeper, but don't be disappointed
if it faces a dark courtyard.

Because Rome's religious importance makes it a year-round
tourist destination, there is never a period when hotels are pre-
dictably empty, so you should always try to make reservations.
If you do arrive without reservations, try one of the following
EPT information offices: Via Parigi 5 (tel. 06/488-3748), Termini Station (tel. 06/487-1270), Leonardo da Vinci Airport (tel.
06/601-1255). All can help with accommodations, and there is
no charge. Students can try the **Protezione Giovanni** office at
Termini Station; it specializes in finding low-cost accommodations for girls, but will help all students if it is not too busy. **CTS**
(tel. 06/467-9254) is a student travel agency with a bureau in
Termini Station. Avoid official-looking men who approach tour-

ists at Termini Station: They tout for the less desirable hotels around the train station.

Room rates in Rome are on a par with, or even higher than, those in most other European capitals. Some hotels quote separate rates for breakfasts—an extra charge of between 7,000 and 27,000 lire, depending on the hotel category. If you object to paying extra for breakfast, remember that you're not obliged to pay, but make it clear when you check in that you will not be having breakfast. Air-conditioning in lower-priced hotels may cost extra; in more expensive hotels it will be included in the price. All hotels have rate cards on the room doors or inside the closet. These specify exactly what you have to pay and detail any extras.

Highly recommended lodgings are indicated by a star ★.

Category	Cost*
Very Expensive	over 450,000 lire
Expensive	300,000–450,000 lire
Moderate	150,000–300,000 lire
Inexpensive	under 150,000 lire

All prices are for a standard double room for two, including tax and service.

Very Expensive **Grand.** A 100-year-old establishment of class and style, this CIGA-owned hotel caters to an elite international clientele. It's located only a few minutes from Via Veneto. Off the richly decorated, split-level main bar—where afternoon tea is served every day—there are a smaller, intimate bar and a buffet restaurant. The spacious bedrooms are decorated in gracious empire style, with smooth fabrics and thick carpets in tones of blue and pale gold. Crystal chandeliers and marble baths add a luxurious note. The Grand also offers one of Italy's most beautiful dining rooms, called simply Le Restaurant (*see* Dining, *above*). *Via Vittorio Emanuele Orlando 3, tel. 06/4709, fax 06/ 474–7307. 170 rooms and suites with bath. Facilities: bar, 2 restaurants. AE, DC, MC, V.*

★ **Hassler.** Located at the top of the Spanish Steps, the Hassler boasts what is probably the most scenic location of any hotel in the city. The front rooms and penthouse restaurant have sweeping views of Rome; other rooms overlook the gardens of Villa Medici. The hotel is run by the distinguished Wirth family of hoteliers. They assure a cordial atmosphere and magnificent service from the well-trained staff. The public rooms are memorable—especially the first-floor bar, a chic rendezvous, and the glass-roofed lounge, with gold marble walls and a hand-painted tile floor. The elegant and comfortable guest rooms are decorated in a variety of classic styles; some feature frescoed walls. The penthouse suite has a mirrored ceiling in the bedroom and a huge terrace. *Piazza Trinità dei Monti 6, tel. 06/ 678–2651, fax 06/678–9991. 101 rooms and suites with bath. Facilities: bar, restaurant. AE, MC, V.*

Majestic. In the 19th-century tradition of grand hotels, this establishment on Via Veneto offers sumptuous furnishings and spacious rooms, with up-to-date accessories such as CNN-TV, mini-bars, strongboxes, and white marble bathrooms. There are authentic antiques in the public rooms, and the excellent

Rome Lodging

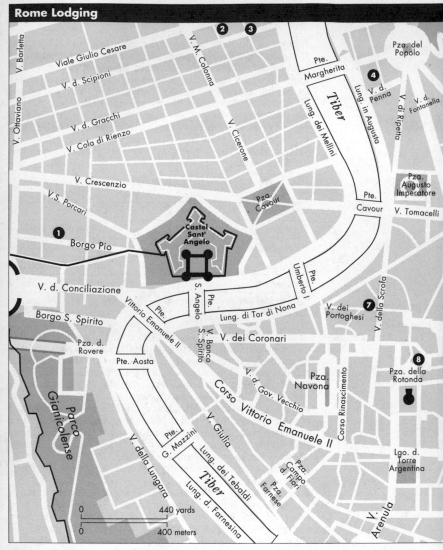

0 ——— 440 yards
0 ——— 400 meters

restaurant looks like a Victorian conservatory. *Via Veneto 50, tel. 06/486841, fax 06/488–0984. 86 rooms and suites with bath, many with whirlpool baths. Facilities: restaurant, bar with terrace, garage. AE, DC, MC, V.*

Expensive **Albergo del Sole al Pantheon.** This small hotel has been in its central location opposite the Pantheon since the 15th century. It was entirely renovated in 1989 and has been tastefully decorated with a blend of modern and antique furnishings. Ceilings are high, floors are tiled in terra-cotta, and there is a charming courtyard for al fresco breakfasting in good weather. *Piazza della Rotonda 63, tel. 06/678–0441, fax 06/684–0689. 26 rooms with bath. Facilities: bar, nearby garage. AE, DC, MC, V.*

Farnese. A turn-of-the-century mansion, totally renovated in 1991, the Farnese is located near the Metro and within walking distance of St. Peter's. Furnished with great attention to detail in Art Deco style, it has dazzling modern baths and charming fresco decorations. Room rates are low for the category and include a banquet-size breakfast. *Via Alessandro Farnese 30, tel. 06/321–2553, fax 06/321–5129. 24 rooms with bath. Facilities: parking, bar, roof garden. AE, DC, MC, V.*

Flora. With its Old-World decor and style, now largely refurbished with entirely new bathrooms, the Flora has a solid position among Via Veneto hotels. The rooms are ample and comfortable, and many have fine views of Villa Borghese. Potted plants are featured in the public rooms and marble-lined hallways. Period furniture, Oriental rugs, and old paintings add character to the rooms. Service is attentive, with a personal touch; this, together with the unostentatious comfort, is what keeps its regular clientele coming back year after year. The management is especially proud of the lavish breakfasts, served either in your room or in the old-fashioned dining room, which is complete with crystal chandelier, oil paintings, and red-velvet chairs. *Via Veneto 191, tel. 06/497821, fax 06/482–0359. 175 rooms with bath. AE, DC, MC, V.*

★ **Forum.** A centuries-old palace converted into a fine hotel, the Forum is on a quiet street within shouting distance of the Roman Forum and Piazza Venezia. Although it seems tucked away out of the mainstream, it's actually handily located for all the main sights. The wood-paneled lobby and street-level bar are warm and welcoming. The smallish bedrooms are furnished in rich pink and beige fabrics; the bathrooms are ample, with either tub or shower. What's really special about the Forum, though, is the rooftop restaurant: The view toward the Colosseum is superb. Breakfast on the roof or a nightcap at the roof bar can be memorable. *Via Tor dei Conti 25, tel. 06/679–2446, fax 06/678–6479. 76 rooms with bath. Facilities: bar, restaurant. AE, DC, MC, V.*

Giulio Cesare. An aristocratic townhouse in the residential, but central, Prati district, the Giulio Cesare is a 10-minute walk across the Tiber from Piazza del Popolo. It's beautifully run, with a friendly staff and a quietly luxurious air. The rooms are elegantly furnished, with thick rugs, floor-length drapes, rich damasks in soft colors, and crystal chandeliers. Public rooms have Oriental carpets, old prints and paintings, and marble fireplaces. *Via degli Scipioni 287, tel. 06/321–0751, fax 06/321–1736. 90 rooms with bath. Facilities: bar, garden, terrace. AE, DC, MC, V.*

★ **Victoria.** Considerable luxury in the public rooms, solid comfort throughout, and impeccable management are the main features of this hotel near Via Veneto. Oriental rugs, oil paintings, welcoming armchairs, and fresh flowers add charm to the public spaces, and the homey rooms are decorated in soothing combinations of peach, blue, and green. American businessmen, who prize the hotel's personalized service and restful atmosphere, are frequent guests. Some upper rooms and the roof terrace overlook the majestic pines of Villa Borghese. The restaurant offers à la carte meals and a good-value fixed-price menu featuring Roman specialties. *Via Campania 41, tel. 06/473931, fax 06/462343. 110 rooms with bath. Facilities: bar, restaurant. AE, DC, MC, V.*

Moderate **Britannia.** Located close to Termini Station and next to St. Paul's Episcopal Church, the Britannia is a bright, quiet, and compact hotel. The rooms are small but well planned; 401 and 402 both have terraces. Rooms are decorated in blue-gray or beige, and all have luxurious marble bathrooms. *Via Napoli 64, tel. 06/488-3153, fax 06/488-2343. 32 rooms with bath. Facilities: lounge, bar. AE, DC, MC, V.*

★ **Carriage.** Stay here for the location (by the Spanish Steps), the Old World elegance, and the reasonable rates. Totally renovated over the past few years, the hotel is decorated in soothing tones of blue and pale gold, with subdued Baroque accents adding a touch of luxury. The rooms have antique-looking closets and porcelain telephones. Double room 402 and single room 305 have small balconies; elegant room 302 is spacious, with an oversize bathroom. Alternatively, try for one of the two rooms adjoining the roof terrace. *Via delle Carrozze 36, tel. 06/699-0124, fax 06/678-8279. 27 rooms and suites with bath. AE, DC, MC, V.*

★ **Internazionale.** With an excellent location near the top of the Spanish Steps, the Internazionale has long been known as one of the city's best mid-size hotels. It's in a totally renovated building on desirable Via Sistina and is within easy walking distance of many downtown sights. Doubly thick windows ensure peace and quiet in the compact rooms. Rooms on the fourth floor have terraces; the fourth-floor suite has a private terrace and a frescoed ceiling. The decor throughout is in soothing pastel tones, with some antique pieces, mirrors, and chandeliers heightening the English country-house look. Guests relax in small, homey lounges downstairs and begin the day in the pretty breakfast room. *Via Sistina 79, tel. 06/679-3047, fax 06/678-4764. 40 rooms with bath. AE, DC, MC, V.*

Locarno. The central location off Piazza del Popolo helps keep the Locarno a favorite among the art crowd, which also goes for its intimate mood, though some of Locarno's fine *fin de siècle* character has been lost in renovations. An attempt has been made to retain the hotel's original charm, however, while modernizing the rooms. The latest additions are electronic safes and air-conditioning. The decor features coordinated prints in wallpaper and fabrics, lacquered wrought-iron beds, and some antiques. *Via della Penna 22, tel. 06/361-0841, fax 06/321-5249. 38 rooms with bath. Facilities: bar, lounge. AE, V.*

★ **Portoghesi.** In the heart of Old Rome, facing the so-called Monkey Tower, the Portoghesi is a fine small hotel with considerable atmosphere and low rates for the level of comfort offered. From a tiny lobby, an equally tiny elevator takes you to the quiet bedrooms, all decorated with floral prints and handsome pieces of old furniture. There's a breakfast room but no restaurant. *Via dei Portoghesi 1, tel. 06/686–4231, fax 06/687–6976. 27 rooms, most with bath. MC, V.*

★ **La Residenza.** In a converted town house near Via Veneto, this hotel is a good value, offering first-class comfort and atmosphere at reasonable rates. The canopied entrance, spacious well-furnished lounges, and the bar and terrace are of the type you would expect to find in a deluxe category. Rooms have large closets, color TV, fridge-bar, and air-conditioning; bathrooms have heated towel racks. The decor includes a color scheme of aquamarine and beige, combined with bentwood furniture. The clientele is mostly American. Rates include a generous American-style buffet breakfast. *Via Emilia 22, tel. 06/ 460789, fax 06/485721. 27 rooms with bath or shower. Facilities: bar, rooftop terrace, parking. No credit cards.*

Sant'Anna. If there were any doubts that the picturesque Borgo neighborhood in the shadow of St. Peter's was becoming fashionable, this stylish hotel goes some way toward dispelling them. Decorated with a flair that at times seems overdone, especially in the ample art deco bedrooms, the mood here is nonetheless soothing and welcoming. There is a frescoed breakfast room; the courtyard terrace boasts a fountain. There's no elevator to take you up the four floors, but it's worth the climb to the top floor to stay in one of the spacious blue-and-white attic rooms, each with a little terrace. *Borgo Pio 134, tel. 06/654– 1882, fax 06/654–8717. 19 rooms with bath or shower. AE, DC, MC, V.*

Inexpensive **Ausonia.** This small pension's big advantages are its location on Piazza di Spagna and its helpful management and family atmosphere. Six rooms face the famous square (quieter now that most through-traffic has been banned); all others face the inner courtyard. Furnishings are simple, but standards of cleanliness are high and rates are low. The hotel has many American guests; make sure you reserve well in advance. *Piazza di Spagna 35, tel. 06/679–5745. 10 rooms without bath. No credit cards.*

★ **Margutta.** This small hotel is centrally located on a quiet side street between the Spanish Steps and Piazza del Popolo. Lobby and halls are unassuming, but rooms are a pleasant surprise, with light walls, a clean and airy look, attractive wrought-iron bedsteads and modern baths. Three rooms on the roof terrace are much in demand for their views of the city's domes, bell towers, and the pines of the Pincian hill, but their rates nudge into Moderate category. Though it's in an old building, there is an elevator. *Via Laurina 34, tel. 06/322–3674. 21 rooms with bath or shower. AE, DC, MC, V.*

★ **Suisse.** This homey and simple hotel has an unbeatable location—five minutes' walk from the Spanish Steps. Clean and comfortable rooms and reasonable rates make the Suisse an excellent value. The mood in the public rooms is old-fashioned— the check-in desk is distinctly drab—but the rooms, though small, are cheerful, with bright bedspreads, framed prints, and old furniture. The lounge has large windows and well-upholstered armchairs. Some rooms face the fairly quiet courtyard. There's an upstairs breakfast room, but no restaurant. *Via Gregoriana 56, tel. 06/678–3649. 28 rooms, 14 with bath. No credit cards.*

The Arts and Nightlife

The Arts

Rome offers a vast selection of music, dance, opera, and film. Schedules of events are published in daily newspapers; in the "Trovaroma" Thursday supplement of *La Repubblica;* in the *Guest in Rome* booklet distributed free at hotel desks; and in the monthly *Carnet*, available free from EPT offices.

Concerts
Rome has long been a center for a wide variety of classical music concerts, although it is a common complaint that the city does not have adequate concert halls or a suitable auditorium. Depending on the location, concert tickets can cost from 8,000 to 45,000 lire. The principal concert series are those of the **Accademia di Santa Cecilia** (offices at Via dei Greci, box office tel. 06/654–1044), the **Accademia Filarmonica Romana** (Teatro Olimpico, Via Gentile da Fabriano 17, tel. 06/396–2635), the **Instituzione Universitaria dei Concerti** (San Leone Magno auditorium, Via Bolzano 38, tel. 06/361–0051), and the **RAI** Italian Radio-TV series at Foro Italico (tel. 06/368–6625). There is also the internationally respected **Gonfalone** series, which concentrates on Baroque music (Via del Gonfalone 32, tel. 06/687–5952). The **Associazione Musicale Romana** (tel. 06/656–8441) and **Il Tempietto** (tel. 06/481–4800) organize music festivals and concerts throughout the year. There are also many small concert groups. Many concerts are free, including all those performed in Catholic churches, where a special ruling permits only concerts of religious music. Look for posters outside churches announcing free concerts.

Rock, pop, and jazz concerts are frequent, especially in summer, although even performances by big-name stars may not be well advertised. Tickets for these performances are usually handled by **Orbis** (Piazza Esquilino 37, tel. 06/482–7403).

Opera
The opera season runs from November to May, and performances are staged in the **Teatro dell'Opera** (Via del Viminale, information in English: tel. 06/675–95725; ticket reservations in English: tel. 06/675–95721). Tickets go on sale two days before a performance, and the box office is open 10–1 and 5–7. Prices range from 20,000 to 60,000 lire for regular performances; they can go much higher for special performances, like an opening night or an appearance by an internationally acclaimed guest singer. Standards may not always measure up to those set by Milan's fabled La Scala, but, despite strikes and shortages of funds, most performances are respectable.

As interesting for its spectacular location as for the music is the summer opera season in the ruins of the ancient **Baths of Caracalla.** Tickets go on sale in advance at the Teatro dell'Opera box office, or at the box office at the Baths of Caracalla, 8–9 PM on the evening of the performance. Take a jacket or sweater and something to cover bare legs: Despite the daytime heat of a Roman summer, nights at Caracalla can be cool and damp.

Dance
The **Rome Opera Ballet** gives regular performances at the Teatro dell'Opera (*see* above), often with leading international guest stars. Rome is regularly visited by classical ballet companies from Russia, the United States, and Europe; performances are at Teatro dell'Opera, Teatro Olimpico, or at one of

the open-air venues in summer. Small classical and modern dance companies from Italy and abroad give performances in various places; check concert listings for information.

Film Rome has dozens of movie houses, but the only one to show exclusively English-language films is the **Pasquino** (Vicolo del Piede, just off Piazza Santa Maria in Trastevere, tel. 06/580–3622). Films shown here have subtitles and are not dubbed. Programs change frequently, so pick up a weekly schedule at the theater or consult the daily papers. Occasionally, certain film clubs and movie theaters also show English-language films in English; consult the newspapers.

Nightlife

Although Rome is not one of the world's most exciting cities for nightlife (despite the popular image of the city as the birthplace of *La Dolce Vita*), discos, live-music spots, and quiet late-night bars have proliferated in recent years. This has been true in the streets of the old city and in far-flung parts of town. The "flavor of the month" factor works here, too, and many places fade into oblivion after a brief moment of popularity. The best source for an up-to-date list of late-night spots is the weekly entertainment guide "Trovaroma," published every Thursday in the Italian daily newspaper *La Repubblica*.

Bars Rome has a range of bars offering drinks and background music. Jacket and tie are in order in the elegant **Blue Bar** of the Hostaria dell'Orso (Via dei Soldati 25, tel. 06/686–4250) and in **Le Bar** of the Grand hotel (Via Vittorio Emanuele Orlando 3, tel. 06/482931). **Harry's Bar** (Via Veneto 150, tel. 06/474–5832) is popular with American businessmen and Rome-based journalists. **Little Bar** (Via Gregoriana 54a, tel. 06/679–6386) is open from 9 PM until very late; it's in the Piazza di Spagna area.

Informal wine bars are popular with Romans who like to stay up late but don't dig disco music. Near the Pantheon is **Spiriti** (Via Sant'Eustachio 5, tel. 06/689–2499), which also serves light lunches at midday and is open until 1:30 AM. The same atmosphere prevails at **Cavour 313** (Via Cavour 313, tel. 06/678–5496), near the Roman Forum. Both are closed Sunday.

"In" places around the Piazza Navona and the Pantheon include **Antico Caffe della Pace** (Via della Pace 3, tel. 06/686–1216), and **Hemingway** (Piazza delle Coppelle 10, tel. 06/654–4135), which attracts a crowd from the movies, TV, and fashion worlds. Both are open evenings only, until very late.

Beer halls and pubs are popular with young Italians. **Birreria Marconi** (Via di Santa Prassede 9c, tel. 06/486636), near Santa Maria Maggiore, is also a pizzeria. It is closed Sunday. **Birreria Santi Apostoli** (Piazza Santi Apostoli 52, tel. 06/678–8285), is open every day until 2 AM. Among the pubs, **Fiddler's Elbow** (Via dell'Olmata 43, no phone) is open 5 PM–midnight but is closed Monday. **Four Green Fields** (Via Costantino Morin 42, off Via della Giuliana, tel. 06/359–5091) features live music and is open daily from 8:30 PM to 1 AM.

Music Clubs Jazz, folk, pop, and Latin music clubs are flourishing in Rome, particularly in the picturesque Trastevere neighborhood. Jazz clubs are especially popular, and talented local groups may be joined by visiting musicians from other countries. As admission, many clubs require that you buy a membership card for about 10,000–20,000 lire. The Rome EPT sponsors a Rome By Music pass that costs about 30,000 lire and will admit you to several of the best clubs. It is sold at major hotels. For information call 06/0578–3309.

In the Trionfale district near the Vatican, **Alexanderplatz** (Via Ostia 9, tel. 06/372–9398) has both a bar and a restaurant, and features nightly live programs of jazz and blues played by Italian and foreign musicians. For the best live music, including jazz, blues, rhythm and blues, African, and rock, go to **Big Mama** (Vicolo San Francesco a Ripa 18, tel. 06/581–2551). There is also a bar and snack food. Latin rhythms are the specialty at **Clarabella** (Piazza San Cosimato 39, tel. 06/581–7654), a live music club in the heart of Trastevere. There are usually two shows nightly. It's closed Monday.

In the trendy Testaccio neighborhood, **Caffè Latino** (Via di Monte Testaccio 96, tel. 06/574–4020) attracts a thirtysomething crowd with concerts (mainly jazz) in one room and a separate video room and bar for socializing. **Music Inn** (Largo dei Fiorentini 3, tel. 06/654–4934) is Rome's top jazz club and features some of the biggest names on the international scene. Open Thursday through Sunday evenings.

Live performances of jazz, soul, and funk by leading musicians draw celebrities to **St. Louis Music City** (Via del Cardello 13a, tel. 06/474–5076). There is also a restaurant. Closed Thursday.

Discos and Nightclubs Most discos open about 10:30 PM and charge an entrance fee of around 25,000–30,000 lire, which sometimes includes the first drink. Subsequent drinks cost about 10,000–15,000 lire. Some discos also open on Saturday and Sunday afternoons for under-16s.

There's deafening disco music at **Tatum** (Via Schiaparelli 29–30, tel. 06/322–1251) for the under-30 crowd, which sometimes includes young actors. Special events, such as beauty pageants, fashion shows, and theme parties, are featured, and there is a restaurant. Despite the address, the entrance is actually on Via Luciani 52. It's closed Monday.

Casanova (Piazza Rondanini 36, tel. 06/654–7314) is a disco for the under-25 crowd. Located near the Pantheon, there's live music and a cabaret to entertain before the deejay takes over. Roman yuppies mingle with a sophisticated show biz crowd while dancing to disco music at **Fabula** (Via Arco dei Ginnasi 14, Largo Argentina, tel. 06/679–7075). **Fonclea** (Via Crescenzio 82a, tel. 06/689–6302), near Castel Sant'Angelo, has a pub atmosphere and live music ranging from jazz to Latin American to rhythm-and-blues, depending on who's in town. The kitchen serves Mexican and Italian food.

Gilda (Via Mario dei Fiori, near Piazza di Spagna, tel. 06/678–4838) is the place to spot famous Italian actors and politicians. Formerly the Paradise supper club, this hot nightspot now has a new piano bar, as well as a restaurant and live music. It's closed Monday. **Hysteria** (Via Giovanelli 12, tel. 06/855–4587) attracts a very young crowd who come to enjoy the variety of music: disco, funk, soul, and hard rock. It's located off Via Salaria near the Galleria Borghese. It's closed Monday, also. A glittering disco, piano bar, and restaurant attracts over-25s to the **Open Gate** (Via San Nicolo di Tolentino 4, tel. 06/474–6301). Dancing starts at midnight.

One of Rome's first discos, **The Piper** (Via Tagliamento 9, tel. 06/841–4459) is an "in" spot for teenagers. It has disco music, live groups, and pop videos. Occasionally, there's ballroom dancing for an older crowd. It opens weekends at 4 PM and is closed Monday and Tuesday. Funky music and huge video screens make **Scarabocchio** (Piazza Ponziani 8, tel. 06/580–0495) another popular spot. It's closed Monday.

Veleno (Via Sardegna 27, tel. 06/493583) is one of the few places in Rome to offer black dance music, including disco, rap, funk, and soul. It attracts sports personalities and other celebrities.

For singles Locals and foreigners of all nations and ages gather at Rome's cafés on **Piazza della Rotonda** in front of the Pantheon, at **Piazza Navona,** or **Piazza Santa Maria** in Trastevere. The cafés on **Via Veneto** and the bars of the big hotels draw mainly tourists and are good places to meet other travelers in the over-30 age group. In fair weather, under-30s will find crowds of contemporaries on the **Spanish Steps,** where it's easy to strike up a conversation.

Excursion 1: Ostia Antica

One of the easiest excursions from the capital takes you west to the sea, where tall pines stand among the well-preserved ruins of Ostia Antica, the main port of ancient Rome. Founded around the 4th century BC, it gives you an idea of what Rome itself must have been like then. Ostia Antica conveys the same impression as Pompeii, but on a smaller scale and in a prettier, parklike setting. The city was inhabited by a cosmopolitan population of rich businessmen, wily merchants, sailors, and slaves. The great *horrea* (warehouses), were built in the 2nd century AD to handle huge shipments of grain from Africa; the *insulae*, forerunners of the modern apartment building, provided housing for the growing population. Under the combined assaults of the barbarians and the anopheles mosquito, the port was eventually abandoned, and it silted up. Tidal mud and windblown sand covered the city, and it lay buried until the beginning of this century. Now extensively excavated and excellently maintained, it makes for a fascinating visit on a sunny day.

Tourist Information

There is an overall charge for entrance to the excavation complex **Scavi di Ostia Antica,** and it includes entrance to the Ostiense Museum, which is on the grounds and observes the same opening hours. *Via dei Romagnoli, tel. 06/565–1405. Admission: 8,000 lire. Open daily 9–one hour before sunset.*

Escorted Tours

Tourvisa (Via Marghera 32, tel. 06/455–3224) offers boat excursions three days a week from March to December to Ostia Antica, with a guided visit to the excavations.

Getting Around

By Car The Via del Mare leads directly from Rome to Ostia Antica; the ride takes about 35 minutes.

By Train There is a regular train service from Ostiense train station, near Porta San Paolo, which is connected with the Piramide stop on Metro Line B. Trains leave every half-hour, and the ride takes about 30 minutes.

Exploring

Numbers in the margin correspond to points of interest on the Rome Environs map.

Near the entrance to the *Scavi* (excavations) is a fortress built in the 15th century for Pope Julius II. The hamlet that grew up around it is charming. However, your visit to **Ostia Antica** itself starts at **Via delle Tombe,** lined with sepulchers from various periods. From here, you enter the **Porta Romana,** one of the city's three gates. This is the beginning of the **Decumanus Maximus,** the main thoroughfare crossing the city from end to end.

About 300 yards up on the right are the **Terme di Nettuno** (Baths of Neptune), decorated with black-and-white mosaics representing Neptune and Amphitrite. Directly behind the baths is the barracks of the fire department, which played an important role in a town with warehouses full of valuable goods and foodstuffs.

Just ahead, and also on the right side of Decumanus Maximus, is the beautiful **Theater,** built by Augustus and completely restored by Septimus Severus in the 2nd century AD. Behind it, in the vast Piazzale delle Corporazioni, where trade organizations similar to guilds had their offices, is the **Temple of Ceres:** This is appropriate for a town dealing in grain imports, since Ceres, who gave her name to cereal, was the goddess of agriculture. Next to the theater, where there is a coffee bar, you can visit the **House of Apuleius,** built in Pompeiian style—containing fewer windows, and built lower, than those in Ostia. Next to it is the **Mithraeum,** with balconies and a hall decorated with symbols of the cult of Mithras. This men-only religion, imported from Persia, was especially popular with legionnaires.

On the Via dei Molini, 200 yards beyond the theater, there is a mill, where grain for the warehouses next door was ground with the stones you see there. Along Via dei Molini, a left turn 50 yards up Via dei Molini, you'll come upon a **thermopolium** (bar) with a marble counter and a fresco depicting the fruit and foodstuffs that were sold here. Turn right at the end of Via di Diana onto Via dei Dipinti; at the end is the **Museo Ostiense,** which displays some of the ancient sculptures and mosaics found among the ruins.

Retrace your steps along Via dei Dipinti and turn right just before Via di Diana for the **Forum,** with monumental remains of the city's most important temple, dedicated to Jupiter, Juno, and Minerva; other ruins of baths; a basilica (in Roman times a basilica served the secular purpose of a hall of justice); and smaller temples.

A continuation of Decumanus Maximus leads from the Forum. From the crossroads, about 100 yards on, Via Epagathiana, on the right, leads down toward the Tiber, where there are large warehouses, erected in the 2nd century AD to deal with enormous amounts of grain imported into Rome during that period, the height of the Empire.

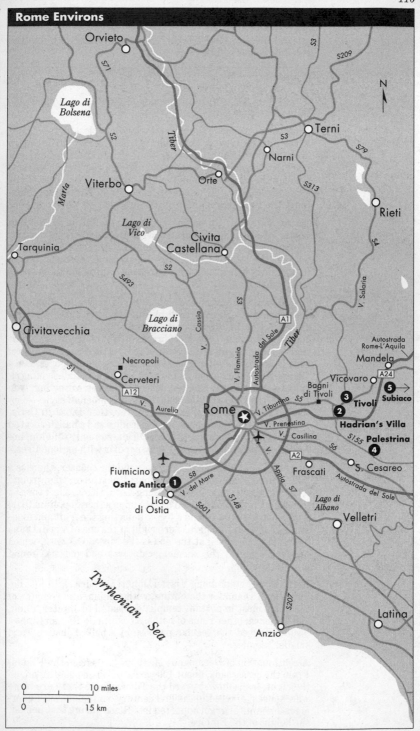

Rome Environs

Orvieto

S71

S3

S209

Lago di Bolsena

S2

Tiber

Terni

S3

Narni

N

Viterbo

Orte

S313

S79

Rieti

Lago di Vico

Civita Castellana

S4

Maria

Tarquinia

S493

S2

Cassia

S3

V. Salaria

Civitavecchia

Lago di Bracciano

A1

Tiber

Autostrada Rome-L'Aquila

S1

V. Flaminia

Autostrada del Sole

Mandela

Necropoli

V.

V. Aurelia

A12

Cerveteri

Vicovaro

A24

Bagni di Tivoli

3 **Tivoli**

5 **Subiaco**

Rome

S5

2

V. Tiburtina

Hadrian's Villa

V. Prenestina

S155

Palestrina

V. Casilina

S6

4

Fiumicino

A2

Frascati

S. Cesareo

Ostia Antica **1**

S8

V. del Mare

Appia

Autostrada del Sole

Lido di Ostia

S7

S601

S148

Lago di Albano

Velletri

Tyrrhenian Sea

S207

Anzio

Latina

0   10 miles

0   15 km

Take the street opposite the entrance to the warehouses to the **House of Cupid and Psyche,** a residential house named for a statue found there; you can see what remains of a large pool in an enclosed garden decorated with marble and mosaic motifs. It takes little imagination to notice that house building even then put a premium on water views: The house faces the shore, which would have been only about a quarter-mile away. Take Via del Tempio di Ercole left and then go right on Via della Foce to see (on the left) the **House of Serapis,** a 2nd-century multi-level dwelling, and the **Baths of the Seven Wise Men,** named for a fresco found there.

Take Via del Tempio di Serapide away from Via della Foce and then the Cardo Degli Aurighi, where you'll pass—just up on the left—another apartment building. The road leads back to the Decumanus Maximus, which continues to the **Porta Marina.** Off to the left, on what used to be the seashore, are the ruins of the **Synagogue,** one of the oldest in the Western world. This is where you begin your return; Porta Marina is the farthest point in the tour. Go right at the **Bivio del Castrum,** past the slaughterhouse and the large round temple. You'll come to the **Cardine Massimo,** a road lined with ruined buildings. From here, turn left onto Via Semita dei Cippi to see the **House of Fortuna Annonaria,** the richly decorated house of a wealthy Ostian. This is another place to marvel at the skill of the mosaic artists and, at the same time, to realize that this really was someone's home. One of the rooms opens onto a secluded garden.

Continue on Via Semita dei Cippi for about 150 yards until you turn right on Decumanus Maximus to retrace your last leg of the tour back to the entrance.

Dining

Monumento. Handily located near the entrance to the excavations, this attractive trattoria serves Roman specialties and seafood. *Piazza Umberto I, tel. 5650021. Reservations advised in the evening. Dress: casual. AE, DC, MC, V. Closed Mon. and Aug. 20–Sept. 7. Moderate.*

Sbarco di Enea. Also near the excavations, this restaurant is heavy on ancient-Roman atmosphere, with Pompeiian-style frescoes and chariots in the garden. On summer evenings you dine outdoors by torchlight, served by waiters in Roman costume. You'll probably come for lunch, when you can enjoy *farfalle con granchio* (pasta with crab sauce) or *linguine con aragosta* (with lobster sauce) and other seafood specialties, without all the hoopla. *Via dei Romagnoli 675, tel. 06/565–0034. Reservations advised in the evening. Dress: casual. AE, MC. Closed Mon. and Feb. Moderate.*

Excursion 2: Tivoli, Palestrina, and Subiaco

East of Rome lie some of the region's star attractions, which could be combined along a route that loops through the hills where ancient Romans built their summer resorts. The biggest attraction is Tivoli, which could be seen on a half-day excursion from Rome. But if you continue eastward to Palestrina, you can see a vast sanctuary famous in ancient times. And you could also fit in a visit to the site on which St. Benedict founded the hermitage that gave rise to Western monasticism. The monastery of St. Benedict is in Subiaco—not easy to get to unless you have a car, but you may want to make the effort to gain an insight into medieval mysticism.

Tourist Information

Tivoli (Giardino Garibaldi, tel. 0774/293522).
Subiaco (Via Cadorna 59, tel. 0774/85397).

Escorted Tours

American Express (tel. 06/67641) and **CIT** (tel. 06/47941) have half-day excursions to Villa d'Este in Tivoli. **Appian Line** (tel. 06/488-4151) and **Carrani Tours** (tel. 06/482-4194) have morning tours that include Hadrian's Villa.

Getting Around

By Car For Tivoli, take the Via Tiburtina or the Rome–L'Aquila autostrada (A24). From Tivoli to Palestrina, follow signs for the Via Prenestina and Palestrina. To get to Palestrina directly from Rome, take either the Via Prenestina or Via Casilina or take the Autostrada del Sole (A2) to the San Cesareo exit and follow signs for Palestrina; this trip takes about one hour. To get to Subiaco from either Tivoli or Palestrina or directly from Rome, take the autostrada for L'Aquila (A24) to the Vicovaro-Mandela exit, then follow the local road to Subiaco; from Rome, the ride takes about one hour.

By Train The FS train from Termini station to Palestrina takes about 40 minutes; you can then board a bus from the train station to the center of town.

By Bus ACOTRAL buses leave every 15 minutes from the terminal at the Rebibbia stop on Metro Line B for Tivoli, but not all take the route that passes near Hadrian's Villa. Inquire which bus passes closest to Villa Adriana and tell the driver to let you off there. The ride takes about 60 minutes. For Palestrina, take the ACOTRAL bus from the Anagnina stop on Metro Line A. There is local bus service between Tivoli and Palestrina, but check schedules locally. From Rome to Subiaco, take the ACOTRAL bus from the Rebibbia stop on Metro Line B; buses leave every 40 minutes and those that take the autostrada make the trip in 70 minutes, as opposed to an hour and 45 minutes by another route.

Exploring

Numbers correspond to points of interest on the Rome Environs map.

The road east from Rome to Tivoli passes through some unattractive industrial areas and burgeoning suburbs. You'll know you're close when you see vast quarries of travertine marble and smell the sulphurous vapors of the little spa, Bagni di Tivoli. This was once green countryside; now it's ugly and overbuilt. But don't despair because this tour takes you to two of the Rome area's most attractive sights: Hadrian's Villa and Villa d'Este. Villa d'Este is a popular destination; fewer people go to

Hadrian's Villa. Both are outdoor sights, which entail a lot of walking, and in the case of Villa D'Este, stair climbing. That also means that good weather is a virtual prerequisite for enjoying the itinerary.

❷ Visit **Hadrian's Villa** first, especially in the summer, to take advantage of the cooler morning sun: There's little shade. Hadrian, who succeeded Trajan as emperor in AD 117, was a man of genius and intellectual curiosity. Fascinated by the accomplishments of the Hellenistic world, he decided to re-create it for his own enjoyment by building this villa over a vast tract of land below the ancient settlement of Tibur. From AD 118 to 130, architects, laborers, and artists worked on the villa, periodically spurred on by the emperor himself, as he returned from another voyage full of ideas for even more daring constructions. After Hadrian's death in AD 138, the fortunes of his villa declined. The villa was sacked by barbarians and Romans alike; by the Renaissance, many of his statues and decorations had ended up in Villa d'Este. Still, it is an impressive complex.

Study the exhibits in the visitor center at the entrance and the scale model in the building adjacent to the bar, close by. They will increase your enjoyment of the villa itself by helping you make sense out of what can otherwise be a maze of ruins. It's not the single elements, but the peaceful and harmonious effects of the whole, that make Hadrian's Villa such a treat. Oleanders, pines, and cypresses growing among the ruins heighten the visual impact. *Villa Adriana. Admission: 8,000 lire. Open daily 9–90 minutes before sunset.*

Time Out The **Adriano** restaurant, at the entrance to Hadrian's Villa, is a handy place to have lunch and to rest before heading up the hill to Villa d'Este. The food is good, and the atmosphere is relaxing. *AE, DC, MC, V. Closed Mon. Moderate.*

❸ From Hadrian's Villa, catch the local bus up to **Tivoli**'s main square, Largo Garibaldi. Take a left onto Via Boselli and cross Piazza Trento, with the church of Santa Maria Maggiore on your left, to reach the entrance to **Villa d'Este.** Ippolito d'Este was an active figure in the political intrigues of mid-16th-century Italy. He was also a cardinal, thanks to his grandfather, Alexander VI, the infamous Borgia pope. To console himself at a time when he saw his political star in decline, Ippolito tore down part of a Franciscan monastery that occupied the site he had chosen for his villa. Then the determined prelate diverted the Aniene River into a channel to run under the town and provide water for Villa d'Este's fountains. Big, small, noisy, quiet, rushing, and running, the fountains create a late-Renaissance playground, now run-down, with fountains spouting polluted water. *Villa d'Este. Admission: 5,000 lire. Open daily 9–90 minutes before sunset.*

Only 27 kilometers (17 miles) south of Tivoli on S636 and 37 kilometers (23 miles) outside Rome along Via Prenestina, ❹ **Palestrina** is set on the slopes of Mount Ginestro, from which it commands a sweeping view of the green plain and distant mountains. It is surprisingly little known outside Italy, except to students of ancient history and music lovers. Its most famous native son, Giovanni Pierluigi da Palestrina, born here in 1525, was the renowned composer of 105 masses, as well as madrigals, magnificats, and motets. But the town was celebrated long before the composer's lifetime.

Ancient Praeneste, modern Palestrina, was founded much earlier than Rome. It was the site of the Temple of Fortuna Primigenia, which dates from the beginning of the 2nd century BC. This was one of the biggest, richest, and most frequented temple complexes in all antiquity. People came from far and wide to consult its famous oracle, yet in modern times, no one had any idea of the extent of the complex until World War II bombings exposed ancient foundations that stretched way out into the plain below the town. It's since become clear that the temple area was larger than the town of Palestrina is today. Now you can make out the four superimposed terraces that formed the main part of the temple; they were built up on great arches and were linked by broad flights of stairs. The whole town sits on top of what was once the main part of the temple.

Large arches and terraces scale the hillside up to **Palazzo Barberini,** built in the 17th century along the semicircular lines of the original temple. It's now a museum containing a wealth of material found on the site, some dating back to the 4th century BC. The collection of splendid engraved bronze urns was plundered by art thieves in 1991, but they couldn't carry off the chief attraction, a 1st century BC mosaic representing the Nile in flood. This delightful work is a large-scale composition in which form, color, and innumerable details captivate the eye. It's worth making the trip to Palestrina just for this. But there's more: a perfect scale model of the temple as it was in ancient times, which will help you appreciate the immensity of the original construction. *Museo Nazionale Archeologico, Palazzo Barberini. Admission: 6,000 lire. Open Tues.–Sun., spring and fall 9–6, summer 9–7:30, winter 9–4.*

⑤ If you are driving or if you don't mind setting out on a roundabout route by local bus, you could continue on to **Subiaco,** tucked away in the mountains above Tivoli and Palestrina. Take S155 east for about 40 kilometers (25 miles) before turning left on S411 for 25 kilometers (15 miles) to Subiaco. Its inaccessibility was undoubtedly a point in its favor for St. Benedict: The 6th-century monastery that he founded here became a landmark of Western monasticism.

This excursion is best made by car because it's nearly a 3-kilometer (2-mile) walk from Subiaco to Santa Scholastica, and another half-hour by footpath up to San Benedetto. If you don't have a car, inquire in Subiaco about a local bus to get you at least part of the way.

The first monastery you come upon is that of **Santa Scholastica,** actually a convent, and the only one of the hermitages founded by St. Benedict and his sister Scholastica to have survived the Lombard invasion of Italy in the 9th century. It has three cloisters, the oldest dating back to the 13th century. The library, which is not open to visitors, contains some precious volumes; this was the site of the first print shop in Italy, set up in 1474. *Admission free. Open daily 9–12:30, 4–7.*

Drive up to the **monastery of St. Benedict,** or take the footpath that climbs the hill. The monastery was built over the grotto where St. Benedict lived and meditated. Clinging to the cliff on nine great arches, the monastery has resisted the assaults of man and nature for almost 800 years. You climb a broad, sloping avenue and enter through a little wooden veranda, where a Latin inscription augurs "peace to those who enter." You find yourself in the colorful world of the upper church, every inch of it covered with frescoes by Umbrian and Sienese artists of the 14th century. In front of the main altar, a stairway leads down to the lower church, carved out of the rock, with yet another stairway down to the grotto, or cave, where Benedict lived as a hermit for three years. The frescoes here are even earlier than those above; look for the portrait of St. Francis of Assisi, painted from life in 1210, in the Chapel of St. Gregory, and for the oldest fresco in the monastery, in the Shepherd's Grotto. *Admission free. Open daily 9–12:30, 3–6.*

Back in town, if you've got the time, stop at the 14th-century **church of San Francesco** to see the frescoes by Il Sodoma. *Ring for admission.*

Dining

Palestrina **Coccia.** In this dining room of a small, centrally located hotel in
★ Palestrina's public garden, you'll find scenic views, a cordial welcome, and local dishes with a few interesting variations. The fettucine is light and freshly made, served with a choice of sauces. A more unusual item on the menu is the *pasta e fagioli con frutti di mare* (thick bean and pasta soup with shellfish). *Piazzale Liberazione, tel. 06/953–8172. Reservations not needed. Dress: casual. AE, DC, MC, V. Moderate.*

Subiaco **Belvedere.** This small hotel on the road between the town and the monasteries is equipped to serve crowds of skiers from the slopes of nearby Mount Livata, as well as pilgrims on their way to St. Benedict's hermitage. The atmosphere is homey and cordial. Specialties include homemade fettuccine with a tasty *ragú* sauce and grilled meats and sausages. *Via dei Monasteri 33, tel. 0774/85531. No reservations. Dress: casual. No credit cards. Inexpensive.*

Mariuccia. This modern barnlike restaurant, located close to the monasteries, caters to weddings and other functions but is calm enough on weekdays. There's a large garden and a good view from the picture windows. House specialties are homemade fettuccine with *porcini* mushrooms and *scaloppe al tartufo* (truffled veal scallops). In the summer you dine outdoors under bright umbrellas. *Via Sublacense, tel. 0774/84851. Reservations advised for lunch. Dress: casual. No credit cards. Closed Mon. and Nov. Inexpensive.*

Tivoli **Del Falcone.** A central location—on the main street leading off Largo Garibaldi—means that this restaurant is popular and often crowded. In the ample and rustic dining rooms, you can try homemade fettuccine and cannelloni. Country-style grilled meats are excellent. *Via Trevio 34, tel. 0774/22358. Reservations advised. Dress: casual. No credit cards. Inexpensive.*

4 Florence

By George
Sullivan

Florence is one of the preeminent treasures of Europe, and it is a time-honored Mecca for sightseers from all over the world. But as a city, it can be surprisingly forbidding to the first-time visitor. Its architecture is predominantly Early Renaissance and retains many of the harsh, implacable, fortresslike features of pre-Renaissance palazzi, whose facades were mostly meant to keep intruders out rather than to invite sightseers in. With the exception of a very few buildings, the stately dignity of the High Renaissance and the exuberant invention of the Baroque are not to be found here. The typical Florentine exterior gives nothing away, as if obsessively guarding secret treasures within.

The treasures, of course, are very real. And far from being a secret, they are famous the world over. The city is an artistic treasure house of unique and incomparable proportions. A single historical fact explains the phenomenon: Florence gave birth to the Renaissance. In the early 15th century the study of antiquity—of the glory that was Greece and the grandeur that was Rome—became a Florentine passion, and with it came a new respect for learning and a new creativity in art and architecture. In Florence, that remarkable creativity is everywhere in evidence.

Prior to the 15th century, Florence was a medieval city not much different from its Tuscan neighbors. It began as a Roman settlement, laid out in the first century BC, and served as a provincial capital when the Roman Empire was at its height. Its rise to real power, however, did not begin until the era of the medieval Italian city-states, beginning in the 11th century.

From the 11th to the 14th centuries, northern Italy was ruled by feudal lords, and by the 13th century Florence was a leading contender in the complicated struggle between the Guelphs and the Ghibellines. Florence was mostly Guelph, and its Ghibelline contingent ruled the city only sporadically (which did not, however, keep the Florentine Guelphs from squabbling among themselves). In those bloody days Florence was filled with tall defensive towers built by the city's leading families on a competitive anything-you-can-build-I-can-build-bigger basis; the towers (and the houses below them) were connected by overhead bridges and catwalks, constructed to allow the members of allied families access to each other's houses without venturing into the dangerous streets below. The era gave rise, possibly for the first time in history, to the concept of turf, and its urban conflicts were at times just as vicious and irrational as the gang warfare within cities today.

The Guelph-Ghibelline conflict ended, finally, with the victory of the Guelphs and the rise of the Medici in the 15th century. The famous dynasty (which ruled Florence, and later all Tuscany, for more than three centuries) began with Giovanni di Bicci de' Medici and his son Cosimo, who transformed themselves from bankers into rulers. The dynasty reached its zenith with Cosimo's grandson Lorenzo the Magnificent (1449–92), patron and friend of some of Florence's most famous Renaissance artists. The towers were torn down, and the city assumed a slightly softer aspect. It still looks today much as it did then.

The history of modern Florence was shaped by its six years as the capital of the Kingdom of Italy. In 1861 Tuscany united with most of the other states on the Italian peninsula, and in

1865 Florence became the new nation's capital. In 1871 Florence relinquished the honor, when the final unification of Italy was effected by the capitulation of Rome.

But the city's history was equally influenced by the flood of November 4, 1966. The citizens of Florence went to bed the night before in a heavy downpour after three days of rain and a particularly wet autumn; they awoke the next morning to confront the worst disaster in the city's history. Florence was entirely under water. The Piazza del Duomo became a rushing river; the church of Santa Croce was battered by a torrent more than 20 feet deep; the Ponte Vecchio disappeared completely as the Arno broke into the walls of its shops and flowed through. Only toward midnight did the flood begin to recede.

The Ponte Vecchio—amazingly—survived. But the damage to the rest of the city, including some of its greatest artistic treasures, was horrific. Technologically and financially ill-equipped to cope with such a disaster, Florence asked for, and received, advice and help from an army of international experts. Today, most of the damage to the city has been repaired. But little has been done to keep this kind of ruin from happening again.

Essential Information

Arriving and Departing by Plane

Airports and Airlines The local airport, called **Peretola** (tel. 055/373498) is 10 kilometers (6 miles) northwest of Florence. Although expanding to accommodate flights from Milan, Rome, and some European cities, it is still a relatively minor airport. **Galileo Galilei** airport in Pisa (tel. 050/28088) is 80 kilometers (50 miles) west of Florence and is used by most international carriers.

International travelers flying on Alitalia through Rome's **Leonardo da Vinci Airport** can go directly nonstop to Florence's Santa Maria Novella train station via Alitalia's twice-daily Airport Train. Luggage is checked through to Florence, and meals and extras are available on the train. Airport Train arrangements must be made when you buy your plane ticket. The service also operates in the other direction, returning from Florence to the da Vinci airport.

Between the Airports and Downtown **By Car:** From Peretola take Autostrada A11 directly into the city. Driving from Pisa airport, take S67, a direct route to Florence.

By Train: A scheduled service operates on the one-hour connection between the station at Pisa airport and Santa Maria Novella train station in Florence. Trains start running about 7 AM from the airport, 6 AM from Florence, and continue service every hour until about 11:30 PM from the airport, 8 PM from Florence. You can check in for departing flights at the air terminal at Track 5 of the train station (tel. 055/216973).

By Bus: Don't think you can make the connection from **Pisa** airport because there is no direct service to Florence. Buses do go to Pisa itself, but then you have to change to a slow train service. There is a local bus service from Peretola to Florence (*see* Getting Around By Bus, *below*).

Arriving and Departing by Car, Train, and Bus

By Car   Florence is connected to the north and south of Italy by Autostrada A1. It takes about an hour's scenic drive to reach Bologna and about three hours to get to Rome. The Tyrrhenian coast is an hour away on A11 west. Upon entering the city, abandon all hope of using a car, since most of the downtown area is a pedestrian zone. For traffic information in Florence, call 055/577777.

By Train   Florence is on the principal Italian train route between most European capitals and Rome and within Italy is served quite frequently from Milan, Venice, and Rome by the new nonstops called Intercity (IC). The **Santa Maria Novella** station is near the downtown area; avoid trains that stop only at the Campo di Marte station in an inconvenient location on the east side of the city. For train information in Florence, call 055/278–785.

By Bus   Long-distance buses run by **SITA** (Via Santa Caterina da Siena 15/r, tel. 055/211487) and **Lazzi Eurolines** (Via Mercadante 2, tel. 055/215154) offer inexpensive if somewhat claustrophobic service between Florence and other cities in Italy and Europe.

Getting Around

By Bus   ATAF, the local city bus company, operates an efficient, extensive network of buses within the city and the outlying area. Maps and timetables are available for a small fee at the ATAF booth in the station or at the office at Piazza Duomo 57r, or for free at the main tourist office (*see* Important Addresses and Numbers, *below*). There are two types of tickets valid for one or more rides on all lines. One costs 1,000 lire and is valid for 60 minutes; the other costs 1,300 lire for 120 minutes. A 24-hour tourist ticket costs 5,000 lire. They must be purchased in advance at tobacco stores, newsstands, or ATAF booths next to the train station or near the cathedral. You have to cancel them on the small validation machines immediately on boarding the bus. Buses displaying a sign of a hand holding a coin have ticket-dispensing machines that accept exact change. Long-term visitors or frequent users of the bus should look into the monthly passes sold at the ATAF office.

By Taxi   Taxis usually wait at stands throughout the city (such as in front of the train station and in Piazza della Repubblica), or they can be called by dialing 055/4390 or 055/4798.

By Moped   Those who want to go native and rent a noisy Vespa (Italian for wasp) or other make of motorcycle or moped may do so at **Motorent** (Via San Zanobi 9/r, tel. 055/490113) or **Alinari** (Via Guelfa 85r, tel. 055/280500). Helmets are mandatory and can be rented here.

By Bicycle   Brave souls many also rent bicycles at easy-to-spot locations at Fortezza da Basso, Santa Maria Novella train station, and Piazza Pitti, or from an organization called **Ciao e Basta** (Via Alamanni, next to the station, tel. 055/256555).

By Foot   This is definitely the best way to see the major sights of Florence, since practically everything of interest is within walking distance along the city's crowded, narrow streets or is otherwise accessible by bus.

Important Addresses and Numbers

Tourist Information The city information office is at Via Cavour 1/r (next to Palazzo Medici Riccardi), tel. 055/276–0382. Open 8:30–7.

The **APT** (tourist office) is just off Piazza Beccaria, at Via Manzoni 16, tel. 055/22320. Open weekdays 8:30–1:30 and 4–6:30, Sat. 8:30–1:30. There is an information office next to the train station and another near Piazza della Signoria, at Chiasso dei Baroncelli 17/r (tel. 055/230–2124).

Consulates **U.S.** Lungarno Vespucci 38, tel. 055/298276. Open weekdays 8:30–noon and 2–4.
British. Lungarno Corsini 2, tel. 055/284133. Open weekdays 9:30–12:30 and 2:30–4:30.
Canadians should contact their embassy in Rome.

Emergencies **Police.** Tel. 113. The main police station is located at Via Zara 2, near Piazza della Liberta.

Doctors and Dentists For English-speaking doctors and dentists, get a list from the U.S. consulate, or contact **Tourist Medical Service** (Viale Lorenzo Il Magnifico, tel. 055/475411). **Ambulance.** Misericordia (Piazza del Duomo 20, tel. 055/212222).

Late-Night Pharmacies. The following are open 24 hours a day, seven days a week. For others, call 055/110.

Comunale No. 13 (train station, tel. 055/263435).

Molteni (Via Calzaiuoli 7/r, tel. 055/263490).

Taverna (Piazza San Giovanni 20/r, tel. 055/284013).

English-Language Bookstores **Paperback Exchange** (Via Fiesolana 31/r, tel. 055/2478154) will do just that, besides selling books outright. **BM Bookshop** (Borgo Ognissanti 4/r, tel. 055/294575) has a fine selection of books on Florence. **Seeber** (Via Tornabuoni 68, tel. 055/215697) has English-language books alongside the other titles. *All are open 9–1 and 3:30–7:30. Closed Mon. morning, Sun.*

Travel Agencies **American Express** (Via Guicciardini 49/r, near Piazza Pitti, tel. 055/278751) is also represented by **Universalturismo** (Via Speziali 7/r, off Piazza della Repubblica, tel. 055/217241). **CIT** has a main office (Via Cavour 56 tel. 055/294306) and also a branch near the train station (Piazza Stazione 51, tel. 055/284–145). **Wagon-Lits Turismo/Thomas Cook** (Via del Giglio 27/r, tel. 055/218851). *All agencies are open weekdays 9–12:30 and 3:30–7:30, Sat. 9–noon.*

Guided Tours

Orientation Visitors who have a limited amount of time in Florence may find guided tours an efficient way of covering the city's major sights. The major bus operators (*see* Arriving and Departing by Car, Train, and Bus, *above*) offer half-day itineraries, all of which generally follow the same plan, using comfortable buses staffed with English-speaking guides. Morning tours begin at 9, when buses pick visitors up at the main hotels. The first stop is the cathedral complex, with its bapistry and bell tower, and the Accademia to see Michelangelo's famous statue of David. Next is the Piazzale Michelangelo for a fine view of Florence, then on to the Pitti Palace (or the Museo del Opera del Duomo on Mondays, when the Pitti is closed) for a guided tour of the art. The tours usually end at about 12:30 PM. Afternoon tours stop at the main hotels at 2 PM, begin in Piazza della Signoria, visit the Uffizi Gallery (or the Palazzo Vecchio on Mondays, when the Uffizi is closed), the nearby town of Fiesole, and return to Florence to see the church of Santa Croce, generally ending at about 6 PM.

Excursions   Contact the above operators a day in advance, if possible, because excursions are popular. Comfortable buses with English-speaking guides make full-day trips from Florence to Siena and San Gimignano (departure 9 AM, return 6 PM, lunch not included) and afternoon excursions to Pisa (departure 2 PM, return 7 PM), with pickup and return from the main hotels.

Exploring Florence

No city in Italy can match Florence's astounding artistic wealth. Important paintings and sculptures are everywhere, and art scholars and connoisseurs have been investigating the subtleties and complexities of these works for hundreds of years. But what makes the art of Florence a revelation to the ordinary sightseer is a simple fact that scholarship often ignores: An astonishing percentage of Florence's art is just plain beautiful. Nowhere in Italy—perhaps in all Europe—is the act of looking at art more rewarding.

But a word of warning is in order here. For some years now, Florentine psychiatrists have recognized a peculiar local malady to which foreign tourists are particularly susceptible. It's called "Stendhal's syndrome," after the 19th-century French novelist, who was the first to describe it in print. The symptoms can be severe: confusion, dizziness, disorientation, depression, and sometimes persecution anxiety and loss of the sense of identity. Some victims immediately suspect food poisoning, but the true diagnosis is far more outlandish. They are suffering from art poisoning, brought on by overexposure to so-called Important Works of High Culture. Consciously or unconsciously, they seem to view Florentine art as an exam (Aesthetics 101, 10 hours per day, self-taught, pass/fail), and they are terrified of flunking.

Obviously, the art of Florence should not be a test. So if you are not an inveterate museum goer or church collector with established habits and methods, take it easy. Don't try to absorb every painting or fresco that comes into view. There is second-rate art even in the Uffizi and the Pitti (*especially* the Pitti), so find some favorites and enjoy them at your leisure. Getting to know a few paintings well will be far more enjoyable than seeing a vast number badly.

And when fatigue begins to set in, stop. Take time off, and pay some attention to the city itself. Too many first-time visitors trudge dutifully from one museum to the next without really seeing what is in between. They fail to notice that Florence the city (as opposed to Florence the museum) is a remarkable phenomenon: a bustling metropolis that has managed to preserve its predominantly medieval street plan and predominantly Renaissance infrastructure while successfully adapting to the insistent demands of 20th-century life. The resulting marriage between the very old and the very new is not always tranquil, but it is always fascinating. Florence the city can be chaotic, frenetic, and full of uniquely Italian noise, but it is alive in a way that Florence the museum, however beautiful, is not. Do not miss the forest for the trees.

The three walking tours outlined in the following pages are best taken a day at a time. Attempts to complete them in fewer than three days will prove frustrating, for many (if not most) Florentine museums and churches close sometime between noon and 2, and only the churches reopen in the late afternoon.

Highlights for First-time Visitors

Duomo (Cathedral of Santa Maria del Fiore) (Tour 1: From the Duomo to the Boboli Gardens).

Battistero (Baptistery) (Tour 1: From the Duomo to the Boboli Gardens).

Museo dell'Opera del Duomo (Tour 1: From the Duomo to the Boboli Gardens).

Bargello (Museo Nazionale) (Tour 1: From the Duomo to the Boboli Gardens).

Piazza della Signoria (Tour 1: From the Duomo to the Boboli gardens).

Galleria degli Uffizi (Tour 1: From the Duomo to the Boboli Gardens).

Galleria dell'Accademia (Tour 3: From the Duomo to Santa Croce and Beyond).

Ponte Vecchio (Tour 1: From the Duomo to the Boboli Gardens).

Santa Croce (Tour 3: From the Duomo to Santa Croce and Beyond).

Tour 1: From the Duomo to the Boboli Gardens

Numbers in the margin correspond to points of interest on the Florence map.

The first tour begins with the Cathedral of Santa Maria del Fiore, more familiarly known as the **Duomo,** located in the Piazza del Duomo, with its accompanying **Battistero** (Baptistery), the octagonal building that faces the Duomo facade. The Baptistery is one of the oldest buildings in Florence, and local legend has that it was once a Roman temple of Mars; modern excavations, however, suggest its foundation was laid in the sixth or seventh century AD, well after the collapse of the Roman Empire. The round-arched Romanesque decoration on the exterior probably dates from the 11th or 12th century. The interior ceiling mosaics (finished in 1297) are justly famous, but—glitteringly beautiful as they are—they cannot outshine the building's most renowned feature: its bronze Renaissance doors decorated with panels crafted by Lorenzo Ghiberti (1378–1455). The panels are located on the north and east doors of the building (the south door panels are Gothic, designed by Andrea Pisano in 1330), and Ghiberti spent most of his adult life (from 1403 to 1452) working on them. The north doors depict scenes from the life of Christ; the later east doors (the ones facing the Duomo facade) depict scenes from the Old Testament.

The two sets of doors are worth close examination, for they are very different in style and illustrate with great clarity the artistic changes that marked the beginning of the Renaissance. Look, for instance, at the far right panel of the middle row on the earlier north doors *(Jesus Calming the Waters)*. Ghiberti here captured the chaos of a storm at sea with great skill and economy, but the artistic conventions he used are basically pre-Renaissance: Jesus is the most important figure, so he is the largest; the disciples are next in size, being next in importance; the ship on which they founder, being least important, is a mere toy. But you can sense Ghiberti's impatience with these artificial spatial conventions. The Cathedral Works Committee made him retain the decorative quatrefoil borders of the south doors for his panels here, and in this scene Ghiberti's storm seems to want to burst the bounds of its frame.

On the east doors, the decorative borders are gone. The panels are larger, more expansive, more sweeping, and more convincing. Look, for example, at the middle panel on the left-hand door. It tells the story of Jacob and Esau, and the various episodes of the story (the selling of the birthright, Isaac ordering Esau to go hunting, the blessing of Jacob, and so forth) have been merged into a single beautifully realized street scene. A perspective grid is employed to suggest depth, the background architecture looks far more convincing than on the north door panels, the figures in the foreground are grouped realistically, and the naturalism and grace of the poses (look at Esau's left leg) have nothing to do with the sacred message being conveyed. Although the religious content remains, man and his place in the natural world are given new prominence and are portrayed with a realism not seen in art since the fall of the Roman Empire, more than a thousand years before.

When Ghiberti was working on these panels, three of his artist friends were bringing the same new humanistic focus to their own very different work. In sculpture, Donato di Niccolo Betto Bardi, known as Donatello, was creating statuary for churches all over town; in painting, Tommaso di Ser Giovanni, known as Masaccio, was executing frescoes at the churches of Santa Maria del Carmine and Santa Maria Novella; in architecture, Filippo Brunelleschi was building the Duomo dome, the Ospedale degli Innocenti, and the church interiors of San Lorenzo and Santo Spirito. They are the fathers of the Renaissance in art and architecture—the four great geniuses who created a new artistic vision—and between them, they began a revolution that was to make Florence the artistic capital of Italy for more than a hundred years.

As a footnote to Ghiberti's panels, one small detail of the east doors is worth a special look. Just to the lower left of the Jacob and Esau panel, Ghiberti placed a tiny self-portrait bust. From either side, the portrait is extremely appealing—Ghiberti looks like everyone's favorite uncle—but the bust is carefully placed so that there is a single spot in front of the doors from which you can make direct eye contact with the tiny head. When that contact is made, the impression of intelligent life— of *modern* intelligent life—is astonishing. It is no wonder that when these doors were completed, they received one of the most famous compliments in the history of art, from a competitor known to be notoriously stingy with praise: Michelangelo

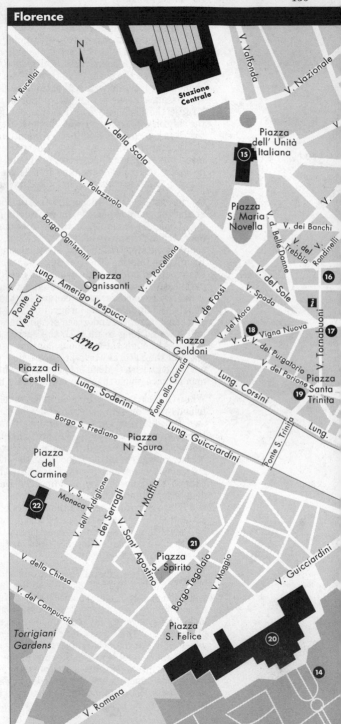

Florence

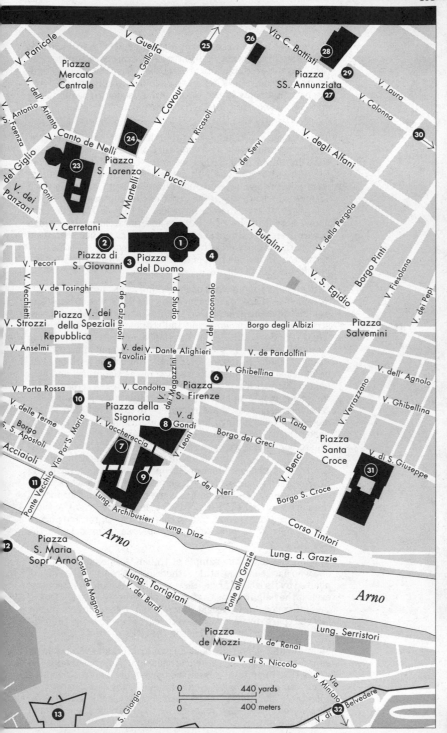

himself declared them so beautiful that they could serve as the Gates to Paradise.

The doors that you see on the Baptistery are exact copies of Brunelleschi's, and they still have the gleam of new bronze. The originals were removed, to protect them from the effects of pollution and acid rain. They have been beautifully restored and are now on display in the Cathedral Museum (to be discussed shortly). *Admission to Baptistery interior free. Open Mon.– Sat. 1–6, Sun. 9–1.*

The immense Duomo—the fourth-largest church in the world—was designed by Arnolfo di Cambio in 1296 but was not consecrated until 1436. The imposing facade dates only from the 19th century; it was built in the neo-Gothic style to complement Giotto's genuine Gothic (14th-century) **Campanile** (Bell Tower), which stands to the right of the church's facade. The real glory of the Duomo, however, is Filippo Brunelleschi's dome, herald of the new Renaissance in architecture, which hovers over the cathedral (and the entire city when seen from afar) with a dignity and grace that few domes, even to this day, can match. It was the first of its kind in the world, and for many people it is still the best.

Brunelleschi's dome was epoch-making as an engineering feat, as well. The space to be enclosed by the dome was so large and so high above the ground that traditional methods of dome construction—wooden centering and scaffolding—were of no use whatever. So Brunelleschi developed entirely new building methods, which he implemented with equipment of his own devising (including the modern crane). Beginning work in 1420, he built not one dome but two, one inside the other, and connected them with common ribbing that stretched across the intervening empty space, thereby considerably lessening the crushing weight of the structure. He also employed a new method of bricklaying, based on an ancient Roman herringbone pattern, interlocking each new course of bricks with the course below in a way that made the growing structure self-supporting. The result was one of the great engineering breakthroughs of all time: Most of Europe's great domes, including St. Peter's in Rome, were built employing Brunelleschi's methods, and today the Duomo has come to symbolize Florence in the same way that the Eiffel Tower symbolizes Paris. The Florentines are justly proud, and to this day the Florentine phrase for "homesick" is *nostalgia del cupolone* (homesick for the dome).

The interior is a fine example of Italian Gothic, although anyone who has seen the Gothic cathedrals of France will be disappointed by its lack of dramatic verticality. Italian architecture, even at the height of the Gothic era, never broke entirely free of the influence of Classical Rome, and its architects never learned (perhaps never wanted to learn) how to make their interiors soar like the cathedrals in the cities around Paris.

Most of the cathedral's best-known artworks have now been moved to the nearby cathedral museum. Notable among the works that remain, however, are two equestrian frescoes honoring famous soldiers: Andrea del Castagno's *Niccolo da Tolentino*, painted in 1456, and Paolo Uccello's *Sir John Hawkwood*, painted 20 years earlier; both are on the left-hand wall of the nave. *Niccolo da Tolentino* is particularly impressive: He rides his fine horse with military pride and wears his even finer hat—surely the best in town—with panache.

If time permits, you may want to explore the upper and lower reaches of the cathedral, as well. Ancient remains have been excavated beneath the nave; the stairway down is near the first pier on the right. The climb to the top of the dome (463 steps) is not for the faint-hearted, but the view is superb; the entrance is on the left wall just before the crossing. *Piazza del Duomo, tel. 055/294514. Excavation admission: 2,000 lire. Ascent admission: 4,000 lire. Duomo open daily 7:30 AM–6:30 PM; open for nonreligious purposes 10–5.*

Leave the Duomo by the right-aisle exit and turn left; at the east end of the piazza, opposite the rear of the cathedral, is the ❹ **Museo dell'Opera del Duomo** (Cathedral Museum). Its major attractions—other than the Ghiberti door panels mentioned earlier—are two: Donatello's *Mary Magdalen* and Michelangelo's *Pietà* (not to be confused with the more famous *Pietà* in St. Peter's, in Rome). The High Renaissance in sculpture is in part defined by its revolutionary realism, but Donatello's *Magdalen* goes beyond realism: It is suffering incarnate. Michelangelo's heart-wrenching *Pietà* was unfinished at his death; the female figure supporting the body of Christ on the left was added by one Tiberio Calcagni, and never has the difference between competence and genius been manifested so clearly. *Piazza del Duomo 9, tel. 055/2302885. Admission: 4,000 lire; free Sun. Open Mar.–Oct., Mon.–Sat. 9–7:30; Nov.–Feb., Mon.–Sat. 9–5:30.*

Return to the Duomo facade, and turn left onto **Via de Calzaiuoli.** This unusually wide street dates from the 14th century and probably represents Florence's first modern city planning. The street received special attention because it ran directly from the city's main religious square to its main civic square, the Piazza della Signoria, where the medieval city hall was located. Both the axis and the city hall remain intact to this day.

A short detour to the west (down Via dei Speziali) leads to the **Piazza della Repubblica.** The piazza's location, if not its architecture, is historically important: Here was located the ancient forum around which lay the original Roman settlement. The street plan in the area around the piazza still reflects the carefully plotted orthogonal grid of the Roman military encampment. The Mercato Vecchio (Old Market), located here since the Middle Ages, was demolished at the end of the last century, and the current piazza was constructed between 1890 and 1917 as a neoclassical showpiece. Nominally the center of town, it has yet to earn the love of most Florentines.

Return to Via de Calzaiuoli and turn right. Just down the street ❺ is the rectangular church of **Orsanmichele,** containing a beautifully detailed 14th-century Gothic tabernacle by Andrea Orcagna. Of particular note here, however, is the building's exterior. Originally a granary, it was transformed in 1336 into a church with 14 exterior niches. Each of the major Florentine trade guilds was assigned its own niche and paid for the sculpture the niche contains. All the statues are worth examining, though many are copies, but one deserves special notice: Andrea del Verrocchio's *Doubting Thomas*, dating from around 1470, in the middle niche on the Via de Calzaiuoli. The composition is beautifully controlled: Christ (like the building's other figures) is entirely framed within the niche, but St. Thomas stands on its bottom ledge, with his right foot completely outside the niche frame. This one detail—the positioning of a single foot—brings the whole composition to life, as if St. Thomas, just a moment ago, had stepped into the niche off the busy street to confront his master. It is particularly appropriate that this is the building's only niche to be topped with a classical triangular Renaissance pediment, for it is the revolutionary vitality of sculpture like this that gave the Renaissance its name.

From Via de Calzaiuoli, follow Via dei Tavolini (which turns into Via Dante Alighieri after one block and passes the fraudulently named Casa di Dante on the left) to the intersection of Via del Proconsolo. The church on the southwest corner is the ancient **Badia Fiorentina,** built in 1285; its graceful bell tower (best seen from the interior courtyard) is one of the most beautiful in Florence. The interior of the church proper was half-heartedly remodeled in the Baroque style during the 17th century; its best-known work of art is Filippino Lippi's delicate *Apparition of the Virgin to St. Bernard* (1486), on the left as you enter. The painting—one of Lippi's finest—is in superb condition and is worth exploring in detail. The Virgin's hands are perhaps the most beautiful in the city. (To illuminate, drop a coin in the box near the floor to the painting's right).

❻ On the opposite side of Via del Proconsolo from the Badia is the **Bargello.** During the Renaissance the building was used as a prison, and the exterior served as a "most-wanted" billboard: Effigies of notorious criminals and Medici enemies were painted on its walls. Today, the building is the **Museo Nazionale,** and houses what is probably the finest collection of Renaissance sculpture in Italy. Michelangelo, Donatello, and Benvenuto Cellini are the preeminent masters here, and the concentration of masterworks, which are beautifully displayed, is remarkable. For Renaissance art lovers, the Bargello is to sculpture what the Uffizi is to painting.

One particular display—easily overlooked—should not be missed. In 1402 Filippo Brunelleschi and Lorenzo Ghiberti competed to earn the most prestigious commission of the day: the decoration of the north doors of the Baptistery in the Piazza del Duomo. For the competition, each designed a bronze bas-relief panel on the theme of the Sacrifice of Isaac; both panels are on display, side by side, in the room devoted to the sculpture of Donatello on the upper floor. The judges chose Ghiberti for the commission; you can decide for yourself whether or not they were right. *Via del Proconsolo 4, tel. 055/210801. Admission: 6,000 lire. Open Tues.–Sat. 9–2, Sun. 9–1.*

Leaving the Bargello, continue south along Via del Proconsolo, to the small Piazza San Firenze. The church of San Firenze, on the left, is one of Florence's few Baroque structures; its steps offer a fine view of the Badia bell tower. From the north end of the piazza, go west on Via Condotta, then left onto Via dei Magazzini, which leads into the **Piazza della Signoria,** recently excavated and then repaved, the most striking square in Florence. It was here, in 1497, that the famous "bonfire of the vanities" took place, when the fanatical monk Savonarola induced his followers to hurl their worldly goods into the flames; it was also here, a year later, that he was hanged as a heretic and, ironically, burned. A bronze plaque in the piazza pavement marks the exact spot of his execution.

Time Out At the west end of the piazza, facing the statuary on the steps of the Palazzo Vecchio, is **Rivoire,** a café famous for its chocolate (both packaged and hot). Its outdoor tables and somewhat less expensive indoor counter are stylish, if pricey, places from which to observe the busy piazza. *Piazza della Signoria.*

❼ The statues in the square and in the 14th-century **Loggia dei Lanzi** on the south side are variable in quality, with the booby prize indubitably going to Bartolommeo Ammannati's gigantic **Neptune Fountain,** dating from 1565, at the corner of the Palazzo Vecchio. Even Ammannati himself considered it a failure, and the Florentines call it *Il Biancone,* which may be translated as "the big white man" or "the big white lump," depending on your point of view. Benvenuto Cellini's famous bronze *Perseus Holding the Head of Medusa* in the Loggia, however, is far from a failure; even the statue's pedestal is superbly executed (although the statuettes in its niches are recent copies of the originals). Other works in the loggia include *The Rape of the Sabine Women* and *Hercules and the Centaur,* both late–16th-century by Giambologna, and, in the back, a row of sober matrons dating from Roman times. The Loggia recently underwent lengthy structural restorations; many of the statues have been replaced by copies.

Back in the piazza, Giambologna's equestrian statue, to the left of the Neptune Fountain, pays tribute to the Medici Grand Duke Cosimo I; occupying the steps of the Palazzo Vecchio are a copy of Donatello's proud heraldic lion of Florence, known as the *Marzocco* (the original is now in the Bargello); a copy of Donatello's *Judith and Holofernes* (the original is inside the Palazzo Vecchio); a copy of Michelangelo's *David* (original now in the Accademia); and Baccio Bandinelli's *Hercules* (1534).

❽ The **Palazzo Vecchio** itself is far from beautiful, but it possesses a more than acceptable substitute: character. The palazzo was begun in 1299 and designed (probably) by Arnolfo di Cambio, and its massive bulk and towering campanile dominate the piazza masterfully. It was built as a meeting place for the heads of the seven major guilds that governed the city at the time; over the centuries it has served lesser purposes, but today it is once again the City Hall of Florence. The interior courtyard is a good deal less severe, having been remodeled by Michelozzo in 1453.

Although most of the interior public rooms are well worth exploring, the main attraction is on the second floor: two adjoining rooms that supply one of the most startling contrasts in Florence. The first is the vast **Sala dei Cinquecento** (Room of the Five Hundred) named for 500 deputies who debated here from 1865 to 1871, when Florence served as the capital of the Kingdom of Italy. The Sala was decorated by Giorgio Vasari, around 1570, with huge frescoes celebrating Florentine history; depictions of battles with neighboring cities predominate. Continuing the martial theme, the Sala also contains Michelangelo's *Victory* group, intended for the never-completed tomb of Pope Julius II, plus miscellaneous sculptures of decidedly lesser quality.

The second room is the little **Studiolo,** entered to the right of the Sala's entrance. This was the study of Cosimo de Medici's son, the melancholy Francesco I, designed by Vasari and decorated by Vasari and Agnolo Bronzino. It is intimate; civilized; and filled with complex, questioning, allegorical art. It makes the vainglorious proclamations next door ring more than a little hollow. *Piazza della Signoria, tel. 055/276-8465. Admission: 8,000 lire. Open weekdays 9–7, Sun. 8–1.*

9 Just south of the Palazzo Vecchio is the **Palazzo degli Uffizi,** a U-shaped building fronting on the Arno, designed by Vasari in 1559. Built as an office building—"uffizi" means "offices" in Italian—the palazzo today houses the finest collection of paintings in Italy. Hard-core museum goers will want to purchase the English guide sold outside the entrance.

The collection's highlights include Paolo Uccello's *Battle of San Romano* (its brutal chaos of lances is one of the finest visual metaphors for warfare ever committed to paint); Fra Filippo Lippi's *Madonna and Child with Two Angels* (the foreground angel's bold, impudent eye contact would have been unthinkable prior to the Renaissance); Sandro Botticelli's *Primavera* (its nonrealistic fairy-tale charm exhibits the painter's idiosyncratic genius at its zenith); Leonardo da Vinci's *Adoration of the Magi* (unfinished and perhaps the best opportunity in Europe to investigate the methods of a great artist at work); Raphael's *Madonna of the Goldfinch* (darkened by time, but the tenderness with which the figures in the painting touch each other is undimmed); Michelangelo's *Holy Family* (one of the very few easel works in oil he ever painted, clearly reflecting his stated belief that draftsmanship is a necessary ingredient of great painting); Rembrandt's *Self-Portrait as an Old Man* (which proves that even Michelangelo could, on occasion, be wrong); Titian's *Venus of Urbino* and Caravaggio's *Bacchus* (two very great paintings whose attitudes toward myth and sexuality are—to put it mildly—diametrically opposed); and many, many more. If panic sets in at the prospect of absorbing all this art at one go, bear in mind that the three tours outlined here are structured so as to offer late-afternoon free time, and the Uffizi is, except Sunday, open late. *Piazzale degli Uffizi 6, tel. 055/218341. Admission: 10,000 lire. Open Tues.–Sat. 9–7, Sun. 9–1.*

Time Out There is a coffee bar inside the Uffizi, near the exit; its terrace offers a fine close-up view of the Palazzo Vecchio. For something more substantial, try lunch at **Cavallino,** a moderately priced restaurant serving Tuscan specialties, overlooking the Piazza della Signoria at Via delle Farine 6/r (closed Wed.).

Leave Piazza Signoria at the southeast corner and follow Via Vacchereccia one block west to Via Por Santa Maria. Just north **10** of the intersection is an open-air loggia known as the **Mercato Nuovo** (New Market). It was new in 1551. Today it harbors mostly souvenir stands; its main attraction is Pietro Tacca's bronze *Porcellino* (Piglet) fountain on the south side, dating from around 1612 and copied from an earlier Roman work now in the Uffizi. Rubbing its drooling snout is a Florentine tradition—it is said to bring good luck.

Follow Via Por Santa Maria toward the river, and you will ar-**11** rive at the **Ponte Vecchio** (the Old Bridge), which is to Florence

what Tower Bridge is to London. It was built in 1345 to replace
an earlier bridge that was swept away by flood, and its shops
housed first butchers, then grocers, blacksmiths, and other
merchants. But in 1593 the Medici Grand Duke Ferdinando I,
whose private corridor linking the Medici palace (the Palazzo
Pitti) with the Medici offices (the Uffizi) crossed the bridge
atop the shops, decided that all this plebeian commerce under
his feet was unseemly. So he threw out all the butchers and
blacksmiths and installed 41 goldsmiths and eight jewelers.
The bridge has been devoted solely to these two trades ever
since.

In the middle of the bridge, take a moment (better yet, several
moments) to study the **Ponte Santa Trinita,** the next bridge
downriver. It was designed by Bartolommeo Ammannati in
1567 (possibly from sketches by Michelangelo), blown up by the
retreating Germans during World War II and painstakingly reconstructed after the war ended. Florentines like to claim it is
the most beautiful bridge in the world. Given the bridge's simplicity, this may sound like idle Tuscan boasting. But if you
commit its graceful arc and delicate curves to memory and then
begin to compare these characteristics with those of other
bridges encountered in your travels, you may well conclude
that the boast is justified. The Ponte Santa Trinita is more than
just a bridge: It is a beautiful piece of architecture.

A few yards beyond the south end of the Ponte Vecchio (on the
⑫ left side of Via del Guicciardini) is the church of **Santa Felicita,**
in the tiny piazza of the same name. Rarely visited by sightseers, the church contains one of Florence's finest Mannerist
masterpieces: Jacopo da Pontormo's *Deposition,* painted
around 1526, above the altar in the Capponi Chapel, just to the
right of the entrance. The subject matter has recently inspired
a particularly droll scholarly debate: Is the body of Christ being lowered from an inexplicably invisible cross, or is it being
raised toward God the Father, who was painted on a ceiling
dome above that no longer exists? Scholarly debate aside, the
painting's swirling design and contorted figures are quintessentially Mannerist. The palette, however, transcends Mannerism: Despite being ill-lit (the lights must be turned on by
the sacristan), the altarpiece's luminous colors are among the
most striking in Florence.

Like most Italian churches, Santa Felicita closes its doors during the early afternoon. So if you have lingered at the Uffizi or
over lunch, you may want to return here at the end of the tour,
after exploring the Belvedere Fortress and the Boboli Gardens.

After leaving Santa Felicita, walk along Costa di San Giorgio,
which starts as a tiny alley to the left of the church, passes a
house once occupied by Galileo (No. 11), and continues on to the
Porta San Giorgio entrance in the old city walls. The walk up
this narrow street is one of Florence's least-known pleasures.
The climb is steep, but just as you begin to wonder when it is
going to end, a remarkable transformation takes place: The city
falls away, the parked cars disappear, vine-covered walls
screening olive trees appear on both sides, birds begin to chirp,
and Florence becomes—of all things—tranquil. A narrow
Florentine street has suddenly turned into a picturesque Tuscan country lane.

Just before the costa ends at Porta San Giorgio, turn onto the short lane on the right (Via del Forte di San Giorgio), which ⑬ leads to the main entrance of the **Belvedere Fortress** (down the steps and through the arch). The fortress, which sometimes holds temporary art exhibitions, was built in 1429 to help defend the city against siege. But time has effected an ironic transformation, and what was once a first-rate fortification is now a first-rate picnic ground. Buses carry view-seeking tourists farther up the hill to the Piazzale Michelangelo, but, as the natives know, the best views of Florence are right here. To the north, all the city's monuments are spread out in a breathtaking cinemascope panorama, framed by the rolling Tuscan hills beyond: the squat dome of Santa Maria Novella, Giotto's proud campanile, the soaring dome of the Duomo, the forbidding medieval tower of the Palazzo Vecchio, the delicate Gothic spire of the Badia, and the crenellated tower of the Bargello. It is one of the best city-views in Italy. To the south the nearby hills furnish a complementary rural view, in its way equally memorable. If time and weather permit, a picnic lunch here on the last day of your stay is the perfect way to review the city's splendors and fix them forever in your memory. *Admission free. Open daily 9–sunset.*

Leave the Belvedere Fortress by the north exit, turn left, and ⑭ you will come to the rear entrance of the **Boboli Gardens,** adjacent to the Pitti Palace. Once inside the entrance, follow the path at the far left. The gardens began to take shape in 1549, when the Pitti family sold the palazzo to Eleanor of Toledo, wife of the Medici Grand Duke Cosimo I. The initial landscaping plans were laid out by Niccolo Pericoli Tribolo; after his death in 1550 development was continued by Bernardo Buontalenti; Giulio and Alfonso Parigi; and, over the years, many others. They produced the most spectacular backyard in Florence. The Italian gift for landscaping—less formal than the French but still full of sweeping drama—is displayed here at its best. A description of the gardens' beauties would fill a page but would be self-defeating, for the best way to enjoy a pleasure garden is to wander about, discovering its pleasures for yourself. One small fountain deserves special note, however: the famous *Bacchino*, next to the garden exit at the extreme north end of the palace, nearest the river. It depicts Pietro Barbino, Cosimo's favorite dwarf, astride a particularly unhappy tortoise. It seems to be illustrating—very graphically, indeed—the perils of too much pasta. *Admission free. Open Tues.–Sun. 9–one hour before sunset.*

Tour 2: From the Duomo to the Cascine

Tour 2 also begins at the Duomo. From the north side of the Baptistery, walk west along the mostly modern Via de Cerretani; after three blocks it forks. Take the middle fork (Via dei Banchi), which leads into the Piazza di Santa Maria Novella, ⑮ dominated by the church of **Santa Maria Novella** on the north side.

The facade of the church looks distinctly clumsy by later Renaissance standards, and with good reason: It is an architectural hybrid. The lower half of the facade was completed mostly in the 14th century; its pointed-arch niches and decorative marble patterns reflect the Gothic style of the day. About a hundred years later (around 1456), architect Leon Battista Alberti was called in to complete the job. The marble decoration of his upper story clearly defers to the already existing work below, but the architectural features he added evince an entirely different style. The central doorway, the four ground-floor half-columns with Corinthian capitals, the triangular pediment atop the second story, the inscribed frieze immediately below the pediment—these are classical features borrowed from antiquity, and they reflect the new Renaissance era in architecture, born some 35 years earlier at the Ospedale degli Innocenti (*see* Tour 3: From the Duomo to Santa Croce and Beyond, *below*). Alberti's most important addition, however, the S-curve scrolls that surmount the decorative circles on either side of the upper story, had no precedent whatever in antiquity. The problem was to soften the abrupt transition between wide ground floor and narrow upper story. Alberti's solution turned out to be definitive. Once you start to look for them, you will find scrolls such as these (or sculptural variations of them) on churches all over Italy, and every one of them derives from Alberti's example here.

The architecture of the interior is (like the Duomo) a dignified but somber example of Italian Gothic. Exploration is essential, however, because the church's store of art treasures is remarkable. Highlights include the 14th-century stained-glass rose window depicting *The Coronation of the Virgin* (above the central entrance door); the Filippo Strozzi Chapel (to the right of the altar), containing late–15th-century frescoes and stained glass by Filippino Lippi; the chancel (the area around the altar), containing frescoes by Domenico Ghirlandaio (1485); and the Gondi Chapel (to the left of the altar), containing Filippo Brunelleschi's famous wooden crucifix, carved around 1410 and said to have so stunned the great Donatello when he first saw it that he dropped a basket of eggs.

One other work in the church is worth special attention, for it possesses great historical importance as well as beauty. It is Masaccio's *Holy Trinity with Two Donors*, on the left-hand wall, almost halfway down the nave. Painted around 1425 (at the same time as Masaccio was working on his frescoes in Santa Maria del Carmine, described later in this tour), it unequivocally announced the arrival of the Renaissance era. The realism of the figure of Christ was revolutionary in itself, but what was probably even more startling to the contemporary Florentines was the coffered ceiling in the background. The mathematical rules for employing perspective in painting had just been discovered (probably by Brunelleschi), and this was one of the first paintings to employ them with utterly convincing success. As art historian E. H. Gombrich expressed it, "We can imagine how amazed the Florentines must have been when this wall-painting was unveiled and seemed to have made a hole in the wall through which they could look into a new burial chapel in Brunelleschi's modern style."

Leave Piazza di Santa Maria Novella by Via delle Belle Donne, which angles off to the south where you entered the square from Via dei Banchi and leads to a tiny piazza. In the center is a curious column topped by a roofed crucifix, known as the **Croce al Trebbio.** The cross was erected in 1308 by the Dominican Order (Santa Maria Novella was a Dominican church) to commemorate a famous victory: It was here that the Dominican friars defeated their avowed enemies the Patarene heretics in a bloody street brawl.

Beyond the piazza, bear left onto the short Via del Trebbio, then turn right onto Via Tornabuoni. On the left side of the street is the church of **San Gaetano**, with a rather staid Baroque facade (and Albertian scrolls), finished in 1645. Florence never fully embraced the Baroque movement—by the 17th century the city's artistic heyday was long over—but the decorative statuary here does manage to muster some genuine Baroque exuberance. The cherubs on the upper story, setting the coat of arms in place, are a typical (if not very original) Baroque motif.

For those who can afford it, **Via Tornabuoni** is probably Florence's finest shopping street, and it supplies an interesting contrast to the nearby Piazza della Repubblica. There, at the turn of the century, the old was leveled to make way for the new; here, past and present cohabit easily and efficiently, with the oldest buildings housing the newest shops. Ironically, the "modern" Piazza della Repubblica now looks dated and more than a little dowdy, and it is the unrenewed Via Tornabuoni, bustling with activity, that seems up to the minute.

Time Out For a mid-morning pickup, try **Giacosa**, at No. 83 Via Tornabuoni, for excellent coffee, cappuccino, and pastries, or **Procacci**, at No. 64, for finger sandwiches and cold drinks. *Both closed Mon.*

Via Tornabuoni is lined with Renaissance buildings. But its most imposing palazzo is the **Palazzo Strozzi**, a block south, at the intersection of Via Strozzi. Designed (probably) by Giuliano da Sangallo around 1489 and modeled after Michelozzo's earlier Palazzo Medici-Riccardi (*see* Tour 3: From the Duomo to Santa Croce and Beyond, below), the exterior of the palazzo is simple and severe; it is not the use of classical detail but the regularity of its features, the stately march of its windows, that marks it as a product of the early Renaissance. The interior courtyard (entered from the rear of the palazzo) is another matter altogether. It is here that the classical vocabulary—columns, capitals, pilasters, arches, and cornices—is given uninhibited and powerful expression. Unfortunately, the courtyard's effectiveness is all but destroyed by its outlandish modern centerpiece: a brutal metal fire escape. Its introduction here is one of the most disgraceful acts of 20th-century vandalism in the entire city.

One block west, down Via della Vigna Nuova, in the Piazza Rucellai, is Alberti's **Palazzo Rucellai,** which goes a step further than the Palazzo Strozzi, and possesses a more representative Renaissance facade. A comparison between the two is illuminating. Evident on the facade of the Palazzo Rucellai is the ordered arrangement of windows and rusticated stonework seen on the Palazzo Strozzi, but Alberti's facade is far less forbidding. Alberti devoted a far larger proportion of his wall space to windows (which soften the facade's appearance) and filled in the remainder with rigorously ordered classical elements borrowed from antiquity. The end result, though still severe, is far less fortresslike, and Alberti strove for this effect purposely (he is on record as stating that only tyrants need fortresses). Ironically, the Palazzo Rucellai was built some 30 years *before* the Palazzo Strozzi. Alberti's civilizing ideas here, it turned out, had little influence on the Florentine palazzi that followed. To the Renaissance Florentines, power—in architecture, as in life—was just as impressive as beauty.

If proof of this dictum is needed, it can be found several short blocks away. Follow the narrow street opposite the Palazzo Rucellai (Via del Purgatorio) almost to its end, then zigzag right and left to reach the Piazza di Santa Trinita. In the center of the piazza is a column from the Baths of Caracalla, in Rome, given to the Medici Grand Duke Cosimo I by Pope Pius IV in 1560. The column was raised here by Cosimo in 1565, to mark the spot where he heard the news, in 1537, that his exiled Ghibelline enemies had been defeated at Montemurlo, near Prato; the victory made his power in Florence unchallengeable and all but absolute. The column is called, with typical Medici self-assurance, the **Colonna della Giustizia,** the Column of Justice.

Halfway down the block to the right (toward the Arno) is the church of **Santa Trinita.** Originally built in the Romanesque style, the church underwent a Gothic remodeling during the 14th century (remains of the Romanesque construction are visible on the interior front wall). Its major artistic attraction is the cycle of frescoes and the altarpiece in the Sassetti Chapel, the second to the altar's right, painted by Domenico Ghirlandaio, around 1485. Ghirlandaio was a conservative painter for his day, and generally his paintings exhibit little interest in the investigations into the laws of perspective that had been going on in Florentine painting for more than 50 years. But his work here possesses such graceful decorative appeal that his lack of interest in rigorous perspective hardly seems to matter. The wall frescoes illustrate the life of St. Francis, and the altarpiece, *The Adoration of the Shepherds*, seems to stop just short of glowing.

From Santa Trinita, cross the Arno over the Ponte Santa Trinita and continue down Via Maggio until you reach the crossroads of Sdrucciolo de Pitti (on the left) and the short Via dei Michelozzi (on the right). Here you have a choice. If the noon hour approaches, you may want to postpone the next stop temporarily in order to see the churches of Santo Spirito and Santa Maria del Carmine before they close for the afternoon. If this is the case, follow the directions given two paragraphs below and return here after seeing the churches. Otherwise, turn left onto the Sdrucciolo de Pitti.

As you emerge from the Sdrucciolo into the Piazza dei Pitti, you will see unfold before you one of Florence's largest (if not one of its best) architectural set pieces: the famous **Pitti Palace.** The original palazzo, built for the Pitti family around 1460, comprised only the middle cube (on the upper floors the middle seven windows) of the present building. In 1549 the property was sold to the Medici, and Bartolommeo Ammannati was called in to make substantial additions. Although he apparently operated on the principle that more is better, he succeeded only in producing proof that enough is enough.

Today the immense building houses four separate museums: the former **Royal Apartments,** containing furnishings from a remodeling done in the 19th century; the **Museo degli Argenti,** containing a vast collection of Medici household treasures; the **Galleria d'Arte Moderna,** containing a collection of 19th- and

20th-century paintings, mostly Tuscan; and, most famous, the **Galleria Palatina,** containing a broad collection of 16th- and 17th-century paintings. The rooms of the latter remain much as the Medici family left them, but, as Mary McCarthy pointed out, the Florentines invented modern bad taste, and many art lovers view the floor-to-ceiling painting displays here as Italy's most egregious exercise in conspicuous consumption, aesthetic overkill, and trumpery. Still, the collection possesses high points that are very high indeed, including a number of portraits by Titian and an unparalleled collection of paintings by Raphael, among them the famous *Madonna of the Chair. Piazza Pitti, tel. 055/210323. Admission: Galleria Palatina, 8,000 lire; Museo degli Argenti, 6,000 lire; Royal Apartments closed for restoration; Galleria d'Arte Moderna: 4,000 lire. Open Tues.–Sat. 9–2, Sun. 9–1.*

Return to Via Maggio from the Pitti, take Via dei Michelozzi, a short street that leads into Piazza Santo Spirito; at the north ㉑ end rises the church of **Santo Spirito.** Its unfinished facade gives nothing away, but, in fact, the interior, although appearing chilly (or even cold) compared with later churches, is one of most important pieces of architecture in all Italy. One of a pair of Florentine church interiors designed by Filippo Brunelleschi in the early 15th century (the other, San Lorenzo, is described in Tour 3: From the Duomo to Santa Croce and Beyond, below) it was here that Brunelleschi supplied definitive solutions to the two main problems of interior Renaissance church design: how to build a cross-shaped interior using classical architectural elements borrowed from antiquity and how to reflect in that interior the order and regularity that Renaissance scientists (of which Brunelleschi was one) were at the time discovering in the natural world around them.

Brunelleschi's solution to the first problem was brilliantly simple: Turn a Greek temple inside out. To see this clearly, look at one of the stately arch-topped arcades that separate the side aisles from the central nave. Whereas the ancient Greek temples were walled buildings surrounded by classical colonnades, Brunelleschi's churches were classical arcades surrounded by walled buildings. This was perhaps the single most brilliant architectural idea of the early Renaissance, and its brilliance overthrew the previous era's religious taboo against pagan architecture once and for all, triumphantly reclaiming that architecture for Christian use.

Brunelleschi's solution to the second problem—making the entire interior orderly and regular—was mathematically precise: He designed the ground plan of the church so that all its parts are proportionally related. The transepts and nave have exactly the same width; the side aisles are exactly half as wide as the nave; the little chapels off the side aisles are exactly half as deep as the side aisles; the chancel and transepts are exactly one-eighth the depth of the nave; and so on, with dizzying exactitude. For Brunelleschi, such a design technique would have been far more than a convenience; it would have been a matter of passionate conviction. Like most theoreticians of his day, he believed that mathematical regularity and aesthetic beauty were opposite sides of the same coin, that one was not possible without the other. The conviction stood unchallenged for a hundred years, until Michelangelo turned his hand to architecture and designed the Medici Chapel and the Biblioteca

Laurenziana in San Lorenzo across town (*see* Tour 3: From the Duomo to Santa Croce and Beyond, *below*), and thereby unleashed a revolution of his own that spelled the end of the Renaissance in architecture and the beginning of the Baroque.

Leave Piazza Santo Spirito by Via Sant'Agostino, diagonally across the square from the church entrance, and follow it to Via de Serragli. You are now in the heart of a working-class neighborhood known as the Oltrarno, which is to Florence what Trastevere is to Rome: unpretentious, independent, and proud. Cross Via de Serragli and follow Via San Monaca to Piazza del Carmine. The church of **Santa Maria del Carmine** at the south end contains, in the Brancacci Chapel, at the end of the right transept, a masterpiece of Renaissance painting, a fresco cycle that changed art forever. Fire almost destroyed the church in the 18th century; miraculously, the Brancacci Chapel survived almost intact.

The cycle is the work of three artists: Masaccio and Masolino, who began it in 1423, and Filippino Lippi, who finished it, after a long interruption during which the sponsoring Brancacci family was exiled, some 50 years later. It was Masaccio's work that opened a new frontier for painting; tragically, he did not live to experience the revolution his innovations caused, for he was killed in 1428 at the age of 27.

Masaccio collaborated with Masolino on several of the paintings, but by himself he painted *The Tribute Money* on the upper-left wall; *Peter Baptizing the Neophytes* on the upper altar wall; *The Distribution of the Goods of the Church* on the lower altar wall; and, most famous, *The Expulsion of Adam and Eve* on the chapel's upper-left entrance pier. If you look closely at the latter painting and compare it with some of the chapel's other works, you will see a pronounced difference. The figures of Adam and Eve possess a startling presence, a presence primarily due to the dramatic way in which their bodies seem to reflect light. Masaccio here shaded his figures consistently, so as to suggest emphatically a single, strong source of light within the world of the painting but outside its frame. In so doing, he succeeded in imitating with paint the real-world effect of light on mass, and he thereby imparted to his figures a sculptural reality unprecedented in its day. To contemporary Florentines his Adam and Eve must have seemed surrounded by light and air in a way that was almost magical. All the painters of Florence came to look.

These matters have to do with technique, but with *The Expulsion of Adam and Eve*, his skill went beyond technical innovation, and if you look hard at the faces of Adam and Eve, you will see more than just finely modeled figures. You will see terrible shame and terrible suffering, and you will see them depicted with a humanity rarely achieved in art. *Admission to Brancacci Chapel: 5,000 lire. Open Mon. and Wed.–Sat. 10–5, Sun. 1–5.*

Time Out A popular spot for lunch on Piazza del Carmine is **Carmine,** a moderately priced restaurant with outdoor tables during the warmer months. It is located at the end of the piazza's northern extension. *Closed Sun.*

From Piazza del Carmine, return to Via de Serragli and walk back across the river over the Ponte alla Carraia (with a fine

view of the Ponte Santa Trinita, to the right) to Piazza Carlo
Goldoni, named for the 18th-century Italian dramatist. Here
you again have a choice: You can turn left to explore the
Cascine, a vast (2-mile-long) park laid out in the 18th century
on the site of the Medici dairy farms (it begins some 10 blocks
downriver, at the Piazza Vittorio Veneto), or, if you have not
overdosed on art, you can turn right and return to the Uffizi,
which is open all day on most days (and which is usually far less
crowded in the late afternoon than in the morning).

Tour 3: From the Duomo to Santa Croce and Beyond

Like the other two tours, Tour 3 begins at the Duomo. From the
west side of the Baptistery, follow Borgo San Lorenzo north
one block to Piazza San Lorenzo, in which stands a bustling outdoor clothing market overlooked by the unfinished facade of the
❷❸ church of **San Lorenzo.** Like Santo Spirito on the other side of
the Arno, the interior of San Lorenzo was designed by Filippo
Brunelleschi in the early 15th century. The two church interiors are similar in design and effect and proclaim with ringing
clarity the beginning of the Renaissance in architecture. (If you
have not yet taken Tour 2, you might want to read its entry on
Santo Spirito now; it describes the nature of Brunelleschi's architectural breakthrough, and its main points apply equally
well here. *See* Tour 2: From the Duomo to the Cascine, above.)
San Lorenzo possesses one feature that Santo Spirito lacks,
however, which considerably heightens the dramatic effect of
the interior: the grid of dark, inlaid marble lines on the floor.
The grid makes the rigorous regularity with which the interior
was designed immediately visible and offers an illuminating
lesson on the laws of perspective. If you stand in the middle of
the nave at the church entrance, on the line that stretches to
the high altar, every element in the church—the grid, the nave
columns, the side aisles, the coffered nave ceiling—seems to
march inexorably toward a hypothetical vanishing point beyond the high altar, exactly as in a single-point-perspective
painting.

The church complex contains two other important interiors,
designed by Michelangelo, which contrast markedly with the
interior of the church proper and which in their day marked the
end of Brunelleschi's powerful influence and the end of the
High Renaissance in architecture. The first is the **Biblioteca
Laurenziana,** the Laurentian Library and its famous anteroom,
entered from the church cloister (exit the church through the
door at the left side of the nave just before the crossing, take an
immediate right, climb the stairs to the cloister balcony, and
enter the first door to the right). Michelangelo the architect
was every bit as original as Michelangelo the sculptor. Unlike
Brunelleschi, however, he was not interested in expressing the
ordered harmony of the spheres in his architecture. He was interested in experimentation and invention and in expressing a
personal vision that was at times highly idiosyncratic.

It was never more idiosyncratic than here. This strangely
shaped anteroom has had scholars scratching their heads for
centuries. In a space more than two stories high, why did Michelangelo limit his use of columns and pilasters to the upper
two-thirds of the wall? Why didn't he rest them on strong ped-
estals instead of on huge, decorative curlicued scrolls, which
rob them of all visual support? Why did he recess them into the

wall, which makes them look weaker still? The architectural elements here do not stand firm and strong and tall, as inside the church next door; instead, they seem to be pressed into the wall as if into putty, giving the room a soft, rubbery look that is one of the strangest effects ever achieved by classical architecture. It is almost as if Michelangelo purposely set out to defy his predecessors—intentionally to flout the conventions of the High Renaissance in order to see what kind of bizarre, mannered effect might result. His innovations were tremendously influential and produced a period of architectural experimentation—the Mannerist era in architecture—that eventually evolved into the Baroque. As his contemporary Giorgio Vasari (the first art historian) put it, "Artisans have been infinitely and perpetually indebted to him because he broke the bonds and chains of a way of working that had become habitual by common usage."

Many critics have thought that the anteroom is a failure and have complained that Michelangelo's experiment here was willful and perverse. But nobody has ever complained about the room's staircase (best viewed head-on), which emerges from the library with the visual force of an unstoppable flow of lava. In its highly sculptural conception and execution, it is quite simply one of the most original and beautiful staircases in the world. *Admission free. Open Mon.–Sat. 9–1.*

The other Michelangelo interior is San Lorenzo's **New Sacristy,** so called to distinguish it from Brunelleschi's **Old Sacristy** (which can be entered from inside the church at the end of the left transept). The New Sacristy is reached from outside the rear of the church, through the imposing **Cappella dei Principi,** the Medici mausoleum that was begun in 1605 and kept marble workers busy for several hundred years.

Michelangelo received the commission for the New Sacristy in 1520 from Cardinal Giulio de Medici, who later became Pope Clement VII and who wanted a new burial chapel for his father, Giuliano, his uncle Lorenzo the Magnificent, and two recently deceased cousins. The result was a tour de force of architecture and sculpture. Architecturally, Michelangelo was as original and inventive here as ever, but it is—quite properly—the powerful sculptural compositions of the side wall tombs that dominate the room. The scheme is allegorical: On the wall tomb to the right are figures representing day and night, and on the wall tomb to the left are figures representing dawn and dusk; above them are idealized portraits of the two cousins, usually interpreted to represent the active life and the contemplative life. But the allegorical meanings are secondary; what is most important is the intense presence of the sculptural figures, the force with which they hit the viewer. Michelangelo's contemporaries were so awed by the impact of this force (in his sculpture here and elsewhere) that they invented an entirely new word to describe the phenomenon: *terribilità* (dreadfulness). To this day it is used only when describing his work, and it is in evidence here at the peak of its power. *Piazza di Madonna degli Aldobrandini, tel. 055/213206. Admission: 8,500 lire. Open Tues.–Sat. 9–2, Sun. 9–1.*

Just north of the Medici Chapel (a block up Via dell'Ariento) is Florence's busy main food market, the **Mercato Centrale.** If a reminder that Florence is more than just a museum is needed, this is the perfect place for it. There is food everywhere, some of it remarkably exotic, and many of the displays verge on the magnificent. At the Mercato Nuovo, near Ponte Vecchio, you will see tourists petting the snout of the bronze boar for good luck; here you will see Florentines petting the snout of a real one, very recently deceased and available for tonight's dinner.

Time Out The **Mercato Centrale** has a number of small coffee bars scattered about; there is even one upstairs among the mountains of vegetables. Have a coffee, watch the activity, and enjoy the fact that for once there is not a painting in sight.

Return to the clothing market in front of San Lorenzo, and from the north end of the piazza follow Via de Gori east one block, and turn left onto Via Cavour. As you turn the corner, **(24)** you will pass **Palazzo Medici-Riccardi** (entrance on Via Cavour). Begun in 1444 by Michelozzo for Cosimo de Medici, the main attraction here is the interior chapel on the upper floor. Painted onto its walls is Benozzo Gozzoli's famous *Procession of the Magi*, finished in 1460 and celebrating both the birth of Christ and the greatness of the Medici family, whose portraits it contains. Like his contemporary Ghirlandaio, Gozzoli was not a revolutionary painter and is today considered less than first rate because of his old-fashioned (even for his day) technique. Gozzoli's gift, however, was for entrancing the eye, not challenging the mind, and on those terms his success here is beyond question. The paintings are full of activity yet somehow frozen in time in a way that fails utterly as realism, but succeeds triumphantly as soon as the demand for realism is set aside. Entering the chapel is like walking into the middle of a magnificently illustrated child's storybook, and the beauty of the illustrations makes this one of the most unpretentiously enjoyable rooms in the entire city. *Via Cavour 11, tel. 055/27601. Admission free. Open Mon., Tues., Thurs.–Sat. 9–12:45 and 3–4:45, Sun. 9–noon.*

From Palazzo Medici-Riccardi, follow Via Cavour two blocks north to Piazza San Marco. At the north end of the square is the church of San Marco; attached to the church (entrance just to the right of the church facade) is a former Dominican monas-**(25)** tery that now houses the **Museo San Marco.** The museum—in fact, the entire monastery—is a memorial to Fra Angelico, the Dominican monk who, when he was alive, was as famous for his piety as for his painting. When the monastery was built in 1437, he decorated it with his frescoes, which were meant to spur religious contemplation; when the building was turned into a museum, other works of his from all over the city were brought here for display. His paintings are simple and direct and furnish a compelling contrast to the Palazzo Medici-Riccardi Chapel (Fra Angelico probably would have considered the glitter of Gozzoli's work there worldly and blasphemous). The entire monastery is worth exploring, for Fra Angelico's paintings are everywhere, including the Chapter House, at the top of the stairs leading to the upper floor (the famous *Annunciation*), in the upper-floor monks' cells (each monk was given a different religious subject for contemplation), and in the gallery just off the cloister as you enter. The latter room contains, among many other works, his beautiful *Last Judgment;* as usual with Last Judgments, the tortures of the damned are far more inventive than the pleasures of the redeemed. *Piazza San Marco*

1, tel. 055/210741. Admission: 6,000 lire. Open Tues.–Sat. 9–2, Sun. 9–1.

From Piazza San Marco, take a short detour a half-block down Via Ricasoli (which runs back toward the Duomo from the square's east side) to the **Galleria dell'Accademia.** The museum contains a notable collection of Florentine paintings dating from the 13th to the 18th centuries, but it is most famous for its collection of statues by Michelangelo—including the unfinished *Slaves*—which were meant for the tomb of Michelangelo's patron and nemesis Pope Julius II (and which seem to be fighting their way out of the marble), and the original *David*, which was moved here from the Piazza della Signoria in 1873. The *David* was commissioned in 1501 by the Opera del Duomo (Cathedral Works Committee), which gave the 26-year-old sculptor a leftover block of marble that had been ruined by another artist. Michelangelo's success with the defective block was so dramatic that the city showered him with honors, and the Opera del Duomo voted to build him a house and a studio in which to live and work.

Today the *David* is beset not by Goliath but by tourists, and seeing the statue at all—much less really studying it—can be a trial. After a 1991 attack upon it by a hammer-wielding frustrated artist (luckily, the only damage was a few minor nicks on the toes), the sculpture is surrounded by a plexiglass barrier. But a close look is worth the effort it takes to combat the crowd. The statue is not quite what it seems. It is so poised and graceful and alert—so miraculously *alive*—that it is often considered the definitive embodiment of the ideals of the High Renaissance in sculpture. But its true place in the history of art is a bit more complicated.

As Michelangelo well knew, the Renaissance painting and sculpture that preceded his work were deeply concerned with ideal form. Perfection of proportion was the ever-sought Holy Grail; during the Renaissance, ideal proportion was equated with ideal beauty, and ideal beauty was equated with spiritual perfection. In painting, Raphael's tender Madonnas are perhaps the preeminent expression of this philosophy: They are meant to embody a perfect beauty that is at once physical and spiritual.

But Michelangelo's *David*, despite its supremely calm and dignified pose, departs from these ideals. As a moment's study will show, Michelangelo did not give the statue ideal proportions. The head is slightly too large for the body, the arms are slightly too large for the torso, and the hands are dramatically too large for the arms. By High Renaissance standards these are defects, but the impact and beauty of the *David* are such that it is the *standards* that must be called into question, not the statue. Michelangelo was a revolutionary artist (and the first Mannerist) because he brought a new expressiveness to art: He created the "defects" of the *David* intentionally. He knew exactly what he was doing, and he did it in order to express and embody, as powerfully as possible in a single figure, an entire biblical story. David's hands *are* too big, but so was Goliath, and these are the hands that slew him. *Via Ricasoli 60, tel. 055/214375. Admission: 10,000 lire. Open Tues.–Sat. 9–2, Sun. 9–1.*

From the Accademia, return to Piazza San Marco and turn right on Via Battisti, which leads into the Piazza della Santissima Annunziata. The building directly across the square as (27) you enter is the **Ospedale degli Innocenti,** or Foundling Hospital, built by Brunelleschi in 1419. He designed the building's portico with his usual rigor, building it out of the two shapes he considered mathematically (and therefore philosophically and aesthetically) perfect: the square and the circle. Below the level of the arches, the portico encloses a row of perfect cubes; above the level of the arches, the portico encloses a row of intersecting hemispheres. The whole geometric scheme is articulated with Corinthian columns, capitals, and arches borrowed directly from antiquity. At the time he designed the portico, Brunelleschi was also designing the interior of San Lorenzo, using the same basic ideas. But since the portico was finished before San Lorenzo, the Ospedale degli Innocenti takes the historical prize: It is the very first Renaissance building.

(28) The church at the north end of the square is **Santissima Annunziata;** it was designed in 1447 by Michelozzo, who gave it an uncommon (and lovely) entrance cloister. The interior is an extreme rarity for Florence: a sumptuous example of the Baroque. But it is not really a fair example, since it is merely 17th-century Baroque decoration applied willy-nilly to an earlier structure—exactly the sort of violent remodeling exercise that has given the Baroque a bad name ever since. The **Tabernacle of the Annunziata,** immediately inside the entrance to the left, illustrates the point. The lower half, with its stately Corinthian columns and carved frieze bearing the Medici arms, was built at the same time as the church; the upper half, with its erupting curves and impish sculpted cherubs (badly in need of a bath), was added 200 years later. Each is effective in its own way, but together they serve only to prove that dignity is rarely comfortable wearing a party hat.

One block east of the entrance to Santissima Annunziata (on (29) the left side of Via Colonna) is the **Museo Archeologico.** If time and interest permit, a visit here is unquestionably worthwhile. The collection contains Etruscan, Egyptian, and Greco-Roman antiquities; guidebooks in English are available. The Etruscan collection is particularly notable—the largest in northern Italy—and includes the famous bronze *Chimera*, which was discovered (without the tail, which is a reconstruction) in the 16th century. *Via della Colonna 36, tel. 055/247–8641. Admission: 6,000 lire. Open Tues.–Sat. 9–2, Sun. 9–1.*

Follow Via Colonna east to Borgo Pinti and turn right, following Borgo Pinti through the arch of San Piero to the small Piazza San Pier Maggiore. The tower at the south end is the (30) **Torre dei Corbizi,** dating from the Middle Ages. During the Guelph-Ghibelline conflict of the 13th and 14th centuries, Florence was a forest of such towers—more than 200 of them, if the smaller three- and four-story towers are included. Today only a handful survive.

Time Out Have lunch at **I Ghibellini** (closed Wed.), a moderately priced restaurant overlooking the Piazza San Pier Maggiore. For dessert, follow Via Palmieri to No. 7/r Via Isola delle Stinche, and have an ice cream at **Vivoli,** Florence's most famous *gelateria*.

From Piazza San Pier Maggiore, Via Palmieri (which becomes Via Isola delle Stinche) leads to Via Torta, which curves around to the left—it takes its shape from the outline of a Roman amphitheater once located here—and opens out onto Piazza Santa Croce.

㉛ Like the Duomo, the church of **Santa Croce** is Gothic, but (also like the Duomo) its facade dates only from the 19th century. The interior is most famous for its art and its tombs. As a burial place, the church is a Florentine pantheon and probably contains a larger number of important skeletons than any church in Italy. Among others, the tomb of Michelangelo is immediately to the right as you enter (he is said to have chosen this spot so that the first thing he would see on Judgment Day, when the graves of the dead fly open, would be Brunelleschi's Duomo dome through Santa Croce's open doors); the tomb of Galileo Galilei, who produced evidence that the earth is not the center of the universe (and who was not granted a Christian burial until 100 years after his death because of it), is on the left wall, opposite Michelangelo; the tomb of Niccolo Machiavelli, the Renaissance political theoretician whose brutally pragmatic philosophy so influenced the Medici, is halfway down the nave on the right; the grave of Lorenzo Ghiberti, creator of the Gates of Paradise doors to the Baptistery, is halfway down the nave on the left; the tomb of composer Gioacchino Rossini, of "William Tell Overture" fame, is at the end of the nave on the right. The monument to Dante Alighieri, the greatest Italian poet, is a memorial rather than a tomb (he is actually buried in Ravenna); it is located on the right wall near the tomb of Michelangelo.

The collection of art within the church and church complex is by far the most important of that in any church in Florence. Historically, the most significant works are probably the Giotto frescoes in the two adjacent chapels immediately to the right of the altar, which illustrate scenes from the lives of St. John the Evangelist and St. John the Baptist (in the right-hand chapel) and scenes from the life of St. Francis (in the left-hand chapel). Time has not been kind to them; over the centuries wall tombs were introduced into the middle of them, whitewash and plaster covered them, and in the 19th century they underwent a clumsy restoration. But the reality that Giotto introduced into painting can still be seen. He did not paint beautifully stylized symbols of religion, as the Byzantine style that preceded him prescribed; he instead painted drama—St. Francis surrounded by grieving monks at the very moment of his death. This was a radical shift in emphasis, and it changed the course of art. Before him, the role of painting was to symbolize the attributes of God; after him, it was to imitate life. The style of his work is indeed primitive, compared with later painting, but in its day (the Proto-Renaissance of the early 14th century), it caused a sensation that was not equalled for another 100 years. He was for his time the equal of both Masaccio and Michelangelo.

Among the church's other highlights are Donatello's **Annunciation,** one of the most tender and eloquent expressions of surprise ever sculpted (located on the right wall two-thirds of the way down the nave); Taddeo Gaddi's 14th-century frescoes illustrating the life of the Virgin, clearly showing the influence of Giotto (in the chapel at the end of the right transept);

Donatello's *Crucifix*, criticized by Brunelleschi for making Christ look like a peasant (in the chapel at the end of the left transept); Giovanni Cimabue's 13th-century *Triumphal Cross*, badly damaged by the flood of 1966 (in the church museum off the cloister); and the *Pazzi Chapel*, yet another of Brunelleschi's crisp exercises in architectural geometry (also off the cloister, at the east end). *Piazza Santa Croce 16, tel. 055/ 244619. Church Cloister and Museum admission: 3,000 lire. Open Mar.–Sept., Thurs.–Tues. 10–12:30 and 2:30–6:30; Oct.–Feb., Thurs.–Tues. 10–12:30 and 3–5.*

After leaving Santa Croce, you have a choice. If you have a fair amount of stamina left, you can cross the river at the Ponte alle Grazie (west of the church complex) and climb the Monte alle Croci above it to investigate the view from the **Piazzale Michelangelo** and the church of **San Miniato al Monte;** the latter is a famous example of Romanesque architecture dating from the 11th century and contains a fine 13th-century apse mosaic. If the climb seems too arduous, you can (as always) return to the Uffizi.

Shopping

Since the days of the medieval guilds, Florence has been synonymous with fine craftsmanship and good business. Such time-honored Florentine specialties as antiques (and reproductions), bookbinding, jewelry, lace, leather goods, silk, and straw attest to that. More recently, the Pitti fashion shows and the burgeoning textile industry in nearby Prato have added fine clothing to the long line of merchandise available in the shops of Florence.

Another medieval feature is the distinct feel of the different shopping areas, a throwback to the days when each district supplied a different product. Florence's most elegant shops are concentrated in the center of town, with Via Tornabuoni leading the list for designer clothing. Borgo Ognissanti and Via Maggio across the river have the city's largest concentration of antiques shops, and the Ponte Vecchio houses the city's jewelers, as it has since the 16th century. Boutiques abound on Via della Vigna Nuova and in the trendy area around the church of Santa Croce. In the less-specialized, more residential areas near the Duomo and in the area south of the Arno, known as the Oltrarno, just about anything goes on sale.

Those with a tight budget or a sense of adventure may want to take a look at the souvenir stands under the loggia of the Mercato Nuovo, the stalls that line the streets between the church of San Lorenzo and the Mercato Centrale, or the open-air market that takes place in the Cascine park every Tuesday morning.

Shops in Florence are generally open from 9 to 1 and 3:30 to 7:30 and closed Sundays and Monday mornings most of the year. During the summer the hours are usually 9 to 1 and 4 to 8, with closings on Saturday afternoons but not Monday mornings. When locating the stores, remember that the addresses with "r" in them will be indicated in red, a separate numbering system from the black residential addresses. Most shops take major credit cards and will ship purchases, though it's wiser to take your purchases with you. If not, try the little man in Vicolo de' Cavallari near the Battistero, who wraps packages with a true Florentine flourish.

Via Tornabuoni **Gucci** (Via Tornabuoni 73/r, 57/r). The Gucci family is practically single-handedly responsible for making designers' initials (in this case the two interlocking "Gs") a status symbol. These Florence stores are the ones that started it all, and prices here are slightly better than elsewhere on their clothing and leather goods.

Casadei (Via Tornabuoni 33/r). The ultimate fine leathers are crafted into classic shapes here, winding up as women's shoes and bags.

Ugolini (Via Tornabuoni 20/r). This shop once made gloves for the Italian royal family, but now anyone who can afford it can have the luxury of its exotic leathers, as well as silk and cashmere ties and scarves.

Settepassi-Faraone (Via Tornabuoni 25/r). One of Florence's oldest jewelers, Settepassi-Faraone has supplied Italian (and other) royalty with finely crafted gems for centuries. Its selection of antique-looking classics has been updated with a choice of contemporary silver.

Ferragamo (Via Tornabuoni 16/r). Born near Naples, the late Salvatore Ferragamo made his fortune custom-making exotic shoes for famous feet, especially Hollywood stars, and so this establishment knows about less-than-delicate shoe sizes. His palace at the end of the street has since passed on to his wife, Wanda, and displays designer clothing, but the elegant footwear still underlies the Ferragamo success.

Via della Vigna Nuova **Il Bisonte** (Via del Parione). The street address is just off Via della Vigna Nuova; Il Bisonte is known for its natural-look leather goods, all stamped with the store's bison symbol.

Filpucci (Via della Vigna Nuova 14/r). This is Italy's largest manufacturer of yarns. Its nearby factories producing skeins of the stuff for Italy's top designers, and the extensive stock of its retail outlet in Florence encourages the talented to create their own designs.

Escada (Via della Vigna Nuova 71/r). An elegant boutique, Escada has a reputation for the quality and understatement that is the hallmark of Florentine women's fashions.

Alinari (Via della Vigna Nuova 46/r). This outlet is one of Florence's oldest and most prestigious photographers, and in this store, next to its museum, prints of its historic photographs are sold along with books and posters.

Et Cetera (Via della Vigna Nuova 82/r). In a city of papermakers, this store has some of the most unusual such items, most of which are handmade and some of which have made it into the design collection of New York's Museum of Modern Art.

Antico Setificio Fiorentino (Via della Vigna Nuova 97/r). This fabric outlet really *is* antique, having been producing antique fabrics for over half a millenium. Reams of handmade material of every style and description are on sale, and the decorative tassels make lovely, typically Florentine, presents as well.

Borgo Ognissanti **Pratesi** (Lungarno Amerigo Vespucci 8/r). The name Pratesi is a byword for luxury, in this case linens that have lined the beds of the rich and famous, with an emphasis on the former.

Giotti (Piazza Ognissanti 3/r). The largest selection of Bottega Veneta's woven-leather bags are stocked at this shop, which carries a full line of the firm's other leather goods, as well as its own leather clothing.

Loretta Caponi (Borgo Ognissanti 12/r). Signora Caponi is synonymous with Florentine embroidery, and her luxury lace, linens, and lingerie have earned her a worldwide reputation.

Fallani Best (Borgo Ognissanti 15/r). The eclectic collection of antiques, while concentrating on 18th- and 19th-century Italian paintings, has enough variety to appeal to an international clientele.

Paolo Ventura (Borgo Ognissanti 16/r). Specialties here are antique ceramics from all periods and places of origin. As with the other shops, the rule of thumb is that the Italian goods are best, and, in this case, such items as a Giacomo Balla coffee service is outstanding.

Alberto Pierini (Borgo Ognissanti 22/r). The rustic Tuscan furniture here is all antique, and much of it dates back to the days of the Medici.

Duomo **Bartolini** (Via dei Servi 30/r). For housewares, nothing beats this shop, which has a wide selection of well-designed, practical items.

Emilio Pucci (Via dei Pucci 6/r). Originally from the Marches, Pucci is another household name in Florence, presiding over the opening ceremonies of the Renaissance *Calcio in Costume* festivities each year. He became an international name during the dolce vita era of the early '60s, when his prints and "palazzo pajamas" were all the rage. His shop in the family palazzo still sells the celebrated silks, and recently he added a line of designer wines (red, white, and rosé) from his estate in Chianti to his stock.

Calamai (Via Cavour 78/r). One of Florence's largest gift shops, Calamai carries everything from inexpensive stationery to housewares in bright, bold colors and designs in its largest of three stores.

Pineider (Piazza della Signoria 14/r and Via Tornabuoni 76/r). Pineider now has shops throughout the world, but it began in Florence and still does all its printing here. Personalized stationery and business cards are its main business, but the stores also sell fine desk accessories.

Casa dello Sport (Via dei Tosinghi 8/r). Here you'll find lines of casual wear for the entire family—sporty clothes by some of Italy's most famous manufacturers.

Santa Croce **Salimbeni** (Via Matteo Palmieri 14/r). Long one of Florence's best art bookshops, Salimbeni specializes in publications on Tuscany; it publishes many itself.

I Maschereri (Borgo Pinti 18/r). Spurred on by the revival of Carnival in recent years, I Maschereri has begun to produce fanciful masks in *commedia dell'arte* and contemporary styles.

Sbigoli Terrecotte (Via Sant'Egidio 4/r). This crafts shop carries a wide selection of terra-cotta and ceramic vases, pots, cups, and saucers.

Leather Guild (Piazza Santa Croce 20/r). This is one of many such shops throughout the area that produce inexpensive, antique-looking leather goods of mass appeal, but here you can see the craftspersons at work, a reassuring experience.

Ponte Vecchio **Gherardi** (Ponte Vecchio 5). The king of coral in Florence has the city's largest selection of finely crafted and encased specimens, as well as other precious materials such as cultured pearls, jade, and turquoise.

Piccini (Ponte Vecchio 23/r). This venerable shop has literally been crowning the heads of Europe for almost a century, and combines its taste for the antique with contemporary jewelry.
Melli (Ponte Vecchio 44/r). Antique jewelry is the specialty here; it is displayed alongside period porcelains, clocks, and other museum-quality objects.
Della Loggia (Ponte Vecchio 52/r). For a contemporary look, try this store, which combines precious and semiprecious stones in settings made of precious and nonprecious metals, such as the gold and steel pieces usually on display in its windows.

Oltrarno **Centro Di** (Piazza dei Mozzi 1). Its name stands for Centro di Documentazione Internazionale, and it publishes art books and exhibition catalogues for some of the most important organizations in Europe. Centro Di stocks its own publications along with many others.
Giannini (Piazza Pitti 37/r). One of Florence's oldest papergoods stores, Giannini is *the* place to buy the marbleized version, which comes in a variety of forms, from flat sheets to boxes and even pencils.
Galleria Luigi Bellini (Lungarno Soderini 5). The Galleria claims to be Italy's oldest antiques dealer. Whether or not it's true, what matters is that the merchandise is genuine, and since father Mario Bellini was responsible for instituting Florence's international antiques biennial, there's a good chance he's right.

Via Maggio **Giovanni Pratesi** (Via Maggio 13/r). This shop specializes in Italian antiques, in this case furniture with some fine paintings, sculpture, and decorative objects turning up from time to time.
Guido Bartolozzi (Via Maggio 18/r). Vying with Luigi Bellini as one of Florence's oldest antiques dealers, Bartolozzi's collection of predominately Florentine objects from all periods is as highly selected as it is priced.
Paolo Paoletti (Via Maggio 30/r). Look for Florentine antiques, with an emphasis on Medici-era objects from the 15th and 16th centuries.
Soluzioni (Via Maggio 82/r). This offbeat store displays some of the most unusual items on this staid street, ranging from clocks to compacts, all selected with an eye for the eccentric.

Sports

Bicycling Bikes are a good way of getting out into the hills, but the scope for biking is limited in the center of town. *See* Getting Around in Essential Information, above, for information on where to rent bicycles.

Canoeing Those who get the urge to paddle on the Arno can try **Società Canottieri Comunali** (Lungarno dei Medici 8, tel. 055/282130) near the Uffizi.

Golf **Golf Club Ugolino** (Via Chiantigiana 3, Impruneta, 055/205–1009) is a hilly 18-hole course in the heart of Chianti country just outside town. It is open to the public.

Jogging Don't even think of jogging on city streets, where tour buses and triple-parked Alfa Romeos leave precious little space for pedestrians. Instead, head for the **Cascine,** the park along the Arno at the western end of the city. You can jog to the Cascine along the Lungarno (stay on the sidewalk), or take bus No. 17

from the Duomo. A cinder track lies on the hillside just below **Piazzale Michelangelo,** across the Arno from the city center. The views of the Florence skyline are inspirational, but the locker rooms are reserved for members, so come ready to run.

Swimming There are a number of pools open to foreigners who want to beat the Florentine heat, among them **Bellariva** (Lungarno Colombo 6, tel. 055/677521), **Circolo Tennis alle Cascine** (Viale Visarno 1, tel. 055/356651), **Costoli** (Viale Paoli, tel. 055/675–744), and **Le Pavoniere** (Viale degli Olmi, tel. 055/367506).

Tennis The best spot for an open court is **Circolo Tennis alle Cascine** (Viale Visarno 1, tel. 055/356651). Other centers include **Tennis Club Rifredi** (Via Facibeni, tel. 055/432552) and **Il Poggetto** (Via Mercati 24/B, tel. 055/460127).

Spectator Sports

Horse Racing You can make your bets at the **Ippodromo Visarno** (Piazzale delle Cascine, tel. 055/360056). Check with the local papers to see when they're running.

Soccer *Calcio* (soccer) is a passion with the Italians, and the Florentines are no exception. A medieval version of the game is played in costume each year on or around June 24, feast day of St. John the Baptist, but if you want to see the modern-day equivalent, go and watch the Fiorentina team at the Stadio Comunale (Viale M. Fanti). The big games are played on Sunday afternoons, and the season runs from about late August to May.

Dining

Florentines are justifiably proud of their robust food, claiming that it became the basis for French cuisine when Catherine de Médici took a battery of Florentine chefs with her when she reluctantly relocated to become Queen of France in the 16th century.

A typical Tuscan repast starts with an antipasto of *crostini* (toasted bread spread with a chicken liver pâté) or cured meats such as *prosciutto crudo* (a salty prosciutto), *finocchiona* (salami seasoned with fennel), and *salsiccia di cinghiale* (sausage made from wild boar). This is the time to start right in on the local wine—Chianti, *naturalmente*. Don't be surprised if the waiter brings an entire straw-covered flask to the table. Customers are charged only for what they consume (*al consumo*, the arrangement is called), but it's wise to ask for a flask or bottle to be opened then and there, since leftover wines are often mixed together.

Primi piatti (first courses) can consist of excellent local versions of risotto or variations of pasta dishes available throughout Italy. Peculiar to Florence, however, are the vegetable-and-bread soups such as *pappa al pomodoro* (tomatoes, bread, olive oil, onions, and basil), *ribollita* (white beans, bread, cabbage, and onions), or, in the summer, *panzanella* (tomatoes, onions, vinegar, oil, and bread). Before they are eaten, these soups are often christened with *un "C" d'olio*, a generous C-shaped pouring of the excellent local olive oil from the ever-present tabletop cruet.

Second to none among the *secondi piatti* (main courses) is *bistecca alla fiorentina*—a thick slab of local Chianina beef, grilled over charcoal, seasoned with olive oil, salt, and pepper, and served rare. *Trippa alla fiorentina* (tripe stewed with tomatoes in a meat sauce) and *arista* (roast loin of pork seasoned with rosemary) are also regional specialties, as are many other roasted meats that go especially well with the Chianti. These are usually served with a *contorno* (side dish) of white beans, sauteed greens, or artichokes in season, all of which can be drizzled with more of that wonderful olive oil.

Tuscan desserts are typically Spartan. The cheese is the hard *pecorino*, and locals like to go for the even tougher *biscottini di Prato*, which provide an excuse to dunk them in the potent, sweet dessert wine called *vin santo*, made of dried grapes, which they say will bring the dead back to life!

Remember that dining hours are earlier here than in Rome, starting at 12:30 for the midday meal and from 7:30 on in the evening. Many of Florence's restaurants are small, so reservations are a must. When going to the restaurants, note that the "r" in some of the following addresses indicates the red numbering system used for Florentine businesses, which differs from the black numbers used for residences.

Highly recommended restaurants are indicated by a star ★.

Category	Cost*
Very Expensive	over 110,000 lire
Expensive	70,000–110,000 lire
Moderate	30,000–70,000 lire
Inexpensive	under 30,000 lire

per person, for a three-course meal, including house wine and taxes

Very Expensive **Enoteca Pinchiorri.** A sumptuous Renaissance palace bursting
★ with bouquets is the setting for this restaurant, considered one of the best in Italy. The "enoteca" part of the name comes from its former incarnation as a wineshop under owner Giorgio Pinchiorri, who still keeps a stock of 70,000 bottles in the cellar. Wife Annie Feolde has recently added her refined interpretations of Tuscan cuisine—*triglie alla viareggina* (mullet with tomato sauce) and *arrosto di coniglio* (roast rabbit)—to a nouvelle menu that includes *ravioli di melanzane* (ravioli stuffed with eggplant), *petto di piccione* (pigeon breast), and *formaggio alle erbette* (cheese with herbs). *Via Ghibellina 87, tel. 055/242777. Reservations required. Jacket and tie required. AE, V. Closed Sun. and Mon. lunch, Aug., Dec. 24–28.*

Expensive **Al Lume di Candela.** Everything from pasta to dessert is home-
★ made here. The menu is Florentine and includes such specialties as a simple soup called *acquacotta*, literally "cooked water" but actually a vegetable soup in a meat broth, and an excellent selection of meat dishes such as ossobuco and bistecca alla fiorentina. Small, attractive, and elegant, it is in a medieval tower. *Via delle Terme 23/r, tel. 055/294566. Reservations required. Jacket and tie required. AE, DC, MC, V. Open evenings only. Closed Sun. and Aug. 10–30.*

★ **La Capannina di Sante.** Florence's best fish restaurant is situ-

Dining

Lodging

Florence Dining and Lodging

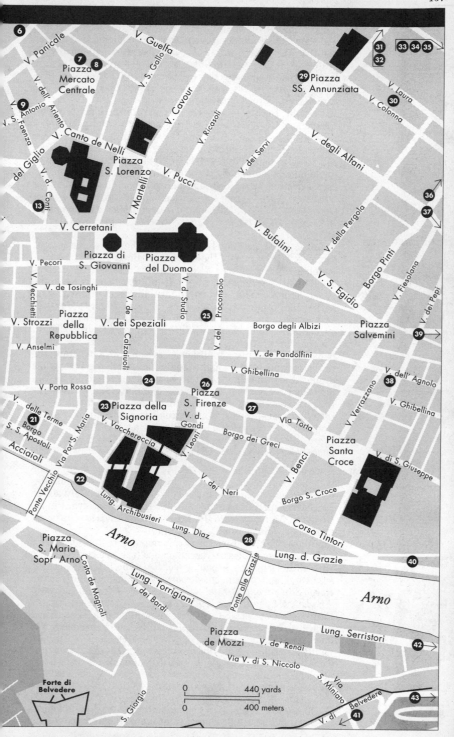

V. Panicale

V. Guelfa

6

7 **8**

Piazza
Mercato
Centrale

V. dell' Ariento

V. S. Gallo

29 Piazza
SS. Annunziata

31

33 **34** **35**

32

V. Laura

V. Colonna

30

9

V. S. Antonio

V. S. Faenza

del Giglio

V. d. Conti

V. Canto de Nelli

Piazza
S. Lorenzo

V. Cavour

V. Ricasoli

V. dei Servi

V. degli Alfani

V. della Pergola

Borgo Pinti

V. Fiesolana

36

37

13

V. Martelli

V. Pucci

V. Cerretani

Piazza di
S. Giovanni

Piazza
del Duomo

V. Bufalini

V. S. Egidio

V. dei Pepi

V. Pecori

V. Vecchietti

V. de Tosinghi

V. de Calzaiuoli

V. d. Studio

Procons olo

V. del

Borgo degli Albizi

Piazza
Salvemini

39

V. Strozzi

Piazza
della
Repubblica

V. dei Speziali

25

V. de Pandolfini

V. dell' Agnolo

38

V. Anselmi

V. Ghibellina

V. Ghibellina

V. Porta Rossa

24

26

Piazza
S. Firenze

27

Via Torta

V. Verazzano

23 Piazza della
Signoria

V. d.
Gondi

Borgo dei Greci

Piazza
Santa
Croce

V. di S. Giuseppe

V. delle Terme

21

Borgo
SS. Apostoli

V. Vacchereccia

V. Por S. Maria

V. Leoni

V. Benci

Acciaioli

22

Ponte Vecchio

Lung. Archibusieri

Lung. Diaz

V. dei Neri

Borgo S. Croce

Corso Tintori

40

Piazza
S. Maria
Sopr' Arno

Costa de Magnoli

Arno

Lung. d. Grazie

28

Lung. Torrigiani

V. dei Bardi

Ponte alle Grazie

Arno

Piazza
de Mozzi

V. de' Renai

Lung. Serristori

42

Via V. di S. Niccolo

V. S. Miniato

Via
al Belvedere

**Forte di
Belvedere**

S. Giorgio

| 0 | 440 yards |
| 0 | 400 meters |

43

V. di

41

ated, not surprisingly, along a quiet stretch of the Arno, with indoor tables in an ample, unpretentious trattoria-type setting and a few tables outdoors under the pergola during the warmer months. Risotto and various types of pasta are combined with seafood, and the *grigliata mista di pesce*, or mixed grill of fish, is among the standouts. *Piazza Ravenna, tel. 055/688345. Reservations advised for dinner. Dress: casual. AE, DC, MC, V. Closed Sun., Mon. lunch, and 1 week in Aug., Dec. 23–30.*

Il Cestello. Located across the Arno from the church of San Frediano in Cestello, the restaurant is part of the Excelsior hotel and moves to the roof during the warmer months to enjoy a stupendous view of the city E. M. Forster would envy. Its Tuscan-based menu features delicious risotto and pasta dishes (including an exemplary *pasta e fagioli*, pasta with beans), a rare selection of seafood, and an ever-changing sampling of whatever is fresh from the market. *Hotel Excelsior, Piazza Ognissanti 3, tel. 055/264201. Reservations recommended for nonguests of the hotel. Jacket and tie required. AE, DC, MC, V.*

Relais le Jardin dell'Hotel Regency. Another hotel restaurant, this one, with a turn-of-the-century, stained-glass-and-wood-paneling setting, stands on its own. Its *crespelle*, or crepes, come highly recommended in their infinite variety, as do the *medaglioni di vitello al rabarbo* (medallions of veal with rhubarb) and other aromatic meat dishes. *Piazza Massimo D'Azeglio 5, tel. 055/245247. Reservations required for nonguests of the hotel. Jacket and tie required. AE, DC, MC, V. Closed Sun.*

Sabatini. A Florentine tradition not without its detractors, the restaurant maintains a high standard of excellence that, while predictable (a recent innovation was its own version of a Bellini, called a Sabatini, made with spumante and strawberry juice), is reassuring in its consistency. *Risotto ai funghi*, or risotto with mushrooms, is one specialty, as are all the Florentine dishes prepared and served with classic Old World style. *Via dei Panzani 9/a, tel. 055/211559. Reservations advised. Jacket and tie required. AE, DC, MC, V. Closed Mon.*

Moderate **Buca dell'Orafo.** One of the best of the Florentine *buca*, meaning hole, restaurants, Buca dell'Orafo is set in the cellar of a former goldsmith's shop near the Ponte Vecchio. It offers all the Florentine specialties and prides itself on its bistecca. *Via dei Girolami 28, tel. 055/213619. Reservations advised. Dress: casual. Closed Sun., Mon., and all Aug.*

Camillo. Bright and bustling, this popular restaurant does a swift business in classic Tuscan dishes (the house has its own olive oil and Chianti), including *fegatini di pollo* (sautéed chicken livers) and porcini mushrooms with parmigiano cheese. *Borgo San Jacopo 57/r, tel. 055/212427. Reservations advised. AE, DC, MC, V. Closed Wed., Thurs., Aug., and Dec.*

Cantinetta Antinori. Set on the ground floor of a Renaissance palace, this is an elegant place for ladies (and gentlemen) who lunch after shopping in nearby Via Tornabuoni. The Antinori family is best known as wine producers, and their wares may be sampled with light salads, bread, sausage, and cheese snacks or more complete meals. *Piazza Antinori 3, tel. 055/292234. Reservations advised. Dress: casual. AE, DC, MC, V. Closed Sat., Sun., and Aug.*

★ **Il Cibreo.** Located near the Sant'Ambrogio market, Il Cibreo uses the freshest ingredients to prepare updated versions of

Florentine classics, presented in an upscale trattoria-style dining room or in a piazza overlooking the market during the warmer months. The *pappa al pomodoro*, presented as a thick red dollop on a sparkling white Ginori plate, and inventive dishes such as *anatra farcita di pinoli e uvetta* (duck stuffed with pine nuts and raisins) are two of many specialties. A café annex serves drinks and snacks all day. *Via dei Macci 118/r, tel. 055/234–1100. Reservations advised for dinner. Dress: casual. Closed Sun., Mon., and Aug. 1–Sept. 10. AE, DC, MC, V.*

Coco Lezzone. The name roughly translates as "big smelly cook," a self-effacing image that this whitewashed, red-checked-tablecloth hole-in-the-wall, a few Gucci-shod steps off Via Tornabuoni, deems appropriate. It serves classic Florentine dishes such as pappa al pomodoro and arista. *Via del Parioncino 26/r, tel. 055/287178. Dress: casual. Closed Tues. dinner, Sun. (in summer, Sat. and Sun.), Christmas week, Aug. No credit cards.*

★ **Le Fonticine.** Owner Silvano Bruci is from Tuscany, wife Gianna from Emilia-Romagna, and the restaurant combines the best of both worlds in a trattoria-type setting liberally hung with Silvano's extensive collection of paintings. Emilia-Romagna specialties such as tortellini ready the taste buds for Tuscan grilled porcini mushrooms so meaty they provide serious competition for the bistecca alla fiorentina. *Via Nazionale 79/r, tel. 055/282106. Reservations advised. Dress: casual. AE, DC, MC, V. Closed Sun., Mon, and July 25–Aug. 25.*

Harry's Bar. Americans love it, and it *is* the only place in town to get a perfect martini or a hamburger or a club sandwich, but it offers two typical Tuscan dishes every day. The small menu also has well-prepared international offerings, and the bar is open until midnight. *Lungarno Vespucci 22/r, tel. 055/239–6700. Reservations required. Dress: casual. AE, V. Closed Sun. and Dec. 15–Jan. 8.*

La Loggia. Though it may be crowded and somewhat rushed, La Loggia is worth the wait for the view of Florence from atop the Piazzale Michelangelo, especially during the summer when there are tables outdoors. The food is almost incidental, but sticking to such Florentine classics as porcini mushrooms and bistecca alla fiorentina makes for a thoroughly memorable evening. *Piazzale Michelangelo 1, tel. 055/234–2832. Dress: casual. AE, DC, MC, V. Closed Wed. and Aug. 10–25.*

Mario da Ganino. On a side street between the Duomo and Palazzo Vecchio, this trattoria is informal, rustic and cheerful. You are offered a taste of mortadella (at no charge) to start off your meal, which might include some of the homemade pasta on the menu. *Gnudoni* (ravioli without the pasta casing) are a specialty, as is cheesecake for dessert. Main courses uphold Florentine tradition, with grilled steak and chops and bean dishes. Get there early; it seats only about 35, and double that number in good weather at outside tables. *Piazza dei Cimatori 4/r, tel. 055/214125. Reservations advised. Dress: casual. AE, DC. Closed Sun. and Aug. 15–25.*

Sostanza detto Il Troia. Equally famous for its brusque service as it is for its bistecca alla fiorentina, Il Troia is Florence's oldest restaurant, founded in 1869. Its menu is still strictly Florentine, and all the local classics are served at communal tables, with no frills, to a clientele of out-of-towners and tourists. *Via del Porcellana 25/r, tel. 055/212691. Reservations advised. Dress: casual. No credit cards. Closed Sat. evening, Sun., and Aug.*

★ **La Vecchia Cucina.** Located in an out-of-the-way part of town near the Campo di Marte, this restaurant draws a loyal crowd of devotees of its highly inventive variations on Italian themes. The menu changes every other week, since it features seasonal foods such as asparagus and porcini mushrooms, but always includes pasta made by the owner's mother, who is from Emilia-Romagna. The olive oil is of the highest quality, the wine list has an excellent selection of Italian wines, and the homemade dessert pastries are miniature masterpieces. *Viale de Amicis 1/r, tel. 055/660143. Reservations necessary. Dress: casual. AE, DC, MC, V. Closed Sun. and Aug.*

Inexpensive **Acqua al Due.** You'll find this tiny restaurant near the Bargello. It serves an array of Florentine specialties in a lively, very casual setting. Acqua al Due is popular with young Florentines, partly because it's air-conditioned in the summer and always open late. *Via dell'Acqua 2/r, tel. 055/284170. No reservations. Dress: casual. AE, DC, MC, V. Closed Mon. and Aug.*

★ **Angiolino.** This bustling little trattoria in the Oltrarno district is popular with locals and visitors. It has a real charcoal grill and an old woodburning stove to keep customers warm on nippy days. The menu offers Tuscan specialties such as *ribollita* (minestrone) and a classic bistecca alla fiorentina. The bistecca can push the check up into the Moderate range. *Via Santo Spirito 36/r, 055/239–8976. Reservations advised in the evening. Dress: casual. No credit cards. Closed Sun. dinner, Mon., and last 3 weeks in July.*

Mario. Clean and classic, this family-run trattoria on the corner of Piazza del Mercato near San Lorenzo offers a genuine Florentine atmosphere and cooking, with no frills. Open for lunch only. *Via Rosina (Piazza del Mercato Centrale). No phone. Dress: casual. No credit cards. Closed evenings and Sun.*

Mossacce. You share a table here and watch the cook in the glassed-in kitchen prepare your order, chosen from a menu of Florentine classics. *Via del Proconsolo 55/r, tel. 055/294361. No reservations. Dress: casual. AE, MC, V. Closed weekends and Aug.*

Za-Za. Slighty more upscale than neighboring trattorias, Za-Za attracts white-collar workers and theater people. Posters of movie stars hang on wood-paneled walls, and classic Florentine cuisine is served at communal tables. *Piazza Mercato Centrale 16/r, tel. 055/215411. Reservations advised. Dress: casual. AE, DC, MC, V. Closed Sun. and Aug.*

Wine Shops In addition, there are many wine shops where you can have a snack or sandwich. Of these, **Le Cantine** (Via dei Pucci) is stylish and popular, as is **Cantinone del Gallo Nero** (Via Santo Spirito 6), which also serves meals in a brick-vaulted wine cellar. More modest are **Borgioli** (Piazza dell'Olio), **Fiaschetteria** (Via dei Neri), **Fratellini** (Via dei Cimatori), **Nicolino** (Volta dei Mercanti), and **Piccolo Vinaio** (Via Castellani).

Lodging

Florence's importance not only as a tourist city but as a convention center and the site of the Pitti fashion collections throughout the year has guaranteed a variety of accommodations, many in former villas and palazzos. However, these very factors mean that reservations are a must at all times of the year.

If you do find yourself in Florence with no reservations, go to the **Consorzio ITA** office in the train station. It's open every day from 8:20 AM to 9 PM. If the office is shut, your best bet is to try some of the inexpensive (but clean) accommodations at a *pensione* or a *locanda* (inn); many are located on **Via Nazionale** (which leads east from Piazza Stazione) and on **Via Faenza,** the second left off Via Nazionale.

Highly recommended lodgings are indicated by a star ★.

Category	Cost*
Very Expensive	over 480,000 lire
Expensive	270,000–480,000 lire
Moderate	150,000–270,000 lire
Inexpensive	under 150,000 lire

*All prices are for a double room for two, including tax and service.

Very Expensive
★ **Excelsior.** Traditional Old World charm finds a regal setting at the Excelsior, a neo-Renaissance palace complete with painted wooden ceilings, stained glass, and acres of Oriental carpets strewn over marble floors in the public rooms. The rooms are furnished with the chaises-longues, classical decorations, and long mirrors of the Empire style. This is characteristic of the CIGA hotel chain that owns it and is especially appropriate here, since Napoleon's sister Caroline was once the proprietress of the property. Plush touches include wall-to-wall carpeting in the rooms and thick terrycloth towels on heated racks in the bathrooms. Its Il Cestello restaurant serves excellent food and in summer moves up to the roof for a wonderful view. *Piazza Ognissanti 3, tel. 055/264201, fax 055/210278. 205 rooms with bath. Facilities: restaurant with piano bar. AE, DC, MC, V.*

Grand Hotel. Across the piazza from the Excelsior, this Florentine classic, also owned by the CIGA chain, provides all the luxurious amenities of its sister. Most rooms and public areas are decorated in sumptuous Renaissance style, many with frescoes. Baths are in marble. Some rooms have balconies overlooking the Arno. *Piazza Ognissanti 1, tel. 055/288781, fax 055/217400. 107 rooms with bath. Facilities: restaurant, winter garden, bar, parking. AE, DC, MC, V.*

Grand Hotel Villa Cora. Built near the Boboli Gardens and Piazzale Michelangelo in the mid-19th century when Florence was briefly the capital of Italy, the Villa Cora retains the opulence of that era. The decor of its remarkable public and private rooms runs the gamut from neoclassical to rococo and even Moorish, and reflects the splendor of such former guests as the Empress Eugénie, wife of Napoleon III, and Madame Von Meck, Tchaikovsky's mysterious benefactress. *Viale Machiavelli 18, tel. 055/2298451, fax 055/229086. 48 rooms with bath. Facilities: restaurant, garden, pool, piano bar, car service. AE, DC, MC, V.*

Regency. Undisturbed sleep is almost guaranteed at this hotel, which is tucked away in a respectable residential district near the synagogue. The rooms are decorated in richly colored and tasteful fabrics and antique-style furniture faithful to the hotel's incarnation in the 19th-century as a private mansion. It has one of Florence's best hotel restaurants. *Piazza Massimo D'Azeglio 3, tel. 055/245247, fax 055/234–2938. 38 rooms with bath. Facilities: garden, restaurant. AE, DC, MC, V.*

Villa San Michele. The setting for this hideaway is so romantic—nestled in the hills of nearby Fiesole—that it once attracted Brigitte Bardot for her honeymoon (even today guests sleep on linen sheets). The villa was originally a monastery whose facade and loggia have been attributed to Michelangelo. The rooms now contain sumptuous statuary, paintings, Jacuzzis, and Savonarola chairs that would put their namesake to shame. Many of the rooms have a panoramic view of Florence, others face an inner courtyard, and a luxuriant garden surrounds the whole affair. The restaurant is excellent, and MAP is mandatory. *Via Doccia 4, Fiesole, tel. 055/59451, fax 055/598734. 28 rooms with bath. Facilities: restaurant, piano bar, pool, garden, courtesy bus service. AE, DC, MC, V. Open mid-Mar.–mid-Nov.*

Expensive **Astoria Pullman.** Decorated with the classic Tuscan *pietra serena* (a gray sandstone), white stucco walls, and terracotta floors, the hotel resembles an ancient Florentine palace (complete with a copy of Botticelli's *Primavera)*, and no wonder, since that's precisely what it was. Parts of the original building go back to 1176, with the Palazzo Gaddi wing a relative newcomer dating from the 17th century. And though John Milton wrote much of *Paradise Lost* here, that would hardly describe the recently remodeled hotel's present condition, with modern, comfortable facilities and rooms with a view on the top floors. *Via del Giglio 9, tel. 055/239–8095, fax 055/214632. 90 rooms with bath. Facilities: garden. AE, DC, MC, V.*

★ **Baglioni.** This large turn-of-the-century building was conceived in the European tradition of grand hotels; it's located between the train station and the cathedral. The charming roof terrace has the best view in Florence and is home to the Terrazza Brunelleschi restaurant. The hotel is spacious and elegant, with well-proportioned rooms decorated tastefully in antique Florentine style, and many have leaded glass windows. Fourth-floor rooms have been completely done over in pastel tones harmonizing with the floral carpeting or mellow parquet. The hotel has a full range of conference facilities, which makes it a favorite of businesspeople. *Piazza dell'Unità Italiana 6, tel. 055/218441, fax 055/215695. 197 rooms with bath. Facilities: roof-garden restaurant. AE, DC, MC, V.*

Beacci Tornabuoni. This is perhaps *the* classic Florentine *pensione* (although by law all lodgings have been reclassified as hotels of various categories). Set in a 14th-century palazzo, it contains a series of quaint, old-fashioned rooms, renovated a few years ago, all presided over by a *signora* full of personality. Half board is required, but the food is good and can also be brought to the rooms, most of which have views of the red-tiled roofs in the neighboring downtown area. *Via Tornabuoni 3, tel. 055/212645, fax 055/283594. 30 rooms with bath. Facilities: restaurant, bar. AE, DC, MC, V.*

Bernini Palace. Located just behind Palazzo Vecchio is this proud and important part of Florence's past. The hotel breakfast room was where the parliament of a newly united Italy met during the brief period that Florence was the nation's capital. The hotel has very recently been entirely refurbished, fitted out with period-style furniture and modern facilities. Many rooms have views of Palazzo Vecchio and are decorated in soothing dusty rose or muted blue tones. *Piazza San Firenze 29, tel. 288621, fax 055/268272. 86 rooms with bath. Facilities: minibar, TV, garage. AE, DC, MC, V.*

Kraft. The efficient and comfortable Kraft has many period-style rooms with balconies overlooking the Arno. Its location near the Teatro Comunale (it is also next to the U.S. consulate) gives it a clientele from the music world. *Via Solferino 2, tel. 055/284273, fax 055/239–8267. 68 rooms with bath. Facilities: rooftop restaurant, pool. AE, DC, MC, V.*

★ **Monna Lisa.** Housed in a Renaissance palazzo, the hotel retains its original *pietra serena* staircase, terra-cotta floors, and painted ceilings and was once the home of Sant' Antonino, who became bishop of Florence. Its rooms still have a rather homey quality, and though on the small side, many have contemplative views of a lovely garden. The ground-floor lounges give you the feel of living in an aristocratic town house. *Borgo Pinti 27, tel. 055/2479751, fax 055/247–9755. 20 rooms with bath. Facilities: garden, bar. AE, DC, MC, V.*

Plaza Hotel Lucchesi. This comfortable hotel, just a short walk beyond the Uffizi along the Arno, was completely renovated recently. Now its modern rooms with wonderful views of the river are soundproof as well, as are the ones overlooking the red-tiled roofs extending toward Santa Croce. *Lungarno della Zecca Vecchia 38, tel. 055/264141, fax 055/248–0921. 97 rooms with bath. Facilities: restaurant. AE, DC, MC, V.*

Moderate **Annalena.** The entrance to the hotel, just beyond the Pitti Palace, faces the Boboli Gardens, while the hotel's rear rooms look out on the largest private garden in Florence. Once part of the Medici holdings, it has been everything from a convent to a hiding place for refugees. Its distinguished past is reflected in an authentic antique decor steeped in character, and it attracts a worldly, bohemian clientele. *Via Romana 34, tel. 055/222402, fax 055/222403. 20 rooms with bath. Facilities: breakfast room on terrace. AE, DC, MC, V.*

Bencistà. Below the luxurious Villa San Michele in Fiesole, this hotel has the same tranquil setting and is even two centuries older. The rooms are furnished with antiques, and half board is required. *Via Benedetto da Maiano 4, Fiesole, tel. 055/59163, fax 055/59163. 40 rooms, 30 with bath. No credit cards.*

★ **Loggiato dei Servi.** A relatively new and charming hotel, the Loggiato dei Servi is tucked away under a historic loggia in one of the city's quietest and loveliest squares. Vaulted ceilings and tasteful furnishings, some of them antiques, make this a hotel for those who want to get the feel of Florence and will appreciate a 19th-century town house look while enjoying modern creature comforts. The hotel has no restaurant. *Piazza Santissima Annunziata 3, tel. 055/289592, fax 055/289595. 29 rooms with bath. AE, DC, MC, V.*

Morandi alla Crocetta. Near Piazza Santissima Annunziata, this charming, family-run hotel is close to the sights but on a quiet street in a building that was once a monastery. It is furnished comfortably, in the classic style of a gracious Florentine home. Very small, it is worth booking well in advance. *Via Laura 50, tel. 055/234–4747, fax 055/248–0954. 9 rooms with bath. AE, DC, MC, V.*

Quisisana e Ponte Vecchio. The hotel gets the first part of its name from the Italian for "here one heals," the second part from its location near the city's most famous bridge. Comfortable rooms furnished in mahogany, a central location, and a loggia with views of the Arno make it a pleasant place to stay. *Lungarno Archibusieri 4, tel. 055/216692, fax 055/268303. 36 rooms, 33 with bath. Facilities: terrace. AE, DC, MC, V.*

La Residenza. Located just down the street from the Beacci, on Florence's most elegant shopping street, is La Residenza: The top floor has a charming roof garden and rooms with even better views for fewer lire. The *signora* here is equally accommodating, the decor equally antique, and the plumbing up to date. *Via Tornabuoni 8, tel. 055/284197. 24 rooms with bath. Facilities: roof garden, garage. AE, DC, V.*

Inexpensive **Bellettini.** You couldn't ask for anything more central; this small hotel occupies two floors of a well-kept but centuries-old building near the church of San Lorenzo, in a neighborhood with plenty of inexpensive eating places. The good-sized rooms have Venetian or Tuscan provincial decor; bathrooms are bright and modern. Air-conditioning is available at an extra charge. *Via dei Conti 7, tel. 055/213561, fax 055/283551. 28 rooms with bath. Facilities: bar, lounge. AE, DC, MC, V.*

Liana. This small hotel, located near the English Cemetery, is in a quiet 19th-century villa that formerly housed the British Embassy. Its clean and pleasant rooms all face a stately garden. *Via Vittorio Alfieri 18, tel. 055/245303, fax 055/234–4596. 23 rooms with bath or shower. AE, MC, V.*

Nuova Italia. Near the train station, within walking distance of the sights, this hotel is run by a cordial, English-speaking family. It has a homey atmosphere; rooms are clean and simply furnished, all with private baths. Some rooms can accommodate extra beds. Low, bargain rates include breakfast. *Via Faenza 26, tel. 055/268430, fax 055/210941. 20 rooms with bath. AE, DC, MC, V.*

Rigatti. Occupying the top two floors of the 19th-century Palazzo Alberti, between Palazzo Vecchio and Santa Croce, this elegantly furnished hotel has wonderful views of the Arno from its tiny front terrace, as well as five quiet rooms overlooking a garden in back. The rooms are spacious and tastefully furnished, with modern bathrooms. *Lungarno Diaz 2, tel. 055/213022. 28 rooms, 14 with bath. No credit cards.*

The Arts and Nightlife

The Arts

Theater **Estate Fiesolana.** From June through August, this festival of theater, music, dance, and film takes place in the churches and the archaeological area of Fiesole (Teatro Romano, Fiesole, tel. 055/599931).

Concerts **Maggio Musicale Fiorentina.** This series of internationally acclaimed concerts and recitals is held in the **Teatro Comunale** (Corso Italia 16, tel. 055/277–9236) from late April through June. During the same period, there is a concert season of the Orchestra Regionale Toscana, in the church of **Santo Stefano al Ponte** (tel. 055/242767). Amici della Musica organizes concerts at the **Teatro della Pergola** (box office Via della Pergola 10/r, tel. 055/247–9652).

Opera Operas are performed in the Teatro Comunale from December through February.

Film **Florence Film Festival.** An international panel of judges gathers in late spring at the Forte di Belvedere to preside over a wide selection of new releases.

Festival del Popolo. This festival, held each December, is devoted to documentaries and is held in the Fortezza da Basso.

Nightlife

Unlike the Romans and Milanese, the frugal and reserved Florentines do not have a reputation for an active nightlife; however, the following places attract a mixed crowd of Florentines and visitors.

Piano Bars Many of the more expensive hotels have their own piano bars, where nonguests are welcome to come for an *aperitivo* or an after-dinner drink. The best view is from the bar at the **Excelsior** (Piazza Ognissanti 3, tel. 055/264201), on a roof garden overlooking the Arno. **Caffé Pitti** (Piazza Pitti 9, tel. 055/239–6241), an informal bar, is a popular afternoon and evening gathering place for Florence's international colony. The accent is on Brazil at **Caffé Voltaire** (Via della Scala 9/r, tel. 055/218255), where there's Latin food and music.

Jazz Clubs The generically named **Jazz Club** (Via Nuova de Caccini 33, tel. 055/247–9700) has live music and closes only on Monday.

Discos The two largest discos, with the youngest crowds, are **Yab Yum** (Via Sassetti 5r, tel. 055/282018) and **Space Electronic** (Via Palazzuolo 37, tel. 055/239–3082). Less frenetic alternatives are **Jackie O'** (Via Erta Canina 24, tel. 055/2342442) and **Full Up** (Via della Vigna Vecchia 21/r, tel. 055/293006).

5 **Tuscany**

*Lucca, Siena, and
the Hill Towns*

Rome may be the capital of Italy, but Tuscany is its heart. Stretching from the Apennines to the sea, midway between Milan and Rome, the region is quintessentially Italian, in both its appearance and its history. Its scenic variety is unmatched in Italy; its past has been ignoble (it produced the Guelph-Ghibelline conflict of the Middle Ages) and glorious (it produced the Renaissance). Its towns are justly famous for their wealth of fine architecture and art, but visitors often come home even more enthusiastic about Tuscany's unspoiled hilly landscapes, about the delicious Chianti wines produced by vineyards on those hills, and about the robust and flavorful Tuscan cooking. Be sure to allot some portion of your time here for leisurely strolls, unhurried meals, and aimless wandering around this peerless countryside, for there is the true soul of Tuscany to be found.

A uniquely creative and beautiful use of the Italian language— the language of Dante, Petrarch, and Boccaccio, all native sons—is a longstanding tradition in Tuscany, of which the Tuscans are justly proud. The tradition was officially recognized and honored when Italy was unified in 1871, and the Tuscan dialect was chosen as the national language. Today the purest Italian is said to be spoken in the area between Siena and Arezzo, and even visitors with limited textbook Italian can often hear the difference. As they enter the region, the language suddenly becomes much easier to understand and takes on a bell-like clarity and mellifluous beauty unequaled throughout the rest of Italy.

It also takes on a notorious wit. As a common proverb has it, "Tuscans have Paradise in their eyes and the Inferno in their mouths" (a wry reference to Dante), and the sting of Tuscan wit is as famous throughout Italy as the beauty of Tuscan speech. Happily, the Tuscans usually reserve their wit for each other and treat visitors with complete and sincere courtesy.

For a long time, the Tuscan hill towns were notorious as well. Even its earliest civilized settlers, the Etruscans, chose their city-sites for defensive purposes (the fortress-town of Fiesole, above Florence, is a fine surviving example). With the end of the Roman Empire, the region fell into disunity, and by the 11th century Tuscany had evolved into a collection of independent city-states, each city seeking to dominate, and sometimes forcibly overpower, its neighbors. The region then became embroiled in an apparently endless international quarrel between a long succession of popes and Holy Roman Emperors. By the 13th century, Tuscany had become a battleground: The infamous conflict between the Guelphs and the Ghibellines had begun.

The Guelphs and the Ghibellines are the bane of Italian schoolchildren; their infinitely complicated, bloody history is to Italy what the Wars of the Roses are to England. To oversimplify grossly, the Ghibellines were mostly allied with both the Holy Roman Emperor (headquartered over the Alps in Germany) and the local aristocracy (dominated by feudal lords); the Guelphs were mostly allied with both the Pope (headquartered in Rome) and the emerging middle class (dominated by the new trade guilds). Florence, flourishing as a trade center, was (most of the time) Guelph; its neighboring city-states Pisa and Siena were (most of the time) Ghibelline. But the bitter struggles that resulted were so Byzantine in their complexity, so full of factional disputes and treachery within, that a dizzying series of conflicts within conflicts resulted. (Dante, for instance, was banished from Florence not for being a Ghibelline but for being the wrong brand of Guelph.)

Eventually the Florentine Guelphs emerged victorious, and in the 15th century the region was united to become the Grand Duchy of Tuscany, controlled from Florence by the Medici Grand Dukes. Today the hill towns are no longer fierce, although they retain a uniquely medieval air, and in most of them the citizens walk the same narrow streets and inhabit the same houses that their ancestors did 600 years ago.

Tuscan art, to most people, means Florence, and understandably so. The city is unique and incomparable, and an astonishing percentage of the great artists of the Renaissance lived and worked there. But there is art elsewhere in Tuscany, and too often it is overlooked in favor of another trip to the Uffizi. Siena, particularly, possesses its own style of architecture and art quite different from the Florentine variety; the contrast is both surprising and illuminating. And even the smallest of the hill towns can possess hidden treasures, for the artists of the Middle Ages and the Renaissance took their work where they could find it. Piero della Francesca's fresco cycle in the church of San Francesco in Arezzo is perhaps the preeminent hidden treasure; tucked away in a small church in a small town, it is artistically the equal of almost anything Florence has to offer and is all the more appealing for its uncrowded isolation.

Essential Information

Important Addresses and Numbers

Tourist Information
Regional information on Tuscany is available in **Florence** (Via di Novoli, tel. 055/439311).

Local information is available in the following tourist offices, which are generally open 9–12:30, 3:30–7:30.

Arezzo (Piazza Risorgimento 116, tel. 0575/20839).
Lucca (Piazza Vittoria Veneto 40, tel. 0583/493639).
Pisa (Piazza Duomo 8, tel. 050/560464).
Pistoia (Palazzo dei Vescovi, tel. 0573/21622).
Prato (Via Cairoli 48, tel. 0574/24112).
Siena (Piazza del Campo 55, tel. 0577/280551).
Volterra (Via Turazza 2, tel. 0588/86150).

Emergencies
Police, Ambulance, Fire, tel. 113. This number will put you in touch with the First Aid Service (Pronto Soccorso).

Travel Agencies
Florence. *American Express* (Via Guicciardini 49/r, tel. 055/278751); *CIT* (Via Cavour 56, tel. 055/294306); *Wagon Lits (Thomas Cook)* (Via del Giglio 27/r, tel. 055/218851).

Car Rentals
Cars may be rented at the airports and in the larger cities in Tuscany, and travelers using the economical Alitalia Jet-Drive package can fly to Pisa to visit the north of Tuscany, including Florence, Siena, and San Gimignano. Alitalia has a tie-in with Jolly Hotels, in which Jet-Drive passengers can get up to a 20% discount; there are Jolly Hotels in Florence and Siena.

Arriving and Departing by Plane

The largest airports in the region are Pisa's **Galileo Galilei** airport and Florence's **Peretola** airport. Flights from New York to Florence also go through Milan. There are direct flights from Paris to Pisa or Florence; from London there are direct flights to Pisa; from the United States, you'll have to get connecting flights from Rome or Milan.

Arriving and Departing by Car and Train

By Car Autostrada A1, the Autostrada del Sole, connects Florence with Bologna, 105 kilometers (65 miles) north, and Rome, 277 kilometers (172 miles) south, and passes close to Arezzo.

By Train The coastal line from Rome to Genoa passes through Pisa and all the beach resorts. The main line from Rome to Bologna passes through Arezzo, Florence, and Prato.

Getting Around

By Car Cars are the best way of seeing Tuscany, making it possible to explore the tiny towns and country restaurants that are so much a part of the region's charm. A11 leads west from Florence and meets the coastal A12 between Viareggio and Livorno. Toll-free superstrade link Florence with Siena and Arezzo. Drivers should be prepared to navigate through bewildering suburban sprawls around Tuscan cities; keep looking for signs to the *Centro Storico* to reach the historic sections where most of the sights are located.

By Train The main rail line runs past Cortona through Arezzo and Florence to Prato. Another main line connects Florence with Pisa. There are a few local lines as well.

By Bus Tuscany is crisscrossed by bus lines that connect the smaller towns and cities on the autostrade and superhighways. They are a good choice for touring the hill-towns around Siena, such as San Gimignano; you can then take a SITA bus from Siena to Arezzo and get back onto the main Rome-Florence train line.

By Boat Boat services link the islands of Tuscany's archipelago with the mainland; passenger and car ferries leave from Livorno and Piombino for Elba. The ferry to Giglio leaves from Porto Santo Stefano on the Argentario peninsula.

Guided Tours

From Florence, **American Express** (Via Guicciardini 49/r, tel. 055/278751) operates one-day excursions to Siena and San Gimignano and can arrange for cars, drivers, and guides for special-interest tours in Tuscany. **CIT** (Via Cavour 56, tel. 055/294306) has a three-day Carosello bus tour from Rome to Florence, Siena, and San Gimignano, as well as a five-day tour that also takes in Venice.

Exploring Tuscany

Since most visitors to Tuscany will also spend some time in Florence (*see* Chapter 4), that city may be considered the starting point for each of these excursions. Tour 1 heads west from Florence toward the Tuscan coast, taking in the historic cities of Lucca and Pisa, among others; Tour 2 goes south through lovely inland valleys to several charming hill towns, with special attention given to Siena, Florence's ancient rival for Tuscan supremacy. No spot on either tour is more than a few hours' drive from Florence, but you would be hard pressed to see all the sights in a day trip—better to allow at least two or three days for each itinerary.

Highlights for First-time Visitors

Lucca (Tour 1: En Route to Pisa).
Piazza del Duomo, in Pisa, including the Leaning Tower (Tour 1: En Route to Pisa).
San Gimignano (Tour 2: South to Siena).
Piazza del Campo, in Siena (Tour 2: South to Siena).
Duomo, in Siena (Tour 2: South to Siena).
Pinacoteca Nazionale, in Siena (Tour 2: South to Siena).
San Francesco, in Arezzo (Tour 2: South to Siena).

Tour 1: En Route to Pisa

Numbers in the margin correspond to points of interest on the Tuscany map.

❶ The tour begins at **Prato,** 21 kilometers (13 miles) northwest of Florence. One of Prato's leading medieval citizens, Francesco di Marco Datini, was the subject of Iris Orogo's 1957 biography *The Merchant of Prato.* Datini was a 14th-century cloth-merchant who built his business, according to one of his surviving ledgers, "in the name of God and of profit"; the city remains to this day one of the world's largest manufacturers of cloth.

Prato's main attraction is its 11th-century **Duomo.** Romanesque in style, it is famous for its Chapel of the Holy Girdle (to the left of the entrance), which enshrines the sash of the Virgin; it is said that the girdle was given to the apostle Thomas by the Virgin herself, when she miraculously appeared after her Assumption. The Duomo also contains 16th-century frescoes by Prato's most famous son, the libertine monk Fra Filippo Lippi; the best known depict Herod's banquet and Salome's dance. *Piazza del Duomo. Open 7–noon and 4–7.*

Sculpture by Donatello that originally adorned the Duomo's exterior pulpit is now on display in the **Museo dell'Opera del Duomo.** *Piazza del Duomo 49, tel. 0574/29339. Admission free. Open Mon. and Wed.–Sat. 9:30–12:30 and 3–6:30, Sun. 9:30–12:30.*

The nearby **Galleria Comunale** contains a good collection of Tuscan and Sienese paintings, mainly from the 14th century. *Palazzo Pretorio, Piazza del Comune, tel. 0574/452302. Open Mon.–Sat. 9–1 and 3–7.*

❷ The town of **Pistoia,** 15 kilometers (9 miles) west of Prato, saw the beginning of the bitter Guelph-Ghibelline conflict of the Middle Ages. Reconstructed after heavy bombing during

World War II, the town contains some fine Romanesque architecture. Its **Cathedral of San Zeno** in the main square (Piazza del Duomo) houses the **Dossale di San Jacopo,** a magnificent silver altarpiece. The two half-figures on its left side are by Filippo Brunelleschi (1377–1446), better known as the first Renaissance architect (and designer of Florence's magnificent Duomo dome). *Illumination of altarpiece: 2,000 lire.*

Other attractions include the **Ospedale del Ceppo** (Piazza Giovanni XII, a short way down the Via Pacini from the Piazza del Duomo), a hospital founded during the 14th century, with a superb early 16th-century ra-cotta frieze by Giovanni della Robbia; the church of **Sant'Andrea** (down the Via Pappe to the Via Sant' Andrea), with a fine early 14th-century pulpit by Giovanni Pisano that depicts the life of Christ; and, back in the Piazza del Duomo, an unusual Gothic baptistery and the 14th-century **Palazzo del Comune,** which now houses two museums: the **Museo Civico,** containing medieval art, and the **Centro Marino Marini,** containing contemporary art. *Palazzo del Comune, Piazza del Duomo, tel. 0573/367871 (Museo Civico) or 0573/368182 (Centro Marino Marini). Admission: 4,000 lire. Open Tues.–Sat. 9–1 and 3–7, Sun. 9–1.*

❸ The town of **Lucca,** 42 kilometers (25 miles) west of Pistoia, was where Caesar, Pompey, and Crassus agreed to rule Rome as a triumvirate in 56 BC; it was later the first town in Tuscany to accept Christianity. Today it still has a mind of its own, and, unlike most of Tuscany, its citizens rarely vote Communist. For a fine overview of the town, take a walk or a drive along its 16th-century ramparts, which are shaded by stately trees.

Numbers in the margin correspond to points of interest on the Lucca map.

❹ Lucca is one of the most picturesque fortress-towns in Tuscany and is worth exploring at length on foot. As usual, the main attraction is the **Duomo** (Piazza del Duomo, on the southern side of town). Its round-arched facade is a fine example of the rigorously ordered Pisan Romanesque style, in this case happily enlivened by an extremely disordered collection of carved columns. The decoration of the facade and of the porch below are worth a close look; they make this one of the most entertaining church fronts in Tuscany. The Gothic interior contains a moving Byzantine crucifix (called the **Volto Santo,** or Holy Face), brought here in the 8th century, and the masterpiece of the Sienese sculptor Jacopo della Quercia, the marble *Tomb of Ilaria del Caretto* (1406).

❺ Slightly west of the center of town is the church of **San Michele** (Piazza San Michele), with a facade even more fanciful than the Duomo; it was heavily restored in the 19th century, however, and somewhat jarringly displays busts of modern Italian patriots such as Garibaldi and Cavour.

Time Out For dessert, try the local sweet cake, *buccellato*, available at **Pasticceria Taddeucci** (Piazza San Michele 34), or a coffee or ice cream at the venerable **Caffe di Simo** (Via Fillungo), a favorite of Lucca's famous son Giacomo Puccini, composer of some of the world's best-loved operas.

❻ The church of **San Frediano** (Piazza San Frediano) is just inside the middle of the north wall; it contains more works by Jacopo

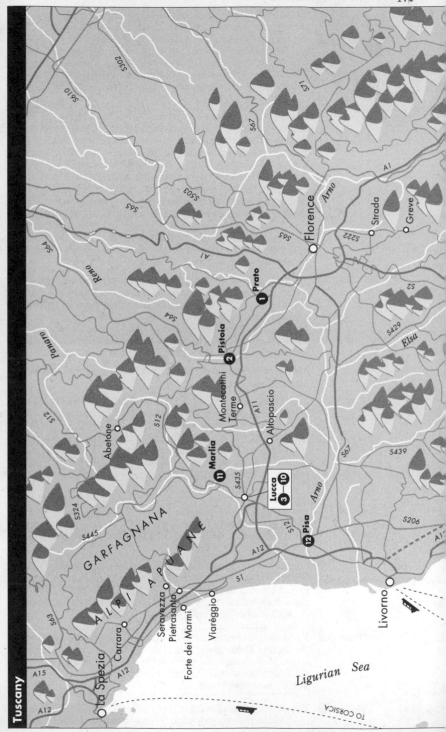

Tuscany

Ligurian Sea

TO CORSICA

Livorno

La Spezia

A15
A12

Carrara

Seravezza
Pietrasanta

Forte dei Marmi

Viaréggio

S63

S445

S324

Abetone

S12

GARFAGNANA

ALPI APUANE

S12

Panaro

Remo

S64

S65

S503

S610

S302

S71

S67

Florence

Arno

Strada

Greve

A1

S222

S2

Elsa

S429

S439

S206

A12

A12

A1

S1

Pisa

12

Arno

S12

S67

Altopascio

Lucca

3 — 10

S435

11

Marlia

Montecatini
Terme

A11

Pistoia

2

Prato

1

S64

S65

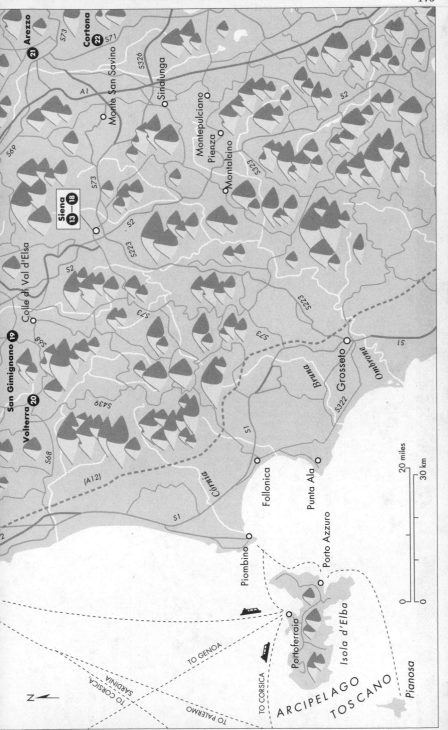

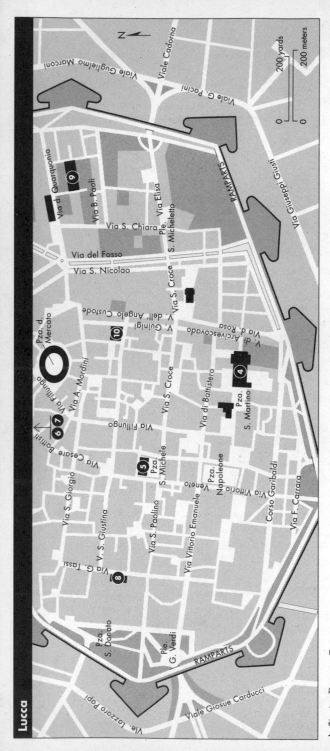

Lucca

Anfiteatro Romano, **7**
Duomo, **4**
Museo Nazionale, **9**
Palazzo Guinigi, **10**
Pinacoteca
   Nazionale, **8**
San Frediano, **6**
San Michele, **5**

7 della Quercia, and, bizarrely, the lace-clad mummy of the patron saint of domestic servants, Santa Zita. Near it, to the southeast, is the site of the ancient **Anfiteatro Romano,** or Roman amphitheater. Its piazza takes its oval shape from the theater, but the seats disappeared when medieval houses were built on top of them.

8 Near the west walls of the old city, the **Pinacoteca Nazionale** is worth a visit to see the Mannerist, Baroque, and Rococo art on display. *Palazzo Mansi, Via Galli Tassi 43, tel. 0583/55570. Admission: 6,000 lire. Open Tues.–Sat. 9–7, Sun. 9–2.*

Time Out For an inexpensive lunch in pleasant surroundings, try **Trattoria da Giulio** (Via delle Conce 47, near Porta San Donato), which serves orzo and *porri* (leek) soups, roasted meats, and other simple Lucchese specialties.

---

9 On the eastern end of the historic center, the **Museo Nazionale** houses an extensive collection of local Romanesque and Renaissance art. *Villa Guinigi, Via della Quarquonia, tel. 0583/46033. Admission: 4,000 lire. Open May–Sept., Tues.–Sat. 9–7, Sun. 9–1; Oct.–Apr., Tues.–Sat. 9–4:30, Sun. 9–1.*

10 Finally, for a fine view of the surrounding countryside, climb the tree-topped tower of the medieval **Palazzo Guinigi,** near the center of town. *Admission: 3,000 lire. Open 10–4, summer 9–7.*

Numbers in the margin correspond to points of interest on the Tuscany map.

11 Eight kilometers (5 miles) north of Lucca is the handsome **Villa Reale** at **Marlia.** Its superb gardens, laid out in the second half of the 17th century and surrounded by a park, are a fine place for a break and a stroll. *Villa Reale, tel. 0583/30108. Admission: July–Oct. 5,000 lire, Nov. and Mar.–June 4,000 lire. Guided visits on the hour, July–Sept., Tues.–Thurs. and Sun. 10, 11, 4, 5, 6; Nov., and Mar.–June, Tues.–Sun. 10, 11, 3, 4, 5.*

12 The town of **Pisa,** southwest of Lucca, reached its glory as a maritime republic during the 12th century; its architects and artists strongly influenced the development of the Romanesque and Gothic styles in Tuscany. Defeated by its arch rival Genoa in 1284 (also a seaport trading center), Pisa went into a gradual decline, its harbor filling with silt from the Arno; in the 15th century it became a satellite to Florence, when the Medici gained full control of Tuscany. During World War II, the city was virtually destroyed by Axis and Allied bombing.

The main attraction is, of course, the **Campo dei Miracoli** (the Field of Miracles) at the northwestern edge of town, on which stand the **Duomo,** the **Baptistery,** and the famous **Leaning Tower.** The Leaning Tower was begun in 1174, the last of the three structures to be built, and the lopsided settling began when construction reached the third story. The Tower's architects attempted to compensate by making the remaining floors slightly taller on the leaning side, but the extra weight only made the problem worse. The settling continues to this day, as do efforts to prop it up; in April 1992, five rings of half-inch steel cable were clamped around the lower stones, hoping to ease the pressure on the stones. Legend holds that Galileo conducted an experiment on the nature of gravity by dropping metal balls from the top of the 187-foot-high Tower; historians hold that this legend has no basis in fact (which is not quite to say that it is false). In early 1990 the Tower was closed for structural reinforcement and will probably remain closed permanently.

The **Duomo** was the first building to use the horizontal marble striping pattern (borrowed from Moorish architecture in the 11th century) so common to Tuscan cathedrals. It is famous for the Romanesque panels on the transept door facing the Tower, which depict the life of Christ, and for its beautifully carved 13th-century pulpit, by Giovanni Pisano (the Baptistery houses a pulpit carved by Giovanni's father, Nicola).

The walled area on the northern side of the Campo dei Miracoli is the **Camposanto,** or cemetery, which is filled, according to legend, with earth brought back from the Holy Land during the Crusades. Its galleries contain numerous frescoes, notably *The Drunkenness of Noah,* by Renaissance artist Benozzo Gozzoli, and the disturbing *Triumph of Death,* whose authorship is disputed. Across the lawn is the **Museo delle Sinopie,** in which an extensive array of preparatory drawings for the frescoes are displayed. *Camposanto. Open daily 9–one hour before sunset. Museo delle Sinopie. Admission: 4,000 lire. Open 9–1, 3–5.*

In the center of town, the **Piazza dei Cavalieri** possesses some fine Renaissance buildings: the **Palazzo dei Cavalieri,** the **Palazzo dell'Orologio,** and the church of **Santo Stefano dei Cavalieri.** The square was laid out around 1560 by Giorgio Vasari, better known for his chronicles of the lives of Renaissance artists that made him the first art historian. Along the Arno, the tiny Gothic church of **Santa Maria della Spina** (on the Lungarno Sonnino, south of the river) merits a visit, and the **Museo di San Matteo,** on the northern side, contains some touching examples of local Romanesque and Gothic art. *Lungarno Mediceo. Admission: 6,000 lire. Open Mon.–Sat. 9–2, Sun. 9–1.*

Tour 2: South to Siena

Depending on how much time you have, choose between two roads leading south from Florence to Siena: the speedy modern highway S2 if you're trying to fit Siena into a day trip from Florence, or the narrower and more meandering Route S222 if you really want to see the countryside. The S222 is also known as the **Strada Chiantigiana** because it runs through the heart of the Chianti wine-producing country. The most scenic section runs between **Strada in Chianti,** 16 kilometers (10 miles) south of Florence, to **Greve in Chianti,** 11 kilometers (7 miles) farther south, where rolling hillsides are planted with vineyards and olive groves. Greve is a busy provincial town that was once a medieval marketplace; around its triangular central piazza you can find a number of restaurants and vintners who offer wine tastings (*degustazioni*).

⑬ Florence's great historical rival, **Siena,** is located 68 kilometers (42 miles) south of Florence. The town was founded by Augustus around the time of the birth of Christ, although legend holds that it was founded much earlier by Remus, brother of Romulus, the legendary founder of Rome. During the late Middle Ages, the city was both wealthy and powerful (it saw the birth of the world's oldest bank, the Monte dei Paschi, still very much in business). It was bitterly envied by Florence, which in

1254 sent forces that besieged the city for over a year, reducing its population by half and laying waste to the countryside. The city was finally absorbed by the Grand Duchy of Tuscany, ruled by Florence, in 1559.

Numbers in the margin correspond to points of interest on the Siena map.

Unlike Renaissance Florence, Siena is a Gothic city, laid out over the slopes of three steep hills and practically unchanged since medieval times. Its main square, the **Piazza del Campo,** is one of the finest in Italy; fan shaped, its nine sections of paving (representing the 13th-century government of Nine Good Men) fan out from a reproduction of Jacopo della Quercia's Gaia Fountain. Twice a year, on July 2 and August 16, the square is the site of the famous **Palio,** a horserace in which the city's 17 neighborhoods compete to possess the cloth banner that gives the contest its name. Unlike many other such in Italy, the Palio is deeply revered by the townspeople, and the rivalries it generates are taken very seriously.

⑭ Dominating the piazza is the **Palazzo Pubblico,** which has served as Siena's Town Hall since the 1300s. It now also contains the **Museo Civico,** its walls covered with pre-Renaissance frescoes, including Simone Martini's early 14th-century *Maesta* and *Portrait of Guidoriccio da Fogliano,* and Ambrogio Lorenzetti's famous *Allegory of Good and Bad Government,* painted from 1327 to 1329 to demonstrate the dangers of tyranny. The original Jacopo della Quercia fountain, moved under cover to protect it from the elements, is also on display. The climb up the palazzo's bell tower is long and steep, but the superb view makes it worth every step. *Piazza del Campo, tel. 0577/292263. Bell Tower admission: 4,000 lire. Open Apr.– Sept., Mon.–Sat. 9:30–7:30; Oct.–Mar., Mon.–Sat. 9:30–1:30. Palazzo Pubblico (Museo Civico) admission: 5,500 lire. Open Apr.–Oct., Mon.–Sat 9:30–7:30, Sun. 9:30–1:30; Nov.–Mar., daily 9:30–1:30.*

Time Out There is a **gelateria** at Piazza del Campo 21, excellent for surveying the piazza while enjoying a refreshing ice cream. More substantial sustenance may be found nearby at **Ristorante Il Verrocchio,** which serves inexpensive Sienese specialties and is located a block east of the northern side of the campo. *Logge del Papa 2. Closed Wed.*

⑮ Siena's **Duomo,** several blocks west of the Piazza del Campo, is beyond question one of the finest Gothic cathedrals in Italy. Its facade, with its multicolored marbles and painted decoration, is typical of the Italian approach to Gothic architecture, lighter and much less austere than the French. The cathedral, as it now stands, was completed in the 14th century, but at the time the Sienese had even bigger plans. They decided to enlarge the building, using the current church as the transepts of the new church, which would have a new nave running toward the southeast. The beginnings of construction of this new nave still stand and may be seen from the steps outside the Duomo's right transept. Unfortunately, the city fell into decline, and the plans were never carried out.

The interior is one of the most striking in Italy and possesses a fine coffered and gilded dome. It is most famous for its unique and magnificent marble floors, which took almost 200 years to

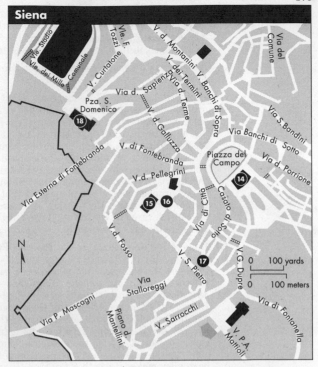

complete (beginning around 1370); more than 40 artists contributed to the work, made up of 56 separate compositions depicting biblical scenes, allegories, religious symbols, and civic emblems. The Duomo's carousel pulpit, which is almost as famous as the floors, was carved by Nicola Pisano around 1265 and depicts the life of Christ, on its rostrum frieze (the staircase is a later addition). Finally, a door in the left-hand aisle just before the crossing leads into the **Biblioteca Piccolomini,** a room painted by Pinturicchio in 1509; its frescoes depict events from the life of native son Aeneas Sylvius Piccolomini, who became Pope Pius II in 1458. The frescoes are in fine repair and have a freshness rarely seen in work so old. *Biblioteca Piccolomini, tel. 0577/283048. Admission: 1,500 lire. Open Apr.–Oct., daily 9:30–1 and 2:30–6; Nov.–Mar., daily 10–1 and 2:30–5.*

16 Next to the Duomo is its museum, the **Museo dell'Opera del Duomo,** containing (among other things) a small collection of Sienese art and the cathedral treasury. Its masterpiece is unquestionably Duccio's *Maesta,* painted around 1310 and magnificently displayed in a room devoted entirely to Duccio's work. *Piazza del Duomo, tel. 0577/283048. Admission: 5,000 lire. Open Apr.–Oct., daily 9–7:30; Nov.–Mar., daily 9–1:30.*

Steps between the cathedral and its museum lead to the **Battistero,** or Baptistery, painted with 15th-century frescoes. Its large bronze baptismal font (also 15th-century) was designed by Jacopo della Quercia and is adorned with bas-reliefs by various artists, including two by Renaissance masters: Lorenzo Ghiberti *(The Baptism of Christ)* and Donatello *(Herod Presented with the Head of St. John).*

⑰ Chief among Siena's other attractions is the **Pinacoteca Nazionale,** several blocks southeast of the entrance to the Duomo; it contains a superb collection of Sienese art, including Ambrogio Lorenzetti's 14th-century depiction of a castle that is generally considered the first nonreligious painting—the first pure landscape—of the Christian era. *Via San Pietro 29, tel. 0577/281161. Admission: 5,000 lire. Open Tues.–Sat. 8:30–7, Sun. 8:30–1.*

⑱ If time permits, a visit to the church of **San Domenico,** northwest of the Duomo, is also worthwhile; its **Cappella di Santa Caterina** displays frescoes by Il Sodoma portraying scenes from the life of Saint Catherine and houses a reliquary containing her head.

Time Out Not far from the church of San Domenico, the **Enoteca Italica** is a fantastically stocked wine cellar in the bastions of the Medici fortress. Here you can taste wines from all over Italy and have a snack, too. *Fortezza Medicea, Viale Maccari, tel. 0577/ 288497. Open 3 PM–midnight.*

Numbers in the margin correspond to points of interest on the Tuscany map.

⑲ The picturesque town of **San Gimignano** is 32 kilometers (20 miles) northwest of Siena. San Gimignano's high walls and narrow streets are typical of Tuscan hill towns, but it is the surviving medieval towers that set the town apart from its neighbors. Only a handful remain today, but at the height of the Guelph-Ghibelline conflict, a forest of more than 70 such towers dominated the city, which the locals like to call a mini-Manhattan. The towers were built partly for defensive purposes—they were a safe refuge and useful for pouring boiling oil on attacking enemies—and partly to bolster the egos of their owners, who competed with deadly seriousness to build the highest tower in town.

Many of the town's most important medieval buildings are clustered around the central Piazza del Duomo. They include the **Palazzo del Podestà,** with its imposing tower; the **Palazzo del Popolo,** now the municipal museum, displaying Sienese and Renaissance paintings; and the Romanesque **Collegiata** (which lost its status as a Duomo when San Gimignano lost its bishop), containing fine 15th-century frescoes by Domenico Ghirlandaio in the Chapel of Santa Fina. *Admission to palazzo and chapel: 5,000 lire. Open 9:30–12:30, 2:30–5:30, summer to 6:30.*

Before leaving San Gimignano, be sure to see its most famous work of art, at the northern end of town, in the church of **Sant' Agostino:** Benozzo Gozzoli's beautiful 15th-century fresco cycle depicting the life of St. Augustine. Also try a taste of Vernaccia, the local white wine, available at the many locations marked *degustazione.*

⑳ Continue on to **Volterra,** 29 kilometers (18 miles) southwest of San Gimignano. D. H. Lawrence, in his *Etruscan Places,* sang the praises of Volterra, "standing somber and chilly alone on her rock." The town has long been known for its alabaster, which has been mined since Etruscan times; today the Volterrans use it to make ornaments and souvenirs sold all over town. A magnificent collection of small alabaster funerary urns that once held the ashes of deceased Etruscans (along with many other Etruscan artifacts) may be seen at the **Museo Etrusco Guarnacci** (Via Don Minzoni). Later art can be found in the **Duomo,** at the **Pinacoteca** (Palazzo Minucci-Solaini, Via dei Sarti 1), and at the **Museo di Arte Sacra** (via Roma). The town's best-known Renaissance works are the 15th-century frescoes in the Duomo by Benozzo Gozzoli and the 16th-century *Deposition* by Rosso Fiorentino in the Pinacoteca. *Combined admission to Museo Etrusco Guarnacci, Pinacoteca, and Museo di Arte Sacra: 8,000 lire. Open Mar. 16–Oct. 14, daily 9:30–6:30 (Museo Etrusco Guarnacci closes 1–3); Oct. 15–Mar. 15, daily 9:30–1 (Museo Etrusco Guarnacci 9–2).*

The walls of Volterra also harbor one of the few pieces of Etruscan architecture that escaped Roman destruction: the **Arco Etrusco,** with its weather-worn Etruscan heads, at the Porta all'Arco.

As you return along S68 to Siena, time permitting, you may want to stop off halfway at **Colle di Val d'Elsa,** yet another walled hill town whose narrow medieval streets have been preserved.

㉑ On the other side of Siena, a major point of interest is **Arezzo,** 88 kilometers (55 miles) northeast of Siena. (You may want to break the drive halfway with a rest stop at **Monte San Savino,** a prosperous-looking small town, with the tiny nearby hill town of **Gargonza** that has been carefully restored into a vacation resort; *see* Dining and Lodging, *below*.) Arezzo was the birthplace of the poet Petrarch; the Renaissance artist and art historian Giorgio Vasari; and Guido d'Arezzo, the inventor of musical notation. Today the town is best known for the magnificent Piero della Francesca frescoes in the church of **San Francesco,** on the Via Cavour in the center of town. Painted between 1452 and 1466, they depict *The Legend of the True Cross* on three walls of the choir. What Sir Kenneth Clark called "the most perfect morning light in all Renaissance painting" may be seen in the lowest section of the right wall, where the troops of the Emperor Maxentius flee before the sign of the cross. To summarize the legend briefly (but incompletely): Adam's son Seth, after Adam's death, plants a branch from the tree of paradise on his grave; the Queen of Sheba, granted a vision, recognizes a beam made from the resulting tree as sacred and explains her vision to Solomon; the beam is used to construct the cross on which Christ was crucified; the cross is later found, after Constantine's victory, by the Empress Helen. Unfortunately, part of the frescoes may be hidden from view while restoration work takes place.

Other attractions in Arezzo include the church of **San Domenico,** just inside the walls to the north of San Francesco (Piazza Fossombroni), which houses a 13th-century crucifix by Cimabue; the **house** that Giorgio Vasari designed and decorated for himself in 1540, just west of San Domenico; and the **Museo Archeologico,** with a fine collection of Etruscan bronzes. *Vasari house: Via XX Settembre. Open Tues.–Sat. 9–2, Sun. 9–1. Museo Archeologico: Via Margaritone 10, tel. 0575/20882. Admission: 6,000 lire. Open Tues.–Sat. 9–2, Sun. 9–1.*

㉒ About 30 kilometers (18 miles) south of Arezzo on S71, the medieval town of **Cortona** is known for its excellent small art gallery and a number of fine antiques shops, as well as for its colony of foreign residents. Cortona has the advantage of being on the main train network, though you will have to take a local bus from the station up into the town, passing the Renaissance church of **Santa Maria del Calcinaio** on the way.

The heart of Cortona is formed by **Piazza della Repubblica** and the adjacent **Piazza Signorelli.** Wander into the courtyard of the picturesque **Palazzo Pretorio,** and, if you want to see a representative collection of Etruscan bronzes, climb its centuries-old stone staircase to the **Museo dell'Accademia Etrusca** (Gallery of Etruscan Art). *Piazza Signorelli 9, tel. 0575/62534. Admission: 5,000 lire. Open Apr.–Sept., Tues.–Sun. 10–1 and 4–7; Oct.–Mar., Tues.–Sun. 9–1 and 3–5.*

The nearby **Museo Diocesano** (Diocesan Museum) houses an impressive number of large and splendid paintings by native son Luca Signorelli, as well as a beautiful *Annunciation* by Fra Angelico, a delightful surprise to find in this small, eclectic town. *Piazza del Duomo 1, tel. 0575/62830. Admission: 5,000 lire. Open Apr.–Sept., Tues.–Sun. 9–1 and 3–6:30; Oct.–Mar., Tues.–Sun. 9–1 and 3–5.*

What to See and Do with Children

Just outside Pistoia is the new **Giardino Zoologico,** especially laid out to accommodate the wiles of both animals and children. *Via Pieve a Celle 160, Pistoia, tel. 0573/571280. Open daily 9–sunset.*

Pinocchio afficionados will be delighted by the **Parco di Pinocchio** in Collodi, near Pescia. A statue of the long-nosed puppet is the centerpiece of a garden containing sculptural groups that depict scenes from Carlo Lorenzini's children's classic, *The Adventures of Pinocchio.* Close by is the beautifully kept Italian garden of Villa Garzoni.

Walking, hiking, and **picnicking** in the inviting, hilly Tuscan countryside are natural attractions for children. In the hills of Garfagnana, above Lucca, is a tennis camp called **Il Ciocco,** especially designed for children; there are horseback riding, swimming, and health facilities, and adults can participate as well. *Centro Turistico Internazionale, Barga, Lucca; tel. 0583/710021.*

Off the Beaten Track

Elba. The largest island in the Tuscan archipelago, Elba is an hour by ferry or a half hour by Hovercraft from Piombino, or a short hop by air from Pisa. Its main port is **Portoferraio,** fortified in the 16th century by the Medici Grand Duke Cosimo I. Victor Hugo spent his boyhood here, and Napoleon his famous exile in 1814–15, when he built (out of two windmills) the **Palazzina Napoleonica dei Mulini** and (a few miles outside town) the **Villa San Martino.** *Palazzina Napoleonica and Villa San Martino. Admission: 5,000 lire for both if visiting on the same day. Open Tues.–Sat. 9–1:30, Sun. 9–12:30.*

The island's main attractions, however, are its rough landscape and pristine beaches offering a full array of sports. From Elba, private visits can be arranged to the other islands in the archipelago, including **Montecristo,** which inspired Alexander Dumas's 19th-century best-seller *The Count of Monte Cristo* and is now a wildlife refuge. Elba's restaurants offer excellent seafood, to be sampled with the local Moscato and Aleatico wines.

Forte dei Marmi. Tuscany's most exclusive beach resort, a favorite of moneyed Tuscans and Milanese, whose villas are neatly laid out in an extensive pine wood, is 65 kilometers (30 miles) northwest of Florence by car. It is near the marble-producing towns of **Carrara** (where Michelangelo quarried his stone), **Serravezza,** and **Pietrasanta.**

Montecatini Terme. One of Europe's most famous health spas, Montecatini Terme is 16 kilometers (10 miles) west of Pistoia by car, train, or Lazzi or Tambellini bus. It is renowned for its **mineral springs,** used to treat liver and skin disorders. Montecatini was heavily developed at the beginning of this century, leaving a wealth of Art Nouveau buildings, the most attractive of which is the **Stabilimento Tettuccio.**

Montepulciano. Some 64 kilometers (40 miles) southwest of Florence by car or bus, Montepulciano is one of Tuscany's loveliest hill towns. Medieval, Renaissance, and Baroque architecture blend here and are best appreciated on a stroll enhanced by the town's famous wine, Vino Nobile di Montepulciano.

Shopping

Specialty Items **Arezzo** is known for its production of gold, as well as a burgeoning cottage knitwear industry. (For sweaters, try *Maglierie, Piazza Grande.*) The olive oil of **Lucca** is exported throughout the world. **Prato** makes hard almond cookies called *biscottini,* ideal for dunking in the beverage of one's choice. **Siena** is known for a variety of medieval desserts: *cavallucci, panforti,* and *ricciarelli.* **Volterra** has a number of shops selling boxes, jewelry, and other objects made from alabaster. For information and directions, contact Cooperativa Artieri Alabastro (Piazza dei Priori 2, tel. 0588/87590).

Flea Markets The first Sunday of each month, a colorful flea market selling antiques and not-so-antiques takes place in Piazza Grande in **Arezzo.** On the second Sunday of the month, another market goes to Piazza San Martino in **Lucca.** In summer, a beachcomber's bonanza takes place Wednesday mornings in **Forte dei Marmi,** near Lucca, when everything from fake designer sunglasses to plastic sandals and terrycloth towels goes on sale.

Sports

Fishing For a license, contact the **Federazione Italiana della Pesca Sportiva** (Via de Neri 6, Firenze). The spot for tuna fishing in Tuscany is at **Punta Ala,** from Sept. to Oct. Fishing trips and charters may be arranged through **Renato Lessi** (Localita Porto, Punta Ala, Grosseto, tel. 0564/922–7693).

Golf Punta Ala is also the site of the **Golf Club Punta Ala,** an 18-hole course on the sea opposite the island of Elba (Via del Golf 1, Punta Ala, Grosseto, tel. 0564/922121).

Horseback Riding Some popular riding sites are **Rendola Riding** (Rendola Valdarno, Arezzo, tel. 0575/987045), **Rifugio Prategiano** (Montieri, Grosseto, tel. 0566/997703), **Le Cannelle** (Parco dell'Uccellina, Talamone, Grosseto, tel. 0564/887020). For more information, contact the **Federazione Italiana Sport Equestre** (Via Paoletti 54, Firenze, tel. 055/480039).

Sailing Charters in Tuscany are available through the **Centro Nautico Italiano** (Piazza Signoria 31/r, Firenze, tel. 055/287045); **Mario Lorenzoni** (Via degli Alfani 105/r, Firenze, tel. 055/284790); and **Renato Lessi** (Localita Porto, Punta Ala, Grosseto, tel. 0564/922793). For more information, contact the **Federazione Italiana Vela** (CP 49, Marina di Carrara, tel. 0585/57323) or the **Federazione Italiana Motonautica** (Via Goldora 16, 55044 Marina di Pietrasanta, tel. 0584/20963).

Skiing The best spot for skiing in Tuscany is **Abetone.** For information, contact the **Federazione Italiana Sports Invernali** (Viale Matteotti 15, Firenze, tel. 055/576987).

Spectator Sports

Horse Racing Besides the racecourses in the **Cascine** in Florence, horse racing takes place in **Montecatini** and **Punta Ala,** as well as **San Rossore** and **Follonica.**

Dining and Lodging

Dining Though Florentine cuisine now predominates throughout Tuscany, the Etruscan influence on regional food still persists, after more than three millenia. As the ancient race was responsible for the introduction of the cypress to the Tuscan landscape, it is also credited with the use of herbs in cooking. Basic ingredients such as tarragon, sage, rosemary, and thyme appear frequently, happily coupled with game, Chianina beef, or even seafood. Each region has its own specialties, usually based on simple ingredients. In fact, Tuscans are disparagingly called *mangiafagioli*, or bean eaters, by other Italians. In the tradition of Tuscan-born Amerigo Vespucci, however, its chefs have recently discovered the rest of the world, and for better or worse, an "international cuisine" has been gradually making its appearance throughout the region.

Fortunately, Tuscany's wines remain unaltered. Grapes have been cultivated here since Etruscan times, and Chianti still rules the roost (almost literally when selected by the *Gallo Nero*, Black Rooster, label, a symbol of one of the region's most powerful wine-growing consortiums; the other is a *putto*, or cherub). The robust red wine's straw flask is still a staple on most tables, and the discerning can select from a multitude of other varieties, including such reds as Brunello di Montalcino and Vino Nobile di Montepulciano, and whites such as Valdinievole and Valdichiana. The dessert wine vin santo is produced throughout the region and is often enjoyed with hard dry almond cookies called *biscottini di Prato*, which are perfect for dunking.

Highly recommended restaurants are indicated by a star ★.

Category	Cost*
Very Expensive	over 110,000 lire
Expensive	70,000–110,000 lire

Moderate	35,000–70,000 lire
Inexpensive	under 35,000 lire

per person, for a three-course meal, including house wine and taxes

Lodging Highly recommended lodgings are indicated by a star ★.

Category	Cost*
Very Expensive	over 300,000 lire
Expensive	220,000–300,000 lire
Moderate	100,000–220,000 lire
Inexpensive	under 100,000 lire

All prices are for a double room for two, including tax and service.

Arezzo
Dining

Buca di San Francesco. A frescoed cellar restaurant in a historic building next to the church of San Francesco, this "buca" (literally "hole," figuratively "cellar") has a medieval atmosphere and serves straightforward local specialties. Vegetarians will like the *ribollita* (vegetable soup thickened with bread) and the *sformato di verdure* (spinach or chard pie), though it may be served *con cibreo* (with a giblet sauce). Meat eaters will find the lean Chianina beef a succulent treat. *Piazza San Francesco 1, tel. 0575/23271. Reservations advised. Dress: casual. AE, DC, MC, V. Closed Mon. evening, Tues., and all July. Moderate.*

Tastevin. Close to San Francesco and to the central Piazza Guido Monaco, Tastevin has introduced creative cooking styles in Arezzo but serves traditional dishes as well, in three attractive dining rooms, two in warm Tuscan provincial style, one in more sophisticated Art Deco. At the small bar the talented owner plays and sings show tunes and Sinatra songs in the evening; there is a 15% cover charge for music. The restaurant's specialties are *risotto tastevin* (with cream of truffles) and seafood or meat *carpaccio* (sliced raw). *Via de Cenci 9, tel. 0575/28304. Reservations advised in the evening. Dress: casual. AE, MC, V. Closed Mon. (Sun. in summer). Moderate.*

Spiedo d'Oro. Cheery red-and-white tablecloths add a bright note to this large, reliable trattoria near the Archeological Museum. This is your chance to try authentic Tuscan home-style specialties, such as *zuppa di pane* (bread soup), *pappardelle all'ocio* (noodles with duck sauce), and *ossobuco aretina* (sautéed veal shank). *Via Crispi 12, tel. 0575/22873. No reservations. Dress: casual. V. Closed Thurs. and July 1–18. Inexpensive.*

Lodging

Continental. Centrally located near the train station and within walking distance of all major sights, the Continental has been a reliable and convenient place to stay since it opened in the 1950s. Recently refurbished, it now has bright white furnishings with yellow accents, gleaming new bathrooms complete with hair dryers, and a pleasant roof garden. Rates are at the low end of the Moderate category. *Piazza Guido Monaco 7, tel. 0575/20251, fax 0575/340485. 74 rooms with bath or shower. Facilities: roof garden, restaurant (closed Sun. eve. and Mon. Inexpensive). AE, DC, MC, V. Moderate.*

Cortona **La Loggetta.** Located above Cortona's main medieval square,
Dining this attractive restaurant occupies a 16th-century wine cellar;
its four ample dining rooms have a relaxing atmosphere and
tasteful decor in keeping with the setting. In fair weather you
can eat outdoors, overlooking the 13th-century town hall, dining on regional dishes and such specialties as *cannelloni*
(crepes filled with spinach and ricotta) and *lombatine al
cartoccio* (veal chops with porcini mushrooms). The owners
pride themselves on their selection of Tuscan wines. *Piazza
Pescheria 3, tel. 0575/603777. No reservations. Dress: casual.
AC, DC, MC, V. Closed Sun. eve. (except summer), Mon., and
Jan. 5–Feb. 10. Moderate.*

Tonino. Deservedly well known and popular with locals and visitors alike, this large modern establishment can be noisy and
crowded on holiday weekends. But it is very satisfactory indeed at all other times, when you can enjoy the view of the
Chiana valley and feast on host Tonino's own *antipastissimo,*
an incredible variety of delectables. This is the place to taste
Chiana beefsteak. *Piazza Garibaldi, tel. 0575/630500. Reservations advised, especially weekends. Dress: casual. AE, DC,
MC, V. Closed Mon. eve., Tues. Moderate.*

Gargonza **Castello di Gargonza.** In a tiny 13th-century hill town with a
Dining and Lodging castle, church, and cobbled streets, all the houses are for rent
by the week and rooms can be had by the night. This enchanting
place in the farmland between Siena and Arezzo has been res-
urrected by a farsighted Florentine count to provide a unique
vacation spot. The houses sleep two to seven people, have one
to six rooms each, and have as many as four baths. A pool and
tennis court are on the way. *52048 Monte San Savino, tel. 0575/
847021, fax 0575/847054. 18 houses with bath. Facilities: restaurant, parking. AE, MC, V. Moderate weekly; inquire about
daily rate. Closed Jan. 10–Feb. 10.*

Lucca **Solferino.** About 6 kilometers (4 miles) outside town, on the
Dining road to Viareggio, this pleasant restaurant serves exquisite
variations of regional favorites, such as *anatra ripiena in
crema di funghi* (stuffed duck with mushroom sauce), made
with ingredients from the family farm. Ask for a piece of
buccellato, a sweet, anise-flavored bread with raisins that is a
specialty of Lucca. *San Macario in Piano, tel. 0583/59118. Reservations required. Dress: casual. AE, DC, MC, V. Closed
Wed., Thurs. lunch, 2 weeks in mid-Aug., Jan. 7–15. Expensive.*

★ **La Mora.** Some 9 kilometers (6 miles) outside Lucca, this former country inn and coach station is worth going out of your
way for. The menu offers a range of local specialties, from *farro*
(wheat soup) with beans to *tacconi* (homemade pasta) with rabbit sauce and lamb from the nearby Garfagnana hills. You'll be
tempted by the variety of *crostini* (canapés) and delicious desserts, as well. *Via Sesto di Ponte a Moriano 1748, tel. 0583/
57109. Reservations advised. Dress: casual. AE, DC, MC, V.
Closed Wed. evening, Thurs., June 25–July 8, and Oct. 10–30.
Moderate–Expensive.*

Buca di Sant'Antonio. Near the church of San Michele, this was
of a rustic inn. The specialties here are local dishes, some unfamiliar but well worth trying, such as *ravioli di ricotta alle
zucchine* (cheese ravioli with zucchini) and roast *capretto* (kid)
or *agnello* (lamb) with savory herb seasoning. *Via della Cervia
3, tel. 0583/55881. Reservations advised in the evening. Dress:*

casual. AE, DC, MC, V. Closed Sun. evening and Mon.; July 9–29. Moderate.

Il Giglio. Located just off Piazza Napoleone and close to the Hotel Universo, this restaurant has quiet, turn-of-the-century charm and classic cuisine. Seafood is a specialty, but it can be expensive. You may prefer to order *crostini* (toast rounds with Tuscan pâté) and *stracotto* (braised beef with mushrooms). *Piazza del Giglio 3, tel. 0583/44058. Reservations advised in the evening. Dress: casual. AE, DC, MC, V. Closed Tues. evening, Wed. Moderate.*

Lodging **Villa La Principessa.** Just outside Lucca, only 3 kilometers (2 miles) from town, this is an exquisitely decorated 19th-century country mansion that has been converted into an exclusive hotel. Some rooms have beamed ceilings, and doors are individually decorated. Antique furniture and portraits give an aura of gracious living but the rooms are in need of sprucing up. The restaurant is known for its creative cuisine. A well-manicured park and large swimming pool lure guests outdoors in fair weather. *Massa Pisana, tel. 0583/370037, fax 0583/379019. 44 rooms and suites with bath. Facilities: park, pool, restaurant (closed Wed.). AE, DC, MC, V. Closed Nov. 5–Mar. 31. Expensive.*

Universo. This hotel retains much of the genteel old-world charm it had when English essayist John Ruskin stayed here. In the spacious, high-ceiling public rooms the decor is in early 1900s style. The hotel was entirely renovated in 1989, when rooms were modernized and endowed with TV, minibars, and sparkling new baths. *Piazza del Giglio 1, tel. 0583/493678. 60 rooms with bath or shower. Facilities: bar, restaurant. V. Moderate.*

Ilaria. A family-run hotel beside a minuscule canal within easy walking distance of the main sights, it was renovated in 1987. The rooms are small but fresh and functional. *Via del Fosso 20, tel. 0583/47558. 17 rooms, most with bath. AE, DC, MC, V. Inexpensive.*

Montalcino **La Cucina di Edgardo.** This tiny restaurant on Montalcino's
Dining main street seats 30 in two charming dining rooms done in off-white and beige with dark wooden beams, a fireplace, and terra-cotta floors. It offers a complete menu, including everything from antipasto to after-dinner sweets, wine, and mineral water, for about 60,000 lire. The specialties of the house are *crema contadina* (bean soup garnished with onion) and *brasato al brunello* (beef braised in the local Brunello wine). *Via Soccorsi Saloni 33, tel. 0577/848232. Reservations advised, especially weekends and summer. Dress: casual. AE, DC, MC, V. Closed Wed. and Jan. 10–30. Moderate.*

★ **Taverna dei Barbi.** A meal at this delightful tavern, set among vineyards and mellow brick buildings on the country estate of the wine producer Fattoria dei Barbi, may well be a highlight of your journey through this part of Tuscany. The rustic dining room features a beamed ceiling, huge stone fireplace, and arched windows with views of the farmland that produces practically all the ingredients used in traditional recipes. Specialties include *zuppa di fagioli* (country-style bean soup with chard) and *scottiglia di pollo* (browned chicken served with garlic bread). The estate-produced Brunello is excellent, and the Taverna serves a range of other wines with the Barbi label. *Fattoria dei Barbi, tel. 0577/849357. Reservations required.*

Dress: casual. No credit cards. Closed Jan. 15–31, and July 1–15, also closed Tues. eve. Oct.–May, Wed. Moderate.

Pisa **Sergio.** In a 900-year-old palazzo on the Arno, Sergio has a clas-
Dining sic provincial elegance and an eclectic collection of paintings on
wood-paneled walls. You can choose among chef-host Sergio's
creations, such as ravioli with porcini mushrooms, seafood in
cartoccio (en papillote), or *portafoglio alla Sergio* (veal
escalopes stuffed with mushrooms, cheese, and prosciutto in
wine sauce). *Lungarno Pacinotti 1, tel. 050/48245. Reservations advised, especially in the eve. Jacket and tie advised. AE,
DC, MC, V. Closed Sun. and Mon. lunch; Jan. Moderate–Expensive.*

Bruno. A pleasant restaurant, with beamed ceilings and the
look of a country inn, Bruno is located just outside the old city
walls, a short walk from the bell tower and cathedral. Dine on
classic Tuscan dishes, from *zuppa alla pisana* (thick vegetable
soup) to *baccalà con porri* (cod with leeks). *Via Luigi Bianchi
12, tel. 050/560818. Reservations advised in the evening. Dress:
casual. AE, DC, MC, V. Closed Mon. eve., Tues., and August
5–15. Moderate.*

Spartaco. Centrally located on the station square, Spartaco is a
well-established trattoria, with contemporary white chairs
contrasting with terra-cotta-tiled floors and fine antique
pieces. It's a large place, and seating doubles in the summer
when tables are set out on the square. Among the specialties
are Tuscan dishes, *farro* (wheat soup) and *baccala alla
livornese* (stockfish with onions). *Piazza Vittorio Emanuele
22, tel. 050/20457. No reservations. Dress: casual. AE, DC,
MC, V. Closed Sun. Moderate.*

Lodging **Cavalieri.** Opposite the railway station, in an unremarkable
1950s building, this CIGA hotel offers functional, modern comforts in completely soundproofed and air-conditioned rooms,
all with color TV and minibar. The restaurant specializes in
homemade pasta and seafood and is open every day. *Piazza della Stazione 2, tel. 050/43290, fax 050/502242. 92 rooms with
bath or shower. AE, DC, MC, V. Expensive.*

Royal Victoria. In a pleasant palazzo facing the Arno, a 10-min-
ute walk from the Campo dei Miracoli, this hotel is about as
close as Pisa comes to Old World ambience. It's comfortably
furnished, featuring antiques and reproductions in the lobby
and in some rooms, in which the decor varies from functional
modern to turn-of-the-century. Renovations in 1988 spruced
up the desk and added an up-to-the-minute phone system.
There's a large restaurant, open every day for hotel guests.
*Lungarno Pacinotti 12, tel. 050/502130. 67 rooms, 46 with bath.
AE, DC, MC, V. Inexpensive.*

Pistoia **La Casa degli Amici.** The name means "the house of friends,"
Dining and that's the atmosphere that the two industrious ladies who
own it succeed in creating in this restaurant located outside
Pistoia's old walls, on the road toward the autostrada A-11 exit.
They offer homey specialties such as *ribollita* (bread and vegetable soup), and *pasta e fagioli*, (pasta and bean soup) and some
creative dishes, too. There's a terrace for outdoor dining in the
summer. *Via Bonellina 111, tel. 0573/380305. Reservation advised. Dress: casual. AE, DC, MC, V. Closed Sun. eve., Tues.,
and Aug. Moderate.*

Rafanelli. *Maccheroni all'anatra* (pasta with duck sauce) and
other game dishes are the specialties, served with careful at-

tention to tradition and quality for more than half a century by the same family. The restaurant is located just outside the old city walls; prices are in the low range of this category. *Via Sant'Agostino 47, tel. 0573/532046. No reservations. Dress: casual. AE, DC, MC, V. Closed Sun. eve., Mon., and Aug. Moderate.*

Prato
Dining

Piraña. Oddly named for the cannibalistic fish swimming in an aquarium in full view of diners, this sophisticated restaurant, decorated in shades of blue with white accents, is a favorite in Prato. Seafood is the specialty and may take the form of *ravioli di pesce* (seafood ravioli with cream of scampi sauce) or *rombo al forno* (baked turbot). It's a bit out of the way for sightseers but handy if you have a car, for it's near the Prato Est autostrada exit. *Via G. Valentini 110, tel. 0574/25746. Reservations advised. Dress: casual. AE, DC, MC, V. Closed Sat. lunch, Mon. lunch, Sun., and Aug. Expensive.*

La Veranda. A large antipasto buffet greets you just inside the door of this restaurant near Prato's 13th-century Frederick castle. The decor is elegant, with pale pink walls, terra-cotta tiled floors, and Venetian glass chandeliers, but the atmosphere is friendly and family-oriented. Although the large menu has several international dishes, including Spanish paella, it does not ignore Tuscan specialties: *agnello alla cacciatora* (lamb with a tangy wine-vinegar sauce) or *tagliata* (sliced beef) with rucola and truffle are two good choices. *Via dell'Arco 10, tel. 0574/38235. Dress: casual. AE, DC, MC, V. Closed Sun. Moderate.*

San Gimignano
Dining

Bel Soggiorno. On the top floor of a 100-year-old inn, this rustic restaurant has a wall of windows from which to view the landscape. Tuscan specialties include *pappardelle alla lepre* (noodles with hare sauce) and *risotto del Bel Soggiorno* (with saffron and nutmeg). *Via San Giovanni 91, tel. 0577/940375. Reservations advised. Dress: casual. AE, DC, MC, V. Closed Mon. and Jan. 7–Feb. 7. Moderate.*

★ **Le Terrazze.** A time-honored inn in the heart of San Gimignano, La Cisterna is justly famous for Le Terrazze restaurant, with a charming view of rooftops and countryside and an ample menu featuring Tuscan dishes in seasonal variations. The specialties are served *alla sangimignanese* (finished off in the oven). *Piazza della Cisterna 23, tel. 0577/940328. Reservations advised. Dress: casual. AE, DC, MC, V. Closed Tues. and Wed. lunch and Nov. 10–Mar. 1. Moderate.*

Lodging
★

Pescille. As an appealing alternative to the simple comforts of the Bel Soggiorno and Cisterna hotels in town (both Inexpensive), this is a rambling farmhouse 8 kilometers (2 miles) outside San Gimignano that has been converted into a handsome hotel, in which restrained contemporary and country classic decors blend well. It also houses the fine *Cinque Gigli* restaurant. *Località Pescille, Strada Castel San Gimignano, tel. 0577/940186, fax 0577/940375. 33 rooms with bath. Facilities: outdoor pool, tennis, park, restaurant (closed Wed.) AE, DC, MC, V. Closed Nov. 6–Apr. 6. Moderate.*

Siena
Dining
★

Al Marsili. Located between Piazza del Campo and the cathedral, this 900-year-old wine cellar is an elegant place to dine, under broad, brick-vaulted ceilings. The menu offers Tuscan and Italian specialties, among them homemade pastas such as *pici* and *tortelloni burro e salvia* (large cheese-filled ravioli with butter and sage). Various meat dishes are cooked in wine, and the wine list features the finest Tuscan and Italian labels, including many from the nearby Chianti country. *Via del Castoro 3, tel. 0577/47154. Reservations advised. Dress: casual. AE, DC, MC, V. Closed Mon. Moderate.*

Le Logge. Near Piazza del Campo, this typically Sienese trattoria has rustic dining rooms on two levels and tables outdoors from June to Oct. The menu features Tuscan dishes, such as *pennette all'osteria* (pasta with creamy herbed sauce) and *coniglio con pignoli* (rabbit with pine nuts). *Via del Porrione 33, tel. 0577/48013. Reservations advised. Dress: casual. DC, MC, V. Closed Sun. and June 1–15, Nov. 1–15. Moderate.*

Tullio Tre Cristi. This is a typical and historic neighborhood trattoria, long ago discovered by tourists and still reliable. The paintings on the walls are by famous local artists of the 1920s, but the culinary tradition here goes back even further. Try *spaghetti alle briciole*, a poor-man's dish of pasta with breadcrumbs, tomato, and garlic, or veal escaloppes subtly flavored with *dragoncello* (tarragon). You can eat outdoors in summer. To find the restaurant, take Via dei Rossi from Via Banchi di Sopra. *Vicolo di Provenzano 1, tel. 0577/280608. Reservations advised. Dress: casual. DC, MC, V. Closed Sun. eve., Mon., and mid-Jan–mid-Feb. Moderate.*

Lodging **Certosa di Maggiano.** A former 14th-century monastery con-
★ verted into an exquisite country hotel, this haven of gracious living is little more than a mile from the center of Siena. The atmosphere is that of an exclusive retreat in which a select number of guests enjoy the style and comfort of an aristocratic villa. *Via Certosa 82, tel. 0577/288180, fax 0577/288189. 14 rooms with bath. Facilities: outdoor pool, tennis, gardens, restaurant (closed Tues. Expensive.). AE, DC, MC, V. Very Expensive.*

Park. Set among olive groves and gardens on a hillside just outside the city walls, this hotel offers solid comfort and spacious rooms with views of the grounds and countryside. A historic 16th-century villa, it has the restful atmosphere and antique charm of Tuscan country life. The Olivo restaurant is known for fine regional cuisine. *Via Marciano 18, tel. 0577/44803, fax 0577/49020. 68 double rooms with bath or shower. Facilities: outdoor pool, 2 tennis courts, riding, park, minibus service into town, 2 restaurants, poolside service, Caminetto bar. AE, DC, MC, V. Very Expensive.*

★ **Palazzo Ravizza.** Individually decorated rooms in a 17th-century town house a short walk from Siena's cathedral offer solid, old-fashioned comforts; many have new bathrooms. The quiet garden is a lovely place to sit and contemplate the rolling landscape, and the vaulted dining rooms are frescoed with delicate motifs. Half board is required from March to November; at other times it's possible to book only bed and breakfast. *Via Pian dei Mantellini 34, tel. 0577/280462, fax 0577/271370. 30 rooms, 21 with bath or shower. Facilities: garden, restaurant. AE, DC, MC, V. Moderate.*

Santa Caterina. This small hotel also has an intimate townhouse look. Converted into a hotel in 1986, its rooms feature floral bedspreads, private bathrooms, and air-conditioning. There's a garden and a glassed-in veranda that is used as a breakfast room. Rates are on the low end of the category. *Via Piccolomini 7, tel. 0577/221105, fax 055/271087. 19 rooms with bath. Facilities: garden. AE, DC, MC, V. Closed Nov. 10–Mar. 1. Moderate.*

Sinalunga
Dining and Lodging
★

Locanda dell'Amorosa. A medieval hamlet set in Tuscan farmland has become a rustic retreat for jaded city folk, who reserve ahead for a meal or weekend in the country. The journey is only a half-hour by car from Siena or Arezzo and even less from Montepulciano, Cortona, and Monteoliveto Maggiore. The stone and brick buildings have been tastefully adapted to their current use, and the restaurant serves regional dishes that seem to taste even better in such apt surroundings. You can take home estate-produced wines and preserves as a souvenir of your stay. *Località Amorosa, Sinalunga, 10 km. (6 mi) from the Valdichiana exit of the Autostrada del Sole (A1), tel. 0577/ 679497, fax 0577/678216. 15 rooms with bath. Facilities: pool, restaurant (reservations required; dress: casual). AE, DC, MC, V. Closed Mon. and Tues. lunch, and Jan. 15–Feb. 28). Very Expensive.*

Volterra
Dining

Etruria. Located on the town's main square, this restaurant serves an excellent *minestra di farro* (wheat soup), a tasty array of local game, and its own version of *panforte*, the dark, hard dessert cake that dates to medieval times. *Piazza dei Priori 8, tel. 0588/86064. No reservations. Dress: casual. AE, DC, MC, V. Closed Thurs., June 10–30, and Jan. Moderate.*

Lodging

San Lino. Located in a former convent, this hotel has modern comforts, a swimming pool, and its own regional restaurant. On top of that, it's centrally located. *Via San Lino 26, tel. 0588/ 85250. 43 rooms with bath. Facilities: pool, restaurant (closed lunch and Wed.). AE, DC, MC, V. Moderate.*

The Arts

Theater
The seasons at **Teatro Metastasio** (which include performances at a converted factory space called the **Capannone**), in Prato, run from January to May and October to December.

Music
The Tuscan hills ring with music from July to September, when music festivals abound. These include **Estate Musicale Lucchese,** in Lucca; the **Festival di Marlia;** and other festivals in Barga and Torre del Lago. In late July and August Siena hosts **Settimane Musicali Senesi.**

6 Venice

Venice is one of those cities you either love or you hate. Some people are repelled by its maze of narrow snaking streets, the faint smell of decay rising from the canals, and the hordes of pigeons and tourists in Piazza San Marco; they feel claustrophobic, longing for more grand vistas crowned with monumental architecture. But the far greater number of travelers are simply bowled over by this incredible treasure of a city. No matter how many times you have seen it in pictures or movies or TV commercials, the real thing is stranger and more lovely than you ever imagined. Its landmarks, the Basilica San Marco and the Palazzo Ducale, are delightfully idiosyncratic, exotic mishmashes of Byzantine, Gothic, and Renaissance styles. Piazza San Marco is a true public gathering space, full of music and laughter and joy, yet only a minute's walk away are streets so quiet that your footsteps echo on the stone pavements and shuttered, crumbling facades. Sunlight shimmers here, and silvery mist softens every perspective. It is a city full of secrets, ineffably romantic, and given over entirely to pleasure.

Venice today is in one important way the same as it was more than 1,000 years ago, when inhabitants from the mainland defied the sea to build a city on forests of tree trunks driven into the mud flats of a treacherous lagoon. The intervening centuries saw the development of some of the world's most inspired architecture, but water remains the city's defining feature.

You must walk everywhere in Venice, and where you cannot walk, you go by water. Occasionally, from fall to spring, you have to walk *in* water, when extraordinarily high tides known as *acque alte* invade the lower parts of the city, flooding Piazza San Marco for a few hours. Unless you're lucky to find one of the makeshift plank bridges that appear from nowhere to keep certain busy routes open, you'll have to take off your socks and shoes, roll up your pantlegs, and wade in with everyone else. The problem of protecting Venice and its lagoon from dangerously high tides has generated extravagant plans and so many committee reports that the city may sink as much under the weight of paper as under that of the water. Pollution, too, threatens the city, although restorers are working with new techniques to preserve historic facades, and the canals' waters smell better than they did a few years ago.

Then there are the hordes of tourists from all over the world that flow through Piazza San Marco and eddy wide-eyed around stern guides imparting succinct history lessons in a babble of languages. Like the Venetians, you will have to adapt to the crowds, visiting the major sights at odd hours, when the tour groups are still at breakfast or have boarded buses on their return to the mainland (most of them are day-trippers). Get away from Piazza San Marco when it's crowded; you'll be surprised to find many areas of Venice practically deserted. Explore the districts of Cannaregio or Castello, quiet areas where you can find the time and space to sit and contemplate the watercolor pages of Venetian history.

The resourceful Venetians who built this island city during Europe's Dark Ages used their navigational and trading talents to turn an out-of-the-way refuge against the marauding Goths into a staunch—and very rich—bulwark of Christendom that held against the tides of Turkish expansion. Early in its history the city called in Byzantine artists to decorate its churches with brilliant mosaics, still glowing today. Then the influence of Lombard-Romanesque architecture from the 11th to 13th centuries gave rise to the characteristic type of palace for which Venice is famous the world over. Many of the sumptuous palaces along the Grand Canal were built at that time, strong reminders of Venice's control of all major trading routes to the East. Subsequently, Gothic styles from elsewhere in Europe were adapted to create a new kind of Venetian Gothic art and architecture. Venice attained a peak of power and wealth in the 15th and 16th centuries. It extended its domain inland to include all of what is now known as the Veneto region and even beyond. In the last half of the 15th century, the Renaissance arrived in Venice, and its artists began to write a new and important chapter in the history of painting. Venice's greatest artists were major figures indeed—Giovanni Bellini in the late 15th century; Titian, Veronese, and Tintoretto in the 16th century—and their work covers walls and ceilings and altars all over the city still today.

The decline of Venice came slowly. For 400 years the powerful maritime city-republic had held sway. After the 16th century the tide changed. The Ottoman Empire blocked Venice's Mediterranean trade routes, and the rest of Europe had to look to new Atlantic routes for its goods. Like its steadily dwindling fortunes, Venice's art and culture began a prolonged decline, leaving only the splendid monuments to recall a glorious past, with the misty paintings of Canaletto and the beautiful frescoes of Tiepolo striking a glorious swan song.

You can see the panoply of history by visiting only the major museums and churches, but if you want a fuller picture of the districts that keep this a living city, get off the beaten track as often as you can. You'll need a detailed map showing most, if not all, street names and *vaporetto* (water bus) routes, but you'll probably get lost anyway (everyone does). Ask directions from shopkeepers or at a café where locals outnumber the tourists; chances are, they will admire your initiative and put you back on the right track.

Essential Information

Arriving and Departing by Plane

Airports and Airlines
Marco Polo airport at Tessera, about 10 kilometers (6 miles) north of the city on the mainland, is served by domestic and international Alitalia flights, including service from London, Amsterdam, Brussels, Frankfurt, Munich, Paris, Vienna, and Zurich. For information, call tel. 041/661262.

Between the Airport and Downtown
By Bus
Blue **ATVO** buses make the 25-minute non-stop trip from the airport to Piazzale Roma, which is where the road ends at the entrance to Venice; from Piazzale Roma you can get a waterbus to the landing nearest your hotel. ATVO fare is 5,000 lire. There are **ACTV** local buses from the airport, but you need a ticket (fare 1,000 lire) before boarding the bus, and there is no ticket office at the airport. You can buy a ticket at the tobacconist stand in the airport, but this is not always open. Also, luggage can be a problem on the ACTV bus, which is usually crowded with local commuters.

By Taxi
A yellow taxi from the airport to Piazzale Roma costs about 40,000 lire.

By Boat Depending on where your hotel is, this may be the best way to get to Venice from the airport. The most direct way is by the **Cooperativa San Marco** launch, with regular scheduled service throughout the day, until midnight; it takes about an hour to get to the landing just off Piazza San Marco, stopping at the Lido on the way, and the fare is 15,000 lire per person, including bags. A **water taxi** (a sleek modern motorboat known as a *motoscafo*) from the airport costs about 100,000 lire, but it is always wise to agree on a water-taxi fare before boarding.

Arriving and Departing by Car, Train, and Bus

By Car You are strongly advised not to bring a car to Venice. You'll have to pay for a garage or parking space during your stay. If there's space, you can park in one of the multistory garages at Piazzale Roma or in the adjacent garage or parking lot of Tronchetto. On holiday weekends, traffic backs up on the causeway between Venice and Mestre; electronic signs advise whether and where parking space is available. From the Tronchetto parking lot you can get a Line 34 vaporetto (water bus) direct to San Marco, or the slower Line 1; otherwise take bus No. 17 or walk about 500 yards to Piazzale Roma, where other vaporetti stop. You can take your car to the Lido, the long, narrow island guarding the Venetian lagoon; the car ferry (Line 17) leaves about every 50 minutes from a landing at Tronchetto.

By Train Venice is served by train from Milan, Turin, Genoa, and Rome, as well as international trains (including the Venice-Simplon Orient Express) from Paris, Nice, Vienna, Munich, Bern, and Zurich.

Santa Lucia station is on the Grand Canal in the northwest corner of the city. Make sure your train is bound for this station. Some through trains to points north leave you at the Venezia-Mestre station on the mainland, where you have to change to a local train to get to the Venezia–Santa Lucia station. For train information, call tel. 041/715555.

By Bus The bus terminal is at Piazzale Roma, near the vaporetto stop of that name. Express buses operated by SITA connect Venice with every major Italian city.

Porters Because cars are not allowed in Venice, many people need porters to help negotiate the footbridges and staircases. Porters wear badges and blue shirts or smocks. You will find them at the airport and train stations and also at some of the principal vaporetto landings. They charge about 8,000 lire for one or two bags, extra at night and on holidays. Since you can't always count on finding a porter when you need one, a folding luggage cart will prove invaluable (suitcases with wheels are not the answer on uneven paving stones and over bridges).

However you arrive in Venice, get information before you arrive on the location of your hotel and exactly how to get there. Depending on its location, regardless of whether you take a vaporetto or water taxi to the nearest landing, you may have to walk some distance from the landing to reach it, with or without the help and guidance of a porter. Be prepared to find your way on your own or to call the hotel for instructions when you arrive.

Getting Around

First-time visitors find that getting around Venice presents some unusual problems: The layout is complex; the waterborne transportation can be bewildering; the house-numbering system is totally illogical; street names in the six districts are duplicated; and often you must walk, whether you want to or not. It's essential that you have a good map showing all street names and vaporetto routes; buy one at a newsstand. In the areas where you're most likely to wander, signs are posted on many corners pointing you in the right direction for the nearest major landmark—San Marco, the Rialto, the Accademia, etc.—but don't count on finding such signs once you're deep into residential neighborhoods. Count on getting lost at least once—it's an essential part of the Venice experience.

By Vaporetto ACTV vaporetti run the length of the Grand Canal and circle the city. You can buy a map and timetable of the network at newsstands. There are more than 20 lines, some of which connect Venice with the major and minor islands in the lagoon. Line 1 is the Grand Canal local. Line 5 takes a circular route skirting Venice, taking in the islands of Murano and the Guidecca. Timetables are posted on all landing stages, where ticket booths are located (open early morning–9 PM). Buy single tickets or books of 10, and stamp your ticket in the machine at the landing. The fare is 2,200 lire on most lines; 3,300 lire for the Line 2 express connecting the train station, Rialto, San Marco, and the Lido. A 24-hour tourist ticket costs 12,000 lire, while a 3-day tourist ticket costs 18,000 lire, but these are not valid on Line 2. Vaporetti run every 10 minutes or so during the day; Lines 1 and 2 run more or less every hour between midnight and dawn. Landing stages are clearly marked with name and line number and serve boats going in both directions.

By Motoscafo These stylish powerboats are expensive, and the fare system is as complex as Venice's layout. A minimum fare of about 50,000 lire gets you nowhere, and you'll pay three times as much to get from one end of the Grand Canal to the other. Always agree on the fare before starting out.

By Traghetto Few tourists know about the two-man gondolas that ferry people across the Grand Canal at various fixed points. They are the cheapest and shortest gondola ride in Venice and can save a lot of walking. The fare is 500 lire, which you hand to the gondolier when you get on. Look for traghetto signs.

By Gondola No visit to Venice is complete without a gondola ride. But not many visitors know that the best time for one is in the late afternoon or early evening hours, when the Grand Canal isn't so heavily trafficked, or that it's best to start from a station on the Grand Canal because the lagoon is usually choppy. Make it clear that you want to see the smaller canals and come to terms on the cost and duration of the ride before you start. Gondoliers are supposed to charge a fixed minimum of about 70,000 lire for up to five passengers for 50 minutes. In practice they ask double that for a 30- to 40-minute ride. After 9 PM the rate goes up. Bargaining may get you a better price.

Important Addresses and Numbers

Tourist Information The main APT tourist office is at Calle Ascensione 71C (tel. 041/522–6356), just off Piazza San Marco, under the arcade in

the far left corner opposite the basilica. *Open Apr.–Oct.,
Mon.–Sat. 8:30–7:30; Nov.–Mar., Mon.–Sat. 8:30–1:30.*

There are other information booths at the Santa Lucia train
station (tel. 041/715016), in the bus terminal at Piazzale Roma
(tel. 041/522–7402), at Marco Polo airport (no phone), and at
Tronchetto parking lot (no phone).

Consulates **U.K.** (Campo della Carita 1051, Dorsoduro, tel. 041/522–7207).
There is no U.S. or Canadian consular service.

Emergencies **Police,** tel. 113.
Ambulance, tel. 041/523–0000.

Doctors and Dial the number for ambulances (*see above*) and ask the **Croce**
Dentists **Azzurra** (Blue Cross) to recommend a doctor or dentist convenient for your location. The British consulate can also recommend doctors and dentists.

Late-Night Venetian pharmacies take turns opening late or on Sundays;
Pharmacies dial 192 for information on which are open. Alternatively, the
daily list of late-night pharmacies is posted on the front of every
pharmacy. Two with English-speaking staff are **Farmacia
Italo-Inglese** (Calle della Mandola 3717, in San Marco district,
tel. 041/522–4837) and **International Pharmacy** (Calle Larga
XXII Marzo 2067, in San Marco district, tel. 041/522–2311).

English-Language Venice's centuries of experience in dealing with foreign visi-
Bookstores tors mean that bookstores and newsstands throughout the city
are well stocked with publications in English. **Fantoni,** on
Salizzada San Luca, specializes in art books and has an excellent selection of collections by famous writers and photographers. **O. Bohm,** just behind Piazza San Marco on Salizzada San
Moisè, has English-language books and a large selection of antique prints of Venice. **Libreria San Barnaba,** on Fondamenta
Gherardini, near Campo San Barnaba, has shelves full of
paperbacks and books on Venice in English.

Good general-interest bookstores include **Serenissima** (San
Zulian), near San Marco; **Studium** (Calle Canonica), off Piazzetta dei Leoncini; and **Zanco** (Campo San Bartolomeo), near
the Rialto Bridge.

Travel Agencies **American Express** (San Moisè 1471, tel. 041/520–0844); **Wagons
Lits/Turismo** (Piazzetta dei Leoncini 289, tel. 041/522–3405).

Guided Tours

Orientation Two-hour walking tours of the San Marco area, taking in the
basilica and the Doge's Palace, can be booked through **American Express** (tel. 041/520–0844) and other travel agencies. The
American Express tour ends with a glass-blowing demonstra-
tion (about 28,000 lire). From March 15 to November 15 American Express offers an afternoon walking tour that ends with a
gondola ride (about 32,000 lire).

Special-Interest American Express, and other operators offer group gondola
rides with serenades, daily from May through October in the
evening (about 30,000 lire).

During July and August, free guided tours (some in English) of
Basilica San Marco are offered several times a day by the Patri-
archate of Venice; information is available in the atrium of the
church. *Tel. 041/520–0333. No tours Sun.*

Bassani (Calle Larga XXII Marzo 2414, near San Marco, tel. 041/520–3644) offers two offbeat tours to help visitors to Venice get the feel of the city. *A Day in Venice* tour takes you to some hidden corners and includes lunch (about 80,000 lire). *A Night in Venice* includes dinner, a gondola serenade, and music at a night spot (about 95,000 lire). Both are available May–October.

Excursions Don't take organized tours to the islands of Murano, Burano, or Torcello. They are annoyingly commercial and emphasize glass-factory showrooms, pressuring you to buy. You can easily visit these islands on your own (*see* Tour 5: Islands of the Lagoon in Exploring Venice, *below*).

American Express offers an excursion by bus to the Venetian villas and Padua (about 65,000 lire. *Tours Apr.–Oct., Tues., Thurs., Sat., Sun.*

An excursion on the Brenta Canal on the Burchiello motor-launch to Padua includes lunch. The return trip is by bus (about 150,000 lire; tours Apr.–Oct., Tues., Thurs., Sat.).

Personal Guides **American Express** and other travel agencies can provide guides for walking or gondola tours of Venice or cars with driver and guide for tours of the mainland. You can get a list of licensed guides and their rates from the main tourist office in Piazza San Marco (tel. 041/522–6356) or contact the Guides' Association (Calle San Antonio 5448/A, Castello, tel. 041/523–9902, fax 041/523–2012).

Exploring Venice

The church of San Marco is unquestionably the heart of Venice, but venturing even 50 yards from it can sometimes lead to confusion. Although the smaller canals (a canal is called a *rio*) are spanned by frequent bridges, the Grand Canal can only be crossed on foot at three points—near the train station, at the Rialto bridge, and at the Accademia bridge—which decidedly complicates matters. It's supremely maddening to find yourself on the wrong bank of a canal with no bridge in sight.

A street is called a *calle*, but a street that runs alongside a canal is called either a *riva* or a *fondamente*. The closed-in streetscapes of Venice make it hard to see any reference point, such as the spire of the Campanile, above the rooftops, and the narrow back streets often take unpredictable turnings that foul up your sense of direction. Streets and canals may look deceptively familiar, only to make sudden dead ends. Keep a map of vaporetto lines with you at all times because the best way back to Piazza San Marco or your hotel may well be along one of these routes.

Our first two tours should help you find your bearings. Tour 1 takes in the sights around the San Marco district, the geographic and spiritual center of the city. Tour 2 takes to the water along the Grand Canal, the main artery of Venice, linking many of its major sights. Tours 3 and 4 take you east and west, respectively, giving you the chance to explore some of the more offbeat sights and areas, as well as the less central churches and art collections. The last two tours take you to the other major islands of the Venetian lagoon, places where the pace of life is slower and the crafts that helped establish Venice's trading reputation are still practiced.

Highlights for First-time Visitors

Accademia Gallery (Tour 4: The Western
and Northern Districts).
Basilica San Marco (Tour 1: The San Marco District).
Campanile of San Marco (Tour 1: The San Marco District).
Campo Santi Giovanni e Paolo (Tour 3: To the Arsenal
and Beyond).
Frari Church (Tour 4: The Western and Northern Districts).
Murano, Burano, and Torcello (Tour 5: Islands of the Lagoon).
Palazzo Ducale (Tour 1: The San Marco District).
Piazza San Marco (Tour 1: The San Marco District).
Ponte di Rialto (Tour 2: The Grand Canal).
San Giorgio Maggiore (Tour 6: San Maggiore and Guidecca).
Scuola di San Rocco (Tour 4: The Western
and Northern Districts).

Tour 1: The San Marco District

*Numbers in the margin correspond to points of interest on the
Venice map.*

1 **Piazza San Marco** (St. Mark's Square) is the heart of Venice, perpetually animated during the day, when it's filled with people and crowds of fluttering pigeons. It can be magical at night, especially in the winter, when melancholy mists swirl around the lampposts and bell tower. Historically and geographically, it's the logical place to start exploring the city. If you stand at the Piazza's far end, facing the basilica, you'll notice that rather than being a strict rectangle it opens wider at the basilica end, enhancing the perspective and creating the illusion of being even larger than it is. On your left, the long arcaded building is the **Procuratie Vecchie,** built in the early 16th century as offices and residences for the powerful Procurators of San Marco, administrators of the basilica. Across the piazza, on your right hand, is the **Procuratie Nuove,** built almost a century later in a more grandiose classical style. The Procuratie Nuove has impeccable architectural lineage: It was originally planned by perhaps Venice's greatest Renaissance architect, Jacopo Sansovino (1486–1570) to carry on the look of his **Libreria Vecchie,** around the corner to the right, across from the Palazzo Ducale, though Sansovino died before the building was begun. The actual designer was Vincenzo Scamozzi (1552–1616), a pupil of Palladio and a devout Neoclassist; later sections were completed by Baldassare Longhena (1598–1682), Venice's other great architect, who belonged firmly to the Baroque tradition.

When Napoleon entered Venice with his troops in 1797, he called Piazza San Marco "the world's most beautiful drawing room"—and promptly gave orders to redecorate it. His architects demolished an old church that stood behind you, at the end of the square farthest from the basilica, and put up the **Ala Napoleonica** (Napoleonic Wing or Fabbrica Nuova) to unite the two 16th-century buildings on either side.

Today the arcades of these three grand buildings shelter shops and cafés. Several of the cafés have their own small orchestras that play outdoors in fair weather; though patrons of the cafés must pay an additional charge for the entertainment, passers-by in the piazza can enjoy it for free. On warm summer nights, the orchestras compete to see which can draw the biggest crowd, and the fun is infectious.

Time Out On the Procuratie Vecchie side is the historic **Café Quadri,** which was shunned by Venetians during the 19th century when the occupying Austrians made it their gathering place; loyal Venetians preferred the venerable **Café Florian,** on the Procuratie Nuove side, where Casanova, Wagner, and Proust were regular customers. Like a gondola ride, eating and drinking at these expensive cafés may be a splurge, but it's a treat you shouldn't miss.

At the basilica end of the piazza, on the left (north) side next to the Procuratie Vecchie, is the **Torre dell'Orologio** (Clock Tower), erected in 1496 and endowed with an enameled timepiece and animated figures of Moors that strike the hour. During Ascension Week and on Epiphany (Jan. 6), an angel and three wise men go in and out of the doors and bow to the Virgin.

❷ Now it is finally time to turn your attention to the Piazza's crowning glory, the **Basilica San Marco,** one of Europe's most beautiful churches. An opulent synthesis of Byzantine and Romanesque styles, it is laid out in a Greek cross topped off with five plump domes. The Basilica did not actually become the cathedral of Venice until as late as 1807, but its role as the church of the doge (the elected head of the Venetian republic), gave it immense power and wealth. It was begun in 1063 to house the remains of St. Mark the Evangelist, which were filched from Alexandria two centuries earlier by two agents of the doge. The story goes that they stole the saint's remains and hid them in a barrel under layers of pickled pork to get them past Islamic guards.

That escapade is illustrated in a mosaic in the lunette (semicircular decoration) over the farthest left of the front doors. This 13th-century mosaic is the earliest one on this heavily decorated facade; look at it closely and you can see a picture of the church as it appeared in the 13th century.

Over the years this church stood as a symbol of Venetian wealth and power, and it was endowed with all the riches the Republic's admirals and merchants could carry off from the Orient, earning it the nickname *Chiesa D'Oro* (Golden Church). The four bronze horses that prance and snort over the central doorway (copies only, but the originals are on view indoors in the Museo Marciano, *see* below) were classical sculptures that victorious Venetians took away from Constantinople in 1204, along with a lot of other loot that you can see inside. Just inside the central front doors in the church porch, look for a medallion of red porphyry set in the floor to mark the spot of another of Venice's political coups: here Barbarossa, the Holy Roman Emperor, was forced to kneel in tribute to Pope Alexander III in 1177.

Entrance to the church is free, but be warned: Guards at the door turn away any visitors, male or female, wearing shorts or inappropriate attire. If you want to take a free guided tour in English (offered Mon.–Sat. at 11 AM), wait on the left in the

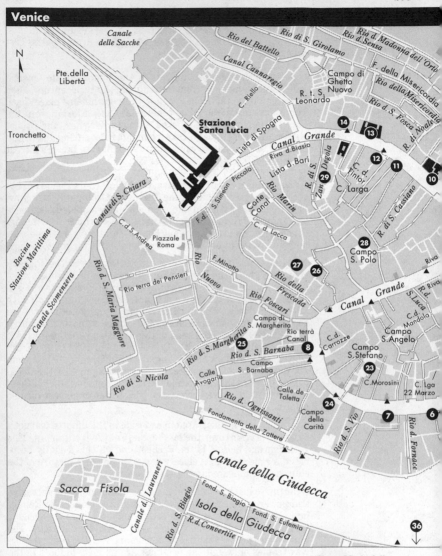

Venice

Sacca
della
Misericordia

Canale delle Navi

31 34

San
Michele

0 — 440 yards
0 — 400 meters

C. Racchetta
Fondamente
Rio S. Caterina
30
R. d. Gesuiti Nuove
Rio della Panada
C. d Squero
dei Mendicanti
R. d. S.
Guistina

Strada
Nuova
Rio d. Santi Apostoli
C. d Tesla

Campo d.
Pescheria
Erberia
16
Campo Santi
Giovanni e Paolo
17
R. Barbaria delle Tole

del Vin
9
Rio d. S. Marina
18
R. d. S.
Francesco
Canale d. Galeazze

del Carbon
R. d. Fava
Sal. di S. Lio
Ruga
Giuffa
Canale d. Galeazze

Merceria
15
R. d. S. Severo
R. d. S. Lorenzo
C. Lion
22
C. d.
Furlani
R. d. Scudi
R. d. Gorne

Campo
Manin
C. d. Bande
Fond.
Osmarin
R. d. Grec
R. d. Pieta

Fabbri
Fond.
Osmarin

1
2
3 **4**
R. d. Palazzo
19
R. d. Arsenale

Frezzeria
5
Molo
Riva degli
Schiavoni

R. d.
S. Moise
7
**Piazza
San Marco**

Darsena
Grande
Rio d. Vergini
21
R. d. S. Daniele
Can. di S.
Pietro

20
V. Garibaldi
Rio della Tana
Rio d. S. Anna

Riva dei Sette Martiri
R. d. S. Giuseppe

Canale di S. Marco

35
*Isola di
S. Giorgio
Maggiore*

Fond.
delle Zitelle

Calle
Michelangelo

Viale Trieste
Rio dei Giardini

▲ Boat stop

porch for a group to form. *Church open Mon.–Sat. 9:30–5:30, Sun. 2:30–5:30.*

One of the innovations of this church was a roof of brick vaulting, rather than wood, enabling the ceiling to be decorated with mosaics. As you enter the basilica, you'll find it surprisingly dark inside, compared to the soaring light-filled Gothic cathedrals of northern Europe, for many of the original windows were filled in and covered with even more mosaics. In the mysterious dusk, candles flicker and the gold tiles of mosaics glitter softly, sensuously. (The tiles were laid on at slight angles to achieve precisely this effect.) The earliest mosaics are from the 11th and 12th centuries; later ones were done as late as the 16th century, such as the Last Judgment on the arch between the porch and the nave, said to be based on drawings by Tintoretto. Go into the chapel of St. Zeno (to the right just off the porch) to see some earlier (13th-century) mosaics, telling the story of the life of St. Mark. Next to it, the **Baptistery** contains a bronze font cover by Jacopo Sansovino and the tomb of Doge Andrea Dandolo (1307–1354), a friend of Petrarch and a writer in his own right. Several of the earlier doges were buried here, while later ones were interred in the church of Santo Giovanni e Paolo (*see* Tour 3, *below*).

Two more chapels, both in the left transept, are worth a special look: the **Chapel of the Madonna of Nicopeia,** which holds a precious icon (part of the loot from Constantinople) that many consider Venice's most powerful protector; and next to it, on the left, a small chapel dedicated to the Virgin Mary with fine 15th-century mosaics depicting her life, possibly based on drawings by Andrea Mantegna.

If you stand in the central aisle facing the main altar, notice the polygonal pulpit to the right, at the intersection of the nave and right transept. After the coronation ceremony, each new Doge stood here for the people to behold him in the glory of his new office.

To enter the **sanctuary,** you must pay a separate admission fee (2,000 lire), but it's well worth it. (It's open basically the same hours as the basilica, but be aware that it does close 90 minutes earlier than the church Oct.–Mar.) The main altar, with its green marble canopy lifted high on carved alabaster columns, covers the tomb of St. Mark. Behind this is the real attraction: the **Pala D'Oro** (Golden Altarpiece), a dazzling gold-and-silver screen encrusted with precious gems and enameled panels. Originally made in Constantinople in the 10th century, it was continually embellished over the next few centuries by master craftsmen in Venice and elsewhere. Invest a few 100-lire coins to listen to a recorded description—otherwise you'll miss some of the incredible detail. The bronze door leading from the sanctuary back into the sacristy is another Sansovino work; check out the top left corner, where the artist included a self-portrait and, above that, a picture of his friend and fellow artist Titian.

The same ticket admits you to the **Treasury,** which contains some exquisite pieces, many of them exotic treasures borne away from Constantinople and other vanquished places.

From the atrium, climb the steep stairway to the **Museo Marciano** (St. Mark's Museum) for a look at the interior of the church from the organ gallery and a sweeping view of Piazza San Marco and the Piazzetta dei Leoncini from the outdoor gallery.

The highlight of the museum is the close-up of the four magnificent gilded bronze horses that once stood outside on the gallery. The originals were probably cast in Constantinople in the 4th century AD, but some hold that they are Greek works of the 3rd century BC. Napoleon hauled them off to Paris after he conquered Venice in 1797, but they were returned after the fall of the French Empire. *Admission: 2,000 lire. Open Apr.–Sept., daily 9:30–5:30; Nov.–Mar., daily 10–4.*

③ Just outside the basilica is the tall brick **Campanile** (Bell Tower), a reconstruction of the original, which stood for 1,000 years before it collapsed one morning in 1912, practically without warning. In the 15th century, clerics found guilty of immoral behavior were suspended in wooden cages from the tower, sometimes to subsist on bread and water for as long as a year, sometimes to starve to death. The pretty marble loggia (covered gallery) at its base was built in the early 16th century by Florentine architect Jacopo Sansovino (1486–1570): It, too, has been carefully restored. The view from the tower on a clear day is worth the price of admission. You get a pigeon's-eye view of the city, the Lido, the lagoon, and the mainland as far as the distant Alps. Oddly, you can't see the myriad canals that snake through the 117 islets on which Venice is built. *Piazza San Marco, tel. 041/522–4064. Admission: 3,000 lire. Open Easter–Oct., daily 10–8; Nov.–Easter, daily 10–4. Closed for maintenance most of Jan.*

The square that leads from Piazza San Marco down to the waters of St. Mark's Basin is called the **Piazzetta San Marco.** This landing stage, now crowded with excursion boats, was once the grand entrance to the Republic. Two tall columns rise here on the waterfront: one is topped by the winged lion, a traditional emblem of St. Mark that became by extension the symbol of Venice itself; the other bears aloft a statue of St. Theodore (the first patron saint of Venice) and his dragon.

④ Above the Piazzetta rises the **Palazzo Ducale** (Doge's Palace), a Gothic-Renaissance fantasia of pink-and-white marble, a majestic expression of the prosperity and power attained by Venice during its most glorious period. Its top-heavy design (the dense upper floors rest on the graceful ground-floor colonnade) has always confounded architectural purists, who insist that proper architecture be set out the other way around. The palace was not only the residence of the doge, but also the parliament house, home of the law courts, and a prison. Venice's government, set up sometime in the seventh century as a participatory democracy, provided for an elected ruler, the doge, to serve for life, but in practice he was simply a figurehead. Power really rested with the Great Council, originally an elected body but, from the 13th century on, an aristocratic stronghold, with members inheriting their seats from their noble ancestors. Laws were passed by the Senate, a group of 200 elected from the Great Council (which could have as many as 1,700 members); executive powers belonged to the College, a committee of 25 leaders. In the 14th century, the Council of Ten was formed to deal with emergency situations; this group's meetings were not open to the public, and eventually they effectively wrested control of the government from the Senate. Plots, intrigues, and corruption were the order of the day, and it scarcely mattered who occupied the doge's seat.

A fortress for the doge existed on this spot in the early ninth century; the building you see today was a product of the 12th century, although, like the basilica next door, it was continually added to and transformed throughout the centuries. You enter the palace at the ornate Gothic **Porta della Carta** (Gate of the Paper, where official decrees were traditionally posted), which opens onto an immense courtyard. Ahead is the **Scala dei Giganti** (Stairway of the Giants), guarded by huge statues of Mars and Neptune by Jacopo Sansovino. Ordinary mortals do not get to climb these stairs, however; after paying your admission fee, walk along the arcade to reach the central interior staircase. Its upper flight is called the **Scala D'Oro** (Golden Staircase), also designed by Sansovino, with its lavish gilded decoration. While it may seem odd that the government's main council rooms and reception halls would be so far upstairs, imagine how effectively foreign emissaries must have been intimidated by this arduous climb.

Visitors must have also been overwhelmed with the sumptuous decoration of these apartments, their walls and ceilings covered with work by Venice's greatest artists. Among the grand rooms you can visit are the **Anticollegio** (a waiting room outside the College's chamber), which features two fine paintings, Tintoretto's *Bacchus and Ariadne Crowned by Venus* and Veronese's *Rape of Europa;* the **Sala del Collegio** (the College Chamber), its ceiling magnificently painted by Veronese; and the **Sala del Senato** (Senate chamber), with Tintoretto's *Triumph of Venice* on the ceiling. The huge *Paradise* on the end wall of the **Great Council Hall** is by Jacopo Tintoretto (1518–94): It is a dark, dynamic masterpiece. This is the world's largest oil painting (23 by 75 feet), a vast work commissioned for a vast hall. Don't miss the gorgeous ceiling, with Veronese's majestic *Apotheosis of Venice* filling one of the center panels. Step onto the balcony of the Great Council Hall for a view of St. Mark's Basin, its waters churning with the wakes of countless boats. Look at the frieze of portraits of the first 76 doges around the upper part of the walls. One portrait is missing: Only a black void near the left-hand corner of the wall opposite Tintoretto's painting marks the spot where the portrait of doge Marin Falier should be. A Latin inscription bluntly explains that Falier was executed for treason in 1355. The Republic never forgave him.

At the ticket office of the doge's Palace you can book a guided tour (unfortunately, only given in Italian) of the palace's secret rooms; it takes you to the doge's private apartments, up into the attic and Piombi prison, and through hidden passageways to the torture chambers, where prisoners were interrogated. The 18th-century writer and libertine, Casanova, a native of Venice, was imprisoned here in 1755, having somehow offended someone in power (the official accusation was of being a Freemason); he made a daring escape 15 months later and fled to France, where he continued his career of intrigue and scandal. From the east wing of the Doge's Palace, the enclosed marble **Ponte dei Sospiri** (Bridge of Sighs) arches over a narrow canal to the cramped, gloomy cell blocks of the so-called New Prison. (The bridge was named for the sighs of those being led to prison.) On your way to the exit on the ground floor of the palace, you can see the **Pozzi Prison**—18 dark, dank cells that were set aside for the most hardened criminals. *Piazzetta San Marco, tel. 041/522–4951. Admission: 8,000 lire. Open daily 8:30–7.*

Secret Itineraries Tour daily 10 AM and noon; reserve at least a day ahead if possible. Cost: 5,000 lire.

Walk back to the far end of Piazza San Marco, where a massive
❺ marble staircase in the Fabbrica Nuova leads to the **Museo Correr,** an interesting and varied collection of historical items and paintings by old masters, once the private collection of the aristocrat Teodoro Correr, who donated them to the city in 1830. Exhibits range from the absurdly high-soled shoes worn by 16th-century Venetian ladies (who had to be supported by a servant on each side in order to walk on these precarious perches) to fine artworks by the talented Bellini family of Renaissance painters. *Piazza San Marco, Ala Napoleonica, tel. 041/522-5625. Admission: 5,000 lire. Open daily 9-4.*

Tour 2: The Grand Canal

Catch Vaporetto Line 1 at the San Marco landing stage for a leisurely cruise along the **Grand Canal,** Venice's main thoroughfare. This 2-mile ribbon of water loops through the city. When the canal is busiest, usually in the morning, large and small craft crisscross its waters, stirring up a maelstrom that sets gondolas rocking and sends green waves slapping at the seaweed-slippery foundations of palaces. The quietest and most romantic time to ride in a gondola along the Grand Canal is about an hour or so before sunset: this is an experience you shouldn't miss. However, for an overall sightseeing tour of the canal, you get a better, more extensive view from the vaporetto—which is both higher in the water and much less expensive. Try to get one of the coveted seats in the prow, where you have a clear view.

The Grand Canal has an average depth of about 9 feet and varies from 40 to 76 yards in width. It winds like an inverted letter *S* through Venice, from the San Marco landing to the landing at the train station (Ferrovia), passing under three bridges and between 200 palaces dating from the 14th century to the 18th century, most of them in Venetian Gothic or Renaissance style.
❻ Starting from San Marco, look left for **Santa Maria della Salute,** the huge, white, domed 17th-century Baroque church designed by Longhena. On the same side is the low white marble wall marking the never-completed **Palazzo Venierdei Leoni,** well
❼ worth a return visit (April through October) to view the **Peggy Guggenheim Collection,** a small but choice gallery of 20th-century painting and sculpture in the heiress's lavish former apartments. Guggenheim (1898–1979) used her wealth and social connections to become a serious patron of art—she was once married to the painter Max Ernst—and her holdings include several works by Picasso, Kandinsky, Ernst, Pollock, and Motherwell, among others. *Entrance on Calle San Cristoforo. Tel. 041/520-6288. Admission: 7,000 lire (Sat. free). Open Apr.-Oct., Sun., Mon., Wed.-Fri. 11-6; Sat. 11-9.*

Across the canal you can see the imposing terraced front of the **Gritti Palace Hotel** (*see* Lodging, *below*), occupying the former Palazzo Pisani. English critic John Ruskin stayed here with his young wife Effie in 1851, while working on his book *Stones of Venice.* **Palazzo Corner,** otherwise known as Ca'Grande, is also on the right bank, just past the Santa Maria del Giglio stop. A Renaissance beauty designed by Sansovino, with classical details, it now houses the Prefecture. **Palazzo Barbaro,** the 15th century Gothic villa on the right bank just before the Accademia Bridge, is where Henry James lived while writing *The Aspern Papers;* later he made it the setting for his novel *Wings of the Dove.* The **Accademia Bridge** is one of only three spanning the Grand Canal—until the first bridge was built here in 1854, in fact, the Rialto was the only bridge over the Grand Canal. The current plain wooden bridge leads on the left bank to the wonderful **Accademia Gallery,** a treasure house of Venetian painting (*see* Tour 4, *below*).

❽ A few minutes farther on, on the left bank at the Ca'Rezzonico stop, is **Palazzo Rezzonico,** a Baroque mansion begun by Longhena in the 1660s, and completed by another architect, Giorgio Massari, in the 1740s. This was English poet Robert Browning's last home, where he died in 1889. Return here to visit the **Museo del Settecento Veneziano** (Museum of 18th-Century Venice). Pictures by the 18th-century Venetian painters Gianantonio Guardi and Pietro Longhi, and a fine series of frescoes by their younger contemporary Giandomenico Tiepolo at the back of the palace, really open a window onto that frivolous social era. *Fondamenta Rezzonico, tel. 041/522-4543. Admission: 5,000 lire. Open Sat.–Thurs. 9–7.*

Just past Palazzo Rezzonico, still on the left bank, are two identical 15th-century Gothic palaces designed by Bartolomeo Bon for the Giustinian family. In the second one, composer Richard Wagner lived in 1858–59 while writing his opera *Tristan und Isolde.* Next door is **Ca'Foscari,** where the second of Venice's two disgraced doges, Francesco Foscari, lived in 1457 when he was deposed by the Council of Ten. Now part of the University, it is adorned with lovely marble columns, tracery, and a frieze.

Turn to the right bank, as you round the bend in the canal, to see **Case dei Mocenigo,** a series of houses built with a single neoclassical facade, decorated with lions' heads. Byron lived in one of these from 1816 to 1819, where he began his satiric epic *Don Juan,* enjoyed several reckless love affairs, and eventually stole Countess Guiccioli from her husband. A couple of years later he wrote historical dramas about the traitor doge Marin Falier and the two Foscari doges. Just past the next vaporetto stop, still on the right bank, stands **Palazzo Corner-Spinelli,** a richly decorated Renaissance palace with arched windows, probably designed by Mauro Coducci (1440–1504). On the right bank across from the next vaporetto stop, look at Renaissance architecture in full flower at the imposing white **Palazzo Grimani,** by Michele Sanmicheli (1484–1559); today the Court of Appeals sits here.

❾ The canal narrows and boat traffic increases as you approach the **Rialto Bridge,** arched high over the canal so that war galleys could sail under it. The windows in the arch belong to the shops inside; plan to return here on foot and walk across to admire fine views up and down the Grand Canal. This is a commercial hub of the city, with open-air vegetable, fruit, and fish markets on the left and on the right, an upscale shopping district. Just beyond the bridge on the right is the 16th-century **Fondaco dei Tedeschi,** originally used by merchants from various Germanic states as warehouses and offices for the all-important trade with Venice. Now that the Giorgione frescoes that once covered its facade have gone, it's a pretty bleak-looking building; today it's the city's main post office.

The Ca'd'Oro landing on the right, just beyond the Rialto, iden-
⑩ tifies the lovely Venetian Gothic palace of **Ca'd'Oro,** adorned
with marble traceries and ornaments that were once embellished with pure gold. Today it houses the **Franchetti Gallery,** a
fine collection of tapestries, sculptures, and paintings. *Calle
della Ca d'Oro, tel. 041/523–8790. Admission: 4,000 lire. Open
Mon.–Sat. 9–2, Sun. 9–1.*

A little farther up from Ca'd'Oro, over on the left bank, is the
⑪ grand Baroque **Palazzo Pesaro,** designed by Longhena. It's
now home to two rather dull art collections, the **Galleria d'Arte
Moderna** (Modern Art Gallery, though "modern" in Venice
means mostly 19th-century work) and **Museo Orientale** (Oriental Art Museum). *Galleria d'Arte Moderna: tel. 041/721172,
admission free, open Tues.–Sun. 9–7. Museo Orientale: tel.
041/524–1173, admission 3,000 lire, open Tues.–Sun. 9–7.*

Not far beyond, on the left, another white church is adorned
⑫ with Baroque statues; this is **San Stae,** and the landing here is a
gateway to a part of Venice that most tourists never see, a
neighborhood of narrow canals, airy squares, and good
trattorie. Back on the right bank, the Renaissance **Palazzo
Vendramin-Calergi** (1509), designed by Coducci in white stone
with red marble medallions and an imposing carved frieze, was
where Wagner died in 1883; it is now the winter home of the
⑬ **Casino** (*see* Nightlife, *below*). Turn to the left bank to see the
Fondaco dei Turchi, built in the Byzantine style because it was
the trade center for the Turks from 1621–1838. Under its portico, the traitorous doge Marin Falier was buried after his execution. The **Museo di Storia Naturale** (Natural History Museum)
occupies the building now. *Tel. 041/524–0885. Admission:
3,000 lire. Open Mon.–Sat. 9–1:30, Sun. 9–1.*

⑭ Another vaporetto stop away is **San Marcuola,** on the right.
This unfinished brick church is guarded by cats and pigeons,
and it marks the edge of another district that is off the beaten
track and well worth exploring: Cannaregio and the old Jewish
ghetto.

Tour 3: To the Arsenal and Beyond

To explore the city's eastern districts and see some of its most
beautiful churches, head out of Piazza San Marco under the
clock tower into the **Merceria,** one of Venice's busiest streets,
which leads more or less directly from Piazza San Marco to the
Rialto bridge. At Campo San Zulian and the church of San
Giuliano, turn right onto Calle Guerra and Calle delle Bande to
⑮ reach the graceful white marble church of **Santa Maria Formosa.** It's on a lively square with a few sidewalk cafés and a small
vegetable market on weekday mornings. Follow Calle Borgo-
loco into Campo San Marina, where you turn right, cross the
⑯ little canal, and take Calle Castelli to the church of **Santa Maria
dei Miracoli.** Perfectly proportioned and sheathed in marble,
it's an early Renaissance gem, decorated inside with exquisite
marble reliefs. Notice how the architect, Pietro Lombardo,
made the church look bigger with various optical illusions:
varying the color of the exterior marble to create the effect of
distance; using extra pilasters to make the building's canal side
look longer; slightly offsetting the arcade windows to make the
arches look deeper. The church was built in the 1480s to house

an image of the Virgin that is said to perform miracles—look for this icon on the high altar.

Behind the church, bear right to Calle Larga Giacinto Gallina, which leads to **Campo Santi Giovanni e Paolo,** site of the massive Dominican church of San Giovanni e Paolo, or San Zanipolo, as it's known in the slurred Venetian dialect. The powerful equestrian **monument of Bartolomeo Colleoni** by Florentine sculptor Andrea del Verrocchio (1435–88) stands in the square. Colleoni had served Venice well as a *condottiere*, or mercenary commander (the Venetians preferred to pay others to fight for them on land and had the money to do it). When he died in 1475, he left his fortune to the city on the condition that a statue be erected in his honor "in the piazza before St. Mark's." The republic's shrewd administrators coveted Colleoni's ducats but had no intention of honoring anyone, no matter how valorous, with a statue in Piazza San Marco. So they commissioned the statue and put it up in the piazza before the Scuola di San Marco, headquarters of a charitable confraternity that happened to have the right name, enabling them to collect the loot.

⑰ The Church of **Santi Giovanni e Paolo** contains tombs of several doges, as well as a wealth of artworks. Don't miss the Rosary Chapel, off the left crossing; with its Veronese ceiling paintings, it's a sumptuous study in decoration, built in the 16th century to commemorate the victory of Lepanto in western Greece in 1571, when Venice led a combined European fleet in destroying the Turkish navy.

⑱ Continue beyond Santi Giovanni e Paolo to another large church, **San Francesco della Vigna,** built by Sansovino in 1534. A pretty cloister opens out from the severely simple gray-and-white interior. Not many tourists find their way here, and local youngsters play ball in the square shadowed by the church's austere classical Palladian facade.

⑲ Go left as you leave the church to begin the 500-yard walk to the **Campo dell'Arsenale,** at the main entrance to the **Arsenal,** an immense dockyard founded in 1104 to build and equip the fleet of the Venetian republic and augmented continually through the 16th century. For a republic founded on sea might, having a huge state-of-the-art shipyard was of paramount importance, and this one was renowned for its skill and size. All subsequent dockyards were named after it (the name comes from the Arabic "d'arsina," meaning workshop). No wonder it has such a grandiose entrance, with four stone lions from ancient Greece guarding the great Renaissance gateway.

⑳ The **Museo Navale** (Naval Museum) on nearby Campo San Biagio has four floors of full-scale boat models, from gondolas and doges' ceremonial boats to Chinese junks, as well as other smaller boats guaranteed to fascinate children—and boat lovers. *Campo San Biagio, tel. 041/520–0276. Admission: 1,000 lire. Open Mon.–Sat. 9–1.*

㉑ If you still have time and energy, go east to the island and church of **San Pietro di Castello.** Two footbridges lead to this island. The church served as Venice's cathedral for centuries; now it presides over a picturesque workaday neighborhood, and its tipsy bell tower leans over a grassy square.

Time Out   If you're this far afield, you may need sustenance to get you back to the center of town. There are several moderately priced snack bars and trattorie on Via Garibaldi, midway between the Arsenal and the island of San Pietro. **Sottoprova** (closed Tues.) has tables outdoors.

About midway between the Arsenal and St. Mark's, on your (22) way back from the eastern district, is the **Scuola di San Giorgio degli Schiavoni,** one of several *scuole* built during the time of the Republic. These weren't schools, as the present-day Italian word would imply, but confraternities devoted to charitable works. Many scuole were decorated lavishly, both in the private chapels and in the meeting halls where work was discussed. The Scuola di San Giorgio degli Schiavoni features works by Vittore Carpaccio (ca. 1465–1525), a local artist who often filled his otherwise devotional paintings with acutely observed details of Venetian life. Study the exuberance of his *St. George* as he slays the dragon or the vivid colors and details in *The Funeral of St. Jerome* and *St. Augustine in His Study. Calle dei Furlani, tel. 041/522–8828. Admission: 4,000 lire. Open Tues.–Sat. 10–12:30, 3:30–6, Sun. 11–12:30.*

Tour 4: The Western and Northern Districts

If churches, art, and sculpture and further ramblings through the back streets and along the old canals of Venice continue to interest you, head out of Piazza San Marco under the arcades of the Fabbrica Nuova at the far end of the square. If you want to make a detour for an expensive drink at the fabled **Harry's Bar,** just turn left down Calle Vallaresso, behind the Hotel Luna (23) Baglioni. Then head for **Campo Morosini,** which everyone calls by its old name, Campo San Stefano, in honor of the 14th-century church off to one side of the square; stop in to see the ship's-keel roof, a type found in several of Venice's older churches and the work of its master shipbuilders.

Time Out **Café Paolin,** with tables occupying most of one end of the square, is reputed to have Venice's best ice cream. It's a pleasant place to sit and watch the passing parade.

Join the stream of pedestrians crossing the Grand Canal on the Accademia Bridge to the district called *Dorsoduro* (literally, "hard back") because of its strong clay foundation. The bridge (24) leads you directly to the **Accademia Gallery,** Venice's most important picture gallery. It has an extraordinary collection of Venetian paintings, attractively displayed and well lit. Highlights include Giovanni Bellini's altarpiece from the church of San Giobbe (notice how he carried the church's architectural details right into the frame of the painting) and his moving *Madonna with St. Catherine and the Madgalen;* a fine *St. George* by Andrea Mantegna, Bellini's brother-in-law from Padua, who was much admired by later Venetian painters; the *Tempest,* by Giorgione (1477–1510); and Veronese's monumental canvas, *The Feast in the House of Levi.* This last painting was commissioned as a Last Supper, but the Inquisition took issue with Veronese's inclusion of jesters and German soldiers in the painting. Veronese avoided the charge of sacrilege by changing the title, and the picture was then supposed to depict the bawdy, but still biblical, feast of Levi. This museum was built on what was originally the Scuole della Carità and the church of Santa Maria della Carità; the body of the church has been preserved in a large room that contains the surviving fragments of

Giorgione's masterful frescoes from the facade of the Fondaco dei Tedeschi (*see* Tour 2, *above*). A room preserved from the Scuole holds on one wall its original masterpiece, Titian's *Presentation of the Virgin*. And don't miss the room containing various views of 15th- and 16th-century Venice by Giovanni Bellini's brother Gentile: Study them to see how much the city has changed since then—and how much it looks the same. *Campo della Carità, tel. 041/522-2247. Admission: 8,000 lire. Open Mon.-Sat. 9-2, Sun. 9-1.*

Time Out Between the Accademia and San Barnaba, on Calle Toletta, is **Ae Meravegie** (closed Sun.), a coffee bar and sandwich shop with a variety of tasty sandwiches, quiches, and beer.

Off Campo San Barnaba, on Fondamenta Gherardini, you'll see a floating fruit and vegetable market tied up in the canal. It's one of the few left in Venice. Continue toward Campo Santa Margherita; on your way you can look for two of Venice's best mask shops (*see* Shopping, *below*). **Cà Macana** is on Calle Boteghe; here you can see how masks are made. **Mondonovo,** on Rio Terrà Canal, displays inventive masks.

At **Campo Santa Margherita,** a busy neighborhood shopping square, stop in to see Giovanni Battista Tiepolo's ceiling paintings in the **Scuola dei Carmini.** The paintings, now displayed on the second floor, were commissioned to honor the Carmelite order by depicting prominent Carmelites in conversation with saints and angels. Of the three great Venetian painters whose names start with T (Titian, Tintoretto, and Tiepolo), Tiepolo came last chronologically (he painted in the 18th century, while the others were 16th-century artists) and achieved the greatest international fame in his own time, though an underlying melancholy in his ethereal, brightly colored paintings betrays a man of sober piety. Tiepolo's vivid techniques transformed some unpromising religious themes into flamboyant displays of color and movement. Mirrors are available on the benches to make it easier to see the ceiling without getting a sore neck. *Campo dei Carmini, tel. 041/528-9420. Admission: 5,000 lire. Open Mon.-Sat. 9-noon, 3-6.*

Continue on to the **Frari,** an immense Gothic church of russet-colored brick, built in the 14th century for the Franciscans. In keeping with the austere principles of the Franciscan order, the Frari is quite stark inside, with much less ornamentation than other Venetian churches. The relative absence of decoration gives a select feeling to the church paintings, such as Bellini's *Madonna and Four Saints* in the sacristy. The most striking is Titian's large *Assumption* over the main altar. Titian cleverly used the design of the church interior to frame his painting. Worldly and polished, Titian also was a fashionable portrait painter, and the Virgin's rapturous rise to heaven here is charged with very real human emotion. The *Pesaro Madonna* over the first altar on the left nave near the main altar is also by Titian; his wife, who died shortly afterward in childbirth, posed for the figure of Mary. Both of these pictures demonstrate Titian's love of robust, brilliant color and dramatic composition. The Madonna was radical for its time because the main figure was not placed squarely in the center of the painting, but look at how dynamic the picture is as a result. On the same side of the church, look at the spooky pyramid-shape tomb of sculptor Antonio Canova (1757–1822). Across the nave is a neoclassical 19th-century monument to Titian, executed by two of Canova's pupils. *Admission: 1,000 lire. Open Mon.–Sat. 9–1:30, Sun. 9–1.*

㉗ Behind the Frari is the **Scuola di San Rocco,** filled with dark, dramatic canvases by Tintoretto. Born some 30 years after Titian, Jacopo Robusti—called Tintoretto because his father was a dyer—was more mystical and devout than the sophisticated Titian. Though his colors are equally brilliant, he carried Titian's love of motion and odd composition to almost surreal effects, in the same Mannerist vein as El Greco (who was at one time a pupil of Titian's!). In 1564, Tintoretto beat other painters competing for the commission to decorate this building by submitting not a sketch but a finished work, which he additionally offered free of charge. The more than 50 paintings took a total of 23 years to complete. These works, depicting Old and New Testament themes, were restored in the 1970s, and Tintoretto's inventive use of light has once more been revealed. *Campo San Rocco, tel. 041/523–4864. Admission: 6,000 lire. Open weekdays 10–1, weekends 10–4.*

The area around San Rocco is well off the normal tourist trail, with narrow alleys and streets winding alongside small canals to little squares, where posters advertising political parties and sports events seem to be the only signs of life. Head back ㉘ past the Frari to **Campo San Polo,** one of Venice's largest squares, and a favorite playground for neighborhood children. From here you take Calle della Madonetta, Calle dell'Olio, Ruga Ravano, and Ruga Vecchia San Giovanni to the **Rialto** shopping district, where you can cross the Grand Canal for the shortcut back to San Marco. Alternatively, you can go north from Campo San Polo by way of Calle Bernardo, Calle dello Scaleter, Rio Terrà Parrucchetta, and Calle del Tintor to ㉙ **Campo San Giacomo dell'Orio,** where the 13th-century church of San Giacomo stands on a charming square that few tourists ever find. Here you're not far from the **San Stae** vaporetto landing, so you can take the boat back along the Grand Canal to the heart of the city.

Tour 5: Islands of the Lagoon

Narrow channels help boats negotiate the shallow waters of the Venetian lagoon, with its islands of Murano, Burano, and Torcello. These islands are famous for their handicrafts—notably glass and lace—but guided tours here usually involve high-pressure attempts to make you buy, with little time left for anything else. It's much cheaper and more adventurous to make your own way around the islands, using the good vaporetto connections. Services to and from Venice use the landing stage at Fondamente Nuove, almost due north of St. Mark's. The most distant island, Torcello, is ideal for picnics but has no food stores. Buy provisions in Venice if you plan to picnic there.

If you're making your way on foot to Fondamente Nuove, stop ㉚ at the church of the **Gesuiti,** which dominates the Campo dei Gesuiti. This 18th-century church is built in an extravagantly Baroque style; the classical arches and straight lines of the Renaissance have been abandoned in favor of flowing, twisting forms. The marble of the gray-and-white interior is used like brocade, carved into swags and drapes. Titian's *Martyrdom of*

St. Lawrence, over the first altar on the left, is a dramatic example of the great artist's feel for light and movement.

From **Fondamente Nuove** you have a choice of vaporetti. Line 5 goes to San Michele and Murano; Line 12, which you can join at Murano, skips Venice's cemetery-island of San Michele and goes to Murano, Burano, and Torcello.

Numbers in the margin correspond to points of interest on the Venetian Lagoon map.

㉛ It's only a five-minute ride to **San Michele,** the smallest of the islands, which is taken up almost completely with the pretty Renaissance church of **San Michele in Isola,** designed by Coducci in 1478, and Venice's **cemetery.** It is a moving experience to walk among the gravestones, with the sound of lapping water on all sides. Poet Ezra Pound, the great Russian impresario and art critic Sergey Diaghilev, and the composer Igor Stravinsky are buried here.

㉜ Another five minutes on Line 5 takes you to **Murano,** which, like Venice, is made up of a number of smaller islands, linked by bridges. Murano is known exclusively for its glassworks, which you can visit to see how glass is made. Many of these line the **Fondamenta dei Vetrai,** the canalside walkway leading away from the landing stage. The houses along this walk are much more colorful—and a lot simpler—than their Venetian counterparts; traditionally they were workmen's cottages. Just before the junction with Murano's Grand Canal—250 yards up from the landing stage—is the church of **San Pietro Martire.** This 16th-century reconstruction of an earlier Gothic church has two works by Venetian masters: the *Madonna and Child,* by Giovanni Bellini, and *St. Jerome,* by Veronese.

Cross the Ponte Vivarini and turn right onto **Fondamenta Cavour.** Follow the Fondamenta around the corner to the **Museo Vetrario** (Glass Museum), with a collection of Venetian glass that ranges from priceless antique to only slightly less expensive modern. The museum gives you a good idea of the history of Murano's glassworks, which were moved here from Venice in the 13th century because they were a fire risk. It's useful, too, to get a clear idea of authentic Venetian styles and patterns if you're planning to make some purchases later. *Admission: 5,000 lire. Open daily 9–4.*

㉝ Make your way back along the same route to the landing stage and take Line 12 to **Burano,** which is about 30 minutes from Murano. It's a small island fishing village with houses painted in cheerful colors and a raffishly raked bell tower on the main square, about 100 yards from the landing stage and clearly visible. Lace is to Burano what glass is to Murano, but be prepared to pay a lot for the real thing. Stalls line the way from the landing stage to **Piazza Galuppi,** the main square; the vendors, many of them fishermen's wives, are generally good-natured and unfamiliar with the techniques of the hard sell.

The **Consorzio Merletti di Burano** (Lace Museum) on Piazza Galuppi is the best place to learn the intricacies of the lace-making traditions of Burano. It is also useful for learning the nature of the skills involved in making the more expensive lace, in case you intend to buy some lace on your way back to the vaporetto. *Piazza Galuppi. Admission: 5,000 lire. Open Tues.–Sat. 9–6, Sun. 10–4.*

Venetian Lagoon

Time Out   Among the pleasant *trattorie* on Piazza Galuppi are **Ai Pescatori** (closed Mon.) and **Romano** (closed Tues.). Both serve seafood specialties à la carte, but keep your eye on the costs.

Vaporetto Line 12 continues from the Burano landing stage to the sleepy green island of **Torcello,** about 10 minutes farther. This is where the first Venetians landed in their flight from the barbarians 1,500 years ago. Even after many settlers left to found the city of Venice on the island of Rivo Alto (Rialto), Torcello continued to grow and prosper, until its main source of income, wool manufacturing, was priced out of the marketplace. It's hard to believe now, looking at this almost deserted island, that in the 16th century it had 20,000 inhabitants and 10 churches.

A brick-paved lane leads up from the landing stage and follows the curve of the canal toward the center of the island. You pass **Locanda Cipriani,** an inn famous for its good food and the patronage of Ernest Hemingway, who often came to Torcello for the solitude. These days Locanda Cipriani is about the busiest spot on the island, as well-heeled customers arrive on high-speed powerboats for lunch.

Just beyond is the grassy square that holds the only surviving monuments of the island's past splendor. The low church of **Santa Fosca,** on the right, dates back to the 11th century. Next to it is the **cathedral,** also built in the 11th century: The ornate Byzantine mosaics are testimony to the importance and wealth of an island that could attract the best artists and craftsmen of its day. The vast mosaic on the inside of the facade depicts the

Last Judgment as artists of the 11th and 12th centuries imagined it: Figures writhe in vividly depicted contortions of pain. Facing it, as if in mitigation, is the calm mosaic figure of the Madonna, alone in a field of gold above the staunch array of Apostles.

The trip back from Torcello retraces the route from Venice. Boats leave approximately every hour, and the trip takes about 50 minutes.

Tour 6: San Giorgio Maggiore and Giudecca

Numbers in the margin correspond to points of interest on the Venice map.

Looking out across the Basin of San Marco, you can see the island of San Giorgio Maggiore, separated by a small channel from the Giudecca. A tall brick campanile on that distant bank perfectly complements the Campanile of San Marco. Behind it looms the stately dome of one of Venice's greatest churches, San Giorgio Maggiore. To reach the island, take a Line 5 or 8 vaporetto from San Zaccaria, which is near San Marco. (Make sure you're going on the clockwise route, designated *circolare destra*.)

A church has been on this island since the late eighth century, with a Benedictine monastery added in the tenth century. The present church of **San Giorgio Maggiore** was begun in 1566 by the greatest architect of his time, Andrea Palladio, whose work is so evident throughout the Venetian Arc (*see* Chapter 7). Two of Palladio's hallmarks are mathematical harmony and architectural elements borrowed from classical Rome, both of which are evident in this superbly proportioned neoclassical church of red brick and white marble. Inside, the church is refreshingly airy and simply decorated. Two important late Titian paintings hang on either side of the chancel: *The Last Supper* and *The Gathering of Manna*. Over the first altar on the right-hand side of the nave is an *Adoration of the Shepherds* by Jacopo Bassano (1517–1592), a painter from Bassano del Grappa on the mainland, who used the techniques of Veronese and Titian to depict the humbler walks of life. Take the elevator up the Campanile outside (admission 2,000 lire) for a fine view of Venice and its harbor. *Open daily 9–12:30 and 2–5.*

The monastery of San Giorgio Maggiore, once the home of Pope Pius VII, later a barracks for the occupying Austrians, now houses an artistic foundation and is usually closed to the public. The gardens contain an open-air theater that is still used in the summer. Palladio designed the monastery's first cloister, and Longhena was the architect for the grand baroque library.

Catch the Line 5 or 8 vaporetto (still *circolare destra*) to reach the island of **Giudecca,** a crescent cupped around the southern shore of Venice. Giudecca has always been seen as a place apart. First it was a colony for Jews in the 13th century (which possibly accounts for its name), and later it became a pleasure garden for wealthy Venetians during the long and luxurious decline of the Republic. Today it has a sleepy middle-class air about it, pleasantly in contrast to the heart of Venice. In one regard it is still the province of the wealthy, however: The exclusive **Cipriani** hotel (*see* Lodging, *below*) lies secluded on its eastern tip.

36 The main attraction here is the church of **Il Redentore,** also by Palladio. Its tranquil, stately facade is actually a series of superimposed temple fronts, topped by a dome and a pair of slim Byzantine bell towers. The interior, like San Giorgio Maggiore's, is perfectly proportioned and airy, in contrast to the dusky clutter of the Basilica San Marco.

Each July, the feast of Il Redentore (the Redeemer) is celebrated with a pontoon bridge being built over the channel to Giudecca, commemorating the doge's annual visit to this church to offer thanks for the end of a 16th-century plague. Fireworks explode over the lagoon, and a good time is had by all.

The vaporetto Lines 5 or 8 will take you back in the other direction *(circolare sinistra)* to San Marco, or you can take Lines 5 or 8 *(circolare destra)* or Line 9 from Giudecca directly across the channel to the **Zattere,** the broad waterfront promenade on Dorsoduro, where there are plenty of inexpensive restaurants and a casual neighborhood atmosphere.

What to See and Do with Children

The whole experience of a visit to Venice should provide excitement for a child. For the parent it means trading one constant warning ("Look both ways before crossing") for another ("Stay away from the edge of that canal"). Wandering over the many footbridges and along narrow alleyways leading nowhere, children get a chance to burn off a lot of excess energy, and sometimes their aimless rambles lead to an unexpected square or little church. But there are not many activities aimed at children.

Glassblowing. Go to one of the showrooms with demonstrations along Fondamenta dei Vetrai in Murano. (*See* Tour 5: Islands of the Lagoon, *above*).

Gondola ride. Your child will probably have suggested this more than once, long before you even arrive in Venice. Gondoliers usually perform well for children, demonstrating how they steer and calling out to other traffic as they near a junction.

Lion Statues. These guardians of the Arsenal are a reminder of Venice's glorious naval past (*See* Tour 3: To the Arsenal and Beyond, *above*). The lions in Piazzetta dei Leoncini, near San Marco, are fine mounts for tots.

Museo Navale (*See* Tour 3: To the Arsenal and Beyond, *above*).

Torre dell'Orologio. The hourly display when the bronze bell is struck always draws a crowd of young and old (*See* Tour 1: The San Marco District, *above*).

Winter Carnival. Children enjoy dressing up in masks or full costume during the carnival festivities during the two weeks before Ash Wednesday.

Off the Beaten Track

The Ghetto. In 1516, Venice's Great Council ordered all Jews to be confined to a small island in Cannaregio. They were not allowed to leave this area after sunset, when the huge gates were barred until dawn. Jewish physicians, whose services were favored by the aristocrats, were the only exception. The ghetto expanded to Ghetto Vecchio and Ghetto Novissimo. In 1797 Napoleon's troops pulled down the Ghetto's gates, but by that time their synagogues and homes were rooted in these neighborhoods. The **Museo Ebraico** is in one corner of Campo Ghetto Nuovo, a pretty square with a fountain and a few trees. From the museum, you can join a guided tour of the synagogues; tours are in English and are given several times a day. *Campo del Ghetto Nuovo, tel. 041/715359. Open June–Sept., weekdays and Sun., 10–7; Oct.–May, weekdays and Sun., 10–4. Closed Sat. and Jewish holidays.*

Lido. This island, forming the north–south barrier for the Lagoon, has the best beaches for sunbathing, but although thousands swim here and at nearby Jesolo, the Adriatic is reputedly polluted. There are tennis courts, a golf course, flying club, and a horse-riding club. Hotels Des Bains and Cipriani have exclusive clubs with lovely swimming pools. The famous Lido Casino operates during the summer months only (in the winter it returns to its palahal home on the Grand Canal—*see* Tour 2, *above*). The church and monastery of San Nicolo are on the northern end of the island; during the week, this is a pleasant place for a walk and lunch. Avoid the Sunday crowds; most restaurants are closed on Monday. *Take vaporetto Line 1 or 2 to the Piazzale Maria Elisabetta on the Lido. From there Bus A goes north to San Nicolo.*

Madonna dell'Orto. In the residential Cannaregio district, north of the first loop of the Grand Canal, this was Tintoretto's parish church; he was buried just to the right of the main altar. On each side of the altar are his paintings *The Last Judgment* and *Adoration of the Golden Calf.* In the latter, he supposedly painted his own face (with a black beard) on one of the pagans holding the calf. There are several more of his paintings and work by other artists here. *Cannaregio district, Fondamenta Madonna dell'Orto.*

Palazzo Labia. This 18th-century palace, once the home of the wealthy Labia family, is not regularly open to the public, but by prior arrangement you can view the masterpieces decorating its ballroom: some of Tiepolo's most magnificent frescoes, a series telling the story of Antony and Cleopatra. The Palace is in Cannaregio, between the Ghetto and the train station, just off the Grand Canal. *Campo San Geremia. To arrange a visit, call tel. 041/781111, or inquire at desk at entrance.*

Shopping

Shopping in Venice is part of the fun of exploring the city, and you're sure to find plenty of interesting shops and boutiques as you explore. It's always a good idea to mark on your map the location of a shop that interests you; otherwise, you may not be able to find it again in mazelike Venice. Shops are usually open 9–1 and 3:30 or 4–7:30 and are closed Sunday and on Monday morning. However, many tourist-oriented shops are open all day, every day. Food shops are closed Wednesday afternoon, except in July and August, when they close Saturday afternoon. Some shops close for both a summer and a winter vacation.

Shopping Districts   The main shopping areas are the **Mercerie,** the succession of narrow and crowded streets winding from Piazza San Marco to the Rialto, and the area around Campo San Salvador, Calle del Teatro, Campo Manin, and Campo San Fantin. If you can't face the crowds on the Mercerie, go a little out of the way to the **Strada Nuova,** between Santi Apostoli and the train station, where many Venetians shop. The **San Marco** area is full of shops and top-name boutiques, such as Missoni, Valentino, Fendi, and Versace.

Department Stores The only thing approximating a department store here is **Coin,** at the Rialto bridge, featuring men's and women's fashions. The **Standa** stores on Campo San Luca and Strada Nuova have a wide range of goods at moderate prices.

Food Markets The open-air fruit and vegetable market at **Rialto** is colorful and animated throughout the morning, when Venetian housewives come to pick over the day's offerings and haggle with vendors. The adjacent fish market offers a vivid lesson in ichthyology, presenting some species you've probably never seen (open mornings Mon.–Sat.). At the other end of Venice, in the Castello district, is **Via Garibaldi,** the scene of another lively food market on weekday mornings.

Specialty Stores Glass, most of it made in Murano, is Venice's number-one prod-
Glassware uct, and you'll be confronted by mind-boggling displays of traditional and contemporary glassware, often kitsch. Take your time and be selective. Should you buy glass in Venice's shops or in the showrooms of Murano's factories? You will probably find that prices are pretty much the same; showrooms in Venice that are outlets of Murano glassworks sell at the same prices as the factories. However, because of competition, shops in Venice stocking wares from various glassworks may charge slightly lower prices.

In Venice, **Venini** (Piazzetta dei Leoncini 314), **Pauli** (Calle dell'Ascensione 72), and **Salviati** (Piazza San Marco 78 and 110) are reliable and respected firms. For chic, contemporary glassware, **Carlo Moretti** is a good choice; his signature designs are on display at **Isola** (Campo San Moisè). For stunning glass beads and jewelry, go to **Archimede Seguso** (Piazza San Marco); **Vetri d'Arte** (Piazza San Marco) offers moderately priced glass jewelry. In a category all his own is **Gianfranco Penzo** (Campo del Ghetto Nuovo 2895), who decorates Jewish ritual vessels in glass, makes commemorative plates, and takes special orders.

In Murano, most of the glass factories have showrooms where glassware is sold. The **Domus** shop (Fondamenta dei Vetrai) has a selection of smaller objects and jewelry from the best glassworks.

Lace Venice's top name is **Jesurum,** with a shop at Piazza San Marco 60 and a much larger establishment at Ponte Canonica, behind the Basilica San Marco. **Martinuzzi, Fabris,** and **Tokatzian,** all on Piazza San Marco, also have a good selection. Remember that much of the lace and embroidered linen sold in Venice and on Burano is made in China or Taiwan. For the same sumptuous brocades, damasks, and cut velvets used by the world's most prestigious decorators, go to **Lorenzo Rubelli** (Campo San Gallo 1089), just off Piazza San Marco. At **Norelene** (Campo San Maurizio 2606), you'll find stunning hand-printed fabrics.

Masks These are a tradition in Venice; they were worn everywhere during the lengthy Carnival season in the 18th century. Shops throughout the city sell masks of all types. Among the most interesting are **Mondonovo** (Rio Terrà Canal), **Cà Macana** (Calle delle Botteghe, near San Barnaba), and **Laboratorio Artigiano Maschere** (Barbaria delle Tole, near Santi Giovanni e Paolo).

Prints An old print of Venice makes a distinctive gift or souvenir. There's an excellent selection at **O. Bohm** (Salizzada San Moisè, just off Piazza San Marco). Hand-printed paper and desk accessories, memo pads, and address books abound at the well-known **Piazzesi** shop (Campiello della Feltrina, near Santa Maria del Giglio).

Sports

Golf The **Golf Club Lido di Venezia,** an 18-hole course, is located on the Lido island. *Via del Forte, Alberoni, Lido, tel. 041/731333.*

Horseback Riding **Circolo Ippico Veneziano** (tel. 041/526–5162) is located at Ca' Bianca on the Lido. It is open all year.

Jogging The best spot to jog is past the public gardens (Giardini) in the Castello district and over to the pine wood on Sant'Elena; you get a magnificent view of the city as you jog back toward the center.

Swimming Considering the polluted state of the Adriatic, the best place to swim is at a pool. Venice's only public pool is the **Piscina Gandini** (tel. 041/528–5430), located on the island of Sacca Fisola, at the far end of Giudecca (take Line 5 vaporetto to Sacca Fisola). The deluxe hotels **Excelsior** (tel. 041/526–0201) and **Hotel des Bains** (tel. 041/526–5921) are both located on Lungomare Marconi on the Lido; their pools are open to nonguests for a fee.

Tennis The **Hotel des Bains** (*see* Swimming, *above*) and the exclusive **Sea Gull Club** of the Hotel Cipriani (tel. 041/520–7744) will let nonguests play for a fee. There are tennis clubs on the Lido: **Lido Tennis Club** (tel. 041/526–0954) and the **Tennis Union** (tel. 041/968134).

Dining

The general standard of Venetian restaurants has suffered from the onslaught of mass tourism. It is very difficult to eat well in Venice at moderate prices. Although seafood is a specialty here, it's no bargain, and you will find some fish dishes very expensive, especially those that are priced by weight (mainly baked or steamed fish). Under the auspices of the restaurant association, most of the city's restaurants offer special tourist menus, moderately priced according to the level of the restaurant and generally representing good value. It's always a good idea to reserve your table or have your hotel *portiere* do it for you. Dining hours are short, starting at 12:30 or 1 for lunch and ending at 2:30–3, when restaurants close for the afternoon, opening up again to start serving at about 8 and closing again at 11 or midnight. Most close one day a week and are also likely to close without notice for vacation or renovation. Few have signs on the outside, so when the metal blinds are shut tight, you can't tell a closed restaurant from a closed TV-repair shop. This makes them hard to spot when you are exploring the city. You may not find a cover charge *(pane e coperto),* but a service charge of 10%–15% will almost surely be on the check.

Venetian cuisine is based on seafood, with a few culinary excursions inland. Antipasto may take the form of a seafood salad, *prosciutto di San Daniele* (cured ham) from the mainland, or pickled vegetables. As a first course Venetians favor risotto, a creamy rice dish that may be cooked with vegetables or shellfish. Pasta, too, is good with seafood sauces; Venice is *not* the place to order spaghetti with tomato sauce. *Pasticcio di pesce* is pasta baked with fish, usually *baccalà* (dried cod). A classic first course is *pasta e fagioli* (thick bean soup with pasta). *Bigoli* is strictly a local pasta, made of whole wheat, usually served with a salty *tonno* (tuna) sauce. Polenta, made of cornmeal, is another pillar of regional cooking. It's often served as an accompaniment to *fegato alla veneziana* (liver with onion, Venetian style). Local seafood includes *granseola* (crab) and *seppie* or *seppioline* (cuttlefish).

The dessert specialty in Venice is *tiramisù* (a heavenly concoction of creamy cheese, coffee, and chocolate with pound cake); the recipe originated on the mainland, but the Venetians have adopted it enthusiastically. Local wines are the dry white Tocai and Pinot from the Friuli region and bubbly white Prosecco, a naturally fermented sparkling white wine that is a shade less dry. The best Prosecco comes from the Valdobbiadene; Cartizze, which is similar, is considered superior by some but is expensive. Popular red wines include Merlot, Cabernet, Raboso, and Refosco. You can sample all of these and more in Venice's many wineshops, where wine is served by the glass and accompanied by *cicchetti* (assorted tidbits), often substantial enough for a light meal.

Highly recommended restaurants are indicated by a star ★.

Category	Cost*
Very Expensive	over 150,000 lire
Expensive	90,000–150,000 lire
Moderate	50,000–90,000 lire
Inexpensive	under 50,000 lire

per person, including three courses, wine, and service

Very Expensive **Antico Martini.** A Venetian institution known for good food,
★ Antico Martini has an elegant look, neoclassical columns, and a pretty pink-accented dining terrace overlooking La Fenice theater. In the winter you dine in cozy wood-paneled salons. Specialties are seasonal and might include *petti di pollo San Giorgio* (breast of chicken with cream and mushrooms), kidneys flambé, and vegetarian ravioli. A four-course *menu gastronomico* (fixed-price menu) is an excellent value at about 66,000 lire, including cover and service charges. *Campo San Fantin 1983, tel. 041/522–4121. Reservations advised. Jacket and tie required. AE, DC, MC, V. Closed Tues., Wed. lunch, Dec.–Feb. but open for Christmas and Carnival seasons.*

Danieli Terrace. The famous Danieli Hotel provides a superlative location for a very special meal, which you can enjoy on the terrace in fair weather or in the pastel-toned dining room. Either way you have a picture-postcard view of San Giorgio and

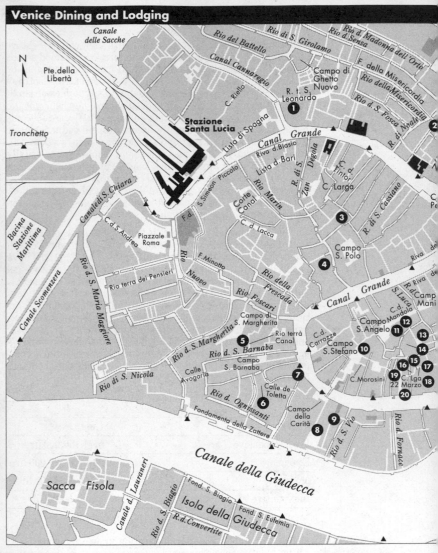

Venice Dining and Lodging

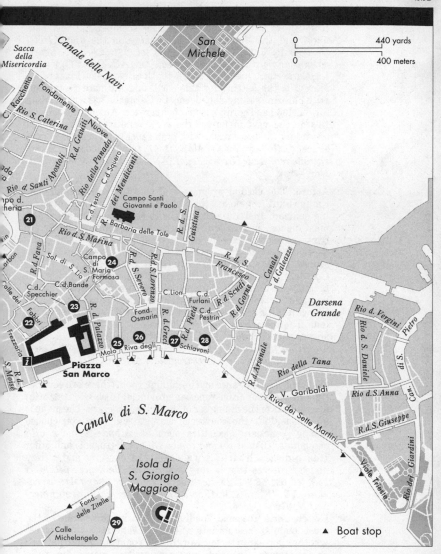

Sacca
della
Misericordia

Canale delle Navi

San
Michele

0   440 yards
0   400 meters

Racchetta
Fondamente
Rio S. Caterina
R.d. Gesuiti
Fondamente Nuove
Rio della Panada
C. d. Squero
C.d. Tiesta
dei Mendicanti
Rio a' Santi Apostoli
Rio d'Santi Apostoli

21

Rio d. S. Marina

Campo Santi
Giovanni e Paolo
Ri Barbaria delle Tole

R.d. S.
Giustina

Campo di
S. Maria
Formosa
24
R.d. S. Lorenzo
R.d. S. Severo
R.d. S.
Francesco

Sal. di S. Lio
C.d. Bande
C. Lion
C.d.
Furlani
R.d. Scudi
R.d. Gorna

Canale d. Galeazze

Darsena
Grande

Rio d. Vergini

R.d. Fava
C.d.
Specchier
Fond.
Osmarin
C.d. Pestrin

Rio d. S. Daniele

Can. di S. Pietro

23
R.d. Palazzo
R.d. Greci
R.d. Pietà

Calle dei
22
Fobbri
Frezzaria

25
Molo
Riva degli
26
27
Schiavoni
28

R.d. Arsenale

Rio della Tana

V. Garibaldi

Rio d. S. Anna

Piazza
San Marco

R.d. S. Moisè

i

Riva dei Sette Martiri

R.d. S. Giuseppe

Viale Trieste

Rio dei Giardini

Canale di S. Marco

Isola di
S. Giorgio
Maggiore

Fond.
delle Zitelle

Calle
Michelangelo

29

▲ Boat stop

the lagoon. Cuisine and prices are on a par with the ambience. *Branzino al forno* (baked sea bass) and scampi take the honors here, and the desserts are as dreamy as the view. *Hotel Danieli, Riva degli Schiavoni 4196, tel. 041/522-6480. Reservations advised. Jacket and tie required. AE, DC, MC, V.*

La Caravella. One of Venice's top locales, near Piazza San Marco, is the setting for this small and intimate restaurant with old-time sailing-ship decor. La Caravella has a reputation for fine food and cordial, courteous service. Among the specialties on the vast menu are the very Venetian *taglierini alla granseola* (delicate pasta with crab sauce) and scampi in port sauce. *Calle Larga XXII Marzo 2397, tel. 041/5208901. Reservations required. Dress: casual. AE, DC, MC, V. Closed Wed. Nov.–Apr.*

Expensive   **Arturo.** The cordial proprietor of this tiny restaurant near Campo Sant'Angelo has the distinction (in Venice) of not serving seafood. Instead, spaghetti with seasonal vegetables and meat dishes, such as *braciolona di maiale* (pork chop in vinegar), are tasty, as are the *porcini* mushrooms, in season. *Calle degli Assassini 3656, tel. 041/528-6974. Reservations required. Dress: casual. No credit cards. Closed Sun., Aug.*

Cortile. Set in a lovely garden court shaded by awnings and bright with blossoms, this open-air restaurant is refreshing by day and romantic by night, when you dine by candlelight. In the winter it moves indoors to wood-paneled Venetian-style salons. The specialties are *crespelle* (crepes) and flambé dishes; it shares the kitchen of La Caravella but its prices are a notch lower. *Calle Larga XXII Marzo 2402, tel. 041/520-8938. Reservations not necessary. Dress: casual. AE, DC, MC, V. Closed Wed.*

Do Forni. The entrance and one dining room (there are several, ranging in decor from Venetian provincial to classic trattoria) are replicas of the dining car of the *Orient Express*. The menu is enormous, but the courteous waiters will help you choose among Venetian specialties such as *zuppa di mare alla chioggiotta* (fish stew) and *rombo Do Forni* (turbot) and other Italian dishes. There's a wide choice of desserts and a fizzy house Prosecco that is very pleasant. *Calle degli Specchieri 468, tel. 041/523-7729. Reservations not necessary. Dress: casual. AE, DC, MC, V. Closed Thurs. (open daily in summer) and Nov. 20–Dec. 6.*

★ **Fiaschetteria Toscana.** You'll soon see why this is one of the most popular restaurants with the Venetians themselves, whether you eat in the upstairs dining room or under the arbor on the square. Cheerful, courteous waiters may suggest the delicate *tagliolini alla buranella* (thin noodles with shrimp) or *rombo* (turbot) with capers. The local clientele appreciates the food's excellent quality and the friendly atmosphere. *Campo San Giovanni Crisostomo, tel. 041/528-5281. Reservations advised. Dress: casual. AE, DC, MC, V. Closed Tues., July 1–15.*

★ **Noemi.** Centrally located, near Piazza San Marco, this attractive restaurant is in the tourist mainstream but maintains high standards of cuisine and service. The menu gastronomico (about 65,000 lire) offers several choices in a four-course framework, and there's a three-course lunch menu of Venetian specialties (about 43,000 lire). Otherwise you order à la carte. Specialties are *cannelloni allo smeraldino* (with chopped chicken, cheese, and spinach) and veal chop *alla zingara* (with olives and capers). *Calle dei Fabbri, tel. 041/522-5238. Reser-*

*vations advised. Dress: casual. AE, DC, MC, V. Closed Sun.
and Mon. lunch, Dec. 15–Jan. 31.*

Moderate **Da Fiore.** Long a favorite with Venetians, Da Fiore has been discovered by tourists, so it's imperative to reserve for an excellent seafood dinner, which might include such specialties as *pasticcio di pesce* (fish pie) and *seppioline* (cuttlefish). Not easy to find, it's near Campo San Polo. *Calle dello Scaleter 2202, tel. 041/721308. Reservations necessary. Dress: casual. AE, DC, MC, V. Closed Sun., Mon., Aug. 10–early Sept., Dec. 25–Jan. 15.*

Da Ignazio. Smallish, pleasant, and handy to the Rialto district, Ignazio is reliable for good food at reasonable prices, barring expensive fish dishes. The cuisine is classic Venetian here, from pasta or risotto with seafood sauce to *fegato alla veneziana* (liver with onions), but there are standard Italian items as well. *Calle dei Saoneri 2749, tel. 041/523–4852. Reservations advised. Dress: casual. AE, DC, MC, V. Closed Sat.*

Da Raffaele. Near Santa Maria del Giglio, this tavern has wood-beamed ceilings and serves classic Venetian specialties, such as *fegato alla Veneziana* (liver with onions). In warm weather tables are set outdoors, alongside a canal. *Fondamenta delle Ostreghe 2347, San Marco, tel. 041/523–2317. Reservations advised. Dress: casual. AE, DC, MC, V. Closed Thurs.*

Montin. On a quiet canal in the Dorsoduro district, this old inn is popular with Venetians and tourists alike. Inside, walls are covered with paintings; outside, you dine under an elongated arbor. The specialties are *rigatoni ai quattro formaggi* (with cheese, mushrooms, and tomato) and *antipasto Montin* (seafood antipasto). *Fondamenta di Borgo 1147, tel. 041/522–7151. Reservations advised. Dress: casual. AE, DC, MC, V. Closed Tues. evening, Wed., 15 days in Jan., 15 days in Aug.*

Inexpensive **Ai Cugnai.** The "management," a bevy of friendly and efficient ladies, lends a homey air to proceedings in this popular neighborhood tavern near the Accademia. You eat in the modest dining room and "garden" courtyard. The limited menu offers such Venetian specialties as spaghetti *alle seppie* (with cuttlefish sauce) and *granseole* (crabs). *Calle Nuova Sant'Agnese 857, tel. 041/528–9238. Reservations advised in evening. Dress: casual. No credit cards. Closed Mon. and all Jan.*

Antica Adelaide. This informal tavern serves a limited range of well-prepared dishes such as *pasticcio alla gorgonzola* (pasta baked with cheese) and *fritto di pesce* (fried fish). In fair weather you dine in a garden courtyard. To find this inconspicuous establishment, look for the barrel in front of the entrance. *Calle Priuli 3728, off Strada Nuova, tel. 041/520–3451. Reservations advised in evening. Dress: casual. No credit cards. Closed Mon.*

★ **Gazebo.** You'll find Gazebo near the train station and Ponte delle Guglie. It is a friendly trattoria that's several cuts above the others on this main pedestrian route. It offers outdoor dining in a garden courtyard and courteous service. Spaghetti *al cartoccio* (steamed in foil with seafood) is the specialty, and there's pizza, too. *Rio Terrà San Leonardo 1333/A (Strada Nuova), tel. 041/716380. Reservations advised. Dress: casual. AE, DC, MC, V. Closed Thurs.*

L'Incontro. This trattoria has a faithful clientele of Venetians and visitors, attracted by generous servings, friendly waiters, and reasonable prices. Menu choices include *calamari* (squid) either fried or in a wine sauce and a reliable spaghetti with seafood sauce. It is near San Barnaba and Campo Santa Margherita. *Rio Terrà Canal 3062/A, Dorsoduro, tel. 041/522–2404. Reservations advised. Dress: casual. MC, V. Closed Mon.*

Vino Vino. The annex of the famous Antico Martini restaurant (*see above*), this is a highly informal wine bar where you can sample Italian vintages and munch on a limited selection of dishes from the kitchens of its upscale big sister, next door. It's open nonstop 10 AM–1 AM. *Calle del Caffettier 2007/a, near Campo San Fantin, tel. 041/523–7027. No reservations. Dress: casual. AE, DC, MC, V. Closed Tues.*

Lodging

Most of Venice's hotels are in renovated palaces. The top hotels are indeed palatial, although some "Cinderella" rooms may be small and dowdy. In lower categories, space is at a premium; some rooms may be cramped, and not all hotels have lounging space. Because of conservation laws, some cannot install elevators. Air-conditioning is essential for survival in summer heat; many hotels charge a hefty supplement for it. Although it has no cars, Venice does have boats plying the canals and pedestrians chattering in the streets, even late at night. Don't be surprised if your room is noisy (earplugs help).

The busiest times for hotels are spring and autumn; December 20–January 2; and the two-week Carnival period leading up to Ash Wednesday, usually in February. Book well in advance. If you don't have reservations, you can almost always get a room in any category by going upon arrival to the AVA (Venetian Hoteliers Association) booths at the train station, airport, and at the municipal parking garage at Piazzale Roma. The 10,000, 20,000, or 30,000-lire deposit (depending on the category of the hotel) is rebated on your bill. The booths are open daily 9–9.

Most hotels quote rates inclusive of breakfast. Rates are generally higher than in Rome or Florence, but you can save considerably in the off season. Remember that it is essential to know how to get to your hotel when you arrive in Venice.

Highly recommended lodgings are indicated by a star ★.

Category	Cost*
Very Expensive	over 400,000 lire
Expensive	220,000–400,000 lire
Moderate	100,000–220,000 lire
Inexpensive	under 100,000 lire

*All prices are for a standard double room for two, including taxes and service.

Very Expensive
★

Cipriani. It's impossible to feel stressed in this sybaritic oasis of stunningly decorated rooms and suites, some with garden patios. The Cipriani is located on the Giudecca, across St. Mark's Basin from the heart of Venice, with views of San Giorgio and the lagoon. The hotel launch whisks you back and forth to San Marco at any hour of the day or night, but the Cipriani is not for anyone who wants to feel Venice's heartbeat. Cooking courses and fitness programs help keep guests occupied. *Giudecca 10, tel. 041/520–7744, fax 041/5203930. 98* *rooms or suites with bath. Facilities: outdoor pool, gardens, tennis courts. AE, DC, MC, V. Closed Dec.–mid-Feb.*

Danieli. This famous hotel is a collage of newer buildings around a 15th-century palazzo, which is loaded with sumptuous Venetian decor and atmosphere. Some of the suites are positively palatial, but lower-priced rooms may not be. The salons and bar are chic places to relax and watch the celebrities go by, and the dining terrace, like many rooms, has a fabulous view of San Giorgio and St. Mark's Basin. *Riva degli Schiavoni 4196, tel. 041/522–6480, fax 041/5200208. 230 rooms or suites with bath. Facilities: bar, restaurant, terrace. AE, DC, MC, V.*

Gritti Palace. The atmosphere of an aristocratic private home pervades this quietly elegant hotel. Fresh flowers, fine antiques, sumptuous appointments, and Old World service give guests the feeling of being very special people. The dining terrace on the Grand Canal is best in the evening when the boat traffic dies down. *Campo Santa Maria del Giglio 2467, tel. 041/794611, fax 041/5200942. 98 rooms or suites with bath. Facilities: bar, restaurant, canalside terrace. AE, DC, MC, V.*

Expensive **Londra Palace.** This grand hotel commands a fine view of San Giorgio and St. Mark's Basin and has a distinguished ambience. The rooms are decorated in dark paisley prints, with sophisticated touches, and the rooftop suite is a honeymooner's dream. The Deux Lions restaurant offers fine Venetian and French cuisine, and the piano bar is open late. Guest perks include a complimentary Mercedes for one-day excursions and free entrance to the city Casino. *Riva degli Schiavoni 4171, tel. 041/520–0533, fax 041/5225032. 69 rooms and suites with bath. Facilities: piano bar, restaurant, terrace, solarium. AE, DC, MC, V.*

★ **Metropole.** Everything about the Metropole has the distinctive atmosphere of a small, exclusive hotel. It is decorated with subtle color-coordinated fabrics and run with careful attention to detail. It overlooks St. Mark's Basin, but the quiet, spacious rooms on the garden are especially inviting. You can step from your watertaxi or gondola directly into the hotel lobby. *Riva degli Schiavoni 4149, tel. 041/520–5044, fax 041/522–3679. 73 rooms with bath. Facilities: bar, buffet restaurant. AE, DC, MC, V.*

Saturnia Internazionale. There's lots of Old World charm in this historic palace, which is quietly but centrally located near Piazza San Marco. Its beamed ceilings, damask-hung walls, and authentic Venetian decor impart real character to the solid comfort of its rooms and salons. Many rooms have been extensively redecorated and endowed with more glamorous—and much larger—bathrooms. *Calle Larga XXII Marzo 2398, tel. 041/520–8377, fax 041/520–7131. 95 rooms with bath. Facilities: bar, 2 restaurants. AE, DC, MC, V.*

Moderate **Accademia.** One of Venice's most charming hotels, the Accad-
★ emia is also one of its most popular, so early reservations are a must. It is located in a 17th-century villa near the Accademia Gallery and the Grand Canal. Lounges, bar, and wood-paneled breakfast room are cheery, with fresh flowers everywhere. You can even have breakfast outside on the garden terrace in good weather. Bedrooms are ample and comfortably furnished, whether in the traditional wood-paneled style or in the bright, contemporary look of the air-conditioned top floor. A gracious private-home atmosphere and reasonable rates in this category make this one a gem. *Fondamenta Bollani 1058, tel. 041/523–*

7846, fax 041/523-9152. 28 rooms, most with bath or shower. Facilities: bar, 2 gardens, landing on canal. AE, DC, MC, V.

La Fenice et des Artistes. The hotel takes its name from the Fenice Theater, which is nearby. There is a slightly bohemian air to the place, perhaps because of the theatrical clientele, so don't be shocked to find other guests in 18th-century costume if you arrive during the Carnival season. Rooms are individually decorated; those in the older wing have more character. *Campiello della Fenice 1936, tel. 041/523-2333, fax 041/520-3721. 65 rooms with bath. MC, V.*

Flora. This hotel has what many in this category lack: plenty of sitting rooms and a pretty garden with wrought-iron coffee tables. It's in a quiet, though central, location near San Moisé and Piazza San Marco. Rooms have Venetian period decor, which some might find a bit dark; some are rather small, with tiny bathrooms. But the location and relaxing atmosphere should be enough to make up for these shortcomings. *Calle Bergamaschi 2283 (off Calle Larga XXII Marzo), tel. 041/520-5844, fax 041/522-8217. 44 rooms with bath or shower. Facilities: garden. AE, DC, MC, V. Closed mid-Nov.-Jan.*

Scandinavia. Glass chandeliers shed their light on dizzying combinations of Venetian damask patterns on walls, floor, divans, and chairs. The somewhat overpowering decor confirms that you're in the heart of Venice, just off charming Campo Santa Maria Formosa, near Piazza San Marco. The hotel is up a steep flight of stairs, and there's no elevator. *Campo Santa Maria Formosa 5240, tel. 041/522-3507, fax 041/523-5232. 35 rooms with bath or shower. AE, DC, MC, V.*

Torino. This compact hotel is not for claustrophobics, but its fine location near Santa Maria del Giglio makes it an excellent base for sightseeing. The rooms have all the basics, neatly arranged for maximum efficiency in a small space, and are decorated in pastels. There's a comfortable little sitting room; breakfast is served in your room. *Calle delle Ostreghe 2356, tel. 041/520-5222, fax 041/522-8227. 20 rooms with bath or shower. AE, DC, MC, V.*

Inexpensive **Alboretti.** Redecorated in 1986, this small hotel is simply but attractively furnished. Despite its size and central location, the Alboretti has a little garden courtyard off the breakfast room and a sitting room upstairs from the tiny lobby and bar area. There is no elevator. The hotel restaurant has creative Venetian cuisine. In all, the Alboretti offers good value. *Rio Terrà A. Foscarini 882, tel. 041/523-0058, fax 041/521-0158. 19 rooms with bath or shower. Facilities: restaurant. AE, MC, V.*

La Residenza. A little out of the way, this hotel in a Gothic palace is worth the 10-minute walk from San Marco (or the vaporetto ride to the San Zaccaria stop). Breakfast is served in an authentic Venetian salon, and the rooms are well furnished. The atmosphere is subdued, almost staid. *Campo Bandiera e Moro 3608, tel. 041/528-5315, fax 041/523-8859. 16 rooms, 15 with bath. AE, DC, MC, V. Closed 2nd week of Jan.-mid-Feb., 2nd week of Nov.-1st week of Dec.*

San Stefano. Here is a hotel in miniature, from the tiny reception area to the minuscule courtyard and breakfast room and skinny elevator. However, its 11 rooms are well furnished in Venetian style, with optional air-conditioning and TV. It's an excellent value and centrally located, too. *Campo San Stefano 2957, tel. 041/520-0166, fax 041/522-4460. 11 rooms with shower. MC, V.*

The Arts and Nightlife

The Arts

You'll find a list of current and upcoming events in the "Guest in Venice" booklet, free at your hotel. Keep an eye out for posters announcing concerts and other events. Venice hosts important temporary exhibitions in the Doge's Palace, in Palazzo Grassi at San Samuele on the Grand Canal and in other venues. The **Biennale,** a cultural institution, organizes many events throughout the year, including the film festival, beginning at the end of August. In even-numbered years, the big Biennale international art exhibition is held from the end of June to the end of September; exceptionally, the 1992 event has been shifted to 1993.

Concerts   A Vivaldi festival is held in September; concerts of classical and contemporary music are performed in the city's theaters and churches throughout the year. Watch for posters, or check with the Venice tourist information office at Piazza San Marco. The **Kele e Teo Agency** (San Marco 4930, tel. 041/520–8722) handles tickets for many musical events.

Opera and Ballet   **Teatro La Fenice,** on Campo San Fantin, is one of Italy's oldest opera houses. The opera season lasts from December to May or June. Concerts, ballets, and other musical events are held there throughout the year, except in August. For programs and tickets, write Biglietteria, Teatro La Fenice, Campo San Fantin, 30121 Venice, or call 041/521–0161, fax 041/522–1768. Tickets for opera performances go on sale at the box office about one month in advance. The box office is open Monday–Saturday 9:30–12:30, 4–6. If there is a performance on Sunday, the box office remains open, closing on Monday instead.

Nightlife

Except for the scene at Piazza San Marco in fair weather, when the cafés stay open late and the square is a meeting place for visitors and Venetians, there's practically no nightlife in Venice.

Bars and Nightclubs   The **Martini Scala Club** is an elegant piano bar with restaurant. *Calle delle Veste (Campo San Fantin), tel. 041/522–4121. Open Wed.–Mon. 8 PM (10 PM in summer)–3:30 AM.*

The top hotel bars stay open late if the customers want to linger. **Ai Speci** (Calle degli Specchieri 648, tel. 041/520–9088) is an American-style bar with a relaxing, intimate atmosphere.

One of the most popular meeting places for young Venetians is **Paradiso Perduto** (Fondamenta Misericordia 2540, Cannaregio, tel. 041/720581), which serves good pizzas and other hot dishes, at low prices, and has live music on Monday night. It's usually open until 1 AM or later.

Casino   The city-operated gambling casino is open April–September in a modern building on the Lido (Lungomare Marconi 4, tel. 041/529–7111) and in the beautiful Palazzo Vendramin Calergi (same phone) on the Grand Canal during the other months. Both are open daily 3 PM–about 4:30 AM.

Discos The disco scene is dismal. **El Souk,** near the Accademia, gets a fairly sophisticated young crowd. *Calle Contarini 1056a, tel. 041/520–0371. Open daily 10PM–3AM.*

7 The Venetian Arc

Verona to Trieste

The Venetian Arc encompasses the coastal crescent and inland plain that stretches from the mouths of the Rivers Po and Adige on the west along the Gulf of Venice to Trieste and the Slovenian border on the east. It is mainly flat green farmland spotted with low hills that swell and rise steeply inland in a succession of plateaus and high meadows to the snow-tipped Alps. The entire area basks in the reflected splendor of Venice, its long-time ruler, and is studded with some of Italy's most interesting cities. All of them came under Venice's domination at one time or another, and Venetian influence is evident in their art and architecture, though there's a touch of German *gemütlichkeit* (congeniality) in the mountain towns, and there are stately shades of Hapsburg grandeur in cosmopolitan Trieste.

Much of the pleasure of exploring this area comes from discovering the individual differences, the variations on an overall Venetian theme, that confer special charm on each of the towns you'll visit. Some, such as Verona, Treviso, and Udine, have a solid medieval look; Asolo has an idyllic setting; Bassano combines a bit of both these qualities. If you're interested in architecture, you'll seek out the scores of villas built by Venetian aristocrats on their country estates. Several of these were designed by the architect Andrea Palladio (1508–80), and some were decorated with frescoes by Tiepolo or Veronese. If you are a confirmed or fledgling oenophile, you'll enjoy tasting local wines within view of the vineyards that produce some of the best-known Italian vintages—among them, Soave, Valpolicella, Bardolino, and Prosecco. You'll find art everywhere, from Giotto's frescoes in Padua and the great Venetian masters in Verona to single, perfect gems such as Giorgione's solemn altarpiece in Castelfranco, and Veronese's lighthearted frescoes in Villa Barbaro at Maser.

Essential Information

Important Addresses and Numbers

Tourist Information
Padua (Stazione Ferrovie [Train Station], tel. 049/875–2077). Treviso (Via Toniolo 41, tel. 0422/547632). Trieste (Stazione Centrale, tel. 040/420182). Udine (Piazza Primo Maggio 6, tel. 0432/295972). Verona (Via Dietro Anfiteatro 6, tel. 045/592828; Piazza Erbe 42, tel. 045/803–0086). Vicenza (Piazza Matteotti, tel. 0444/320854; Piazza Duomo 5, tel. 0444/544122).

Emergencies
Police, Ambulance, Fire, tel. 113. This number will also put you in touch with the First Aid Service (Pronto Soccorso).

Doctors and Dentists. Telephone 112, or go to the Ospedale Civile e Policlinico dell'Universita, Padua, tel. 049/821–1111.

Late-Night Pharmacies. Pharmacies take turns staying open late and on Sundays. For up-to-date information on which pharmacy is open, call 192.

Travel Agencies
The largest area offices of American Express and WagonsLits are located in Venice (*see* Essential Information in Chapter 6). Local offices in the Venetian Arc include the following:

Padua (American Express, Via Risorgimento 20, tel. 049/666133).

Trieste (Paterniti Viaggi [American Express representative], Corso Cavour 7, tel. 040/65222).

Car Rentals **Padua.** *Avis* (Piazza Stazione 1, tel. 049/664198); *Hertz* (Piazza Stazione 5, tel. 049/657877).

Trieste. *Avis* (Via San Nicolo 12, tel. 040/68243); *Hertz* (Via Mazzini 1, tel. 040/60650).

Udine. *Avis* (Via Europa Unita 23, tel. 0432/22149); *Hertz* (Via Europa Unita 127, tel. 0432/293033).

Verona. *Avis* (Stazione FS [Train Station], tel. 045/26636); *Hertz* (Stazione FS, tel. 045/25832).

Getting Around

By Plane The main airport serving the Venetian Arc is **Marco Polo** in Venice (*see* Essential Information in Chapter 6), which handles international and most domestic flights to the region. Two other airports serve domestic routes. **Ronchi dei Legionari** airport, 35 kilometers (21 miles) north of Trieste, is linked with Via Miramare in the center of town by a regular bus service. **Villafranca** airport, 11 kilometers (7 miles) west of Verona, is connected with Porta Nuova train station by regular bus service. Charter flights also land at **Treviso** airport (about 20 miles north of Venice).

By Car The main highway in the region is A4, which connects Verona, Padua, and Venice with Trieste. The distance from Verona, in the west, to Trieste is 263 kilometers (163 miles). Branches link A4 with Treviso (A27), Pordenone (A28), and Udine (A23).

By Train The main lines from Milan (via Verona and Vicenza) and from Rome (via Florence and Bologna) meet at Padua, where cars for Venice are shunted off if the train is to continue to Treviso and Gorizia or to Trieste. From Venice, it's about 20 minutes by train to Padua, about two hours to Trieste, and 1½ hours to Verona.

By Bus An efficient bus network serves the smaller centers, and frequent buses for Padua and Treviso leave Venice's bus terminal at Piazzale Roma.

Guided Tours

Orientation Many of the best tours begin and end in Venice because so much of the region is accessible from there. For Venice addresses of operators, *see* Essential Information in Chapter 6. **American Express** and other agencies offer half-day guided tours by air-conditioned bus to some Venetian villas and Padua. The **Burchiello excursion boat** makes an all-day tour along the Brenta Canal, including lunch and visits to several villas. The American Express office suggests itineraries for individual tours of the Veneto region by rented car. You may opt to tour with or without a driver.

Special-Interest Throughout the region, local tourist information offices propose individual wine itineraries. One such itinerary winds through the vineyards where Prosecco and Cartizze wines are produced, between Conegliano and Valdobbiadene: This 50-kilometer (30-mile) route can easily be covered in a day. For information, inquire at the Treviso Information Office (*see* Tourist Information, *above*).

Exploring the Venetian Arc

This exploring section covers the broad Adriatic sweep of the Venetian Arc from west to east, beginning at Venice. Many of the first towns visited can be seen on one- or two-day excursions from Venice itself, although it is far better to give yourself time to appreciate the more remote spots by planning a few overnight stops en route.

The first three tours head westward, in the direction of the ancient university city of Padua, Palladio's Vicenza, and the Roman city of Verona. Tour 4 goes northeast into the foothills of the Alps and the Dolomites, where market towns cling to steep hillsides and streams rage down from the mountains. Moving farther east and then southeast, Tour 5 passes the medieval trading city of Udine before continuing on into Trieste, formerly the principal port of the Hapsburg Empire and still very much a multicultural city. Trieste is Italy's easternmost outpost, bordered on three sides by Slovenia and the Adriatic, with only a narrow strip of Italian territory connecting it with the rest of the country.

Highlights for First-time Visitors

Arena di Verona (Tour 3: Verona).
Asolo (Tour 4: High Road to Treviso).
Bassano del Grappa (Tour 4: High Road to Treviso).
Cappella degli Scrovegni (Tour 1: Villa Pisani and Padua).
Castello di San Giusto (Tour 5: East to Trieste).
La Rotonda (Tour 2: Palladian Vicenza).
Miramare Castle (Tour 5: East to Trieste).
Strada del Vino Rosso (Tour 4: High Road to Treviso).
Teatro Olimpico (Tour 2: Palladian Vicenza).
Villa Pisani (Tour 1: Villa Pisani and Padua).

Tour 1: Villa Pisani and Padua

Numbers in the margin correspond to points of interest on the Venetian Arc map.

❶ About 30 kilometers (20 miles) west of Venice, along the A4, **Villa Pisani** (or Villa Nazionale), in Strà, is typical of the stately residences built for wealthy Venetians on their country estates. An imposing 18th-century edifice, it once belonged to Napoleon, who appreciated the similarities with Versailles. See the grandiose frescoes by Giambattista Tiepolo on the ceiling of the ballroom and explore the park; also climb to the top of the little tower for a good look at the maze. *Admission: 6,000 lire. Open Tues.–Sun. 9–1:30.*

❷ Only 7 kilometers (4 miles) beyond is **Padua** (Padova in Italian), well worth a one-day stopover. It's a bustling city with a medieval nucleus, the seat of a famous university founded in 1222, but now surrounded by unattractive modern business districts. Pick up a map and brochures at the tourist office in the train

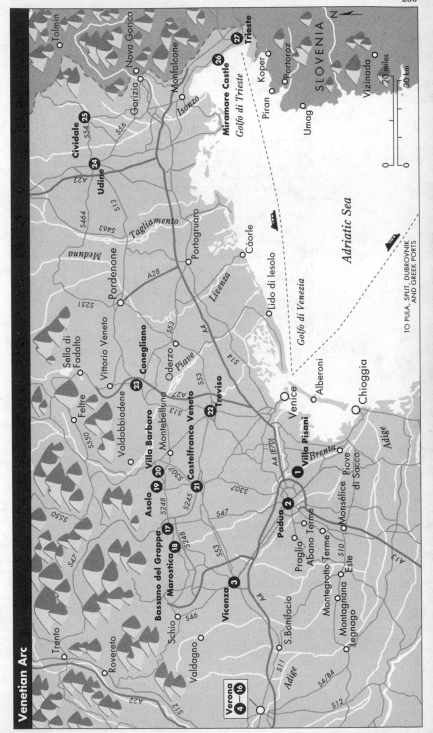

Venetian Arc

station and head straight down **Corso del Popolo,** which changes its name to Corso Garibaldi about 400 yards on, when it crosses the Bacchiglione River.

To the left just across the river is **Cappella degli Scrovegni** (Scrovegni Chapel), built in the 13th century near the site of an ancient Roman arena. The chapel was erected by a wealthy Paduan, Enrico Scrovegni, in honor of his deceased father. Scrovegni called on Giotto to decorate its interior, a task that occupied the great artist and his helpers from 1303 to 1305. They created a magnificent fresco cycle, arranged in typical medieval comic-strip fashion, illustrating the lives of Mary and Christ. The frescoes were freshly restored in 1991. *Corso Garibaldi, tel. 049/875–1153. Admission: 5,000 lire includes admission to Musco Civico degli Eremitani, tel. 049/875–2321 (see below).* Both open Apr.–Sept., Tues.–Sun. 9–7; Oct.–Mar. 9–5:30.

Turn left from the chapel entrance and cross the gardens that now occupy the area of the original Roman arena to reach Piazza Eremitani and the 13th-century church of the **Eremitani.** It contains some fragments of frescoes by Andrea Mantegna (1431–1506), the brilliant locally born artist whose masterpieces are in nearby Mantua: Most of these frescoes, however, were destroyed in the Allied bombing of 1944. The **Museo Civico** (Civic Museum) here has its quota of works by Venetian masters. A small road leads diagonally left from the church back to Corso Garibaldi.

Time Out   About a quarter-mile farther along Corso Garibaldi is the **Caffè Pedrocchi** (Piazzetta Pedrocchi), a monumental 19th-century neoclassical coffeehouse that looks like a cross between a museum and a stage set. You couldn't ask for a more impressive place to have a cappuccino.

Just to the left, on a side street leading off the other side of the Corso, is the 16th-century **University** building. This is worth a visit to see the exquisite and perfectly proportioned anatomy theater and a hall harboring a lectern used by Galileo. *Via VIII Febbraio. Admission free. Guided visits only. Scheduled to reopen in 1993 after restorations.*

The **Municipio** (city hall) faces the University from the Caffè Pedrocchi side of the Corso. Behind it are three adjacent historic squares that form the heart of the city and are constantly crisscrossed by students on bicycles. In the largest square, scene of the city's outdoor market in the morning, is **Palazzo della Ragione** (also called **Il Salone**), which was built in the Middle Ages as seat of Padua's parliament. Today its street-level arcades shelter shops and cafés. In the frescoed Great Hall on the upper level is an enormous wooden horse, a 15th-century replica of the bronze steed in Donatello's equestrian statue of Gattamelata (*see* below). The hall is often used for exhibitions, and on those occasions is open to the public.

Take a look at the 15th- and 16th-century buildings on Piazza dei Signori and the cathedral a few steps away. Then return to the University and take the second street east of the Corso— via del Santo—south to the huge basilica of **Sant'Antonio,** one of Padua's major attractions. Standing in front of the church is Donatello's powerful statue of the *condottiere* (mercenary general) Gattamelata, which was cast in bronze—that alone was a monumental technical achievement—in about 1450 and was to have an enormous influence on the development of Italian Renaissance sculpture. A cluster of Byzantine domes and slender, minaretlike towers gives the church an Oriental look, reminiscent of San Marco in Venice. The interior is sumptuous, too, with marble reliefs by Tullio Lombardo, the greatest in a talented family of marble carvers who decorated many churches in the area—among them, Santa Maria dei Miracoli in Venice. The artistic highlights here, however, all bear Donatello's name; the 15th-century Florentine master did the remarkable series of bronze reliefs illustrating the life of Saint Anthony, as well as the bronze statues of the Madonna and saints on the high altar.

Saint Anthony's feast day, June 13, brings pilgrims from all parts of Italy and Europe to Padua.

Take a left outside the museum and walk along Via Belludi to **Prato della Valle,** an unusual and attractive piazza laid out in 1775, with a wooded oval park at the center, surrounded by a canal. At the southeast end of this immense square is the church of **Santa Giustina,** with finely inlaid choir stalls and Veronese's colossal altarpiece, *The Martyrdom of St. Justine.*

Tour 2: Palladian Vicenza

Another 32 kilometers (20 miles) west of Padua by rail or autostrada is **Vicenza,** the city that bears the distinctive signature of the 16th-century architect Andrea Palladio. The architect, whose name is the basis of the term "Palladian," gracefully incorporated elements of classical architecture—columns, porticoes, and domes—into a style that reflected the Renaissance celebration of order and harmony. His elegant villas and palaces were influential in propagating classical architecture in Europe, especially Britain, and later in America. (Thomas Jefferson's Monticello is an homage to the master.)

In the mid-16th century Palladio was given the opportunity to rebuild much of Vicenza, which had suffered great damage during the bloody wars waged against Venice by the League of Cambrai, an alliance of the Papacy, France, the Holy Roman Empire, and several neighboring city-states. He imposed upon the city a number of his grand Roman-style buildings—rather an overstatement, considering the town's status. With the Basilica, begun in 1549 in the very heart of Vicenza, he ensured his reputation and embarked on a series of lordly buildings, all of which proclaim the same rigorously classical harmony and elegance.

From the train or bus station, Viale Roma leads straight north to Porta Castello, a gateway through a fragment of the old city wall and the starting point of the broad main avenue of Vicenza, **Corso Palladio.** Before strolling down the Corso, however, you may want to turn right just past the gate, go one block south, and turn left to see the Gothic **Duomo,** which contains a gleaming altarpiece by Lorenzo Veneziano, a 14th-century Venetian painter.

Corso Palladio is a memorable avenue, lined with a succession of imposing palaces and churches that run the gamut from Venetian Gothic to Baroque, including the striking **Palazzo del Comune,** about halfway along. Make a side trip left down Contrà Porti for a look at other splendid palaces and, back on Corso Palladio, stop in at the church of **Santa Corona** to see the exceptionally fine *Baptism of Christ* (1500) by Giovanni Bellini over the altar on the left just in front of the transept. **Palazzo Chiericati,** on a square at the end of the Corso, is an exquisite and unmistakably Palladian building. The palace houses the **Museo Civico,** with a representative collection of Venetian paintings. *Piazza Matteotti, tel. 0444/321348. Admission: 5,000 lire, including admission to Teatro Olimpico (see below). Open Tues.–Sat. 9:30–noon, 2:30–5; Sun. 10–noon.*

On the other side of the square is the **Teatro Olimpico,** Palladio's last, and perhaps finest, work. Based closely on the model of the ancient Roman theater, it represents an important development in theater and stage design and is noteworthy for its acoustics and the cunningly devised false perspective of a classical street in the permanent backdrop. *Piazza Matteotti, tel. 0444/323781. Admission: 5,000 lire. Open Mar. 16–Oct. 15, Mon.–Sat. 9:30–12:30, 3–5:30, Sun. 9:30–noon; Oct. 16–Mar. 15, Mon.–Sat. 9:30–noon, 2–4:30, Sun. 9:30–noon.*

Retrace your steps along Corso Palladio and, halfway back, turn left onto the elongated **Piazza dei Signori,** the heart of the city. This is the site of Palladio's **Basilica,** a confusing name not for a church but for a courthouse, the Palazzo della Ragione. Almost as remarkable as the graceful two-story galleries on the exterior is the skill with which the architect wedded his exterior structure to an already existing Gothic one. He also designed, but never completed, the **Loggia del Capitaniato,** opposite.

Time Out **Gran Caffè Garibaldi** is a classic coffeehouse with a good restaurant upstairs. It looks out on the Basilica. *Piazza dei Signori 5. Closed Tues. evening, Wed.*

Two of the most interesting villas of the Veneto region are a little more than a mile from the center of Vicenza, on the Este road to the southeast. You can walk to both, but it is easier to take the No. 8 bus from Corso Palladio to the Via San Bastiano bus stop. From the bus stop you climb gently a quarter-mile until you reach **Villa Valmarana dei Nani,** an 18th-century country house decorated with a series of marvelous frescoes by Giambattista Tiepolo: These are fantastic visions of a mythological world. The guest house holds more frescoes, these by Tiepolo's son, Gian Domenico. *Via San Bastiano 8, tel. 0444/321803. Admission: 5,000 lire. Open Mar.–Sept., Wed. and Thurs., weekends 10–noon; Tues.–Sat. 3–6 (Tues.–Sat. 2:30–5:30 Mar.–Apr.).*

From Villa Valmarana, continue along Via San Bastiano (which narrows to the size of a path) for a few hundred yards to reach **La Rotonda,** the most famous Palladian villa of all. Serene and symmetrical, it was the model for Jefferson's Monticello. Take the time to admire it from all sides, and you'll see that it was the inspiration not just for Monticello, but for nearly every state capital in the United States. The interior is a bit of a disappointment, but that's not why you came here anyway. *Via della Rotonda 33, tel. 0444/321793. Admission: to grounds, 3,000 lire; to interior, 5,000 lire. Open Mar. 15–Oct. 15. Grounds open Tues.–Thurs. 10–noon, 3–6; interior open Wed. 10–noon, 3–6.*

Tour 3: Verona

Only about 60 kilometers (38 miles) from Vicenza on the main
autostrada and rail line is **Verona**. This attractive city, on the
banks of the fast-flowing Adige river, ranks with Venice as a
top attraction in the region and rivals other Italian art cities. It
has considerable charm; classical and medieval monuments; a
picturesque town center where bright geraniums bloom in window boxes; and a romantic reputation, thanks to Shakespeare's
Romeo and Juliet, which is set here. It is one of Italy's most
alluring cities, despite extensive industrialization and urban
development in its newer sections. Inevitably, with its lively
Venetian air, proximity to Lake Garda, and renowned summer
opera season, it attracts hordes of tourists, especially vacationing Germans and Austrians, who drive through the Brenner
Pass just to the north.

Verona grew to power and prosperity within the Roman Empire as a result of its key commercial and military position in
northern Italy. After the fall of the Empire, Verona continued
to flourish, under the guidance of Barbarian kings such as Theodoric, Alboin, Pepin, and Berenger I, reaching its cultural and
artistic peak in the 13th and 14th centuries, under the Della
Scala dynasty. (You'll see the *scala*, or ladder, emblem all over
town.) In 1404, however, Verona traded its independence for
security and placed itself under the control of Venice. (The
other recurring architectural motif is the lion of Saint Mark,
symbol of allegiance to Venice.) Verona remained under Venetian protection until 1797, when Napoleon invaded. In 1814 the
entire region of Venetia was won by the Austrians, and it was
finally united with the rest of Italy in 1866.

*Numbers in the margin correspond to points of interest on the
Verona map.*

The obvious place to start your visit is at **Piazza Brà**, the vast
and airy square at the center of the city, where the **Arena di Verona** is located. Built by the Romans in the 1st century AD, it is
one of the largest and best preserved Roman amphitheaters
anywhere. Only four arches remain of the outer rings, but the
main structure is so complete that it takes little imagination to
picture it as the site of the cruel deaths of countless gladiators,
wild beasts, and Christians. Today, it hosts Verona's summer
opera, famous for spectacular productions and audiences of as
many as 25,000. An informal, picnicky spirit adds to the fun.
The best operas to see here are the big splashy ones that demand huge choruses, "Cinerama" sets, lots of color and movement, and, if possible, camels, horses, and/or elephants. The
music can be excellent, and the acoustics are fine, too. If you go,
be sure to bring or rent a cushion—four hours on 2,000-year-
old marble can be an ordeal (*see* The Arts and Nightlife, *below*).
*Arena di Verona 045/590109. Admission: 6,000 lire. Open
Apr.–Sept., Tues.–Sun. 8–6:30; Oct.–Mar., Tues.–Sun. 8–
5:30. Closed occasionally for rehearsals during July and Aug.*

Via Mazzini, an old and fashionable thoroughfare, leads off Piazza Brà to **Piazza delle Erbe** (Vegetable Market Square), site
of the ancient Roman forum and today a colorful market in the
morning, when huge rectangular umbrellas are raised to shade
the neat ranks of fruits and vegetables. Off Piazza delle Erbe is
Piazza dei Signori, enclosed on all sides by stately public buildings. The 12th-century **Palazzo della Ragione** has a somber-

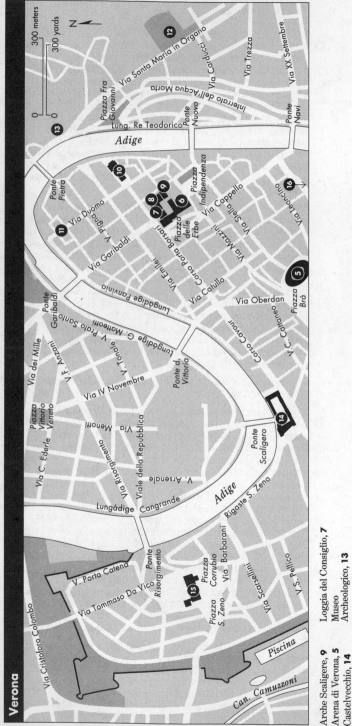

Verona

Arche Scaligere, **9**
Arena di Verona, **5**
Castelvecchio, **14**
Duomo, **11**
Giusti Gardens, **12**
Juliet's Tomb, **16**

Loggia del Consiglio, **7**
Museo
Archeologico, **13**
Palazzo del Governo, **8**
Palazzo della
Ragione, **6**
San Zeno Maggiore, **15**
Sant' Anastasia, **10**

looking courtyard, Gothic staircase, and medieval tower. Op-
7 posite is the graceful **Loggia del Consiglio,** built in the 12th
century to house city council meetings. At the end of the
8 square is **Palazzo del Governo,** the medieval stronghold from
which the Della Scalas ruled Verona with an iron fist.

9 Just off this end of the square are the **Arche Scaligere,** the magnificent Gothic tombs of the Della Scalas, behind a 14th-cen-
tury wrought-iron fence bearing the family's ladder emblem.
The tomb over the door of the church is the resting place of
Cangrande I, protector of Dante and patron of the arts; the
equestrian statue is a copy of the one on view at the Castelvecchio Museum (*see* below). In the same neighborhood are the
10 11 Gothic church of **Sant'Anastasia** and the Romanesque **Duomo**
(Cathedral). The square by Sant' Anastasia leads onto a shady
riverside walkway along the swift-flowing but shallow Adige,
which always has a refreshingly cool breeze blowing from it,
thanks to its origins in the Alpine glaciers.

12 Cross the Adige at Ponte Nuovo to see the **Giusti Gardens,** laid
out on several levels around a 16th-century villa. There's a formal Italian garden, an 18th-century maze, and a fine view of the
city from the terrace, from which Johann von Goethe, the
German poet and dramatist, drew inspiration. *Via Santa Maria in Organo. Admission: 5,000 lire. Open daily 9–sunset.*

Time Out **Cacciatore,** in the Piazza Isolo section at this end of Ponte
Nuovo, is one of Verona's historic *osterie* (wine shops). The fine
local wines are still a big draw for habitués, but some inexpensive dishes are also available. *Via Seminario 4. Closed Sun.*

On the same bank of the river, you can also get some good views
13 from the terraces of the **Museo Archeologico,** located in an old
monastery above the Roman Theater, which was built in the
same era as the arena. The Roman Theater is in the museum
grounds and is sometimes used for dramatic productions.
*Rigaste del Redentore, tel. 045/33974. Admission: 5,000 lire.
Open Apr.–Sept., Tues.–Sun. 8–6:45; Oct.–Mar., Tues.–Sun.
8–1:30.*

Cross the Adige on Ponte Pietra and head for Corso Porta
Borsari. It begins right by Sant'Anastasia and becomes Corso
Cavour, which is lined with attractive old buildings and palaces
14 and leads to **Castelvecchio,** a 14th-century castle built for
Cangrande II Della Scala. A crenellated building in russet
brick with massive walls, towers, turrets, and a vast courtyard, it looks like a fairy-tale castle guarding a bridge across
the Adige. Inside is the **Museo Civico,** which gives you a good
look at the castle's vaulted halls and the treasures of Venetian
painting and sculpture that they contain. *Corso Cavour, tel.
045/8005157. Admission: 5,000 lire. Open Tues.–Sun. 8–6:45;
hours and admission cost may change when museum houses
temporary exhibitions.*

From the castle it's a short walk upstream along Rigaste San
Zeno and Via Barbarani to one of Italy's finest Romanesque
15 churches, **San Zeno Maggiore.** It's set between two medieval
bell towers and has a 13th-century rose window and 12th-centu-
ry portal. Inside, look for Mantegna's *Madonna* over the main
altar; there's a peaceful cloister off the left nave.

Romantic souls may want to see what the astute tourist office
16 says is **Juliet's Tomb,** on the other side of the old town; it's a
pretty spot, though hardly a major attraction in this city of
world-class monuments. Authentic or not, it is still popular
with lovesick Italian teenagers, who leave notes for the tragic
lover. *Via del Pontiere. Admission: 5,000 lire. Open Tues.–
Sun. 8–6:45.*

Tour 4: High Road to Treviso

*Numbers in the margin correspond to points of interest on the
Venetian Arc map.*

If you're coming from Venice or Padua, take S47 north from the
A4 for 37 kilometers (22 miles); from Vicenza, take S248 north-
17 east into the foothills of the Alps, toward **Bassano del Grappa,** a
beautifully located town directly above the swift-flowing waters of the Brenta River at the foot of the Mount Grappa massif
(5,880 feet). Bassano's old streets are lined with low buildings
sporting wooden balconies and eye-catching flowerpots. Bright
ceramic wares produced here and in nearby Nove are displayed
in shops along byways that curve uphill toward a centuries-old
square, and, even higher, to a belvedere with a good view of
Mount Grappa and the beginning of the Valsugana valley.

Bassano's most famous landmark is the covered bridge that has
spanned the Brenta since the 13th century. Floods are frequent, and the bridge has been rebuilt countless times. The
present-day bridge is a postwar reconstruction using Andrea
Palladio's 16th-century design. The great architect astutely
chose to use wood as his medium, knowing that it could be replaced quickly and cheaply. The bridge still displays his devo-
tion to balance, harmony, and simplicity. Almost as famous is
the characteristic Nardini liquor shop at one end of the bridge;
it's redolent of the grappa that has been distilled here for more
than a century. Stop in for a sniff or a snifter.

A side trip of only 7 kilometers (4 miles) west takes you to
18 **Marostica,** where a castle on the hillside overlooks the town.
The main square is paved in checkerboard fashion, and a game
of chess is acted out here by people in medieval costume on the
second weekend in September in even-numbered years.

The most romantic and charming of the towns in the vicinity is
19 **Asolo,** 11 kilometers (7 miles) east of Bassano along S248. This
hillside hamlet was the consolation prize of an exiled queen. At
the end of the 15th century, Venetian-born Caterina Cornaro
was sent here by Venice's doges to keep her from interfering
with their administration of her former kingdom of Cyprus,
which she had inherited. To soothe the pain of exile, she established a lively and brilliant court in Asolo. Over the centuries,
Venetian aristocrats continued to build gracious villas on the
hillside, and in the 19th century Asolo once again became the
idyllic haunt of musicians, poets, and painters. In the center of
town you can explore Piazza Maggiore, with its Renaissance
palaces and turn-of-the-century cafés, and then continue uphill, past Caterina's ruined castle and some Gothic-style
houses, to the Roman fortress that stands on the summit. Other walks will take you past the villas once inhabited by Robert
Browning and the actress Eleanora Duse. Be warned that
Asolo's dreamy Old World atmosphere disappears on holiday
weekends when the crowds pour in.

⑳ Seven kilometers (4 miles) northeast of Asolo, in Maser, is **Villa Barbaro,** a gracious Renaissance creation, the work of Palladio. Easy to reach by car, it's also accessible by bus from Bassano. The fully furnished villa is still inhabited by its owners, who make you slip heavy felt scuffs over your shoes to protect the highly polished floors. The elaborate stuccos and opulent frescoes by Paolo Veronese bring the 16th century to life. This Venetian villa is worth going out of your way to see. *Admission: 5,000 lire. Open Apr.–Sept., Tues., weekends 3–6; Oct.–Mar., Tues., weekends 3–5. Closed Nov.–Dec. 8, Dec. 23–Jan. 6.*

On your way to Treviso, you can make a slight detour south
㉑ down S307 to see **Castelfranco Veneto,** girdled by crenellated walls and a moat. There's a superb Giorgione *Madonna* in the cathedral. *Open daily 8–noon, 4–7.*

㉒ Only 30 kilometers (20 miles) north of Venice, **Treviso** acts as an attractive gateway to the Italian mainland. It has arcaded streets, frescoed houses, and channeled streams that run through the center of town. You can explore Treviso on foot in half a day; its restaurants are good places to stop for lunch. The most important church here is **San Nicolò,** on Via San Nicolò, a few blocks north and across the river from the train station. An impressive Gothic building with an interesting vaulted ceiling, San Nicolò has frescoes of the saints by 14th-century artist Tommaso da Modena on the columns. But the best is yet to come: In the chapter house of the seminary next door is a remarkable series of 40 portraits of Dominican friars by the same artist. They are astoundingly realistic, considering that some were painted as early as 1352. *Via San Nicolò. For admission, inquire at the custodian's desk at the seminary entrance.*

As you explore the town, you'll see lots of old houses with decorated facades, many of them built in the 15th century. Go left from the front of the Seminary a quarter-mile to the **Duomo** (Cathedral). Inside, on the altar of one of the chapels to the right, is an *Annunciation* by Titian. Running alongside the cathedral are Via Canova and Via Calmaggiore, lined with some well-preserved medieval buildings. Via Calmaggiore leads to **Piazza dei Signori,** the heart of medieval Treviso and still the town's social center, with outdoor cafés and some impressive public buildings facing it. One of these, the Palazzo di Trecento, has a small alley leading behind it. Follow the alley for about 200 yards, to the **Pescheria** (Fish Market), on an island in one of the small rivers that flow through town.

㉓ A 23-kilometer (14-mile) drive north on S13 takes you to **Conegliano,** in the heart of wine-producing country. Conegliano itself is attractive, with Venetian-style villas and frescoed houses, but the real attraction is the wine. Well-marked and leading southeast from Conegliano, the **Strada del Vino Rosso** (Red Wine Road) winds its way through Cabernet and Merlot country. The road leads down along the Piave River, and there are dozens of places to stop, sample, and buy the red—and some rosé—wines. The wine road ends at **Oderzo,** where S53 takes you to the main east–west route for the Venetian Arc, A4.

Tour 5: East to Trieste

About 100 kilometers (65 miles) east of Venice on the A4, take A23 north for 18 kilometers (10 miles) to reach the city of
㉔ **Udine,** which commands a view of the surrounding plain and the

Alpine foothills. Legend has it that Udine stands on a mound erected by Attila the Hun so he could watch the burning of the important Roman center of Aquileia to the south. Udine flourished in the Middle Ages, thanks to its good location for trade routes, and the rights it gained from the local patriarch to hold regular markets. There is a distinct Venetian feel to the city, noticeable in the architecture of the Piazza della Libertà, under the stern gaze of the lion of St. Mark, symbol of Venetian power.

㉕ Take a 17-kilometer (9-mile) excursion east along Route 54 to **Cividale,** a city that dates from the time of Julius Caesar. It is popularly supposed (particularly by locals) that Cividale was built by Caesar when he was commander of Roman legions in the area. The city straddles the river Natisone and contains many examples of Venetian Gothic buildings, particularly the **Duomo** (Cathedral) and the **Palazzo Comunale.**

The **Museo Archeologico Nazionale** is the best place to trace the history of the area and the importance of Cividale and Udine in the formative period following the collapse of the Roman Empire. Among the interesting exhibits is a large collection of Lombard artifacts, including weapons, jewelry, and domestic wares from this warrior race that swept into what is now Italy in the 6th century. *Piazza del Duomo. Admission: 5,000 lire. Open Tues.–Sat. 9–1:30, Sun. 9–12:30. Closed Mon.*

Time Out Stop for a moderately priced lunch of local favorites, especially mushrooms and game. **Al Fortino** is located in an old castle with vaulted ceilings and an open hearth. *Via Carlo Alberto 46. Closed Tues., Jan. 1–15, Aug.*

You'll have to backtrack through Udine to get back to A4 for the rest of the trip eastward to Trieste. The road follows the coast and is under the shadow of the huge geological formation called the Karso, a large, barren expanse of limestone that forms a giant ledge, most of which is across the border in Slovenia. Italian territory goes only a few miles inland in this strip, and Italy's small Slovenian minority ekes out an agricultural existence in the region, which has changed hands countless times since the final days of Imperial Rome.

㉖ Little more than 7 kilometers (4 miles) before Trieste, at the eastern end of the Venetian Arc, is **Miramare Castle,** a 19th-century extravaganza in white stone, built on the seafront for the Archduke Maximilian of Hapsburg (brother of Emperor Franz Josef). Maximilian spent a brief, happy time here until Napoleon III of France took Trieste from the Hapsburgs and sent the poor archduke packing. He was given the title of Emperor of Mexico in 1864 as a compensation, but met his death before a Mexican firing squad in 1867. You can visit the lush grounds and admire the memorable views over the Adriatic. *Admission: 5,000 lire; guided tour of castle costs another 1,500 lire. Grounds open daily 9–one hour before sunset. Castle open weekdays 9–1:30, weekends 9–12:30.*

㉗ Surrounded by rugged countryside and beautiful coastline, **Trieste** is built on a hillside above what was once the chief port of the Austro-Hungarian Hapsburg Empire. Typical of Trieste are its turn-of-the-century cafés, much like Vienna's coffeehouses; these are social and cultural centers of the city.

The sidewalk cafés on the vast seaside Piazza dell' Unità d'Italia are the popular meeting places in the summer months. The square is similar to Piazzetta San Marco in Venice; both are focal points of architectural interest that command the best views of the sea. The Palazzo Comunale (Town Hall) is at the end of the square, away from the sea; behind it, steps lead uphill, following the pattern of upward expansion of the city from its roots as a coastal fishing port in Roman times. About a hundred yards beyond Palazzo Comunale, you pass two churches in dramatically different styles. The first, **San Silvestro,** is a solid Romanesque construction dating to the 11th century; just beyond it is the Baroque extravagance of **Santa Maria Maggiore,** which backs onto a network of yet more alleys (closed to traffic) heading farther up the hill.

At the top is the **Cattedrale di San Giusto,** a 14th-century church that incorporates two much older churches, one dating as far back as the 5th century. The exterior adds even more to the jumble of styles involved by using fragments of Roman tombs and temples: You can see these most clearly on the pillars of the main doorway. The highlights of the interior are the mosaics and frescoes dating back to the 13th century.

Some of the best views from the hilltop are from the **Castello di San Giusto,** which is next to the church. This 15th-century castle was built by the Venetians, who always had an eye for the best vantage point in the cities they conquered or controlled. The Hapsburgs, subsequent rulers of Trieste, enlarged it to its present size. Some of the best exhibits in the Castle **Museum** are the displays of weaponry and armor. *Piazza Cattedrale 3. Admission: 2,000 lire. Open Tues.–Sun. 9–12:45.*

Time Out Two vaulted halls within the castle walls are occupied by the **Bottega del Vino,** which has a separate entrance, so it is open much later than those of the castle. It is open only in the evening, from about 6 PM. For supper, try the gnocchi with porcini mushrooms while sitting on a terrace overlooking the bay. *Piazza Cattedrale 3. Closed Tues. and Jan.*

Return downward to the port, along Via della Cattedrale, passing the **Arco di Riccardo,** a 1st-century AD Roman arch honoring Augustus. Retrace your steps toward Piazza dell' Unità d'Italia, but just before you reach it, turn right to the **Piazza della Borsa,** the square containing Trieste's original stock exchange, the **Borsa Vecchia,** a neoclassical building now serving as the chamber of commerce. The statue of Leopold I, at one end of the Piazza, marks the beginning of **Corso Italia,** the busy shopping street of Trieste. As you walk along this main street, you'll notice an international variety of shops and goods. This reflects not just the varied series of rulers who have presided over this important port, but also the fact that many of the present-day shoppers in Trieste are visitors from what used to be Yugoslavia—Slovenes, Croats, Serbs—intent on stocking up on Western consumer goods. A Slav buying American records from an Italian in a city once ruled by Austrians and Hungarians seems a fitting scenario for this city, which wears its internationalism comfortably.

What to See and Do with Children

The Venetian Arc bears the distinct stamp of culture—or, in the case of Trieste, cultures—so it would be a shame not to combine a little learning with the pleasures of exploring new places. **La Rotonda** (*see* Tour 2: Palladian Vicenza, *above*) is a unique blend of classical architectural principles and Palladio's Renaissance sensibilities, but for a child it's the prototype of Monticello. Similarly, Palladio's bridge at **Bassano del Grappa** is an example of these same design ideas, but this time given a very practical purpose. And the maze at **Villa Pisani** (*see* Tour 1: Villa Pisani and Padua, *above*) should provide a good energy outlet for youngsters who are surfeited with old masters. The Roman **Arena** in Verona (*see* Tour 3: Verona, *above*) evokes the era of gladiators; children who like medieval castles will enjoy visits to **Castelvecchio** in Verona (*see* Tour 3: Verona, *above*) and **Castello di San Giusto** in Trieste (*see* Tour 5: East to Trieste, *above*).

Off the Beaten Track

Abano Terme and **Montegrotto Terme.** These two spas, about 12 kilometers (8 miles) south from Padua, are set in the dreamy landscape of the Euganean Hills. Colorful gardens and fresh summer breezes make them havens for those seeking a break from city life.

Montagnana. Take A13 then S10 southwest from Padua 50 kilometers (30 miles) to reach this medieval city. Its surrounding walls are remarkably well preserved, and there are 24 towers, a moat, and four city gates. Its former rivals, Este and Monselice, are only 20 kilometers (12 miles) east on the same road.

Santa Maria in Organo. This medieval church in Verona is on the same road as the Giusti Gardens. Make a point to visit the choir and refectory to see the inlaid-wood masterpieces of the 15th-century monk Fra Giovanni. A series of wood panels depicts varied scenes—local buildings, an idealized Renaissance town, wildlife, and fruit—and the works radiate enthusiasm and a love of life, aided by the artist's eye for detail and his grasp of the latest technique (perspective).

Praglia. This Benedictine monastery, hidden in the hills 12 kilometers (7 miles) southwest of Padua, provides guided tours of its evocative 15th-century halls and cloisters. You can also buy wine and honey produced here by the monks. *Offerings appreciated. Open Tues.–Sun. noon–5. Closed major religious holidays.*

Check locally with the EPT and AAST offices for the opening days of the countless villas in the Venetian Arc. Many are privately owned but are open to the public at certain times or by special request. These gracious country homes give insight into the way wealthy Venetians used to—and still do—vacation.

Shopping

Many of the goods normally associated with Venice are actually produced in the surrounding areas of the Venetian Arc—which means that with a bit of diligence or luck you can pick up a bargain from the source. Mountain towns and villages—Bassano del Grappa is one—have the strongest handicraft tradition, and you can find a wide range of goods in artisans' shops on the side streets. The main towns on the coastal plain are often associated with one or two specialties, either because of traditional skills or because of ancient trading rights that set a pattern of importing specific items from other parts of the Mediterranean.

Flea Markets Verona's **Piazza delle Erbe** market has a changing selection of food, wines, clothing, some antiques, and even pets. (Open daily.)

Padua has three Saturday-only markets featuring a wide range of goods: **Piazza Barbato, Piazza di Brenta,** and **Prato di Valle.** On the second Sunday of every month, there is an antique market in the center of **Asolo**; get there early for any real bargains.

Specialty Stores
Antiques The area around the church of Sant' Anastasia in **Verona** is full of antiques shops, most of them catering to serious collectors.

Ceramics **Bassano del Grappa** and nearby **Nove** are the best bets for ceramic items (*see* Tour 4: High Road to Treviso, *above*).

Jewelry **Vicenza** is one of Italy's leading centers for the production and sale of jewelry. Each year, in January and in June, it plays host to an international trade fair for goldsmiths.

Liqueurs You can buy some of Trieste's famous **Stock** (Via L. Stock 2, tel. 040/7350) liqueur from the headquarters.

Wrought-iron Goods Shops in **Bassano del Grappa** and **Treviso** feature wrought-iron and copper utensils, many of them made on the premises.

Sports

The Adriatic coastline and Alpine foothills provide multiple opportunities for exercise, to burn off those pasta calories. Swimming is possible at most of the ports along the Venetian Arc, but pollution has made the prospect risky at most beaches. Most towns of even moderate size have public swimming pools. Below are some other sporting options.

Golf **Golf Club Condulmer** (Via Zermanese, Treviso, tel. 041/457062); **Padriciano** (Trieste, tel. 040/226159).

Hang Gliding **Scuola Monte Grappa** (Via Ca' Diego, Rosa [5 km, or 3 mi, south of Bassano del Grappa], tel. 0424/848210).

Horseback Riding **Via Libia 30** (Padua, tel. 049/654635); **Lancenigo** (6 km, or 3½ mi, northwest of Treviso, tel. 0422/63357).

Tennis **Via Col Fagheron 24** (Bassano del Grappa, tel. 0424/31853); **Via Col Galliano** (Verona, tel. 045/566372); **Via Monte Zebio 42** (Vicenza, tel. 0444/565547).

Sailing **Club Vela d'Altura** (Via Pigafetta 7, Santa Margherita, Caorle [23 km, or 14 mi, south of A4 from S. Stino], tel. 0421/83346).

Dining and Lodging

Dining In the main cities of the Venetia region, restaurants are in the middle-to-upper ranges of each price category, but in smaller towns and in the countryside you can find some real bargains in comfortable accommodations and good eating. At the eastern end of the Arc, prices are generally lower. Seafood is the specialty along the coast, of course, but inland the cuisine varies from the delicate risotto, radicchio, and asparagus of the Venetia region to the more decisively flavored cooking of the Trieste area, heavily influenced by Austria. San Daniele del Friuli, near Udine, is famous for its delicious prosciutto. Polenta, made of cornmeal, is a staple throughout the area; it is served with thick, rich sauces or grilled as an accompaniment to meat dishes. In Trieste, the city's position near the Austrian and Slovenian borders has fostered a varied—and somewhat heavier—cuisine reflecting the tastes of those countries. The best local wines are Soave, Tocai, Prosecco, Riesling, and Pinot—all white; Bardolino, Valpolicella, Merlot, Cabernet, and Pinot Nero—reds. The Collio designation indicates wines from vineyards in the eastern portion of the Venetian Arc. One of the best known and rarest wines produced here is the Sauterne-like Picolit, made in very limited quantities. Grappa is a locally distilled aquavit.

Category	Cost*
Very Expensive	over 95,000 lire
Expensive	70,000–95,000 lire
Moderate	35,000–70,000 lire
Inexpensive	under 35,000 lire

per person, including house wine, service, and tax

Highly recommended restaurants are indicated by a star ★.

Lodging The area around Venice has been playing host to visitors for centuries, and the result is a range of comfortable accommodations at every price. As with dining, common sense should tell you that the slightly out-of-the-way small hotel will cost you less than its counterpart in a stylish Adriatic resort. Expect to pay more as you approach Venice, since many of the mainland towns absorb the overflow during the times when Venice becomes most crowded, such as Carnival (the two weeks preceding Lent) and throughout the summer.

Category	Cost*
Very Expensive	over 250,000 lire
Expensive	140,000–250,000 lire
Moderate	90,000–140,000 lire
Inexpensive	under 90,000 lire

Prices are for a standard double room for two, including IVA and service.

Highly recommended lodgings are indicated by a star ★.

Asolo **Hosteria Ca'Derton.** The location is an attraction here: Ca'Der-
Dining ton is right on the main square. It has a pleasant, old-fashioned
ambience, with early photos of Asolo on the walls and bouquets
of dried flowers on each table. The friendly proprietor takes
pride in the homemade pasta and desserts and in offering a
good selection of both local and international dishes. *Piazza
D'Annunzio 11, tel. 0423/952730. Reservations advised. Dress:
casual. AE, DC, MC, V. Closed Mon. evening and Tues.; Feb.
15–28, Aug. 17–31. Moderate.*

Lodging **Villa Cipriani.** A distinguished member of the CIGA chain, this
★ historic old villa is set in a romantic garden on the hillside and
surrounded by other gracious country homes. Tastefully furnished with 19th-century antiques, it offers Old World atmosphere, all creature comforts, and attentive service. The
excellent restaurant has a terrace overlooking the garden. *Via
Canova 298, tel. 0423/952166, fax 0432/952095. 31 rooms with
bath or shower. Facilities: garden, garage, restaurant (reservations advised; jacket and tie required). AE, DC, MC, V. Expensive.*

Bassano del **Al Ponte–Da Renzo.** An ample family-run establishment on the
Grappa Brenta River, this popular restaurant has big picture windows
Dining with a vista of the old town and the famed covered bridge. The
tree-shaded garden for outdoor dining has the same view. The
specialty of the house is seafood, with seafood antipasto and
grilled fish fresh from the Adriatic featured on the menu,
where you'll also find regional dishes according to the season.
*Via Volpato 60, tel. 0424/503055. Reservations advised in sum-
mer. Dress: casual. V. Closed Mon. evening, Tues., and all
Jan. Moderate.*
Restaurant Belvedere. Spacious and attractive, with wood paneling and a large hearth, the Belvedere is known for regional
and creative cuisine. Local specialties include *bigoli di Bassano*
(homemade pasta) and *toresani* (roast squab). *Viale delle Fosse
1, tel. 0424/26602. Reservations advised. Jacket and tie advised. AE, DC, MC, V. Closed Sun. Moderate.*

Lodging **Belvedere.** Totally renovated in 1985, this historic hotel has
★ richly decorated public rooms with period furnishings and Oriental rugs. A fireplace and piano music in the lounge and an excellent restaurant with a garden make for a very pleasant stay.
The bedrooms are decorated in traditional Venetian or chic contemporary style. *Piazzale G. Giardino 14, tel. 0424/29845, fax
0424/29849. 95 rooms with bath or shower. Facilities: air-conditioning, color TV. AE, DC, MC, V. Moderate.*

Conegliano **Canon d'Oro.** The town's oldest inn, Canon d'Oro, is in a 15th-
Dining century building in a central location near the train station.
Restful classic decor lets you concentrate on the good food,
mainly regional specialties such as risotto, *gnocchi alla Canon
d'Oro* (potato dumplings), *baccala alla vicentina* (creamy cod),
and *fegato alla veneziana* (liver with onions). *Via XX
Settembre 129, tel. 0438/34246. Reservations not required.
Dress: casual. AE, MC, V. Closed Sat. Moderate.*

Maser **Agnoletti.** About 19 kilometers (12 miles) from Treviso in the
Dining town of Giavera del Montello near Maser, Agnoletti is an 18th-
★ century inn with Old World atmosphere and decor. The kitchen
can produce an all-mushroom menu; but if you order something
else, at least try the mushroom *zuppa* (soup) or *crostata* (tart).
In the summer you eat in the garden. *Giavera del Montello, Via*

della Vittoria 131, tel. 0422/876009. Reservations advised. Dress: casual. No credit cards. Closed Mon., Tues., Jan. 1–20, July 1–15. Moderate.

Da Bastian. A good place to stop for lunch before visiting the Villa Barbaro, this establishment has a contemporary look, a pleasant garden for outdoor dining, and an interesting menu featuring a varied antipasto of pâtés, homemade vegetarian ravioli, and broiled meat with tasty sauces. *Via Cornuda, tel. 0423/565400. Dress: casual. No credit cards. Closed Wed. evening, Thurs., and Aug. Moderate.*

Padua
Dining

El Toulà. The Padua branch of a prestigious restaurant chain bearing the same name is decorated with a flair in stylish black and creamy tones. The ambience is sophisticated and elegant. The cuisine has a Venetian accent, and specialties include risotto with radicchio or other seasonal vegetables and *tortelli di zucca* (squash-filled ravioli). The wine list offers a fine selection of the area's best bottles. *Via Belle Parti 11, tel. 049/875–1822. Reservations advised. Dress: jacket and tie or elegantly casual. AE, DC, MC, V. Closed Sun., Mon. lunch, Aug. Expensive.*

Cavalca. A family-run establishment with a long tradition, Cavalca is just off Piazza dei Signori in the heart of Padua. Classic decor and simple but courteous service are hallmarks here. The specialties are *pasta e fagioli* (pasta and bean soup), roast *capretto* (kid), or a platter of *arrosti misti* (assorted roast meats). *Via Manin 8, tel. 049/876–0061. Reservations required. Dress: casual. AE, DC, MC, V. Closed Tues. evening, Wed. July 1–21, Jan. 12–22. Moderate.*

Fagiano. Located near the basilica of Sant'Antonio, Fagiano is a popular trattoria with locals and tourists. The specialties are hearty standbys: *pasta e fagioli* and *fagiano farcito* (stuffed pheasant). *Via Locatelli 45, tel. 049/652913. Reservations advised. Dress: casual. MC, V. Closed Mon. and July 15–Aug. 15. Inexpensive.*

Lodging

Donatello. Directly opposite the basilica of Sant'Antonio, the Donatello is central and popular with tourists. About half the rooms have a view of the square and church but can be noisy. The decor is contemporary; rooms have minibars and color TV. *Via del Santo 102, tel. 049/875–0634, fax 049/875–0829. 42 rooms, 40 with bath or shower. Facilities: garage, restaurant (closed Wed., Moderate). AE, DC, MC, V. Closed mid-Dec.–mid-Jan. Moderate.*

Europa. Located right in the center of town, the Europa is handy for sightseeing: It's a reliable '60s commercial hotel and is furnished in undistinguished modern style. All rooms have air-conditioning, minibar, and color TV; marble-sheathed bathrooms add a touch of dated luxury. Parking space in front of the hotel is reserved for guests. *Largo Europa 9, tel. 049/661200. 59 rooms with bath or shower. Facilities: Zaramella restaurant (closed Sat. evening, Sun. Moderate). AE, DC, MC, V. Moderate.*

Treviso
Dining
★

El Toulà. Clones of this, the original Toulà, have sprouted up in unlikely places—even Japan. This is your chance to enjoy the art-nouveau decor and classic international cuisine for which it became famous. There are regional dishes as well, among them *risotto con funghi* (with mushrooms) or asparagus in season. For cooking, ambience, and service, it's one of the region's best. *Via Collalto 26, tel. 0422/540275. Reservations advised.*

Jacket and tie preferred. AE, DC, MC, V. Closed Sun. evening, Mon., and July 25–Aug. 25. Expensive.

★ **Beccherie.** In a town known for good eating, this rustic inn is a favorite. It's in the heart of old Treviso, behind the main square. Wooden beams, copper utensils, and Venetian provincial decor set the tone inside, and there are tables outside for fair-weather dining under the portico. Specialties vary with the season. In winter, look for *crespelle al radicchio* (crepes with radicchio) and *faraona in salsa pearada* (guinea hen); spring brings risotto with spring vegetables, *stinco di vitello* (roast veal shin), and *pasticcio di melanzane* (eggplant casserole). *Piazza Ancilotto 10, tel. 0422/540871. Reservations advised. Dress: casual. AE, DC, MC, V. Closed Thurs., Fri. lunch, and July 12–30. Moderate.*

Lodging **Continental.** You'll find this hotel within the old city walls, between the train station and the sights. It is a traditional four-star hotel offering solid comfort. The rooms have minibar, color TV, and air-conditioning. Rich fabrics and Oriental rugs lend an air of opulence. There is no restaurant. *Via Roma 16, tel. 0422/411216, fax 0422/55054. 82 rooms with bath or shower. AE, DC, MC, V. Moderate–Expensive.*

Al Fogher. Located on the outskirts, Al Fogher is handy if you're traveling by car. It has a bright contemporary look, with lots of modern art on the walls and room decor about equally divided between classic and modern. All rooms are equipped with minibar and color TV, and all are air-conditioned. *Viale della Repubblica 10, tel. 0422/20686, fax 0422/430391. 55 rooms with bath or shower. Facilities: parking, restaurant (closed Sun., Moderate). AE, DC, MC, V. Moderate.*

Trieste **Suban.** Despite its location in the hills on the edge of town, this
Dining historic trattoria is worth the taxi ride. The rustic decor is rich
★ in dark wood, stone, and wrought iron, and you'll find typical regional fare with imaginative variations. You can eat under an arbor in fair weather. Among the specialties are *jota carsolina* (typical local minestrone made of cabbage, potatoes, and beans) and duck breast in Tokay sauce. *Via Emilio Comici 2, tel. 040/54368. Reservations advised for evening and Sun. lunch. Dress: casual. AE, DC, MC, V. Closed Mon., Tues., Aug. 1–20. Moderate.*

Lodging **Duchi d'Aosta.** Located on the spacious Piazza dell'Unità d'Italia, this hotel is beautifully furnished in period style and lavish with Old World atmosphere. Its restaurant, Harry's Grill, is one of the city's most elegant. *Piazza dell'Unità d'Italia 2, tel. 040/7351, fax 040/366092. 50 rooms with bath or shower. Facilities: restaurant (Expensive), bar. AE, DC, MC, V. Expensive.*

Colombia. With a convenient location near the train station, Colombia is also within walking distance of the major sights and the cog railway to Opicina. Unpretentious but adequate, it caters mainly to businessmen. There is no restaurant, but there's a typical beer cellar restaurant close by. *Via della Geppa 18, tel. 040/369333, fax 040/369644. 40 rooms with bath or shower. AE, DC, MC, V. Moderate.*

Udine **Alla Buona Vite.** This classic restaurant in the center of town
Dining specializes in seafood. *Tagliolini dello chef* (with a creamy scampi sauce) and *rombo al limone e capperi* (turbot with lemon and capers) are among the many choices here. *Via Treppo*

10, tel. 0432/21053. Reservations advised. Dress: casual. AE, DC, MC, V. Closed Sun. evening, Mon., and Aug. Moderate.

★ **Antica Maddalena.** Just a few steps from Udine's pretty Piazza dell'Unità you'll find this elegant eating place, defined by its owner as a deluxe trattoria. Lots of warm wood tones, fresh flowers, and stained glass create a distinctive ambience to complement a menu of regional and Italian specialties, among them *zuppa di funghi porcini* (wild mushroom soup), *gnocchi con zucca e ricotta* (with squash and ricotta cheese), and *carpaccio di salmone con rucola* (chopped salmon with lemon and rugola). *Via Pellicccerie 4, tel. 0432/25111. Reservations advised. Dress: casual. AE, DC, MC, V. Closed Sun., Mon., lunch, 2 weeks in Feb., 2 weeks in Aug. Moderate.*

Trattoria al Lepre. A characteristic *focolare* (hearth) in one of the dining rooms is a symbol of traditional local cooking, and that's what you'll enjoy in this simple establishment. The specialties include *tagliatelle con funghi* (homemade pasta with mushrooms) and *stinco di maiale* (roast pork shin served with polenta). *Via Poscolle 27, tel. 0432/295798. Reservations advised. Dress: casual. AE, DC, MC, V. Closed Sun. and 10 days in Aug. Moderate.*

Lodging **Astoria Hotel Italia.** Centrally located, the Italia offers soundproofed, air-conditioned rooms furnished in traditional style, all with minibars and color TV. Public rooms feature Venetian glass chandeliers and comfortable armchairs. *Piazza XX Settembre 24, tel. 0432/505091, fax 0432/509070. 80 rooms with bath or shower. Facilities: garage, restaurant (Moderate). AE, DC, MC, V. Expensive.*

Verona **Le Arche.** True to its name, this elegant yet informal restaurant
Dining is in a medieval building a step away from the Della Scala
★ tombs. The dining room is furnished in art nouveau style, featuring candlelight and flowers, and it has an elegant turn-of-the-century air. Only seafood is served, absolutely fresh and superlatively prepared in the Venetian tradition. The specialties are *ravioli di branzino con vongole* (ravioli stuffed with sea bass with clam sauce) and *scorfano con olive nere* (baked sea scorpion with black olives). *Via Arche Scaligere 6, tel. 045/800–7415. Reservations advised. Dress: casual. AE, DC, MC, V. Closed Sun., Mon. lunch, and July 1–21. Expensive.*

Dodici Apostoli. Vaulted ceilings, frescoed walls, and a medieval ambience make this an exceptional place to enjoy classic local and regional dishes. Near Piazza delle Erbe, it stands on the foundations of a Roman temple. Specialties include *zuppa scaligera* (a soup of meat stock with vegetables and bread) and *vitello lessinia* (veal with mushrooms, cheese, and truffles). *Corticella San Marco 3, tel. 045/596999. Reservations advised. Dress: casual. AE, DC, V. Closed Sun. evening, Mon., and June 15–July 7, Jan. 1–7. Expensive.*

La Greppia. The classic decor with vaulted ceilings sets the tone in this popular restaurant off Via Mazzini between the Arena and Piazza delle Erbe. The kitchen produces fine versions of local and regional dishes, especially *tortelli di zucca* (ravioli filled with squash) and *bolliti* (assorted boiled meats served with a choice of sauces). Service is courteous and efficient. *Vicolo Samaritana 3, tel. 045/800–4577. Reservations advised. Dress: casual. AE, DC, V. Closed Mon. and June 15–30. Moderate.*

Lodging **Gabbia d'Oro.** A historic building off Piazza Erbe in the ancient
★ heart of Verona was fully and tastefully restored in 1990 to
house this intimate, deluxe hotel, where guests get personalized attention. Public rooms and individually furnished guest
rooms have frescoes, beamed ceilings, and antique prints and
furnishings. Some rooms have wrought-iron balconies. Guests
can relax outdoors in the medieval courtyard, on the roof terrace, or indoors in a bar with 18th-century carved wood panel-
ling. *Corso Porta Borsari 4A, tel. 045/800–3060, fax 045/
590293. 27 rooms with bath. Facilities: courtesy taxi to 24-hr
garage, bar, roof terrace; restaurant for guests only planned
by 1993. AE, DC, MC, V. Very Expensive.*

★ **Colomba d'Oro.** This attractive four-star hotel, located right by
the Arena, occupies a historic building dating to the 14th century. Repeatedly renovated over the past few years, it has re-
tained a clubby atmosphere and European charm while
providing up-to-date comfort. Warm wood furniture and floors;
an unsparing use of good fabrics in tones of green, blue, or yellow; and bright, tiled baths make for a cheery ambience. There
is no restaurant. Rates are low in the category. *Via Cattaneo
10, tel. 045/595300, fax 045/594974. 47 rooms with bath or shower, 2 suites with twin baths. Facilities: garage. AE, DC, MC, V.
Expensive.*

Giulietta e Romeo. A value-for-the-money choice in the medieval part of Verona and very handy for sightseeing, this is a
simple but comfortable hotel with an irresistibly romantic
name. The hotel was extensively renovated in 1991. *Vicolo Tre
Marchetti 3, tel. 045/800–3554, fax 045/801–0862. 30 rooms
with bath or shower. AE, MC, V. Moderate.*

Vicenza **Da Remo.** Located about a mile outside town, Da Remo is worth
Dining the taxi ride simply because it is one of Vicenza's best restaurants. In an attractive country-house setting, with light, airy
dining rooms and a garden terrace, you can enjoy a relaxing
meal of Venetian specialties, among them *faraona al radicchio*
(guinea hen with radicchio) and risotto with seasonal vegetables. *Via Ca'Impenta 14, tel. 0444/911007. Reservations advised. Dress: casual. AE, DC, MC, V. Closed Sun. evening,
Mon., Aug., Christmas holidays. Moderate.*

★ **Scudo di Francia.** A Gothic palace in the heart of town houses
the white vaulted dining rooms of Scudo di Francia. Minimal
but highly effective decor makes this restaurant aesthetically
pleasing, and it's highly satisfactory from the culinary point of
view, as well, since the regional cuisine features specialties
such as *bignè caldi al prosciutto e tartufo* (hot pastry puffs with
ham and truffles), *pasta e fagioli* (pasta and bean soup), and
baccalà alla vicentina (creamed cod). *Contrà Piancoli 4, tel.
0444/323322. Reservations advised. Dress: casual. AE, DC,
MC, V. Closed Sun. evening, Mon., and Aug. Moderate.*

Lodging **Campo Marzio.** Centrally located, Campo Marzio is between
the train station and the historic center, within walking distance of the sights. This stylish contemporary hotel has functionally furnished rooms in neutral tones with bright spreads,
big windows, color TV, and minibars. The buffet breakfast is
abundant. *Viale Roma 21, tel. 0444/545700, fax 0444/320495. 35
rooms with bath or shower. Facilities: parking, restaurant.
AE, DC, MC, V. Moderate.*

The Arts and Nightlife

The Arts

Most of this region is within striking distance of Venice, with its own wide range of cultural attractions (*see* The Arts and Nightlife in Chapter 6), but the Arc does offer ample opportunities to satisfy a hunger for Italian culture.

Concerts and Opera
Pride of place must go to the spectacular summer opera season in the **Arena di Verona** (*see* Tour 3: Verona in Exploring the Venetian Arc, *above*). The season lasts from July to September, and the 22,000 in the audience sit on the original stone terraces, which date back to the time when gladiators fought to the death. The opera stage is huge and best suited to grand operas such as *Aida*, but the experience is memorable no matter what is being performed. *For tickets, contact Ente Lirico Arena di Verona, Piazza Brà 28, 37100 Verona, tel. 045/590109. The box office is at Arch 6 of the Arena. Open weekdays 8:40–12:20, 3–5:50, Sat. 8:40–12:20.*

Trieste holds an open-air operetta festival each summer (July–Aug). For dates, times, and prices, contact the main tourist office (*see* Important Addresses and Numbers in Essential Information, *above*).

Theater
Even if your Italian is dismal, it's probably worth it to attend a performance of classical drama (in Italian) in the **Teatro Olimpico** in Vicenza (*see* Tour 2: Palladian Vicenza in Exploring the Venetian Arc, *above*). Palladio's masterpiece was designed to be used, not just admired. For details, contact Teatro Olimpico (Vicenza, tel. 0444/323781).

Nightlife

Many people in the Veneto area are willing to make the trip into Venice for a big night out, but it can be more enjoyable to stay put and soak up the atmosphere where you are. Most towns have central squares where the slow ritual of the *passeggiata* (promenade) takes place. As for cities, Padua is perhaps the liveliest, given its large student population, with Verona a close second, thanks to all the tourists.

Bars
Caffè Pedrocchi (*see* Tour 1: Villa Pisani and Padua in Exploring the Venetian Arc, *above*) in Padua is probably the best-known café in the Venetian Arc. Have your drink inside or out while you admire the uninhibited mixture of architectural styles. **Piazza Brà** in Verona and **Piazza dell'Unità d'Italia** in Trieste are standout squares surrounded by outdoor cafés. Sometimes, while sipping a drink in a café at Piazza Brà, you can overhear the opera being performed inside the adjacent Arena. Historic **Caffè San Marco** on Via Battisti in Trieste is a shrine of Old World atmosphere.

Discos
The best bets are in Padua: **Big Club** (Via Armistizio, tel. 049/680934) and **Ippopotamus** (Via Savonarola 149, tel. 049/42108).

Jazz Club
Video Club Sisma (Via Chiesanuova 106, Padua, tel. 049/871-6577).

8 Liguria

Genoa and the Rivieras

The region of Liguria is contained in a narrow strip of coastline stretching 349 twisting kilometers (217 miles) from the French border to Tuscany and never more than 40 kilometers (25 mi) wide. The sea that beats upon these shores has given them their character and their history. Every American schoolchild knows that Genoa, set in the heart of this rocky coast, is the birthplace of Christopher Columbus. That famous explorer was only one, and not the first or the last, in a long line of seafaring men whose activity centered in the ports of the two Rivieras of Italy.

Liguria is favored by a mild climate year-round; this, and the ease with which it can be reached from the rest of western Europe, has helped to make it one of the most popular regions in Italy for visitors. An impressive number of foreigners—British, American, French—have permanent residences here. For centuries, its charm has inspired poets and artists, many of whom came for a brief visit and stayed on. Italians from inland cities flock to its beaches in summer or maintain their villas along its length, and some areas of the western coast have become especially popular with German and other European package-tour operators, almost swamping what were once attractive small seaside towns. The flavor of the area is cosmopolitan, a mellow blend of rustic and sophisticated, provincial and smart set, primitive and old-fashioned and luxurious and up-to-date. The eye is caught, the attention is held, by the contours of the coastline curving serpentinely in an east–west arc from Ventimiglia to La Spezia; by the Ligurian Alps, plunging in sheer cliffs or sloping gradually to the sea; by the glamour and color of the resorts, the busy ports, the stately yachts against the skyline, and the grandiose view across the Gulf of Genoa from a hairpin curve on the highway.

Liguria's narrow strip of coastline, protected by mountains, varies considerably between the two Rivieras. The Riviera di Ponente, from the French border to Genoa, has some protected bays and wide sandy beaches. From Genoa to the east, the coastline of the Riviera di Levante becomes rockier and steeper, punctuated by small bays and inlets, and the less accessible coastal villages have a more traditional way of life. Two rugged peninsulas jut out from the Levante coastline. The first is the famous Portofino promontory, a rocky outcrop 40 million years old and covered with olives, pines, and cypresses. A network of nature and hiking trails crosses the peninsula, rewarding the energetic with sweeping views of the Ligurian coastline. Farther along the coast is the second peninsula, where the road goes inland, leaving the visitor to hike or take a train or boat to explore the Cinque Terre, five fishing villages clinging to cliff faces or perched on bluffs overlooking the sea.

As Italy's largest port, Genoa itself is a bustling city, with a proud history of trade and navigation that predates Columbus. Modern container ships unload at docks that centuries before served galleons and vessels bound for the spice routes. By the 3rd century BC, when the Romans conquered Liguria, Genoa was already an important trading station. The Via Aurelia was built to link Rome with what is now France. The Middle Ages and the Renaissance saw the rise of Genoa as a great seaport, and the city—jumping-off place for the Crusades, commercial center of tremendous wealth and prestige, strategic bone of international contention—was of key importance to Europe.

Thereafter, Genoa declined in rank as a sea power. Napoleon reduced all Liguria to an ineffective "family estate of the Bonapartes," as Tolstoy speaks of it in *War and Peace*. When the emperor was finally defeated at Waterloo, the region became part of Piedmont, and reacquired its separate identity only after the unification of Italy.

People today come to Liguria less for its history and its art than for its mild climate, its fine seafood, and coastal villages, many of which remain unspoiled. Tennis and *bocce* (Italian lawn-bowling) are played all year, while during the summer the coast sees colorful flotillas of yachts and smaller sailboats, often moored next to the boats of the hard-working local fishermen. The Mediterranean vegetation along the coast—myrtle, heather, broom, rosemary, pine, and olives—gives way to chestnut groves and terraced vineyards on the hills. Relaxed Liguria is the sort of place where knowing the difference between scrub pine and cypress means more than knowing your Rococo from your Renaissance.

Essential Information

Important Addresses and Numbers

Tourist Information The main EPT (provincial tourist board) office for Genoa is in the center of town (Via Roma 11, tel. 010/581407), just off Piazza De Ferrari. There are information offices at Principe Station (tel. 010/262633) and at the airport (tel. 010/2415247). The helpful local tourist offices (listed below) are sometimes known as "Pro Loco." *EPT and Pro Loco offices usually open Mon.-Thurs. 8–2, 2:30–5:30, Fri. and Sat. 8–1.*

Alassio (Palazzo Hanbury, Via Gibb, tel. 0182/40346).
Albenga (Via Martiri della Liberta, tel. 0182/50475).
Bordighera (Palazzo del Parco, tel. 0184/262322).
Camogli (Via XX Settembre 33r, tel. 0185/771066).
Genoa (Piazza Verdi 18/r, tel. 010/562056).
Imperia (Via Matteotti 22, tel. 0183/60730).
La Spezia (Via Mazzini 47, tel. 0187/36000).
Lerici (Via Roma 47, tel. 0187/967346).
Rapallo (Via A. Diaz 9, tel. 0185/51282).
San Remo (Corso Nuvoloni, tel. 0184/571571).
Varazze (Viale Nazioni Unite, tel. 019/97007).
Ventimiglia (Via Cavour 61, tel. 0184/351183).

Emergencies **Police**, tel. 113; Genoa municipal police, tel. 010/53631. **Ambulance**, tel. 010/595951.

Doctors and Dentists In case of accident, go to the public hospital in Genoa, **Ospedale Generale Regionale San Martino** (Viale Benedetto XV, tel. 010/354021). For information on dentists and night-duty and Sunday-duty doctors, call tel. 010/354022.

Late-Night Pharmacies **Europa** (Corso Europa 676, Genoa, tel. 010/380139). **Ghersi** (Corso Buenos Aires 74/r, Genoa, tel. 010/541661).

Car Rentals **Genoa.** *Avis* (Via Balbi 190r, tel. 010/155598); *Budget* and *Kemwel* (at the airport, tel. 010/603–822); *Hertz* (Via delle Casacce 3, tel. 010/564412).
La Spezia. *Avis* (Via Fratelli Rosselli 86/88, tel. 0187/33345); *Hertz* (Via San Bartolomeo 665, tel. 0187/516712).

San Remo. *Avis* (Corso Imperatrice 96, tel. 0184/73897); *Hertz* (Via XX Settembre 17, tel. 0184/85618).

Arriving and Departing by Plane

Cristoforo Colombo International Airport, at Genoa Sestri (tel. 010/2411) is only 6 kilometers (4 miles) from the center of Genoa. It has regular service to all main European cities. The nearest airport for U.S. flights is Nice, in France, about 2½ hours west of Genoa. Bus services from Cristoforo Colombo connect with Genoa's air transit terminal on Via Petrarca (tel. 010/581316).

Arriving and Departing by Car, Train, Bus, and Boat

By Car Autostrada (highway) A12 south from Genoa links up with the autostrada network for all southern destinations; Rome is a six-hour drive from Genoa. The 150-kilometer (90-mile) trip north to Milan on A7 takes two hours. Nice is 2½ hours west on A10.

By Train Frequent and fast train services connect Liguria with the rest of Italy. Genoa is 1½ hours from Milan and five hours from Rome. Many services from France (in particular, the French Riviera) pass along the Ligurian Coast on the way to all parts of Italy.

By Bus Buses operated by **SITA** (tel. 010/313851) provide connections along both Ligurian coasts to Genoa, linking the region with the French Riviera and other parts of Italy. The main station is at Piazza di Principe. The **Pesci** line (Piazza della Vittoria 94r, Genoa, tel. 010/564936) specializes in services from Genoa to all other parts of Italy, with frequent connections to Rome and Milan.

By Boat Genoa is Italy's largest port and can be reached from the United States as well as other parts of Liguria and Italy (Sardinia, La Spezia, and Savona). Ships berth in the heart of Genoa, including cruise ships of the Genoa-based **Costa Cruise Line** (Via Gabriele D'Annunzio 2, tel. 010/54831) and ferries to various ports around the Mediterranean, operated by **Tirrenia Navigazione** (Stazione Marittima, tel. 010/258041).

Getting Around

By Car Two good roads run parallel to each other along the coast of Liguria. Closer to shore and passing through all the towns and villages is S1, which has excellent views at almost every turn but which gets crowded in July and August. More direct and higher up than S1 is the autostrada, known as A10 west of Genoa and A12 to the east. This route saves a lot of time on weekends, in summer, and on days when festivals slow traffic in some resorts to a standstill.

By Train Regular service, connecting all parts of Liguria, operates from Genoa's two stations, **Stazione Principe** (for points west) and **Stazione Brignole** (for the east). All the coastal resorts are on this service, and many international trains stop along the coast west of Genoa on their way from Paris to Milan or Rome.

By Bus SITA and **Pesci** (*see* Arriving and Departing By Bus, *above*) buses run the length of the Ligurian Coast in both directions. Local buses serve the steep valleys that run to some of the towns along the western coast. Tickets may be bought at local bus stations or even newsstands (in the case of local buses). Buy your ticket before you board the bus.

By Boat This is the most pleasant (and, in some the cases, the only) way to get from place to place within Liguria. A busy network of local services connects many of the resorts. For general information about availability of services in Liguria, contact **Servizio Marittimo del Tigullio** (Calata Zingari, Genoa, tel. 010/ 265712), which connects Genoa with most of the ports to the west and provides links to the east to Cinque Terre and Portovenere. Or contact **Camogli–San Fruttuoso Maritime Services** (Societa Golfo Paradiso, Via Scalo 2, Camogli, tel. 0185/ 772091), which runs between Camogli and San Fruttuosa (on the Portofino promontory), as well as between Recco and Punta Chiappa, two other towns close to Camogli. Summer excursions link both ports with the Cinque Terre and Portovenere.

Guided Tours

Orientation One of the joys of visiting even the tiniest of the Ligurian coastal resorts is the chance to take an informal **harbor cruise** or excursion to the next town along the coast. Some of these tours are scheduled and operated by the main ferry lines (*see* Getting Around by Boat, *above*), but you can have as much fun—if not more—negotiating a price with a boat owner at one of the smaller ports. You're likely to get someone whose English is rudimentary at best, but that shouldn't affect your appreciation of the rugged and colorful coastal scenery.

There is a three-hour **bus tour** available in Genoa, operated by the tourist office. Buses have English-speaking guides and are the best way to get to know the city. Buses leave from Piazza Acquaverde every afternoon at 2:30 (Oct.–Mar.) or 3:30 (Apr.– Sept.) Tickets (about 20,000 lire) can be purchased on the bus; for information, inquire at the tourist booth at **Stazione Principe** (Piazza Acquaverde, tel. 010/262633).

You can also take a **boat tour** of the harbor in Genoa. The tour lasts about an hour and includes a visit to the Lanterna, the breakwater outside the harbor, the Bacino delle Grazie, and the Molo Vecchio (Old Pier). You can see extensive views of the city throughout the tour. For information, contact the **Cooperativa Batellieri** (Marine Station), Ponte dei Mille, Genoa, tel. 010/265712.

Exploring Liguria

Our three exploring tours follow the coast from west to east. The scenic coastal road, S1, links every attraction discussed in this chapter, except for those villages that are inaccessible from any road and have to be reached by foot or by boat.

Tour 1 covers the Riviera di Ponente from its western border with France, at Ventimiglia, along the coast toward Genoa at the head of the broad Ligurian Gulf. Tour 2 explores Genoa itself, starting with a bird's-eye view of the city, from the top of the Granarolo funicular, and continuing through the old and new sections before finishing with the port itself. Tour 3, along the Riviera di Levante, snakes its way southward along this rocky coastline, abandoning S1 only when it explores the remoter parts of the Portofino Peninsula and the Cinque Terre.

Highlights for First-time Visitors

Camogli (Tour 3: Riviera di Levante).
Cinque Terre (Tour 3: Riviera di Levante).
Giardino Hanbury (Tour 1: Riviera di Ponente).
Museo del Tesoro di San Lorenzo, Genoa (Tour 2: Genoa).
Palazzo Balbi Durazzo, Genoa (Tour 2: Genoa).
Portofino (Tour 3: Riviera di Levante).
Portovénere (Tour 3: Riviera di Levante).
San Remo (Tour 1: Riviera di Ponente).
Via Garibaldi, Genoa (Tour 2: Genoa).

Tour 1: Riviera di Ponente

Numbers in the margin correspond to points of interest on the Liguria map.

The **Riviera di Ponente** is a narrow coastal strip punctuated by rocky outcrops jutting out between wide bays and sandy coves. Its other name is Riviera dei Flori (Riviera of Flowers) because flower cultivation is a major industry here. Just past the French border, stop at Mórtola Inferiore to visit the world-famous **Giardino Hanbury** (Gardens of Hanbury Villa), one of the largest botanical gardens in Italy. Planned and planted by a wealthy English merchant, Sir Thomas Hanbury, and his botanist brother, Daniel, in 1867, the gardens contain a variety of species from five continents—including many palms and succulents (plants of the cactus group). There are panoramic views of the sea from the gardens. *Giardino Hanbury, Mórtola Inferiore, tel. 0184/39507. Admission: 8,500 lire. Open June–Sept., daily 9–6; Oct.–May, Thurs.–Tues. 10–4.*

On the ocean side of the road are the famous **Balzi Rossi** (Red Rocks), caves in the sheer rock, in which prehistoric man left traces of his life and magic rites. You can visit the caves and a small museum containing some of the objects found there. *Admission: 4,000 lire. Open Tues.–Sun. 9–1, 2:30–6.*

❷ **Ventimiglia,** about 9 kilometers (6 miles) from the French border, was once a pre-Roman settlement known as Albintimilium and contains some important archaeological remains, such as a 2nd-century AD amphitheater. A vital trade center for hundreds of years, Ventimiglia declined in prestige as Genoa grew and is now little more than a frontier town that lives on tourism and the cultivation of flowers. The town is divided in two by the Roia River. The **Citta Vecchia** (Old City), on the western side, is what you'll see first: It is a well-preserved and typical medieval town. The 11th-century **Duomo** (Cathedral) has a Gothic portal dating from 1222. Walk up Via del Capo to the ancient walls, which offer fine views of the coast. S1 crosses the river into the new part of town, famous for its large flower market. Avoid Ventimiglia on Friday, a chaotic market day that draws crowds of bargain hunters from France.

Time Out While you're in the heart of the Citta Vecchia, stop at the **Cuneo** (closed Wed. and July) for a lunch of fresh shellfish or pasta. *Via Aprosio 16.*

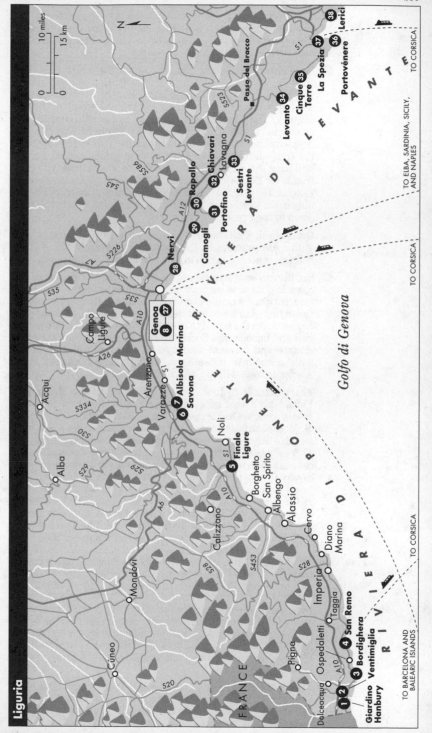

Liguria

10 miles
15 km

TO CORSICA

TO BARCELONA AND
BALEARIC ISLANDS

TO ELBA, SARDINIA, SICILY,
AND NAPLES

TO CORSICA

TO CORSICA

Golfo di Genova

FRANCE

Cúneo

Mondoví

Alba

Acqui

Campo
Ligure

Arenzano

Varazze

Calizzano

Pigna

Dolceacqua

Ospedaletti

Taggia

Imperia

Cervo

Alassio

Albengo

Borghetto
San Spirito

Diano
Marina

R I V I E R A   D I   P O N E N T E

R I V I E R A   D I   L E V A N T E

Noli

Passo del Bracco

1 2 Giardino
Hanbury
3 Ventimiglia
Bordighera
4 San Remo
5 Finale
Ligure
6 Savona
7 Albisola Marina
8 — 27 Genoa
28 Nervi
29 Camogli
30 Rapallo
31 Portofino
32 Chiavari
Lavagna
33 Sestri
Levante
34 Levanto
35 Cinque
Terre
36 Portovénere
37 La Spezia
38 Lerici

From Ventimiglia, a provincial road swings up the Nervia River valley to the lovely sounding medieval town of **Dolceaqua** (Sweetwater), with its ruined castle, and to **Pigna,** also of Roman times.

❸ **Bordighera,** just a few minutes down the coast from Ventimiglia, is a famous winter resort dominating a broad promontory with lush vegetation. A large English colony, still very much in evidence, developed here in the second half of the 19th century. The English were attracted to the mild climate. It is an elegant town with a *fin de siècle* atmosphere; expect to find people taking afternoon tea in the cafés. This garden spot was the first town in Europe to grow date palms, and its citizens still have the exclusive right to provide the Vatican with palm fronds for Easter celebrations. Walk along the **Lungomare Argentina,** the magnificent mile-long seafront promenade, beginning in the western end of the town, for a good view to the west, down to the French Côte d'Azur.

Ospedaletti, 6 kilometers (4 miles) east, is an unspoiled town with a fine promenade, the **Corso Regina Margherita.** A horticultural center, it is rich in palms, eucalyptus, and pines.

❹ Six kilometers (4 miles) east is **San Remo,** the capital of this coast and its most elegant resort. Renowned for its royal visitors, its famous casino (one of only four in Italy), and its romantic setting, San Remo still maintains some of the glamour of its heyday from the late 19th century to World War II. Among the rich and famous who flocked to San Remo, drawn by the mild climate and pleasant countryside, were Alfred Nobel, who built a summer house here, and Russian Empress Maria Alexandrovna, wife of Czar Alexander II.

From October to June, get up early to visit the **Mercato dei Fiori,** Italy's most important flower market (open 6 AM–8 AM), held in a market hall between Piazza Colombo and Corso Garibaldi. More than 20,000 tons of carnations, roses, mimosa, and innumerable other cut flowers are dispatched from here each year. There are some elegant world-class hotels in San Remo where you can stop to have a drink, as well as exotic gardens and imposing *corsos* (promenades). The old part of San Remo, **La Pigna** (meaning pine cone) is a warren of alleyways leading up to **Piazza Castello,** with a splendid view of the town. The Russian Orthodox church of **San Basilio,** with its onion domes, stands at one end of the **Corso dell' Imperatrice** and, like that imposing seafront promenade, is a memento of the Empress Maria.

Time Out Join the fishermen and other locals for a lunch of freshly caught seafood at **Porto-Da Nico,** a small family-run trattoria near the harbor. *Piazza Bresca 9. Closed Tues. and Nov.–Dec. 28.*

Imperia, 26 kilometers (16 miles) along the coast, actually consists of two towns: Porto Maurizio, a medieval town built on a promontory, and Oneglia, now an industrial center for oil refining and pharmaceuticals. Porto Maurizio has a virtually intact medieval center and some imposing 17th- and 18th-century palaces.

Just a few kilometers east of Oneglia is **Diano Marina,** the heart of Liguria's olive-growing industry. At one time it was surrounded by woods consecrated to the Ligurian god Bornmanus, who evolved into the Roman goddess of hunting, Diana, giving the town its present name. The Knights of Malta built a castle that still stands over the town (closed to the public). Diano Marina was badly damaged in an earthquake in 1887, and most of the center dates from the late 19th century.

❺ The countryside around **Finale Ligure,** 20 kilometers (12 miles) northeast along the coast, is pierced by deep, narrow valleys and caves; the limestone outcroppings provide the warm pinkish stone found in many buildings in Genoa. Here there are rare reptiles and rare species of flora. Finale Ligure itself is made up of three villages: Borgo, Marina, and Pia. The last two have fine sandy beaches and modern resort amenities. About two kilometers (1 mile) inland is the old village of **Finalborgo,** a medieval settlement planned to a rigid blueprint, with 15th-century walls. The village is crowned by the impressive ruins of the huge **Castel Gavone.** The Baroque Church of **San Biagio** houses many works of art, and the 14th- to 15th-century Dominican convent of **Santa Caterina** can be visited for the shade of the courtyard or to see the museum of paleontology and natural history, which houses prehistoric remains found in the area. *Museo Civico. Open May–Sept., Tues.–Fri., 10–noon, 3–6, weekends 9–noon; Oct.–Apr., Tues.–Fri., 9–noon, 2:30–4:30.*

Time Out   Develop your taste for homemade *pesto* (pasta sauce made from basil and pine nuts) at the **Torchi** restaurant (closed Tues. and Jan.–Feb.), located in the center of Finalborgo. *Via dell' Annunziata 12, tel. 019/690531.*

❻ **Savona,** 25 kilometers (13 miles) farther east, is the fifth largest seaport in Italy and handles vast oil and coal cargoes, as well as car and truck ferries. Much of the town is modern and not very interesting, although a small, austere older quarter near the harbor contains some fine homes of the town's merchant class. The large **Palazzo della Rovere,** on Via Pia, was designed for Pope Julius II by the Florentine Giuliano da Sangallo in 1495; there is also the 14th-century **Palazzo degli Anziani** and three 12th-century towers. Every year on Good Friday wooden carvings depicting the Passion of Christ are carried in procession. Watch for shops selling crystallized fruit, which is a local specialty.

❼ Just outside Savona, to the east, is **Albisola Marina,** which preserves its centuries-old tradition of ceramic making. Numerous shops here sell these distinctive wares. A whole sidewalk, **Lungomare degli Artisti,** has been transformed by the colorful ceramic works of local artists. It runs along the beachfront. The 17th-century **Villa Faraggiana,** located by the parish church on Via dell'Oratorio, has interesting antique ceramics and exhibits on the history of the craft. *Admission free. Open Apr.–Sept., Wed.–Mon. 3–7.*

If you'd like to take a break for a little sea and sun, stop in **Varazze,** 12 kilometers (7 miles) east, known for its fine sandy beach. The town also has well-preserved ancient ramparts, with a 10th-century church facade built into one of the rampart walls.

From Varazze, it is about 35 kilometers (22 miles) to Genoa. Just before you get to the city, you'll pass **Pegli,** a popular summer home for many patrician Genovese families. Some of the grand villas, with their well-tended gardens and parks, also function as museums.

Tour 2: Genoa

⑧ Visitors who come to Liguria for the sun and the sea generally avoid the busy, sprawling city of **Genoa,** which stretches for 20 kilometers (12 miles) along the coast. Yet Genoa can offer a fascinating, rich, and colorful experience. Known as La Superba (The Proud), Genoa was from the 13th century a great maritime center that rivaled Venice and Pisa in power and splendor. Its bankers, merchants, and princes adorned the city with palaces and churches and amassed impressive collections of art. Genoa's lively medieval center is one of Europe's largest. While brimming with historical curiosities and buildings, Genoa is also a thoroughly modern and prosperous city. Its port (Italy's largest) is being equipped to keep up with new technologies; the city is also advanced in communications, electronics, and general commerce.

Europe's biggest boat show takes place here, as does the Euroflora flower show (held every five years—next in 1996). Classical dance and music are richly represented; the Nervi Park, just outside the city, offers a unique setting for a ballet festival usually held here (*see* The Arts and Nightlife, *below*) and the annual Niccolò Paganini Violin Contest, internationally renowned, also takes place in Genoa.

The historic harbor area was given a face-lift for the Columbus celebrations in 1992, and some of the fair installations, such as the Bigo elevator ride with harbor view, have become a permanent part of the city scene.

Numbers in the margin correspond to points of interest on the Genoa map.

⑨ Immediately above the coast the terrain rises steeply: Dotted around the circumference of the city are a number of huge fortresses. Start your tour of Genoa with an aerial view of the city. Take the **Granarolo funicular,** actually a cog railway, up to one of the fortified gates in the 17th-century city walls. It takes 15 minutes to hoist you from Piazza Principe, behind the Principe Station on Piazza Acquaverde, to **Porta Granarolo,** 1,000 feet above, where you can get a good sense of the size of Genoa. *Fare: 1,000 lire. Leaves every ½-hour, on the ¼-hour, 6AM–midnight.*

⑩ A good way to begin exploring Genoa, once you're back on street level, is to start on **Via Balbi,** which runs southeast from the train station toward the medieval town. On the right, at No. 10, is the **Palazzo Balbi Durazzo,** formerly the royal palace. The palace, which dates from the 17th century, now houses Genoa's Department of Fine Arts and Antiquities and contains paintings, sculptures, tapestries and Oriental ceramics. The building was bought by the Royal House of Savoy in the early 19th century and has some magnificent rooms decorated in the lavish and frivolous rococo style. The gallery of mirrors and the ballroom on the upper floor are particularly good examples. There are also works by Sir Antony Van Dyck, who lived in Genoa for six years, from 1621, and painted many fine portraits of the Genovese nobility. *Tel. 010/247–0640. Admission: 4,000 lire. Open daily 9–1:30.*

⑪ Opposite is the **Palazzo dell' Università,** built in the 1630s as a Jesuit college and the site of a university since 1803. Climb the stairway flanked by lions to visit the elegant courtyard, with its portico of double Doric columns.

A few minutes' walk along the Via Balbi, in the Piazza della Nunziata, is the 16th- to 17th-century church of the **Santissima Annunziata,** which has exuberantly frescoed vaults and is an excellent example of Genovese Baroque architecture.

Continue down Via Cairoli to **Via Garibaldi,** once known as the "Strada Nuova" (New Street). Genoa's leading patrician families built their residences here from 1554 onward to escape the cramped conditions of the medieval section of town; 13 palaces were built along the street in just 10 years. Via Garibaldi is one of the most impressive streets in Italy, and its palaces house some of the finest art collections in the country.

⑫ You come to the 17th-century Baroque **Palazzo Rosso** (Red Palace), at No. 18, one of the last palaces to be erected here. Named after the red stone used in its construction, it now contains, apart from a number of lavishly frescoed suites, works by Titian, Veronese, Caravaggio, Rubens, and Van Dyck. *Tel. 010/282641. Admission: 4,000 lire. Open Tues.–Sun. 9–12:30.*

⑬ Opposite, at No. 10, is **Palazzo Bianco.** Originally white, as its name suggests, Palazzo Bianco has become considerably darkened with age and grime. It has a fine art collection, with the Dutch and Flemish schools well represented. *Tel. 010/291803. Admission: 4,000 lire. Open Tues.–Sat. 9–7, Sun. 9–noon.*

⑭ **Palazzo Tursi** (No. 9) is Genoa's Town Hall, built in the 16th century by the wealthy Nicolò Grimaldi. The palace, also known as Palazzo Municipale, is made from pink stone quarried in the region. Visitors are welcome to view the richly decorated rooms and the famous Guarnerius violin that belonged to Paganini and is played once a year on Columbus Day (October 12). However, when the rooms are in use by Genoa's officials, as is often the case, they are closed to the public. *Tel. 010/20981. Admission free. Open Mon.–Sat.; call for hours.*

Most of the other palaces on Via Garibaldi can be visited only by special application, but many have courtyards that are open to the public.

⑮ At the end of Via Garibaldi, on Piazza Portello, take the elevator to **Castelletto** for a good view of the old city. *Fare: 1,000 lire one-way. Continuous service 6 AM–10:30 PM.*

Turn right at the end of Via Garibaldi onto the narrow streets that zigzag down into the **medieval city.** The caruggi district is also the city's most disreputable. Don't go there after dark, or on holidays when shops are closed and the alleys deserted. These winding, picturesque alleys—known as *caruggi*—contain many medieval buildings, some decorated with typically Ligurian black-and-white facades, on a more intimate scale than the grand, airy palaces of Via Garibaldi.

⑯ Make your way west toward the harbor and **San Siro,** Genoa's oldest church. The edifice was rebuilt in the 16th and 17th-centuries on the site of a pre–9th-century cathedral; it contains a

⑰ 5th-century chapel. Nearby, just off Via San Luca, is the **National Gallery, housed in the richly adorned Palazzo Spinola.** The collection contains, among other fine works, masterpieces

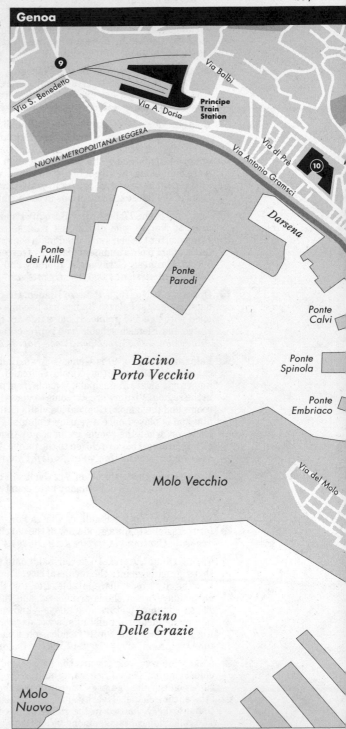

by Luca Giordano (1634–1705) and Guido Reni (1575–1642). The *Ecce Homo,* by Antonello da Messina (1430–79), is a hauntingly beautiful painting and is also of historical interest because it was the Sicilian da Messina who first brought Flemish oil paints and techniques to Italy from his voyages in the Low Countries. *Piazza Pelliceria 1, tel. 010/294661. Admission: 4,000 lire. Open May–Sept., Tues–Sat. 9–7, Sun. 9–1; Oct.–Apr., Tues–Sat. 9–5, Sun. 9–1.*

Walk south down Via San Luca to Piazza Banchi to see the **⑱ Loggia dei Mercanti** (covered market). Then head back to the heart of the medieval quarter, to Via Soziglia, a street lined with shops selling handicrafts and tempting foods.

Time Out You may want to rest your feet at the **Klanguti Tearoom** (tel. 010/296502), at the end of the street in Piazza Soziglia. Try the excellent homemade cakes and ice creams.

South of the Piazza Soziglia is the quarter where wealthy Genovese built their homes in the 16th century. Prosperous guilds, such as the goldsmiths for whom Vico Indoratori and Via Orefici were named, also set up shop here. The **Piazza San Matteo** is an excellently preserved medieval square, for 500 years the seat of the Doria family. The Dorias ruled Genoa and much of Liguria from the 16th to the 18th century and built fine palaces all over the city. The square is bounded by 13th- to 15th-century houses decorated with portals and loggias (open **⑲** galleries). The black-and-white church of **San Matteo** dates from the 12th century; its crypt contains the tomb of Andrea Doria, who framed a constitution for the city in 1529 and began his family's reign. Doria won his fame as an admiral, serving, in turn, the French and Spanish crowns, but managing to maintain the independence of his native city.

Leaving Piazza San Matteo, continue down toward the cathe**⑳** dral of **San Lorenzo,** at the heart of medieval Genoa's political and religious center. The cathedral is embellished inside and out with the contrasting black slate and white marble so common in Liguria. It was consecrated in 1118 to St. Lawrence, who passed through the city on his way to Rome in the 3rd century; the last campanile dates from the early 16th century. For hundreds of years the building was used for state, as well as religious, purposes: Civic elections, court rulings, and religious ceremonies and festivals all took place here. Note the lively 13th-century Gothic portal and the 15th- to 17th-century frescoes inside. The **Museo del Tesoro di San Lorenzo** (San Lorenzo Treasury Museum), located in the cathedral, contains some stunning medieval pieces. The art of goldsmiths and silversmiths, for which medieval Genoa was renowned, is particularly well represented here. *Admission: 1,000 lire. Open Tues., Thurs., Sat. 9:30–11:45, 3–5:45.*

㉑ Across the Piazza San Lorenzo is the **Palazzo Ducale,** built in the 16th century over a medieval hall: Its facade was rebuilt in the late 18th century. Cross over the 19th-century thoroughfare Via San Lorenzo, and head southwest into the old city center, where a settlement has existed since the 6th century BC **㉒** **Santa Maria di Castello,** one of Genoa's greatest religious buildings, was an early Christian church. It was rebuilt in the 12th century and finally completed in 1513. You can visit the adjacent cloisters by special request and see the fine artwork contained in the museum (open Wed., Sat., and Sun. 8–noon, 3–6).

Take the little lane left from behind the church to reach the

(23) 12th-century Romanesque church of **San Donato,** with its original portal and octagonal campanile. The 13th-century Gothic

(24) church of **Sant'Agostino,** almost directly behind it, was damaged during World War II, but still has a fine campanile and two well-preserved cloisters, which now house an excellent sculpture museum.

At the southeastern end of the old city, the twin-towered, 12th-

(25) century **Porta di Sant'Andrea** stands at the old gateway to the Roman road that led through Genoa. Nearby, in Piazza Dante,

(26) is the ruined, ivy-covered house where **Christopher Columbus** spent his childhood.

Taking Via Dante northwest, you'll hit **Piazza de Ferrari,** the center of modern Genoa. The World War II–ravaged opera

(27) house, **Teatro Carlo Felice,** was finally rebuilt. It reopened in 1991, with a massive, much-criticized tower. It stands next to the **Academy of Fine Arts,** which contains a collection of Ligurian paintings from the 13th to the 19th century. The piazza, which also contains the Stock Exchange and part of the Ducal Palace, leads into Via XX Settembre, Genoa's chic modern shopping center. The spacious 19th-century urban layout of this part of town strongly contrasts with the narrow, crowded alleys of the medieval quarter, only a few minutes away.

A fitting end to your tour of Genoa could be a visit to the **harbor,** the layout of which dates to Roman times. The Genoa inlet, the only one of its size along the Italian Riviera, was also used by the Phoenicians and Greeks as a harbor and a vantage point from which they could penetrate inland to form settlements and to trade.

The **Lanterna,** a lighthouse more than 360 feet high, stands in the middle of the harbor. It was built in 1544 at the height of Andrea Doria's career. It is one of Italy's oldest lighthouses and a traditional emblem of Genoa. You can get a closer view of the Lanterna, the Molo Vecchio (the historic dock, restored for 1992 events), and all Genoa's harbor from one of the informative harbor tours (*see* Guided Tours in Essential Information, *above*).

Tour 3: Riviera di Levante

Numbers in the margin correspond to points of interest on the Liguria map.

Of the two Ligurian Rivieras, the Riviera di Levante is the wilder and more rugged. Here the hills drop sharply to the sea and are pierced by compact bays and inlets. You may want to choose a base and take short day-trips or explore the area by boat from the larger towns.

(28) **Nervi,** 10 kilometers (6 miles) east of Genoa, is an elegant turn-of-the-century resort. It's famous for the **Anita Garibaldi** promenade, with its splendid sea views, palm-lined roads, and 300 acres of parks rich in orange trees and exotics. In these grounds stand the villas Gropallo, Grimaldi, and Serra, the last of which contains the **Galleria d'Arte Moderna.** *Via Capolungo*

*3, tel. 010/326025. Admission: 4,000 lire. Open Tues.–Sat. 9–
1:15, 3–6, Sun. 9:15–12:45.*

Also worth seeing is the **Museo di Villa Luxoro.** It has 17th- and
18th-century Genoese furnishings, furniture, ceramics, and ornaments; Flemish and Genoese paintings and drawings; old silver and lace; and antique clocks. *Via Aurelia 29, tel. 010/
322673. Admission: 4,000 lire. Open Tues.–Sat. 9–5, Sun. 9–
12:30.*

㉙ Camogli, at the edge of the large promontory and nature reserve known as the Portofino peninsula, is the first unspoiled
port you reach, about 20 kilometers (12 miles) from Genoa.
Camogli has always been a town of sailors, and by the 19th century this small village was leasing its ships throughout the Continent. The festival of San Fortunata, held on the second
Sunday of May each year, is noteworthy for the public—and
free—feast of freshly caught fish cooked in pans 12-feet wide.
The village has multicolored houses, a huge 17th-century sea
wall in the harbor, and Dragone Castle, built onto the sheer
rock face by the harbor. Within the castle is the impressive
Acquario, with good displays of local marine life. The tanks are
actually built into the ramparts. *Admission: adults 3,000 lire,
children under 10 1,500 lire. Open May–Sept., daily 10–noon
and 3–7; Oct.–Apr., daily 10–noon and 2–6.*

From Camogli you can reach, by foot or boat, the hamlets of
San Rocco, San Nicolò, and **Punta Chiappa,** with their remarkable sea views. They lie along the western coast of the peninsula and are more natural and less fashionable than those facing
south on the eastern coast. The small Romanesque church at
San Nicolò was where sailors who survived dangerous voyages
came to offer thanks.

㉚ Rapallo lies at the extreme eastern edge of the peninsula,
about 10 kilometers (6 miles) from Camogli on S1. Rapallo was
one of Europe's most fashionable resorts, but it passed its heyday before World War II and has suffered from the building
boom brought on by tourism. Ezra Pound and D. H. Lawrence
lived here, and many other writers, poets, and artists have
been drawn to it. Today, the town's natural harbor is filled with
yachts. A single-span bridge on the eastern side of the bay is
named after Hannibal, who is said to have passed through the
area after crossing the Alps. Two ancient buildings are highlights in the center of town: The Cathedral of **Santi Gervasio
and Protasio,** at the western end of Via Mazzini, was founded in
the 6th century; across the road is the **Leper House of San Lorenzo,** which still retains parts of its original medieval frescoes
on its exterior walls. Behind the bay, which is lined with palms
and orange trees, you can explore the medieval sections of the
town and browse for antique lace, for which Rapallo is famous.
The **Museo Civico** has a collection of the handiwork. *Admission:
3,000 lire. Open 9–noon.*

From Rapallo, you can take the road onto the Portofino peninsula for about 3 kilometers (2 miles) to visit **Santa Margherita
Ligure,** a quieter and more sedate resort, and then 5 kilometers
㉛ (3 miles) farther to **Portofino** itself, one of the most picturesque
villages along the coast.

Known as the "Pearl of the Riviera," this enchanting fishing village is the refuge of some of Europe's wealthiest and most discerning pleasure-seekers. From the harbor, follow the signs

for the climb to the **Castello di San Giorgio,** with its medieval relics and excellent views. *Admission: 3,000 lire. Open Apr.–Sept., Tues.–Sun. 10–6; Oct.–Mar., Tues.–Sun. 10–5.*

Across a small square is the church of **San Giorgio,** which is supposed to contain the saint's relics, brought back from the Holy Land by the Crusaders. Other excellent views can be seen from the lighthouse on the **Punta del Capo,** a quarter hour's walk along a marked path from Portofino. The best vantage point is from *Monte Portofino,* which looms 2,000 feet over the village. The climb is worth it: From here you can see as far as Corsica or explore the beautiful peninsula.

The popularity of the village is understandable, but trying to reach Portofino by the single narrow road can be a nightmare in the summer. Cars are not allowed in the center (parking outside); an alternative is to take a boat from Santa Margherita. It is not surprising that Portofino enthusiastically celebrates San Giorgio's Day (April 23).

③② Return to the Riviera di Levante coast for the 12-kilometer (8-mile) drive from Rapallo to **Chiavari,** another fishing village with narrow, twisting streets and a good harbor. Chiavari's citizens were energetic explorers, and many emigrated to South America in the 19th century. The town boomed, thanks to the wealth of the returning voyagers, but Chiavari still retains many medieval traces in its buildings. There is an interesting **Museo Archeologico** in the center of town. Here you can see finds from an 8th-century BC necropolis (tomb city), which was excavated nearby. *Palazzo Rocca, Piazza Matteotti. Admission free. Open Tues.–Sun. 2–5; closed Mon.*

③③ About 6 kilometers (4 miles) along the coast is the town of **Sestri Levante,** situated at the base of another, tiny, peninsula. Follow the signs for the footpath to the **Parco Castelli** on the peninsula. From here you have excellent views of the town and the coast; the lawns are the perfect spot for a picnic. *Admission free. Open May–Sept., daily 8–noon, 2–7; Oct.–Apr., weekends 8–noon, 2–5.*

Although the center of Sestri is industrial, with steelworks and shipyards, there is a small medieval district surrounding what is known as the **Baia del Silenzio** (Bay of Silence), the small harbor just behind Piazza Matteotti at the base of the peninsula. Walk up one of the alleyways to see some of the worked slate doorways of the older houses.

From Sestri, S1 turns inland past the spectacular Passo del Bracco and does not reach the coast again until the large port of La Spezia, more than 60 kilometers (40 miles) away. The towns that lie on the less accessible coastal strip between Levanto and Portovénere (near La Spezia) are reached by narrow roads that wind down from the hills; until about 50 years ago, they could be reached only by boat. Visits can still be made by boat or by the small local train that runs from Levanto to Riomaggiore and stops at each station. You can drive only as far as Levanto or Riomaggiore, but not between the two.

③④ It's best to make **Levanto** your base for exploring this area. Levanto is a secluded town with good beaches and graceful buildings that date from the 13th century. Many of the buildings are adorned with clever trompe l'oeil paintings that give the impression that real town folk are looking at you from their windows.

Some of the best attractions near Levanto are within walking distance—but the walk can be a hike of up to five hours. Make sure you wear comfortable, sturdy shoes and carry a water bottle, since it can be very hot in the summer. Your goal is the group of almost inaccessible coastal villages known as the ❸❺ **Cinque Terre,** built against steep cliffs and linked by walks.

The first and largest is **Monterosso,** with a 12th-century church in the Ligurian style, lively markets, and small beaches. Next is **Vernazza,** a charming village of narrow streets, small squares and arcades, and the remains of forts dating to the Middle Ages. **Corniglia,** the middle village, is perched on a hillside amid vineyards; it offers excellent views of the entire coastal strip. The last two villages, **Manarola** and **Riomaggiore,** sit on tiny harbors hemmed in by sheer cliffs. It's an adventure to visit these five villages, and the reward for your exertion is a sense of tranquillity amid the dramatic coastal scenery.

❸❻ **Portovénere's** small colorful houses, some dating from the 12th century, were once all connected to the 12th- to 16th-century citadel, so that in times of attack the villagers could reach the safety of the battlements. The town has a strategic position at the end of a peninsula that extends southeast from the Cinque Terre and forms the western border of the Gulf of Spezia. Lord Byron is said to have written *Childe Harold* here. The huge, strange grotto at the base of the seaswept cliff is named after the poet, whose strength and courage were much admired after he swam across the gulf to the village of San Terenzo to visit his friend Shelley. Above the grotto, on a formidable solid mass of rock, is **San Pietro,** a 13th-century Gothic church built on the site of an ancient pagan shrine. With its black-and-white-striped exterior, it is a landmark recognizable from far out at sea.

❸❼ About 8 kilometers (5 miles) from Portovénere is **La Spezia,** a large industrialized naval port. La Spezia lacks the charm of the smaller towns, but it does have the remains of the massive 13th-century **Castel San Giorgio.** There is also an interesting Civic Museum, which houses some remarkable Bronze and Iron Age statues, as well as a collection of traditional local costumes and household implements. *Via Curtatone 9. Open Mon. 9–1, Tues.–Sat. 9–1 and 3–5.*

❸❽ The road to **Lerici,** the last Ligurian town before you reach Tuscany, passes through a magnificent unspoiled coastline of gray cliffs and pine forests. The town once belonged to Tuscan Pisa, and the medieval castle that stands above the splendid bay, which has attracted lovers of nature for centuries, is 13th-century Pisan. Shelley was one of Lerici's best-known visitors and spent some of the happiest months of his life in the lovely white village of **San Terenzo,** 2 kilometers (1 mile) away. The Villa Magni, where he lived, has a collection devoted to him. After Shelley drowned at sea here in 1822, the bay was renamed Golfo dei Poeti, in honor of him and Byron.

What to See and Do with Children

Liguria itself is an attraction for children because its charm and popularity are based more on the scenery of the coastline than on museums and galleries. Watching the local fishermen can be a captivating experience for many children, and the best villages for watching nets being mended or hauls being dragged in are **Camogli, Santa Margherita Ligure,** and **Sestri Levante.** Children might also want to burn off energy with some hiking along the coastal paths; these walks provide lots of opportunities for budding naturalists to examine the local flora. The area around Portofino is ideal for these activities.

Monte di Portofino. The footpaths up to and around the mountain have a wide variety of plant species, as well as excellent views of the Riviera di Levante.

Paraggi. Walk around this eastern stretch of the Portofino peninsula to see some of the plant and tree species that are known as "living fossils" because they survived the glaciers of the Ice Ages.

Acquario del Tirreno. You can combine a trip to a castle with an interesting visit to the aquarium, where there are displays of local fish and plant life in their natural habitat. *Castel Dragone, Camogli. Admission: adults 3,000 lire, children under 10 1,500. Open May–Sept., daily 10–noon and 3–7.*

Villa Doria. This villa near the train station at Pegli (just west of Genoa) has a large park that is a great place for children to run freely. The villa itself, which has been converted into a naval museum, is closed indefinitely for renovation. *Villa Doria, Piazza Bonavino 7, Pegli. Park admission free. Open Oct.– Apr., daily 10–noon and 2–6.*

Villa Durazzo Pallavicini. Also in Pegli, these 19th-century gardens feature temples and artificial lakes arranged to delight children and parents. The villa has an archaeological museum. *Via Pallavicini 11, Pegli. Admission to villa: 3,000 lire; park is free. Open Tues.–Fri. 9–5, Sat. 9–12:30.*

Off the Beaten Track

We have followed the west–east format of the three exploring tours in arranging these sights and attractions.

Galleria Rambaldi. This small gallery contains paintings by Guido Reni, Diego Velázquez, and Veronese. It's worth the side trip just to see the tiny village of **Coldirodi,** inland on A10 between Bordighera and San Remo. *Ring for admittance. Open daily 3–5.*

Museo Spaghetti. This is a serious museum devoted to the history and production of pasta. Its chief artifact is a document, dated 1279, mentioning macaroni. The date is important: It is 16 years before Marco Polo returned from the Far East, proving that Italy did invent spaghetti after all. The museum is located in Pontedassio, about 9 kilometers (6 miles) north of Diano Marina. *Museo Spaghetti. Admission: 2,000 lire. Open daily 2–5.*

Bardinetto. Take the inland road 25 kilometers (15 miles) from Borghetto to reach this attractive village in the middle of an area rich in mushrooms, chestnuts, and raspberries, as well as local cheese. A ruined castle stands high above the village.

Museo d'Arte Orientale Chiossone. The museum, with one of Europe's most extensive collections of Oriental art, stands in a relaxing green park. The Japanese, Chinese, and Thai collections are noteworthy. *Villetta di Negro, Piazza Corvetto, Genoa, tel. 010/542285. Admission: 4,000 lire. Open May–Sept., Tues.–Sat. 9–7, Sun. 9–12:30. Oct–Apr., Tues.–Sat. 9–5, Sun. 9–12:30.*

Shopping

Liguria is famous for its fine laces, its silver and gold filigree work, and its ceramics. Look also for bargains in velvet, macramé, olive wood, and marble. Genoa is the best spot for finding all these specialties, but the coastal towns and villages along the two Ligurian Rivieras have bazaar-style markets in the central squares or along the harborfront. In these markets you can succeed with a bit of bargaining, and your chances improve if you're able to clinch your deal with a word or two in Italian.

Genoa   **Codevilla** (Via Orefici 53, tel. 010/20657). This well-established shop is one of the best jewelers on a street devoted to goldsmiths.

Pescetto (Via Scurreria 8, tel. 010/593637). You'll find designer clothes, perfumes, and gifts in this elegant shop located near Codevilla.

Pietro Romanengo fu Stefano (Via Soziglia 74, tel. 010/297869). Judge for yourself whether the handmade chocolates here are the best in Genoa (the management says they are).

L'Enoteca (Via Porta degli Archi 3 [next to the tourist office], tel. 010/564071). The wine connoisseur will appreciate the selection of rare Ligurian wines on sale in this wine shop.

La Rinascente (Via Vernazza 5) and **Coin** (Via XII Ottobre 4) are Genoa's two major department stores.

Via XX Settembre and **Via Luccoli** are famous for their wide range of small, exclusive shops.

Riviera di Ponente   **Taggia.** There is an antiques market held here on the fourth weekend of the month. *7 km (4 mi) east along S1 from San Remo, then 3 km (2 mi) inland from Armi di Taggia.*

Millesimo. Little rum chocolates known as *millesimi* are produced here. Look for bargains, too, in wrought-iron work, relief work on copper plate, and pieces in local sandstone. *4 km (2½ mi) west of Savona on A10, then 36 km (21 mi) inland on A6.*

Albisola. This is the center of the Ligurian ceramics industry; shops around the central square all have ceramic ware. *3 km (2 mi) inland from Albisola Marina, off S334.*

Campo Ligure. Silver filigree is the specialty of this market town in the attractive Stura Valley. *27 km (17 mi) inland from Voltri on A26 and S456.*

Riviera di Levante   **Zoagli.** This attractive coastal village is famous for its silk velvet. *On S1, 4 km (2½ mi) east of Rapallo.*

Chiavari. The famous straw Campanino chairs are produced here, as well as macramé lace. *On S1, 12 km (7 mi) east of Rapallo.*

Sports

In Liguria, water sports are popular all along the coast. Most resorts have good facilities for swimming, waterskiing, and sailing. The mild climate means that tennis can be played all year, and every town has public courts (usually next to the bocci area).

Biking **Albisola Marina.** *Velo Club Albisola*, (Albisola Superiore, Via Italia 1).
Genoa. *Quito al Mare* (Piazza SanPietro 3r). *Alta Val Bisogno Sports Club* (Via Benedetto da Porto 2/A, tel. 010/804771).
Levanto. *Genoa Club Levanto* (Piazza Staglieno 1, tel. 0187/808160).
Ventimiglia. *Ventimiglia Cycling Club* (Corso Genova 112, tel. 0184/352879).

Bowling **Albenga** (Piazza Corridoni, tel. 0182/52241).
Genoa (Piazza Rizzolio, tel. 010/466671; Via Gobetti 8/A, tel. 010/314102).

Fishing There is good fresh water fishing in most of the remote inland areas. Try the streams around Calizzano. Underwater spearfishing is best at Zoagli, Bordighera, and Nervi. For information about restrictions and licenses, contact **Federazione Italiana della Pesca Sportiva e Attivita Sub-acquee** (Galleria Mazzini 7/1, Genoa, tel. 010/565273).

Golf **Alassio.** *Garlenda Club* (18 holes) (17030 Garlenda, tel. 0182/580012).
Arenzano. *Pineta di Arenzano* (nine holes) (16011 Arenzano, tel. 010/911–1817).
San Remo. *Campo Golf* (18 holes) (Via Campo Golf, tel. 0184/557093).

Horseback Riding **Arenzano** (Via Aurelia 21, tel. 010/911–0616).
Chiavari. *Rivarola Carasco* (Via Veneto 212, tel. 0185/382204). *Boschetto Horse-Riding Club* (Salita Ceiva, tel. 0185/301785).
Genoa. *Ligurian Horse-Riding Club* (Via Bosco 57/7, tel. 010/588872).
Rapallo. *Rapallo Riding Club* (Via Santa Maria Campo 196, tel. 0185/50462).

Tennis Tennis is extremely popular throughout Liguria all year long. It would be impossible to list every court because each town has at least one set of public courts or a private club that welcomes visitors. Local Pro Loco tourist offices (*see* Important Addresses and Numbers in Essential Information, *above*) can provide information on the availability of courts and short-term membership in local clubs.

Waterskiing **La Spezia.** *La Spezia Motorboat Club* (Via della Marina 224, tel. 0187/50401).

Beaches

Along both Ligurian Rivieras, the beaches are protected by mountains, so the climate is mild and the foliage lush. The Riviera di Ponente, from Genoa west to the French border, has both sandy and pebbly beaches with some quiet bays. **Alassio** has a long sandy beach at the head of a bay. The villages of **Diano Marina** and **Pia** (near Finale Ligure) have fine sandy beaches with all the amenities of modern resorts. **Varazze** has a wide, sandy beach and many tall palm trees. **Arenzano,** 22 kilometers (14 miles) west of Genoa, is perhaps the last pleasant beach resort on the Riviera di Ponente before greater Genoa's industrial influence takes over. Arenzano's beach is large and broad; along it you'll find nearly every sports facility.

The Riviera di Levante includes Genoa and the coast east as far as Portovénere. Beaches on this coast are rocky, with many spectacular cliffs near the sea. There are small coves *(ciazze)* where you can dock your boat and swim in relatively calm water. The combination of sea, foliage, and rocks is enticing. **Portofino Promontory** has one sandy beach, on the east side, at **Paraggi.** From Chiavari to Cavi di Lavagna, the coast becomes a bit gentler, with a few sandy areas. From Sestri Levante down to Portovénere, the coast is rugged; however, these areas are good for sailing and skin diving.

Dining and Lodging

Dining Liguria makes the best of its coastal location by utilizing all sorts of seafood. Anchovies, sea bass, squid, and octopus are popular ingredients in the cuisine, which uses liberal amounts of olive oil and garlic. *Datteri*, tiny razor clams unique to Liguria, figure in *zuppa di datteri* (a type of chowder) and in many pasta dishes. Another famous Ligurian pasta sauce is *pesto*, made from pine nuts, garlic, oil, cheese, and a type of basil that grows only along the coastal hills. *Vitello* (veal) is the most popular meat and is often served stuffed, as in *cima*. You should also try the succulent *agnello* (lamb).

When not snacking on pizza sold by the slice or by weight, Genoans and other Ligurians eat *focaccia*, a salty, pizzalike bread that goes well with a cool glass of wine. Local vineyards tend to produce mainly light and refreshing whites, such as Pigato, Vermentino Ligure, and Cinque Terre. Rossese and Dolceacqua are good reds. Desserts are less rich than those in other Italian regions, and the Ligurians often finish a meal with fresh fruit. Homemade *gelato* (ice cream) is another favorite.

Highly recommended restaurants are indicated by a star ★.

Category	Cost*
Very Expensive	over 85,000 lire
Expensive	65,000–85,000 lire
Moderate	35,000–65,000 lire
Inexpensive	under 35,000 lire

per person, including house wine, service, and tax

Lodging There are fewer Ligurian bargains in lodging than in dining. Constant demand combines with a limited choice to create a high average price, at least in comparison with other Italian regions. Genoa, the largest city in the region, has surprisingly few hotels, and these tend to be mainly expensive establishments geared more to the needs of business clients than to tourists. Visitors prefer to stay in the towns and resorts along the coast, where there is a better range of accommodations. Here, though, you should try to have reservations, particularly during the peak summer period. The best bargains are in the less-visited inland areas: There are few hotels in this part of Liguria, but many of them are family-run and welcoming.

Highly recommended lodgings are indicated by a star ★.

Category	Cost*
Very Expensive	over 300,000 lire
Expensive	170,000–300,000 lire
Moderate	110,000–170,000 lire
Inexpensive	under 110,000 lire

All prices are for a standard double room for two, including service and 9% IVA (19% for luxury establishments).

Alassio
Dining

Palma. Centrally located near the train station, La Palma is an exclusive, elegant little place seating only 30. It specializes in Ligurian seafood dishes as well as the basic Italian specialties, for those who prefer meat. Try the *soglia in vino rosso* (sole in red wine) or *branzino con carciofi* (sea bass with artichokes). *Via Cavour 5, tel. 0182/640314. Reservations advised. Dress: casual. AE, DC, MC, V. Closed Wed. and Nov. Expensive.*

Lodging

Eden. This small but well-maintained and friendly hotel has a beachfront location in a quiet part of town, about a 10-minute walk along the beach from the center. Many rooms have sea views, and the beachfront terrace has a seafood restaurant for guests only. *Passeggiata Cadorna 20, tel. 0182/640281. 29 rooms, most with bath or shower. Facilities: restaurant, bar, beach facilities. MC, V. Closed Nov.–Jan. Inexpensive.*

Bordighera
Dining

Le Chaudron. The charming rustic interior, with ancient Roman arches, has the look of restaurants across the French border in Provence. Ligurian specialties are featured on the predominantly seafood menu of this centrally located restaurant: Try the *branzino al sale grosso* (sea bass baked in a mold of sea salt) or *spaghetti con aragosta* (with tiny lobsters). Other specialties, such as the *coquilles St. Jacques*, reflect the French influence. *Piazza Bengasi 2, tel. 0184/263592. Reservations advised. Dress: casual. AE, DC, MC, V. Closed Mon. and Feb. 1–15, July 1–15. Moderate.*

La Reserve Tastevin. This traditional and informal trattoria has access to the beach and excellent views of the sea from the dining room. There are even changing rooms for anyone who wants a postlunch dip. Concentrate on the seafood here: *Muscoli alla marinara* (mussel soup) is a hearty concoction that can be ordered as a starter or a main course. *Via Arziglia 20, tel. 0184/261322. No reservations. Dress: casual. AE, DC, MC, V. Closed Sun. evenings, Mon. (except July and Aug.), and Oct. 20–Dec. 20. Expensive.*

Lodging

Grand Hotel del Mare. Located at the top of a steep hill rising from the beach, this elegant hotel lives up to its name; the service and facilities are impeccable. The large rooms have panoramic views of the coastline; ask for one facing the water. The hotel restaurant enjoys a fine reputation. *Via Portico della Punta 34, tel. 0184/262201, fax 0184/262394. 109 rooms with bath. Facilities: beach, saltwater pool, garden, tennis courts, restaurant, piano bar. AE, MC, V. Closed Oct.–Dec. 22. Expensive.*

Grand Hotel Capo Ampelio. This hotel occupies a converted villa on a hill overlooking the town and the coastline; recent refurbishing has maintained the traditional architectural features in the reception rooms and staircases but added convenient modern features to the rooms. The hotel is somewhat outside the town center, so rooms are quiet; ask for a room with a sea view. *Via Virgilio 5, tel. 0184/264333, fax 0184/264244. 104 rooms with bath. Facilities: bar, restaurant, garden, pool. AE, DC, MC, V. Closed Nov. 20–Dec. 20. Expensive.*

Camogli
Dining

Vento Ariel. This tiny but friendly restaurant is located right on the port, and it has informal but elegant decor and place settings. It serves seafood only and regularly runs out of items because it relies on the day's catch. Try the *spaghetti alle vongole* (with clams) or the grilled mixed fish, which differs according to the day's haul. *Calata Porto, tel. 0185/771080. Reservations advised. Dress: casual. AE, DC, MC, V. Closed Wed. and Feb. Expensive.*

Lodging
★

Cenobio dei Dogi. Although this hilltop villa perched over the town was once the summer home of Genoa's doges (medieval elected rulers), it now has a modern appearance. The rooms have TV and air-conditioning, and the hotel facilities make it a compound that many visitors never wish to leave. Guests can relax in the colorful park gazing out on the outstanding views of the Portofino peninsula, or they can enjoy numerous sporting activities. Although the rooms are not lavishly appointed, many have balconies with panoramic views. *Via Cuneo 34, tel. 0185/770041, fax 0185/772796. 88 rooms with bath. Facilities: private beach, pool, tennis courts, park, bar, restaurant. AE, MC, V. Closed Jan. 7–Mar. 7. Expensive.*

Diano Marina
Dining

Il Caminetto. Seafood and regional dishes are featured in this simple, cheerful restaurant with a homey feel. Make sure the waiter lets you know about the daily special, which can sometimes be an unusual item such as *gnocchetti* (dumplings) or *anguille in salsa piccante* (grilled baby eels in a spicy sauce). *Via Olanda 1, tel. 0183/494700. Reservations advised weekends and in summer. Dress: casual. AE, DC, MC, V. Closed Mon. and Feb. 25–Mar. 10, Nov. 6–20. Moderate.*

★

Candidollo. Take the valley road just a couple of miles north to find this charming and good-value restaurant, which uses locally grown ingredients as well as freshly caught seafood. *Carciofi* (artichokes), peaches, and apricots—all grown on neighboring farms—accompany a selection of fish and meat dishes that vary according to the season. Portions are large. *Diano Borello, tel. 0183/43025. Reservations advised. Dress: casual. No credit cards. Closed Mon. lunch, Tues. and Nov.–Apr. (except several days around Christmas and Easter). Inexpensive.*

Lodging

Diana Majestic. This quiet hotel provides a respite from the otherwise noisy resort: In midsummer the only sounds you hear are the cicadas in the neighboring olive groves and the songs of birds. The rooms are on the small side but bright, and many of them have balconies where you can have breakfast or a drink looking out over the beautiful coastline. *Via degli Oleandri 15, tel. 0183/495445. 80 rooms with bath or shower. Facilities: private beach, extensive garden, pool, restaurant. No credit cards. Closed Nov.–May. Moderate.*

Genoa
Dining

Gran Gotto. Classic regional dishes are served in this small, elegant restaurant near Stazione Brignole in the modern part of town. The service is quick and helpful; the waiter will proudly detail the ingredients of the day's specials. Try the *ripieni* (stuffed vegetables) and the *antica torte di mele* (apple pie), one of the many excellent homemade desserts. *Via Fiume 11r, tel. 010/564344. Reservations advised. Jacket and tie required. AE, DC, MC, V. Closed Sat. lunch, Sun., and Aug. 10–31. Expensive.*

★ **Zeffirino.** The five Belloni brothers share the chef's duties at this remarkable restaurant, which is full of odd combinations. The decor is a mixture of styles and materials, ranging from rustic wood to modern metallic. Try the *passutelli* (ravioli stuffed with ricotta cheese and fruit) or any of the homemade pasta dishes. *Via XX Settembre 20, tel. 010/591990. Reservations advised. Jacket and tie required. AE, DC, MC, V. Closed Wed. Expensive.*

Da Genio. On a byway in old Genoa, near Piazza Dante, this classic trattoria serves equally classic Genoese dishes, including *trenette al pesto* (pasta with pesto sauce) and minestrone, also laced with a dollop of pesto. *Salita San Leonardo 61r, tel. 010/546463. Reservations advised. Dress: casual. No credit cards. Closed Sun. and Aug. 1–30. Moderate.*

Melograno. Tuscan specialties figure prominently on the menu of this small restaurant decorated in art-nouveau style. It is located in the southern part of Genoa and overlooks the harbor. In addition to the Tuscan specialties, such as *bistecca alla fiorentina* (charcoal-grilled steak, Florence-style), there are many homemade items, including gelato and pesto. *Via Maccaggi 62r, tel. 010/546407. Reservations required. Dress: casual. No credit cards. Closed Sun. and Aug. 8–31. Moderate.*

7 Nasi. The historic Quarto dei Mille district is the setting for this small establishment, proudly supervised by its chef, Enrico Nasi, who specializes in a wide range of Ligurian seafood dishes. Homemade desserts are also recommended. Summertime meals are served on the terrace, which has an excellent view of the bustling harbor. Try the *zuppa di datteri* (Ligurian clam chowder) if you see it on the menu. *Via Quarto 16, tel. 010/337357. No reservations. Dress: casual. AE, DC, MC, V. Closed Tues. Moderate.*

Marinella. This restaurant is located in Nervi, a suburb 10 kilometers (6 miles) east of the center of Genoa. It has a waterside location, which attracts regular customers as much as do its seafood specialties. (There's an inexpensive hotel annex, too.) Try *trofie al pesto* (fresh pasta with pesto, potatoes, and green beans); main dishes change from day to day, according to the fishermen's catch. *Passeggiata Anita Garibaldi 18, Nervi, tel. 010/321429. Reservations advised weekends. Dress: casual. AE, DC, MC, V. Closed Fri. and Nov. Moderate.*

Trattoria Walter. This unpretentious family-run restaurant is in the heart of the city, near Palazzo Spinola. The service is simple and straightforward, and the price is right for a good, inexpensive sampling of genuine Genoese specialties. *Via Colalanza 2, corner of Via San Luca, tel. 010/290524. No reservations. Dress: casual. No credit cards. Closed Sun. and Aug. 1–21. Inexpensive.*

Lodging **Bristol Palace.** This grand hotel, located on a fashionable downtown shopping street, was built in the last century and maintains the old-fashioned traditions of courtesy and discretion. The rooms are large, with high ceilings, and paintings decorate the large reception rooms. There's no restaurant, but the hotel is in the heart of the downtown area. *Via XX Settembre 35, tel. 010/592541, fax 010/561756. 130 rooms with bath. Facilities: bar, no-smoking rooms. AE, DC, MC, V. Very Expensive.*

President. This member of the Starhotel chain of comfortable and reliable business hotels is also well located for tourists. The high-rise hotel opened in 1991 as part of a large new commerical and convention center near Brignole station. The rooms have big windows and modern decor in tones of dusty rose and blue-gray, with sparkling white baths. There's a large bar area between the desk and the terrace, which becomes an outdoor café in fair weather. *Corte Lambruschini 4, tel. 010/5727, fax 010/553-1820. 198 rooms with bath or shower. Facilities: bar, restaurant, parking. AE, DC, MC, V. Very Expensive.*

★ **Pagoda Residence.** If you want to stay at a top-quality hotel outside the center of Genoa, try this unusual establishment in Nervi, 10 kilometers (6 miles) east of Genoa. It occupies a 19th-century building designed to look like a pagoda, built at a time when Europe was fascinated by the exotic Orient. Inside, the rooms have modern decorations and furnishings. Reception rooms are decorated in a combination of Venetian and Baroque styles, with an emphasis on dark wood. It's set next to a large, shady park. *Via Capolungo 15, Nervi, tel. 010/326161, fax 010/321218. 21 rooms with bath. Facilities: bar, restaurant, private beach, garden. AE, DC, MC, V. Expensive.*

★ **Agnello d'Oro.** The central location in Genoa's old quarter, about 100 yards from Stazione Principe, makes this modest hotel a good choice for budget travelers who want to be in the thick of things. The simple room furnishings have been improved by the recent renovations, which include air-conditioning. Full-board rates (rates that include all meals, which are eaten at the hotel) make staying here a good bargain. *Vico delle Monachette 6, tel. 010/262084. 40 rooms, 37 with bath. Facilities: bar, terrace, restaurant (guests only; closed Oct.–Mar.). DC, MC, V. Inexpensive.*

Rio. Located by Ponte Calvi in the old harbor area, the sturdy, comfortable Rio was built during the 19th-century hotel boom. Marble floors and bright rooms give the hotel an airy feel, in refreshing contrast to the narrow streets that surround it. There is no restaurant, but Continental breakfast is available. *Via al Ponte Calvi 5, tel. 010/290551, fax 010/290554. 47 rooms with shower. AE, DC, MC, V. Closed Jan. Inexpensive.*

Levanto
Dining

Araldo. Arches and frescoes add to the atmosphere of this elegant little restaurant that opened in 1991. Food and service are outstanding; the menu, featuring creative Mediterranean cuisine, changes with the seasons and offers more than 100 wines. *Via Jacopo 24, tel. 0187/807253. Reservations advised. Jacket preferred. Closed Mon. AE, DC, MC, V. Moderate–Expensive.*

Lodging
★

Stella Maris. Located in the center of Levanto and only a 10-minute walk from the beach, the Stella Maris is a real find. It takes up one floor of a 19th-century *palazzo* (the ground floor now houses the palatial offices of a bank). Seven rooms are decorated with original frescoes and 19th-century furniture and seven are modern; the couple who run the hotel have an infectious enthusiasm for the building's history and decoration. You must stay on a half-board plan in the summer, but it's no sacrifice because the home cooking features Ligurian seafood specialties; you can have your homemade ice cream in the sunny garden. *Via Marconi 4, tel. 0187/808258. 14 rooms with bath (showers). Facilities: garden, restaurant. No credit cards. Closed Nov. Inexpensive.*

Monterosso **Il Gigante.** A good introduction to Ligurian seafood is the
(Cinque Terre) *zuppa di pesce* (fish soup) served at this traditional trattoria in
Dining one of the fishing villages of the Cinque Terre. This soup is usually served as a first course, but is filling enough to be an entrée. The waiters are happy to advise you on the daily specials,
which can include *risotto di frutti di mare* (shellfish risotto) and
spaghetti with an octopus sauce. *Monterosso al Mare, tel. 0187/
817401. Reservations advised. Dress: casual. AE, DC, MC, V.
Closed Tues. and Oct. 15–Mar. 15. Moderate.*

Lodging **Porto Roca.** Five minutes out of town and located on a hill with
★ excellent sea views, Porto Roca is removed from the crowds
who visit the village, especially on weekends. It has the look of
a well-kept villa, interiors with authentic antique pieces, and
ample terraces. The rooms are bright and airy, with sea
breezes that visitors to the town below often miss. Porto Roca
is located on a network of not-too-demanding hill walks.
*Monterosso al Mare, tel. 0187/817502, fax 0187/817692. 43
rooms with bath or shower. Facilities: bar, terrace, gardens,
restaurant. AE, MC, V. Closed Nov.–Mar. 15. Expensive.*

Portofino **Il Pitosforo.** A chic, tan clientele, many with luxury yachts in
Dining the harbor, give this waterfront restaurant a glamorous atmosphere. *Spaghetti di frutti di mare* (with a mixed seafood sauce)
is recommended; adventurous diners might want to try *lo
stocco accomodou* (dried cod in a savory sauce of tomatoes, raisins, and pine nuts). *Portofino, tel. 0185/269020. Reservations
required. Jacket required. AE, DC, MC, V. Closed Tues. and
all Jan. and Feb. Very Expensive.*

Taverna del Marinaio. Relatively moderate prices in this costly
village are not the only thing this small, family-run restaurant
has to offer. Located under vaulted porticoes on the harbor,
with tables outside in fair weather, it serves homemade
taglierini con gamberi (fresh noodles with shrimp sauce) and
fish with capers and olives or baked with onions. *Piazza
Martiri Olivetta 36, tel. 0185/269103. Reservations advised.
Dress: casual. MC, V. Closed Tues., and Nov.–Dec. Moderate.*

Lodging **Splendido.** Most people resort to superlatives when trying to
★ describe this luxury hotel, built in the '20s on a hill overlooking
the sea. The abiding impression is one of color, from the coordinated fabrics and furnishings of the rooms to the fresh flowers
in the reception rooms and the large terrace below the hotel.
It's like a Jazz Age film set, and you almost expect to see a
Bugatti or Daimler roll up the winding drive from Portofino below. A network of footpaths leads away from the wooded
grounds. The Splendido's relatively small size means you get
even more personal attention than at other luxury hotels. *16034
Portofino, tel. 0185/269551, fax 0185/269614. 65 rooms with
bath. Facilities: pool, tennis court, garden, terrace, bars, restaurant. AE, DC, MC, V. Closed Nov.–Mar. Very Expensive.*

Piccolo Hotel. This modern hotel is located farther down the
same hill occupied by the Splendido, so it shares many of the
advantages of its more luxurious (and expensive) neighbor.
Many rooms look out over the Portofino harbor or onto the well-
tended gardens surrounding the hotel. The Piccolo draws a
younger clientele than the Splendido, and there is a lively atmosphere in the bar. *Portofino, tel. 0185/69015. 26 rooms with*

bath. Facilities: bar, garden. AE, DC, MC, V. Closed Nov.– Mar. Moderate.

Portovénere **Da Iseo.** Try to get one of the tables outside at this waterfront
Dining restaurant, which is decorated in the style of a local fishing hut,
with nets and buoys along the walls. Seafood is the only choice:
It's fresh and plentiful. Try the *zuppa di datteri* (Ligurian clam
chowder), *spaghetti ai datteri* (with Ligurian clams), or the
fritto misto di frutti di mare (mixed grilled seafood).
*Portovénere, tel. 0187/900610. Reservations advised in sum-
mer. Dress: casual. AE, DC, MC. Closed Wed. and Jan.–Feb.
Moderate.*

Lodging **Royal Sporting.** Appearances are deceptive at this modern ho-
★ tel, which is located on the beach, about a 10-minute walk from
the village. From the outside, the stone construction seems
austere and unwelcoming, but the courtyards and interior are
colorful and vibrant. There are fresh flowers and potted plants
in the reception rooms and terraces, and the cool, airy rooms all
have sea views. The sports facilities are among the best in the
area. *Via dell' Olivo 345, tel. 0187/900326, fax 0187/529060. 62
rooms with bath. Facilities: bar, restaurant, pool, private
beach, tennis court, gardens. AE, DC, MC, V. Closed Oct. 15–
Apr. (open Easter Week). Moderate–Expensive.*
Locanda San Pietro. This good-value inn occupies a castle at
the edge of the village and is five minutes from the beach. The
rooms, decorated in art-nouveau style, are quiet. Most have
good views of the coastline around Portovénere. The restaurant features local cuisine and stresses seafood. *Portovenere,
tel. 0187/900616. 31 rooms with bath or shower. Facilities: bar,
restaurant. AE, MC. Closed Jan. 2–Mar. 14. Inexpensive.*

Rapallo **Da Ardito.** This lively trattoria is in the village of San Pietro di
Dining Novella, which is just north of Rapallo. It's extremely popular
with wine lovers, who appreciate the attention given to the
wine list. For a change from seafood, try the *pansotti*, pasta
served with creamy walnut sauce. *Via Canale 9, San Pietro di
Novella, tel. 0185/51551. Reservations advised. Dress: casual.
MC, V. Closed Mon. and Feb. Moderate.*
Savoia. People-watching and pizzas are the attractions of this
modern restaurant occupying a sunny position just off the
beach. There's a good view of the promenade from nearly every
table, and you can relax, knowing that you won't break the
bank with any of the excellent pizzas. Wash it down with a cool
glass of Pigato. *Piazza IV Novembre 3, tel. 0185/247021. No
reservations. Dress: casual. No credit cards. Closed Sun. Inexpensive.*

Lodging **Eurotel.** On the old coast road, but in an elevated position above
the harbor, the Eurotel is a modern building set in a garden,
with a large swimming pool. The decor is functional rather than
charming, but rooms are bright, with balconies and sea views.
*Via Aurelia Ponente 22, tel. 0185/60981, fax 0185/50635. 65
rooms with bath. Facilities: pool, garden, bar, restaurant. AE,
DC, MC, V. Closed Jan. 8–Feb. 15. Expensive.*
Moderno e Reale. This converted 19th-century villa is surrounded by shady gardens, giving it a surprisingly quiet atmosphere, considering its central location near the port. The
rooms are bright and decorated with colorful fabrics and modern pictures: Ask for a room facing the sea. The train station is
less than a quarter mile down Corso Matteotti. *Via Gramsci 6,*

tel. 0185/50601. 49 rooms, 38 rooms with bath or shower. Facilities: garden, bar, restaurant. DC, MC, V. Inexpensive.

San Remo **Bagatto.** Centrally located on San Remo's main thoroughfare,
Dining Bagatto has a good selection of classic Italian and regional
★ dishes, including *trenette al pesto* (pasta with pesto sauce) and
seafood. Excellent local wines include Pigato and Rossese. *Via
Matteotti 145, tel. 0184/85500. Reservations advised. Dress:
casual. AE, DC, MC, V. Closed Sun. and June. Moderate.*

Lodging **Royal.** It would take a dedicated hedonist to determine wheth-
★ er this deluxe hotel or the Splendido in Portofino is the most
luxurious in Liguria. One major difference is the location: Only
a few paces from the Casino and the train station, the Royal is
definitely part of San Remo, unlike the Splendido, which is set
above Portofino. Try for a room facing the sea or one of the new
penthouse rooms and suites, with terrific views. The rooms
have a mixture of modern appliances and antique furnishings;
each has a unique feel. It is claimed that there is nearly always a
member of European royalty in residence; the best place to find
out is on the terrace, where an orchestra plays each night under the stars in season. *Corso Imperatrice 80, tel. 0184/5391,
fax 0184/61445. 149 rooms and suites with bath. Facilities: bar,
restaurant, terrace, pool, tennis courts. AE, DC, MC, V.
Closed Oct. 9–Dec. 18. Very Expensive.*

Paradiso. This small hotel is almost directly behind the Royal,
so it shares some of the advantages of its grander neighbor. A
quiet, palm-fringed garden gives it an air of seclusion, which is
a plus in this sometimes hectic city. The rooms are modern and
bright, and many have a little terrace. The hotel restaurant has
a good fixed-price menu. *Via Roccasterone 12, tel. 0184/571211,
fax 0184/578176. 41 rooms with bath or shower. Facilities: bar,
restaurant, garden. AE, DC, MC, V. Moderate.*

Santa Margherita **Cesarina.** The menu of this popular restaurant concentrates on
Ligure locally caught fish, accompanied by an excellent selection of Li-
Dining gurian wines such as Pigato. The daily specials are usually
★ baked fish, but the menu also includes *acciughe ripiene* (stuffed
anchovies) and *salmone marinato* (marinated salmon). *Via
Mameli 2/c, tel. 0185/286059. Reservations required. Jacket required. AE, DC, MC, V. Closed Wed. and Mar. 5–17, Dec. 12–
27. Expensive.*

La Bassa Prora. This waterfront restaurant is a popular spot,
partly because of its central location and partly because of the
fresh fish specials, usually grilled. The *antipasto misto di
frutti di mare* (mixed seafood antipasto) is excellent, and the
main courses provide good value for the money. *Via Garibaldi
7, tel. 0185/286586. No reservations. Dress: casual. AE, V.
Closed Mon. evenings, Tues. and mid-Sept.–mid-Oct. Inexpensive–Moderate.*

Lodging **Grand Hotel Miramare.** Take the shore road south from town to
reach this palatial turn-of-the-century hotel overlooking the
bay. It has a lush garden and swimming pool, and a private
swimming area on the sea. The bright and airy rooms are decorated in colonial or late-19th-century style. The best have
ocean views, as do the hotel terraces. *Lungomare Milite Ignoto
30, tel. 0185/287013, fax 0185/284651. 83 rooms with bath. Facilities: bar, restaurant, garden, pool, private beach, waterskiing. AE, MC, V. Very Expensive.*

Imperial Palace. Via Pagana climbs north out of Santa
Margherita Ligure on its way toward Rapallo; just outside

town it passes this Old World luxury hotel, which is set in an extensive park. The rooms are furnished with antiques; many overlook the shore drive to the sea. The reception rooms are elegantly decorated with tall windows, plush chairs, and potted plants. *Via Pagana 19, tel. 0185/288991, fax 0185/284223. 96 rooms with bath. Facilities: private beach, pool, golf, restaurant, bar, garden. AE, DC, MC, V. Closed Nov.–Apr. 15. Very Expensive.*

Ventimiglia
Dining

La Mortola. Take the coast road about five minutes west from Ventimiglia, until you reach Mortola Inferiore, where you will find this elegant restaurant opposite the famous Hanbury Gardens. The menu is a sophisticated mixture of Italian, Scandinavian, and international dishes, with smorgasbord every Sunday noon, and *rombo al vapore* (steamed turbot, served with butter and radishes). *Mortola Inferiore, tel. 0184/38482. Reservations advised. Jacket and tie required. AE, DC, MC, V. Closed Sun. evening, Mon., and Nov. Moderate.*

Lodging
★

La Riserva. Just 3 miles west of Ventimiglia, but more than 1,100 feet above sea level, is the village of Castel d'Appio, where you'll find this innlike establishment. The staff is very helpful, providing, for example, regular lifts into town for those without cars. But there's no real need to leave La Riserva; apart from its excellent restaurant, it offers numerous activities and a lovely terrace for drinks or sunbathing. Full-board rates are a bargain. Try for a room facing the sea. *Castel d'Appio, tel. 0184/229533, fax 0184/229712. 29 rooms with bath or shower. Facilities: tennis, garden, terrace bar, restaurant, pool, well-marked walks. AE, DC, MC, V. Closed Sept. 20–Easter (except Dec. 18–Jan. 6). Moderate.*

The Arts and Nightlife

The Arts

Music

Alassio. Each September sees a **jazz festival,** with internationally renowned musicians and local bands creating a lively atmosphere in various venues around town.

Cervo. There is an **International Festival of Chamber Music** in July and August.

Dance

Nervi. The grounds of Villa Gropallo provide the setting for an **International Festival of Ballet** (tel. 010/542792) usually held throughout July.

Opera

Genoa. The opera season (Oct.–May) of **Teatro Carlo Felice** (Via XXV Aprile, tel. 010/591697) attracts many lavish productions and occasionally sees the debut of a new work.

Nightlife

Even Genoa, Liguria's largest city, cannot compare with Milan or Rome in the field of organized evening entertainment, but that isn't a problem because a lot of the fun of staying in Liguria is its informal and easygoing atmosphere. It's hard to imagine a more enjoyable activity than sipping local wine outside a café on a warm summer evening, knowing that your eardrums and wallet won't be damaged.

Casinos The **San Remo Casino** is one of only four in Italy. It is a sophisticated establishment reminiscent of the turn of the century. The view over the Ligurian coast is free, even if nothing else is. *Corso Inglese, San Remo. Open daily 2 PM–2 AM.*

Bars **Bordighera.** Have a quiet drink in the piano bar of the **Grand Hotel del Mare** (*see* Dining and Lodging, *above*).

Nightclubs **San Remo.** The casino (*see above*) has a nightclub and restaurant, as well as gaming tables.

Discos **San Remo.** *Nabila* (Giardina Vittorio Veneto 74, tel. 0184/80959).

Santa Margherita Ligure. *Covo di Nord Est* (Lungomare Rossetti 1, tel. 0185/286558).

9 Piedmont/ Valle d'Aosta

From Turin to the Alps and Across the Po Plain

From Alpine valleys hemming the highest mountains in Europe to the mist-shrouded lowlands skirting the Po River, from pulsating industrial centers turning out the best of Italian design to tiny stone villages isolated above the clouds, from hearty peasant cooking in farmhouse kitchens to French-flavored delicacies washed down by some of the finest wines in Italy, Piedmont and the spectacular Valle d'Aosta offer the traveler a store of historical, cultural, and natural riches.

Piedmont's Italian Alps afford excellent skiing and climbing at famous resort towns such as Courmayeur and Breuil-Cervinia. In the lowlands, Turin, the regional capital, is a historical and spiritual center that today also serves as the heart of Italy's booming auto industry. Nearby are Alba, home of the famous Italian white truffles, seasonal delicacies that sell for more than $1,000 per pound; Asti, Barolo, and Barbaresco, the famous wine centers; and the modern business hubs Ivrea, Novara, and Alessandria.

Tucked away at the foot of the Pennine, Graian, Cottian, and Maritime Alps mountains (the name Piemonte, in Italian, means "foot of the mountains"), Piedmont and the autonomous region of Valle d'Aosta just north of it seem more akin to neighboring France and Switzerland. You'll hear the word *madama* more often than *signora* spoken to the well-dressed women in the elegant cafés of Turin, and French is often used in the more remote mountain hamlets.

Piedmont was originally inhabited by Celtic tribes who were absorbed by the Romans. As allies of Rome, the Celts held off Hannibal when he came down through the Alpine passes with his elephants but were eventually defeated, and their capital—Taurasia, the present Turin—was destroyed. The Romans rebuilt the city, giving its streets the grid pattern that survives today. Roman ruins can be found throughout the regions and are particularly abundant in the town of Aosta.

With the fall of the Roman empire, Piedmont suffered the fate of the rest of Italy and was successively occupied and ravaged by barbarians from the east and the north. In the 11th century, a feudal French family named Savoy ruled Turin briefly; toward the end of the 13th century they returned to the area, where they would remain, almost continuously, for 500 years. In 1798 the French Republican armies invaded Italy, but when Napoleon's empire fell, the House of Savoy returned to power in Piedmont.

Beginning in 1848, Piedmont was one of the principal centers of the Risorgimento, the movement for Italian unity. In 1861 the Chamber of Deputies of Turin declared Italy a united kingdom. Rome became the capital in 1870, marking the end of Piedmont's importance in the political sphere. Nevertheless, the architectural splendors of Turin continued to draw travelers.

Piedmont became one of the first industrialized regions in Italy, and the automotive giant FIAT—the Fabbrica Italiana Automobili Torino—was established here in 1899. Today the region is the center of Italy's automobile, metalworking, chemical, and candy industries, having attracted thousands of workers from Italy's impoverished south.

The Valle d'Aosta, to the north, is famous for its impressive fortified castles and splendid Alpine beauty. It was settled in the

3rd millennium BC by people from the Mediterranean and later by a Celtic tribe known as the Salassi, who eventually fell to the Romans. The Saracens were here in the 10th century; by the 12th century, the Savoy family had established itself, and the region's feudal nobles moved into the countryside, building the massive castles that still stand. Valle d'Aosta enjoyed relative autonomy as part of the Savoy kingdom and was briefly ruled by the French four separate times. The province is still officially French-Italian bilingual.

Essential Information

Important Addresses and Numbers

Tourist Information **Alessandria** (Via Savona 26, tel. 0131/51021).
Aosta (Piazza E. Chanoux 8, tel. 0165/35655).
Asti (Piazza Alfieri 34, tel. 0141/50357).
Bardonecchia (Viale Vittoria 44, tel. 0122/99032).
Courmayeur (Piazzale Monte Bianco, tel. 0165/842060).
Ivrea (Corso Vercelli 1, tel. 0125/49687).
Novara (Via Dominioni 4, tel. 0321/23398).
Turin (Via Roma 222, tel. 011/535901; Porta Nuova Train Station, tel. 011/531327).

Emergencies **General Emergencies,** tel. 113. **Police,** tel. 112.

Doctors and Dentists Call 113 and ask for "Pronto Soccorso" (First Aid); this will put you in touch with someone who can recommend a doctor or dentist.

Late-Night Pharmacies **Aosta.** *Farmacia Centrale* (Piazza E. Chanoux 35, tel. 0165/362205). **Turin.** *Farmacia Internazionale* (Via C. Alberto 24, tel. 011/535144). Pharmacies in these cities and throughout the region take turns staying open late and on Sundays. Call 192 for the latest information on which are open.

Car Rental **Ivrea.** *Avis* (Corso Nigra 78, tel. 0125/422091).
Turin. *Avis* (Corso Turati 15, tel. 011/501107; Caselle Airport, tel. 011/470–1528). *Hertz* (Corso Marconi 19, tel. 011/650–4504; Caselle Airport, tel. 011/470–1103).

Arriving and Departing by Plane

The region's only international airport, **Aeroporto Caselle,** is 18 kilometers (11 miles) north of Turin. Alitalia, TWA, and some charter operators offer flights to Turin from the United States via Rome or Milan. The airport is notoriously foggy in winter, and many flights are diverted to Genoa, on the coast, with bus connections provided to Turin. Buses from Caselle Airport to Turin arrive at the bus station on Corso Inghilterra in the center of the city.

Arriving and Departing by Car, Train, and Bus

By Car Italy's *autostrada* (superhighway) network links the region with the rest of Italy and neighboring France. Aosta, Turin, and Alessandria all have autostrada connections, with the A4 heading east to Milan and the A6 heading south to the Ligurian coast and Genoa. If you drive in from France or Switzerland, you pass through either the Mount Blanc or Grand St. Bernard tunnels: These are two of the most dramatic entrances to Italy.

By Train   Turin is on the main Paris–Rome express line and is also connected with Milan, only 90 minutes away on the fast train. The fastest trains cover the 667-kilometer (400-mile) trip to Rome in about six hours, but most of the services take about nine.

By Bus   Two Turin-based lines, **SADEM** (Via della Repubblica 14, Grugliasco, Turin, tel. 011/301616) and **SAPAV** (Corso Torino 396, Pinerolo, Turin, tel. 011/794277), offer services along the autostrada network to Genoa, Milan, and more distant destinations in Italy. **SITA** buses, part of the nationwide system, also connect Turin with the rest of Italy. The main bus station for all these services is on the corner of Corso Inghilterra and Corso Vittorio Emanuele.

Getting Around

By Car   Turin is the hub of all the transportation systems in Piedmont, with autostrada connections to the north, south, and east. Well-paved secondary roads run through the rest of the region, following the course of mountain valleys in many places. Sudden winter storms can close off some of the mountain stretches: For information on road conditions, call tel. 011/5711.

By Train   Services to the larger cities east of Turin are part of the extensive and reliable train network serving the Lombard Plain. West of the region's capital, however, the train services soon peter out in the steep mountain valleys. Continuing connections by bus serve these valleys, and information about train/bus mountain services can be obtained from train stations.

By Bus   **SADEM** and **SAPAV** (*see* Arriving and Departing by Bus, *above*) are the specialists in bus transportation in Piedmont and the Valle d'Aosta. **SAVDA** (Strada Ponte Suaz 6, Aosta, tel. 0141/361244) specializes in mountain service, providing frequent links between Aosta, Turin, and Courmayeur.

Guided Tours

Turin's guided tours are organized by the city's tourist office at Via Roma 222 (tel. 011/535901). The range of tours is extensive, from group tours by bus, to see the main sights of Turin and its surroundings, to specialist tours led by personal guides.

Alpine guides are not only recommended, they're essential if you're planning to traverse some of the dramatic ranges outside Saint-Vincent, Courmayeur, or Breuil-Cervinia. Before embarking on an excursion (however short) into the mountains in these areas, contact the representative of the CAI (Club Alpinisti Italiani) about the risks involved and the availability of an experienced guide. CAI information is available at each tourist information office.

Exploring Piedmont/Valle d'Aosta

While certain parts of this region remain inaccessible by car or train, the roads that do exist are good and, in most cases, direct. This exploring chapter takes you along rushing streams and into the highest reaches of the mountains, as well as through cities that have borne the imprint of humans for millennia.

The first tour is a detailed examination of Turin and some of the sights that make easy day trips from the regional capital. Tour 2 begins in Turin and winds its way northeast into the Valle d'Aosta, passing Europe's most distinctive peak (the Matterhorn) before taking you to the highest (Mont Blanc). In between are the castles of the Valle d'Aosta (sometimes called Italy's Loire) and the Roman city of Aosta itself. The last tour, which also begins in Turin, heads east across the fertile and historical Po plain, visiting major cities and ancient towns, such as Asti, Alessandria, and Novara.

Highlights for First-time Visitors

Breuil-Cervinia (Tour 2: The Valle d'Aosta, the Matterhorn, and Mont Blanc)
Cloister of Sant'Orso, Aosta (Tour 2: The Valle d'Aosta, the Matterhorn, and Mont Blanc).
Courmayeur (Tour 2: The Valle d'Aosta, the Matterhorn, and Mont Blanc).
Fenis Castle (Tour 2: The Valle d'Aosta, the Matterhorn, and Mont Blanc).
Mole Antonelliana, Turin (Tour 1: Turin and Its Outskirts).
Sacra di San Michele (Tour 1: Turin and Its Outskirts).

Tour 1: Turin and Its Outskirts

Numbers in the margin correspond to points of interest on the Piedmont/Valle d'Aosta and Turin maps.

① **Turin**—in Italian, Torino—is roughly in the center of Piedmont–Valle d'Aosta; it is situated on the Po River, in the middle of the plain that marks the beginning of the Po Valley and stretches eastward all the way to the Adriatic. Apart from its role as northwest Italy's major industrial, cultural, and administrative hub, Turin is also the nucleus of education, science, and the arts. It also has a reputation as Italy's main center for mysticism and the supernatural. This distinction is enhanced by the presence of Turin's most controversial, fascinating, and unsettling relic, the Sacra Sindone (Holy Shroud), still believed by many Catholics to be the cloth in which Christ's body was wrapped when He was taken down from the cross. The shroud, an ancient piece of linen more than four yards long, is rarely on view to the public. In 1988, after centuries of public debate about the authenticity of the cloth—which clearly shows the imprint of a human body—the Vatican agreed to have samples dated by scientists in the United States, Britain, and Italy. The tests showed the shroud to be a medieval fake, though how the human image became fused into it remains a mystery and the shroud continues to be revered as a holy relic.

② Start your tour of Turin at the 15th-century **Duomo** (Cathedral), where the **Holy Shroud** is housed. The building, with its white marble facade and campanile (bell tower), stands in the heart of town on the Piazza San Giovanni, adjacent to the Royal Palace. Inside, two monumental black marble staircases lead to the shadowy black marble–walled **Cappella della Sacra Sindone** (Chapel of the Holy Shroud), designed by the priest and architect **Guarino Guarini** (1604–83), a genius of the Baroque style who was official engineer and mathematician to the court of Duke Carlo Emanuele II of Savoy. Unfortunately, the chapel has been closed indefinitely for restoration and will probably remain closed through 1993.

③ Adjoining the cathedral is the 17th-century **Palazzo Reale** (Royal Palace). The former Savoy royal residence, it is an imposing work of brick, stone, and marble that stands on the site of Turin's ancient Roman city gates. In contrast to its austere exterior, the palace's interior is characterized by luxurious, mostly Rococo decor, including tapestries, gilded ceilings, and sumptuous 17th- to 19th-century furniture. *Tel. 011/542664. Admission: 6,000 lire. Open Tues.–Sun. 9–2.*

④ Pass through wrought-iron gates in the adjacent Piazza Castello to **Palazzo Madama,** named for the French queen Maria Cristina, who made it her home in the 17th century. The castle incorporates the remains of a Roman gate, as well as medieval and Renaissance additions. The architect Filippo Juvarra (1678–1736) designed the castle's elaborate Baroque facade in the early 18th century: He was intent on dispelling the idea that Italy's importance as a producer of contemporary art and architecture was in decline. Juvarra's bold use of the Baroque is also evident in the interior of the castle, where the huge marble staircase heralds his patron's wealth and prestige. The large assembly hall was the scene of the first Italian Senate meetings in the mid-19th century. Today the castle houses the **Museo Civico d'Arte Antica** (Civic Museum of Ancient Art), which has a rich collection of Gothic, Renaissance, and Rococo sculpture and paintings, as well as medieval illuminated manuscripts. This museum has been closed for some time for extensive restorations, and it is not likely to reopen in 1993.

⑤ In the same square is the church of **San Lorenzo,** built by Guarini from 1668 to 1680. Guarini was in his mid-60s when he began work on the church, but the sprightly collection of domes, columns, and florid Baroque features seems more the work of a younger architect cutting his teeth with a daring display of mathematical invention. The cupola and the vividly painted interior are standouts.

Time Out   **Baratti e Milano,** located just to the east of Piazza Castello in the glass-roofed gallery between Via Lagrange and Via Po, is one of Turin's charming Old World cafés. It's famous for its chocolates, so you can indulge your sweet tooth here or buy some *gianduiotti* (hazelnut-flavored chocolates) or candied chestnuts to take home to friends.

From Piazza Castello, the porticoed Via Roma, one of the city's main thoroughfares, leads half a mile south to Piazza Carlo Felice, a landscaped park and fountain in front of the train station. First opened in 1615, Via Roma was largely rebuilt in the 1930s, during the time of Premier Benito Mussolini. Halfway

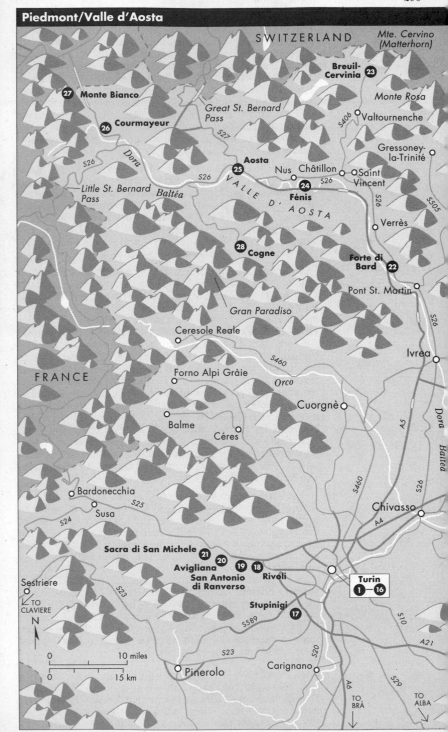

Piedmont/Valle d'Aosta

SWITZERLAND

Mte. Cervino
(Matterhorn)

Monte Rosa

Breuil-Cervinia 23

Valtournenche

S406

Gressoney-la-Trinité

27 **Monte Bianco**

Great St. Bernard Pass

S27

26 **Courmayeur**

S26

Dora

25 **Aosta**

Nus   Châtillon

Saint Vincent

S26

24 **Fénis**

S26

S505

Baltéa

VALLE D'AOSTA

Verrès

Little St. Bernard Pass

28 **Cogne**

Forte di Bard **22**

Pont St. Martin

Gran Paradiso

Ceresole Reale

S460

Ivrea

S26

FRANCE

Forno Alpi Gràie

Orco

S26

Cuorgnè

A5

Dora Baltea

Balme

Céres

Bardonecchia

S25

Chivasso

Susa

S24

A4

Sacra di San Michele **21**

20

19

18

Rivoli

Turin
1 — **16**

Sestriere

TO CLAVIERE

N

Avigliana
San Antonio di Ranverso

S23

Stupinigi

17

S20

S10

0 ——— 10 miles

0 ——— 15 km

S589

S23

Pinerolo

Carignano

A6

TO BRÀ

A21

S29

TO ALBA

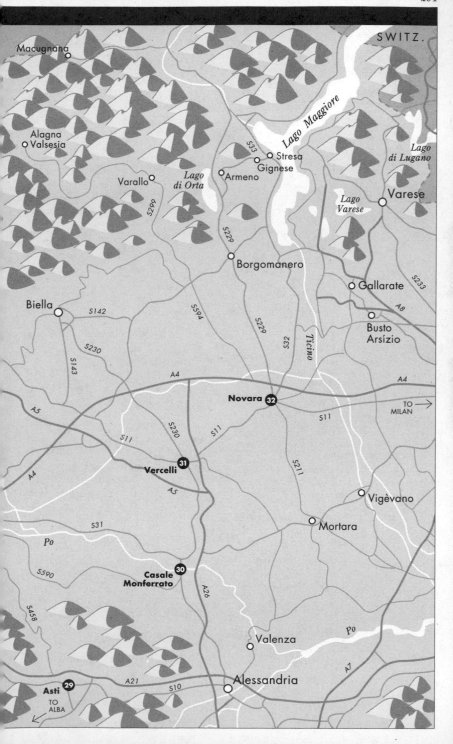

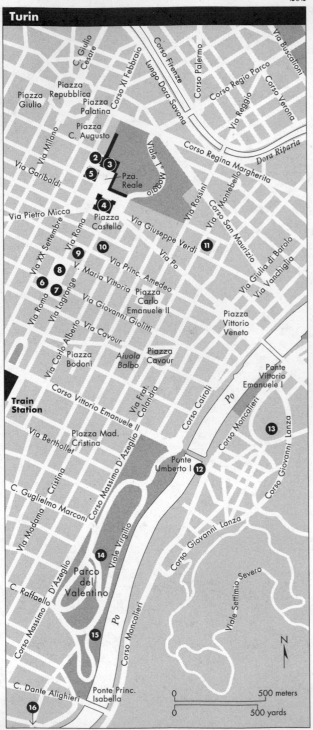

6 **7** down are the churches of **San Carlo** and **Santa Cristina,** the latter with its ornate Baroque facade. The churches flank the **8** entrance to **Piazza San Carlo,** a stately, formal expanse considered by many to be the grandest square in Italy. In the center stands a statue of Duke Emanuele Filiberto of Savoy, victor of the 1557 battle of San Quintino, which heralded the peaceful resurgence of Turin under the Savoys, after years of bloody dynastic fighting. The fine bronze statue, erected in the 19th century, is one of Turin's symbols: The duke is returning his sword to its sheath at the end of the fight and is looking to the prosperous future of his family and the city.

Time Out **Cafe San Carlo,** located under the arcades running alongside the square, is another historic coffeehouse where locals love to stop for coffee and pastry at tiny marble-topped tables under the huge crystal chandelier. On the opposite side of the square is **Stratta,** one of Turin's best-known chocolate shops; locals swear by the homemade candies here.

9 Just off Via Roma is Guarini's **Palazzo dell'Accademia delle Scienze** (Palace of the Academy of Sciences). This large Baroque building, prefiguring the 18th century's preoccupation with logic and science, houses two of Turin's most famous museums. The **Museo Egizio** (Egyptian Museum) is considered by many to be the finest in scope outside Cairo. Its superb collection includes statues of pharaohs, mummies, and whole frescoes taken from royal tombs. Equally fascinating are the papyrus, art objects, and day-to-day utensils taken from the tombs of less noble ancient Egyptians. Look for the papyrus *Book of the Dead* and the 13th-century BC statue of Ramses II, which still glistens in its original colors. *Tel. 011/537581. Admission: 10,000 lire. Open Tues–Sun. 9–2.*

The **Galleria Sabauda,** in the same building as the Egyptian Museum, was built around the collections brought together by the house of Savoy. It is particularly rich in 16th- and 17th-century Dutch and Flemish paintings: Note Jan Van Eyck's *Saint Francis with Stigmata,* with the saint receiving the marks of Christ's wounds while a companion cringes beside him as if feeling it all himself. Other Dutch masterpieces include paintings by Anthony Van Dyck and Rembrandt. Simone del Pollaiuolo's *Tobias and the Angel* is showcased, and other Italian artists featured include Fra Angelico, Andrea Mantegna, and Paolo Veronese. *Tel. 011/547440. Admission: 6,000 lire. Open Tues.–Sun. 9–2.*

Diagonally across the square is another of Guarini's Baroque **10** triumphs, the dark red **Palazzo Carignano,** built from 1679 to 1685. This is one of the great historical buildings of Turin and Italy itself. Kings of Savoy Carlo Alberto (1798–1849) and Vittorio Emanuele II (1820–78) were born within its walls; Italy's first parliament met here from 1860 to 1865.

Take the little road behind the palazzo about 50 yards to Via Po, turn right and take the fourth left (Via Montebello) to the **11** striking **Mole Antonelliana.** You will probably have noticed this Turin landmark already: Its unusual square dome and thin, elaborate spire jut well above the city's rooftops. This odd structure, built between 1863 and 1897, was originally intended to be a synagogue, but costs escalated and eventually it was bought by the city of Turin. In its time it was the tallest building in the world. There is an excellent view of the city, the plain surrounding it, and the Alps beyond from a terrace at the top of the dome. Take the elevator to the top. *Tel. 011/668–9372. Admission: 3,000 lire. Open Tues.–Sun. 9–7.*

Via Po leads to the large Piazza Vittorio Veneto, which slopes down to the Po River and the stone bridge, **Ponte Vittorio Emanuele.** Immediately across the bridge is the 19th-century church of **Gran Madre di Dio** (Great Mother of God), built in a ⑫ neoclassical style based on the Pantheon in Rome. Turn right, along the Corso Moncalieri, to climb the Monte dei Cappuccini. At the top of this 150-foot hill are the church and convent of ⑬ **Santa Maria del Monte,** which date from 1583. This is a good spot to look back across the Po to the center of Turin. Don't be surprised if you find yourself in the middle of a wedding party: Local couples often come here to have their pictures taken.

Return to Corso Moncalieri and cross the next bridge downstream, Ponte Umberto I. Running along this cityside bank of the river is the **Parco del Valentino,** opened in 1856 and one of the most beautiful in Italy. The park has many pedestrian avenues, one of which, **Viale Virgilio,** goes right along the river ⑭ bank and leads to the **Castello del Valentino.** The design of this 17th-century castle, built more for appearance than for defense, is based on models of 16th-century French châteaus. The interior is particularly elaborate, with frescoed walls and rich decoration, but the real attraction of the castle is its riverside setting amid the greenery of the park. *Tel. 011/669–9372. Admission: 3,000 lire, free Fri. Open Apr.–Oct., Tues.–Sat. 9:30–4, Sun. 10:30–4.*

Follow the riverside to the southern edge of the park, where ⑮ you'll find the **Borgo Medioevale** (Medieval Village), one of the most tranquil spots in Turin. The village, a faithful reproduction of medieval Piedmontese buildings, was created for the Turin Exposition of 1884. A visit here is like stepping back into the Middle Ages, with craftsmen's shops, houses, churches, and stores clustered along narrow streets and lanes. *Admission free. Open daily 8–7.*

No visit to car-manufacturing Turin would be complete without ⑯ out a pilgrimage to the **Museo dell'Automobile** (Car Museum). Here you'll get an idea of the importance of FIAT—and automobiles, in general—to Turin's economy. A collection of antique cars dates to 1893, and displays show how the city has changed over the years as a result of its premier industry. *Corso d'Unita d'Italia, tel. 011/677666. Admission: 7,000 lire. Open Tues.–Sun. 10–6:30.*

The next five sights are west of the city. Start at the train station and follow Via Sacchi as it heads southwest. The road changes its name several times within the city boundaries before becoming Corso Unione Sovietica. About 8 kilometers (5 miles) out of Turin, after passing the FIAT plant (visible on the ⑰ right), you come to **Palazzina di Caccia** in the town of **Stupinigi.** This elaborate building was built by Juvarra in 1729 as a hunting lodge for the House of Savoy. It is more like a royal villa, with its many wings, landscaped gardens, and surrounding forests. This regal aspect was not lost on Napoleon, who lived here before claiming the crown of Italy. The castle interior is sumptuously decorated and today houses a collection of art and furniture in the appropriately named **Museo d'Arte e Ammo-**

biliamento. *Tel. 011/358-1220. Admission: 6,000 lire. Open Tues.-Sat. 9:30-5, Sun 10-1, 2-5.*

The next sight is best reached by going back to Turin and taking Corso Francia west from Piazza Rivoli. After 13 kilometers (8 miles), you reach **Rivoli,** where the Savoy court was based in the Middle Ages. The 14th- to 15th-century **Casa del Conte Verde,** right in the center of town, is a good example of medieval architecture of the transitional period, when its defensive function was giving way to the decorative. The 18th-century Savoy castle, built in the Baroque style under the direction of Juvarra, now houses the **Museo d'Arte Moderna** (Modern Art Museum), which contains many examples of 20th-century Italian art. The Futurist movement is particularly well represented. *Tel. 011/958-1547. Admission: 8,000 lire. Open Tues.-Sun. 10-7.*

Roads west from Rivoli begin to climb the broad Valle di Susa, which narrows as it heads toward France. Take the road marked "Rosta" from Rivoli; at Rosta, about 6 kilometers (4 miles) west, you can park and walk to the abbey **San Antonio di Ranverso.** This building was an abbey hospital, founded in the 12th century by the Hospitalers of Saint Anthony to care for victims of Saint Anthony's Fire, a crippling disease contracted by eating contaminated grains. Pilgrims came here over the centuries for cures or, sometimes, to offer thanks for a miraculous recovery, and the 15th-century terra-cotta decorations, with their lifelike depictions of pilgrims and saints, retain the color of the originals.

Six kilometers (4 miles) farther along the same road that led from Rivoli, you reach the medieval town of **Avigliana.** With its attractive lakeside setting, Avigliana was a favorite of the Savoys up to the mid-15th century. Medieval houses still line the twisting and narrow streets. **Casa della Porta Ferrata,** on the street of the same name, is a well-preserved example of Piedmont Gothic domestic architecture: Notice how the fascination with narrow pointed arches is carried through even to private houses.

Make sure to take the twisting, narrow road that leads south from Avigliana and is marked for the **Sacra di San Michele** (Abbey of Saint Michael). You leave Avigliana and pass between two glacier-fed lakes before going right for the rest of the 14-kilometer (8-mile) climb to the abbey. San Michele was built here in the 11th century to stand out: The location, on Monte Pirchiriano, is the most prominent for miles around. When monks came to enlarge the abbey, they had to build part of the structure on supports more than 90 feet high—an engineering feat that was famous in medieval Europe. By the 12th century, this important abbey controlled 176 churches in Italy, France, and Spain. St. Michael was also honored in one of the abbeys under its influence—Mont St-Michel in France. Because of the abbey's strategic position, it came under numerous attacks over the next five centuries, having been claimed by the armies that swept up through the valley, and it was eventually abandoned in 1622. It was restored in the late 19th and early 20th centuries.

From Porta dello Zodiaco, a splendid Romanesque doorway decorated with the signs of the Zodiac, you climb 150 steps, past 12th-century sculptures, to reach the church. The interior has 16th-century frescoes on the walls: On the left are religious subjects representing New Testament themes, while on the right are stories depicting the founding of the church. Go down to the crypt to see the 9th- to 12th-century chapels. *Donation requested. Open Apr.–Sept., daily 9–noon, 3–7; Oct.–Mar., daily 9–noon, 2–dusk.*

Tour 2: The Valle d'Aosta, the Matterhorn, and Mont Blanc

Take Autostrada A5 north from Turin; at Ivrea, 50 kilometers (30 miles) along, join S26 on its way north. The road takes you through countryside that becomes hillier and hillier, passing through steep ravines guarded by brooding, romantic castles. Another change that you may not notice from your car is the beginning of French-speaking territory, as you enter the Aosta region, about 18 kilometers (11 miles) north of Ivrea. Pont St-Martin is the first village of the region; a few minutes afterward you pass through the narrow Gorge de Bard. Tower-

㉒ ing above the gorge is the **Forte di Bard** (closed to the public), a 19th-century reconstruction of a fort that stood for eight centuries, serving the Savoys for six of them. In 1800 Napoleon entered Italy through this valley and used the cover of darkness to get his artillery units past the castle unnoticed. Ten years later he remembered this inconvenience and had the fortress destroyed.

Continue on S26, through the town of **Saint Vincent,** a popular resort since the late 18th century. Its main claim to fame these days is the Casino de la Vallée, Europe's largest gambling site. A few kilometers farther on S26, turn right, at Chatillon, for the 30-kilometer (19 mile) detour up a dramatic mountain val-

㉓ ley to **Breuil-Cervinia,** the Italian-Swiss village at the base of the Matterhorn (Monte Cervino, in Italian; Mont Cervin in French). Like the village, the famous peak straddles the border between Italy and Switzerland, and all sightseeing and skiing facilities are operated jointly. Serious climbers can make the ascent of the Matterhorn from Breuil-Cervinia (having registered with the local mountaineering officials at the tourist office), but this climb is for serious and experienced climbers only. You get splendid views of the peak from Plateau Rosa and the Cresta del Furggen, both of which can be reached by cable car from the center of Breuil-Cervinia. While many locals complain that the tourist facilities and the condominiums in the village have changed the face of their beloved Breuil, most would agree that the cable car has given them access to climbing and off-trail skiing in ridges that were once inaccessible.

Return to S26 and continue west toward Aosta. About 12 kilometers (7 miles) from Chatillon is the best-preserved fortress in the Valle d'Aosta, which many call "Italy's Loire" because of

㉔ the many castles. The many-turreted castle of **Fénis** was built in the mid-14th century by Aimone di Challant, another member of the prolific family that was related to the Savoys. This castle is the sort imagined by schoolchildren, with pointed turrets, portcullises, and spiral staircases. The 15th-century courtyard has a stairway leading to a loggia (open walkway) with wooden balconies. Inside you can see the medieval kitchen, with much of the original cooking equipment, and a collection of weapons in the armory. If you have time to visit only one castle in the Valle d'Aosta, this is it, though it may be partly closed for restoration. *Tel. 0165/764263. Admission: 4,000 lire. Open Mar.–Oct., Wed.–Mon. 9–7 (group tours every half-hour); Nov.–Feb., Wed.–Mon. 9:30–noon, 2–5 (group tours every hour).*

S26 continues climbing through the Valle d'Aosta for the last 14 kilometers (9 miles) to Aosta itself. The road at this point is heading almost due west, with rivulets from the Parco Nazionale del Gran Paradiso (a wilderness reserve) streaming down from the left to join the Dora Baltea. Be careful driving here in late spring, when melting snow can turn some of these ❷❺ streams into torrents. **Aosta** stands at the junction of two important trade routes from France to Italy—from the valleys of the Rhône and the Isère. Its significance as a trading post was recognized by the Romans, who built a garrison here in the 1st century BC. The present-day layout of streets in this small city, which is tucked away in the Alps more than 400 miles from Rome, is the clearest example of Roman street planning in Italy. Well-preserved Roman walls form a perfect rectangle around the center of Aosta, and the regular pattern of streets reflects its role as a military stronghold.

At the eastern entrance to town, in a square that commands a fine view over Aosta and the mountains, is the **Arco di Augusto** (Arch of Augustus), built in 25 BC to mark Rome's victory over the Celtic Salassi tribe. Across the square, and then a right turn off Via San Anselmo, is the **Collegiata di Sant'Orso** (Collegiate Church of Saint Orso): the sort of church that has layers of history in its architecture. Originally there was a 6th-century chapel on this site, founded by the Archdeacon Orso, a local saint. Most of this structure was destroyed or hidden when an 11th-century church was erected over it. This church, in turn, was replaced by Gothic, and later Baroque, features, leaving the church a jigsaw puzzle of styles, but—surprisingly—not a chaotic jumble. The 11th-century features are almost untouched in the crypt, and if you go up the stairs on the left from the main church you can see the 11th-century frescoes (ask the sacristan for entrance). These frescoes, recently restored, depict the life of Christ and the Apostles: Although only the tops are visible, you can see the expressions on the faces of the disciples. Take the doorway by the entrance to the crypt to see the crowning glory of Sant' Orso—the 12th-century **cloister.** Pairs of white marble columns, with black capitals, run along the side of the church, to form the cloister. At one side are frescoes of the same period, depicting Old and New Testament themes, as well as scenes from the life of St. Orso.

Continue down Via Anselmo (named for St. Anselm, who was born in Aosta and later became archbishop of Canterbury in England) through the huge Roman **Porta Pretoria.** Turn right after this three-arch gateway to see the 72-foot-high ruin of the facade of the **Teatro Romano** (Roman Theater). Just ahead are the ruins of the 1st-century BC amphitheater, which once held 20,000 spectators. Only seven of its original 60 arches remain, and these are built onto the facade of the adjacent convent of **Santa Caterina.** The convent usually allows visitors in to see these arches (ask at the entrance).

About 100 yards west of the Roman theater (down Via Monsignor de Sales) is Aosta's **Cattedrale,** which dates from the 10th century, although all that remains from that period are the campaniles (bell towers). The decoration inside is mainly

Gothic, but the main attraction of the cathedral predates that era by 1,000 years: the carved ivory diptych (devotional work with two images) showing the Roman Emperor Honorius and dating from AD 406. *For admission to the treasury, contact the Sacristan at the Piccolo Seminario, 2 Piazza Giovanni XXIII (behind the cathedral).*

Take Via Stati Generali about 50 yards down to Piazza Chanoux, the center of Aosta and the scene of a permanent craft exhibition, in one of its arcades. Aosta and the surrounding countryside are famous for wood carvings and wrought-iron work, and this exhibition is a good place to pick up a bargain. Each year, on the last two days of January, the whole town turns out for the Sant' Orso Fair, when all sorts of handicrafts are on sale, including handmade lace from nearby Cogne, carved stonework, and brightly colored woolens.

Having made a detour to see the Matterhorn on your way up from Turin, you probably won't want to leave the Valle d'Aosta without seeing Europe's tallest peak, Mont Blanc (Monte Bianco in Italian). Follow S26 west for about 40 kilometers (25 miles) from Aosta, turning right on S26D when you see the signs for ❷❻ **Courmayeur,** about a mile outside town.

The jet-set celebrities who flock here, particularly in winter, are following a tradition that dates back to the late 17th century, when Courmayeur's natural springs first began to draw visitors. The scenic spectacle of the Alps gradually surpassed the springs as the biggest drawing point (the Alpine letters of the English poet Shelley were almost advertisements for the region), but the biggest change in the history of Courmayeur came in 1965, when the Mont Blanc tunnel opened. Now Courmayeur stands on one of the main routes from France into Italy, although the planners have managed to maintain some restrictions on wholesale development within the town.

Take S26D north about 3 kilometers (2 miles) beyond Courmayeur to **La Palud,** where you can catch the cable car up to ❷❼ **Monte Bianco.** The cable car crosses into France, so you should have your passport ready. Remember, too, that the cable car depends on the weather, and that can mean stuck on the French side, sometimes overnight: Have French money with you, in case. You ride up to the viewing platform at **Punta Helbronner** (over 11,000 feet), which is also the border post with France. The view is outstanding, but you realize that Mont Blanc's attraction is not so much its shape (it is much less distinctive than the Matterhorn), but the expanse of the massif and the vistas from the top. The next stage, as you pass into French territory, is particularly impressive: You dangle over a huge glacial snow field (more than 2,000 feet below) and make your way slowly to the viewing station above **Chamonix.** From this point you're looking down into France, and if you change cable cars, you can make your way down to Chamonix itself. The return trip covers the same route, and the total time should be 90 minutes, although this is entirely weather dependent.

As you make your way back toward Aosta, take time to explore the **Parco Nazionale del Gran Paradiso.** Take the right turn at Aymavilles, about 6 kilometers (4 miles) west of Aosta, to climb ❷❽ into the Val di Cogne. The village of **Cogne** itself, about 20 kilometers (12 miles) up the valley, is the best place to stop and sample the peace and solitude of this huge park, once the do-

main of King Vittorio Emanuele II and bequeathed to the nation after World War I. Gran Paradiso is one of Europe's most
rugged and unspoiled wilderness areas, with wildlife and many
plant species protected by law. Try to visit in May, when
spring flowers are in bloom and most of the meadows are clear
of snow. This is one of the few places in Europe where you can
see the ibex (the mountain goat with horns up to three feet
long) or the chamois (the small antelope whose soft skin nearly
drove it to extinction).

If you're in a hurry to return to Turin, you can go back along
superhighway A5, which runs parallel with S26 down to Ivrea,
to Turin.

Tour 3: Fortified Cities of the Po Plain

Take Autostrada A6 south from Turin for about 5 kilometers (3
miles), to the Torfarello exit, where you join A21 east (left turn)
for the 50-kilometer (30-mile) drive to the famous wine city of
Asti. The last few miles of this trip take you into the **Monferrato,** a hilly wooded area, rich in vineyards and truffles. Asti
is one of the main cities of the Monferrato. It is known to Americans mainly because of its wines (there are excellent reds as
well as the famous sparkling white spumante), but its strategic
position on trade routes between Turin, Milan, and Genoa has
given it a broad economic base. In the 1100s Asti began to develop as a republic, at a time when other Italian cities were also
flexing their economic and military muscles. It flourished in the
following century, when the inhabitants began erecting lofty
towers for its defense. Some of these towers remain, giving the
city a medieval look.

Arriving on the autostrada, you enter Asti through Piazza Torino. Directly ahead is Corso Vittorio Alfieri, which runs
west–east across the city. This road, known in medieval times
as Contrada Maestra, was built by the Romans. About 100
yards up on the right is the 18th-century church of Santa
Caterina, which has incorporated one of the medieval towers,
the **Torre Romana** (itself built on an ancient Roman base), as its
bell tower.

Turn left at Piazza Cairoli, about a two-minute walk ahead, and
take the small road that leads to the **Duomo** (Cathedral). Here
is a good chance to see the evolution of the Gothic style of architecture. The cathedral, built in the early 14th century, is decorated mainly in a Gothic style that emphasizes geometry and
verticality: Pointed arches and narrow vaults are counterbal-
anced by the earlier, Romanesque, attention to balance and
symmetry. Then look at the porch, on the south side of the cathedral, facing the square. This addition, built in 1470, represents Gothic at its most florid and excessive.

Return to the Corso and continue to the Piazza Roma, where
there is another of Asti's 13th-century towers, **Torre Comen-
tini.** Asti's best-preserved medieval tower, **Torre Troyana,** is up
Via Morelli, the third left off the Corso after Piazza Roma. This
tall, thin tower is attached to the Palazzo Troya, in Piazza Medici. Go back to the Corso and take the small street opposite Via
Morelli; just ahead is the Gothic church of **San Secondo.** San Secondo is the patron saint of Asti and of the city's favorite sporting event, the annual *palio*, the colorful medieval-style horse

race held each year on the third Sunday of September in the Campo del Palio to the south of the church.

Take the small Via Garibaldi from the right of the church for the few steps it takes to reach Piazza Libertà, which forms the southwest edge of the large triangular **Piazza Alfieri.** This square is the heart of Asti, with its tourist office and civic administrative offices.

Time Out   The **Bottega del Vino,** located on the Piazza Alfieri (just to the left of Corso alla Vittoria), is a wine center and shop, where you can try the range of Asti vintages, buy some as souvenirs or picnic ingredients, or sample a light snack. *Open Mon.–Sat. 9–4:30.*

Take Corso Alfieri, at the northern end of Piazza Alfieri, right (east) to join S10 on its way 36 kilometers (22 miles) east to Alessandria. The road is straight, lying mainly in the southern edge of the Po plain, but for the first half of the drive you see the green hillsides covered with vineyards. If you find yourself driving along this road during a thunderstorm (quite common in late summer afternoons) don't be surprised by the sound of man-made explosions. Wine growers will often let off cannons loaded with blanks to force heavy clouds to rain, rather than build up and develop destructive hailstones.

30   From Alessandria, S31, a direct secondary route that was originally a military supply route for the Romans, goes almost due north. Thirty kilometers (18 miles) from Alessandria is **Casale Monferrato,** strategically situated on the southern banks of the Po. The town was held by the Gonzagas, rulers of Mantua, before falling into the hands of the Savoys: The 16th-century **Torre Civica,** marking the heart of Casale Monferrato in Piazza Mazzini, commanded extensive views up and down the Po. Casale's most enlightening sight is the **Museo Israelitico** (Jewish Museum), located in the women's section of the synagogue on Via Alessandria. Inside is a collection of documents and sacred art of a community that was vital to the prosperity of this mercantile city. The synagogue dates from the late 16th century, and neighboring buildings on the same street formed the Jewish ghetto of that period. *Admission: 3,000 lire. Open Aug.–June, weekdays and Sun. 10–noon and 3–5. Apply to the caretaker.*

31   S31 continues north from Casale Monferrato; the 23-kilometer (14-mile) stretch from there to **Vercelli** goes past rice fields. Vercelli is the rice capital of Italy, and of Europe itself: Northern Italy's mainstay, risotto, owes its existence to the crop that was introduced to this fertile area in the late Middle Ages. Arriving from Casale, you enter town along Corso De Rege. Turn left along Via Massaua to reach the parking area in the grassy square of Piazza Camana. Take Via Manzoni, and then the first left after the post office, to reach **Piazza Cavour,** the heart of the medieval city and former market square. It was to this small square that merchants across northern Italy came in the 15th century to buy bags of the novelty grain from the east— rice. Rising above the low rooftops around the square is the **Torre dell'Angelo** (Tower of the Angel), whose forbidding military appearance reflects its original purpose as watchtower for the heart of the town.

Vercelli has an unusual guided tour of the **Borsa Merci,** the rice exchange where the grain has been traded for centuries. It's best to call first to check on tour times (Via Zumaglini 4, tel. 0161/5981).

Via Gioberti goes east from the square, leading to Via del Duomo, up on the left. Ahead of you is the campanile of the **Duomo,** which is at the end of the street, on Piazza D'Angennes. The building, mainly a late–16th-century construction on the site of what was a 5th-century church, contains tombs of several Savoy rulers in an octagonal chapel along the south (right) wall. The cathedral's *biblioteca* (chapter library—apply in the cathedral for entrance) contains the "Gospel of St. Eusebius," a 4th-century document, and the *Code Sassone*, an 11th-century book of Anglo-Saxon poetry.

Cross Piazza San Eusebio, which is directly in front of the cathedral, and follow Corso De Gasperi to the **Basilica di Sant' Andrea,** on the left. This Cistercian abbey church, built in the early 13th century with funds from another Abbey of St. Andrew (in England), witnessed the growing influence of northern Europe on Italy. Sant'Andrea is one of the earliest examples of Gothic architecture in Italy, which spread from the north but ran out of steam before getting much farther south than the Po plain. The interior of the church is a soaring flight of Gothic imagination, with slender columns rising up to the ribbed vaults of the high ceiling. Tombs along the side aisle continue the preoccupation with stylized decoration and relief work. The gardens on the north (Corso De Gasperi side) of the basilica hold the remains of the abbey itself and some of the secondary buildings. It is only here that the unadulterated Gothic style is interrupted. The remains of the buildings surround a cloister in which you can see the pointed Gothic arches resting on the severe and more solid 12th-century Romanesque column bases.

Wander back to Piazza Camana through the **Città Vecchia,** a collection of narrow streets and alleys reached by taking Via Galileo (left from the basilica) and then making your way left into the narrow streets, using the Torre dell'Angelo in Piazza Cavour as your landmark. Many of the houses are five centuries old, and you can see partly hidden gardens and courtyards beyond the wrought-iron gates.

Leaving Vercelli, follow Corso De Gregori and then Corso Palestro from the parking lot at Piazza Campana. Corso Palestro leads into S11, which turns right out of town at Piazza Cugnolio. The road from Vercelli heads northeast to **Novara,** 23 kilometers (14 miles) away, past intensively farmed rice fields. Novara is the easternmost city in Piedmont, only about 6 miles west of the Ticino River, which forms the border with Lombardy. Milan is only 20 miles beyond the border, and over the centuries the opposing attractions of this neighboring giant and those of its provincial capital, Turin, have made Novara a bit schizophrenic. In the Middle Ages, Novara's pivotal position between these two cities actually made it a battlefield. A major engagement took place as recently as 1849, when the Austrian forces from the east defeated the Piedmontese armies.

Things settled down after that last battle, and much of the present city dates from the late 19th and early 20th centuries, although there are interesting buildings from earlier periods scattered around Novara. Just after you enter Novara, bear left up Corso Torino for about half a mile and turn right onto Corso 20 Settembre, where there are parking lots on each side of the road. From here it's impossible to miss Novara's famous landmark, the tall, slender cupola of **San Gaudenzio,** which you can reach by taking a left on Baluardo Quintino Sella. The church itself, built between 1577 and 1690, conforms to a Baroque design, with twisted columns and sumptuous statues. The main attraction for most people, though, is the cupola, which was built from 1840 to 1888 and soars to a height of just under 400 feet. This spire is visible from everywhere in the city and the surrounding countryside, and has become as much a symbol of Novara as the Mole Antonelliana (built around the same time) is of Turin.

Take a left immediately after leaving the front door of San Gaudenzio and follow the small street south (against the flow of the one-way traffic). You soon pass Corso Italia. Immediately to the left, after you've crossed this main street, is the **Broletto,** a cluster of well-preserved late-medieval buildings. Inside is the **Museo Civico,** which is full of Piedmontese military and social records from the Middle Ages through the 18th century. There are also some archaeological items going back to the Roman and early-Christian (4th–5th century) periods. *Admission: 3,000 lire. Open Apr.–Sept., Tues.–Sun. 10–noon, 3–6; Oct.–Mar., Tues.–Sun. 10–noon, 2–5.*

Novara's **Duomo** is next to the Broletto. The Romanesque origins of this cathedral are impossible to detect because of the major reconstruction undertaken in the past century, leaving the building with an austere neoclassical appearance. You can delve into history more easily at the **Battistero** (Baptistery), which is just outside the entrance to the cathedral. This rotunda-shaped building dates from the 5th century, although it was substantially enlarged in the 10th and 11th centuries. Recent restoration work has uncovered some frescoes decorating the inside walls. These pre-Romanesque frescoes are over 1,000 years old. Their flat, two-dimensional style reflects the influence of Byzantine icons. Now that the frescoes have been restored, the colors add a frightening feel to the depictions of scenes from the Apocalypse.

Just north of Novara, the A4 autostrada will take you back east to Turin (91 kilometers/56 miles) or west to Milan (51 kilometers/32 miles).

What to See and Do with Children

The Alpine landscapes of the Valle d'Aosta will impress youngsters, especially excursions to the **Matterhorn** and **Mont Blanc.** In the vast wilderness of **Parco Nazionale del Gran Paradiso,** there's plenty of wildlife to observe. Among Valle d'Aosta's many castles, the one at **Fénis** most satisfies a young person's image of what a castle should look like. Kids who are interested in ancient times can explore a number of Roman ruins in the city of **Aosta.** In **Turin,** children generally enjoy the model medieval village (Borgo Medioevale), the vintage cars in the Museo dell'Automobile, and the mummies in the Museo Egizio.

Off the Beaten Track

Alba. This moderate-sized town, about 30 kilometers (18 miles) southwest of Asti, is the wine and truffle capital of the area. Visit in October for the National Truffle Fair and the Cento Torri Joust and donkey races. For information on these and other events, contact Tourist Information (Piazza Medford, tel. 0173/35833).

Cinzano Wine Cellars. Brà, about 50 kilometers (30 miles) south of Turin and only 16 kilometers (10 miles) west of Alba (*see* above), is the home of this world-famous wine and vermouth company. You can take a guided tour of the plant and sample some of the product at the end. *Call tel. 0172/47041 for information. Admission free.*

Shopping

Turin is the major city of Piedmont/Valle d'Aosta, and it has all the shopping that you expect to find in a metropolis. Wines and vermouths, from the famous brands of Cinzano and Martini-Rossi, are particular favorites, while salamis, cheeses, and delicious *gianduiotti* (hazelnut-flavored chocolates) are also appreciated as gifts. Elsewhere in the region you'll find more handicrafts, such as Borsalino hats from Alessandria and wrought-iron goods from Aosta. Another good source of bargains is the field of antiques, and many towns and villages have regular antiques markets.

Alessandria The borsalino hat factory is 6 kilometers (4 miles) southeast of town. *Spinetta Marengo, tel. 0131/61880.*

Aosta The capital of the Valle d'Aosta region is a handicrafts center, especially for wood carvings, stone and wrought-iron work, handmade lace, and colorful wool fabrics. There is a permanent craft exhibition in the arcade of the Piazza Chanoux in the center of town, and the annual St. Orso Fair, held on the last two days of January, is a good time to find handicrafts.

Asti The Arazzeria Scassa (tel. 0141/271352) is a craft workshop specializing in tapestries.

Nizza Monferrato Take S456 southeast for 28 kilometers (17 miles) from Asti to reach this attractive medieval town, which has an antiques market every third Sunday of the month.

Turin
Antiques Piazza San Carlo, Via Po, and Via Maria Vittoria are lined with antiques shops, some—but not all—specializing in 18th-century furniture and domestic items.

Boutiques Most people know that Turin produces more than 75% of Italy's cars, but they don't realize that it is also a clothing manufacturing city. Top-quality boutiques stocking local, national, and international lines are clustered along Via Roma and Via Garibaldi.

Food and Flea Markets Go to the famous Balon Flea Market (Piazza Repubblica) on a Saturday morning for some excellent bargains in secondhand books and clothing and some stalls selling local specialties such as gianduiotti.

Valenza Take S494 northeast from Alessandria for 13 kilometers (8 miles) to reach this historic town on the Po. Valenza is one of the world's major producers of gold and silver work, and there is a permanent display of jewelry at Piazza Don Minzoni 1 (tel. 0131/953643).

Sports

Boating The **Lega Navale di Torino** (Turin Boating League) (Corso Unione Sovietica 316, tel. 011/530979) organizes courses and special races throughout the summer.

Clay-Pigeon Shooting Shooting is popular in this mountainous part of Italy, and you can join in the practice at clay-pigeon centers in **Asti** (Valmanera, tel. 0141/271807) or **Turin** (Strade Bramafame 41, tel. 011/254137).

Fishing The streams and rivers around northern Piedmont and Valle d'Aosta are good spots for trout fishing. For information on regulations and licenses, contact the **Federazione Italiana di Pesca Sportiva,** in Turin (Via Giolitti 24, tel. 011/546732).

Golf **Avigliana, Fiano** (near Turin), and **Sestriere** have championship 18-hole courses; nine-hole courses are located in **Claviere, Turin,** and **Valenza.**

Mountaineering/ Rock Climbing Beginner and advanced courses are taught in Macugnana, sponsored by CAI Macugnana Monte Rosa (tel. 0324/65119).

Skiing This is the major sport in both Piedmont and the Valle d'Aosta. Resorts with excellent facilities abound near the highest mountains in Europe—Mont Blanc, Monte Rosa, the Cervino (Matterhorn), and the Gran Paradiso.

Breuil-Cervinia Because its slopes border the Cervino glacier, this resort at the foot of the Matterhorn offers year-round skiing.

Claviere This quaint village, with slate-roofed houses, is one of Italy's oldest ski resorts. Its slopes overlap with those of the French resort of Montgenevre.

Courmayeur This famous spot for the well heeled is well equipped and easy to reach, just outside the Italian end of the Mont Blanc tunnel. The skiing around Mont Blanc is particularly good, and the off-piste options are among the best in Europe.

Sestriere At 6,670 feet, this famous resort near the French border (and just 50 kilometers [30 miles] west of Turin) is popular. It gets good snow from November until May.

Spelunking Cave explorations are organized by CAI Speleological Groups (tel. 011/537983) in Turin. Contact the group for information on trips from Turin or the classes it holds on caving from January to May.

Tennis Tennis is popular throughout the region, and it would be impossible and misleading to try to list all the courts. Most towns and villages have public courts as well as private clubs that offer temporary membership to visitors. Contact the tourist office in each town.

Dining and Lodging

Dining These two regions offer rustic specialties from a farmhouse hearth or fine cuisine with a French accent—and everything in between. Piedmont cooking reflects the geography of the region. The favorite form of pasta is *agnolotti* (similar to ravioli), filled with meat, spinach, or cheese. Another regional specialty is *fonduta*—a local form of fondue, made with melted *Fontina* (a cheese from the Valle d'Aosta), eggs, and sometimes grated truffles. Alba is the home of *tartufi bianchi* (white truffles), much rarer and more expensive than black ones and considered the tastiest and most aromatic by connoisseurs. They sell for at least $1,000 a pound wholesale.

Another local dish is *cardi in bagna cauda*, made of edible thistles *(cardi)* chopped raw, and then dipped in a hot sauce *(bagna cauda* means hot bath), made from butter, oil, anchovies, cream, and shredded garlic.

Turin is also known for delicate pastries and fine chocolates, especially for *gianduiotti*. Valle d'Aosta is famous for a variety of schnappslike brandies made from fruits or herbs.

Piedmont is one of Italy's most important wine-producing regions. Most of the wines are full-bodied reds, such as Barolo, Nebbiolo, Freisa, Barbera, and Barbaresco. Asti Spumante (Italian champagne) comes from the region, as does vermouth, which was developed in Piedmont by A. B. Carpano in 1786.

Highly recommended restaurants are indicated by a star ★.

Category	Cost*
Very Expensive	over 85,000 lire
Expensive	60,000–85,000 lire
Moderate	30,000–60,000 lire
Inexpensive	under 30,000 lire

per person, including house wine, service, and tax

Lodging There is a good variety of accommodations in Piedmont and Valle d'Aosta, but remember that outside of the cities, many people see the area as a two-season resort. Summer and winter occupancy rates are usually quite high, since skiers and mountaineers add to the competition for rooms in the two seasons. The following list features establishments in each price category, and we have mentioned when a hotel or chalet offers attractive half-board or off-season rates. Using these deals can sometimes reduce the overall cost by a full Fodor's category.

In the mountain resorts, many of the hotels cater primarily to half- or full-board guests only, for stays of at least a week. It's better to take a package deal if you're coming for a ski vacation. The following list represents the range of accommodations in Piedmont and Valle d'Aosta—from five-star luxury in the cities to chalet informality in the Alps.

Highly recommended lodgings are indicated by a star ★.

Category	Cost*
Very Expensive	over 300,000 lire
Expensive	140,000–300,000 lire
Moderate	80,000–140,000 lire
Inexpensive	under 80,000 lire

All prices are for a standard double room for two, including service and 9% IVA (19% for luxury establishments).

Aosta

Dining

★ **Piemonte.** A small restaurant in the center of town, the Piemonte has a comfortable, rustic decor and offers *crespelle Valdostana* (crepes with cheese) and *filletto alla provencale* (beef fillet with porcini mushrooms). *Via Porta Pretoria 13, tel 0165/40111. Reservations advised for lunch. Dress: casual. MC, V. Closed Fri. Moderate.*

Vecchio Ristoro. Local and Italian dishes predominate in this old mill, furnished with antiques, in the city center. Try the *trota affumicata* (smoked trout) or the *uova walzer* (eggs cooked with cream and cheese on a bed of crusty baked polenta seasoned with wild herbs). *Via Tourneuve 4, tel. 0165/33238. Reservations advised. Dress: casual. AE, DC, MC, V. Closed Sun., Mon. lunch, and July, Feb. Moderate.*

La Brasserie du Commerce. Small, lively, and informal, it is in the heart of Aosta, near central Piazza Chanoux. On a sunny summer day try to get a table on the terrace. Typical valley dishes, such as *fonduta* (fondue made with fontina cheese) are on the menu, together with a wide range of vegetable dishes and salads. *Via de Tillier 10, tel. 0165/35613. No reservations. Dress: casual. No credit cards. Closed Sun. Inexpensive.*

La Croisee. This big modern restaurant is outside town on the way to the French and Swiss borders and specializes in local Valdostana dishes, such as mixed antipasto, *crepes Valdostana* (crepes made with cheese and ham served as a pasta course), and *carbonata con polenta* (veal chunks in a subtle wine sauce served with polenta). *Viale Gran San Bernardo 5, tel. 0165/362441. Reservations advised. Dress: casual. AE, DC, MC, V. Closed Mon. Inexpensive.*

Lodging

Valle D'Aosta. You'll find this comfortable, modern four-star hotel on the outskirts of town. Half the rooms have recently been remodeled. A few rooms on the fifth floor have balconies, but virtually all rooms have big windows and splendid views of the mountains. There are rooms suitable for disabled people. There is no restaurant, but there is a pleasant garden. *Corso Ivrea 146, tel. 0165/41845, fax 0165/236660. 104 rooms with bath. AE, DC, MC, V. Closed mid-Nov.–mid-Dec. Expensive.*

Europe. This five-story hotel, extensively renovated in 1991, is located in the center of town, near the grandiose Porta Pretoria, an ancient Roman gate. The large rooms are decorated in a comfortable modern style. The hotel restaurant serves local specialties. *Piazza Narbonne 8, tel. 0165/236363, fax 0165/40566. 71 rooms with bath. Facilities: garage, fitness center. AE, DC, MC, V. Moderate.*

Rayon du Soleil. Saraillon, a residential district in the hills above Aosta, is the setting for this traditional red-brick mountain hotel set in a park. There are excellent views from the rooms, which are large, bright, and quiet. The hotel interior is decorated in traditional dark wood. There are rooms suitable for disabled people. *Saraillon 16, tel. 0165/362247, fax 0165/ 236085. 45 rooms with bath. Facilities: garage, pool. AE, DC, MC, V. Closed Nov. 1–mid-Mar. Moderate.*

Asti
Dining
★

Gener Neuv. Family-run and one of Italy's top restaurants, the Gener Neuv offers a sumptuous menu of regional specialties in a warm, welcoming atmosphere of rustic-style elegance, highlighted by excellent service, fine linen, silver, and crystal. The position in a park on the bank of the Tanaro River is splendid. Choice, which is limited to a "small" prix-fixe menu and another "grand" and more expensive one, may include *agnolotti d'anatra* (with duck filling and brown sauce), roast lamb, and, for dessert, *zabaglione* made with sweet moscato d'Asti wine and served with almond cake. *Lungo Tanaro 4, tel. 0141/57270. Reservations required. Dress: casual. AE, MC, V. Closed Sun. evening, Mon., and Aug. Very Expensive.*

Falcon Vecchio. There's been a restaurant in this ancient house in the historic center of Asti since the year 1670. Today, in intimate surroundings, the Falcon Vecchio serves rich local dishes that vary with the season. In fall and winter there are mushroom, truffle, and game dishes. Otherwise, there's a big selection of antipasti; grilled vegetables; and mixed, boiled, or grilled meats *(bollito misto* or *arrosto misto)*. *Vicolo San Secondo 8, tel. 0141/53106. No reservations. Dress: casual. MC, V. Closed Sun. evening, Mon., and Aug. Moderate.*

Lodging

Hotel Salera. Centrally located, this modern hotel is set in a small park in a residential neighborhood, with rooms decorated in classic modern hotel style. Many rooms have lovely views, and there is a big hotel terrace on the top floor. *Via Marello 19, tel. 0141/211815, fax 0141/211818. 54 rooms with bath. Facilities: bar, restaurant, parking. AE, DC, MC, V. Moderate.*

Rainero. An older hotel in the town center, near the station, Rainero has been under the same family management for three generations. It's been remodeled many times and is fitted with modern furnishings. There is no restaurant. *Via Cavour 85, tel. 0141/353866, fax 0141/353866. 49 rooms with bath. AE, DC, MC, V. Inexpensive–Moderate.*

Bardonecchia
Lodging
★

Asplenia. Skiers love this small, modern version of a mountain chalet, located near the center of town and the ski lifts. The ample rooms are comfortably furnished, with a small entryway and a balcony looking out onto beautiful views. *Viale della Vittoria 31, tel. 0122/9870. 25 rooms with bath. MC, V. Closed Easter–May, Sept.–Nov. Moderate.*

Des Geneys-Splendid. One of the best hotels in the area, this establishment is set in a private park near the center of town. Its 1930s style is evident in the arched windows on the ground floor, the stucco walls, and the long metal-rail balconies. The public rooms are spacious and comfortable, and there's a playroom for children. *Via Einaudi 21, tel. 0122/99001, fax 0122/ 999295. 57 rooms with bath. Facilities: bar, restaurant, solarium. MC, V. Closed Apr. 15–June 25, mid-Sept.–mid-Dec. Moderate.*

Riky. This centrally located modern hotel has good service; comfortable, spacious rooms; a good restaurant; and pleasant public rooms, including a children's playroom equipped with video games. There's a solarium and a piano bar with a cozy fireplace, and almost all rooms have terraces with panoramic views. Catering mainly to longer stays at pension rates, it has excellent low-season rates (nearly half price) for people staying at least a week. *Via della Vittoria 22, tel. 0122/9353. 76 rooms with bath. Facilities: bar, restaurant, solarium. AE, DC, V. Closed April–June, Sept.–Dec. 15. Moderate.*

Breuil-Cervinia
Lodging

Cristallo. An elegantly modern hotel high above town, the Cristallo has spectacular views. The two restaurants serve local specialties, such as fonduta and *bistecca Valdostana* (chops cooked with cheese and ham). Facilities and decorations contribute to an overall feeling of pampering and comfort. *Via Piolet 6, tel. 0166/943411, fax 0166/948377. 100 rooms with bath. Facilities: bar, 2 restaurants, fitness center, Olympic-size indoor and outdoor pools, tennis courts. AE, DC, MC, V. Closed May–June, Sept.–Nov. Expensive–Very Expensive.*

Bucaneve. This small, centrally located hotel is decorated in typical mountain style, with lots of wood paneling, flowers, and terraces. Some rooms have balconies. For après-ski activities, there's a restaurant and a cozy bar with a big fireplace. The hotel caters to longer stays at half-board rates. *Tel. 0166/949119, fax 0166/948308. 28 rooms with bath. Facilities: bar, restaurant, sauna, hydro-massage. AE, MC, V. Closed May–June, Sept.–Oct. Moderate.*

Hermitage. Skiers prefer this small, rustic hotel, located outside town near the ski lifts. There's lots of wood decoration and country touches, including a big fireplace in the hall. Some rooms have balconies with beautiful mountain views. The restaurant serves local specialties. Like many mountain hotels, this one caters to longer stays at half-board rates. *Strada Cristallo, tel. 0166/948998, fax 0166/949032. 32 rooms with bath. Facilities: bar, restaurant, indoor pool, sauna. AE, MC, V. Closed May–early July and Sept.–Oct. Moderate.*

Dining and Lodging
★

Neiges D'Antan. Located in a pine wood at Perrères, just outside Cervinia, this small, rustic family-run inn is quiet and cozy, with lots of wood decor and three big fireplaces. There is no TV in rooms: "It disturbs the atmosphere," says one of the proprietors. There's an excellent restaurant serving local specialties, such as fonduta, *zuppa Valpulinentza* (a peasant soup of bread, cabbage, and Fontina cheese), and polenta served with *fressa* (stuffed cabbage). *Perrères, 2 mi outside Cervinia, tel. 0166/948775, fax 0166/948852. 28 rooms with bath. Facilities: bar, restaurant (reservations advised). V. Closed May 4–June 25, Sept. 15–Dec. 5. Inexpensive.*

Courmayeur
Dining

Maison de Filippo. Here you'll find country-style home cooking in a character-filled mountain house furnished with antiques. Reserve in advance, for it's one of the most popular restaurants in the Valle D'Aosta. In summer, you can eat outside, surrounded by stunning views. There is a set menu only, featuring a daily selection of specialties, including a wide choice of antipasti and pasta dishes, such as *tortelloni Valdostana* (ravioli baked with Fontina cheese and butter); agnolotti in various sauces; and *spaghetti affumicata* (spaghetti with salami and bacon). The inn provides ample parking. *Entreves, tel. 0165/89968. Reservations required. Dress: casual. AE, MC, V. Closed Tues.; June 1–July 15, Nov. Moderate.*

Lodging

Royal. A classical mountain hotel in the center of town, the Royal is decorated with terraces, flowers, and wood paneling. Informal but elegant, its modern rooms were freshly renovated in 1987. There's a restaurant and evening piano bar. The hotel caters to longer stays with half- or full-board service. *Via Roma 83, tel. 0165/846787, fax 0165/842093. 93 rooms with* *bath. Facilities: bar, restaurant, outdoor pool, health center with massage, sauna, whirlpool. AE, DC, MC, V. Closed 1 week after Easter–June; mid-Sept.–mid-Dec. Very Expensive.*

Palace Bron. A posh, comfortable hotel, Palace Bron is set in a pine wood at Plan Gorret, above the town itself. There are beautiful views, and it's ideal for relaxing. The rooms are comfortably furnished with period pieces. The restaurant has a fireplace. *Plan Gorret, tel. 0165/846742, fax 0165/844015. 27 rooms with bath. DC, V. Facilities: bar, restaurant, garden, parking. Closed May–June, Oct.–Nov. Expensive.*

Pavillon. This is a modern version of a rustic chalet, complete with wood paneling, nostalgic decoration, and friendly service. Some rooms have views of Mont Blanc. Near cableways, it attracts a lively crowd. The atmosphere and facilities are reminiscent of old-fashioned spas. The hotel offers money-saving full-board rates. *Strada Regionale 62, tel. 0165/846120, fax 0165/846122. 50 rooms with bath. Facilities: bar, restaurant, heated indoor pool, health center with massage and sauna. AE, DC, MC, V. Closed May 1–June 20, Sept. 3–Dec. 1. Expensive.*

Cresta et Duc. A bright, modern Alpine hotel in the center of town, the Cresta features plenty of wooden terraces, flowers, and wooden furnishings. For relaxation there's a good restaurant, bar, billiards room, and lounges. The rooms are large and warm, and the hotel offers good full- and half-board rates. *Via Circonvallazione 7, tel. 0165/842585, fax 0165/842591. 39 rooms (no singles) with bath. Facilities: bar, restaurant. AE, DC, MC, V. Closed Easter–June, mid-Sept.–Dec. 20, Christmas. Moderate.*

Croux. This bright, comfortable hotel is located near the town center on the road leading to Mont Blanc. Many rooms have balconies with great views of the town and towering Alps. There is no restaurant. *Via Circonvallazione 94, tel. 0165/846735, fax 0165/845180. 30 rooms with bath. Facilities: bar, parking. AE, DC, MC, V. Closed May–June, Oct. 1–Dec. 20. Moderate.*

Novara
Lodging

Italia. This modern hotel in the center of the city features comfortable rooms and efficient service; the facilities cater mainly to businessmen. There is a restaurant, and some rooms have extensive views of the town. *Via Solaroli 8, tel. 0321/399316, fax 0321/399310. 62 rooms with bath. Facilities: bar, restaurant (closed Fri.), sauna, solarium. AE, DC, MC, V. Expensive.*

Saint Vincent
Dining
★

Batezar. This tiny, elegant restaurant has only eight tables. It's furnished with local antiques and fine crystal and silver place settings. Just a few steps from the casino, it is considered one of Italy's best restaurants. There's an extensive à la carte menu, but also recommended are the set menus: one of local specialties, the other of international gourmet treats. The menu changes with the season. Try the ravioli stuffed with *caprino* (goat cheese) or *castagne* (chestnuts); *capriccio d'anatra* (boned duck with olives); or *trota* (trout) cooked with lettuce and a basil sauce with grilled radicchio. *Via Marconi 1, tel. 0166/3164. Reservations required. Jacket and tie required. AE, DC, MC, V. Closed weekday lunch, Wed., and Feb. 20–Mar. 7. Very Expensive.*

Lodging

Billia. A luxury Belle Epoque hotel with pseudo-Gothic touches, the Billia is set in a park in the middle of town and connected directly with the casino by a special passageway. Half the rooms are done in modern style and half with period decor, and all creature comforts are attended to. There's a bar, three restaurants (open-air dining in summer), and a nightclub with dancing and a midnight floor show. The hotel also offers a fully equipped conference center—not to mention a private fishing reserve on a nearby mountain stream. *Viale Piemonte 18, tel. 0166/3446, fax 0166/201799. 250 rooms with bath. Facilities: heated outdoor pool, tennis courts, billiards, fully equipped fitness center with sauna and gym. AE, DC, MC, V. Very Expensive.*

Elena. The central location is the selling point of this hotel near the casino. The spacious rooms are decorated in a comfortable modern style, with color-coordinated fabrics and air-conditioning. *Via Biavaz 2, tel. 0166/512140, fax 0166/37459. 48 rooms with bath. Facilities: bar, restaurant. AE, DC, MC, V. Closed Nov. Moderate–Inexpensive.*

Sestriere
Lodging

Grand Sestriere. Large, elegant, and modern, the Grand Sestiere was built in 1980 near the ski lifts. Some rooms have terraces, where you can have breakfast or just a drink while soaking up the sunshine. There is a restaurant and cozy bar for après-ski relaxation. *Via Assietta 1, tel. 0122/76476, fax 0122/76700. 93 rooms with bath. AE, DC, MC, V. Closed Easter–June, Sept.–Dec. 21. Expensive.*

Miramonti. Nearly every room has a terrace at this pleasant, centrally located modern chalet. The ample, comfortable rooms are done in traditional mountain style, featuring lots of wood paneling and flowers, inside and out. *Via Cesana 3, tel. 0122/77048, fax 0122/77295. 30 rooms with bath. Facilities: bar, restaurant. No credit cards. Closed Easter–June, Sept. 10–Oct. Moderate.*

Turin
Dining

Cambio. It's hard to match the setting and atmosphere of this restaurant in the heart of Turin, set in a palace that dates from 1757. It is probably one of the most beautiful and historic restaurants in Europe, with decorative mouldings and mirrors and hanging lamps that look just as they did when Italian national hero Cavour dined here a century ago. The cuisine draws heavily on Piedmont tradition and is served with a wide choice of fine Piedmont wines. Recommended are pastas, such as the agnolotti in an *arrosto* (roast veal) sauce, and other traditional dishes, such as *veal carbonada* (stew). *Piazza Carignano 2, tel. 011/546690. Reservations required. Jacket and tie required. AE, DC, MC, V. Closed Sun. and Aug. Very Expensive.*

Vecchia Lanterna. Sumptuously decorated with brocades, old paintings, and rich carpets, this elegant, intimate restaurant in the center of town serves classic food, made from antique regional recipes. For a first course, try *savarin di riso al Dogaressa*, a rice dish made with seafood. For a second course, *filetto di branzino al Barolo* is a surprising combination of fish and full-bodied red wine. *Corso Re Umberto 21, tel. 011/537047. Reservations required. Jacket and tie required. AE, DC, MC, V. Closed Sat. lunch, Sun. Very Expensive.*

Bue Rosso. Centrally located in an old building decorated in elegant rustic style, this popular restaurant serves Italian cuisine and a few local specialties, such as agnolotti in truffle sauce and meat grilled over an open fire. There is a friendly atmosphere, and the waiters are helpful. *Corso Casale 10, tel. 011/830753. Reservations recommended. Dress: casual. AE, DC, V. Closed Mon., Sat. lunch, and Aug. Expensive.*

Due Lampioni. Join the stylish clientele of this elegant Baroque-style restaurant in a 17th-century palace in the heart of the city. It serves fine classic cuisine and an excellent selection of French and Italian wines. Try the agnolotti, filled with *anatra* (duck) and cooked with *tartufi bianchi* (white truffles); the terrine of fish; tournedos with a purée of olives; or the *carré di cervo* (roast venison). *Via Carlo Alberto 45, tel. 011/839–7409. Reservations advised. Jacket and tie required. AE, MC, V. Closed Sun. and all Aug. Expensive.*

★ **La Smarrita.** A small flower garden shields this intimate, elegant restaurant from the traffic of central Turin. Proprietor Moreno Grossi, with chefs Rolando Rolandi and Idilio Soragi, serves a set menu showcasing what he calls "La Cucina Nuova Italiana": simple, light Mediterranean dishes prepared with fresh herbs and other ingredients, using little fat, that attract the cream of Turin's high society. Grossi recommends the *fantasia di mare*—mixed fish topping mixed vegetables, steamed and seasoned with olive oil, lemon, fresh herbs, and raw tomato. Also, try the fresh homemade pasta with a sauce of *ortiche* (nettle shoots), *tagliatelli con fagiolini e pomodori* (noodles with green beans and tomatoes), or *spaghetti alle vongole* (with clams). There is an excellent wine cellar. *Corso Unione Sovietica 244, tel. 011/390657. Reservations required. Jacket and tie required. AE, DC, MC, V. Closed Mon. and Aug. 8–22. Expensive.*

Da Mauro. Try the Tuscan dishes in this lively, popular family-run trattoria. Specialties include *cannelloni alla Mirella* (stuffed rolls of noodle dough baked with mozzarella cheese), prosciutto and raw tomatoes, *castellana allo prosciutto* (a thin cut of veal baked with Fontina cheese and prosciutto) and famous Florentine grilled beef. *Via Maria Vittoria 21, tel. 011/8397811. No reservations. Dress: casual. No credit cards. Closed Mon. and July. Moderate.*

Ostu Bacu. You'll find this small rustic-style restaurant on the edge of town near the autostrada that goes to Milan. It specializes in regional Piedmont dishes, such as agnolotti and *fritto misto di carne*, a typical Piedmont specialty of fried mixed meats. *Corso Vercelli 226, tel. 011/264579. Reservations advised. Dress: casual. DC, MC, V. Closed Sun. and Aug. Moderate.*

Taverna delle Rose. Piedmont and Veneto cooking dominate in this character-filled restaurant near the train station. One dining room has walls covered with paintings; the other is done in old bricks and candlelight. Piedmont specialties include agnolotti and *brasato* (braised veal), cooked in Barolo wine. Veneto dishes include *pasta e fagioli* (pasta and bean soup) and *baccala* (salt cod, Venice style). *Via Massena 24, tel. 011/545275. Reservations advised for evening. Dress: casual. AE, DC, MC, V. Closed Sat. lunch, Sun. and Aug. Moderate.*

Lodging **Principi di Piemont.** The Principi is one of the best hotels in town, with 50 years of experience. It underwent a major restoration in 1988. The rooms, elegantly furnished in antique style, are spacious and light, with high ceilings. It's centrally located and popular with famous guests. *Via Gobetti 15, tel. 011/562–9693, fax 011/562–0270. 107 rooms with bath. Facilities: bar, restaurant, parking. AE, DC, MC, V. Very Expensive.*

Turin Palace. You're right across from the train station at this century-old building in the center of town. Quiet, spacious, and well-furnished rooms have high ceilings and feature either leather-and-wood classic modern style or Imperial Louis XV furnishings. It's the classiest in town. *Via Sacchi 8, tel. 011/ 562–5511, fax 011/5612187. 123 rooms with bath. Facilities: bar, restaurant, garage. AE, DC, MC, V. Very Expensive.*

Jolly Ligure. This comfortable hotel occupies a centrally located 300-year-old building that was totally renovated and restored in 1985. The rooms are large and airy, with particularly big beds (even in singles) and lots of space for clothes. The location is ideal for sightseeing or business. *Piazza Carlo Felice 85, tel. 011/55641, fax 011/535438. 156 rooms with bath. Facilities: bar, restaurant, parking. AE, DC, MC, V. Expensive.*

Genio. This 120-year-old building in the center of town has recently been redecorated in a smart modern style. The rooms are large and bright, with big, comfortable beds. There's no restaurant, but plenty are within easy walking distance. *Corso Vittorio Emanuele 47, tel. 011/650–5771, fax 011/6508264. 75 rooms with bath. Facilities: bar, parking. AE, DC, MC, V. Moderate.*

Victoria. This is a centrally located modern hotel with some unique touches. Most of the rooms are decorated in classic style with personalized touches. Room 316 has Indian motifs; 310, Old England; 206, Arabian; and so on. Some rooms have canopied beds and 15 rooms on the top floor have terraces. *Via Nino Costa 4, tel. 011/561–1909, fax 011/5611806. 65 rooms with bath. Facilities: bar, parking. AE, DC, MC, V. Moderate.*

The Arts and Nightlife

The Arts

Turin—and to a lesser extent, Aosta—dominate the world of the arts in this northwest corner of Italy. Music is especially popular among the population as a whole, with entire towns and villages plunging enthusiastically into concerts, recitals, and special exhibitions. In the Valle d'Aosta, you can hear French folk songs in Alpine surroundings, while Piedmont itself (and especially Turin) is on the Genoa–Milan concert trail. The best source of information about the arts is Piedmont's daily paper, *La Stampa.*

Music **Aosta.** Each summer there is a series of concerts held in different venues around the city. Organ recitals in July and August attract performers of world renown.

Asti. September is a month of fairs and celebrations in this famous wine city, and the Asti Competition in the middle of the month brings musicians, who perform in churches and halls in the city. For information, contact the tourist information office (Piazza Alfieri 34, tel. 0141/50357).

Turin. Classical music concerts are held in the famous **Conservatorio Giuseppe Verdi** (Via Mazzini 11) throughout the year, but mainly in the winter months. Sacred music and some modern religious pieces are performed in the **Duomo** on Sunday evening; these are usually advertised in the vestibule or in Turin's daily newspaper, *La Stampa.*

Opera **Turin.** The **Teatro Regio,** one of Italy's leading opera houses, begins its season in December. You can buy tickets for most performances (premieres are sold out well in advance) at the box office facing Piazza Castello.

Nightlife

As is the case with the arts, Turin is the major center for after-hours entertainment, although it has some competition from the swanky ski resorts of Courmayeur and Breuil-Cervinia. Elsewhere in Piedmont and Valle d'Aosta you'll find it best to limit yourself to sipping an after-dinner drink in a café on a busy city square or joining in the sometimes-boisterous songfests in the mountain hotel bars.

Casino **Saint Vincent.** The Casino de la Vallée, Europe's largest gambling house, operates in this spa resort near Chatillon in the Valle d'Aosta. Remember to pack your black tie—and a lot of lire.

Bars **Asti.** There is an excellent view from the terrace bar on the top floor of the **Hotel Salera** (*see* Dining and Lodging, *above*).

Breuil-Cervinia. Go to the bar of the hotel **Bucaneve** (*see* Dining and Lodging, *above*) for an après-ski atmosphere, with a blazing fire and wood paneling.

Courmayeur. There is a hushed, sophisticated feeling about the piano bar of the **Royal** hotel (*see* Dining and Lodging, *above*), in the center of town.

Nightclubs **Saint Vincent.** There is a nightly floor show at midnight and a lively nightclub at the **Billia Hotel** (*see* Dining and Lodging, *above*).

Discos The large hotels of Breuil-Cervinia, Courmayeur, and Saint-Vincent all have discos catering to the young, fashionable crowd that comes to these posh resorts. The names of the individual discos change as often as the latest music craze, but all of them have a cover charge (sometimes including the first drink) and a dress code that is best described as neat but eccentric.

Turin. Two good spots for unwinding to the rhythm of a disco beat are **Pick Up** (Via Barge 8) and **Patio** (Corso Moncalieri 346/14). Both are open late and cater to a mixed crowd of young Turinese, university students, and visitors.

10 Milan, Lombardy, and the Lakes

One is tempted to describe Lombardy as a place with something for everyone—Milan, capital of all that is new in Italy; the great Renaissance cities of the plain, Pavia, Cremona, and Mantua, where even the height of summer can be comparatively peaceful; and the Lakes, where glacial waters framed by the Alps have been praised by writers as varied as Virgil, Tennyson, and Hemingway.

The truth, of course, is more complicated. Milan can be disappointingly modern—rather too like the place you have come here to escape, but it is also the perfect blend of old and new, with historic buildings and art collections rivaling those in Florence and Rome. The Lakes, home to dozens of fashionable resorts, have preserved an astonishingly unspoiled beauty, often enhanced by sumptuous summer palaces and exotic formal gardens. Still, one cannot imagine Catullus returning to his "jewel" Sirmione, on Lake Garda, without being a little daunted by its development as a lively resort town. The great towns of the Lombardy plain are rich in history, but their art and architecture pale before the staggering wealth of Rome, Florence, and Venice.

More than 3,000 years ago—the date and the details are lost in the mysteries of Etruscan inscriptions—explorers from the highly civilized realm of Etruria in central Italy wandered northward beyond the river Po. The Etruscans extended their dominance into this region for hundreds of years but left little of their culture. They were succeeded by the Cenomanic Gauls, who, in turn, were conquered by the legions of Rome in the latter days of the Republic.

The region became known as Cisalpine Gaul, and under the rule of Augustus it became a Roman province. Its warlike, independent people became citizens of Rome. Virgil, Catullus, and both the Plinys were born in the region during this relatively tranquil era.

The decline of the Roman Empire was followed by the invasions of the Huns and the Goths. Attila and Theodoric, in turn, gave way to the Lombards, who ceded their iron crown to Charlemagne as the emblem of his vast but unstable empire.

Even before the fragile bonds that held this empire together had begun to snap, the cities of Lombardy were erecting walls in defense against the Hungarians and against each other. These communes did, however, form the Lombard League, which in the 12th century finally defeated Frederick Barbarossa.

Once the invaders had been defeated, new and even more bloody strife began. In each city the Guelphs (bourgeois supporters of the popes) and the Ghibellines (noble adherents to the so-called emperors) clashed with each other. The communes declined, and each fell under the yoke of powerful local rulers. The Republic of Venice dominated Brescia and Bergamo. Mantua was ruled by the Gonzaga, and the Visconti and Sforza families took over Como, Cremona, Milan, and Pavia.

The Battle of Pavia in 1525, when the generals of Charles V defeated the French (and gave Francis I the chance to coin the famous phrase "All is lost save honor"), brought on 200 years of Spanish occupation. The Spaniards were, on the whole, less cruel than the local tyrants and were hardly resisted by the Lombards.

The War of the Spanish Succession, in the early years of the 18th century, threw out the Spaniards and brought in, instead, the Austrians, whose dominion was "neither liked or loathed" during the nearly 100 years of its existence.

Napoleon and his generals routed the Austrians. The Treaty of Campoformio resulted in the proclamation of the Cisalpine Republic, which quickly became the Republic of Italy and, just as rapidly, the Kingdom of Italy, which lasted only until Napoleon's defeat brought back the Austrians. But Milan, as the capital of Napoleon's republic and of the Kingdom of Italy, had had a taste of glory, and the city's inherently independent citizens, along with those of the other Lombardian cities, were not slow to resent and combat the loss of "national" pride.

From 1820 on, the Lombards joined the Piedmontese and the House of Savoy in a long struggle against the Hapsburgs and, in 1859, finally defeated Austria and brought about the re-creation of the Kingdom of Italy two years later.

Milan and other cities of Lombardy have not lost their independence and their hatred of domination. Nowhere in Italy was the partisan insurrection against Mussolini (to whom they first gave power) and the German regime better organized or more successful. Milan was liberated from the Germans by its own partisan organization before the entrance of Allied troops; escaping Allied prisoners could find sanctuary there when fighting was still going on far to the south.

Lombards are a forthright people. They are as much inclined to taciturnity as any Italian is ever apt to be, and, when they do talk, they mean exactly what they say. When they quote a price, there is little use haggling about it. A Milanese is inclined to be courteous but probably has little time for pleasantries; his or her compatriot on the rice farm or in the mountains may be less talkative, but may take more interest in you as an individual.

Our three Lombardy tours—of Milan, the cities of the plain, and the lakes—are arranged as a circuit, running counterclockwise, starting and finishing in Milan. Even without a car, it should be possible to complete all three tours in a hard-paced week. A sensible alternative would be to use Milan as a base and to approach any of our tours' single destinations as a day's or weekend's excursion.

Essential Information

Important Addresses and Numbers

Tourist Information   **Bellagio** (Piazza della Chiesa 14, tel. 031/950204).
Bergamo (Vicolo Aquila Nera, at Piazza Vecchia, tel. 035/232730); in lower Bergamo, Viale Papa Giovanni 106, tel. 035/242226).
Brescia (Corso Zanardelli 34, tel. 030/43418).
Como (Piazza Cavour 16, tel. 031/274064; Stazione FF. SS, tel. 031/267214).
Cremona (Piazza del Comune 8, tel. 0372/23233).
Desenzano (Via Porto Vecchio, tel. 030/914–1510).

Malcesine (Via Capitanato del Porto 6, tel. 045/740–0044).
Mantua (Piazza A. Mantegna 6, tel. 0376/350681).
Milan (Via Marconi 1, tel. 02/809662; Stazione Centrale, tel. 02/669–0432).
Pavia (Via Fabio Filzi 2, tel. 0382/22156).
Riva del Garda (Giardine di Porta Orientale 8, tel. 0464/554444).
Sabbioneta (tel. 0375/52039).
Sirmione (Viale Marconi 2, tel. 030/916245).
Stresa (Via Principe Tomaso 70, tel. 0323/30150).

Consulates Most nations maintain consulates in Milan. **Canada** (Via Pisani 19, tel. 02/669–7451); **United Kingdom** (Via San Paolo 7, tel. 02/869–3442); **United States** (Largo Donegani 1, tel. 02/652841); **Australia** (Via Turati 40, tel. 02/659–8727).

Emergencies **Como: Police,** tel. 031/272366; **Medical Emergency,** tel. 031/113.
Cremona: Police, tel. 0372/2333; **Medical Emergency,** tel. 0372/4051.
Desenzano: Police, tel. 030/113; **Medical Emergency,** tel. 030/914–4761.
Malcesine: Police, tel. 0464/552326; **Medical Emergency,** tel. 0464/554004.
Mantua: Police, tel. 0376/326341; **Medical Emergency,** tel. 0376/329261.
Milan: Police, tel. 02/113; **Carabinieri,** tel. 02/112; **Ambulance,** tel. 02/7733; **Medical Emergency,** Fatebenefratelli Hospital, Corso di Porta Nuova 23, tel. 02/63631.
Pavia: Police, tel. 0382/301204; **Medical Emergency,** tel. 0382/3901.
Sirmione: Police, tel. 0365/20179; **Medical Emergency,** tel. 0365/40361.

Late-Night Pharmacies The pharmacy on the upper level of Milan Central Station is open 24 hours. Others take turns staying open late and on weekends; call 02/192 for the location of the nearest one, or check the rota published in the *Corriere della Sera.*

English-Language Bookstores In **Milan: The American Bookshop** (Largo Cairoli at Via Camperio, tel. 02/870944), **The English Bookshop** (Via Mascheroni 12, tel. 02/469–4468), **Feltrinelli Bookstore** (Via Manzoni 12, tel. 02/700386).

Travel Agencies In **Milan: Compagnia Italiana Turismo** (CIT) (Galleria Vittore Emanuele, tel. 02/866661), **American Express Travel Agency** (Via Brera 3, tel. 02/85571), **Chiariva & Sommariva** (Via Dante 10, tel. 02/85041); **Thomas Cook** (Via Larga 13, tel. 02/5830–3986).

Arriving and Departing by Plane

Milan has two principal airports. **Malpensa,** located about 50 kilometers (31 miles) northwest of the city, handles all intercontinental air traffic, and **Linate,** located less than 10 kilometers (6 miles) east of the city, handles international and domestic air traffic. For air traffic information for both airports, call 02/74852200.

Between the Airports and Downtown
From Malpensa By Car: Take Route S336 east to the autostrada A8 southeast toward Milan. The drive takes about 40 minutes, depending on traffic and destination. **By Taxi:** A taxi stand is located directly outside the arrivals building doors. Approximate fare is 100,000 lire. **By Bus:** There is bus service to Milan's Central

Station. Buses usually leave every half-hour between 8:15 AM and 11:15 PM. Cost is 8,000 lire. The trip takes about one hour. Buy your ticket inside before embarking.

From Linate **By Car:** Take what was once the Old Brescia Road west into the central downtown area. **By Taxi:** A taxi stand is directly in front of the arrivals building. Approximate fare is 20,000 lire. The duration of the journey is less than 20 minutes. **By Bus:** Buses leave every 20 minutes for Milan's Central Station. The trip takes about 20 minutes. Cost is 2,500 lire. You can also take ATM municipal bus No. 73 to Piazza San Babila (every 15 minutes). Cost is 1,000 lire.

Arriving and Departing by Car, Train, and Bus

By Car Two major autostrada routes cross at Milan: the A1, which leads south to Bologna, Florence, and Rome, and the A4, which runs east-west from Turin to Venice. A7 angles southwest down to Genoa from Milan. The city is ringed by a bypass road (the Tangenziale).

By Train Although Milan claims a bewildering number of railway stations, only one need concern you, unless you are traveling on local routes at peculiar hours—in which case service can begin or terminate in suburban stations (most notably Milano Lambrate for Bergamo, and Stazione Nord for Como). **Milano Centrale** (a bombastic neo-Babylonian creation, from what is now politely termed the era of "rational" architecture) has, since opening in 1931, been Milan's main railway station. Premium international ("EC") service and premium ("IC") domestic service connect Milan with all major European cities. The station is located northeast of the historic center of Milan, about 5 kilometers (3 miles) from the Duomo and Galleria. Metro line 3 links it with Piazza Duomo. For train information, call 02/67500.

By Bus Italian bus service is best avoided on intercity routes, since it is neither faster, cheaper, nor more convenient than the railways. Most bus companies use the Piazza Castello. Milan has no central bus terminal. For bus information, call Autostradale (tel. 02/801161) or Zani Viaggi (tel. 02/867131).

Getting Around

By Car The A4 autostrada is the main east–west highway for this region, with various other major highways—A8 from the northwest, A7 from the southwest, A1 from the southeast—converging at Milan. A21 runs roughly parallel to the A4 until it curves north through Cremona and Brescia to feed into the A4. The A22 is a major north–south highway running just east of Lake Garda. Although these major highways will allow you to make good time between the cities of the plain, you'll have to follow secondary roads—often of great beauty—around the lakes. S572 goes along the southern and western shores of Lake Garda, S45bis along the northernmost section of the western shore, and S249 along the eastern shore. Around Lake Como, follow S340 along the western shore, S36 on the eastern coast, and S583 on the lower arms. S33 and S34 trace the western shore of Lake Maggiore.

Car rental agencies in Milan include **Avis** (tel. 02/6981), **Hertz** (tel. 02/20483), **Europcar** (tel. 02/607–1053), or **Budget** (tel. 02/

670–3151), or try "Autonoleggio" in the Yellow Pages. The major international companies have offices at both airports.

By Train From Milan, there is frequent direct service to Cremona, Bergamo, Pavia, Breschia, Mantua, Desenzano del Garda–Sirmione, and Como.

By Bus Trains are generally better than buses for getting around the cities of the plain. There is regular bus service between the small towns on the lakes, which tends to be a cheaper way of getting around than ferry or hydrofoil service. The bus service around Lake Garda serves mostly towns on the western coast.

By Boat There is frequent daily ferry and hydrofoil service between towns on the lakes. Call **Navigazione Lago di Garda** (tel. 030/914–1321) for Lake Garda, **Navigazione Lago di Como** (Piazza Cavour, Como, tel. 031/272278) for Lake Como, and **Navigazione Lago Maggiore** (Piazza Matteotti, Stresa, tel. 0323/30393) for Lake Maggiore. In addition, steamer tours can often be arranged by private launches at lakeside hotels.

Milan

Milan's history as a capital city goes back at least 2,500 years. Its fortunes ever since, both as a great commercial trading center and as the object of regular conquest and occupation, are readily explained by its strategic position at the center of the Lombard plain. Directly south of the central passes across the Alps, Milan is bordered by three highly navigable rivers—the Po, the Ticino, and the Adda—which for centuries were the main arteries of an ingenious network of canals crisscrossing all Lombardy (and ultimately reaching most of northern Italy).

Virtually every invader in European history—Gaul, Roman, Goth, Longobard, and Frank—as well as every ruler of France, Spain, and Austria, has taken a turn at ruling the city and the region. Milan's glorious heyday of self-rule proved comparatively brief, from 1277 until 1500, when it was ruled by its two great family dynasties, the Visconti and subsequently the Sforza. These families were known, justly or not, for a peculiarly aristocratic mixture of refinement, classical learning, and cruelty, and much of the surviving grandeur of Gothic and Renaissance art and architecture is their doing. Be on the lookout in your wanderings for the Visconti family emblem—a viper, its jaws straining wide, devouring a child.

If you are wondering why so little seems to have survived from Milan's antiquity, the answer is simple—war. Three times in the city's history, partial or total destruction has followed conflict—in AD 539, 1157, and 1944.

Getting Around Serious pollution is responsible for a rigorously enforced effort
By Car to ban all unnecessary traffic from the city's center. Cars lacking a special resident's permit will be stopped and ticketed. Parked cars may be towed. For taxi service, call 02/6767, 02/8585, or 02/8388. For limousine service, call 02/657-5166. If age or infirmity ought to entitle you to special dispensation, and both taxis and other forms of cars with drivers are inadequate or unsuitable for your needs, inquire of your rental agency or hotel concierge about car permits for special cases.

By Public Milan has an excellent system of public transport, consisting of
Transport trolley cars, buses, and a subway system, the Metropolitana,

which runs on three lines. Tickets for each must be purchased before you board and must be canceled by machines located at underground station entrances and mounted on poles inside trolleys and buses. Tickets cost 1,000 lire and can be purchased from news vendors, tobacconists, and machines at larger stops. Buy several at once—they remain valid until canceled.

By Bicycle As part of its campaign to ban cars from Milan's center, the city government has begun to set up a network of one-way bicycle rental stations. At first, rentals were free; now there is a small charge. Though the bicycles are clearly intended for residents who would otherwise use cars, current opinion is that tourists may use them, too (though doubtless individual proprietors of stands may arbitrarily decide to disagree, especially if you are unable to explain your rights in Italian). Look for yellow stands filled with yellow bicycles.

By Taxi Taxi fares seem expensive compared with those in American cities: A short downtown hop runs on average 8,000 lire. But drivers are honest here (to an extreme, compared with some cities).

Guided Tours Once our entire Lombardy Tours itinerary could have been accomplished by barge, weaving from district to district via canals and rivers. Boat travel in Milan was apparently a legacy of the Romans, and it continued to work remarkably well with very little maintenance for about 1,700 years. Railways were the final blow. Recently, tourist interest has revived, and there are now guided boat trips through some of the city's Navigli canals. Contact the Tourist Information Office (EPT) for further information (*see* Important Addresses and Numbers in Essential Information, *above*).

Highlights for First-time Visitors

Pinacoteca di Brera
Duomo
Santa Maria delle Grazie (for the *Last Supper*)
Galleria Vittorio Emanuele

Exploring Milan

Numbers in the margin correspond to points of interest on the Milan map.

There's only one logical place to begin a walking tour of **①** **Milan**—the **Duomo** (Cathedral), which has been fascinating and exasperating visitors and conquerors alike since it was begun by Galeazzo Visconti III, first duke of Milan, in 1386. Consecrated in 1577, and not wholly completed until 1897, it is the third-largest church in the world and the largest Gothic building in Italy.

Whether you concur with travel writer H. V. Morton, writing 25 years ago, that the cathedral is "one of the mightiest Gothic buildings ever created," or regard it as a spiny pastiche of centuries, there is no denying that for sheer size and complexity it is unequaled. Its capacity—though it is hard to imagine the church filled—is reckoned to be 40,000. Usually it is empty, a perfect sanctuary from the frenetic pace of life outside and the perfect place for solitary contemplation. The poet Shelley swore by it—claiming it was the only place to read Dante.

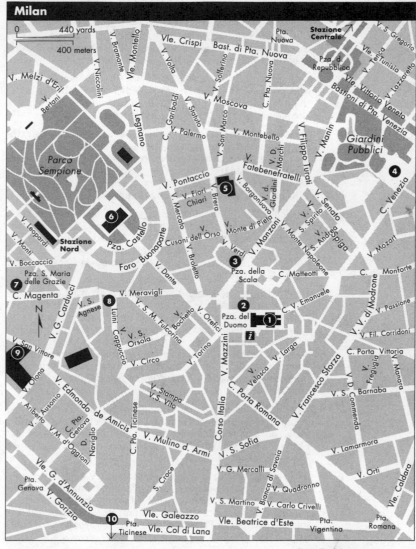

Milan

0   440 yards
400 meters

V. Melzi d'Eril
V. Bertani
Parco Sempione
V. Bramante
V. Niccolini
V. Legnano
V. Montello
Vle. Crispi
V. Volta
V. Solferino
Bast. di Pta. Nuova
Pta. Nuova
Stazione Centrale
V. S. Gregorio
Vle. e Tunisia
V. Lazzaretto
Pza. d. Repubblica
Vle. Vittorio Veneto
Bastioni di Pta. Venezia
V. Garibaldi
C. Statuto
V. Palermo
V. San Marco
V. Moscova
V. Montebello
C. Pta. Nuova
V. Filippo Turati
V. Manin
Giardini Pubblici
C. Venezia
V. Pontaccio
V. Fiori Chiari
V. Brera
V. Borgonuovo
V. d. Giardini
Fatebenefratelli
V. d. Marchi
V. Senato
V. Spirito S.
V. Mozart
Stazione Nord
V. Leopardi
V. Monti
Pza. Castello
Foro Buonaparte
Mercato
Cusani dell'Orso
V. Broletto
Monte di Pietà
V. Manzoni
V. Verdi
V. Monte N.S. Andrea
V. Napoleone
Spiga
C.
Monforte
C.
V. Boccaccio
Pza. S. Maria delle Grazie
C. Magenta
V. Meravigli
V. Dante
Pza. della Scala
C. Matteotti
C. V. Emanuele
C. Porta Vittoria
V. di Modrone
V. Passione
N
V. G. Carducci
V. S. Agnese
Luini
V. Cappuccio
V. S. M. Fulcorina
V. S. Orsola
V. Bocchetto
V. Orefici
Pza. del Duomo
C. V. Emanuele
V. Fil. Corridoni
V. San Vittore
V. Carrobbio
V. Torino
V. Mazzini
V. Velasca
V. Larga
C. Porta Vittoria
Freguglia
V. Manara
V. Circo
Stampa
V. S. Vito
C. Pta. Ticinese
V. Edmondo de Amicis
C. Porta Romana
V. Francesco Sforza
V. D. Commenda
V. S. Barnaba
Aribetto Ausonio
Pta. Genova
V. M. d'Oggiono
Naviglio
V. Mulino d. Armi
V. S. Sofia
V. S. Croce
Corso Italia
V. G. Mercalli
V. Lamarmora
V. Orti
Vle. Caldara
Pta. Genova
Vle. G. d'Annunzio
V. Gorizia
Vle. Galeazzo
Pta. Ticinese
Vle. Col di Lana
Vle. Beatrice d'Este
V. S. Martino
Bianca di Savoia
V. Quadronno
V. Carlo Crivelli
Pta. Vigentina
Pta. Romana

Castello Sforzesco, **6**
Civico Museo di Storia Naturale, **4**
Duomo, **1**
Galleria Vittorio Emanuele, **2**
La Scala, **3**
Museo Archeologico, **8**
Museo Nazionale della Scienza e della Tecnica, **9**
Navigli district, **10**
Pinacoteca di Brera, **5**
Santa Maria delle Grazie, **7**

The building is adorned with 135 marble spires and 2,245 marble statues. The oldest part is the apse (the end of the cruciform opposite the portals). Its three colossal bays of curving and counter-curved tracery, especially the bay adorning the exterior of the stained-glass windows, should not be missed.

Step inside and walk down the right aisle to the southern transept, to the tomb of Gian Giacomo Medici. The tomb owes something to Michelangelo, but is generally considered its sculptor's (Leone Leoni's) masterpiece; it dates from the 1560s.

Directly ahead is the Duomo's most famous sculpture, the rather gruesome but anatomically instructive figure of St. Bartolomeo, whose glorious martyrdom consisted of being flayed alive. It is usually said the saint stands "holding" his skin, but this is not quite accurate. It would appear more that he is luxuriating in it, much as a 1950s matron might approach a new fur stole.

As you enter the apse to admire those splendid windows, glance at the sacristy doors to the right and left of the altar. The lunette on the right dates from 1393 and was decorated by Hans von Fernach. That on the left also dates from the 14th century and is ascribed jointly to Giacomo da Campione and Giovanni dei Grassi.

Don't miss the view from the Duomo's roof: Walk outside the left (north) transept to the stairs and elevator. Sad to say, late–20th-century air pollution has, on all but the rarest days, drastically reduced the view. But even in fog, the roof itself has a fairy-tale quality. As you stand among the impossible forest of marble pinnacles, remember that virtually every inch of this gargantuan edifice, including the roof itself, is constructed of precious white marble. *Admission: 3,000 lire for stairs, 5,000 lire for elevator.*

Should you wish to learn more about the cathedral's history and see some of the treasures removed for safety from the exterior, visit the **Duomo Museum.** *Museo del Duomo, Piazza del Duomo 14B, tel. 02/860358. Admission: 5,000 lire. Open Tues.–Sun. 9:30–12:30, 3–6.*

The subterranean ruins of a fourth-century **baptistry** are located beneath the Duomo's piazza. Though opinion remains divided, it is widely believed that this may have been where Ambrose (Milan's first bishop and patron saint) baptized Augustine Battistero Paleocristiano. *Access through the Cathedral. Admission free. Open Tues.–Sun. 10–noon, 3–5.*

Time Out The best alternative to a conventional restaurant is **Peck,** one of Italy's, if not the world's, most irresistible food emporiums. In the Duomo area, it is something better than a shop—it's six shops. Best for a quick stand-up lunch is **Bottega del Vino** (Via Victor Hugo 4, tel. 02/861040), which offers almost 200 wines by the glass. **Peck Rosticceria** (Via Cantu 3, tel. 02/693017, closed Mon.) offers grilled takeout; for a more relaxed lunch, try **Il Restaurant** (Via Victor Hugo 4, tel. 02/876774, closed Sun. and 2 weeks in Jan.); for do-it-yourself, try the **Delicatessen** (Via Spadari 9).

The great glass-topped, barrel-vaulted tunnel beckoning from just beyond the northern tip of the cathedral's facade is **②** **Galleria Vittorio Emanuele.** Anyone who has grown up on the periphery of a contemporary American city should recognize this spectacularly extravagant late–19th-century creation for what it is—one of the planet's earliest and most elegant shopping malls, rivaled perhaps only by G.U.M., off Red Square in Moscow, for sheer Belle Époque splendor. Its architect, Giuseppe Mengoni, accidently lost his footing and tumbled to his death on the floor of his own creation, just days before its opening.

Like its suburban American cousins, the Galleria fulfills a variety of social functions vastly more important than its ostensible commercial purpose. If you had only a half hour to spend in Milan, this would be the place to spend it. This is the city's heart, midway between the cathedral and La Scala opera house, and it is sometimes called *Il Salotto* (The Living Room). For all but a few hours of the week, it positively teems with life. If you're a bit weary from your exploration of the Duomo, stop here to enjoy that most delightful of spectator sports—people-watching. Pull up a chair at one of the strategically situated tables that spill from the Galleria's bars and restaurants, and prepare to enjoy one of those monstrously surcharged coffees that are the modest price of a front-row seat at one of the best shows in Italy.

Like the cathedral, the Galleria is cruciform in shape. The space at the crossing, however, forms an octagon. If this is where you're standing, don't be afraid to look up and gawk. Even in poor weather, the great glass dome makes a splendid sight. And the mosaics, usually unnoticed, are a vastly underrated source of pleasure, even if they are not to be taken too seriously. They represent Europe, Asia, Africa, and America; those at the entrance arch are devoted to science, industry, art, and agriculture.

Books, clothing, food, wine, pens, jewelry, and myriad other goods are all for sale in the Galleria, and one of Milan's most correct and traditional restaurants, Savini, is located here. There is, in addition, one of those curious Italian institutions, an *Albergo Diurno* (Daytime Hotel), where you can take an hour's nap or a bath, get a haircut or a pedicure, and have your suit pressed or a button replaced. Most of its patrons are Italian, but it is hard to think of a better oasis for a vacationer who's worn out from sightseeing.

❸ Continue across the transepts of the Galleria and head north into the Piazza della Scala, home of the Teatro della Scala, or **La Scala,** where Verdi's fame was established. It was completely renovated after its World War II destruction by Allied bombs in 1943 and reopened at a performance led by Arturo Toscanini in 1946.

You need know nothing of opera to sense that, like Carnegie Hall, La Scala is something rather more than an auditorium. It looms as a symbol—both for the performer dreaming one day to sing here and for the buff who knows every note of *Rigoletto* by heart. For some, a visit to La Scala will be—even more than the Duomo—a solemn but pleasurable act of pilgrimage.

If you are lucky enough to be here during the opera season, which runs for approximately six months beginning each December, you should do whatever is necessary to obtain a ticket—even if it requires perching among the rafters in one of the dreaded gallery seats. Hearing a Verdi or Puccini opera sung in

Italian by Italians in Italy is a magical experience. For now, whet your appetite with a quick stroll through the theater's small museum, **Museo Teatrale alla Scala.** *Tel. 02/805–3418. Admission: 5,000 lire. Open year-round, Mon.–Sat. 9–noon, 2–6, plus May–Oct., Sun. 9:30–noon, 2:30–6. Closed occasionally during rehearsals.*

At the northern end of Piazza della Scala, Via Manzoni leads straight into the heart of Milan's most luxurious shopping district, perhaps the most luxurious shopping district in all of Italy. Right here, in a few small streets laid out like a game of hopscotch—Via Monte Napoleone, Via Sant'Andrea, Via della Spiga—lie the shops of the great Italian designers, such as Armani, Versace, and Gianfranco Ferre. Don't come here looking for affordable fashion—that has been relegated to the other side of the Duomo—but even though the prices are high, it costs nothing to stroll around and drink in the distinctive look and style that makes shopping in Milan special. Milan's fortissimo is ready-to-wear, and twice a year, in March and October, the world's fashion elite descends upon the city for the famous ready-to-wear designer shows that invariably set next season's styles around the globe.

At the northern end of Via Manzoni, you'll reach **Giardini Pubblici,** a good park for young children. On the eastern side of the park, facing Corso Venezia, is the **Civico Museo di Storia Naturale,** with exhibits that appeal to animal and nature lovers. *Corso Venezia 55. Admission free. Open Mar.–Oct., Tues.– Sat. 9:30–12:30, 2:30–5:30, Sun. 9:30–7; Nov.–Feb., Tues.– Sat. 9:30–12:30, 2–5, Sun. 9:30–7.*

From the southwestern corner of the park, follow Fatebenefratelli and then Via Pontaccio to Via Brera, where you'll find the **Pinacoteca di Brera,** on the right at No. 28. The picture collection here is star studded, even by Italian standards. As everyone knows, the only way to "do" a large collection is to start with the best, while you're still fresh, eager, and observant, and leave the charming minor masterpieces for afterward. We suggest you begin by ignoring the 20th-century work displayed along the long corridor that you enter and walk to the large, well-patrolled room (No. 22) with only two big paintings, both behind glass.

There is only one depressing fact to be noted about Raphael's *Betrothal of the Virgin*—he painted it when he was 22, a time when many of us are still struggling with the question of what to do in life. The other painting, Piero della Francesca's *Madonna with Saints and Angels*, is earlier, but just as lovely, much aided by its recent and skillful restoration and cleaning.

The gallery's best-known painting is probably the somber, beautiful, and moving *Dead Christ* by Mantegna, in Room 18. Though it is by far the smallest painting in the room, it dominates, with its sparse palette of gray and terra-cotta. Mantegna's shocking, almost surgical, precision in the rendering of Christ's wounds, the face propped up on a pillow, the day's growth of beard—tells of an all-too-human agony. It is one of Renaissance painting's most quietly wondrous achievements, finding an unsuspected middle ground between the excesses of conventional gore and beauty in representing the Passion's saddest moment.

On your way out, pause a moment to view the fine Carlo Carras (especially *La Musa Metafisica*, or *Metaphysical Muse*), suggesting Italy's confident and stylish response to the likes of Picasso and Max Ernst and to the schools of Cubism and Surrealism. *Tel. 02/864–63501 Admission: 8,000 lire. Open Tues.–Sat. 9–2, Sun. 9–1.*

Take time to wander around the lively quarter surrounding the Pinacoteca di Brera. The narrow streets, lined by boutiques, craft shops, cafés, restaurants, and music clubs, comprise what is often referred to as Milan's Greenwich Village. Longtime haunt of artists and musicians, it has a number of clubs and cafés offering live music until late at night.

❻ The **Castello Sforzesco,** a little more than two blocks west, along Via Pontaccio, is the next stop. For the serious student of Renaissance military engineering, the imposing Castello must be something of a travesty, so often has it been remodeled or rebuilt since it was begun in 1450. It was built by the condottiere founder of the city's second dynastic family, Francesco Sforza, fourth duke of Milan. As for the rest of us, children of all ages, it's clearly everything a storybook castle ought to be. Huge, for one. It is also just across the road from what is claimed to be the best gelateria in all northern Italy: **Viel** (Largo Cairoli) is at the right of the intersection in front of the Castello's southeast face.

Though today the word "mercenary" has a strongly pejorative ring, during the Renaissance all Italy's great soldier-heroes were professionals hired by the cities and principalities that they served. Of them—and there were thousands—Francesco Sforza is considered to have been one of the greatest and most honest. It is said he could remember not only the names of all his men, but of their horses. And it is with his era, and the building of the Castello, that we know we have entered the enlightened age of the Renaissance. It took barely half a century before it and the city were under foreign rule.

Today, the Castello houses municipal museums devoted variously to Egyptian and other antiquities, musical instruments, paintings, and sculpture. Highlights are the Salle delle Asse, a frescoed room still sometimes attributed to Leonardo da Vinci, and Michelangelo's unfinished *Rondanini Pietà*, believed to be his last work: an astounding achievement for a man nearly 90, but a sad memorial to genius at the end. *Piazza Castello. Tel. 02/6236, ext. 3947. Admission free. Open daily 9:30–5:30. Closed last Tues. of month.*

H.V. Morton noted that Milan might well be the only city on earth where you could give a taxi driver the title of a painting as your destination. If this appeals to you, flag one down and say, "*L'ultima Cena*, per favore," since this is how the *Last Supper* is known here. If not, you can walk to the church and former **❼** Dominican monastery of **Santa Maria delle Grazie,** and what is now called the **Cenacolo Vinciano,** which used to be the order's refectory. It is a few blocks southwest on the Corso Magenta.

The *Last Supper* has had an almost unbelievable history of bad luck and neglect—its near destruction in an American bombing raid in August 1943 being only the latest chapter in a series of misadventures, including, if one 19th-century source is to be believed, being whitewashed by the monks. Well-meant but disastrous attempts at restoration have done little to rectify the problem of the work's placement: It is situated on a wall unusually vulnerable to climatic dampness. Yet the artist chose to work slowly and patiently in oil pigments—which demand dry plaster—instead of using the conventional fresco technique of proceeding hastily on wet. Aldous Huxley called it "the saddest work of art in the world." After years beneath a scaffold, with restorers patiently shifted from one square centimeter to another, Leonardo's famous masterpiece still is in a sad state, and studies in methods of further restorations and of preserving this great fresco continue. However, it is nearer to its original glory than it has been at any time since the artist's death in 1519.

Despite Leonardo's carefully preserved preparatory sketches, in which the apostles are clearly labeled by name, there still remains some small debate about a few identities in the final arrangement. But there can be no mistaking Judas, small and dark, his hand calmly reaching forward toward the bread, immured from the terrible confusion that has taken the hearts of the others. One critic, Professor Frederick Hartt, offers an elegantly terse explanation for why the composition works: It combines "dramatic confusion" with "mathematical order." Certainly, the amazingly skillful and unobtrusive repetition of threes, when first you see it—in the windows, in the grouping of the figures, and in their placement—adds a mystical aspect to what at first seems simply the perfect observation of spontaneous human gesture. *Cenacolo Vinciano, tel. 02/498-7588. Admission: 10,000 lire. Open Tues.–Sun. 9–1:15, but hours may vary.*

Take at least a moment to visit the Santa Maria delle Grazie itself. It's a handsome church, with a fine dome by Bramante, which was added along with a cloister about the time that Leonardo was commissioned to paint the *Last Supper.* If you're wondering how it was that two such giants came to be employed decorating and remodeling the refectory and church of a comparatively modest religious order, and not, say, the Duomo, the answer lies in the ambitious but largely unrealized plan to turn Santa Maria delle Grazie into a magnificent Sforza family mausoleum. Though Ludovico Il Moro Sforza, seventh duke of Milan, was but one generation away from the founding of the Sforza dynasty, he was its last ruler. Two years after Leonardo finished the *Last Supper,* Ludovico was defeated and was imprisoned in a French dungeon for the remaining eight years of his life.

Time Out For those who don't scream for ice cream, a venerable neighborhood institution, **The Bar Magenta** (Via Carducci 13 at Corso Magenta) provides an excellent alternative en route. Luncheon, beer, or coffee provides only an excuse for coming here; the real attraction is its casual but civilized, quintessentially Milanese ambience.

8 Go east on Corso Magenta, across Via Carducci, to visit the city's **Museo Archeologico.** Housed in a former monastery, there are some enlightening relics from Milan's Roman past here, from everyday utensils and jewelry to several fine examples of mosaic pavement. *Corso Magenta 15. tel. 02/806598. Admission free. Open Wed.–Mon. 9:30–12:15 and 2:30–5:15.*

You've Let Your Imagination Go, Now Get Up And Follow Your Dreams.

For The Vacation You're Dreaming Of, Call American Express® Travel Agency At 1-800-YES-AMEX.*

American Express will send more than your imagination soaring. We'll fly you, sail you, drive you to any Fodor's destination and beyond. Because American Express believes the best vacations happen from Europe to the Orient, Walt Disney® World to Hawaii and everywhere in between.

For dependable service, expert advice, and value wherever your dreams take you, call on American Express. After all, the best traveling companion is a trustworthy friend.

It's easy to recognize a good place when you see one.

American Express Cardmembers have been doing it for years.

The secret? Instead of just relying on what they see in the window, they look at the door. If there's an American Express Blue Box on it, they know they've found an establishment that cares about high standards.

Whether it's a place to eat, to sleep, to shop, or simply meet, they know they will be warmly welcomed.

So much so, they're rarely taken in by anything else.

Always a good sign.

Next to the Museo Archeologico, Via Santa Agnese leads to the church of **Sant'Ambrogio.** Across from the church's main doors, turn left on Via San Vittore to see the **Museo Nazionale della Scienza e della Tecnica,** which has models based on technical projects by Leonardo da Vinci and collections of locomotives, planes, and cars. *Via San Vittore 21, near Sant'Ambrogio, tel. 02/480-0040. Admission: 6,000 lire adults, 4,000 lire children under 18. Open Tues.–Sun. 9:30–4:30, Mon. holidays.*

If you have time, walk back to Via Carducci, which becomes Via Edmondo de Amicis, and follow it southeast until you can turn right on Corso Porta Ticinese, which ends at the impressive early 19th-century arch of Porta Ticinese. Beyond lies the picturesque **Navigli district** in the southern part of the city. In medieval times a network of navigable canals, called *navigli,* crisscrossed Milan. Almost all have been covered over, except for two long canals, Naviglio Grande and Naviglio Pavese, and part of a third, Darsena. The canals are lined by quaint shops, art galleries, cafés, pubs, restaurants, and clubs. Much of Milan's nightlife is centered here, and the neighborhood has a romantic, bohemian atmosphere.

Shopping

Always beautiful, impeccably groomed, wrapped in fur and glittering jewels, the Milanese woman, the *gran signora,* is possessed of an understated elegance unequaled anywhere in the world.

Her habitat is **Via Monte Napoleone,** where she can be found lining up for fresh pasta and quail eggs in aspic at Il Salumaio (just a few steps from the spot where Verdi wrote his opera *Nabucco*), sipping cappuccino around the pink-lace-covered tables of the Bar Cova, or dropping into Ars Rosa for an embroidered silk-satin nightdress or a hand smocked dress for her little girl. Via Monte Napoleone has 10 top-notch jewelers and a profusion of antique stores and designer fashion boutiques, as well. It's also prime shopping territory for shoes—all beautifully made, classic, fashionable, and expensive. Within a few steps of one another, you'll find shops for Ferragamo at No. 3; Lario 1898 at No. 21; Carrano, also at No. 21; Beltrami at No. 16; Valeriano Ferario at No. 6; and Fausto Santini at No. 1.

Her tailored suit may come from Giorgio Armani, just a few steps away on **Via Sant'Andrea,** or from Gianni Versace, or Gianfranco Ferre, around the corner on the tiny but luxurious **Via della Spiga.** For amusing items for her house, there is L'Utile e il Dilettevole, also on Via della Spiga, with its enchanting Italian country style.

An Armani or Ferre ensemble can set you back several thousand dollars, but similar Italian taste and styling can be found at more affordable prices at **Fiorucci** (in the Galleria Passarella) **Benetton,** and **Emporio Armani** or the department stores **La Rinascente** (in the Piazza Duomo) and **Coin** (Piazza Loreto). In between are covetable but sensible Italian fashion buys at shops like **Biffi, Komlas, Gemelli,** and **Max Mara.**

Canny Milanese regularly make the rounds of the dozens of factory outlets and discount stores in the city, often finding designer labels at 30 to 70% off. Stock changes daily, and not all accept credit cards. Some of the better known discount stores

for men's and women's fashion (and in some cases, shoes) are **Il
Salvagente** (Via Fratelli Bronzetti 16, tel. 02/761–10328),
Leuce (Via Panizzi 6, tel. 02/489–50907), **San Laurent-Rive
Gauche** (Piazza Sant'Erasmo 3, tel. 02/655–7795), **Stockhouse**
(Via Alunno 10, tel. 02/403–6748), **Niki** (Via Fontana 19, tel. 02/
551–81284), and **Floretta Coen** (Via San Calogero 3, tel. 02/839–
7708). You can find designer shoes at whopping discounts at the
outdoor market at **Piazzale Martini** Wednesday morning and
Saturday.

Shops are usually open 9–1 (closed Mon. morning) and 4–7:30;
many are closed in August.

Here are some other possibilities:

Brera is an area with many unique shops. Walk along Via
Brera, Via Solferino, Corso Garibaldi, and Via Paolo Sarpi.

Corso Buenos Aires is a wide avenue with a variety of shops,
several offering moderately priced items.

Corso Vittorio Emanuele has clothing, leather goods, and shoe
shops, some with items at reasonable prices.

Prada (Galleria Vittorio Emanuele, tel. 02/876979) is a smart
leather goods store with a cycle of heroic turn-of-the-century
travel murals (downstairs in the main sales area).

Lenci (Galleria Vittorio Emanuele, tel. 02/870376) is among the
world's foremost doll shops and doubtless the only one bran-
dishing a Latin motto from which we all can learn—*"Ludus est
nobis constanter industria"* (play is our constant work).

Flea markets are popular in Milan and all over Lombardy. Food
and a vast array of items, new and old, are displayed in open-air
stalls. In many markets, bargaining is no longer the custom.
You can try to haggle, but if you fear getting ripped off, go to
the stalls where prices are clearly marked. On Saturdays,
there is a huge market on Viale Papiniano and on Via
Calatafimi, the Fiera di Senigallia, with old and new bargains.
If you collect coins or stamps, go on Sunday morning to Via
Armorari, near Piazza Cordusio, where there is a specialized
market. The best antiques markets are held on the last Sunday
of each month along the Navigli and the third Saturday of each
month on Via Fiori Chiaria, near Via Brera. *Antiques markets
closed Aug.*

Cities of the Plain

This tour takes in some of the great Lombard cities of the Po
River plain south of Milan—Pavia (for its celebrated Certosa,
or charterhouse), which is an easy day's excursion from Milan
or can be the first stop on our trans-Lombardy tours' itinerary;
Cremona, where history's great violin makers lived and
worked; Sabbioneta, a diminutive utopian Renaissance city,
built from one man's life-long obsession; and Mantua, home for
almost 300 years of the fantastically wealthy Gonzaga dynasty.

*Numbers in the margin correspond to points of interest on the
Lombardy and the Lakes map.*

Located at the confluence of the Ticino and Po rivers, about 38
kilometers (24 miles) south of Milan on E62, **Pavia** was once
Milan's chief local rival. The city dates at least to the Roman era

and was the capital of the Lombard kings for two centuries (572–774). Pavia came to be known subsequently as "the city of a hundred towers" (of which only a handful have survived). Its prestigious **university** was founded in 1361 on the site of a 10th-century law school but has claims dating to antiquity. The 14th-century **Castello Visconteo** (Piazza Castello) now houses the local Museo Civico (Civic Museum), which has an interesting archaeological collection and a picture gallery featuring works by Correggio (admission 5,000 lire, open Tues.–Sun. 9–1:30). Go right from the castle entrance and turn right, off Via Matteotti, to visit the tomb of Christianity's most celebrated convert, St. Augustine, housed in a Gothic marble ark on the high altar of the Romanesque church of **San Pietro in Ciel d'Oro**.

The main reason for stopping in Pavia, however, is to see the **Certosa** (the Carthusian monastery), 8 kilometers (5 miles) from the city center. Its facade is stupendous, anticipating by several hundred years, with much the same relish as the Duomo in Milan, the delightful first commandment of Victorian architecture: Always decorate the decoration.

The Certosa's extravagant grandeur was due, in part, to the plan to have it house the tombs of the family of the first duke of Milan, Galeazzo Visconti III (he died during a plague, at age 49, in 1402). And extravagant it was—almost unimaginably so in an age before modern roads and transport. Only the very best marble was used in construction, transported, undoubtedly by barge, from the legendary quarries of Carrara, roughly 150 miles away. Though the ground plan may be Gothic—a cruciform planned in a series of squares—the gorgeous fabric that rises above it is triumphantly Renaissance. On the facade, in the lower frieze, are medallions of Roman emperors and Eastern monarchs; above them are low reliefs of the life of Christ, as well as that of Galeazzo Visconti III. What other age has dared to blend the elements of pagan, religious, and daily life in a single scheme?

The first duke was the only Visconti to be interred here, and then only some 75 years after his death, in a tomb designed by Gian Cristoforo Romano. Look for it in the right transept. In the left transept is a tomb of greater human appeal—that of a rather stern middle-aged man and a beautiful young woman. The man is Ludovico Il Moro Sforza, seventh duke of Milan, who commissioned Leonardo da Vinci to paint the *Last Supper*. The woman is his wife, one of the most celebrated women of her day, Beatrice D'Este, the embodiment of brains, culture, birth, and beauty. Married when he was 40 and she was 16, they had enjoyed six happy years of marriage when she died suddenly, giving birth to a stillborn child. Ludovico commissioned the sculptor Cristoforo Solari to design a joint tomb for the high altar of Santa Maria delle Grazie, in Milan, that would be an accurate portrait of them as they were in life. Originally the tomb was much larger and for some years occupied the honored place before the high altar of Santa Maria delle Grazie as was planned. For reasons that are still mysterious, the Dominican monks seemed to care no more for their former patron than they did for their faded Leonardo fresco and sold the tomb to their Carthusian brothers to the south. Sadly, part of the tomb, and its remains, were lost. *Certosa, tel. 0382/925613. Admission free, donation requested. Open Sept.–Apr., Tues.–Sun. 9–11:30 and 2–5:30; May–Aug. 9–11:30 and 2–8.*

Lombardy and the Lakes

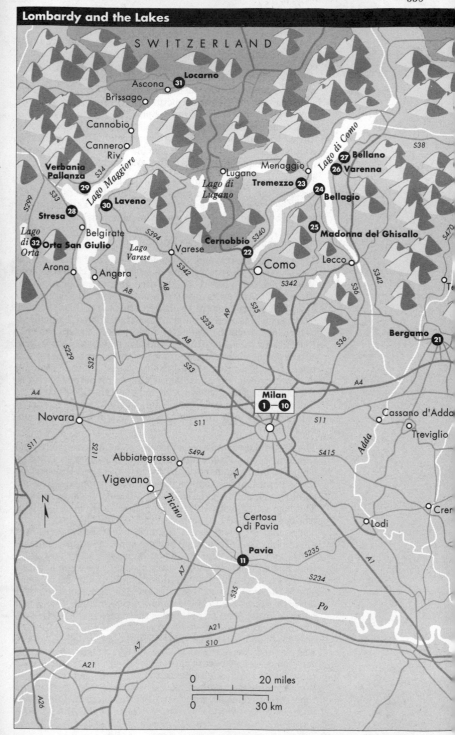

SWITZERLAND

Locarno **31**
Ascona
Brissago

Cannobio

Cannero
Riv.

Verbania
Pallanza **29**

Lago Maggiore

S34

Lago di
Lugano

Lugano

Menaggio

Lago di Como

Bellano **27**
Varenna **26**

Tremezzo **23**

Stresa **28**

Laveno **30**

Bellagio **24**

S38

Lago
di
Orta **32** Orta San Giulio

Belgirate

Lago
Varese

S394

Cernobbio
22

S340

Madonna del Ghisallo **25**

Arona

Angera

Varese

Como

Lecco

S470

S342

S229

A8

S233

A8

A9

S35

S36

S36

Bergamo **21**

Te

Novara

S11

Milan
1 — **10**

S11

A4

Cassano d'Adda

Treviglio

S211

Abbiategrasso

S494

A7

S415

Adda

Vigevano

N

Ticino

Certosa
di Pavia

Pavia **11**

S235

Lodi

Crer

S234

A1

S35

Po

A21

S10

A7

A21

0   20 miles

0   30 km

A26

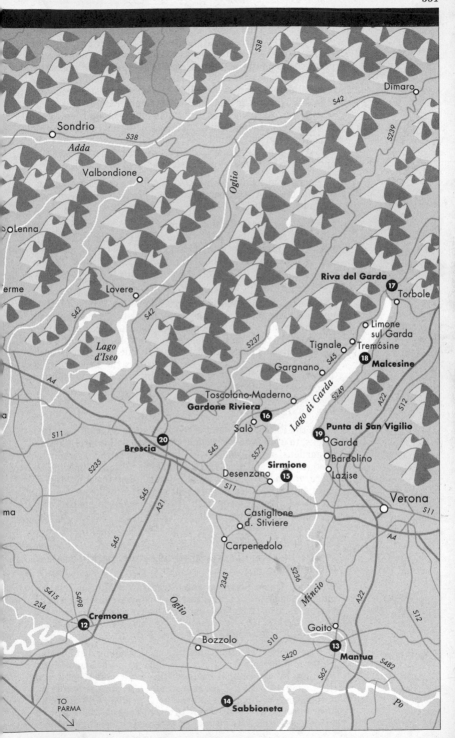

⑫ If there is only one place in Italy to buy a violin, it's **Cremona**—as true today as when Andrea Amati (1510–80) opened up shop here in the middle of the 16th century. Though cognoscenti continue to revere the Amati name, it was the apprentice of Amati's nephew, Nicolo (1596–1684), for whom the fates had reserved a wide and lasting international fame. In a career that spanned an incredible 68 years, Antonio Stradivari (1644–1737) made more than 1,200 instruments—including violas, cellos, harps, guitars, and mandolins, in addition to his fabled violins. Labeled simply with a small printed slip, "Antonius Stradivarius Cremonensis. Faciebat anno. . . ." (the date added in a neat italic hand), they remain the best, most coveted, and most expensive stringed instruments in the world.

Cremona is about 93 kilometers (58 miles) southeast of Milan, via the A1 and A21 autostradas. From Pavia, it's 86 kilometers (53 miles) east on S234.

If you would like to see the original Stradivarius instruments, go to the second floor of the **Palazzo del Comune** (City Hall), where five masterpieces by Cremonese *liutai* (violin makers), dating from the 16th to the 18th centuries, are on view. *Piazza del Comune, tel. 0372/4071. Open weekdays 9–noon and 3–5, weekends 9–noon.*

The **Piazza del Comune** has impressed visitors as one of Italy's loveliest: The cathedral, campanile, baptistery, and City Hall are particularly distinctive and harmonious. The combination of old brick, rose- and cream-colored marble, terra-cotta and old copper roofs brings Romanesque, Gothic, and Renaissance together with unusual success. Don't miss the **Torrazzo** (Big Tower), perhaps the tallest campanile in the country, visible for a considerable distance across the Po's plains. *Admission: 3,000 lire. Open Mar.–Nov., Mon.–Sat. 10:30–noon and 3–6, Sun. 10–12:30.*

From the Piazza del Comune continue along Via Solferino two blocks, to what is now **Piazza Roma.** Here, in this lovely square of gardens, trees, and lawns, at No. 1, Antonio Stradivari lived, worked, and died. It is said that in addition to knowing all there was to know about woods, varnish, and the subtleties of assembling the 70-odd component parts that make up a violin, Stradivari liked to keep each new instrument in his bedroom for a month before varnishing it. This way, he claimed, by virtue of some mysterious somnolent transmigration, he gave a soul to each of his creations.

In the center of the park is **Stradivari's grave,** marked by a simple tombstone.

The small **Museo Stradivariano** (Stradivarius Museum) has an informative display of Stradivari's plans and models, as well as violins made by Cremona's more modern masters. *Via Palestro 17, tel. 0372/23349. Admission: 1,000 lire, free on Sun. Open Tues.–Sat. 9:30–12:30 and 3–6, Sun. 9:30–12:30.*

You may notice, strolling about town, that violin making continues to flourish here. There are, in fact, more than 50 liutai working by traditional methods in small shops scattered throughout Cremona. Most have graduated from the **Scuola Internazionale di Liuteria** (International School of Violin Making). Some have returned there to teach. The school, too, can be an instructive place to visit and is especially welcoming to those contemplating the acquisition of their own ready-made or custom-built Cremonese violin. *Piazza Marconi, tel. 0372/386689. Open Mon.–Sat. 8–1.*

Time Out   There are two fine restaurants in Cremona—one just in front of, the other just behind, the cathedral, both elegant and moderately priced. **Aquila Nera** (Via Sicardo 3, tel. 0372/25646; closed Sun. eve., Mon.) specializes in dishes made with liver; **Ceresole** (Via Ceresole 4, tel. 0372/23322; closed Sun. eve., Mon.) is older and considered slightly better.

⑬   Our next stop is **Mantua,** the real Gonzaga seat, 89 kilometers (55 miles) east of Cremona on S10. The Gonzagas, like the Visconti and Sforza of Milan (with whom they intermarried), lived with the regal pomp and circumstance befitting one of Italy's richest family dynasties. Their reign, first as marquesses, and later as dukes, was a long one—stretching from the first half of the 14th century into the beginning of the 18th.

Even if you've had enough of decrepit, publicly maintained palaces, you may still wish to come to Mantua. First, Virgil was born near here. Second, Mantegna (painter of the poignant *Dead Christ* in Milan's Brera) was the Gonzaga court painter for 50 years, and his best-known and only large surviving fresco cycle can be seen here. In addition, there are two fine churches by Leon Battista Alberti (1404–72): **Sant'Andrea** (1471, some sections earlier or later) and **San Sebastiano** (1461). Both (much like Mantegna's work here) proved highly influential and were widely emulated by lesser architectural lights later in the Renaissance.

Our tour begins at the 500-room complex that centuries of Gonzagas thought of, somehow, as home. The fortress and castle of the **Palazzo Ducale** (Ducal Palace), located at the northeast end of Mantua's Piazza Sordello, gives one the sense that the palace took centuries to build. From a distance, the group of buildings dwarfs the old town skyline. The effect is fascinating. As with Sabbioneta's palazzo, the interiors of Mantua's Palazzo Ducale may be seen today only on a rigorous guided tour conducted in Italian by the municipality. *Piazza Sordello, tel. 0376/320283. Admission: 10,000 lire. Open Mar.–Sept., Tues.–Sat. 9–1 and 2:30–5, Sun. and Mon. 9–1; Oct.–Feb., Tues.–Sat. 9–1 and 2:30–4, Sun. and Mon. 9–1.*

In addition to the 14th-century fortress, the complex includes a 16th-century palace, the Castello San Giorgio, and the ducal chapel. Highlights of the tour include the following:

The **Appartamento dei Nani** (Dwarfs' Apartments) were literally that, dwarf-collecting being one of the more amusing occupations of Renaissance princes. According to historians, the dwarfs were not mistreated but were considered something between members of the family and celebrity comics. The apartments were built both for the dwarfs' delight and for that of the court.

The **Appartamento del Paradiso** (Paradise) is usually praised for its view but is somewhat more interesting for its decorator and first resident, Isabella d'Este. Not only was she married at 16, rather like her younger sister Beatrice (the beautiful young woman of the tomb in the Certosa at Pavia), she was apparently also Ludovico Il Moro Sforza's first and original choice for a wife—until he learned she was already affianced to a Gonzaga rival. Isabella, too, is regarded as one of the great patrons of the Renaissance. She survived her sister by more than 40 years, and the archives of her correspondence, totaling more than 2,000 letters, are regarded as some of the most valuable records of the era.

The high point of all 500 rooms, if not of the city, is the **Camera degli Sposi** (literally, "Bridal Chamber," but actually a hall for receiving audiences). It was painted by Mantegna over a nine-year period, when he was at the height of his power, and finished when he was 44. Here, Mantegna made a startling advance in painting by organizing the picture's plane of representation in a way that systematically mimics the experience of human vision. Even now, more than five centuries after the event, you can almost sense the excitement of a mature artist, fully aware of his painting's great importance, expressing his vision with a masterly, joyous confidence.

The most serious Mantegna fancier will want to visit his house, **Casa di Andrea Mantegna** (Via Acerbi 47, tel. 0376/360506, admission free), not otherwise of great intrinsic interest. It is located diagonally across from the church of San Sebastiano, and you must phone to arrange a visit. It is occasionally open for temporary art exhibitions, too (daily 9–12:30, 3:30–6:30). The artist's tomb is located in the first chapel on the left of another church, **Sant'Andrea,** which itself is considered Mantua's most important Renaissance creation. *Piazza delle Erbe, south of Piazza Sordello. Open daily 8–12:30, 3–7.*

Due south, just beyond the town walls, is the **Palazzo Te,** built for Isabella d'Este's son, Federico II Gonzaga, between 1525 and 1535. Reopened in 1989 after restoration, it is the singular Mannerist creation of artist/architect Giulio Romano, decorated with mythological trompe l'oeil frescoes that are not to every visitor's taste. Whatever its faults, the palace does not skimp on pictorial drama. *Admission: 5,000 lire. Open Tues.– Sun. 10–6.*

About 34 kilometers (21 miles) southwest of Mantua on S420 lies **Sabbioneta.** Vespasiano Gonzaga (1531–91), Sabbioneta's lord, founder, and chief architect, was not a particularly sympathetic man. The glory of his attainments in a life of public service is said to have been excelled only by the ignominy of his treatment of three wives and his only son. Upon retiring from military life at 47, he resolved to turn an old castle and a few squalid cottages into the Perfect City—a tiny, urbane metropolis where the most gifted artists and greatest writers would live in perfect harmony with a perfect patron. After some five years of planning and another five of work, the village was transformed into an elegant, star-shaped, walled fortress, with a rational grid of streets, two palaces, two squares, two churches, an exquisite theater (said to be the first in Europe with a roof), by Vincenzo Scamozzi and a noble Gallery of Antiquities (a forerunner of today's art galleries). Gonzaga died four years later, survived only by the last of his wives.

When Aldous Huxley and his wife visited Sabbioneta in 1924, the town had reached an appalling state of neglect and decay. The Huxleys were given a tour (still the only way of seeing the interiors of most of Sabbioneta's buildings) much like the tour you take today. It began in the **Palazzo Ducale,** where they admired the four fine remaining equestrian figures of Vespasiano and his Gonzaga forebears. They were led through what had once been the Cabinet of Diana, the ducal saloon, and other rooms, only to discover that the rooms had been converted to serve the structure's new function as the town hall. They were shown the little **theater** (an adaption of Palladio's, at Vicenza, by the man who helped him build it), but it lacked its stage, and its frescoes were covered with whitewash. Today you will find the theater restored and its frescoes uncovered. The third building on the tour, the **Palazzo del Giardino,** has a dusty but impressive gallery of antique sculptures. *Open Mar.–Oct., daily 10–noon and 3–6; Nov.–Apr., Tues.–Sat. 10:30–noon and 2:30–4, Sun. 10:30–noon and 2:30–4:30. Tours (4,000 lire) begin whenever enough of the willing are assembled. Apply at the Ufficio Turistico, Via Gonzaga 15 (daily 9:30–noon and 2:30–5:30, tel. 0375/52039) or at the Bar Ducale.*

The sole surviving trace of Sabbioneta's prosperous 16th-century Jewish community is a now-shuttered and derelict **synagogue,** near the center of town. You will have to ask someone to point it out.

From Sabbioneta, S420 heads southwest another 28 kilometers (17 miles) to Parma (*see* Chapter 12), the A1 shoots northwest from Parma to Milan, a 122-kilometer (76-mile) drive.

The Lakes

"The Lakes" actually denotes a vast region spread over the middle third of the northern border region. Though our tour is limited to the four lakes of Garda, Como, Maggiore, and Orta, the best way to see the lake country is to rent a car in fall or spring and thread a path, at as leisurely a pace as possible, along the small mountain roads linking the lakes' least-spoiled northern tips. This is splendid mountain-driving country, with some of the most beautiful and challenging roads in the world.

It is important to remember that the lakes are extremely popular seasonal resort areas. If your wish is not only to see the lakes but actually to stay at them, the throngs that descend in July and August (particularly on weekends) make reservations absolutely essential. As a rule of thumb, if you are not fond of vacation crowds, head north.

Exploring Lake Garda

Of all the curious things to be noted about Lake Garda, one is its perennial attraction for writers. Even the 16th-century essayist Michel de Montaigne, whose 15 months of travel journals contain not a single other reference to nature, paused to admire the view down the lake from Torbole, which he called "boundless."

Lake Garda is 50 kilometers (31 miles) long, ranges from 1½ to 10 miles wide, and is as much as 346 meters (1,135 feet) deep. The terrain is flat at the lake's southern base, mountainous at its northern tip. As a consequence, the standard descriptions of it vary from stormy inland sea to crystalline Nordic fjord. It is the biggest lake in the region and by most accounts the cleanest.

⓯ Our tour begins at **Sirmione,** an enchanting town on the south-west shore. The ruins here, at the water's edge, are a reminder that Garda has been a holiday resort for the pleasure-seeking well-to-do since the height of the Roman era. The locals will almost certainly tell you that the so-called **Grotte di Catullo** (Grottoes of Catullus) were once the site of the villa of Catullus, one of the greatest pleasure-seeking poets of all time. Present archaeological wisdom, however, does not concur, and there is some consensus that this was the site of two villas of slightly different periods, dating from about the 1st century AD. But never mind—the view through the cypresses and olive trees is lovely, and even if Catullus didn't have a villa here, he is closely associated with the area and undoubtedly did have a villa somewhere nearby. *Open Tues.–Sun. 9–6.*

Rocca Scaligera, the castle, was built, along with almost all the other castles on the lake, by the Della Scala family. As hereditary rulers of Verona for more than a century before control of the city was seized by the Visconti in 1402, they counted Garda among their possessions. You may wish to go inside (particularly if you have children with you), since there is a nice view of the lake from the tower. The old part of town, in the shadow of the fortress, is still medieval in appearance. Or you may want to go for a swim at the nearby beach before continuing on the brief clockwise circuit of Lake Garda's shore. *Open summer, Tues.– Sat. 9–8; winter, Tues.–Sat. 9–noon, 3–6:30; year-round Sun. 9–noon.*

Time Out **Vecchia Lugana,** at the base of the peninsula, specializes in fish from the lake; grilled trout and fillet of perch with artichokes are especially good. There's also an elegant garden. *Via Lugana Vecchia, Lugana di Sirmione, tel. 030/919012. Reservations advised. AE, DC, MC, V. Closed Mon. eve., Tues., and Jan. Expensive.*

⓰ Passing Desenzano and Salò (the tiny last-ditch republic of Mussolini's final hours), you come to **Gardone Riviera,** a once-fashionable turn-of-the-century resort, now delightfully faded, and the former home of the flamboyant Gabriele d'Annunzio (1863–1938), one of Italy's greatest modern poets. D'Annunzio's estate, the **Vittoriale,** is an elaborate memorial to himself, clogged with souvenirs of conquests in art, love, and war (of which the largest is a ship's prow in the garden), and complete with a mausoleum. *Admission: 7,000 lire, including guided tour. Open Tues.–Sun. 9–12:30, 2–5:30.*

Time Out **Villa Fiordaliso** is as pretty a restaurant as you will find anywhere. Grilled fish and meats are the specialty. The restaurant is in Gardone Riviera, near the Vittoriale. *Via Zanardelli 132, tel. 0365/20158. AE, DC, MC, V. Closed Sun. eve., Mon., and Jan.–Feb. Expensive.*

Just before the village of **Toscolano-Maderno,** turn left and drive about 3 kilometers (1.8 miles) up the hill to the charming Romanesque church of **Santa Maria de Gaino.** Return to the lake and continue north to the **Villa Feltrinelli** at **Gargnano,** where Mussolini lived. Take the fork to the left about 5 kilometers (3 miles) north of Gargnano and head to **Tignale.** The view from the **Madonna di Monte Castello** church, some 2,000 feet above the lake, is spectacular. Adventurous travelers will want to follow this pretty inland mountain road to **Tremosine** and **Limone sul Garda,** back on the lake, where it is said the first lemon trees in Europe were grown.

⑰ Riva del Garda is the next town to the north. It is large and prosperous, and if you're there in summer, you may want to lodge there if the towns farther south seem too crowded. Many of the town's public buildings date from the 15th century, when it was a strategic outpost of the Venetian Republic. The heart of town, the lakeside **Piazza 3 Novembre,** is surrounded by medieval palazzi. The **Torre Apponale,** predating the Venetian period by three centuries, looms above these houses: Its crenellations recall its defensive purpose. Standing in the piazza and looking out onto the lake, you can understand Riva del Garda's importance as a windsurfing center. Mountain air drafts ensure good breezes on even the sultriest of midsummer days.

Time Out Several hotels and cafés line the sides of Piazza 3 Novembre. **Hotel Centrale,** at the foot of the Torre Apponale, has tables outside, where you can have a cool drink while watching the boating and windsurfing activity offshore.

About 4 kilometers (2.4 miles) north of town, on the road to Tenno, is an attractive waterfall, the 295-foot **Cascata del Varone.** Continue along the northernmost tip of the lake and head south along the eastern shore.

⑱ Continue past Torbole to **Malcesine,** one of the loveliest areas along the northern shore of Lake Garda, and visit the 13th–14th-century **Castello Scaligero** (built, like the one in Sirmione, by the Della Scalas). You're in the Veneto now, and if you are fond of cable cars, take the *funivia* to the top of Monte Baldo **⑲** (5,791 feet). Continue to **Punta di San Vigilio,** which just about everyone agrees is the prettiest spot on Garda's eastern shore, with cypresses, the gardens of the 15th-century Villa Guarienti di Brenzone, and more fine views.

To the south is **Garda,** a very old port, and **Bardolino,** which makes undistinguished but famous red wine. Here, if you are feeling guilty about not entering a single church all day, there are two handsome Romanesque examples—**San Severo,** from the 11th century, and **San Zeno,** from the 9th. **Lazise,** the next town south, has another Della Scala castle, which brings you to the final few, lovely kilometers of Garda's eastern shore.

⑳ Brescia is a mere 19 kilometers (12 miles) west of Lake Garda. The ruins of the **Capitolino,** a Capitoline Temple built by the Emperor Vespasian in AD 73, testify to Brescia's Roman origin. Outstanding among the sculptures in the adjoining **Museo Romano** is the famed 1st-century bronze *Winged Victory. Via dei Musei, tel. 030/46031. Admission: 2,000 lire. Open Oct.–May, Tues.–Sun. 9–12:45 and 2–5; June–Sept., Tues.–Sun. 10–12:45 and 2–6.*

More relics are in the **Museum of Christian Art** (also in the Via dei Musei), including a remarkable collection of early-medieval pieces, but the museum is only open for temporary exhibitions. Check with the tourist office (Corso Zanardelli 34, tel. 030/43418). Otherwise, to the southeast of the center, the **Pinacoteca Tosio-Martinengo** accommodates—besides the works of the Brescia School—pictures by Raphael, Tintoretto, Tiepolo, and Clouet. Closed for renovation in 1992, it should be open by 1993. *Piazza Moretto, tel. 030/59120. Admission: 2,000 lire. Open Oct.–May, Tues.–Sun. 9–12:45 and 2–5; June–Sept., Tues.–Sun. 10–12:45 and 2–6.*

A network of squares in the center of town contains much that is worth savoring. Palladio and Sansovino contributed to the splendid marble **Loggia,** the great Lombard-Venetian palace overlooking the Piazza della Loggia. Another palazzo is topped by the 16th-century **Torre dell'Orologio** (Clock Tower), modeled on the campanile in Venice's Piazza San Marco. On the Piazza del Duomo the 17th-century Baroque **cathedral** sits beside the simple stone 12th-century **Rotonda.** Among the churches worth visiting is the **Madonna del Carmine,** behind which a flight of stairs climbs to the ramparts of the Venetian **Castello,** high enough to give a panoramic view over the town and across the plain to the distant Alps.

㉑ From Brescia, head 43 kilometers (27 miles) west to **Bergamo,** en route to Lake Como. The old city of Bergamo lies at the foot of the Bergamese Alps. Actually, Bergamo is two cities—Bergamo Bassa (Lower Bergamo) and Bergamo Alta (Upper Bergamo), connected by a funicular railway. High up on the hillside, walled in by the ruins of ancient Venetian fortifications, surmounted by a fortress, is Bergamo Alta. The principal monuments here—the 12th-century **Palazzo della Ragione,** the massive **Torre del Comune,** the **Duomo of Bergamo,** the church of **Santa Maria Maggiore,** the **Colleoni Chapel,** and the **baptistery**—are in or near the Piazza Vecchia. The dome and the sanctuary of the Colleoni Chapel are decorated by Tiepolo's frescoes of the life of St. John the Baptist.

In Bergamo Bassa, just below the city walls, in the **Accademia Carrara,** you will find one of Italy's greatest and most important art collections. Many of the Venetian masters are represented—Mantegna, Carpaccio, Tiepolo, Guardi, Canaletto—and there are some magnificent Bellinis and Botticellis as well. *Piazza Carrara, tel. 035/399426. Admission 6,000 lire. Open Wed.–Mon., 9:30–12:30, 2:30–5:30.*

Exploring Lake Como

When somebody next asks you where to spend a honeymoon, an eminently sensible thing to say would be, "Lake Como," and leave it at that. Though summer crowds do their best to vanquish the lake's dreamy mystery and civilized, slightly faded, millionaire's-row gentility, they fail. Como remains a place of consummate partnership between the beauties of nature and those of humanity. Accordingly, our tour of the lake is of gardens and villas (of which a couple of the finest are now hotels). Like so many of Italy's most beautiful villa gardens, those of Como owe their beauty to the landscape architecture of two eras: the Renaissance Italian, with its taste for order, and the 19th-century English, with its fondness for illusions of natural wildness. The two are often framed by vast areas of the most picturesque farmland—notably olive groves, fruit trees, and vineyards.

Como is some 47 kilometers (30 miles) long, measured north to south, and is also Europe's deepest lake (almost 411 meters, or 1,350 feet). Virgil liked Como at least as much as Garda, calling it simply our "greatest" lake.

㉒ **Cernobbio** is the first town you come to as you head north from the town of Como, where the lake's remarkable beauty can be seen. Though most of the villas of the southwest branch (the lake's most fashionable district) remain private and closed to the public, they can be enjoyed from a boat. From the old square at the center of Cernobbio, all paths seem to lead to the **Grand Hotel Villa d'Este.** If you're planning to say "budget be damned" in only one place, this should be it. If you possibly can, stay for a few days at this legendary lakeside resort hotel. If not, then call ahead and ask to see the grounds or enjoy a wonderful meal in one of the hotel's two restaurants (*see* Dining and Lodging, *below*).

Originally built for Cardinal Tolomeo Gallio (who began life humbly as a fisherman) over the course of approximately 45 years (it was completed in 1615), the Villa d'Este has had a colorful and somewhat checkered history, swinging wildly between extremes of grandeur and dereliction. Its tenants have included the Jesuits, two generals, a ballerina, the disgraced and estranged wife of a future king of England (Caroline of Brunswick and George IV, respectively), a family of ordinary Italian nobles, and, finally, a czarina of Russia. Its life as a private summer residence ended in 1873, when it was turned into the fashionable hotel it has remained ever since. The name is not, as you might imagine, derived from some connection with Lombardy's famous d'Este sisters, but from a distant ancestral tie of Caroline Brunswick, called Guelfo d'Este (whose name, for some reason, she evidently liked).

Though the gardens are not so grand as they are reputed to have been during the villa's best days as a private residence and though they have suffered some modification in the course of the hotel's building of tennis courts and swimming pools, they still possess an aura of stately, monumental dignity. The alley of cypresses is a fine example of a proudly repeated Italian garden theme. The fanciful pavilions, temples, miniature forts, and mock ruins make for an afternoon's walk of quietly whimsical surprises—especially once you stray from the more structured and Italian sections of the lower gardens.

If you are lucky enough to visit in late spring or very early summer, you will find the **Villa Carlotta** (just up the road in ㉓ **Tremezzo**) a riotous blaze of color, when more than 14 acres of azaleas and dozens of varieties of rhododendron are in full bloom. The range of the garden's collection is remarkable, particularly when you consider the difficulties of transporting delicate, exotic vegetation before the age of aircraft. Palms, banana trees, cactus, eucalyptus, a sequoia, orchids, and camellias are only the beginning of a list that includes more than 500 species. The villa itself, built between 1690 and 1743 for the luxury-loving Marquis Giorgio Clerici, is slightly newer than the Villa d'Este.

According to local lore, one motive for the Villa Carlotta's magnificence was a keeping-up-with-the-Joneses sort of rivalry between the marquis's ambitious, self-made son-in-law, who inherited the estate, and the son-in-law's arch rival, who built *his* summer palace directly across the lake. Whenever either added to his villa and garden, it was tantamount to taunting the other in public. Eventually the son-in-law's insatiable taste for self-aggrandizement prevailed. The villa's last (and final) owners were Prussian royalty (including the "Carlotta" of the villa's name), and the property was confiscated during the First World War.

The villa's interior is worth a visit, particularly if you have a taste for Antonio Canova's most romantic sculptures. The best known is his *Cupid and Psyche,* which depicts the lovers locked in an odd but graceful and passionate embrace, with the young god above and behind, his wings extended, while Psyche, her lips willing, waits for a kiss that will never come.

㉔ Take the ferry from the pleasant resort town of Menaggio, just north of Tremezzo, to **Bellagio,** sometimes called the prettiest town in Europe. The garden of the **Villa Melzi** is open to the public, and you should go there after a stroll along the cobblestoned streets of the town. **Villa Serbelloni,** a property of the Rockefeller Foundation, is another villa to visit for its celebrated gardens. *Villa Serbelloni. Gardens open Apr.–Oct., Tues.–Sun.*

㉕ If you have a car, take the panoramic drive south through the mountains between Como's two southern branches, to the church of the **Madonna del Ghisallo** (the patroness of bicyclists), and then back to Bellagio, along the edge of the lake. The mountain road goes from Bellagio to Civenna, Asso, and Valbrona and then joins the main shore road at Onno, about 10 kilometers (6 miles) south of Bellagio.

㉖ Another lovely trip is by ferry from Bellagio to **Varenna.** The principal sight here is the lovely garden of the **Villa Monastero,** which, as its name suggests, was a monastery before it was a ㉗ villa. Now it's an international science center. At **Bellano,** a few miles north of Varenna, is a dramatic gorge called the **Orrido.**

Exploring Lake Maggiore

The most beautiful and idyllic of the Italian lakes, Lake Maggiore has its less mountainous eastern shore in Lombardy, its higher western shore in the Piedmont, and its northern tip in Switzerland. Never more than 5 kilometers (3 miles) wide, the lake is almost 50 kilometers (30 miles) long. The better-known resorts are on the Piedmontese shore, particularly Stresa, a well-established tourist town that is just the place to unwind and drift into a siesta, to be awakened only by a cool late-afternoon lake breeze.

㉘ **Stresa** is a small town with a lot going for it. While capitalizing on its central lakeside position, with good connections to the Borromean islands in Lake Maggiore, it has managed to retain a welcoming, relaxing atmosphere that can only be described as charming. Its period of development was about a century ago, and the architecture reflects a genteel, languorous attitude that blends in with the subtropical vegetation. Hemingway's *A Farewell to Arms* was partly set here. Your first duty, if you've driven, is to park and make your way on foot down to the water's edge. Stop at one of the two adjacent waterfront squares, Piazza Marconi or Piazza Matteotti.

Time Out Have a drink or an ice cream in one of the several cafés in Piazza Marconi. You can sit back and relax, watching the Borromean island steamers preparing to set off from the landing stage, a few yards away.

Make your way away from the shore toward Corso Umberto 1, the main road that runs along the length of the lake. The buildings on each side of you are decorated in a playful fashion, with mock windows painted onto blank walls, sometimes with what appears to be nosy locals giving you the eye. Turn left and just about 50 yards up on the right is the entrance to the gardens of **Villa Pallavicino,** a stately residence built on the hill rising from the lake. As you wander around the grounds, with their palms and semitropical shrubs, don't be surprised if you're followed by a peacock or even an ostrich: They're part of the zoological garden, and they are allowed to roam almost at will. From the top of the hill you can see the gentle hills of the Lombardy shore of Lake Maggiore and, nearer and to the left, the jewellike Borromean islands (Isole Borromee). *Admission: adults 8,000 lire, 6,000 children 4–14. Open mid-Mar.–Oct. 30, daily 9–6.*

Boats for the **Borromean Islands** leave every few minutes from the landing stage by Piazza Matteotti: Just look for the signs for "Navigazione Lago Maggiore." Although you can hire a boatman to take you to any (or all) of the islands, it's cheaper and just as convenient to use the regular service. Make sure to buy a ticket allowing you to visit all the islands—Bella, Dei Pescatori, and Madre.

The islands take their name from the Borromeo family, which has owned them since the 12th century. **Isola Bella** (Beautiful Island) is the most famous of the three, and the first that you'll visit. Its name is actually a shortened form of Isabella, wife of the 16th-century Count Carlo III Borromeo who built the palace and terraced gardens for her. Few wedding presents anywhere have been more romantic. Wander up the 10 terraces of the gardens, where peacocks roam among the scented shrubs, statues, and fountains. The view of the lake is splendid from the top terrace. Before Count Carlo began his project, the island was rocky and almost devoid of vegetation, and the soil for the garden had to be transported from the mainland. Visit the **Palazzo** to see the rooms where famous guests—including Napoleon and Mussolini—stayed in 18th-century splendor. *Admission to garden and palazzo: 9,000 lire. Open Apr.–Oct., daily 9–noon, 1:30–5.*

Stop for a while at the second island, tiny **Isola dei Pescatori** (Island of the Fishermen), which is less than 100 yards wide and only about a quarter of a mile long. Of the three islands, this is the one that has remained closest to the way they all were before the Borromeos began their building projects. Little lanes twist through the island, which is nothing more than a tiny fishing village, crowded with souvenir stands in high season.

Isola Madre (Mother Island) is the largest of the three and, like Isola Bella, has a large **botanical garden** (Orto Botanico). There's not much to the island except the garden, but even dedicated nongardeners should stop to appreciate the profusion of exotic trees and shrubs running down to the shore in every direction. Two special times to visit are April (for the camelias) and May (when azaleas and rhododendrons are in bloom). *Admission: 9,000 lire. Open Apr.–Oct., daily 9–noon and 1:30–5.*

㉙ Across the Gulf of Pallanza, in the town of **Verbania Pallanza,** the 17th-century **Palazzo Dugnani** has a splendid collection of peasant costumes. The **Villa Taranto** has magnificent botanical gardens containing some 20,000 species. Created by an enthusiastic Scotsman, Captain Neil McEachern, these gardens rank among Europe's finest. *Admission: 8,000 lire. Open Apr.– Oct., daily 8:30–7:30.*

㉚ From Stresa, you can take a steamer to **Laveno,** on the Lombardian side of the lake. From Laveno, there also are several other
㉛ trips available. Go up to **Locarno** by way of Griffa, Porto Valtravaglia, and Cannero Riviera. You'll stop, too, at the village of **Cannobio** before you enter Switzerland's waters, then at **Brissago** and **Ascona,** and finally at Locarno.

Exploring Lake Orta

A mountainous strip of land separates Lake Maggiore from Lake Orta, its smaller neighbor to the west, in the Piedmont. Orta attracts fewer visitors than the three big lakes described above, and consequently a tour around this lake can be a pleasant alternative in the summer. If you're coming from Stresa, take the twisting mountain road past Mottarone, the tallest peak between the lakes, to Gignese, where you'll be about 2,300 feet above sea level and can take in a last dramatic view of Maggiore. Follow the road down to Orta, through the town of Armeno, shaded first by forests of evergreens, then oaks. In the late summer and early fall, you're likely to see whole families out in these woods, crouched down in their hunt for wild mushrooms, or—if they're particularly lucky—truffles.

㉜ When you reach the lake shore, you'll be in the town of **Orta San Giulio,** at the end of a small peninsula that juts out into Lake Orta about a third of the way up its eastern shore. Intricate wrought-iron balustrades and balconies adorn the 18th-century buildings of this small and charming resort town. Small cafés and shops line the shady main square, which looks out across the lake and the small island of San Giulio. There are few more relaxing experiences than sipping a drink at one of these cafés and looking out at the languid waters being stirred by a mountain breeze, with sailboats busily making their way nowhere in particular.

Enjoy the interesting hike from Orta to the top of the **Sacro Monte** (Sacred Mountain), rising up behind Orta and looking down on the lake. Take the little street past the church of the Assumption, and just ahead you see a gateway marked "Sacro Monte." This leads to the path up the hill, a not very difficult climb taking about 40 minutes for the round-trip. As you approach the top, you pass 20 17th-century chapels, all devoted to Saint Francis of Assisi and decorated with frescoes and striking 17th- and 18th-century life-size terra-cotta statue groups, a total of almost 400 figures, illustrating incidents in the saint's life. You can climb the campanile (bell tower) of the last chapel for a panoramic view over the whole lake and the town, about 350 feet below.

Back down at the lake shore you can hire a boatman to take you across to the island of **San Giulio,** about ⅓ kilometer (½ mile) offshore. Each boat has its fare posted, but most charge about 10,000 lire for up to four people to make the round-trip. The island takes its name from the 4th-century St. Julius, who—like St. Patrick, in Ireland—is said to have banished snakes from the island. Julius is also said to have founded the **Basilica** in AD 390, although the present building shows more signs of its renovations in the 10th and 15th centuries. Inside, there is a black marble pulpit (12th century) with elaborate carvings, and downstairs you'll find the crypt containing relics of the saint. In the sacristy of the church is a large bone, which is said to be from one of the beasts destroyed by the saint, but which on closer examination seems to be a whalebone.

It only takes a few minutes to walk around the parts of the island that are open to the public: Much of the area is taken up by the grounds of private villas. The view back across the lake to Orta, with Sacro Monte behind it, is memorable, particularly in the late afternoon, when the light picks up the glint of the wrought-iron traceries.

Follow the shore drive from Orta San Giulio north to **Omegna,** at the head of Lake Orta. A couple of miles west of Omegna, in the village of **Quarna Sotto,** there's a musical instrument factory that's worth a stop. The shore drive continues around the rest of the lake, and at the southern end you can pick up S229, which will take you back to the A4 autostrada.

What to See and Do with Children

Cruises on the lakes are fun for all ages. Arrange a boat trip through local tourist offices or contact the **Gestione Navigazione Laghi** in Milan (Via L. Ariosto 21, tel. 02/481–2086).

Gardaland Amusement Park is in Castelnuovo, in the hills south of Lake Garda. *Admission: 2,000 lire adults, 16,000 children 2–10. Open Sept. 17–Nov. 4 and Mar. 24–June 29, daily 9–dusk; June 30–Sept. 16, daily 9–midnight.*

Minitalia Park, between Milan and Bergamo, has a relief model of Italy, on a scale of 1:500, with about 200 replicas of the most important monuments. *On the A4 autostrada to Bergamo, 35 km (21 mi) from Milan, at Capriate San Gervasio, tel. 02/909-1341. Admission: 7,000 lire adults, 5,000 lire children 3–10. Open daily 8:30–dusk.*

Parco della Preistoria, 25 kilometers (15 miles) east of Milan on the road to Brescia, has a 4-kilometer (2½-mile) path with 20 full-size replicas of prehistoric animals. Children will be delighted by the 70-foot-long brontosaurus and the fierce tyrannosaurus. There is a picnic area and, for the adults, two bars. *On SS11, near Cassano d'Adda, tel. 0363/78184. Admission: 9,000 lire adults, 7,000 lire children 4–14. Open Mar.–Nov., daily 9–dusk.*

Tremosine, known as the "Garda Terrace," is a mountain forest area that is an ideal place for nature hikes. For more information, write or call the Ufficio Comunale (Via Papa Giovanni XXIII, tel. 0365/953185).

Sports

Participant Sports

Fishing The rivers of Lombardy are known for good fishing. Check with the local tourist office or your hotel for license regulations.

Golf The **Parco di Monza,** 15 kilometers (9 miles) from Milan, contains a 27-hole course. Contact the Pro Monza office (Piazza

Carducci, tel. 039/323222). There are also seven courses near Lake Como.

Health Spas On the peninsula of Sirmione, facing Lake Garda, is the Sirmione thermal spring Boiola. Three hotels offer thermal halls with various treatments: **Grand Hotel Terme** (tel. 030/916261); **Hotel Sirmione** (tel. 030/916331); and **Hotel Fonte Boiola** (tel. 030/916431).

Hiking Hiking is particularly good in the **Parco Nazionale dello Stelvio** and the **Val Malanca,** both in the northern province of Valtellina. *EPT, Sondrio, tel. 0342/214463.*

Horseback Riding In the Como area, contact **Centro di Equitazione Comasco,** Frazione Barella (Grandate) (tel. 031/450235).

Mountain Climbing There is good climbing in the northern province of Valtellina (*see* Hiking, *above*).

Water Sports Schools for sailing, scuba diving, and windsurfing are located in Riva del Garda, on Lake Garda. Torbole, 5 kilometers (3 miles) east of Riva del Garda on S240, is a prime spot for windsurfing; contact **Centro Windsurf** (Colonia Pavese, tel. 0464/505385). At Lake Como, there are well-equipped sailing and windsurfing schools.

Sea Planes Contact the **Seaplane Club Como** (Via Masia 44, tel. 031/559882).

Skiing Facilities are good in the mountains near **Bergamo** (APT, Bergamo, tel. 035/242226). In the province of **Como,** fine ski facilities abound: Valsassina, Val d'Esino, Valvarrone, Valassina, Valcavargna, and Val d'Intelvi (APT, Como, Piazza Cavour 17, tel. 031/274064). Another well-equipped resort is **Malcesine,** on the east side of Lake Garda, with 6 lifts and more than 11 kilometers (7 miles) of runs of varying difficulty (IAT, Malcesine, tel. 045/7400044).

Sport Center The best equipped of Milan's many sport centers is the **Centro Saini,** in the vast Parco Forlanini. Much like a municipal gym, it offers squash and volleyball facilities and weight rooms. It's outside the city center; take bus No. 38. *Via Corelli 136, tel. 02/7380841.*

Waterskiing Numerous facilities for waterskiing and all water sports can be found on Lombardy's lakes. *APT, Como, Piazza Cavour 17, tel. 031/274064.*

Spectator Sports

Auto Racing A Formula 1 race is held in Monza, 15 kilometers (9 miles) from Milan, every September. The track was built in 1922, in the Parco di Monza, where there is also a hippodrome, golf course, and other facilities.

Horse Racing There are tracks near Lake Garda at Maderno and at Padenghe.

Soccer Milan's soccer teams, AC Milan and Inter Milan, are two of the best in Europe. Matches are played on Sunday, and information is available from the city tourist offices.

Dining and Lodging

Dining Unlike most Italian regions, Lombardy exhibits a northern European preference for butter rather than oil as its cooking medium, which imparts a rich and distinctive flavor to the cuisine. Among the most popular specialties is *ossobucco alla milanese*, veal knuckle served with risotto, rice that has been cooked until almost all the liquid has evaporated and a creamy sauce remains. *Risotto milanese* uses chicken broth and has saffron added, which gives the dish a rich yellow color. The lakes are a good source of fish, particularly trout and pike.

Gorgonzola, the rich veined cheese, and *panettone*, a raised fluffy fruitcake with raisins and candied fruit, both come from Milan and can be enjoyed throughout Lombardy. Although most of the wines in Lombardy are good accompaniments to the cuisine, try in particular to have the red wines Grumello or Sangue di Giuda (blood of Judas) or the delicious light sparkling whites from the Franciacorta area.

Highly recommended restaurants are indicated by a star ★.

Category	Milan	Other Areas
Very Expensive	over 120,000 lire	over 90,000 lire
Expensive	80,000–120,000 lire	60,000–90,000 lire
Moderate	45,000–80,000 lire	35,000–60,000 lire
Inexpensive	under 45,000 lire	under 35,000 lire

*per person, including a first course, main course, dessert or fruit, and house wine

Lodging Lombardy is one of Italy's most prosperous regions, and hotels cater to a clientele that demands high standards and is willing to pay for extra comfort. Most of the famous lake resorts are expensive, although more basic—and reasonably priced—accommodations can be found in the smaller towns and villages. Milan may seem to have fewer tourists than other large Italian cities, but there is always competition for rooms, generated by the nearly year-round trade fairs and other business-related bookings. It is best—and almost essential in spring and summer—to make reservations.

Many Lombardy hotels are converted from beautiful old villas and have well-landscaped grounds. Try to visit one or two, even if they are out of your price range as accommodations.

Highly recommended hotels are indicated by a star ★.

Category	Cost*
Very Expensive	over 320,000 lire
Expensive	175,000–320,000 lire
Moderate	110,000–175,000 lire
Inexpensive	under 110,000 lire

*Prices are for standard double room for two, including tax and service.

Bellagio **La Pergola.** Located in Pescallo, less than a .6 kilometer (1 mile)
Dining from Bellagio, La Pergola is a popular lakeside restaurant featuring traditional dishes of Lombardy and the Como region.
Those in the know reserve a table on the lakeside terrace and
order the daily special of freshly caught lake fish (baked or
grilled). You can also stay in one of the inn's 13 rooms. *Pescallo,
tel. 031/950263. Reservations advised. Jacket advised. AE,
DC, MC, V. Closed Nov.–Feb. Moderate.*

Lodging **Grand Hotel Villa Serbelloni.** A large park surrounds this luxury establishment facing the lake. The atmosphere is one of
19th-century luxury that has not so much faded as mellowed:
The rooms are immaculate and plush. The public rooms are a
riot of gilt, marble, and thick, colorful carpets. Service is discreet, and the staff is particularly good about arranging transportation across and around the lake. Ask for a room facing the
lake and the mountains beyond. *Lungolago Bellagio, Via Roma
1, tel. 031/950216, fax 031/951529. 95 rooms with bath or shower. Facilities: private park, private beach, tennis court, pool,
bar, restaurant, terrace. AE, DC, MC, V. Closed Oct. 21–Apr.
14. Very Expensive.*

Du Lac. Located in the center of Bellagio, by the Lake Como
landing dock, Du Lac is a comfortable medium-size hotel. Most
rooms have views of the lake and mountains, and there is a rooftop terrace garden for drinks or just unwinding. *Piazza Mazzini 32, tel. 031/950320, fax 031/951624. 48 rooms with bath or
shower. Facilities: bar, roof garden, restaurant. AE, DC, MC,
V. Closed Oct. 16–Apr. 14. Moderate.*

Bergamo **Dell Angelo–Antico Ristorante.** High marks could be awarded
Dining here in equal measure for the atmosphere (it's a 17th-century
★ inn) and for the excellent cuisine. The restaurant is located just
outside the city walls, a 15-minute walk from the Accademia
Carrara. In good weather there is dining outside in the attractive courtyard. Fish plays a prominent role on the menu: Try the
ravioli di branzino al basilico fresco (stuffed with bass in fresh
basil) and the *zuppa di porcini* (wild mushroom soup). *Via
Borgo Santa Caterina 55, tel. 035/237103. Reservations advised. Jacket advised. AE, DC, MC, V. Closed Mon., 1 week in
Jan., and Aug. Very Expensive.*

La Taverna del Colleoni. Located in Piazza Vecchia, in the heart
of Bergamo's historic Upper Town, this restaurant blends perfectly with the 16th-century surroundings. There is service on
the terrace facing the square, and the specialties include
insalata di gamberi agli agrumi (shrimp in citrus sauce),
tagliatelle ai porcini (freshly made pasta with wild mushrooms), and herbed lamb. *Piazza Vecchia, tel. 035/232596. Reservations advised. Jacket advised. AE, DC, MC, V. Closed
Mon. and Aug. 1–20. Expensive.*

La Trattoria del Teatro. Traditional regional food tops the bill at
this good-value restaurant in the Upper Town. Polenta (northern Italy's answer to corn pudding) makes an appearance as an
accompaniment and as an alternative to pasta. Game is recommended in season. *Fettuccine con funghi* (fettuccine with
mushrooms) is a deceptively simple but rich and memorable
specialty. *Piazza Mascheroni 3, tel. 035/238862. Reservations
advised weekends. Jacket advised. No credit cards. Closed
Mon. and July 15–30. Moderate.*

Lodging **Cristallo Palace.** Located on the periphery of town, the
Cristallo Palace offers the amenities of a modern, efficient ho-

tel, as well as the bonus of good parking and a convenient position on the *tangenziale* (the road that bypasses the center). The rooms are large and well equipped, and the service is polished and prompt. The hotel's restaurant, L'Antica Perosa, is very good, and its prices are at the lower range of this category. *Via Betty Ambiveri 35, tel. 035/311211, fax 035/312031. 90 rooms with bath or shower. Facilities: bar, restaurant, parking, conference facilities. AE, DC, MC, V. Expensive.*

Excelsior San Marco. The most comfortable hotel in the lower part of Bergamo, the Excelsior San Marco is only a short walk from the walls of the Upper Town. The rooms are surprisingly quiet, considering the central location of the hotel. Its restaurant, Tino Fontana, features a rooftop terrace. *Piazza della Repubblica 6, tel. 035/232132, fax 035/223201. 151 rooms with bath or shower. Facilities: bar, restaurant (closed Sun., Moderate), terrace, parking, conference facilities. Expensive.*

★ **Agnello d'Oro.** A gem on a small piazzetta in the heart of the Upper Town, Agnello d'Oro is a tall, narrow inn where everything seems to be on a reassuringly human scale. The rooms are done in different colors and have lots of old prints on the walls, and many have small balconies with good views of the rest of the Upper Town. The lively restaurant is small but popular. *Via Gombito 22, tel. 035/249883, fax 035/235612. 20 rooms with bath or shower. Facilities: restaurant (closed Mon. and mid-Jan.–mid-Feb., Moderate). AE, DC, MC, V. Inexpensive.*

Brescia **La Sosta.** Located centrally, just south of Brescia's cathedral,
Dining La Sosta occupies a 17th-century building. The cuisine and service suggest a more expensive establishment, and the ambience is refined. A local Brescian specialty is *casonsei* (large ravioli). *Capreto alla Bresciana* (roast kid with polenta) is an outstanding main course, but make sure you have room for it. *Via San Martino della Battaglia 20, tel. 030/295603. Reservations advised. Jacket advised. AE, DC, MC, V. Closed Mon., Dec. 24–Jan. 7, Aug. 6–30. Expensive.*

Lodging **Vittoria.** Centrally located and set among 16th-century buildings, Vittoria has more than its share of atmosphere. Built in 1933, the hotel is in the Venetian style, with a hint of Byzantium and the Spice Routes in its pointed arches and windows. The rooms have been renovated recently and are decorated with antiques. *Via delle X Giornate 20, tel. 030/280061, fax 030/280065. 65 rooms with bath or shower. Facilities: bar, restaurant, conference facilities. AE, DC, MC, V. Expensive.*

Cassinetta di **L'Antica Osteria del Ponte.** Make your way 20 kilometers (12
Lugagnano miles) southwest of Milan to one of Italy's finest restaurants,
Dining located in an attractive agricultural village. The Naviglio
★ Grande (Grand Canal) flows nearby: It was built to carry the area's produce to Milan. Luckily, enough of this produce stays put to form the basis of a rich and imaginative menu that changes each season to follow the harvest cycle and sometimes the whim of chef Ezio Santin. The restaurant is located in a traditional country inn, and the inside is a cozy combination of wooden ceiling beams and a blazing fire. Inventive recipes include *ravioli di aragosta* (summer only—filled with lobster meat) and, in the fall, a range of specialties featuring porcini, the prized wild mushroom. *Cassinetta di Lugagnano (3 km, or 5 mi, north of Abbiategrasso), tel. 02/942–0034. Reservations required. Jacket and tie required. AE, DC. Closed Sun., Mon., and Jan. 1–15, Aug. Very Expensive.*

Cernobbio
Dining and Lodging
★

Grand Hotel Villa d'Este. One of the most luxurious hotels in Italy (less cautious folk could extend that to Europe or even the whole world), Villa d'Este caters to just about every conceivable comfort. The villa was built in the late 16th century, and the setting and decorations are enough to indulge the fantasies of a card-carrying hedonist. A broad veranda sweeps out to the lakefront, where a large swimming pool juts out above the water. Across the lake are blue, snowcapped mountains gradually blending into the deep green of the slopes that lead down to the shore. Inside, sparkling chandeliers cast their light on broad marble staircases, and the rooms are furnished in the discreet color-coordinated manner of wealthy Italians. The restaurant is on a par with every other aspect of Villa d'Este, and you can eat in the sumptuous grillroom or outside on the veranda. *Via Regina 40, tel. 031/511471, fax 031/512027. 158 rooms with bath. Facilities: indoor and outdoor pools, 8 tennis courts, sauna, gym, squash court, Turkish bath, massage room, large secluded park, restaurant, cocktail bars. AE, DC, MC, V. Closed Nov.–Mar. Very Expensive.*

Como
Dining

Da Angela. Reservations are a must at this small and intimate restaurant serving Piedmontese specialties. The service is attentive, and the waiters will help you select from a menu that includes various homemade pasta dishes and tasty *coniglio ai capperi* (rabbit with capers). *Via Ugo Foscolo 16, tel. 031/304656. Reservations required. Jacket advised. AE, DC, MC, V. Closed Sun. and Aug. Expensive.*

Lodging
★

Barchetta Excelsior. Piazza Cavour, the address of this welcoming and comfortable hotel, is some of the choicest real estate in Como. The Barchetta Excelsior exploits this lakefront (and central) position; many of its rooms look directly across the well-tended piazza and over Lake Como, which is only about 100 yards away. The recently refurbished rooms are airy and spacious, with those on the upper floors commanding the best views. Make sure to ask for a lake view because not all rooms have one. *Piazza Cavour 1, tel. 031/3221. 85 rooms with bath or shower. Facilities: bar, restaurant (closed Sun.), parking. AE, DC, MC, V. Expensive.*

Tre Re. Located only a block west of the central Piazza del Duomo, this clean, spacious, and welcoming hotel is just a few steps from the cathedral. While the exterior gives away the age of the building (it was a 16th-century palazzo), the rooms inside are airy, comfortable, and modernized. The moderately priced restaurant, which shares an ample terrace with the hotel, is popular with locals for Sunday lunch. *Via Boldoni 20, tel. 031/265374. 32 rooms, 29 with bath or shower. Facilities: bar, restaurant (closed Mon. and Dec. 10–Jan. 9), parking. MC, V. Closed Dec. 10–Jan. 15. Moderate.*

Gardone Riviera/
Fasano del Garda
Dining
★

Villa Fiordaliso. Seeing its function as a high-quality restaurant, the pink-and-white lakeside Villa Fiordaliso also has seven rooms for weary travelers. The menu is tied closely to the availability of fresh local produce, with seasonal treats such as zucchini flowers or porcini mushrooms used in salads or sauces. The villa once belonged to Claretta Petacci, who got it as a present from her lover, Benito Mussolini. You can eat on the lakefront terrace in summer. *Via Zanardelli 132, tel. 0365/20158, fax 0365/290011. Reservations advised. Jacket advised. 7 rooms with bath. AE, DC, MC, V. Closed Sun. evening, Mon., and Jan.–Feb. Expensive.*

Lodging
★
Villa del Sogno. A small winding road takes you from the village to this imposing villa, which surveys the valley and the lake below it. The most popular rooms, inevitably, are those with this view, which can be savored from balconies. The large hotel terrace and the quiet surrounding grounds add to the feeling of getting away from it all, and you'll probably think twice about a busy sightseeing itinerary once you've settled into position in the sun, with a cool drink in hand. *Corso Zanardelli 107, tel. 0365/290181, fax 0365/290230. 34 rooms with bath or shower. Facilities: park, terraces, pool, tennis court, restaurant. AE, DC, MC, V. Closed Oct. 15–Easter. Very Expensive.*

Grand Hotel Fasano. A former 19th-century hunting lodge on the lakefront, the Fasano has matured into a seasonal hotel of a high standard. The staff is friendly, as are most of the guests, who seem to be keen to make the most use of the water sports at their disposal. It's worth paying a bit extra to get one of the larger rooms with a lake view and balcony. *Corso Zanardelli 160, Fasano del Garda, tel. 0365/21051, fax 0365/21054. 77 rooms with bath or shower. Facilities: bar, restaurant, lakefront terraces, private beach, pool, tennis court. MC, V. Closed Nov.–Apr. Expensive.*

Gargnano
Dining
La Tortuga. Gargnano is where the lakeside road leading north from Gardone Riviera begins to weave its way through a series of tunnels: La Tortuga is the best restaurant in this scenic village. Specializing in the cuisine from around Lake Garda, it features *soufflé di verdura* (soufflé of greens) and the excellent *bocconcini di vitello* (tidbits of veal with truffles). From the wine list, try the local red Lugana, which is often served chilled. *Gargnano, tel. 0365/71251. Reservations advised. Jacket advised. AE, V. Closed Mon. eve. (except July–Sept.), Tues., and Jan.–Feb. Expensive.*

Goito
Dining
Al Bersagliere. One of Lombardy's best restaurants can be found in this rustic four-room inn, located in the tiny riverside hamlet of Goito, some 16 kilometers (10 miles) northwest of Mantua on Route 236 (the main Mantua-Brescia road). It is homey and has been run by a single family for more than 150 years. Fish in particular is excellent, including the Mantovese classic, frog soup. The sole terrine and scampi mayonnaise are a bit lighter and less traditional. *Via Goitese 258, Goito, tel. 0376/60007. Reservations required. DC, MC, V. Closed Mon., Tues., AM and 10 days in Jan., 15 days in Aug. Expensive.*

Isola Comacina
Dining
La Locanda dell' Isola. Isola Comacina, five minutes by regular boat from Sala Comacina and Lake Como's only island, is rustic, restful, but at times crowded. The same could be said for the Locanda, but in each case the visit is worth it. Forget any notions of choosing from dozens of items on the menu because here the deal is a set price for a set meal, with drinks included in the price. The good news is that the food is good, the service is friendly, and the setting (eating outdoors on a shady terrace) is relaxing. If recent visits are any guide, you'll have to pace yourself through a mixed antipasto, trout, chicken, salad, and dessert. *Isola Comacina, Sala Comacina, tel. 0344/55083. No reservations. Dress: casual. No credit cards. Closed Tues. (except June–Sept.) and Nov.–Feb. Expensive.*

Mantua
Dining
Il Cigno. With a romantic setting inside a 16th-century palazzo (and featuring some walls frescoed during that period), Il

Cigno scores well with atmosphere. Chef Alessandra Martini steers the menu as far as possible through traditional Mantuan terrain, with local specialties such as *tortelli di zucca* (pasta stuffed with pumpkin), *insalata di cappone* (capon salad), and local variations on the Lombard favorite, risotto. *Piazza Carlo d'Arco 1, tel. 0376/327101. Reservations advised; essential on weekends. Jacket advised. AE, DC, MC, V. Closed Mon., Tues., 10 days in Aug., 7 days in Jan. Expensive.*

L'Aquila Nigra. Located down a small side street opposite the Palazzo Ducale, this popular restaurant is set in a former Medieval convent. Frescoes look down from the walls on diners making their way through local Mantuan dishes, such as *frittata di zucchine* (zucchini omelet) and *faraona al pepe verde* (guinea fowl with green pepper). *Vicolo Bonacolsi 4, tel. 0376/350651. Reservations required. AE, DC, MC, V. Closed Sun. eve., Mon., and Dec. 24–Jan 5. Moderate.*

Lodging **San Lorenzo.** Mantua is a compact city, ideal for covering on foot, and the San Lorenzo is ideally placed in the center of the city. The rooms are large and the decor is authentic early 19th century. Although there is no restaurant, you're within easy walking distance of the two listed above. Some people may find the rooms in the front a little noisy at night, when locals decide that the streets are empty enough of tourists to begin their own *passeggio*, or fashion-conscious constitutional. The San Lorenzo has a rooftop terrace and exudes comfort and individual attention. *Piazza Concordia 14, tel. 0376/220500, fax 0376/ 327194. 41 rooms with bath or shower. Facilities: garage. AE, DC, MC, V. Expensive.*

Milan **Don Lisander.** Walk through the 17th-century courtyard of Pa-
Dining lazzo Trivulzio and turn right at an imposing wrought-iron gate with a garden behind it to enter Don Lisandro, a former chapel. Although the name is a Milanese-dialect reference to Italy's most famous 19th-century novelist, Alessandro Manzoni, who was from Milan and lived close by, there is nothing 19th century or even Milanese about it. Designer lighting, abstract prints on the walls, and a modern terra-cotta tile floor create an uncompromisingly contemporary effect. The creative cuisine is less unflinchingly modern: Try the *terrina di brasato alle verdure* (terrine of braised beef with vegetables) or *gli involtini di pesce spada* (stuffed swordfish on a bed of fresh tomato). There is seating outside in summer, too. *Via Manzoni 12a, tel. 02/ 760–20130, fax 02/784573. Reservations required. Jacket and tie required. AE, DC, MC, V. Closed Sat. eve., Sun., and Dec. 20–Jan. 6, Aug. 7–21. Very Expensive.*

★ **Marchesi.** Gualtiero Marchesi, the manager, has written books on nouvelle cuisine and has a "laboratory" for his new experiments on the premises. Like the food, which is served as though it were an abstract work of art, the dining rooms are aesthetically designed. On each table is a small original sculpture where the salt and pepper would normally be. Your eye, as well as your taste buds, will relish the *raviolo aperto* (two thin layers of pasta with scallops and a ginger sauce) and the *costata di manzo bollita alle piccole verdure* (boiled pork, thinly sliced, with steamed vegetables). Although this restaurant is on a side street to the east of the center of Milan, you'll find it easily, just off Corso XXII Marzo. *Via Bonvesin de la Riva 9, tel. 02/ 741246. Reservations advised. Jacket and tie required. AE, DC, MC, V. Closed Sun. and Mon. lunch, Good Fri.–Easter Mon., Dec. 24–28, July–Aug. Very Expensive.*

Scaletta. The name means "little stairway" in Italian, and the steps leading up to the Scaletta restaurant are a little stairway to culinary paradise. This tiny restaurant could be the dining room of a gracious home, with cool pastel colors, book-lined walls, and a superb collection of blown glass. Host/sommelier Aldo Bellini and genius cook Mamma Pina in the kitchen treat their guests with cordiality and take time to discuss wines and menus with you, if you like. Pina's cooking is a light, personalized version of traditional Italian cuisine; menus change frequently. Reserve two weeks ahead. *Piazzale Stazione Porta Genova 3, tel. 02/581–00290. Reservations required. Jacket and tie preferred. No credit cards. Closed Sun., Mon., and Christmas, Easter, Aug. Very Expensive.*

★ **Boeucc.** This restaurant (pronounced "birch") is Milan's oldest. It's located in the same square as novelist Alessandro Manzoni's house, not far from La Scala. Subtly lit, with cream-colored fluted columns, chandeliers, thick carpets, and a garden for warm-weather dining, it has come a long way from the time when it was simply a basement "hole" (*boeucc* is old Milanese for *buco*, or hole). It serves not only typical Milanese food, but also a wide range of other dishes, including *penne al branzino e zucchine* (pasta with sea bass and zucchini sauce) and *gelato di castagne con zabaglione caldo* (chestnut ice cream with hot zabaglione). *Piazza Belgioioso 2, tel. 02/760–20224. Reservations required. Jacket advised. AE. Closed Sat., Sun. lunch, and Aug., Dec. 24–28. Expensive.*

Savini. Red carpets and glass chandeliers characterize the classy Savini, in the Galleria Vittorio Emanuele. It's a typical old-fashioned Milanese restaurant, with dining rooms on three floors, including a "winter garden," where you can watch the people strolling in the Galleria. This is a good place to try the Milanese specialty *risotto al salto* (rice cooked as a sort of pancake, flipped in the pan) or *costoletta di vitello* (fried veal cutlets). *Galleria Vittorio Emanuele, tel. 02/720–03433. Reservations advised for evening. Jacket advised. AE, DC, MC, V. Closed Sun., Aug. 10–20, Dec. 23–Jan. 3. Expensive.*

Al Cantinone. Opera goers still come here for an after-theater drink, just as they did a century ago. The decor is classic Milanese trattoria; the service is fast, and the food is homey and reliable. A bonus: homemade pasta. Try the *pappardelle* (noodles) or ravioli with meat sauce, Tuscan style. There's a wide selection of grilled meats and a staggering choice of wines. *Via Agnello 19, entrance on Via Ragazzi del 99, tel. 02/807666. Reservations advised. AE, MC, V. Closed Sat. lunch, Sun., and Aug., Christmas, and 1 week in Jan., Easter. Moderate.*

La Libera. Although this establishment in the heart of Brera bills itself as a *birraria con cucina* (beer cellar with kitchen), its young clientele comes here as much for the excellent food and convivial atmosphere as for the draft beer. A soft current of jazz plays under the gentle ripple of conversation, and the decor is a restful dark green. Sample the imaginative cooking— *insalata esotica* (salad with avocado, chicken, rice, and papaya) or *rognone di vitello con broccoletti e ginepro* (veal kidneys with broccoli and juniper berries). *Via Palermo 21, tel. 02/805–3603. No reservations. Jacket advised. No credit cards. Closed Sat., Sun. lunch, and Aug., Dec. 22–Jan. 1. Moderate.*

Nabucco. This is a smart restaurant in the Brera district, tastefully furnished, whose menu offers such delights as *risotto con porcini* (wild-mushroom risotto), an excellent range of salads, and homemade pastries and desserts. Although moderately priced, the good prix fixe lunches take it into the lower category. *Via Fiori Chiari 10, tel. 02/860663. Reservations advised. Jacket advised. AE, DC, MC, V. Closed Sun., Mon. lunch. Moderate.*

★ **Tencitt.** Coming in from a quiet street near the university, you enter through a curved door and step through an arched entrance into a chic dining room, decorated in black and white, with suffused wall lighting. Nouvelle cuisine dishes are popular with the academic and professional clientele. *Via Laghetto 2, tel. 02/795560. Reservations required. Jacket advised. AE, DC, MC, V. Closed Sat. lunch, Sun., and Aug., Dec. 24–28. Moderate.*

La Bruschetta. You'll find this tiny, busy pizzeria off Corso Vittorio Emanuele, behind the Duomo; it is run by a partnership of Tuscans and Neapolitans. The wood stove is in full view, so you can see your pizza cooking in front of you, although there are plenty of nonpizza dishes available, too, such as *spaghetti alle cozze e vongole* (spaghetti with clam and mussel sauce). *Piazza Beccaria 12, tel. 02/802494. Reservations advised, but fast service means you never wait long. Dress: casual. No credit cards. Closed Mon., Aug. 1–21, Dec. 24–28, Good Fri.–Easter Mon. Inexpensive–Moderate.*

★ **Summertime.** Here is a value-for-money choice within easy walking distance of the Castello Sforzesco. Summertime is a spacious restaurant decorated in an appealing modern version of art nouveau—a combination of mirrors, black columns, and a gray marble floor with a pink-and-white flower motif. You can dine well on *tagliatelle con salmone e funghi* (pasta with salmon and mushrooms), choose from a list of imaginative pizzas, and finish with *pesche all'amaretto* (peaches with amaretto liqueur). There's a small garden for outdoor dining in the summer. *Via Vincenzo Monti 33, tel. 02/498–8747. Reservations advised. Dress: casual. MC, V. Closed Mon. and Good Fri.–Easter Mon., Aug. 1–15, Dec. 24–28. Inexpensive–Moderate.*

La Giara. In this Pugliese restaurant you eat tavern style, at wooden tables and benches in simple surroundings. Yet the quality of the food from the limited menu is a revelation. Start with the *sott'olio antipasto* (eggplant, artichoke, mushroom, and tomato preserved in olive oil), and try one of the grilled meat courses, cooked on a range at the front of the restaurant and eaten with nothing but the excellent Pugliese bread and olive oil provided. *Viale Monza 10, tel. 02/285–3835. Reservations not necessary, though you may be asked to share a table at busy times. Dress: casual. No credit cards. Closed Wed. Inexpensive.*

San Tomaso. The atmosphere of an informal beer hall, a trendy young clientele, and a self-service counter add up to pleasant, easy eating. Very busy at lunch, it's usually quieter at night. *Via San Tomaso 5, tel. 02/874510. Reservations advised in evening. Dress: casual. No credit cards. Closed Sun. Inexpensive.*

Taverna Moriggi. Near the stock exchange, it's a dusky, wood-paneled wine bar serving a fixed-price lunch for about 25,000 lire, or cold cuts and cheeses in the evening. *Via Moriggi 8, tel. 02/864–50880. No reservations. Dress: casual. No credit cards. Closed Sat. lunch and Sun. Inexpensive.*

Lodging **Duomo.** This is the obvious choice if a central location is your priority: You're only 20 yards from the cathedral itself. Rooms on the second, fourth, and fifth floors look out onto the Gothic gargoyles and pinnacles of the Duomo. The hotel is spacious and modern, with air-conditioned rooms and duplex suites, snappily furnished in golds, creams, and browns. The guests' comfort is the important thing here; celebrities may be turned away if it's thought they will attract noisy fans and paparazzi. *Via San Raffaele 1, tel. 02/8833, fax 02/864–62027. 160 rooms with bath. Facilities: cable TV, bar, restaurant. MC, V. Closed Aug. Very Expensive.*

Hotel de la Ville. This is a modern hotel in the center of town that has recently been redone in pleasingly subtle, pale colors with silk-hung walls in the guest rooms. Many of the rooms have small balconies, and some have a view of the spires of the Duomo. *Via Hoepli, 6, tel. 02/867651, fax 02/866609. 105 rooms with bath. Facilities: sitting room, bar, 5 conference rooms. AE, DC, MC, V. Very Expensive.*

★ **Pierre Milano.** No expense was spared to furnish each room of this luxury hotel in a different style with the most elegant color-coordinated fabrics and a variety of modern and antique furniture. Everything is electronic. You can open the curtains, turn off the lights, have personal messages from the front desk appear on your TV screen—all by pressing the buttons on your remote control. The Pierre is located on the inner beltway, near the medieval church of Sant'Ambrogio. *Via De Amicis 32, tel. 02/720–00581, fax 02/805–2157. 47 rooms with bath or shower. Facilities: restaurant, bar, convenient parking. AE, DC, MC, V. Very Expensive.*

Principe di Savoia. Of the three deluxe Ciga hotels in Milan renovated in 1991, this is the most sumptuously elegant. Behind the neoclassical facade, the decor is in 19th-century Lombard style, with lavish mirrors, drapes, and carpets. Bedrooms have been enlarged and are more comfortable than ever. In the same general location, near the central station, are Ciga's **Palace**, with interiors in Empire style, and the **Duca di Milano**, suites only, with Edwardian decor. *Piazza della Repubblica 17, tel. 02/6230, fax 02/659–5838. 287 rooms with bath. Facilities: restaurant, bar, parking, indoor pool, fitness center. AE, DC, MC, V. Very Expensive.*

Carlton-Senato. This is the ideal choice for visitors who intend to spend time shopping—or even window shopping—in the nearby high-fashion streets, Via della Spiga, Via Sant' Andrea, and Via Montenapoleone. The hotel is very light and airy, with air-conditioning, double-thickness windows, a garage with direct access to the hotel, and lots of little touches (such as free chocolates and liqueurs in the rooms), to make up for the rather functional room furnishings. Some rooms have terraces large enough for a table, chair, and potted shrubs. *Via Senato 5, tel. 02/760–15535, fax 02/783300. 79 rooms with bath. Facilities: bar, restaurant, garage. AE, MC, V. Closed Aug. Expensive.*

Gritti. The Picassos, Matisses, and Van Goghs in the lobby are originals—so the manager will tell you—except that they were painted quite recently "in the spirit." The Gritti is a bright hotel with a cheerful atmosphere, adequate rooms, and good views (from the inside upper floors) of tiled roofs and the gold Madonnina statue on top of the Duomo, only a few hundred yards away. *Piazza Santa Maria Beltrade 4 (north end of Via Torino), tel. 02/801056, fax 02/89010999. 48 rooms with bath or shower. Facilities: bar, restaurant. AE, DC, MC, V. Moderate–Expensive.*

★ **Antica Locanda Solferino.** It's advisable to make reservations as early as possible for this establishment, which calls itself a *locanda* (inn) because of its size, but whose comforts far surpass such a modest designation. The 19th-century building is located in the Brera district; in 1987 the rooms were all redecorated and feature peasant-print bedspreads, low bedside lamps draped with lace-edged cloths, attractive dried-flower arrangements on the tables, and 19th-century prints on the walls. The rooms are air-conditioned and have color TV. *Via Castelfidardo 2, tel. 02/657–0129, fax 02/656460. 11 rooms with bath. Facilities: restaurant. No credit cards. Closed Aug. 7–17, Dec. 24–Jan. 4. Moderate.*

King. Within easy walking distance of Leonardo's *Last Supper* at Santa Maria delle Grazie and close to the Castello Sforzesco and Sant'Ambrogio, the King is a bright, roomy hotel with high ceilings and an imposing mock-Louis XIV lobby. It was built in 1966 in pseudo-antique style and furnished with aptly regal red rugs, armchairs, and bedsteads. Windows have extra-thick glass to cut down on noise. *Corso Magenta 19, tel. 02/864–50230, fax 02/890–10798. 48 rooms, 44 with bath. Facilities: bar, restaurant. AE, MC, V. Moderate.*

London. Close to the Duomo, the London has clean, spacious rooms and an English-speaking staff. It has an arrangement with the Opera Prima restaurant in the same building, if you want to take your meals there. *Via Rovello 3, tel. 02/720–20166, fax 02/805–7037. 29 rooms with shower. MC, V. Closed Dec. 25–Jan. 3 and Aug. Inexpensive.*

★ **Pensione Rovello.** You pay in advance for your room in this tiny hotel. The accommodations are simple, verging on the spartan, with warm terra-cotta-tile floors and plain white walls. It's a favorite with young travelers and American fashion models. *Via Rovello 18A, tel. 02/873956. 12 rooms, 10 with bath. AE, DC, MC, V. Inexpensive.*

Orta San Giulio
Dining and Lodging

Hotel San Rocco. A converted 17th-century convent in a lakeside garden on the edge of town, the San Rocco has recently completed a major renovation. Half of the rooms have views of the lake, garden, and surrounding mountains. Many have balconies and are furnished in modern style. The restaurant features international cuisine and beautiful views of the lake. Among the specialities is *pesce persico* (perch). *Via Gippini da Verona 11, tel. 0322/905632, fax 0322/905635. 74 rooms with bath. Facilities: bar, restaurant (reservations advised), pool, health club. AE, DC, MC, V. Expensive.*

Pavia
Dining
★

Bixio. Centrally located in an 18th-century building opposite the Castello Visconto, Bixio carries on the Pavian tradition of utilizing whichever vegetables are most plentiful from the rich farmlands surrounding the city. In fact, vegetables play a large part in even the main courses, with two hearty dishes that would figure on a vegetarian menu with no compunction: *torta rustica di verdure* (vegetable pie) and *lasagne di verdure* (lasagna with vegetable filling). Carnivores needn't feel neglected, though, since there is a large selection of local roast meats and some special sausages. *Piazza X Castello 1, tel. 0382/25343. Reservations not needed. Jacket advised. AE, DC, V. Closed Sun. evening, Mon., and all Aug. Moderate.*

Ranco
Dining
★

Ristorante del Sole. Chef Carlo Brovelli presides over this lakeside inn (there are also nine apartments) with a cheerfulness that is infectious. You'll probably feel the same way if you get there early enough to snag one of the tables in the arbor and enjoy one of the best views of Lake Maggiore. The lake figures in the menu, also: The *carpaccio* is made up of fine slices of raw trout and perch. Pigeon is usually served caramelized in honey, while much of the menu changes with the season—artichoke, for example, in many forms in the spring, and eggplant in the summer. Take our advice on reservations to ensure the best table possible because this restaurant is memorable. *Piazza Venezia 5, Ranco (near Angera), tel. 0331/976507, fax 0331/ 976620. Reservations advised. Jacket advised. AE, DC, MC, V. Closed Mon. eve., Tues., and Jan. 1–Feb. 15. Very Expensive.*

Sirmione **Osteria del Pescatore.** The specialty of this simple and popular
Dining restaurant is lake fish. The restaurant is located in town, on the road that leads to the Grotte di Catullo, and has a rustic look. Try grilled trout with a bottle of local white wine. *Via Piana 20, tel. 030/916216. Reservations advised. Dress: casual. DC, MC, V. Closed Jan. and Wed. Oct.–May. Moderate.*

Lodging **Hotel Sirmione.** Just inside the city walls, near the Castello, this charming hotel, which is also a spa, sits amid gardens and terraces beside the lake. The guest rooms are newly decorated, with comfortable Scandinavian slat beds. Some have matching draperies and wall coverings in spriggy prints, some have superbly executed white built-in furniture, and many have balconies. The corner dining room overlooks the lake and garden, and there is outdoor dining in fine weather. Many of the guests have been coming for years, and there's a homelike feeling about the place and the attentiveness of its staff. Full and half-pension are offered. *Piazza Castello 19, tel 030/916331, fax 030/ 916558. 76 rooms with bath. Facilities: restaurant, bar, meeting room, pool, landing stage, parking, spa treatments. AE, DC, MC, V. Moderate.*

Continental. A conveniently located hotel, on the lakefront, right next to the spa, the Continental operates on a demi-pension basis only. This works to keep the cost in check, and the hotel has the amenities and feel of a much more expensive establishment. Most rooms have balconies, but you should ask specifically for a lake view. *Via Punta Staffalo 7, tel. 030/ 916031. 53 rooms with bath and shower. Facilities: lakeside terraces, swimming pool, private beach. AE, DC, MC, V. Closed Dec.—Feb. Expensive (Moderate off-season: Mar.–June, Oct., Nov.).*

★ **Villa Cortine Palace.** An imposing former private villa set in a secluded park and entered through large iron gates, Villa Cortine treads the fine line between being ornately imposing and just plain ostentatious. It dominates a low hill, and the grounds—a colorful mixture of lawns, trees, statues, and fountains—go down to the lake. The villa itself dates back to the early part of the 19th century, although a new wing (1952) has been added: The trade-off is between the more charming Old World decor in the older rooms and the better lake views from those in the new wing. Either way you'll have the benefit of the extensive grounds and diverse facilities, as well as the attention of the well-trained and friendly staff. *Via Grotte 6, tel. 030/ 916021. 57 rooms with bath or shower. Facilities: spacious park-style grounds, lakefront beach, pool, tennis court, restaurant, terrace bar. AE, DC, MC, V. Closed Oct. 26–Mar. Expensive.*

Stresa **Monferrato.** Centrally located, off Piazza Cadorna and close to
Dining the imbarcadero, this hotel restaurant serves *risotto con filetti*

di persico (rice with perch fillets) and typical Piedmontese meat dishes, such as beef braised in Barolo wine. *Via Mazzini 14, tel. 0323/31386. Dress: casual. AE, DC, MC, V. Moderate.*

Lodging **Grand Hotel et des Iles Borromees.** A palatial Old World hotel, this princely establishment has catered to a demanding European clientele since 1863. And though it still has the spacious salons and lavish decor of the turn of the century, it has also been discreetly modernized; rooms have new and luxurious bathrooms, and there is a fitness center, as well as convention facilities. *Lungolago Umberto I 167, tel. 0323/30431. 167 rooms with bath. Facilities: bar, restaurant, pool, tennis courts, fitness center, park. AE, DC, MC, V. Very Expensive.*
Milan e Speranza. The result of the fusion of two of Stresa's traditional hostelries, this large hotel overlooks the imbarcadero, where the lake boats come in and out, and has views of the Borromean islands and lake. The decor is pleasantly old-fashioned, and many rooms have that romantic view, but they also get some noise from the dock. *Piazza Imbarcadero, tel. 0323/31190, fax 0323/32729. 159 rooms with bath. Facilities: bar, restaurant. AE, DC, MC, V. Moderate.*
La Fontana. A small hotel with a friendly management, the Fontana is on the main road through town, about 20 minutes on foot from the imbarcadero. Some rooms have good views of the lake, but the noise factor may make it advisable to take a back room. There is a pleasant garden, but no restaurant. *SS33 (Sempione road), tel. 0323/32707. 20 rooms with bath. AE, MC, V. Inexpensive.*

The Arts and Nightlife

The Arts

Opera The season at Milan's famous **La Scala** opera house runs from December through May. Seats are sold out well in advance, but if you are prepared to pay the desk clerk at your hotel, you will probably be able to get hold of a pair of tickets. For information on schedules and the (unlikely) possibility of box-office tickets, contact Teatro alla Scala (Piazza della Scala, tel. 02/807041). For reservations, call 02/809126. From abroad you can book in advance by mail or fax (02/887–9297) or at CIT or other travel agencies (at agencies, no more than 10 days before performance). Consult the weekly *Viva Milano* for listings.

Concerts La Scala opera house in Milan (*see above*) features a two-month season of **classical concerts** in October and November.

Brescia's **Teatro Grande** (tel. 030/59448) has a series of **classical music** concerts from November to May.

In Gardone Riviera, **Il Vittoriale,** the home of the Italian poet Gabriele d'Annunzio, has a series of concerts in its outdoor theater during July and August. For information, call 0365/20347.

Bergamo's **International Piano Festival,** held in Teatro Donizetti (Piazza Matteotti, tel. 035/249631) attracts world-class musicians in July and August.

Events Each year, on the feast of the Assumption (Aug. 15), there is a **contest** held in Mantua to determine who is the best *madonnaro* (street artist). Some of the painters can re-create masterpieces in a matter of minutes. During the first half of

September, Pavia's **Settembre Pavese** festival presents street processions, displays, and concerts.

Theater Milan's **Piccolo Teatro** (Via Rovello 2, tel. 02/877663) and **Teatro Manzoni** (Via Manzoni 40, tel. 02/790543) are noted for their excellent productions, but you'll need to speak Italian to appreciate them.

Nightlife

Jazz **Le Scimmie** (Via Ascanio Sforza 49, Milan, tel. 02/894–02874) is a good spot for cool jazz in a relaxed atmosphere.

Nightclubs The following Milan clubs are good bets for an evening of dinner and dancing, but don't expect this entertainment to come cheap: **Stage** (Galleria Manzoni, off Via Montenapoleone, tel. 02/760–21071, closed Mon.) and **Nepentha** (Piazza Diaz 1, tel. 02/804837, closed Sun.).

Discos **Lizard** (Largo La Foppa, Milan, tel. 02/659–0890) is trendy, loud, and expensive—a formula that doesn't deter the young Milanese crowd. *Closed Mon.*

Contatto (Corso Sempione 76, Milan, tel. 02/331–4904, open daily midnight–dawn) and **After Dark** (Via Certosa 134, Milan, tel. 02/305585, closed Tues.) are gay clubs/discos for men only.

Bars **Gershwin's,** in Milan (Via Corrado il Salico 10, tel. 02/849–7722), is a relaxed piano bar, where Cole Porter and Noel Coward, along with the bar's namesake, figure in the repertoire.

El Brellin (Vicolo Lavandai at the corner of Alzaia Naviglio Grande, Milan, tel. 02/5810–1351, closed Sun.) is one of the many bars in the Navigli district.

In the Brera quarter, **Momus** (Via Fiori Chiari 8, tel. 02/805–6227) is upscale and intimate.

11 The Dolomites

Bolzano, Trento, and Cortina d'Ampezzo

Unlike other famous Alpine ranges, this vast mountainous domain in northeast Italy has remained relatively undeveloped. The virginal landscape is the ultimate playground for the family or traveler on a quest for an original adventure. Ski fanatics travel across the world to dare some of the steep slopes that test even Olympic champions. Mountaineers risk the climb up sheer rock faces. For calmer souls there is the seduction of a landscape painted from a palette of extreme colors. The lowland valleys are laced with rivers spanned by awkward bridges and are filled with secluded villages and unexpected historic sites.

The Dolomites, sprawling over the Trentino–Alto Adige region and into parts of Lombardy by the Swiss border and the Veneto along the Austrian border, became known to Americans as a winter sports center after Cortina d'Ampezzo catapulted to fame by hosting the Winter Olympics of 1956. Today, scores of funiculars, chair lifts, and ski lifts give access to 600 miles of ski runs, as well as ski jumps and bobsled runs.

Then there are the "untouchable" zones—inaccessible by means of chair lift or ski lift. These are the famous plateaus topping some of the highest mountains, from which you can see Italy on one side and Austria or Switzerland on the other. To enjoy such a rare spectacle, you must spend arduous hours climbing beyond where the lifts leave you, and when you reach the top, you will probably see cows casually grazing on the grass. It can make you dizzy just thinking of how they got there, but contradictions are common in the Dolomites.

This expansive land of rocks and valleys has long attracted Italians and other Europeans looking for a varied natural environment. What they—and you—find is a confusion of colors, architectural styles, and languages. At sunset, the colors of the rocks are highlighted by purples and pinks, with even the snowcapped peaks reflecting the pink glow. A meander through the valleys becomes a botanical escapade, with rare plant species abounding; high above you on the cliffs are castles, protected by their size and position. The serious climber will get a closer view of these remote fortresses. There, on the higher levels, are some rarely seen animals: bears, deer, mountain goats, and birds of prey. It's perhaps not surprising that Reinhold Messer, the first man to climb Everest without oxygen, lives in the Dolomites.

Straddling the Brenner Pass—the main access point to Italy from Central Europe—the Dolomites play host to a mixture of cultures and languages. The people of Alto Adige (also known as South Tyrol), who have been Italian citizens since World War I, continue to speak German as their mother tongue. Their crafts and food still reflect their Austrian origins. In addition to this blend of Germanic and Italian cultures, there is a small Ladin community, an isolated people who speak a language called Ladin, an offshoot of Latin.

In this chapter, we have given place-names in Italian, with their German equivalents (where relevant) in parentheses. Signs throughout much of the Dolomites are bilingual.

Essential Information

Important Addresses and Numbers

Tourist Information The Tourist Board for the Trentino–Alto Adige region is located on Piazza Parrocchia 11–12, Bolzano (tel. 0471/993808). The following are local tourist boards.

Bolzano (Piazza Walther 8, tel. 0471/970660).
Bormio (Via Stelvio, tel. 0342/903300).
Bressanone (Via Stazione 9, tel. 0472/36401).
Chiusa (Piazza Timme 40, tel. 0472/47424).
Cortina d'Ampezzo (Piazzetta San Francesco 8, tel. 0436/3231).
Madonna di Campiglio (Via Pradalago 4, tel. 0465/42000).
Merano (Via del Libertà 45, tel. 0473/35223).
Rovereto (Via Dante 63, tel. 0464/430363).
Trento (Via Alfieri 4, tel. 0461/983880).

Emergencies **Police, Ambulance,** tel. 113. This is also the best number to dial for first aid: Ask for "Pronto Soccorso," and be prepared to give your address.

Late-Night Pharmacies Pharmacies take turns staying open late or on Sundays; for the latest information, consult the current list posted on the front door of each pharmacy or ask at the local tourist office.

Car Rentals **Bolzano.** *Avis* (Piazza Verdi 18, tel. 0471/971467); *Hertz* (Via Alto Adige 30, tel. 0471/977155).

Arriving and Departing by Car and Train

By Car The most important route in the region, A22, is the main north–south autostrada linking Italy with northern Europe via the Brenner Pass.

By Train The express train line that links the towns of Bolzano, Trento, and Rovereto connects with other main lines when it meets Verona, just south of the region.

Getting Around

By Car Autostrada A22 connects Bressanone, Bolzano, Trento, and Rovereto. Roads in the broad mountain valleys are usually wide two-lane routes, but the roads up into the highest passes can be narrow and subject to sudden closure, even in the months when they are open to drivers. A Bolzano number (tel. 0471/49000) provides information on weather-related closures.

By Train An express train line follows the course of the Adige Valley from Brenner Pass southward past Bolzano, Trento, and Rovereto. Branch lines from Trento and Bolzano go to some of the smaller valleys, but most of the mountain attractions described in this chapter are beyond the reach of trains.

By Bus Local buses connect the train stations at Trento, Bolzano, and Merano with the mountain resorts. The service is fairly frequent between most main towns during the day, though some parts of the region remain out of the reach of public transportation.

Guided Tours

Orientation   If you are visiting the region without a car or if you don't care to drive over mountain roads, guided tours from Bolzano or Trento can show you the Dolomites the easy way. However, the sudden and frequent snowfalls mean that tours are offered in summer only.

In **Bolzano,** city sightseeing and guided tours of the region are organized by the **SAD** bus company (Via Perathoner, near the train station, tel. 0471/971259). Through July and August, full-day tours of the mountains are offered; they include a **Great Dolomites Tour** from Bolzano to Cortina and a tour of the **Venosta Valley** that climbs over the Stelvio Pass into Switzerland. A tour of the **Val Gardena** and the Siusi Alps is available from April to October.

In **Trento,** city sightseeing can be arranged through the **Azienda Autonoma** tourist office (Via Alfieri 4, tel. 0461/983880). Tours around Trento are provided by **Calderari e Moggioli** travel agency (Via Manci 46, tel. 0461/980275). These include a full-day guided bus tour of the **Brenta Dolomites** and the **Great Dolomites Tour,** a full-day drive over the Pordoi and Falzarego passes to Cortina d'Ampezzo and Lake Misurina. These tours are offered from June to September only.

Exploring the Dolomites

The best—and only—way to get around in this mountainous region is by following the course of the valleys that find their way to the heart of the massifs that compose the Dolomites. The most important are the valleys formed by the Adige River, beginning near the Swiss border and running to Bolzano, then continuing almost due south, and by the Isarco River, beginning at the Brenner Pass and running southward to Bolzano, where it flows into the Adige. Italy's main road and rail connections to north central Europe run along the Adige through Rovereto to Trento and Bolzano, continuing along the Isarco through Bressanone to the Brenner Pass.

The first tour stays close to the Adige Valley, devoting most of its time to Bolzano Trento, and Rovereto, the two main towns. Tour 2 sets off west from Bolzano along the Venosta Valley, climbing to panoramic views from the Stelvio Pass before swinging south to visit the lofty Brenta massif.

The last tour goes east from Bolzano, following the Great Dolomite Road to the chic ski resort of Cortina d'Ampezzo. It then goes north to the lesser-known town of Dobbiaco, gateway to the Pusteria Valley and the best way west toward the Isarco Valley. Before completing a circuit and returning to Bolzano, the tour makes a slight detour eastward into the Val Gardena, the valley where you'll have the best chance of hearing Ladin spoken.

Highlights for First-time Visitors

Brunico (Tour 3: The Great Dolomites Road).

Cappella di San Giovanni, Bolzano (Tour 1: Bolzano to Trento).

Castello di Buonconsiglio, Trento (Tour 1: Bolzano to Trento).

Cornedo and the view of the Catinaccio range
(Tour 3: The Great Dolomites Road).

Cortina d'Ampezzo (Tour 3: The Great Dolomites Road).

Merano (Tour 2: West to the Stelvio Pass).

Museo Diocesano, Bressanone (Tour 3: The Great
Dolomites Road).

Passo dello Stelvio (Tour 2: West to the Stelvio Pass).

Val Gardena (Tour 3: The Great Dolomites Road).

Tour 1: Bolzano to Trento

*Numbers in the margin correspond to points of interest on the
Dolomites and Bolzano maps.*

❶ **Bolzano** (Bozen), the capital of the Italian province of Alto Adige, is an ideal base for your exploration of the surrounding Dolomites. It is protected by the mountains to the north and the
east and is located on the main north–south artery between
northern Europe and Italy. This quiet city lies at the confluence of the Isarco (Eisack) and Talvera rivers. Bolzano has re-
tained a provincial appeal, but contradicts its country image
with commercial features acquired to cater to the needs of tourists. The high rises of New York will never crop up here, but
McDonald's can be seen—housed, of course, in a more archaic
building.

Bolzano's heart is pedestrians-only **Piazza Walther,** the square
named after the 12th-century German wandering minstrel
Walther von der Vogelweide, whose songs lampooned the papacy and praised the Holy Roman Emperor. Today it serves as an
open-air living room for the town. Locals and tourists alike can
be found at all hours sipping a drink (perhaps a glass of chilled
local Riesling) at the café tables.

Time Out The bar at the **Hotel Grifone** (Grief), on Piazza Walther, is one
of the best places for a view of the square. Tables are set up outside, but the cozy interior is enticing if the weather turns bad.

❷ At one corner of the piazza is the city's Gothic **Duomo** (Cathedral), built between the 12th and 14th centuries. Its lacy spire
looks down on the mosaiclike tiles covering its pitched roof. Inside the church are 14th- and 15th-century frescoes and an in-
tricately carved stone pulpit dating from 1514.

❸ Via Posta leads from the other side of the square to **Piazza
Domenicani,** with its 13th-century **Dominican church,** renowned as Bolzano's main repository for paintings, especially
frescoes. In the adjoining **Cappella di San Giovanni** you can see
frescoes of the Giotto school, one of which is the *Triumph of
Death* (ca. 1340). Despite its macabre title, this fresco shows
the birth of a pre-Renaissance sense of depth and individuality:
It was completed at a time when other European religious art
was anonymous and two dimensional.

❹ From here the narrow Via Goethe leads to **Piazza delle Erbe,**
where a bronze statue of Neptune presides over a bounteous
fruit and vegetable market (Mon.–Sat. 8–1). The stalls spill
over with colorful displays of locally grown produce. Bakeries
and grocery stores showcase hot breads, pastries, cheeses, and

delicatessen meats: It's a complete range of picnic supplies. Take some advice from the locals—try the *speck* (smoked ham) and the Tyrolean-style apple strudel.

The market is at the beginning of Bolzano's main shopping street, **Via dei Portici** (Lauben), lined with long, narrow arcades. The shops specialize in Tyrolean handicrafts and clothing—lederhosen, loden goods, linen suits, and dirndls.

Via del Museo leads in the opposite direction from the market to the **Museo Civico,** about 100 yards away. This museum houses a rich collection of traditional costumes, wood carvings, and archaeological exhibits. The mixture of styles is a reflection of the region's cultural cross-fertilization. *Via del Museo 45. Admission: 2,000 lire. Open Tues.–Sat. 9–noon, 2:30–5:30, Sun. 10–1.*

Just across the road is **Ponte Talvera,** a bridge that extends over the Talvera River to the district of Gries. Cross over to visit the **Parrocchiale** (parish church) of Gries, with its elaborately carved 15th-century wooden altar, and the Benedictine abbey and Baroque church of **San Agostino.** The churches are about a half mile beyond the bridge, along Corso Libertà. Just beyond the parish church is the Passeggiata, a pathway that leads up to the **Guncina** hill, where you get a panoramic view of Bolzano.

Recross the river and go immediately left, along the Lungotalvera Promenade, upstream to the 13th-century **Castel Mareccio** (Schloss Maretsch), nestled under the mountains and surrounded by vineyards. *Restaurant open to public; admission to castle by appointment only. Call tel. 0471/976615 or contact the Bolzano tourist office.*

Fifteen kilometers (9 miles) south of Bolzano is the vineyard village of **Caldaro,** located on the Strada del Vino (Wine Route). From here you get clear views of castles high up on the surrounding mountains. The backdrop reflects the centuries of battle and division that forged the unique character of the area. The Caldaro architecture is famous for the way it blends Italian Renaissance elements of balance and harmony with the soaring windows and peaked arches of the local Gothic tradition. Santa Caterina church, on the main square, is a good example of this mixture.

The Wine Route traces its way through foothills and small villages where the vineyards rise up the terraced hillsides. Eight kilometers (5 miles) beyond Caldaro is **Termeno,** where there is a **Wine Museum** at Ringberg Castle just as you enter the village. Here you can taste or buy some of the specialties of the region. *Admission: 2,000 lire. Open Easter–Oct., Tues.–Sat. 10–noon and 2–6, Sun. 2–6.*

Time Out   In the fall, join the locals in the popular tradition of going into the hills to little taverns to taste the new wine and eat roast chestnuts. These jaunts are known as *toergglen* (from the German *toergl,* meaning winepress).

About 10 minutes past Termeno is **Ora** (Auer), where the Adige Valley broadens and you can join the autostrada A22 heading south. Half an hour of easy driving through the orchard-lined valley takes you to **Trento,** capital of Trentino Province. Somehow this city has escaped the ravages of commercialization and

The Dolomites

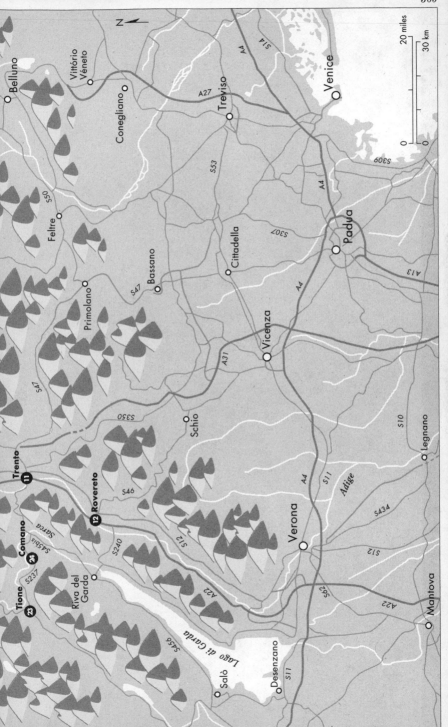

Bolzano

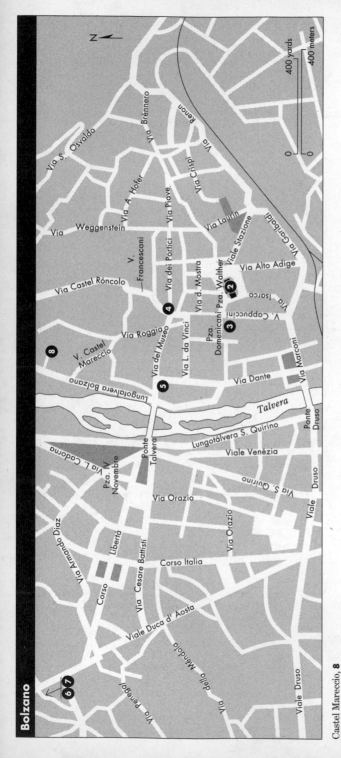

Castel Mareccio, **8**
Dominican Church, **3**
Duomo, **2**
Museo Cívico, **5**
Parrocchiale, **6**
Piazza delle Erbe, **4**
San Agostino, **7**

retains its architectural charm, artistic attractions, and historic importance.

It was here, from 1545 to 1563, that the structure of the Catholic Church was redefined, in the famous Council of Trent. This was the starting point of the Counter-Reformation, which brought half of Europe back to Catholicism. Until 1803, Trento itself was ruled by prince-bishops. Everywhere in Trento you'll see the word *Consiglio* (Council)—in hotel, restaurant, and street names, and even on wine labels. The locals are still proud of their two decades in the limelight.

Trento is worth a visit anytime but is especially attractive in the spring, at blossom time, or during the fall harvest. The city hosts many festivals in both seasons, ranging from the agricultural fair in early spring to the *festival internazionale Film della Montagne* (festival of Mountain and Exploring films) in May. A summer bonus is the week-long San Vigilio Fair, culminating on June 26, when townspeople don medieval clothing in honor of the patron saint of Trento.

Like Bolzano, Trento has at its heart a square—**Piazza del Duomo.** In the center is a Baroque fountain of Neptune; the massive, low, Romanesque **Duomo** forms the southern edge of the square. Before entering the cathedral, pause to savor the view of the mountaintops ranged majestically around the city and visible above the rooftops in every direction. The mountain weather can change within minutes, and you can never be sure of the same visibility when you reemerge from the cathedral.

Step inside to see the unusual arcaded stone stairways on either side of the austere nave. Ahead of you is the *baladacchino* (altar canopy), a clear copy of Bernini's masterpiece in St. Peter's in Rome. In a small chapel to the right is a mournful 15th-century Crucifixion, with Mary and the Apostle John. This crucifix was a focal point of the Council of Trent: Each decree agreed on during the two decades of deliberations was solemnly read out in front of it. Later, walk behind the back of the cathedral to see an exquisite display of 14th-century stonemasons' art, from the small porch to the intriguing knotted columns on the graceful apse.

The crenellated **Palazzo Pretorio,** which seems to be a wing of the cathedral, was built in the 13th century as the prudently fortified residence of the prince-bishops. Endowed with considerable power and autonomy, these clerics enjoyed a unique position in the medieval hierarchy. From the beginning of the 11th century, they wielded a twofold authority, administering civil and military affairs on behalf of the Holy Roman Emperor, and at the same time acting as the pope's representatives in ecclesiastical matters. This was at a time when other parts of Italy were at war, with sides pledging their loyalty to one of these two powers. This delicate balancing act continued for 800 years, ending when Austria secularized the principality in 1802.

The Palazzo Pretorio now houses the **Museo Diocesano Tridentino,** where you can see paintings showing the seating plan of the prelates during the Council of Trent; early–16th-century tapestries by Pieter van Aelst, the Belgian artist who carried out Raphael's designs for the Vatican tapestries; carved wood altars and statues; and an 11th-century sacramentary, or book of services. These and other precious objects all come from the Cathedral's treasury. *Piazza Duomo 18. Admission: 2,000* *lire. Open mid-Feb.–mid-Nov., Mon.–Sat. 9:30–12:30 and 2:30–6.*

Time Out Locals love the ice cream and snacks at **Bertelli,** an attractive café with tables outdoors on Piazza Lodron. It's located a few steps down Via Garibaldi from the rear of the cathedral. *Via Oriola 29. Closed Mon.*

Return to the Piazza del Duomo to reach **Via Cavour,** which leads off from the northwest side. About 100 yards down this narrow street is the Renaissance church of **Santa Maria Maggiore,** where many sessions of the Council of Trent were held. From here it's an easy 50-yard walk up the lane behind the church to **Via Belenzani,** famous for its Renaissance *palazzi,* whose frescoed facades add a colorful note to the walls facing the street. Locals sometimes call this stretch of road Trento's outdoor gallery.

Turn right on Via Manci and begin a pleasant 200-yard climb past souvenir shops and glassware outlets. The road reaches the moated **Castello del Buonconsiglio** (Castle of Good Counsel). This huge castle was the stronghold of the prince-bishops; its position and size made it easier to defend than the Palazzo Pretorio. As you stand facing it, you can see the evolution of architectural styles, starting with the medieval fortifications of the Castelvecchio section on the far left, down to the more decorative Renaissance Magno Palazzo, built three centuries later in 1530. The Castello now houses the **Museo Provinciale d'Arte** (Provincial Art Museum), where exhibits of art and archaeology are displayed in medieval halls or under Renaissance coffered ceilings. The 13th-century **Torre dell'Aquila** (Eagle's Tower) holds the highlight of the museum, a fresco cycle of the months of the year. It is full of charming and informatively detailed scenes of 15th-century life in both court and countryside. *Via B. Clesio 5. Admission: 4,000 lire. Open Tues.–Sun. 9– noon and 2–5.*

Walk along the front of the Castello to the Castelvecchio end, on the left, and cross onto Piazza Raffaello Sanzio. The **Torre Verde** (Green Tower), part of Trento's 13th-century fortifications, stands here, alongside other fragments of the walls. You can take Via Torre Verde from this square back to the center of Trento: The road changes its name to **Via Torre Vanga** as it reaches the tower of that name, another 13th-century fortification, this time guarding the medieval bridge across the Adige, Ponte San Lorenzo.

From a cable car station at the bridge, you can get a lift to **Belvedere di Sardagna,** a vantage point 1,200 feet above Trento.

⑫ Continue down A22 another 24 kilometers (15 miles) to reach **Rovereto,** a medieval town in the main north–south valley of the Adige. A 15th-century castle looks down on the town from the nearest of the foothills of this valley, but this district has more recent memories of warfare. Some of the fiercest fighting of the First World War took place in the wooded hills around Rovereto, with Italian and Austrian troops bogged down in prolonged and costly conflict. Every night you're reminded of the thousands who fell: At sunset the bells of the **Campana dei Caduti** (Bell of the Fallen) toll to commemorate war victims throughout the world.

Tour 2: West to the Stelvio Pass

The high mountain road running through the Stelvio Pass is closed from November to May, so if you're traveling during that period, you won't be able to follow this tour all the way. The leg from Merano to Naturno can be driven from Bolzano year-round; to pick up the tour at Bormio, you'll have to take S42 west from Bolzano 126 kilometers (78 miles) to Tresenda, in Lombardy, and head northeast on S38 another 48 kilometers (30 miles).

Only 28 kilometers (17 miles) north of Bolzano, along the Adige Valley, is **Merano** (Meran), the second largest town in the Alto Adige. Merano has been famous as a spa town for 150 years, and people come to it for its thermal waters, which, like those in many health spas, have natural radioactivity. It is also renowned for its "grape cure"—which is made with local grape juice, not wine. Sheltered by mountains, Merano has an unusually mild climate, with summer temperatures rarely exceeding 80° F and winters that usually stay above freezing, despite the skiing that is within easy reach. (Chair lifts and cable cars connect Merano with the high Alpine slopes of Avelengo and San Vigilio.)

Along the narrow streets of Merano's old town, houses capped with little towers open their huge wooden doors into squares where the pointed arches of the Gothic sit with surprising harmony next to neoclassical and Art Nouveau buildings. In the heart of the old town, the **Piazza del Duomo**, is the 14th-century Gothic cathedral, with a crenellated facade and an ornate *campanile* (bell tower). The Cappella di **Santa Barbara**, just behind the cathedral, is an octagonal church containing a 15th-century *Pietà*.

Merano's main shopping street, the narrow, arcaded **Via dei Portici** (Lauben), runs west from the cathedral. A good place for souvenir shopping, it features most of the best regional products: wood carvings, Tyrolean-style clothes, embroidery, cheeses, salami, and fruit schnapps. Turn left when it ends on Via di Corse and head down to the river, about a quarter-mile away. Cross the Passirio River over Ponte del Teatro to reach the **Terme** (Municipal Baths), just on the other side. This huge complex is the nerve center of the spa facilities, although some hotels have their own treatments. Technicians are trained to treat you with mud packs, massages, inhalation and sauna routines, or just with the thermal waters, which are said to be especially good for coronary and circulatory problems. You can try other cures, including the famous grape cure at harvest time in the fall, when a two-week diet of fresh grapes has since Roman times been seen as a successful way to tone up digestive, liver, and urinary tract functions.

From Merano, follow S38 west along the course of the Adige into the Val Venosta district. Tiny churches, some 1,200 years old, dot the hillsides: Distances play tricks on the eye, making some of the higher churches appear to be toys. Stop at **Naturno**, about 15 kilometers (9 miles) west of Merano, to look at the church of **San Procolo.** This small church, which is frescoed inside and out, has wall paintings that are the oldest in the German-speaking world, dating from the 8th century.

The road climbs higher as it follows the upstream course of the Adige, which is more often called by its German name, the Etsch, in this German-speaking area. The peaks to the left are in the National Park of the Stelvio, part of the Italian government's long-term project to protect the Dolomites from the rapid development that spoiled mountainous regions in neighboring countries.

⑮ **⑯** About 35 kilometers (21 miles) beyond Naturno, follow S38 as it turns sharply left at the village of **Spondigna** (Spondinig). This next stretch of road is well paved and open from June to October, but can be a bit hair-raising for anyone who doesn't like mountain driving. Your goal is the **Passo dello Stelvio** (Stelvio Pass), at just over 9,000 feet the second-highest pass in Europe. Between Spondigna and the pass is 30 kilometers (18 miles) of winding road, with 48 hairpin turns before you reach the top. The view from the top is worth the effort because the pass connects the Venosta Valley with the Valtellina in neighboring Lombardy. Just to the right of the road as you enter is Switzerland. Stelvio is well known as a summer skiing center.

Time Out You'll probably want a breather once you've made it to the top of the pass. A good place for a drink is the bar of the **Hotel Passo dello Stelvio** (tel. 0342/903162), where you can savor the view of two valleys.

⑰ Continue along S38 as it begins its descent toward **Bormio**, the famous Lombard skiing center just 21 kilometers (13 miles) along. The road has its share of hairpins and tunnels, but is less intimidating than the road to Stelvio. At Bormio you turn left onto S300; this begins a spectacular drive southward along the western border of the Stelvio National Park. The road is good but narrow and twisting, and for long stretches your only company will be the complacent cows in the Alpine meadows. About 25 kilometers (15 miles) beyond Bormio, you reach the **⑱** **Passo di Gavia**, a magnificent pass more than 8,500 feet above sea level. Just to your right are the cold waters of **Lago Nero** (Black Lake). This is the source of the River Messi, whose course you follow for the next 18 kilometers (10 miles) as you **⑲** descend to **Ponte di Legno**. About halfway down this part of S300, the road meets the fast-flowing river, at the tiny village of Sant' Apollonia, at the top of a series of hairpin turns.

At Ponte di Legno you turn left along S42 to head east along the Val Vermiglio. The signs will tell you you're heading back to Bolzano, but some of the best parts of this tour, the Brenta Dolomites, are off this direct route to home base. Turn right at **⑳** **Dimaro**, 37 kilometers (23 miles) east of Ponte di Legno, to begin the climb on S239 into the Brenta Dolomites. In the space of a few miles, you climb more than 2,000 feet, once more getting steering practice on the hairpin turns and switchbacks. The strange, rocky pinnacles of the Dolomites, which jut straight up like chimneys and look at times more like Monument Valley in Utah than any European ranges, loom over scattered mountain lakes.

Just above the **Carlo Magno Pass,** where Charlemagne is said to have stopped in AD 800 on his way to Rome to be crowned emper-**㉑** or, is **Madonna di Campiglio**, a chic winter resort with more than 20 ski runs and 30 lifts. The resort itself is 5,000 feet up, but some of the runs (and summer hiking routes) approach the heights of the surrounding peaks, including Pietra Grande, at over 9,700 feet.

㉒ At **Pinzolo**, 14 kilometers (8 miles) south of Madonna di Campiglio, you can see a remarkable 16th-century fresco on the side of a small village church. Follow the signs for the church of **San Vigilio:** After a short walk through the pines, you come across the church. On an exterior wall, the vivid fresco describes the Dance of Death, with ghoulish figures offering a stern rebuke to potential sinners.

㉓ S239 continues its descent to the Sarca Valley, where you pick up S237 east at **Tione.** There are more signs of habitation in this lower valley, with ruins of castles looking down on modern **㉔** farming settlements. **Comano**, a small but locally renowned spa, is 20 kilometers (12 miles) along. You may want to turn south on S45bis to visit the famous **Lake Garda** (*see* The Lakes in Chapter 10 for an exploring route around Lake Garda). Otherwise, continue east on S237 until it meets A22 at Trento.

Tour 3: The Great Dolomites Road

This tour also begins in Bolzano but explores the area to the north and east, following an itinerary known as **La Grande Strada delle Dolomiti** (Great Dolomites Road) to the mountain resort of Cortina d'Ampezzo. The route, opened in 1909, now comprises 110 kilometers (70 miles) of easy grades and smooth driving between the two cities.

㉕ La Grande Strada begins just 6 kilometers (4 miles) east of Bolzano, at **Cornedo**, the beginning of the Ega Valley (Eggental). Before starting off on S241, pull over to savor the view of the Catinaccio Mountains to the left. Their craggy peaks seem to be props for a lighting display, as pink and purple reflections dance over the huge rocks. These rocks are the protagonists in a German legend of a rose garden that turned to stone. The local legend tells of King Laurin, who lived in a vast palace on the Catinaccio, with dwarfs to serve him. At that time the mountain was covered entirely with roses. But King Laurin became infatuated with the daughter of a neighboring king, Similde, and kidnapped her. Similde set out to search for his daughter and recognized her place of imprisonment by the red roses that had grown there. He freed the girl and made Laurin his prisoner. When Laurin finally escaped from Similde's prison, he decreed that the roses that had betrayed him should be turned to rocks, so that they could be seen neither by day nor by night. Today, the spectacular pinkish-red display is at its best at dawn and at sunset.

㉖ Continue along S241 as it climbs the Val d'Ega. About 20 kilometers (12 miles) along, just before you reach the **Passo di Costalunga** (Karerpass), you begin to see the near-vertical rock displays of the Dolomites reflected in the clear waters of **Lake Carezza.** You can view the needlelike range on your right as the road descends into the valley. At **Vigo di Fassa** you join S48 to head left into the heart of the Dolomites.

The road snakes its way through narrow valleys and crosses a series of passes that are all over a mile high. The scenery is outstanding, but the rocky terrain means the soil is too poor for agriculture; miles go by with no farms in sight. As the road continues through the high mountain valleys of the **Cordelove** and then the **Dores** rivers, you start to see chair lifts and runs of the famous Dolomite skiing centers. Some of these, such as Nuvolau, by the **Passo di Falzarego**, are immediately off the road. The Passo di Falzarego also marks the point at which S48 begins its descent. There are more curves and steep-sided turns; the best view comes when you emerge from the Crepa Tunnel and see Cortina and the cross-shaped Ampezzo valley for the first time.

Cortina d'Ampezzo, known as the "Pearl of the Dolomites," is set in a lush meadow 4,000 feet above sea level. Dense forests adjoin the town, and mountains encircle the whole valley. The town sprawls on the slopes along a fast-moving stream; a public park extends along one bank. Luxury hotels and the villas of the rich are conspicuously scattered over the slopes above the town—identifiable, ironically, by their attempts to hide behind stands of firs and spruces.

The bustling center of Cortina has little nostalgia for old-time atmosphere, despite its alpine appearance. The tone is set by elegant shops and stylish cafés, as opulent as their well-dressed patrons, whose corduroy knickerbockers may well have been tailored by Armani. Cortina is the place to go for a whiff of the heady aroma of wealth and sophistication; if you want authentic Tyrolean *gemütlichkeit* (knee-slapping conviviality), pass through Cortina and stop at one of the resorts later on the tour.

The Great Dolomites Road ends at Cortina d'Ampezzo, but our tour goes north and then west, to complete a great loop back to Bolzano. From Cortina continue along S48 for an 11-kilometer (7-mile) climb over the **Passo di Tre Croce** and down again as you head toward the jewellike **Lake Misurina** below. Turn left as you reach the lake to join S48bis, which leads northward to S51, to **Dobbiaco** (Toblach), 34 kilometers (20 miles) north of Cortina. At Dobbiaco, you really begin to feel the influence of Austria, which is just 12 kilometers (7 miles) to the east along the Drau Valley. Italian is spoken grudgingly here, Austrian money is accepted at most shops and restaurants, and the locals appear more blond and blue-eyed than the average Italian. It is not surprising that Gustav Mahler (1860–1911), the great Austrian composer, should have felt at home here; he often came to Dobbiaco for inspiration.

At Dobbiaco, head west along S49 as it runs beside the fast-flowing Rienz River in the **Pusteria** (Puster) Valley. This valley is broader than others in this tour, so you make good time on the 26-kilometer (16-mile) drive west to **Brunico** (Bruneck), with its medieval quarter nestling below the 13th-century bishop's castle. Here, in the adjacent district of Teodone, just to the right of town as you enter from the Dobbiaco side, is the **Museo degli Usi e Costumi della Provincia di Bolzano** (Ethnographic Museum). This re-creation of a typical local village, built around an authentic 300-year-old mansion, reveals the functions and significance of traditional architecture. The wood-carving displays are particularly interesting. *Via Herzog Diet 24, Teodone. Admission: 3,000 lire. Open Apr. 15–Oct., Tues.–Sat. 9:30–5:30, Sun. 2–6.*

Continue west on S49 to **Bressanone** (Brixen), 35 kilometers (21 miles) away. Bressanone is an important artistic center of the Alto Adige district and for centuries was the seat of prince-bishops. Like their counterparts in Trento, these medieval administrators had the delicate problem of serving two opposing masters—the pope (the ultimate spiritual supervisor) and the Holy Roman Emperor (the civil and military leader). Since the Papacy and the Holy Roman Empire were virtually at war throughout the Middle Ages, Bressanone's prince-bishops had to become experts at tact and diplomacy in order to survive. As you arrive from Brunico, you enter the town on Via Mercato Vecchio, a broad road leading to the large **Duomo**, the most imposing building in town. It was built in the 13th century but acquired a Baroque facade 500 years later. Its 14th-century cloister is decorated with medieval frescoes. The adjacent **Museo Diocesano** (Diocesan Museum) is a treasure house of local medieval art, particularly Gothic wood carving. The wooden statues and liturgical objects were all collected from the cathedral treasury. During the Christmas season the curators highlight displays of the museum's large collection of antique Nativity scenes: Look for the shepherds wearing Tyrolean hats. *Admission: 4,000 lire. Open Mar. 15–Oct., Mon.–Sat. 10–5; nativity scenes open Dec. 15–Feb. 10, Mon.–Sat. 2–5. Closed Dec. 24, 25.*

Casa Pfaundler, a Renaissance mansion located next to the parish church to the left of the Duomo, is a fitting reminder of the cultural mix of the region. The architecture, a blend of Italian and German elements, is as much a hybrid as the name.

At Bressanone you are no more than 45 kilometers (27 miles) north of Bolzano. The autostrada (A22) provides the best connection, but there are two more important stops before you return. At **Chiusa** (Klausen), 18 kilometers (10 miles) south along A22, stop to see the narrow streets lined with houses built in the 15th and 16th centuries. Geraniums and begonias fill window boxes beneath the carved wooden shutters. Above the town is the Benedictine monastery of **Sabiona** (Saeben), built as a castle in the 10th century but occupying a site that was fortified in Roman times. The monastery buildings date from the late Middle Ages and are a mixture of Romanesque and Gothic architecture, surrounded by walls and turrets.

Just south of Chiusa on the autostrada, take a short detour east along S242 into the **Val Gardena** (Groedner Tal). Val Gardena provides some of the best views of the Dolomites and is one of Italy's most popular ski resorts. It is also home of the Ladini, descendants of soldiers sent by the Roman Emperor Tiberius to conquer the Celtic population of the area in the 1st century AD. Forgotten in the narrow cul-de-sacs of isolated mountain valleys, the Ladini have developed their own folk traditions and speak an ancient dialect that is derived from Latin and is similar to Romansch, which is spoken in some high valleys in Switzerland. Follow the valley for the 13 kilometers (8 miles) to **Ortisei** (St. Ulrich), the best spot to catch a few phrases of Ladin. Back again on the autostrada, a 20-kilometer (12-mile) drive will return you to Bolzano.

What to See and Do with Children

It's hard to go wrong with children in the Dolomites: The open spaces and the mountains are real attractions for them. The Italians love children, and many of the sporting facilities (both summer and winter) have special children's facilities. Most ski resorts have ski schools for even very young children, and the multilingual teaching staffs make the learning experience enjoyable (*see* Sports, *below*).

The 12th-century castle at **Tirolo** near Merano (*see* Tour 2: West to the Stelvio Pass, *above*) introduces children to the history of the region and teaches the value of strategic locations and fortifications.

The **Museo degli Usi e Costumi** (Ethnographic Museum) at Teodone near Brunico (*see* Tour 3: The Great Dolomites Road, *above*) is a hands-on museum designed to familiarize visitors with local customs and traditions.

No winter visit is complete without a visit to the nativity scenes at the **Museo Diocesano** (Diocesan Museum) in Bressanone (*see* Tour 3: The Great Dolomites Road, *above*).

Off the Beaten Track

On the **Renon** (Ritten) plateau, just above Bolzano and reachable by the funicular to Soprabolzano, are the **Earth Pyramids,** a bizarre geological formation where erosion has left a forest of tall, thin, needlelike spires of rock, each topped with a boulder. *The Soprabolzano funicular leaves from Via Renon, about 300 yards left from the Bolzano train station. At the top an electric train takes you to Collalbo, where you find the Earth Pyramids.*

Five kilometers (3 miles) past Spondigna (Spondinig) in the Venosta Valley, turn left off S40 as it heads toward the Austrian border. A little road leads you to **Glorenza** (Glurns), a tiny village that looks much as it did in the Middle Ages, still surrounded by a high wall and turreted watchtowers. Local building ordinances set strict limits on new construction, and many streets are for pedestrians only.

From July to September at the pretty village of **Fie** (Voels), just off A22, north of the Bolzano Nord exit, you can take the "Hay Cure" at Hotel Heubad (which means Hay Bath in German), a well-equipped hotel in a 16th-century building. The cure consists of burying yourself in warm hay composed of mountain herbs and grasses—a treatment devised by local peasants. The experience is said to be like having a sauna or mud bath, but be warned: This cure is under no circumstances to be taken by people with heart and circulation problems or people with pollen allergies. *Hotel-Pension Heubad, 39050 Fie allo Scillar (Voels am Schlern), tel. 0471/725020.*

Shopping

Shopping is fun in the Dolomites, where larger towns, such as Bolzano, Bressanone, and Brunico, have shops clustered in arcaded shopping streets designed to keep shoppers dry on rainy or snowy days. The ethnic mixture, with its strong Tyrolean influence, makes for local products and handicrafts that are quite different from those elsewhere in Italy. Tyrolean clothing—loden goods, lederhosen, dirndls, and linen suits with horn buttons—is a good buy and costs less than in neighboring Austria. Local handicrafts, such as embroidered goods, wood carvings, figures for nativity scenes, pottery, and handcrafted copper and iron objects, make good gifts.

Antiques	**Trento** is the local center for antiques. The main dealers are **Antiquariato Corti** (Via Mantova 30), **Gasperetti** (Via Torre Verde 52), and **Antichità** (Piazza Santa Maria Maggiore 27).
Handicrafts	In **Bolzano** the best store for locally made goods is **Artigiani Atesini** (Via Portici 39).

In **Trento,** go to **Il Pozzo** (Piazza Pasi 14/L) for handcrafted wooden objects; **Il Laboratorio** (Via Roma 12) specializes in terra-cotta pieces by local artists.

Food and Flea Markets In **Bolzano,** the outdoor fruit and vegetable market is held in the central **Piazza delle Erbe** every morning (8–1) except Sunday. The big weekly flea market takes place Saturday morning in **Piazza della Vittoria,** just across from the center of town.

Trento's small morning market is held in the center of town at **Piazza Lodron,** but the big shopping day is Thursday, when the weekly market spreads out around **Piazza d'Arogno,** next to the cathedral. A flea market is held in **Piazza d'Arogno** every third Sunday of the month; the same piazza is the scene of a handicrafts market every Friday and Saturday.

Sports

Cross-Country Skiing The Dolomites are an ideal place to learn or improve your cross-country skiing (*sci di fondo* in Italian). The major Alpine resorts, and even many out-of-the-way villages, have prepared trails (usually loops marked off by kilometers) catering to differing degrees of ability. Two of the best are at **Ortisei** and **Dobbiaco.** You can have a lot of fun blazing new trails across virgin snow fields; you can usually get permission by asking at the nearest farmhouse or by inquiring at local tourist offices.

Golf **Campo Carlo Magno** (tel. 0465/41003) is a nine-hole course set in the mountains by Madonna di Campiglio, open July 1–September 15.

Hiking The Dolomites have a well-maintained network of trails for hiking and rock climbing, with *rifugi* (huts) located on the most difficult ascents. It is important that you follow safety procedures and have all the latest information on trails and conditions. Two helpful organizations are **Societa degli Alpinisti Tridentini** (Via Manci 109, Trento, tel. 0461/21511) and **Club Alpino Italiano** (Piazza Erbe 46, Bolzano, tel. 0471/978172). Local tourist offices can provide information on less-demanding trails.

Skiing The Dolomites offer some of the best skiing in Europe, with some centers equipped for summer skiing. Generally the ski season runs from late November to April, by which time some people prefer to ski in shirtsleeves. The most comprehensive centers are **Cortina d'Ampezzo,** in the heart of the Dolomites to the east of Bolzano, and **Madonna di Campiglio,** west of Trento. These resorts are unashamedly upscale, but for your money you get the extras you expect from world-class centers: miles of interconnecting runs linked by cable cars and lifts, plus skating rinks, heated indoor pools, and lively après-ski activities.

For some of Cortina's charm, but at a fraction of the price, try the **Monte Rota** slopes, accessible from **Dobbiaco.**

Another comparatively inexpensive area is the **Badia Valley,** reached by heading south on S244 from Brunico.

Ortisei (St. Ulrich), just a few miles up the Val Gardena from the Adige Valley, is a popular skiing center, with lifts linking it to the Siusi range.

Stelvio, the focal point of Tour 2, is a year-round skiing center, with summer skiing on many of its runs.

Resorts call their bargain periods *settimane bianche* (white weeks); these are usually in January and February. Pre-Christmas, a period of unpredictable snow conditions, is also a time when bargains can be found in lift prices and accommodations.

Tennis Courts can be found in **Bressanone** (Lungoisarco Sinistro, tel. 0472/22992), **Brunico** (Lungofiume San Giorgio, tel. 0474/20444), **Cortina d'Ampezzo** (Via Sopiazes, tel. 0436/2937), and **Ortisei** (Roncadizza, tel. 0471/76019).

Dining and Lodging

Dining Encompassing the mainly German-ethnic Alto Adige province, the Dolomites region offers culinary adventures combining Italian cuisine with local Tyrolean specialties, which are much like Austrian and central European country cooking. Local delicatessens teem with regional cheeses, pickles, salami, and smoked meats, while local bakeries present a wide selection of crusty dark rolls, caraway rye bread, and the like—perfect for picnics. Local dishes vary from one isolated mountain valley to the next. Don't miss trying *speck*, the local smoked ham. Other specialties include *canederli*, or *knoedel*, a type of dumpling with many variations, served either in broth or with a sauce; hot sauerkraut; ravioli made from rye flour, stuffed with spinach and fried; and apple or pear strudel. And—as befitting a wine-producing region—the local vintages (and fruit brandies) are delicious. In the fall in the South Tyrol, when autumn colors are beautiful on the mountains, it's a tradition to make a tour of the cozy country wine taverns to drink the new wine and eat hot roast chestnuts. This pleasant pastime is known as *toergglen*, from the word *toergl*, meaning winepress.

Highly recommended restaurants are indicated by a star ★.

Category	Cost*
Very Expensive	over 85,000 lire
Expensive	60,000–85,000 lire
Moderate	25,000–60,000 lire
Inexpensive	under 25,000 lire

per person, including house wine, service, and tax

Lodging Accommodations in the Dolomites range from refurbished castles to spic-and-span chalet guest houses, from stately 19th-century hotels to chic modern ski resorts. Even a small village may have scores of lodging places, many of them very inexpensive. Hotel information offices at train stations and tourist offices can help sort through the language problem if you arrive without reservations: Bolzano train station has a 24-hour hotel service, and tourist offices will give you a list of all the hotels in the area, arranged by location and price. We've tried to mention here a few hotels in towns that make good bases for travel, as well as some notable hotels you can find on the road. Please remember that many hotels in ski resorts cater primarily to longer stays at full or half-pension: It's wiser to book ski vacations as a package in advance. And a word of warning: While spring and fall are wonderful times to travel in the region, many mountain hotels are closed for a month or two after Easter and for about six weeks before Christmas.

Highly recommended lodgings are indicated by a star ★.

Category	Cost*
Very Expensive	over 300,000 lire
Expensive	140,000–300,000 lire
Moderate	80,000–140,000 lire
Inexpensive	under 80,000 lire

All prices are for a standard double room for two, including service and 9% IVA (19% for luxury hotels).

Bolzano (Bozen)
Dining

Abramo. Although outside Bolzano's attractive old center, this restaurant is the best in town. Chef Abramo Pantezi offers a variation of nouvelle cuisine in an attractive, elegantly modern setting designed to reflect Renaissance themes. Tables are set with crystal and silver. Specialties include fish dishes, such as *salmone allo champagne* (salmon in champagne sauce) and *tagliarini agli scampi* (thin noodles with shrimp). There's a vegetarian antipasto selection and a daily dietetic menu selected for calorie control. There's also an extensive wine cellar, which features even some top-quality California vintages. *Piazza Gries 16, tel. 0471/280141. Reservations advised. Dress: casual. AE, MC, V. Closed Sun. Moderate.*

Belle Epoque. This is the fashionable restaurant of Park Hotel Laurin. Its furnishings live up to its name and include potted palms and chandeliers. During the summer months, the restaurant expands to include a grill restaurant in the hotel's lush, extensive park. The menu includes Italian and international cuisine, as well as local specialties, and the kitchen prides itself on serving seasonal dishes. In spring, you can sample half a dozen asparagus dishes, for example, while in the fall the menu offers game, including hare and venison served in a variety of ways. *Park Hotel Laurin, via Laurino 4, tel. 0471/980500. No reservations. Jacket and tie advised. AE, DC, MC, V. Closed Sun. Moderate.*

★ **Grifone/Greif.** More than just a routine hotel restaurant, the Grifone is a continuing favorite in its own right, known for fine food and service. It's especially pleasant to eat outside at tables set up on Piazza Walther. The menu, which changes daily, includes various local specialties, such as wine soup *(weinzuppe)*, made with consommé, cream, white wine, and cinnamon; *herrngroestl* (bite-size pieces of veal sautéed with potatoes and onions), served in the pan with cabbage salad; or *spinatspaetzli* (tiny spinach dumplings), served with butter and grated Parmesan cheese. The grilled fish is also good. *Hotel Grifone/Greif. Piazza Walther, tel. 0471/977056. No reservations. Dress: casual. Closed Sun. AE, DC, MC, V. Moderate.*

Kaiserkron. Join the locals at this solid standby in the center of town. You'll find city burghers and their families eating well-prepared Italian, international, and South Tyrolean dishes under a low, vaulted ceiling or outdoors on an attractive summer terrace. The menu is heavy on grilled-meat dishes, but appetizers are interesting—especially the artichoke *(carciofo)* pâté, a delicious dark-green treat. The house wine is excellent. *Piazza della Mostra 1, tel. 0471/970770. No reservations. Dress: casual. AE, DC, MC, V. Closed Sat. evening, Sun. Moderate.*

Flora's. In a medieval tower on Bolzano's market square, this tiny place has been a tavern for centuries, and it has been lovingly restored. There is no menu; you choose from a limited number of typical homey Tyrolean specialties, different every day. They may include *canederli* (savory dumplings) or *schlutzkrapfen* (ravioli). The desserts are homemade, too. The young owner takes pride in a selection of good wines. *Piazza delle Erbe 17, tel. 0471/974086. No reservations. Dress: casual. No credit cards. Closed Sun. Inexpensive–Moderate.*

Batzenhausl. A medieval building in the center of town houses this crowded *stube* (Tyrolean-style drinking hall). It's a popular hangout for the local intellectual set, who hold long, animated conversations over glasses of local wine and tasty local South Tyrolean specialties, such as *herrengröstl* (meat, potatoes, and herbs) and apple pancakes with ice cream. Try the fried Camembert. *Via Andreas Hofer 30, tel. 0471/976183. Reservations advised. Dress: casual. No credit cards. Closed lunch, Tues., and 2 wks in July. Inexpensive.*

Cavallino Bianco/Weisses Roessl. This is another typical Tyrolean stube in the center of town, decorated with dark wood paneling, carved furniture, frescoes, and stuffed hunting trophies. A popular spot for local intellectuals and young people, it's also one of the few Bolzano restaurants that stays open until midnight. Waitresses in modified *trachten* (Tyrolean costume) serve local specialties, such as *kaseknoedel* (light cheese dumplings), *leberknoedel* (liver dumpling) soup, *wurstel*, and *palaschinken* (sweet pancakelike crepes). *Via dei Bottai (Bindergasse) 6, tel. 0471/973267. No reservations. Dress: casual. Closed Sat. evening, Sun. No credit cards. Inexpensive.*

Lodging **Grifone/Greif.** For at least five centuries, there's been a hotel on
★ this spot, perfectly situated in the center of town on pedestrians-only Piazza Walther, looking across to the cathedral. You'll find a friendly atmosphere combined with old-fashioned elegance and a sense of history. The older wings have antique-style Tyrolean furnishings in some rooms, pleasant modern furnishings characterize the newer parts, and some back rooms have balconies looking past the hotel garden to the mountains. Room 45, a beautiful corner room overlooking the square, is especially attractive. The hotel bar and restaurant are popular and provide excellent food and service; both set up tables and chairs right on Piazza Walther in the summer months. *Piazza Walther, tel. 0471/977056, fax 0471/980613. 130 rooms, 110 with bath. Facilities: garage, use of park and pool of Park Hotel Laurino. AE, DC, MC, V. Expensive.*

Park Hotel Laurino/Laurin. This big turn-of-the-century hotel, done in opulent art-nouveau style, is set in a large, shady park, in the middle of town. It's a short walk from the station and the main shopping district and sights. Most rooms have stunning views of the park and the mountains beyond. Some rooms carry through the Belle Epoque decor; others are furnished in a classic modern hotel style. The Belle Epoque restaurant (*see above*), with outdoor buffet in the summer, serves local specialties. *Via Laurino 4, tel. 0471/980500, fax 0471/970953. 110 rooms with bath. Facilities: garage, pool, restaurant, park. AE, DC, MC, V. Expensive.*

★ **Schloss Korb.** It's worth the 5-kilometer (3-mile) drive west from Bolzano to reach this remarkable hotel. It's set in a romantic 13th-century castle with crenellated roof and massive central tower, perched in a park amid vine-covered hills. Much of the ancient decor is preserved, and the public rooms are filled with Tyrolean antiques, elaborate wood carvings, old paintings, and attractive plants. The rooms are comfortably furnished—some tower rooms have the old Romanesque arched windows. *Missiano (5 km. southwest of Bolzano), tel. 0471/636000, fax 0471/636033. 56 rooms with bath. Facilities: sauna, heated indoor and outdoor pools, tennis courts. No credit cards. Closed Nov.–Easter. Expensive.*

Luna/Mondschein. This central yet secluded hotel, built in 1798, has been run by the Mayr family for nearly 200 years. Set in a lovely garden, it provides a tranquil, friendly atmosphere. The rooms are furnished in a comfortable, classic hotel style using wood paneling throughout. Some rooms overlooking the garden have balconies, but even the rooms overlooking the garage have good views of the mountains. The two restaurants include a typical Tyrolean *weinstube* that serves inexpensive local specialties in a cozy, convivial setting. *Via Piave 15, tel. 0471/975642, fax 0471/975577. 75 rooms with bath. Facilities: private garage, 2 restaurants, garden. DC, MC, V. Moderate.*

Bressanone (Brixen)
Dining

Elefante. The fine restaurant of the hotel of the same name is one of the region's best, serving regional and international dishes in a centuries-old inn. One dining room is furnished with antique elegance; another offers the cozy intimacy of a typical local stube. Specialties include *gnocchi* (dumplings) with cheese, tortellini stuffed with spinach and ricotta, and local Isarco River Valley trout. *Via Rio Bianco 4, tel. 0472/32750. Reservations advised. Jacket and tie required in the evening. V. Closed Mon. (except for hotel guests), Nov. 15–Dec. 28, Jan. 10–Feb. 28. Expensive.*

Fink. Don't be discouraged by the name: This popular restaurant, under the arcades in the pedestrians-only center of town, has a friendly staff and features a good-value daily set menu. It has a rustic ambience, with lots of wood paneling, and serves international as well as hearty Tyrolean specialties. Try the *carré di maiale gratinato* (pork roasted with cheese and served with cabbage and potatoes) or the *castrato alla paesana*, a kind of beef stew. *Via Portici Minori 4, tel. 0472/34883. Reservations advised. Dress: casual. Closed Thurs. and June. V. Inexpensive–Moderate.*

Lodging

Dominik. Well equipped and modern, this hotel is centrally located but has a quiet garden and dining terrace. Most doubles are spacious and modern, with comfortable armchairs, ample baths, and balconies. The superior restaurant features local trout (in season). *Via Terzo di Sotto 13, tel. 0472/30144, fax 0472/36554. 29 rooms with bath. Facilities: indoor pool, park, garage, sauna. AE, MC, V. Closed Nov. 4–Easter. Expensive.*

★ **Elefante.** One of the best and most famous hotels in the region, this cozy inn is located in a historic 15th-century building: There's been a hotel on the site for more than 500 years. The hotel takes its name from an incident in 1550, when King John of Portugal stopped here for a few days while leading an elephant over the Alps as a present for Austria's Emperor Ferdinand. Each room is different, and many are decorated with antiques and paintings. The hotel is centrally located but is set in a large park with a swimming pool. Also in the park is the separate Villa Marzari, with 14 rooms. *Via Rio Bianco 4, tel. 0472/32750, fax 0472/36579. 44 rooms with bath. Facilities: pool, park. V. Closed Nov. 15–Dec. 28, Jan. 10–Feb. 28. Expensive.*

Brunico (Bruneck)
Lodging

Andreas Hofer. There's a Tyrolean feel to this comfortable hotel set in a large garden outside the center of town. Traditional chalet-style terraces and balconies overlook the Pusteria Valley. The rooms have modern furnishings, and there are several rooms with special features for the handicapped. The hotel restaurant is recommended. *Campo Tures 1, tel. 0474/31469, fax 0474/31283. 54 rooms with bath. Facilities: garden, restaurant, sauna, solarium. MC, V. Closed 2 weeks in May, Nov. 25–Dec. 12. Inexpensive–Moderate.*

Post. The best choice for lodging in the center of town is this homey old traditional hotel, recommended by locals, who also like its restaurant, café, and pastry shop. It has its own parking, which is important because of the pedestrians-only rules in effect throughout much of the central area. *Via Bastioni 9, tel. 0474/85127. 60 rooms, 50 with bath. No credit cards. Closed Nov. Inexpensive.*

Cortina d'Ampezzo
Dining

De la Poste. The exclusive restaurants of the hotel on Cortina's main square have a casually chic clientele and a lively atmosphere. There's an elegant main restaurant where you can dine on soufflés and nouvelle cuisine dishes (every Friday fresh fish is served) in a high-ceiling dining room with three big chandeliers. There's also a more informal grill room with wood paneling and the family pewter collection. In ski season it's always crowded. *Piazza Roma 14, tel. 0436/4271. Reservations required. Jacket and tie in the evening in both restaurants. AE, DC. Moderate–Expensive.*

★ **Cristallo.** The Hotel Cristallo has two good restaurants. The elegant main restaurant serves international and Italian dishes, such as *tagliolini primavera* (thin noodles in vegetable sauce), *risotto di funghi* (mushroom risotto), *spaghetti Ampezzano* (spaghetti the local Ampezzo valley way, made with smoked speck ham), and game meats. There is also the Monkey, a lively hangout for the après-ski crowd, where you can drink beer and nibble on local dishes, such as speck, salami, and *fonduta* (fondue), in a relaxed Tyrolean *bierkeller* (beer hall) atmosphere. *Via R. Menardi 42, tel. 0436/4281. No reservations. Dress: jacket and tie at main restaurant; casual for the Monkey. AE, DC, MC, V. Moderate.*

Fanes. This restaurant in the Hotel Fanes outside town serves homey food in rustic elegance. Game is a specialty, with dishes including *camoscio* (chamois) cooked several ways and *capriolo in salmi con polenta* (roe deer stewed in red wine and served with polenta). *Via Roma 136, tel. 0436/3427. Reservations advised. Dress: casual. AE, MC, DC, V. Closed Mon. Moderate.*

Lodging

Europa. This traditional mountain hotel, in the center of town, has the warm family-style atmosphere typical of a chalet. Antiques including an antique wood stove decorate the interior. A roaring fire enlivens the bar. There's also a nightclub, disco, and grill room. *Corso Italia 207, tel. 0436/3221, fax 0436/*

868204. 54 rooms with bath. AE, DC, MC, V. Closed mid-Oct.–mid-Dec. Very Expensive.

Miramonti. This imposing and luxurious hotel, nearly a century old, has a magnificent mountain valley location about .6 kilometer (1 mile) south of town. There's a touch of Old World formality in keeping with the Imperial Austrian design. The interior decor carries the period style throughout; most of the rooms have balconies and were entirely redecorated in 1992. There's a restaurant, and in the cozy bar there's always a roaring fire in the hearth. *Localita Pezzie 103, tel. 0436/4201, fax 0436/867019. 106 rooms with bath (also 7 suites and 5 junior suites). Facilities: shuttle bus every 15 min to town, pool, tennis courts, golf course, fitness center with sauna, massage, inhalation treatment. AE, DC, MC, V. Closed Easter–June 30, Sept. 15–Nov. 30. Very Expensive.*

Cristallo. The CIGA chain owns this large, imposing century-old hotel, built around the same time as the Miramonti and set in a big park in the forest a half mile southeast of town. There's lots of wood paneling, and many of the spacious, comfortable rooms have fancy terraces or wrought-iron balconies which offer fine views. The restaurant is good and the stube is especially cozy (*see above*). Entertainment includes a nightclub and piano bar. *Via R. Menardi 42, tel. 0436/4281, fax 0436/868058. 81 rooms with bath. Facilities: pool, tennis courts, 2 restaurants, nightclub, piano bar. AE, DC, MC, V. Closed Easter–June, Sept–Dec. 19. Expensive (pension or half-pension only).*

De la Poste. Skiers who want to be seen keep returning to this lively hotel on the main square in a pedestrian zone. It's been under the same family management since 1826, and the furnishings feature antiques in characteristic Dolomite style. Almost all rooms have wooden terraces. The hotel's main terrace bar, on the square, is always crowded and is one of Cortina's social centers. *Piazza Roma 62, tel. 0436/4271, fax 0436/868435. 83 rooms with bath. Facilities: bar, restaurant, safe in each room. AE, DC. Closed Oct. 20–Dec. 19. Expensive.*

Fanes. If you find Cortina's sophistication overbearing, get away from it all in this rustic-style hotel, which is set in a garden in the countryside at the southern outskirts of town. Many rooms have wooden balconies with fine views of the Campo range, and there's lots of wooden decor. Room rates are for full- or half-board only. *Via Roma 136, tel. 0436/3427, fax 0436/5027. 25 rooms with bath. AE, DC, MC, V. Closed Easter–June, Nov. 5–Dec. 21. Moderate.*

Dobbiaco (Toblach)
Lodging

Villa Santer. Take the Cortina Road to the mountains at the southern edge of town to reach this modern hotel. It's built and furnished in traditional Tyrolean style, with lots of wooden decoration and a balcony in every room. The restaurant and bar are dedicated to local specialties; there's more local color at the Tyrolean party held for guests once a week. *Via Alemagna 4, tel. 0474/72142, fax 0474/72797. 47 rooms with bath. Facilities: pool, sauna, bar, restaurant. MC, V. Closed Easter–May 18, Oct. 15–Dec. 18. Moderate.*

★ **Alpino Monte Rota Alpengasthof Ratsberg.** To reach this hotel, you take the 10-minute cable car ride to Monte Rota. It is in traditional style, with the timeless look of local chalets. Front rooms have stunning mountain views from balconies, while those in the back look out over the dense mountain forest. You needn't take the cable car back down for sustenance: The Alpino has a good restaurant (which serves even some low-calorie dishes), a bar, and a Tyrolean-style stube. *Monte Rota 10, tel. 0474/72213, fax 0474/72916. 25 rooms with bath. Facilities: pool, sauna, restaurant, bar, lounge. MC, V. Closed Easter–May 15, Sept. 20–Dec. 20. Inexpensive–Moderate.*

Cristallo. Wood beams and paneling lend an Old Tyrolean tone to this small hotel set in a garden just outside town. The architecture and furnishings reflect the local preference for combining traditional chalet design with functional, but comfortable, modern furniture. Most rooms enjoy the panoramic view of the local valley, but some of the best rooms have terraces. Guests relax in the cozy and informal stube. *Viale Roma 11, tel. 0474/72138, fax 0474/72755. 30 rooms with bath. Facilities: pool, bar, restaurant. MC, V. Closed Easter–May 15, mid-Oct.–mid-Dec. Inexpensive–Moderate.*

Madonna di Campiglio
Lodging
★

Golf. You'll have to make your way up to Campo Carlo Magno, the famous pass just north of town, to reach this grand hotel, which is the former summer residence of Austrian Hapsburg Emperor Franz Joseph. A modern wing has been added on to the more-than-a-century-old original structure, but Old World charm remains: Rooms 114 and 214 are still decorated in the old imperial style. Other rooms are also elegantly maintained, and throughout the hotel are verandas, Persian carpets, and bay windows. The hotel is practically on the fairway of a golf course that draws a sophisticated summer crowd. There's a restaurant and piano bar. *Campo Carlo Magno, tel. 0465/41003, fax 0465/40294. 120 rooms (plus 4 suites) with bath. Facilities: golf course, solarium, game room, shuttle bus to town. AE, DC, MC, V. Closed Apr.–June, Sept.–Nov. Very Expensive.*

Savoia Palace. A major renovation in 1988 strengthened the Savoia Palace's reputation as the premier hotel in the center of this fashionable ski resort. The owners knew enough not to tamper with the decor—mountain-style furnishings with lots of carved wood—or the intimate atmosphere of the reception rooms. Two fireplaces blaze away in the bar, where guests recall the day's exploits on the ski slopes. The elegant restaurant serves a mixture of local specialties and hearty dishes drawing on Italian and Austrian influences. Guests stay on full- or half-board terms only. *Via Dolomiti di Brenta, tel. 0465/41004, fax 0465/40549. 55 rooms with bath. Facilities: bar, restaurant. AE, DC. Closed Easter–June, Sept.–Nov. Very Expensive.*

Grifone. A comfortable hotel that catches the sun, the Grifone has distinctive wood paneling on the outside, around flower-decorated terraces, and rooms have views of the forested slopes. The restaurant serves home cooking as well as international dishes. *Via Vallesinella 7, tel. 0465/42002, fax 0465/40540. 60 rooms with bath. Facilities: restaurant, bar, solarium. AE, MC, V. Closed Apr. 15–June 30, Sept. 15–Dec. 4. Expensive.*

Merano (Meran)
Dining
★

Tiffany Grill/Schloss Maur. Stained-glass lamps and wood paneling create a warm art-nouveau effect in these two restaurants of the Hotel Palace. The main restaurant is the height of elegance, with huge marble columns, high ceilings, and crystal chandeliers. In the summer, meals are served outdoors on the terrace overlooking the lovely park. The emphasis in both is on Italian and international cuisine, such as house specialty *spaghetti Schloss Maur* (spaghetti served with a sauce of zucchini, sage, and green pepper) or roast saddle of lamb and lobster. The Tiffany Grill, which offers gourmet menus, is open only in the evening. *Hotel Palace. Via Cavour 2/4, tel. 0473/211300.*

Reservations required. Jacket and tie required. AE, DC, MC, V. Closed Sun. and July. Expensive.

Andrea. This elegant showcase for fine cuisine and service is just off Merano's main shopping street, via Portici, and right by a cable car station. In an atmosphere of relaxed modern elegance, enlivened by wood paneling and lots of green plants, you can dine on eye-pleasing specialties of both local and international cuisine, such as *risotto alle erbe* (with herbs), *filetto di vitello con salsa di alloro* (veal fillet with bay leaf sauce), or *canederli di ricotta su purea di frutta mista* (ricotta dumplings served with pureed fruit). A set menu (about 90,000 lire) offers a complete five-course dinner, including wines—and the wine cellar is also excellent. *Via Galilei 44, tel. 0473/37400. Reservations required. Jacket and tie advised. AE, DC, MC, V. Closed Mon. and 2 weeks in Feb. Moderate–Expensive.*

Flora. There's room for only about 20 diners in this intimate candlelit restaurant under the historic arched arcades of Merano's ancient center. Chef Louis Oberstolz describes his imaginative cooking as "fresh, spontaneous, and natural, using only the finest ingredients." He offers a seven-course set menu. Among the specialties are *quaglia ripiena con fegato d'oca grasso* (boned quail stuffed with foie gras), an antipasto of various types of fish, and *pasta nera con seppiolini* (pasta made with cuttlefish ink and served with a sauce of tiny cuttlefish). *Via Portici 75, tel. 0473/31484. Reservations required. Dress: casual. AE, DC, MC, V. Closed at lunch and Sun. and mid-Jan.–mid-Feb. Moderate.*

Terlano Putz. This local favorite is an old rustic stube under the arcades of Merano's old town. The wide menu focuses on seasonal dishes and offers Tyrolean specialties. Try *zuppa al vino bianco* (soup with white wine); crepes with *radicchio;* or the various risottos, including one made with asparagus in the spring, and with Barolo wine later in the year. *Via Portici 231, tel. 0473/35571. Reservations advised. Dress: casual. No credit cards. Closed Wed. and mid-Feb.–mid-Mar. Inexpensive–Moderate.*

Lodging
★ **Palace Hotel.** Merano's grandest hotel is an opulent turn-of-the-century establishment providing top service and comfort. It is set in an extensive garden with an indoor-outdoor pool, and all rooms on the south side have balconies overlooking the park. The rooms are spacious, decorated in a stately modern classic design in restful colors. The public rooms are attractive and comfortable—there's a new nonsmoking lounge—with Art Nouveau touches, Tiffany glass, marble pillars, and high ceilings. The hotel is a spa center equipped with an impressive health unit, featuring all sorts of baths, massages, mud treatments, and other cures. There is a lovely fountain serving thermal Merano water. *Via Cavour 2/4, tel. 0473/211300, fax 0473/34181. 120 rooms with bath. Facilities: indoor-outdoor pool, spa center, bar, restaurant, garden. AE, DC, MC, V. Closed Jan.–Feb. Very Expensive.*

Castel Freiburg. Set in a wooded valley about 3 kilometers (5 mi) south of town, Castel Freiburg is a romantic hideaway where guests feel pampered and welcome. It's set in a converted 14th-century castle, complete with tower, and is surrounded by its own park, stretching up to the forest. Reception rooms are full of antiques, and the guest rooms are individually furnished with color-coordinated fabrics and decorations. Although only some have terraces, all the rooms have good views of the mountains. A combination of an excellent restaurant and extensive sports facilities means that many guests remain on the premises for days on end. *Via Monte Franco, tel. 0473/ 244196, fax 0473/244488. 38 rooms with bath. Facilities: indoor and outdoor pools, children's playroom, bar, restaurant. AE, DC, MC, V. Closed Nov. 5–Apr. 15. Expensive.*

Schloss Rundegg. A romantic converted 12th-century castle with an original tower, Schloss Rundegg is furnished with antiques and rich fittings, such as Persian carpets. It's set in a park and functions as a fully equipped thermal spa. The restaurant even provides special dietetic eating for weight loss and other cures. Room 32, in the tower, has an interior staircase and 360-degree views. *Via Scena 2, tel. 0473/34100, fax 0473/ 37200. 30 rooms with bath. Facilities: pool, gym, sauna, spa, bar, restaurant. AE, DC, MC, V. Closed Jan. 6–31. Expensive.*

Bristol Hotel. This big 1950s modern-style hotel in the center of town has an open-air swimming pool on its roof, and on a sunny summer day, what could be more pleasant than floating in the pool and gazing up at the mountains surrounding the town? The rooms and public halls are spacious and decorated in a classic modern style enriched by authentic Venetian touches, such as Murano glass mirrors and light fixtures. Most rooms have a terrace. The hotel has a discotheque, and there is also a large and well-appointed spa center, utilizing Merano's thermal water. Baths, sauna, massage, and other health treatments are offered. *Via O. Huber 14, tel. 0473/49500, fax 0473/49299. 138 rooms with bath. Facilities: garden, pool, bar, restaurant, spa center. AE, DC, MC, V. Closed Nov.–Feb. Moderate–Expensive.*

Castel Labers. Located on a hilltop amid forested slopes about 3 kilometers (1.8 miles) east of Merano's center, this hotel has a view of the town's gabled roofs and gardens. Actually a castle set in its own well-kept grounds, its red-tiled gables, towers and turrets give it an unmistakably Tyrolean look, heightened on the interior by dark ceiling beams, painted fresco decorations, and even crossed halberds on the walls. The hospitable Stapf-Neubert family owns the hotel and takes an active part in its management. In summer guests dine outdoors on the terrace and can enjoy a game of tennis or a dip in the hotel pool. *Via Labers 25, tel. 0473/34484, fax 0473/34146. 32 rooms with bath. Facilities: Garden, tennis court, pool, restaurant, AE, DC, MC, V. Closed Nov.–Mar. Moderate.*

Minerva. Recommended by locals as a good spot for budget travelers, this is another turn-of-the-century hotel, built in 1909 and furnished in traditional period style. Set in a garden, it's about 10 minutes by foot from the town center, near several of the luxury hotels. Almost all rooms have balconies with views of the mountains. Full-board rates are economical. *Via Cavour 95, tel. 0473/36712. 44 rooms with bath. Facilities: restaurant, pool. AE, DC. Closed Nov.–Mar., but reopens for 1 week Dec. 24–Jan.1. Moderate.*

Naturno (Naturns)
Lodging

Feldhof. You can savor the full splendor of the Venosta Valley, with its meadows and forests, from most rooms in this small, friendly hotel. The Feldhof is a modern hotel built in the traditional style and furnished in rustic elegance with antique furniture and lots of flowers. All rooms have a private safe, and most have balconies looking out over the hotel garden. The restaurant is for guests only. *Via Municipio 4, tel. 0473/87264, fax*

0473/87263. 27 rooms with bath. Facilities: pool, sauna, solarium, thermal treatment center. No credit cards. Closed Nov. 5–Mar. 20. Moderate–Expensive.

Ortisei (St. Ulrich)
Lodging

Aquila/Adler. Since 1810 there has always been a Hotel Aquila under the same family management in this popular Val Gardena sports center. Today it is regarded as one of the best in the valley. Set in a large park, the original building has been enlarged and renovated several times in the intervening 180 years, but retains a lot of the old atmosphere, looking something like a turreted castle. The Tyrolean character is carried through in special Tyrolean night parties held once a week for guests. The rooms are spacious, and many have balconies or little terraces; some are suitable for disabled persons. *Via Rezia 7, tel. 0471/796203, fax 0471/796210. 85 rooms, most with bath. Facilities: pool, sauna, solarium, massage, tennis courts, fitness and beauty center, bar, restaurant. DC, MC, V. Closed Easter–June 1, mid-Oct.–mid-Nov. Expensive.*

Trento
Dining

Accademia. The excellent restaurant of the Accademia hotel serves innovative Italian nouvelle cuisine in a smartly restored ancient building just off Piazza del Duomo. Specialties include *sformato di grana Trentino* (a type of cheese soufflé), *gnocchetti di ricotta ai pinoli ed uvetta* (ricotta dumplings with pine nuts and raisins), and *filetto di trota salomonata al vino* (trout fillets in wine sauce). *Vicolo Colico 4/6, tel. 0461/981580. Reservations required. Jacket and tie required. AE, DC, V. Closed Mon. Moderate.*

★ **Alla Mora.** What was once an unpretentious trattoria is now an attractive restaurant with a touch of class and a luminous, airy courtyard for outdoor dining under market umbrellas. The menu offers something for all tastes, including such local specialties as *finferle con polenta* (wild mushrooms with polenta and local cheese) and a classic *pasta e fagioli* (pasta and bean soup); salad plates and seafood also are featured. *Via Roggia Grande 8, tel. 0461/984675. Reservations advised, especially for indoor dining. Dress: casual. No credit cards. Closed Mon. Moderate.*

Chiesa. Located near the castle in a building dating back to about 1400, Chiesa is furnished with antiques and serves interesting dishes, some from centuries-old recipes. The *taglieri di Bernardo Cles*, for example, is coin-shaped pasta in a sauce of veal and lettuce—but no tomatoes: When the recipe was devised, tomatoes were not yet eaten in Italy. Other specialties include *risotto alle mele* (risotto with apples), a hearty minestrone soup made of vegetables and barley, and the *Tonco de Pontesel*—a stew of mixed meat served with polenta, made according to a 15th-century recipe. *Via San Marco 64, tel. 0461/238766. Reservations advised. Jacket and tie required. AE, DC, MC, V. Closed Sun, Wed. evening, Aug. 15–31. Moderate.*

Lodging

Accademia. This friendly character-filled hotel occupies an ancient house in the historic center of Trento, close to Piazza del Duomo. The public rooms retain the ancient vaulting, but the bedrooms, renovated five years ago, are modern and comfortably equipped. There's a good restaurant and a courtyard garden. *Vicolo Colico 4/6, tel. 0461/233600, fax 0461/230174. 43 rooms with bath. Facilities: bar, restaurant, garden. AE, DC, MC, V. Expensive.*

The Arts and Nightlife

The Arts

Essentially rural in character, the Dolomites offer a rich selection of folk festivals, harvest fairs, and religious celebrations. Chief among these is Trento's week-long festival of San Vigilio (the last week of June), when marching bands and choirs in costumes perform in the streets and squares of the heart of the city. The other major towns have similar festivals, but equally enjoyable are the more informal and low-key celebrations in the villages of the many valleys, sometimes amounting to nothing more than excuses for hard-working mountain farmers to get together for some local wine and song.

Folk Festivals   **Bolzano.** Spring is heralded each May with large flower markets and with spin-off events, including concerts and folklore and art exhibits. Later, on August 24, is the Bartolomeo Horse Fair on Renon Mountain just northeast of the town. Hundreds of farmers converge for a day of serious trading and frivolous merriment.

Brunico. January 22 sees a dogsled race; locals turn up with flasks of hot mulled wine to back their favorites.

Merano. Local farmers put their horses to the test in the highly charged horse race that is the highlight of Easter Monday. On the second Sunday of October, Merano has a Grape Festival, with parades (complete with townspeople in costumes, floats, and bands) and wine tastings.

Ortisei. The Val Gardena comes alive with a parade of horse-drawn sleighs on January 1.

Concerts   **Bolzano** hosts the International Busoni Piano competition in late August. Concerts and recitals are held in halls and churches. Internationally acclaimed performers usually head the panel of judges.

Film   **Trento** plays host each May to a month-long festival of films devoted to mountains and mountaineering.

Nightlife

The usual form of nightlife in this mountain region is to soak up the atmosphere in a Tyrolean-style stube, often the core of a hotel's entertainment or the focal point of an entire village. Wood-paneled and stocked with a range of local beers and wines, these establishments reflect the synthesis of Austrian and Italian cultures in the Dolomites. Beer is matched by wine, schnitzel by pasta, and zither-accompanied Austrian folk songs by the occasional Verdi aria. More-sophisticated options are limited to the two chic ski resorts, Madonna di Campiglio and Cortina d'Ampezzo.

Discos   **Cortina d'Ampezzo.** You can expect to mingle with the designer-clothing set at the VIP disco at the hotel Europa (*see* Dining and Lodging, *above*); nonguests are welcome, but don't expect to spend less than 35,000 lire.

Merano. The **Bristol Hotel** (*see* Dining and Lodging, *above*) is popular with locals as well as visitors.

Nightclubs **Cortina d'Ampezzo.** The **Cristallo** hotel (*see* Dining and Lodging, *above*) has a nightclub that is open to nonguests.

12 Emilia-Romagna

Bologna to Rimini along the Via Emilia

Emilia-Romagna owes its beginnings to a road. In 187 BC the Romans laid out the Via Aemelia, a long highway running straight from the Adriatic port of Rimini to the central garrison town of Piacenza, and it was along this central spine that the primary towns of the region developed. The old Roman road still exists, and a modern superhighway (A14 and A1) runs parallel to it. Most of the exploring in this chapter will be along either the old road or its modern counterpart.

Despite the unifying factor of the Via Emilia (which the highway is now called), the region has had a fragmented history. The eastern portion of the region, roughly the area from the city of Faenza to the coast, known as Romagna, has looked first to the east, and then to Rome, for art, political power, and, some say, national character. The western portion, Emilia, from Bologna to Piacenza, had a more northern, rather dour, sense of self-government and dissent. Italians say that in Romagna a stranger will be offered a glass of wine; in Emilia, a glass of water—if anything at all.

The principal city of the region is Bologna. It was founded by the Etruscans, but eventually came under the influence of the Roman Empire. The Romans established a garrison there, renaming the old Etruscan settlement Bononia, the Bologna of today.

It was after the fall of Rome that the region began its fragmentation. Romagna, centered in Ravenna, was ruled from Constantinople. Ravenna eventually became capital of the empire in the West, in the 5th century, passing to papal rule in the 8th century. The city today, however, is still filled with reminders of two centuries of Byzantine rule.

The other cities of the region, from the Middle Ages on, became the fiefs of important noble families—the Este in Ferrara and Modena, the Pallavicini in Piacenza, the Bentivoglio in Bologna, and the Malatesta in Rimini. Today all these cities bear the marks of their noble patrons. When in the 16th century the papacy managed to exert its power over the entire region, some of these cities were divided among the families of the reigning popes—hence the stamp of the Farnese family on Parma, Piacenza, and Ferrara.

The region was one of the first to join the quest for a unified Italy in the 19th century, pledging itself to the king of Italy and the forces of Garibaldi in the 1840s. Loyalty to the crown did not last long, however. The Italian socialist movement was born in the region, and throughout Italy Emilia-Romagna has been known for rebellion and dissent. Benito Mussolini was born here, although, in keeping with the political atmosphere of his home state, he was a firebrand socialist during the early part of his career. Despite being the birthplace of Il Duce, Emilia-Romagna did not take to fascism: It was in this region that the antifascist resistance was born, and during the war the region suffered terribly at the hands of the Fascists and the Nazis.

Despite a long history of bloodletting, turmoil, and rebellion, the arts—both decorative and culinary—have always flourished in Emilia-Romagna. The great families financed painters, sculptors, and writers (Dante found a haven in Ravenna after being expelled from his native Florence). In modern times, Emilia-Romagna has given to the arts famous sons like painter Giorgio Morandi, author Giorgio Bassani (author of *Garden of the Finzi-Continis*), filmmaker Federico Fellini, and tenor Luciano Pavarotti.

Gourmets the world over would argue that Emilia-Romagna's greatest contribution to mankind has been gastronomic. Bologna is the acknowledged leading city of Italian cuisine. It is home to two of the most famous Italian delicacies—foods that, sadly, have been poorly treated outside their native city. What the world calls "baloney" the Bolognese call *mortadella*, a robust pork sausage spiced with whole peppercorns (if there aren't peppercorns in it, then it isn't mortadella), which bears no resemblance to the stuff sliced at the typical U.S. deli counter. The other famous dish is *spaghetti al ragu*, known to the world as *spaghetti Bolognese*. The spaghetti with meat sauce dished around the world is a far cry from the real thing. In Bologna a *ragu* sauce is made with onions, carrots, minced pork and veal, butter, and fresh tomatoes, and is cooked for five or six hours in a special earthen pot. It is, in a word, exquisite. Few dining experiences in Italy can match the satisfaction of a properly cooked ragu.

Bologna is also the home of tortellini, lasagna, and *vitello alla Bolognese*, a veal cutlet smothered with prosciutto and Parmesan cheese. The rest of the province has made substantial contributions to the kitchen. Parma is the home of Parma ham and the most famous of all Italian cheeses, Parmesan. Modena is the birthplace of *zampone* (stuffed pigs' feet, which tastes much better than it sounds) and *aceto balsamico*, the jet-black, fragrant herb vinegar that is now a must on the shelves of any self-respecting gourmet.

Essential Information

Important Addresses and Numbers

Tourist Information **Bologna** (Via Marconi 45, tel. 051/237413; Gugliemo Marconi airport, tel. 051/381732 railway station, tel. 051/246541; Piazza Maggiore 6, 1d, tel. 051/239–660).
Ferrara (Piazza Municipio 19, tel. 0532/209370 or 419269).
Modena (Via Scudari 30, tel. 059/222–482).
Parma (Piazza Duomo 5, tel. 0521/234735).
Piacenza (Piazzetta Mercanti 10, tel. 0523/29324).
Ravenna (Via Salara 8, tel. 0544/35404).
Rimini (Piazzale Cesare Battisti, railway station, tel. 0541/51480; Piazzale Independenza, waterfront, tel. 0541/51101).

Travel Agencies **Bologna** (American Express, Via Marconi 47, tel. 051/235783 or 051/267600).
Rimini (American Express, Viale Vespucci 127, tel. 0341/23–779).

Emergencies **Police**, tel. 112. **Ambulance**, tel. 113. **Doctors and Dentists**, tel. 113. **Late-Night Pharmacies**, tel. 051/192 for information.

Arriving and Departing by Plane

Bologna is an important business and convention center and is therefore served by air routes that link it with other Italian cities, as well as by direct flights to European capitals. The airport, Bologna–Borgo Panigale, is 7 kilometers (4 miles) from town. Bus service connects it with a downtown air terminal at the central railway station in Bologna proper. For air-traffic information call 051/311578.

519 M.P.H.

190 M.P.H.

S:HS 7469

75 M.P.H.

0 M.P.H.

WE LET YOU SEE EUROPE AT YOUR OWN PACE.

Regardless of your personal speed limits, Rail Europe offers everything to get you over, around and through anywhere you want in Europe. For more information, call your travel agent or **1-800-4-EURAIL.**

Rail Europe

Arriving and Departing by Train

Bologna is an important rail hub for the entire northern part of Italy and has frequent, fast train service to Rome, Milan, Florence, and Venice. For information about train departures call 051/246490.

Getting Around

By Car The Via Emilia runs through the heart of the region. It is a straight, modern low-lying road, the length of which can be traveled in a few hours. Ferrara, Ravenna, and the tiny Republic of San Marino are joined to it by good modern highways.

By Train The railway follows the Via Emilia, and all the cities mentioned here (except San Marino) can be reached by train.

By Bus Private bus service links all the cities of Emilia-Romagna, with Bologna being the central hub. The Autostazione (bus terminal) is in Piazza XX Settembre, at the top of Via dell' Indipendenza; for information call 051/248374. City-run bus routes connect major towns with smaller villages and hamlets in the district, but routes are roundabout, and schedules vary from place to place.

Exploring Emilia-Romagna

A tour through Emilia-Romagna has something for everyone: great art, stirring history, fabulous food—even a day at the beach at the seaside resort of Rimini. The best way to see the region is to begin your tour in the west, in Piacenza, and then to proceed east along the Via Emilia to the sea. The major towns are either on that route or just off it, the longest detours being no more than 30 or 40 miles off the main road.

Highlights for First-time Visitors

Mosaics in church of San Vitale, Ravenna (Tour 2: Rimini, Ravenna, and Ferrara).

Tomb of Galla Placidia, Ravenna (Tour 2: Rimini, Ravenna, and Ferrara).

Tempio Malatestiano, Rimini (Tour 2: Rimini, Ravenna, and Ferrara).

Castello Estense, Ferrara (Tour 2: Rimini, Ravenna, and Ferrara).

Piazza del Duomo (including the Duomo, the Baptistery, and the church of San Giovanni), Parma (Tour 1: From Piacenza to the Rubicon).

Farnese Theater and Palazzo della Pilotta, Parma (Tour 1: From Piacenza to the Rubicon).

Tour 1: From Piacenza to the Rubicon

Numbers in the margin correspond to points of interest on the Emilia-Romagna map.

1 The city of **Piacenza** has always been associated with industry and commerce. Its position on the river Po has made it an im-

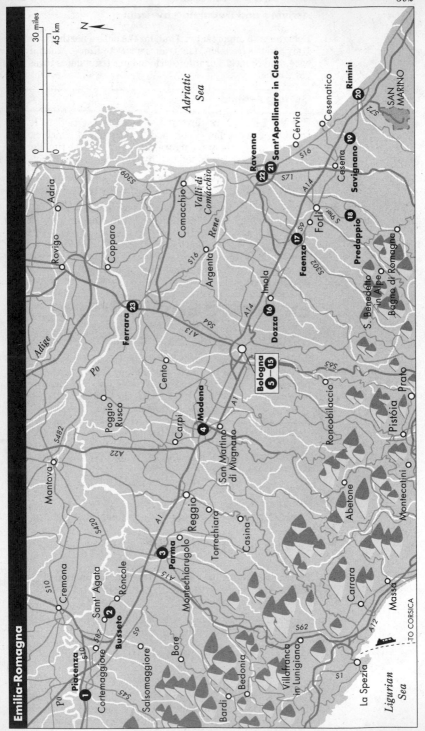

Emilia-Romagna

portant inland port since the earliest times—the Etruscans, then the Romans, had thriving settlements on this site. As you approach the city today, you could be forgiven for thinking that it holds little of interest. Piacenza is surrounded by ugly industrial suburbs (with a particularly unlovely oil and gas refinery), but these enclose a delightfully unspoiled medieval downtown.

The heart of the city is the **Piazza dei Cavalli** (Square of Horses), dominated by the massive Palazzo del Comune, a severe turreted and crenellated Gothic building of the 13th century. It was the seat of town government during those times when Piacenza was not under the iron fist of a ruling family. The equestrian statues from which the Piazza dei Cavalli takes its name are images of members of the last greatest of the rulers of Piacenza. The statue on the right is Ranuccio Farnese; on the left is his father, Alessandro Farnese. Alessandro was a beloved ruler, enlightened and fair; Ranuccio, his successor, was less successful. Both statues are the work of Francesco Mochi, a master sculptor of the Baroque period.

Walk out of the piazza on Via XX Settembre, which leads to Piacenza's impressive **cathedral,** a rather grim-looking building dating from the mid-12th century. Attached to the massive bell tower is a *gabbia* (iron cage), where evildoers were exposed naked to the scorn (and missiles) of the crowd in the marketplace below. The interior of the cathedral is an odd mixture of Gothic and Baroque. Fine medieval stonework decorates the pillars and the crypt, and there are extravagant frescoes by 17th-century artist Guercino in the dome of the cupola. *Open daily 7–noon, 4–7.*

The **Museo Civico,** the city-owned collection of Piacenzan art and antiquities, is housed in the vast Palazzo Farnese, which was started by the ruling family in 1558 but never completed. The museum was closed for many years but, after the restoration and the reordering of the collections, it is again open to the public. The highlight of this rather eclectic collection is the Etruscan Fegato di Piacenza, a bronze tablet in the shape of a *fegato* (liver), with the symbols of the gods of good and ill fortune marked on it. By comparing this master "liver" with one taken from the body of a freshly slaughtered sacrifice, the priests could predict the future. On a more humanistic note, the collection also contains a painting by Botticelli, the *Madonna with St. John the Baptist,* and a series of Roman bronzes and mosaics. There is also a collection of carriages, arms and armor, and other paraphernalia owned by the Farnese, giving a good idea of the splendor of that powerful family. *Piazza Cittadella. Admission: 3,500 lire. Open Tues., Wed., Fri., 9–12:30, Thurs. 9–12:30 and 3:30–5:30, Sat. 9–12:30 and 3–6, Sun. 9:30–noon and 3:30–6:30.*

The area between Piacenza and Parma, 62 kilometers (37 mi) away, is opera country. In the quiet backwater towns north of the Via Emilia, the great Italian opera composer Giuseppe Verdi lived and worked. The composer of *Aida, Rigoletto, La Traviata,* and *Otello* was born in a very simple farmhouse in the hamlet of Ròncole and built the grand villa of **Sant'Agata** in the nearby town of **Busseto** when he had become world famous.

If you are driving from Piacenza, take Route A10 northeast for Cremona, but turn off it just a few miles out of Piacenza and follow the signs for Route 587 to the town of Cortemaggiore.

From Cortemaggiore, turn onto a smaller rural road (not numbered) and follow the signs for Busseto, some 10 kilometers (6 miles) away. If you plan to visit all the area's Verdi's sights, invest in a 5,000-lire ticket valid for Villa Pallavicino, Palazzo Orlandi, Teatro Verdi, and Verdi's birthplace (but not Villa Sant'Agata).

In Busseto you can visit the **Villa Pallavicino,** where Verdi worked and lived with his mistress (later wife), Giuseppina Strepponi. There is a small Verdi museum here that displays such relics of the maestro as his piano, scores, composition books, walking sticks, and other bits of memorabilia. *Admission: 2,500 lire. Open Apr.–Sept., Tues.–Sun. 9:30–12:30 and 3–7; Oct.–Mar., Tues.–Sun. 9:30–noon and 2:30–5.*

In the center of town is the lovely **Teatro Verdi,** dedicated, as one may expect, to the works of the hamlet's famous son. Currently under restoration, it is a well-preserved 19th-century-style theater, and it's worth a look to get a feel for a place where Verdi worked. *Admission: 2,500 lire. Open Apr.–Sept., Tues.–Sun. 9:30–12:30 and 3–7; Oct.–Mar., Tues.–Sun. 9:30–noon and 2:30–5.*

Palazzo Orlandi, owned for the past century by the Orlandi family, was also Verdi's home for a few years. Only a few of its stately rooms are open to the public. *Admission: 2,500 lire. Open Apr.–Sept., Tues.–Sun. 9:30–12:30 and 3–7; Oct.–Mar., Tues.–Sun. 9:30–noon and 2:30–5.*

Five kilometers (3 miles) north of Busseto is **Villa Sant'Agata,** the grand country home Verdi built for himself in 1849, where some of his greatest works were composed. For Verdi lovers, Sant'Agata is a shrine. *Admission: 5,000 lire. Open Apr. 1–Nov. 9, daily 9–11:40 and 3–6:40.*

The town of **Róncole,** the composer's birthplace, is a few kilometers east of Busseto. The simple farmhouse in which he was born is on the edge of town, as is the church in which he took some of his earliest steps in a musical career: He was the church organist here when still in his teens. *Verdi's birthplace. Admission: 2,500 lire. Open Apr.–Sept. Tues.–Sun. 9:30–12:30, 3–7; Oct.–Mar. Tues.–Sun. 9:30–noon, 2:30–5.*

To rejoin Route A1 for the Via Emilia, take Route 588 south from Busseto 15 kilometers (9 miles). Both roads lead directly to Parma, 24 kilometers (15 miles) away.

❸ **Parma** is a delightful, dignified town that stands on the banks of a tributary of the river Po. Much of the historic center has been untouched by modern times, despite heavy damage during World War II, and with the efforts being made by the city fathers to control traffic, strolling Parma's cobbled streets is a charming experience. The traffic regulations, while a boon to pedestrians, are a nightmare for motorists. Every obstacle is put in the way of motor traffic—one-way streets, no-turning zones, and the like—so it is best to leave your car outside the center and see the town on foot.

Almost every major European power has had a hand in ruling Parma at one time or another. The Romans founded the city— it was little more than a garrison on the Via Emilia—and then a succession of feudal lords held sway here. In the 16th century came the ever-avaricious Farnese family (who are still the dukes of Parma), and then, in fast succession, the Spanish,

French, and Austrians, with the Austrians taking over following the upheavals in central Europe after the fall of Napoleon. The French influence is strong. The great French novelist Stendahl lived in the city for several years and set his classic novel *The Charterhouse of Parma* here.

The **Piazza del Duomo**—site of the cathedral, the baptistery, the church of San Giovanni, and the palaces of the bishop and other notables—is the heart of the city. This square and its buildings make up one of the most harmonious, tranquil city centers in Italy. The focal point of the piazza is the magnificent 12th-century **Duomo,** with its two vigilant stone lions standing guard beside the main door. The arch of the entrance is decorated with figures representing the months of the year, a motif repeated inside the baptistery on the right-hand side of the square.

Some of the original artwork of the 1100s still exists in the church, notably the *Descent from the Cross,* a carving in the right transept, by Benedetto Antelami (1150–1230), a sculptor and architect whose masterwork is this cathedral's baptistery (*see* below). You can still feel the emotion the artist wished to convey in the simple figures.

It is odd to turn from this austere work of the 12th century to the exuberant fresco in the dome, the *Assumption of the Virgin,* by the late-16th-century painter Antonio Correggio. The fresco was not well received when it was unveiled in 1530. "A mess of frogs' legs," the bishop of Parma is said to have called it. In contrast to the rather dark, somber interior of the cathedral, though, the beauty and light of the painting in the dome are a welcome relief. *Open daily 7:30–noon, 3–7.*

The **Baptistery,** standing to the side of the Duomo, is a solemn and simple Romanesque building on the exterior and an uplifting Gothic building within. The doors of the Baptistery are richly decorated with figures, animals, and flowers, and the interior is adorned with figures carved by Antelami, showing the months and seasons. *Admission: 3,000 lire. Open daily 9–12, 3–6.*

There is more painting by Correggio in the nearby church of **San Giovanni Evangelista,** a church with an elaborate Baroque facade and a Renaissance interior. Of the several works by Correggio in this church, it is his *St. John the Evangelist* (left transept) that is considered the finest. Also in this church (in the second and fourth chapels on the left) are works by Girolamo Parmigianino, a contemporary of Correggio's and, as his name suggests, a native of Parma. *Open daily 6:30–noon, 3:30–8.*

Next door to the church, in the adjoining monastery, is a **pharmacy** where Benedictine monks used to mix medicines and herbals. The 16th-century decorations still survive, while the potions (the people of Parma swore they would cure almost every ill) are, alas, gone—the pharmacy stopped production in 1881. *Open Tues.–Sun. 9–1.*

The **Galleria Nazionale** of Parma is the primary art gallery of the city, and it is housed in the vast, and rather grim looking, **Palazzo della Pilotta,** on the banks of the river. The palace was built about 1600 and is so big that from the air it is Parma's most recognizable sight—hence, the destruction done to it when it was bombed by Allied forces in 1944. Much of the building has been restored, but not all. The palazzo takes its name from the ballgame *pilotta*, a sort of handball played within the palace precincts in the 17th century.

To enter the art museum, which is on the ground floor of the palace, you pass through the magnificent and elaborately Baroque **Teatro Farnese**, built in 1628 and based on Palladio's theater in the northern Italian town of Vicenza. Built entirely of wood, the theater was burned badly during Allied bombing, but has been faultlessly restored.

The art gallery itself is large and contains many examples of works by the two best-known painters of Parma—Correggio and Parmigianino. There are also works by Fra Angelico, Leonardo da Vinci, El Greco, and Il Bronzino. *Admission: 10,000 lire. Open Tues.–Sat. 9–2, Sun. 9–1.*

Near the Palazzo della Pilotta, on the Strada Garibaldi, is the **Camera del Correggio**, the former dining room of the abbess of the Convent of Saint Paul. It was extensively frescoed by Correggio, and, despite the religious character of the building, the decorations are entirely secular, with very worldly depictions of mythological scenes—the *Triumphs of the Goddess Diana*, the *Three Graces*, and the *Three Fates*. *Admission free. Open Tues.–Sat. 9–2, Sun. 9–1.*

Time Out | Civilization in Parma is more than painting and architecture. To taste the delicacies that put Parma on the world culinary map, have a snack or buy the ingredients for a picnic at **Salumeria Melli** (Via della Repubblica 68) or **Specialità di Parma** (Via Farini 9c).

Near the central Piazza Garibaldi is **Madonna della Steccata**, a delightful 16th-century domed church. It is chiefly famous for a wonderful fresco cycle by Parmigianino. The painter took so long to complete it that his exasperated patrons imprisoned him briefly for breach of contract, before releasing him to complete the work. *Open daily 7:30–noon, 3–6:30.*

❹ **Modena**, 56 kilometers (34 miles) from Parma along Route A1, is an old town that's famous today for three very modern names. The luxury high-performance cars Maserati and Ferrari come from Modena, and so does the world-famous opera star Luciano Pavarotti.

The modern town that encircles the historic center is extensive, and, while the old quarter is small, it is filled with an Old World atmosphere, narrow medieval streets, and pleasant piazzas. Begin your exploration at the **Duomo** in the central Piazza Grande. The church is one of the finest examples of Romanesque architecture in the country and dates from the 12th century. As in Parma, the exterior is decorated with medieval sculptures showing the works of the months, as well as a realistic-looking scene of the sacking of a city by barbarian hordes, a reminder to the faithful to be ever vigilant in defense of the church. The bell tower is made of white marble and is known as *La Ghirlandina* (The Little Garland) because of its distinctive garland-shaped weather vane on the summit of the tower.

The interior of the church is very somber and is divided by an elaborately decorated gallery carved with scenes of the Passion of Christ. The carvings took 50 years to complete and are by an anonymous Modenese master of the 12th century. The tomb of the patron saint of Modena, San Geminiano, is in the crypt. *Open daily 8–6.*

The principal museum of the town is housed in the **Palazzo dei Musei,** a short walk from the Duomo (follow Via Emilia—the old Roman road runs through the heart of the town—to Via di Sant'Agostino. The museum is in the piazza on the left). The collection was assembled in the mid-17th century by Francesco d'Este, Duke of Modena, and the gallery **Galleria Estense** is named in his honor. There is a portrait bust of him in the first room by Bernini.

The duke was a man of many interests, as you can see from the galleries' collections of *objets d'art*—ivories, coins, medals, and bronzes, as well as works of art dating from the Renaissance to the Baroque. There are works here by Correggio, as well as by masters from other parts of Italy, such as the Venetians Tintoretto and Veronese, the Bolognese Reni and the Carracci brothers, and the Neapolitan Salvator Rosa.

The gallery also houses the Duke's **library,** a huge collection of illuminated books, of which the best known is the beautifully illustrated bible of the 15th century, the *Bible of Borso d'Este.* A map, dated 1501, was one of the first in the world to show Columbus's discovery of America. *Admission: 4,000 lire. Open Tues., Wed., Fri., Sun. 9–2; Thurs., Sat. 9–7.*

In the Piazza Roma (follow the curved Via Ramazzini away from the Palazzo dei Musei), you'll find the huge Baroque **palace** of the dukes of Modena. It is now a military academy; once the province of the dukes only, it is still off-limits, except to flocks of cadets in elaborate uniforms. Behind the academy are Modena's large public gardens.

⑤ Bologna, 38 kilometers (23 miles) from Modena, is the principal city of Emilia-Romagna and one of the most important cities in Italy. Through its long history, first as an Etruscan city, then a Roman one, then as an independent city-state in the Middle Ages, Bologna has always been a power in the north of Italy. Through the centuries, the city has acquired a number of nicknames: "Bologna the Learned," in honor of its ancient (the oldest in the world) university; "Bologna the Turreted," recalling the forest of medieval towers that once rose from the city center (two remarkable examples still exist); and "Bologna the Fat," a tribute to the preeminent position the city holds in the world of cuisine.

Wars, sackings, rebellions, and aerial bombing do not seem to have made much of an impression on the old center of the city: The narrow, cobblestoned streets are still there, as are the ancient churches, the massive palaces, the medieval towers, and the famous arcades that line many of the main thoroughfares of the town.

The streets are always bustling with students. The university was founded in the year 1050, and by the 13th century already had more than 10,000 students. It was a center for the teaching of law and theology, and it was ahead of its time in that many of the professors were women. Today the university has one of the most prominent business schools in Italy and has the finest faculty of medicine in the country. Marconi, the inventor of wireless telegraphy, first formulated his ground-breaking theories in the physics labs of the university.

The heart of the city is the Piazza Maggiore and the adjacent Piazza del Nettuno. Grouped around these two squares are the imposing Duomo of San Petronio, the huge Palazzo Comunale, the Palazzo del Podestà, the Palazzo di Re Enzo, and the fountain of Neptune. It is one of the best groupings of public buildings in the entire country.

Numbers in the margin correspond to points of interest on the Bologna map.

❻ The **Duomo** (San Petronio) was started in the 14th century, and work was still in progress on this vast building some 300 years later. It is still not finished, as you can see: The facade is partially decorated and lacks most of the marble facing that the architects planned on several hundred years ago. The main doorway was carved by the great Sienese master of the Renaissance, Jacopo della Quercia. Above the center of the door is a Madonna and Child, flanked by saints Ambrose and Petronius, patrons of the city.

The interior of the cathedral is huge and echoing, 432 feet long and 185 feet wide. It is so vast that it's sobering to note that originally the Bolognans had planned an even bigger church (you can still see the columns erected to support the larger church outside the east end) but decided on this "toned down" version in the interest of economy. The church museum contains models to show how the original, planned church would have looked. The most important artworks in the church are in the left aisle, frescoes by Giovanni di Modena, dating from the first years of the 1400s. In the right aisle, laid out in the pavement of the church, is a huge sundial, placed there in 1655, showing the time, date, and month. *Open daily 8–6. Museo di San Petronio (inside church) open Mon., Wed., Fri.–Sun. 10–12:30.*

❼ The **Palazzo Comunale,** on the right as you face the church, is a mixture of styles and buildings, dating from the 13th to 15th centuries. When Bologna was an independent commune, this huge palace was the seat of government, a function it serves today. Over the door is a giant statue of Pope Gregory XIII, Bologna-born and most famous for his reorganization of the calendar—a system still in use today.

The Palazzo Comunale contains a picture gallery, the Collezioni Communale d'Arte, which has paintings of the Middle Ages, as well as some Renaissance works by Luca Signorelli and Tintoretto. The best reason for seeing the collection, however, is to get a look at the views of the piazza from the upper stories of the palace. *Admission: 5,000 lire. Open Mon., Wed.–Sat. 9–2, Sun. 9–12:30.*

❽ The **Palazzo Podestà,** which faces the Duomo, was built in 1484, and attached to it is the soaring Torre dell'Arengo. The bells in this tower have rung since 1453, whenever the city has celebrated, mourned, or called its citizens to arms.

❾ Next to the Palazzo Podestà is the medieval **Palazzo di Re Enzo,** the building in which King Enzo of Sardinia was imprisoned for 23 years (until his death in 1272). He had been unwise enough to wage war on Bologna and was captured after the fierce battle of Fossalta in 1249. The palace has other unhappy associations:

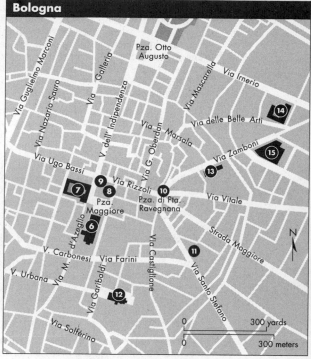

Bologna

Common criminals received the last rites of the church in the tiny chapel in the courtyard before being taken out to execution in the Piazza Maggiore.

Next to the Palazzo di Re Enzo is the elaborate Baroque **fountain** by the sculptor Giambologna. Given Bologna's landlocked position, the choice of subject—the God of the Sea, Neptune, and his attendant sirens and dolphins—seems rather odd. It was sculpted in 1566 and is known by the nickname Il Gigante (The Giant), which certainly fits.

The busy, chic Via Rizzoli runs from the Piazza del Nettuno directly into the medieval section of the city, passing the Piazza di Porta Ravegnana. Here are two of Bologna's famous towers: The taller, the **Torre degli Asinelli,** is 320 feet high and leans an alarming 7½-feet out of the perpendicular; the other tower, the **Torre Garisenda,** was shortened for safety in the 1500s. It is 165 feet high and tilts 10 feet. The Torre degli Asinelli can be climbed (500 steep stairs) and has a fine view of the city. *Admission: 1,000 lire. Open May–Sept., daily 9–6; Oct.–Apr., daily 9–5.*

The towers were built at the same time (1488) and are mentioned by Dante in the *Inferno.* They are the only two that remain of the more than 200 towers that once graced the city—every family of any importance had to have a tower as a symbol of its prestige and power.

From the Piazza di Porta Ravegnana, turn right on Via Santo Stefano. Four blocks along that street is the church of **Santo Stefano,** a remarkable building that is actually several churches contained in one building. The oldest, the church of Santi Vitale e Agricola, dates from the 8th century and contains a 14th-century nativity scene much loved by Bologna's children, who come at Christmastime to pay their respects to the baby Jesus. The church of San Sepolcro (12th century) contains the courtyard of Pontius Pilate, so named for the basin in the center of the court that's said to be the basin Pilate washed his hands in after condemning Christ. *Open daily 9–noon, 3:30–6.*

There is also a museum here displaying various medieval religious works, where you can buy sundry items made by the monks, such as honey, shampoo, or jam. *Admission free. Open Mon.–Sat. 9–noon and 3:30–5:30, Sun. 9–1 and 3:30–5:30.*

Leaving the church, turn right on Via Farini, then, a few blocks farther along, turn left on Via Garibaldi. This leads you to the ⑫ church of **San Domenico,** an interesting church that contains the tomb of Saint Dominic, who died here in 1221. The tomb of the saint, called the Arca di San Domenico, is in the sixth chapel on the right. Many artists contributed to the decoration, notably Niccolò di Bari, who was so proud of his work here that he changed his name to Niccolò dell'Arca to recall this famous work. The young Michelangelo carved the angel on the right. In the right transept of the church is a tablet marking the last resting place of the hapless King Enzo, whose prison you saw in the Piazza Maggiore. In the square in front of San Domenico are two curious tombs raised above the ground on pillars, commemorating two famous 14th-century lawyers.

Returning to the Piazza di Porta Ravegnana, turn up the busy Via Zamboni and stop a few blocks up on the right to see the ⑬ church of **San Giacomo Maggiore.** Inside is the burial chamber of the Bentivoglio family, the leading family in Bologna in the Middle Ages. The crypt is connected by underground passage to the Teatro Comunale, across the street—a rather odd feature, until you realize that the family palazzo of the Bentivoglio used to stand on that spot. The most notable tomb is that of Antonio Bentivoglio, carved by Jacopo della Quercia in 1435. We can tell his profession—lecturer in law—from the group of students carved on the base, each listening intently to their professor. *Open daily 8–noon, 3–6.*

Continuing along the Via Zamboni, you come to the principal art gallery of the city and one of the most important in Italy, ⑭ the **Pinacoteca Nazionale.** The collection here includes many works by the immortals of Italian painting, including Raphael's famous *Ecstasy of St. Cecilia.* There is also a beautiful multipaneled painting by Giotto and a Parmigianino *Madonna and Saints.* The centerpiece of the collection, however, comprises the many rooms devoted to the two greatest Bolognese painters, Guido Reni and Annibale Carracci, both masters of the late 16th century. Some of the most interesting paintings, from a historical point of view, are by Giuseppe Crespi, a Bolognese painter of the 18th century who avoided grand religious or historical themes, preferring instead to paint scenes of daily life in his native city. These small canvases give you an excellent idea of the boisterous, earthy life of Old Bologna. *Via delle Belle Art 56; tel. 051/243222. Admission: 6,000 lire. Open Tues.–Sat. 9–2, Sun. 9–1.*

⑮ The Pinacoteca Nazionale is on the edge of the **university** district, and it is worth a walk through the adjoining streets to get a sense of what an Italian university is like. There is no campus, as such, but a jumble of buildings, some dating as far back as the 15th century, with the bulk of them from the 17th and 18th centuries. This neighborhood, like neighborhoods in most college towns, has lots of bookshops, coffee shops, and cheap snack bars and restaurants. None of them is particularly distinguished, but they all give a good idea of student life in the city. Political slogans and sentiments are scrawled on walls all around the university and tend, for the most part, to be ferociously leftist.

Time Out For wonderful ice cream in the university district, try **Moline,** which has simple but delicious *cioccolata con panna* (chocolate and vanilla with heavy whipped cream) or a series of more adventurous flavors and delicate fruit ices. *Via delle Moline 6. Closed Mon.*

From Bologna there are two choices of itineraries: Head north to Ferrara and then east to Ravenna or continue along the Via Emilia, stopping for short visits at some of the smaller towns en route to Rimini and the sea.

Numbers in the margin correspond with points of interest on the Emilia-Romagna map.

16 If you have chosen the latter, the first port of call out of Bologna, just off A14, is the little hamlet of **Dozza,** 31 kilometers (19 miles) away. It is a small village on a hill crowned with a splendid restored medieval castle. Every other year artists from all over Italy flock to the town to take part in the mural competition—it seems that every square foot of the town has been painted with colorful scenes done with varying degrees of skill. The castle is home to the **Enoteca Regionale,** the wine "library" for the region. Here you can sample the different vintages that come from the surrounding countryside, particularly Dozza's own Albana, a white wine that comes dry or sweet. *Tel. 0542/ 678089. Admission free, tasting 3,000 lire. Open May–Sept., Tues.–Sun. 9–1 and 4–7; Oct.–Apr., Tues.–Sat. 10–noon and 2–5, Sun. 10–noon and 3–6.*

17 Forty-nine kilometers (30 miles) from Bologna, along Via Emilia, is **Faenza,** a town that has been producing ceramics since the 12th century—its "faience" pottery is known the world over. In the central **Piazza del Popolo** are dozens of shops selling the town's product. Faenza is also home to the **Museo delle Ceramiche,** one of the largest ceramics museums in the world, covering the potter's art in all phases of history and in all parts of the world. *Viale Baccarini. Admission: 6,000 lire. Open May–Sept., Tues.–Sat. 9–7, Sun. 9:30–1; Oct.–Apr., Tues.–Sat. 9:30–1 and 3–6, Sun. 9:30–1.*

18 From Faenza continue on A14 to the town of **Forli,** 14 kilometers (9 miles) away, and turn off onto the rural Route 9ter. This leads you through hilly country to the small town of **Predappio,** the birthplace of Benito Mussolini and Il Duce's final resting place. The cemetery on the outskirts of town contains the crypt of the Mussolini family, with the former dictator himself in the place of honor. A spotlit bust glowers at visitors, and glass cases contain some of his decorations and medals. It is a chilling place and has become the object of pilgrimage for the followers of fascism (young and old), who write repugnant political slogans in the visitors' book. *Cimitero Municipale. Open daily, 8–dusk.*

Returning to A14, on Via Emilia you pass through the modern towns of Forlimpopoli, Cesena, and Savignano. At **Savignano,** though, there is a reminder that no matter how new the towns might look, you are still traveling in a place of great history—just outside the town is a small stream, the Rubicone. Cross it and you, too, have crossed the Rubicon, the river made famous by Julius Caesar when, in 49 BC, he defied the Senate of Rome by bringing his army across the river and plunging the country into civil war.

From here, the road leads on to the next three important destinations, Rimini, Ravenna, and Ferrara.

Tour 2: Rimini, Ravenna, and Ferrara

Rimini is the principal summer resort on the Adriatic Coast and one of the most popular holiday destinations in Italy. Every summer, beginning in June, the city is flooded with vacationers, not just from Italy but from France, Austria, Germany, Scandinavia, and Great Britain, as well. The city is given over almost exclusively to tourism, with hundreds of hotels, grand and modest, and restaurants catering to virtually every national palate: You are just as likely to find a *bierkeller* or an English tea shop as you are an Italian restaurant. The waterfront is lined with beach clubs that rent a patch of sand, a deck chair, and an umbrella by the day, week, month, or the entire season. Hotels along the beach front have staked out their own private turf, so the chance of swimming (or even seeing the sea close up) without paying for the privilege is slim.

In the off-season, Rimini, in common with resorts the world over, is a ghost town. Some hotels and restaurants are open, but the majority are closed tight, hibernating until the return of the free-spending tourists. Summers are so crowded here that it is most unwise to go to Rimini without confirmed hotel reservations. For those who like sun by day, disco by night, and hordes of frolicking teenagers, Rimini is the town for you; those who prefer more sedate vacations are advised to stay away.

The new town has just about swallowed the old, but there are signs here and there that tell of Rimini's long and turbulent history. Rimini stands at the junction of two great Roman consular roads: the Via Aemilia and the Via Flaminia. In addition, in Roman times, it was an important port, making it a strategic and commercial center. From the 13th century onward, the city was controlled by the Malatesta family, an unpredictable group, capable of grand gestures and savage deeds. The famous lovers in Dante's *Inferno*, Paolo and Francesca, were Malatestas. Paolo was the brother of Gianciotto Malatesta; Francesca, Gianciotto's wife. Gianciotto murdered them both for having betrayed him. Sigismondo Malatesta, lord of the city in the middle of the 15th century, was a learned man of great wit and culture. He also banished his first wife, strangled his second, and poisoned his third. He lived with his beautiful mistress, Isotta, until her death. He was so grief-stricken that he raised a magnificent monument in her honor, the **Tempio Malatestiano.** It is the principal sight in the town.

The oldest building in the city is the **Arco d'Augustus,** in the Piazzale Giulio Cesare. It was erected in 27 BC, making it the oldest Roman arch in existence, and it marks the meeting of the Via Aemilia and the Via Flaminia. From there, walk along the Corso Augusto to the Piazza Tre Martiri (where, legend says, the mule carrying St. Anthony suddenly stopped and knelt in honor of the Holy Sacrament that was being carried past at the time) and turn right on Via Quattro Novembre. One block up, also on the right side, is Sigismondo's memorial to his great love, Isotta, the Tempio Malatestiano.

Despite the irregular—from a church point of view—nature of Sigismondo's relationship with Isotta, the Tempio is today the **cathedral** of Rimini. The building was in fact originally a Franciscan church before Sigismondo took it over to make it into a monument to his beloved. The facade is a beautiful piece of Renaissance architecture by Leon Battista Alberti. It is in the shape of a Roman triumphal arch, and is considered to be one of Alberti's masterpieces.

The interior is light and spacious and contains the tombs of both the lovers. The intertwined I, for Isotta, and the S, for Sigismondo, are dotted about everywhere and look rather like "$" signs. The carvings of elephants and roses recall the coat-of-arms of the Malatesta family. Sigismondo's tomb, on the right of the entrance door, is some distance from Isotta's in the second chapel. (Her tomb is on the left wall of the chapel; the original inscription in marble had a pagan twist and was covered with another in bronze.) On the right, in what is now the Tempio's book and gift shop, is a wonderful but badly damaged fresco by Piero della Francesca showing Sigismondo paying homage to his patron saint. Over the main altar of the church is a crucifix attributed to Giotto. *Open daily 7–noon, 3:30–7.*

There are two routes from Rimini to Ravenna. The coast road, Route 16, hugs the shoreline as far as Cervia before edging inland. While the distance, 52 kilometers (31 miles), is not great, the going along this route is slow. The coast north of Rimini is lined with dozens of small resort towns, only one having any charm, the seaport of Cesenatico; the others are mini-Riminis, and during the summer the narrow road is hopelessly clogged with traffic. A faster route is to head inland on A14 and then turn off onto the inland Route 71, which leads directly into Ravenna. The distance is 64 kilometers (39 miles).

㉑ About five kilometers (3 miles) southeast of Ravenna stands the church of **Sant'Apollinare in Classe.** It is landlocked now, but when the church was built, it stood in the center of the busy shipping port of Classis. The arch above and the area around the high altar are rich in mosaics. Those on the arch, older than those behind it, are considered superior to the rest. They show Christ in judgment and the 12 lambs of Christianity leaving the cities of Jerusalem and Bethlehem. In the apse is the figure of Sant'Apollinare himself, a bishop of Ravenna, and above him is a magnificent Transfiguration decorated with flowers, trees, and little birds. *Open daily 9–noon, 3–6.*

㉒ **Ravenna** is a stately old city, still living on the dreams of its faded glory. The high point in Ravenna's long history was 1,500 years ago, when the city became the capital of the Roman Empire, but by then the empire was in its period of irreversible decline. The city was taken by the barbarian Ostrogoths in the

5th century; then, in the 6th, it was conquered by the Byzantines, who ruled the city from Constantinople.

Because Ravenna spent much of its history looking to the East, its greatest art treasures show much Byzantine influence: Above all, Ravenna is a city of mosaics, the finest in Western art. A single 6,000-lire ticket will admit you to six of Ravenna's most important monuments: the tomb of Galla Placida, the Church of San Vitale, the Neonian Baptistery, and the church of Sant'Appollinare Nuovo, all described below, as well as the Church of Spirito Santo and the Museo Arcivescovile e Cappella Sant'Andrea.

The **Tomb of Galla Placidia** and the church of **San Vitale** have the best-known, and most elaborate, mosaics in the city. The little tomb and the great church stand side by side, but the tomb predates the church by at least a hundred years. Galla Placidia was the sister of the last emperor of Rome, Honorius, the man who moved the imperial capital to Ravenna in AD 402. She is said to have been beautiful and strong willed, taking an active part in the governing of the crumbling empire. She was also one of the most active Christians of her day, endowing churches and supporting priests and their congregations throughout the realm. This tomb, built for her in the mid-5th century, is her monument. Outside, the tomb is a rather uninspired building of red brick; within, however, the color and clarity of the mosaics that decorate the ceiling are startling. The deep blue and gold catch the light and seem to glitter. The central dome has symbols of Christ and the evangelists, and over the door is a depiction of the Good Shepherd. The Apostles, in groups of two (there are only eight of them, for some reason), ring the inner part of the dome. Notice the small doves at their feet, drinking from the water of faith. In the tiny transepts are some delightful pairs of deer (which represent souls), drinking from the fountain of resurrection. There are three sarcophagi in the tomb, and, it is thought, none of them contains the remains of Galla Placidia. She died in Rome in AD 450, and there is no record of her body having been transported back to the place where she wished to lie.

The mosaics of the Galla Placidia tomb are simple works that have not yet received the full impact of Byzantine influence. Quite the opposite is the case of the mosaics in the church of San Vitale, next door. The church was built in AD 547, after the Byzantines conquered the city, and it is decorated in an exclusively Byzantine style. In the area behind the altar are the most famous works in the church. These show accurate portraits of the Emperor of the East, Justinian, attended by his court, and the Bishop of Ravenna, Maximian. Facing him, across the chancel, is the Emperor's wife, Theodora, with her entourage, holding a chalice containing the communion wine. From the elaborate headdresses and heavy cloaks of the emperor and empress, you can get a marvelous sense of the grandeur of the imperial court.

On the ceiling above the royal couple, ruling over all, is a mosaic of Christ the King. With him is the saint for whom the church is named, Vitale, and the founder of the church, Bishop Ecclesio, who holds a model of the building. *Tomb of Galla Placidia and Church of San Vitale. Via San Vitale off Via Salara, near Piazza del Popolo. Admission: 3,000 lire (ticket also valid for Basilica San Vitale). Open summer, daily 8:30–7; winter, daily 9–4:30.*

Next to the church is the **Museo Nazionale** of Ravenna, housed in a former monastery. The collection contains artifacts of ancient Rome, Byzantine fabrics and carvings, and other pieces of early-Christian art. *Admission: 6,000 lire. Open Tues.–Sun. 8:30–1:30.*

To reach another great mosaic site, the **Neonian Baptistery,** return to the Piazza del Popolo and walk along Via Battistero, toward the Piazza John F. Kennedy. The Baptistery, next door to the 18th-century cathedral, is a few blocks along on the left. In keeping with the purpose of the building, the great mosaic in the dome shows the baptism of Christ, and beneath that scene are the apostles. The lowest band of mosaics contains Christian symbols, the Throne of God and the Cross. *Admission: 3,000 lire (ticket also valid for Museo Arcivescovile e Capella Sant'Andrea). Open daily 9:30–4:30.*

A few blocks away, on Via Ricci, and next door to the large church of St. Francis, is a small neoclassical building containing the **tomb of Dante.** Exiled from his native Florence, the great poet, author of the *Divine Comedy,* died here in 1321. The Florentines have been trying to reclaim their famous son for hundreds of years, but the Ravennans refuse to give him up, arguing that Florence did not welcome Dante in life, so it doesn't deserve him in death. The site contains a small museum. *Admission: 3,000 lire; free on Sun. and holidays. Open Tues.–Sun. 9–noon.*

From the tomb of Dante, walk up Via Guaccimanni toward the busy Via Roma. At the intersection of the two streets, slightly to the left, is the last great mosaic site in the city proper, the church of **Sant'Apollinare Nuovo.** Since the left side of the church was reserved for women, it is only fitting that the mosaic decoration on that side is a scene of 22 virgins offering crowns to the Virgin Mary. On the right wall are 26 men carrying the crowns of martyrdom. They are approaching Christ, who is surrounded by angels. The mosaics in Sant'Apollinare Nuovo date from the early 6th century and are slightly older than the works in San Vitale. *Admission: 3,000 lire (ticket also valid for Basilica dello Spirito Santo). Open May–Sept., daily 9:30–5:30; Oct.–Apr., daily 9:30–4:30.*

㉓ Seventy-four kilometers (44 miles) along Route 16 from Ravenna lies **Ferrara.** It is a city of turrets and towers, of a mighty castle protected by its deep moat, and historic palaces of great grandeur. Although the site has been inhabited since before Christ and was once the possession of Ravenna, the history of Ferrara begins in the 13th century, with the coming of the Este family. From 1259 until 1598 the city was ruled by the dukes of the Este family, and in those three and a half centuries the city was stamped indelibly with their mark.

It was during the Renaissance that the court of the Este came into full flower. In keeping with their time, the dukes could be politically ruthless—brother killed brother, son fought father—but they were avid scholars and enthusiastic patrons of the arts. Duke Nicolo III murdered his wife and her lover but was a man of cultivation. The greatest of all the dukes, Ercole I, tried to poison his nephew, who laid claim to the duchy (and when that didn't work, he beheaded him), but it is to this pitiless man that Ferrara owes its great beauty. One of the most celebrated names in Italian history, Lucrezia Borgia, married into the Este family—and it seems that her infamous reputation is not at all deserved. She was beloved by the Ferrarese people and was mourned greatly when she died. She is buried in the church of Corpus Domini in the city.

Naturally enough, the building that was the seat of Este power dominates the town: It is the massive **Castello Estense,** placed square in the center of the city in the Piazza della Repubblica. It is a suitable symbol for the Este family: cold and menacing on the outside, lavishly decorated within. The public rooms are grand, but deep in the bowels of the fortress are chilling dungeons where enemies of the state were held in wretched conditions—a function these quarters served as recently as 1943, when antifascist prisoners were detained there.

The castle was begun in 1385, but work was going on here as late as the 16th century. The Sala dei Giochi (the Games Room) is extravagantly decorated with walls painted to show pagan athletic scenes, and the Sala dei Aurora to show the times of the day. Oddly enough, the one chapel that is on view is not Catholic, but Protestant (one of the few to survive the Counter-Reformation), placed here for the use of the Protestant Princess Renée of France, who married into the Este family in the 16th century. From the terraces of the castle, and from the hanging garden, reserved for the private use of the duchesses, are fine views of the town and surrounding countryside. *Admission: 5,000 lire. Open Tues.–Sat. 9–1, 2:30–6:30; Sun. 10–1, 2–7.*

A few steps from the castle, along the Corso dei Martiri della Libertà, is the magnificent Gothic **Duomo,** with its facade of three tiers of arches and beautiful carvings over the central door. It was begun in 1135 and took more than a hundred years to complete. The interior does not live up to the expectations fostered by the facade. It was completely remodeled in the 17th century, and none of the original decoration remains in place. *Open daily 8–noon, 3–7.*

The treasures of the old interior are preserved in the **cathedral museum** above the church (entrance inside). Here are some of the lifelike carvings taken from one of the doors of the Duomo, dating from the 13th century and showing the months of the year. Also in the museum are a statue of the Madonna by the Sienese master Jacopo della Quercia and two masterpieces by the Ferrarese painter Cosimo Tura, an *Annunciation* and *St. George Slaying the Dragon. Admission: free, but voluntary offerings taken. Open Mon.–Sat. 10–noon, 3–5.*

The area behind the Duomo, the southern part of the city stretching between the Corso della Giovecca and the ramparts of the city above the river, is the oldest and most characteristic part of Ferrara. In this part of the old town various members of the Este family built themselves pleasure palaces, the most famous of which is the **Palazzo Schifanoia** (*schifanoia* means carefree—literally, "fleeing boredom"). Begun in the 14th century, the palace was remodeled in 1466 and is the first Renaissance palazzo in the city. The interior is lavishly decorated, particularly the Salone dei Mesi, with an extravagant series of frescoes showing the months of the year. The Palazzo now houses the **Museo Civico** (City Museum), with its collection of coins, statuary, and paintings. *Via Scandiana 23. Admission: 2,500 lire, free 2nd Sun. and Mon. of each month. Open daily 9–7.*

Near the Palazzo Schifanoia, on Via XX Settembre, is the **Palazzo di Ludovico il Moro,** a magnificent 15th-century palace built for Ludovico Sforza, husband of Beatrice d'Este. The great, but unfinished, courtyard is the most interesting part of this luxurious palace. It also houses the **Museo Archeologico** for the region and includes relics of early man, the Etruscans, and Romans, found in the country surrounding the city. *Via XX Settembre 124. Admission: 2,500 lire. Open May–Sept., Tues.– Sat. 9–1, 3:30–7; Oct.–Apr., Tues.–Sat. 9–1.*

In the same neighborhood, on Via Scienze, is the peaceful palace called the **Palazzo del Paradiso.** In the courtyard is the tomb of the great writer Ariosto, author of the most popular work of literature of the Renaissance, the poem "Orlando Furioso." The building now houses the city library. *Admission free. Open weekdays 9–7:30, Sat. 9–1.*

The Estes were great patrons of Ariosto, and he passed a good deal of his life in Ferrara. **Ariosto's house** lies in the northern part of the city, at Via Ariosto 67. The interior has been converted into an office building and is not open to the public.

Not far from the Palazzo del Paradiso, on Via Savonarola, is the charming 15th-century house, the **Casa Romei.** Downstairs there are rooms with 15th-century frescoes and several sculptures collected from churches that have been destroyed. *Via Savonarola 30. Admission: 4,000 lire. Open Tues.–Sun. 8:30–2.*

On the busy Corso della Giovecca is the **Palazzina di Marfisa d'Este,** an elegant 16th-century home owned by Marfisa d'Este, a great patron of the arts. The house has painted ceilings, fine 16th-century furniture, and a garden containing a grotto and an outdoor theater. *Corso della Giovecca 170. Admission: 2,000 lire, free 2nd Sun. and Mon. of each month. Open Mon.– Sat. 9–12:30, 2–5; Sun. 9–12:30.*

Time Out   For a good cup of cappuccino, a piece of pastry, or rich ice cream, try **Gelateria Nazionale.** *28 Corso Martiri della Libertà 30, opposite the cathedral. Closed Thurs. and 2 weeks in Aug.*

From the castle, cross the Corso della Giovecca and walk up the wide Corso Ercole d'Este. At the corner of Corso Porta Mare is the **Palazzo dei Diamanti** (the Palace of Diamonds), so called for the 12,600 blocks of diamond-shaped stone that stud the facade. The palace was built in the 15th and 16th centuries and today contains an extensive art gallery devoted primarily to the painters of Ferrara. *Corso Ercole d'Este 21. Admission: 6,000 lire. Open Tues.–Sat. 9–2, Sun. 9–1.*

Sports

Golf   **Chiesa Nuova di Monte San Pietro,** 16 km (10 mi) west of Bologna, tel. 051/969100.

Swimming   There is a public swimming pool at Via Costa 174, Bologna (tel. 051/617–9022). Open May–Sept., daily 9:30–7; Oct.–Apr., weekdays 1:30–3, Sun. 9–1.

Tennis   **Virtus Tennis Club** (Via Galimberti 1, Bologna, tel. 051/412-408).

Dining and Lodging

Dining Bologna's reputation as the culinary capital of Italy is well deserved, but there is much fine dining to be had in the other cities of Emilia-Romagna as well. The inland part of the region takes its cue from Bologna, but each city has a traditional dish of its own. In Piacenza rice dishes predominate, particularly *risotto in padella* (rice simmered with fresh herbs and tomatoes). Parma is most famous for its ham; Modena, for meat products and the delicious balsamic vinegar; Rimini, reflecting its position on the sea, is home to an elaborate fish stew called *brodetto;* Ferrara is famous for simple foods: pears, peaches, asparagus, and zucchini.

The two most important pastas of the region are *pasta al ragu,* usually narrow egg noodles served with what is known the world over as Bolognese sauce, and the stuffed pasta called tortellini, which can be served with the ragu, in a cream sauce, or even in soups. Ravioli stuffed with ricotta cheese and spinach is a specialty of the area, as are the larger versions of the same thing: *agnolotti,* which can be stuffed with cheese but more frequently are filled with minced pork or beef, and *tortelli,* stuffed with squash.

The best-known wine of the region is Lambrusco, a sparkling red that has some admirers and many detractors. Some praise it for its tartness; others condemn it for the same quality. A lesser-known wine is Vino del Bosco, also a sparkling red, which comes from the region around Ferrara.

Highly recommended restaurants are indicated by a star ★.

Category	Cost*
Very Expensive	over 90,000 lire
Expensive	60,000–90,000 lire
Moderate	30,000–60,000 lire
Inexpensive	under 30,000 lire

per person, including first course, main course, dessert or fruit, and house wine

Lodging In Italy, the region of Emilia-Romagna has a reputation for an efficiency that outstrips most of the rest of the country. Consequently, even the smallest hotels are well run, with high levels of service and quality. Bologna is very much a businessperson's city, and most of the hotels cater to travelers of this type. There are, of course, smaller, more intimate hotels that cater to the tourist.

The business of Rimini is tourism. There are hundreds of hotels, grand ones with all sorts of luxury facilities and modest boarding houses with only a few rooms. Many offer full- or half-board plans—an economical alternative to eating in Rimini's many, but not particularly distinguished, restaurants. You should not go to Rimini during tourist season without confirmed hotel reservations: In July and August the city is filled to overflowing.

Highly recommended lodgings are indicated by a star ★.

Category	Cost*
Very Expensive	over 300,000 lire
Expensive	140,000–300,000 lire
Moderate	80,000–140,000 lire
Inexpensive	under 80,000 lire

All prices are for a standard double room for two, including service and tax.

Bologna **San Domenico.** Located about 33 kilometers (20 miles) outside
Dining Bologna, in the town of Imola, San Domenico is the holder of
two Michelin stars and is always counted among the top 10 Italian restaurants—its partisans say it should be number one. It is an elegant place, well worth the trip from Bologna, and reservations must be made days in advance. Specialties of the house are the homemade pâté with truffles and a delicious breast of duck in a sauce of black olives. *Imola, Via Sacchi 1, tel. 054/229000. Reservations required. Jacket required. AE, DC, V. Closed Mon. Very Expensive.*

Al Pappagallo. Located almost directly beneath Bologna's famous towers, Asinelli and Garisenda, the Pappagallo was once synonymous with gourmet eating in the city. Though competition has shifted the spotlight from it in recent years, it retains enough of its reputation and quality cuisine to merit at least one slap-up feast, served in a stylish, semiformal atmosphere. The first course specialty is *lasagna del Pappagallo*, made with veal, sirloin of pork, and wood mushrooms. For main course, sample the poetically named *foglie morte* ("dead leaves," from its shape and appearance once cooked): a turkey dish lightly cooked in butter, white wine, and prosciutto. *Piazza della Mercanzia 3c, tel. 051/232807. Reservations required. Jacket required. AE, DC, MC, V. Closed Sun. and Mon. lunch. Expensive.*

★ **Tre Frecce.** Housed in a 13th-century palace with high windows and ceilings, Tre Frecce doesn't rely on its atmosphere alone. The risotto with mushrooms or artichokes is excellent, as are the black truffle tarts in pepper sauce, and the fresh salmon in basil sauce. *Strada Maggiore 19, tel. 051/231200. Reservations advised. Dress: casual. AE, DC, MC, V. Closed Sun. eve., Mon., Aug., Dec. 24–Jan. 2. Expensive.*

Rosteria Luciano. A changing list of daily specials augments what is already one of Bologna's most varied menus. Some of the best offerings are shrimp with pineapple, wild boar sausage, and excellent pork and veal roasts. Among the desserts is *ricottina al forno*—delicious, charcoal-flavored ricotta baked in the oven. *Via Nazario Sauro 19, tel. 051/231249. Reservations advised. Dress: casual. DC, MC, V. Closed Tues. eve., Wed., Aug., Dec. 23–Jan. 2. Moderate–Expensive.*

Da Carlo. Dining on the medieval terrace in summer is a treat in this attractive restaurant. Make sure to reserve a table outside. Specialties include delicate game, such as braised pigeon with artichokes. *Via Marchesana 6, tel. 051/233227. Reservations advised, especially in summer. Dress: casual. AE, DC. Closed Tues. and Jan. 1–20, Aug. 23–Sept. 3–4. Moderate.*

Da Cesari. Wine made by the owner's family, good pastas such as *spaghetti alla chitarra* (with asparagus and prosciutto), and entrées such as duck with lemon and wild *radicchio* make this one of the best restaurants in Bologna in its price category. *Via de Carbonesi 8, tel. 051/237710. Reservations advised. Dress: casual. AE, DC, MC, V. Closed Sun. and Aug. Moderate.*

Rosteria Antico Brunetti. This old wood-paneled restaurant, founded in 1873, is very close to Piazza Maggiore and serves mainly pizzas to a mixed clientele. The specialty here is fish and seafood, which can go on your pizza or in your pasta. Dining is on two floors, but even then the restaurant fills quickly. *Via Caduti di Cefalonia 5, tel. 051/234441. No reservations. Dress: casual. AE, DC, MC, V. Closed Wed. Moderate.*

Ruggero. Unless it's Thursday or Friday, when fish is the only option, meat is the thing to order at this unassuming trattoria next to the Hotel Due Torri. The *bolliti misti* (mixed boiled meats) is tender and tasty, as are the roasts and the famous Bolognese mortadella. *Via degli Usberti 6, tel. 051/236–056. Reservations advised. Dress: casual. AE, DC, V. Closed Sat. lunch, Sun., and Aug. Moderate.*

★ **Trattoria di Re Enzo.** If you want a break from Bolognese food, try this popular Neapolitan restaurant. Spaghetti with *datteri di mare* (razor clams) and tomato sauce can be a meal in itself. The best second course is grilled swordfish steak with a zesty pepper sauce. *Via Riva di Reno 79, tel. 051/234803. Reservations required. Dress: casual. No credit cards. Closed Sun. and Dec. 24–Jan. 2. Moderate.*

Bertino. Popularity has not spoiled this traditional neighborhood trattoria. Meals are simple but prepared with care: Try the *paglia e fieno* (yellow and green pasta) with sausage, or choose from the steaming tray of bolliti misti. *Via delle Lame 55, tel. 051/522230. Reservations not required. Dress: casual. AE, DC, MC, V. Closed Sun., Mon. eve., Dec. 25–Jan. 1, and Aug. Inexpensive.*

Lodging **Grand Hotel Baglioni.** Sixteenth-century frescoes by the Bolognese Carracci brothers are rarely seen outside a museum or
★ church, but here they provide the stunning backdrop for the public rooms of one of Italy's most glamorous hotels. The rooms are warm and charming, and the staff is extremely attentive. The location is ideal, just a few steps from the central Piazza Maggiore. *Via Independenza 8, tel. 051/225445, fax 051/234840. 125 rooms with bath. Facilities: restaurant, conference rooms, bar. AE, DC, MC, V. Very Expensive.*

Royal Carlton. This is very much a business-traveler's hotel. The lobby is spartan, but the rooms are elegant and attractive: All are air-conditioned and have radios, balconies, and color TV. The hotel is in the heart of the city, near the train station. *Via Montebello 8, tel. 051/249361, fax 051/249724. 250 rooms with bath. Facilities: restaurant, bar, garage, conference rooms. AE, DC, MC, V. Very Expensive.*

★ **Corona d'Oro.** Once a medieval printing house, this centrally located hotel has been in business for more than a century. The public space is a delight, with a lyrical Art Nouveau decor, an atrium, and enough flowers for a wedding. The rooms are comfortable—all are air-conditioned and have color TV. *Via Oberdan 12, tel. 051/236456, fax 051/262679. 35 rooms with shower. Facilities: bar, conference room. AE, DC, MC, V. Closed Aug. Expensive.*

Dei Commercianti. Close to the Duomo and recently renovated, Dei Commercianti provides comfort and a good location at reasonable prices. Ask for one of the rooms with a terrace—those on the upper floors have wonderful views. *Via de Pignattari 11,* *tel. 051/233052, fax 051/224733. 31 rooms with bath or shower. Facilities: bar, parking. AE, DC, MC, V. Moderate.*

Orologio. Under the same management as the Dei Commercianti, the Orologio is located in a quiet pedestrian zone and has been recently renovated. The hotel is a good choice for those who would rather spend their lire dining out. Top-floor rooms have good views of the Duomo. *Via IV Novembre 10, tel. 051/231253, fax 051/260552. 32 rooms with bath or shower. Facilities: parking. AE, DC, MC, V. Moderate.*

Accademia Hotel. This small hotel is right in the middle of the university quarter, a comfortable base for exploring the area. The rooms are adequate, the staff friendly. *Via delle Belle Arti 6, tel. 051/263590 or 232318. 28 rooms, 24 with bath or shower. No credit cards. Closed 2-3 weeks in Aug. Inexpensive–Moderate.*

Ferrara
Dining
★
La Provvidenza. One of the best-known restaurants in Ferrara, Provvidenza is a pleasant country-style inn with a lovely garden for summertime dining alfresco. The local specialties—like fish grilled over charcoal and the bollito misto—are the best. *Corso Ercole l d'Este 92, tel. 0532/205187. Reservations advised. Dress: casual. AE, DC, V. Closed Mon. Expensive.*

Le Grazie. In an atmospheric part of the old town, down a long cobbled street, this restaurant makes its own excellent pasta. Try the *tagliatelle con cuori di carciofo e noci* (pasta with artichoke hearts and nuts). Other dishes are local, as is the wine list. *Via Vignatagliata 61, tel. 0532/761052. Reservations advised. Dress: casual. AE. Closed Tues. Moderate.*

Lodging
Duchessa Isabella. On a quiet street near Piazza Ariostea, this converted 16th-century mansion is the place for those who relish period atmosphere—the staff wears old-world dress, and a landau, drawn by a smart white horse, is available to guests for sightseeing. Each of the sumptuously draped bedrooms and suites is individually named. Every detail of the decor is meticulous, such as the elegant dining room's painted wooden ceiling. Some may find the formality wearying and the tone somewhat bogus, but a stay here will definitely be a memorable experience. *Via Palestro 70, tel. 0532/202121, fax 0532/202638. 28 rooms with bath. Facilities: restaurant, bar, garden, conference rooms, parking. AE, DC, MC, V. Expensive–Very Expensive.*

★
Ripagrande. This hotel is in a meticulously restored 14th-century palace in the heart of old Ferrara. Although the public rooms are authentically restored, the bedrooms are modern—chrome- and-glass-decorated boxes with little appeal. The rooms on the top floor are the exception, however—they have terraces, beamed ceilings, and views of the city. The staff is very attentive. *Via Ripagrande 21, tel. 0532/765250, fax 0532/764377. 40 rooms with bath or shower. Facilities: terrace bar, garage, conference rooms. AE, DC, MC, V. Expensive.*

Modena
Dining
★
Borso d'Este. One of the city's most highly regarded restaurants—particularly with the affluent youth—offers some delicious variations on old themes, like ravioli stuffed with game and Parmesan. Other specialties include risotto *agli asparagi* and a mushroom tart with truffle sauce. *Piazza Roma 5, tel. 059/21114. Reservations required. Dress: casual. AE, DC, MC, V. Closed Sat. lunch, Sun., and Aug. Expensive.*

Fini. A dining institution in Modena, Fini is widely held to be

the best restaurant the city has to offer. It is an elegant, traditional place, serving classics like bolliti misti in a green sauce.
Excellent local wines and homemade desserts. *Largo San
Francesco, tel. 059/214250. Reservations required. Jacket and
tie required. AE, DC, MC, V. Closed Mon., Tues., and July
27–Aug. 25, part of Dec. Expensive.*

Lodging   **Canal Grande.** Once a ducal palace, the Canal Grande offers
large, airy, well-equipped rooms, with TV and minibar. The
hotel's restaurant, La Secchia Rapita, is rated highly. *Corso
Canalgrande 6, tel. 059/217160, fax 059/219669. 78 rooms with
bath or shower. Facilities: restaurant, bar, garden, parking.
AE, DC, MC, V. Expensive.*

Parma   **Croce di Malta.** The historic premises once housed a convent,
Dining   then an inn (there are still inexpensive rooms available here),
before this attractive restaurant with turn-of-the-century decor opened in 1984. It's in the heart of Parma and the food is
traditional local fare. The homemade pasta is light and delicate;
try *tortelli* with squash filling or *tagliatelle* in any fashion. Second courses are well-prepared and filling versions of classic veal
and cheese dishes. *Borgo Palmia 8, tel. 0521/235643. Reservations advised. Dress: casual. AE, MC, V. Closed Sun. Moderate.*

★   **La Greppia.** Here, at the best and most elegant restaurant in
the city, risotto with porcini mushrooms is excellent, as is the
pâté in Marsala wine, the *torta di melanzane* (eggplant pie),
and the fried porcini mushrooms. *Via Garibaldi 39A, tel. 0521/
233686. Reservations required. Jacket required. AE, DC, MC,
V. Closed Thurs., Fri., July and Dec. 24–Jan. 1. Moderate.*

★   **Parma Rotta.** An old inn about 1.6 kilometer (1 mile) from
downtown Parma, the Parma Rotta remains an informal neighborhood trattoria serving hearty dishes like *pasta e fagioli*
(bean-and-pasta soup), roast pork, and spit-roasted lamb. *Via
Langhirano 158, tel. 0521/581323. Reservations advised.
Dress: casual. AE, DC, MC, V. Closed Sun. from June–Sept.,
Mon. Oct.–May. Moderate.*

Sant'Ambrogio. This is an informal restaurant in the center of
town. Roast duck and turkey are the best bets, but try the
cotechino con crauti (boiled pork sausage with pickled cabbage), too. *Vicolo Cinque Piaghe 1A, tel. 0521/34482. Reservations not necessary. Dress: casual. AE, DC, MC, V. Closed
Mon. Moderate.*

Lodging   **Palace Hotel Maria Luigia.** A top-quality hotel convenient to
old Parma and the train station, the Maria Luigia has large,
well-furnished rooms and is popular with business travelers.
*Via Mentana 140, tel. 0521/281032, fax 0521/231126. 105 rooms
with bath or shower. Facilities: bar, garage, restaurant, conference rooms. AE, DC, MC, V. Expensive.*

Park Hotel Stendhal. Completely renovated, the Stendhal is
again one of the best hotels in Parma. It is on the edge of the
historic center of town and convenient for the tourist and business traveler alike. Some rooms have views of the Palazzo della
Pilotta. *Via Bodoni 3, tel. 0521/208057, fax 0521/285655. 63
rooms with bath or shower. Facilities: restaurant, bar, parking, conference rooms. AE, DC, MC, V. Expensive.*

Torino. A warm reception and pleasant surroundings are the
best reasons for staying in this relaxed hotel. It's well run,
comfortable, and located in a quiet pedestrian zone in the heart
of town. *Via Mazza 7, tel. 0521/281046, fax 0521/230725. 33*

rooms with bath or shower. Facilities: air-conditioning, bar, garage. AE, DC, MC, V. Closed Aug. 1–25, Dec. 24–31. Moderate.

Piacenza **Antica Osteria del Teatro.** Set on a lovely piazza in the center of
Dining town, this restaurant is generally held to be the best in Piacen-
★ za. Try the *tortelli* stuffed with ricotta, the roast duck, or the grilled sea bass. *Via Verdi 16, tel. 0523/23777. Reservations advised. Dress: casual. AE, DC, MC, V. Closed Sun. eve., Mon., Aug. 1–Aug. 25, and Jan. 1–Jan. 25. Expensive.*

Ristorante Scai. Roast meat and game are what this restaurant does best, and a changing menu provides diners with pasta stuffed with roe-deer, as well as main courses of venison, duck, pig's feet or rabbit. *Piazza Baracca 22 (close to the church of San Vitale, at the end of Via Cavour), tel. 0544/22520. Reservations not necessary. Dress: casual. AE, DC, MC, V. Closed Mon. Inexpensive.*

Ravenna **Tre Spade.** An old mill has been converted into this fine restau-
Dining rant near the Duomo. The food is inventive and flawlessly
★ served. The *sella di lepre* (hare stuffed with liver paté and polenta) and the roast pheasant are wonderful. *Via G. Rasponi 37, tel. 0544/32382. Reservations required. Dress: casual. AE, DC, MC, V. Closed Sun. eve. in winter, Mon. and July 25–Aug. 20. Expensive.*

Ca de Ven. A vast wine cellar in the heart of the Old City, the Ca de Ven is a wonderful place for a hearty lunch or dinner. You sit at long tables with the other diners and feast on platters of delicious cold cuts; *piadine* (flat Romagna bread); and cold, heady white wine. If you're here in chilly weather, try the wholesome *pasta e fagioli. Via C. Ricci 24, tel. 0544/30163. No reservations. Dress: casual. V. Closed Mon. Inexpensive.*

Lodging **Ravenna.** There are a few more facilities here than at the Miner-
va hotel across the road, but little else to help you choose between them: both are just around the corner from the rail station with identical prices, and both offer the same modern, box-like rooms with functional furnishings. They are highly useful, however, if you've just stepped off a train, and you'll find little else in this price range at such a central location. Reserve in advance in summer. *Via Maroncelli 12, tel. 0544/22204. 25 rooms, 18 with bath. Facilities: bar, garage. MC, V. Inexpensive.*

Rimini **La Bicocca.** This popular trattoria is a good place for an intro-
Dining duction to the cuisine of Romagna. There are tasty pastas in
★ various seafood sauces, cheeses and local salamis, and excellent regional wines—all served in a cheerful atmosphere. *Vicolo Santa Chiara 105, tel. 0541/781148. Reservations advised. Dress: casual. AE, DC, MC, V. Closed Mon. Moderate.*

★ **Zio.** Nothing but seafood is served here, and all of it is good value for the money. The *insalata frutti di mare* is an all-encompassing seafood antipasto; *tortellini alle vongole* (stuffed pasta in a white clam sauce), fish cannelloni, and simple grilled sole are also recommended. *Vicolo Santa Chiara 18, tel. 0541/786160. Reservations advised. Dress: casual. AE, DC, MC, V. Closed Wed. and July. Moderate.*

Rock Island. Formerly a seafood restaurant, now a busy pub and *panineria*, the Rock Island is at the end of a pier right on the sea. You can drink and snack here and take part in Rimini's raucous nightlife. Steamy, loud, and full of young people, it's not for the fainthearted. *Molo di Levante, tel. 0541/50178.*

Dress: casual. No credit cards. Closed weekdays in winter. Inexpensive.

Lodging **The Grand Hotel.** One of the leading resort hotels in Italy, the
★ Grand is a turn-of-the-century hotel set in a quiet park, within
easy reach of its own private beach. The rooms are large and
airy, air-conditioned, and equipped with color TV and minibar.
*Via Ramusio 1, tel. 0541/56000, fax 0541/56866. 128 rooms with
full bath, 6 suites. Facilities: nightclub, sauna, beauty salon, 2
pools, private beach, yacht and tennis clubs, restaurant, bars,
parking. AE, DC, MC, V. Very Expensive.*

Club House Hotel. Ultramodern and right on the sea, the Club
House is a good hotel for summer vacations and is one of the few
open during the off-season. All rooms have balconies, minibar,
and color TV. *Viale Vespucci 52, tel. 0541/391460, fax 0541/
391442. 128 rooms with bath. Facilities: parking, bar, restaurant, private beach. AE, DC, MC. Expensive.*

Annarita. Set back in a leafy, residential road leading off the
main Viale Vespucci, this is a small but comfortable pensione,
mainly frequented by a regular clientele: availability may consequently be limited. Guests are expected to pay full board
during the summer season. Facilities are rudimentary, rooms
are basic, but the main benefits here are its closeness to the
beach promenade and the convenient price. *Viale Misurata 24,
tel. 0541/391044. Facilities: bar, restaurant, parking. No credit
cards. Inexpensive.*

The Arts

Bologna hosts a wide selection of orchestral and chamber music
concerts, as well as an acclaimed opera season. The 18th-century Teatro Comunale presents concerts by Italian and international orchestras throughout the year, but opera dominates
the theater's winter season. All events sell out quickly, so be
sure to reserve seats early (Largo Respighi 1, tel. 051/222999).
The Teatro della Celebrazione is the center for chamber music
(Via Saragozza 236, tel. 051/529011). Also check concert schedules for the Sala Bossi (Piazza Rossini 2, tel. 051/222997) and
the Sala Mozart in the Accademia Filarmonica, the principal
music school of the city (Via Guerazzi 13, tel. 051/235236).

Parma is the region's opera center, with performances held at
the Teatro Regio (tel. 0521/218687) on Via Garibaldi. Opera
here is taken just as seriously as in Milan, although tickets are a
little easier to come by. Playwright Dario Fo helped found
Parma's **Teatro Stábile di Parma** theater (Viale Basetti 12, tel.
0521/208088), whose productions still maintain a mixture of
comedy and politics—though your understanding of the
themes will be limited without a knowledge of Italian.

13 Umbria and the Marches

Perugia, Assisi, Urbino, Spoleto, and Orvieto

Umbria is the green heart of Italy. A region of steep, austere hills, deep valleys, and fast-flowing rivers, Umbria has not yet been swamped by tourism and has escaped the unplanned industrial expansion that afflicts much of central Italy. No town in Umbria boasts the extravagant wealth of art and architecture of Florence, Rome, or Venice, but this lack works in your favor. Cities can be experienced whole, rather than as a series of museums and churches, forced marches through 2,000 years of Western culture; in Umbria the visitor comes to know the towns as people live in them today.

This is not to suggest that the cultural cupboard is bare—far from it. Perugia, the capital of the region, and Assisi, Umbria's most famous city, are rich in art and architecture, as are Orvieto, Todi, and Spoleto. Virtually all the small towns in the region boast a castle, church, or museum worth a stop.

The earliest inhabitants of Umbria, the Umbri, were thought by the Romans to be the most ancient inhabitants of Italy. Little is known about them, since with the coming of Etruscan culture, the tribe fled into the mountains in the eastern portion of the region. The Etruscans, who founded some of the great cities of Umbria, were in turn supplanted by the Romans. Unlike Tuscany and other regions of central Italy, Umbria had few powerful medieval families to exert control over the cities in the Middle Ages—proximity to Rome ensured that Umbria would always be more or less under papal domination.

The relative political stability of the region did not mean that Umbria was left in peace. Located in the center of the country, it has for much of its history been a battlefield, where armies from north and south clashed. Hannibal destroyed a Roman army on the shores of Lake Trasimeno, and the full and bloody course of the interminable Guelph-Ghibelline conflict of the Middle Ages was played out in Umbria. Dante considered it the most violent place in Italy. Trophies of war still decorate the facade of the Palazzo dei Priori in Perugia, and the little town of Gubbio continues a warlike rivalry begun in the Middle Ages—every year it challeges the Tuscan town of San Sepolcro to a cross-bow tournament. Today, of course, the bowmen shoot at targets, but neither side has forgotten that 500 years ago its ancestors shot at each other.

In spite of—or perhaps because of—this bloodshed, Umbria has produced more than its share of Christian saints. The most famous is St. Francis, the decidedly unmartial saint whose life shaped the Church and the history of his time. His great shrine at Assisi is visited by hundreds of thousands of pilgrims each year. St. Clare, his devoted follower, was Umbria born, as were St. Benedict; St. Rita of Cascia; and, ironically, the shadowy patron saint of lovers, St. Valentine.

The Marches—or Marche, in Italian—stretch between the hills of the southern Apennines down to the Adriatic sea. It is a scenic region of mountains and valleys, with great turreted castles standing on high peaks defending passes and roads—silent testament to the region's warlike past. The Marches have passed through numerous hands. First the Romans supplanted the native civilizations; then Charlemagne supplanted the Romans (and gave the region its name: It was divided into "Marks," or provinces, under the rule of the Holy Roman Emperor); then began the seemingly never-ending struggle between popes and local lords. Cesare Borgia succeeded in wrestling control of the Marches from the local suzerains, annexing the region to the papacy of his father, Alexander VI.

Despite all this martial tussling, it was in the lonely mountain town of Urbino that the Renaissance came to its fullest flower; that small town became a haven of culture and learning that rivaled the greater, richer, and more powerful city of Florence, and even Rome itself.

Essential Information

Important Addresses and Numbers

Tourist Information   **Ancona** (Via Thaon de Revel 4, tel. 071/33249; railway station, Piazza Fratelli Rosselli, tel. 071/41703; EPT, Via Marini 14, tel. 071/200313).
Ascoli Piceno (Corso Mazzini 229, tel. 0736/257267; Via Malta, tel. 0736/255250).
Assisi (Piazza del Comune 12, tel. 075/812450).
Gubbio (Piazza Oderisi 6, tel. 075/922–0693).
Loreto (Via Solari 3, tel. 071/977139).
Perugia: Umbria's regional tourist office (Via Mazzini 21, tel. 075/25341); Perugia's city tourist office (Piazza IV Novembre 3, tel. 075/23327).
Spoleto (Piazza della Libertà 7, tel. 0743/49890 or 220311).
Urbino (Piazza Rinascimento 1, tel. 0722/2613).

Emergencies   **Police. Perugia** (Piazza dei Partigiani, tel. 113). **Assisi** (Piazza Matteotti 3, tel. 075/812239). **Spoleto** (Via Cerquiglia 36, tel. 0743/49044). **Orvieto** (Piazza della Repubblica, tel. 0763/40088).

Arriving and Departing

By Car   On the western edge of the region is the Umbrian section of the Autostrada del Sole (A1), the principal north–south highway in Italy. It links Florence and Rome with the important Umbrian town of Orvieto and passes near Todi and Terni. The S3 intersects with A1 and leads on to Assisi and Urbino. The Adriatica superhighway (A14) runs north–south along the coast, linking the Marches to Bologna and Venice.

By Train   The main rail line from Rome to Ancona passes through Narni, Terni, Spoleto, and Foligno. Travel time from Rome to Spoleto is a little less than two hours. The main Rome–Florence line stops at Orvieto, and, with a change of trains at the small town of Orte, one can travel by rail from Rome or Florence to Perugia and Assisi.

By Bus   Rome and Florence are served by private bus services, leaving from Perugia and Orvieto.

Getting Around

By Car   Umbria has an excellent and modern road network. Central Umbria is served by a major highway, 75bis, which passes along the shore of Lake Trasimeno and ends in Perugia, the principal city of the region. Assisi, the most visited town in the region, is well served by the modern highway 75, which connects to Routes 3 and 3bis, which cover the heart of the region.

Major inland routes connect coastal A14 to large towns in the Marches, including Urbino, Jesi, Macerata, and Ascoli Piceno, but inland secondary roads in mountain areas can be tortuous and narrow.

By Train Branch lines link the central rail hub, Ancona, with the inland towns Urbino, Fabriano, and Ascoli Piceno. In Umbria, a small, privately owned railway runs from Città di Castello in the north to Terni in the south.

By Bus There is good local bus service between all the major and minor towns of Umbria. Some of the routes in rural areas, especially in the Marches, are designed to serve as many destinations as possible and are, therefore, quite roundabout and slow. Schedules often change, so consult with local tourist offices before setting out.

Exploring Umbria and the Marches

The steep hills and deep valleys that make Umbria and the Marches so picturesque also make it difficult to get around in. Driving routes must be chosen carefully to avoid tortuous mountain roads; major towns are not necessarily linked to each other by train, bus, or highway. A convenient base for exploring the region might be Perugia, the largest city in Umbria and the hub of Tour 1, but to see the region properly you would still need to stay overnight in other towns along the way. Tour 2 heads east across the Appenines to the region known as the Marches; we begin exploring it in the hilltop city of Urbino, travel down to the Adriatic coast to visit Ancona, then climb back west into the hills to Loreto and Ascoli Piceno. Back in Umbria, Tour 3 concentrates on two memorable towns: Spoleto, site of the famous arts festival, south of Perugia; and Assisi, St. Francis' hometown, just east of Perugia. The final tour centers on Orvieto, built on a huge rock outcropping in western Umbria, southwest of Perugia.

Highlights for First-time Visitors

Basilica of St. Francis, Assisi (Tour 3: Spoleto and Assisi).

Collegio del Cambio, Perugia (Tour 1: Perugia to Gubbio).

Duomo, Orvieto (Tour 4: Orvieto and Environs).

Duomo, Spoleto (Tour 3: Spoleto and Assisi).

Ducal Palace, Urbino (Tour 2: The Marches).

Fontana Maggiore and Palazzo dei Priori, Perugia
(Tour 1: Perugia to Gubbio).

House of the Virgin Mary, Loreto (Tour 2: The Marches).

Palazzo dei Consoli, Gubbio (Tour 1: Perugia to Gubbio).

Piazza del Popolo, Ascoli Piceno (Tour 2: The Marches).

Tour 1: Perugia to Gubbio

Numbers in the margins correspond to points of interest on the Umbria and the Marches and Perugia maps.

❶ Perugia, the largest and richest of Umbria's cities, is an old and elegant place of great charm. Despite a rather grim crust of modern suburbs, Perugia's location on a series of hills high above the suburban plain has ensured that the medieval city remains almost completely intact. Perugia is the best-preserved hill town of its size, and few other places in Italy illustrate better the concept of the self-contained city-state that so shaped the course of Italian history.

The best approach to the city is by train—the station is located in the unlovely suburbs—and there are frequent buses running directly to the Piazza d'Italia, the heart of the old town. If you are driving to Perugia, it is best to leave your car in one of the parking lots near the station and then take the bus or the escalator (which passes through fascinating subterranean excavations of the Roman foundations of the city) to the center of town.

The nerve center of the city is the broad, stately **Corso Vannucci,** a pedestrian street that runs from the Piazza d'Italia to the Piazza IV Novembre. As evening falls, the Corso Vannucci becomes the place where the Perugini gather for their evening *passeggiata*, a pleasant predinner stroll, pausing for an aperitif at one of the many bars that line the street.

Time Out You can enjoy the lively comings and goings of the Corso Vannucci from the vantage point of the **Bar Sandri** (Corso Vannucci 32). This fine old bar is a 19th-century relic with wood-paneled walls and an elaborately frescoed ceiling.

Corso Vannucci runs into Piazza IV Novembre, a pretty, sunny square dominated by the **Duomo** (the Cathedral of San Lorenzo), the medieval **Palazzo dei Priori** (the seat of government), and the **Fontana Maggiore** (a fountain by Giovanni and Nicola Pisano that dates from the 13th century).

❷ The **Duomo** is a large and rather plain building dating from the Middle Ages but with many additions from the 15th and 16th centuries. The interior is vast and echoing, with little in the way of decoration. There are some elaborately carved choir stalls, executed by Giovanni Battista Bastone in 1520. The great relic of the church is kept in a chapel in the left aisle; it is the wedding ring of the Virgin Mary that the Perugians stole from the nearby town of Chiusi. The ring is the size of a large bangle and is kept under lock (15 locks, actually) and key for every day of the year except July 30, when it is exposed to view. *Duomo. Open daily 8–1, 4–7:30.*

In the adjoining **Museum of the Duomo** there is a large array of precious objects associated with the cathedral, including vestments, vessels, manuscripts, and gold work, as well as one outstanding piece of artwork, an early masterpiece by Luca Signorelli, the altarpiece showing the Madonna with St. John the Baptist, St. Onophrius, and St. Lawrence (1484). *Admission: 2,000 lire. Open Wed.–Fri. 9–noon, Sat. 9–noon, 3:30–5:30, Sun. 3:30–5:30.*

❸ The **Palazzo dei Priori** faces the Duomo across the piazza. It is an imposing building, begun in the 13th century, with an unusual staircase that fans out into the square. The facade is decorated with symbols of Perugia's pride and past power: The griffin is the symbol of the city; the lion denotes Perugia's alle-

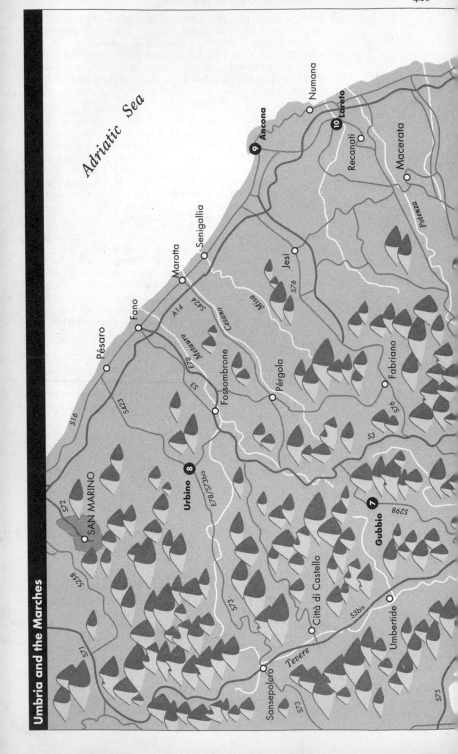

Umbria and the Marches

Adriatic Sea

Numana

Ancona **9**

10 Loreto

Recanati

Macerata

Pésaro

Fano

Marotta

Senigallia

Jesi

Potenza

S16

S423

A14

S424

Metauro

E78

S3

Cesano

Misa

S76

Fossombrone

Pérgola

Fabriano

S72

SAN MARINO

Urbino **8**

E78/S73bis

S73

S3

S76

S258

Gubbio **7**

S298

S71

Città di Castello

S3bis

Umbertide

Sansepolcro

Tevere

S73

S75

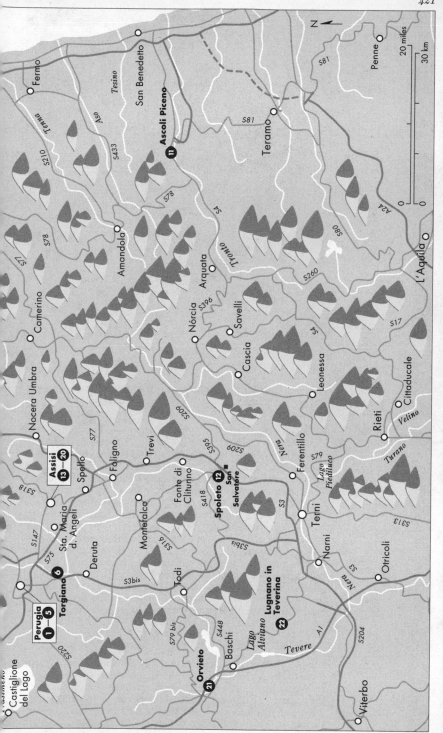

Archaeological
Museum of Umbria, **5**
Collegio del
Cambio, **4**
Duomo, **2**
Palazzo dei Priori, **3**

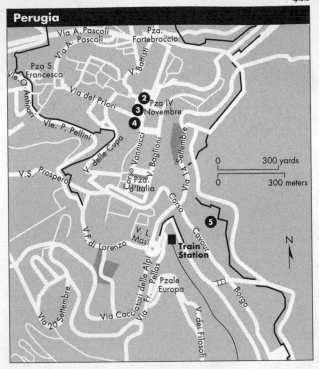

giance to the Guelph (or papal) cause; and both figures support the heavy chains of the gates of Siena, which fell to Perugian forces in 1358.

Attached to the Palazzo dei Priori, but entered from the Corso Vannucci, is the **Collegio del Cambio,** a series of elaborate rooms that housed the meeting hall and chapel of the guild of bankers and money changers. The walls were frescoed from 1496 to 1500 by the most important Perugian painter of the Renaissance, Pietro Vannucci, better known as Perugino. The decorative program in the Collegio includes common religious themes, like the Nativity and the Transfiguration (on the end walls), but also figures intended to inspire the businessmen who congregated here. On the left wall are female figures representing the virtues, and beneath them the heroes and sages of antiquity. On the right wall are the Prophets and Sibyls— said to have been painted in part by Perugino's most famous pupil, Raphael, whose hand, the experts say, is most apparent in the figure of Fortitude. On one of the pilasters is a remarkably honest self-portrait of Perugino surmounted by a Latin inscription and contained in a *faux* frame. *Admission: 2,000 lire. Open Nov.–Feb., Tues.–Sat. 8–2, Sun. 9–12:30; Mar.–Oct., Tues.–Sat. 9–12:30 and 2:30–5:30, Sun. 9–12:30.*

About a 10-minute walk south of the center along Corso Cavour leads to the **Archaeological Museum of Umbria,** which contains an excellent collection of Etruscan artifacts from throughout the region. Perugia was a flourishing Etruscan site long before it fell under Roman domination in 40 BC. (Other than this collection, little remains of Perugia's mysterious ancestors, although the Gate of Augustus, in Piazza Fortebraccio, the northern entrance to the city, is of Etruscan origin.) *Piazza Giordano Bruno. Admission: 4,000 lire. Open Mon.–Sat. 9–1:30 and 3–7; Sun. 9–1.*

❻ Wine lovers are certain to want to visit **Torgiano,** 15 kilometers (9.3 miles) southeast of Perugia. It is home to the famous Lungarotti winery, best known for delicious Rubesco Lungarotti, San Giorgio, and Chardonnay. The town is also home to the fascinating Wine Museum, which has a large collection of ancient wine vessels, presses, documents, and tools that tell the story of viticulture in Umbria and beyond. The museum traces the history of wine in all its uses—for drinking at the table, as medicine, and in mythology. *Corso Vittorio Emanuele 11. Admission: 2,000 lire. Open Apr.–Sept., daily 9–noon and 3–8; Oct.–Mar., daily 9–1 and 3–6.*

The 40-kilometer (25-mile) trip from Perugia northeast to **❼** **Gubbio** follows S298 through rugged, mountainous terrain. There is something otherworldly about Gubbio, a small jewel of a medieval town tucked away in this mountainous corner of Umbria. Even at the height of summer, the cool serenity and silence of Gubbio's streets remain intact. The town is perched on the slopes of Mount Ingino, and the streets are dramatically steep.

Gubbio's relatively isolated position has kept it free of hordes of high-season visitors, but even during the busiest times of year the city lives up to its Italian nickname, The City of Silence. Parking in the central Piazza *dei* Quaranta Martiri (named for 40 hostages murdered by the Nazis in 1944) is easy and secure, and it is wise to leave your car there and explore the narrow streets on foot.

Walk up the main street of the town, Via della Repubblica (a steep climb) to Piazza della Signoria. This square is dominated by the magnificent **Palazzo dei Consoli,** a medieval building designed and built by a local architect known as Gattapone—a man still much admired by today's residents (every other hotel, restaurant, and bar has been named after him).

While the Palazzo dei Consoli is impressive, it is the piazza itself that is most striking. When approached from the thicket of medieval streets, the wide and majestic square is an eye-opener. The piazza juts out from the hillside like an enormous terrace, giving wonderful views of the town and surrounding countryside.

The Palazzo dei Consoli houses a small **museum,** famous chiefly for the Tavole Eugubine, bronze tablets written in an ancient Umbrian language. Also in the museum are the *ceri,* three 16-foot-high poles crowned with statues of saints Ubaldo, George, and Anthony. These heavy pillars are the focal point of the best-known event in Gubbio, the Festival of the Candles ("Ceri"), held every May 15. On that day, teams of Gubbio's young men, dressed in medieval costumes and carrying the ceri, race up the steep slopes of Mount Ingino to the Monastery of St. Ubaldo, high above the town. This festival, enacted faithfully every year since 1151, is a picturesque, if strenuous, way of thanking the patron saints of the town for their assistance in a miraculous Gubbian victory over a league of 11 other towns. *Admission: 2,000 lire. Open Apr.–Sept., daily 9–12:30 and 3:30–6; Oct.–Mar., daily 9–1 and 3–5.*

The **Duomo** and the **Palazzo Ducale** face each other across a narrow street on the highest tier of the town. The Duomo dates from the 13th century, with some Baroque additions—in particular, a lavishly decorated bishop's chapel. *Duomo. Open daily 9–5.*

The Palazzo Ducale is a scaled-down copy of the Palazzo Ducale in Urbino (Gubbio was once the possession of that city's ruling family, the Montefeltro). Gubbio's palazzo contains a small museum and a fine courtyard. There are magnificent views from some of the public rooms. *Palazzo Ducale. Open Tues.–Sun. 9–2.*

Time Out Under the arches that support the Palazzo Ducale is the **Bar del Giardino Pubblico,** a bar set in the tiny public gardens, which seem to hang off the side of the mountain. It is a charming place for a cold drink and a rest after a tiring climb up to the Duomo and Palace. *Open May–Sept., daily 9–7.*

Tour 2: The Marches

An excursion from Umbria into the region of the Marches is recommended for those who want to get off the beaten track and see a part of Italy rarely visited by foreigners. It must be admitted that traveling in the Marches is not as easy as in Umbria or Tuscany. Beyond the narrow coastal plain and away from major towns, the roads are steep and twisting. Train travel in the region is slow, and destinations are limited, although one can reach Urbino and Ascoli Piceno, the principal tourist cities of the region, by rail, if by rather a roundabout route.

8 **Urbino** is a majestic city, sitting atop a steep hill, with a skyline of towers and domes. It is something of a surprise to come upon Urbino—its location is remote—and it is even stranger to reflect that this quiet country town was once a center of learning and culture almost without rival in western Europe.

The town looks much as it did in the glory days of the 15th century, a cluster of warm brick and pale stone buildings, all topped with russet-colored tiled roofs. The focal point of the city is the immense and beautiful Ducal Palace. The tradition of learning in Urbino continues to this day. The city is the home of a small but prestigious Italian state university—one of the oldest in the world—and during term time the streets are filled with hordes of noisy students. It is very much a college town, with the usual array of bookshops, record stores, bars, and coffeehouses. During the summer, the Italian student population is replaced by foreigners who come to study Italian language and arts at several prestigious, private fine-arts academies.

Urbino's fame rests on the reputation of three of its native sons. They are Duke Federico da Montefeltro, the enlightened warrior-patron who built the Ducal Palace; Raphael, one of the most influential painters in history and an embodiment of the spirit of the Renaissance; and the architect Donato Bramante, who translated the philosophy of the Renaissance into buildings of grace and beauty. Why three of the greatest men of the age should have been born within a generation of one another in this remote town has never been explained. Oddly enough, there is little work by either Bramante or Raphael in the city, but the duke's influence can still be felt strongly, even now, some 500 years after his death.

The **Ducal Palace** holds the place of honor in the city, and in no other palace of its era are the principles of the Renaissance stated quite so clearly. If the Renaissance was, in ideal form, a celebration of the nobility of man and his works, of the light and purity of the soul, then there is no place in Italy, the birthplace of the Renaissance, where these tenets are better illustrated. From the moment you enter the peaceful courtyard, you know that you are in a place of grace and beauty, the harmony of the building reflecting the high ideals of the men who built it.

Today the palace houses the **National Museum of the Marches,** with a superb collection of paintings, sculpture, and other *objets d'art,* well arranged and properly lit. It would be hard to mention all the great works in this collection—some originally the possessions of the Montefeltro family, others brought to the museum from churches and palaces throughout the region—but there are a few that must be singled out. Of these, perhaps the most famous is Piero della Francesca's enigmatic work *The Flagellation of Christ.* Much has been written about this painting, and few experts agree on its meaning. Legend has it that the three figures in the foreground represent a murdered member of the Montefeltro family (the barefoot young man) and his two murderers. Others claim the painting is a heavily veiled criticism of certain parts of Christian Europe—the iconography is obscure and the history extremely complicated. All the experts agree, though, that the painting is one of Piero della Francesca's masterpieces. Piero himself thought so. It is one of the few works he signed (on the lowest step supporting Pilate's throne).

Other masterworks in the collection are Paolo Uccello's *Profanation of the Host,* Piero della Francesca's *Madonna of Senigallia,* and Titian's *Resurrection* and *Last Supper.* Duke Federico's study is an astonishingly elaborate, but tiny, room decorated with inlaid wood, said to be the work of Botticelli. *Piazza Duca Federico, tel. 0722/2760. Admission: 8,000 lire. Open Apr.–Sept., Mon.–Sat. 9–7, Sun. 9–1; Oct.–Mar., Mon.–Sat. 9–2, Sun. 9–1.*

The **house of the painter Raphael** really is the house in which he was born and in which he took his first steps in painting (under the direction of his artist father). There is some debate about the fresco of the Madonna that adorns the house. Some say it is by Raphael, others attribute it to the father—with Raphael's mother and the young painter himself standing in as models for the Madonna and Child. Either way, it's an interesting picture. *Via Raffaello. Admission: 3,000 lire. Open Apr.–Sept., Tues.– Sat., 9–1, 3–7, Sun. 9–1; Oct.–Mar., Tues.–Sat. 9–2, Sun. 9–1. Closed Mon.*

❾ To reach **Ancona,** on the Adriatic Coast, from Urbino, a distance of approximately 87 kilometers (54 miles), take the E78 or S3 to the superhighway A14, which runs along the coast but inland by a mile or so. The coast road, Route 16, is a congested two-lane highway with little to recommend it.

Ancona was probably once a lovely city. It is set on an elbow-shaped bluff (hence its name; ankon is Greek for "elbow"), that juts out into the Adriatic. Once in a while (but not often) one does catch glimpses of the old architecture of the city. But Ancona was the object of serious aerial bombing during the Second World War—it was, and is, an important port city—and was reduced to rubble. The city has been rebuilt in the unfortunate postwar poured-concrete style, practical and inexpensive but certainly not pleasing. Unless you are taking a ferry to Yugoslavia or Venice, there is little reason to visit the city—with a few exceptions.

⑩ Loreto is an easy excursion from Ancona. To reach this small inland hill town, take Route A14 to the Loreto turnoff, a 24-kilometer (15-mile) drive south of Ancona.

Loreto is famous for one of the best-loved shrines in the world, that of the **house of the Virgin Mary.** The legend is that angels moved the house from Nazareth, where the Virgin was living at the time of the Annunciation, to this hilltop in 1295. The reason for this sudden and divinely inspired move was that Nazareth had fallen into the hands of Muslim invaders, not suitable landlords, the angelic hosts felt. More recently, following archaeological excavations made at the behest of the church, evidence has come to light proving that the house did once stand elsewhere and was brought to the hilltop by human means around the time the angels are said to have done the job.

The house itself consists of three rough stone walls contained within an elaborate marble tabernacle; built around this centerpiece is the giant basilica of the Holy House, which dominates the town. Millions of visitors come to the site every year (particularly at Easter and on the Feast of the Holy House, December 10), and the little town of Loreto can become uncomfortably crowded with pilgrims. Many great Italian architects have contributed to the design of the basilica. They include Bramante, Sangallo, and Sansovino. The interior contains a great number of mediocre 19th- and 20th-century paintings but also has some fine work by Renaissance masters like Luca Signorelli and Melozzo da Forli.

Nervous air travelers may take comfort in the fact that the Holy Virgin of Loreto is the patroness of air travelers and that Pope John Paul II has composed a prayer for a safe flight—available in the church in a half-dozen languages.

⑪ Ascoli Piceno, 105 kilometers (65 miles) from Ancona, is not a hill town. Rather, it sits in a valley, ringed by steep hills and cut by the fast-racing Tronto River. The town is almost unique in Italy, in that it seems to have its traffic problems—in the historic center, at any rate—pretty much under control; you can drive *around* the picturesque part of the city, but driving *through* it is most difficult. This feature makes Ascoli Piceno one of the most pleasant large towns in the country for exploring on foot. True, there is traffic, but you are not constantly assaulted by jams, noise, and exhaust fumes the way you are in other Italian cities.

The heart of the town is the majestic **Piazza del Popolo,** dominated by the Gothic church of San Francesco and the Palazzo del Popolo, a 13th-century town hall that contains a graceful Renaissance courtyard. The square itself functions as the living room of the entire city. At dusk each evening the piazza is packed with people standing in small groups, exchanging news and gossip as if at a cocktail party.

Time Out There are several bars on the Piazza del Popolo, but two are exceptional. One, **Merletti,** in the corner closest to the Palazzo del Popolo, is a perfectly preserved turn-of-the-century coffeehouse, with a creaky wood floor, marble-topped tables, an ornate bar, and a large selection of homemade pastries. Have a cup of coffee here and feel as if you've stepped back in time. The other bar, **Mix,** is a modern, trendy place with a wonderful array of sandwiches and pizzas, as well as a fine wine list. It's an excellent place for a light lunch or snack.

The 175-kilometer (108-mile) drive to Spoleto takes you out of the Marches and back into Umbria. The route, S4 southwest to Rieti, then Route 79 north to Terni, then Route 3 into Spoleto, is roundabout but vastly preferable to a series of winding mountain roads that connect Ascoli Piceno with Umbria.

Tour 3: Spoleto and Assisi

⑫ **Spoleto** is an enchanting town perfectly situated in wooded countryside. "A little bit of heaven fallen to earth" it was once called, and it is not hard to understand the sentiment. "Quaint" may be an overused term, but it is the most appropriate word to describe this city still enclosed by stout medieval walls. The chief pleasure of Spoleto is that the city itself is the sight. There is no long tramp through museums and churches in store for you here; rather, you can enjoy the simple treat of walking through the maze of twisting streets and up and down cobbled stairways, enjoying the beauty of the town and its wonderful peace and quiet.

Quiet, that is, except when the city is hosting the Festival of Two Worlds, an arts festival, held every year from mid-June to mid-July. During those two months the sleepy town is swamped with visitors who come to see world-class plays and operas, to hear concerts, and to see extensive exhibitions of paintings and sculpture. Hotels in the city and countryside are filled to overflowing, and the streets are packed with visitors. It is unwise to arrive in Spoleto during this period without confirmed hotel reservations. Furthermore, experiencing the city itself, rather than the festival, is very difficult during these months. Those who don't care for crowds are advised to avoid the city during the festival.

Even in the off-season, parking in the Old City is difficult. If you are traveling by car, it is best to park outside the walls. There is usually ample parking available near the Piazza della Vittoria.

Spoleto is dominated by a huge castle that was built in 1359–63 by the Gubbio-born architect Gattapone. It was until recently a high-security prison, but is now undergoing restoration and is sometimes open to the public. The castle was built to protect the city's most famous monument, the massive bridge known as the **Ponte delle Torri** (Bridge of the Towers), built by Gattapone on Roman foundations. This massive structure stands 262 feet above the gorge it spans and was built originally as an aqueduct. The bridge is open to pedestrians, and a walk over it affords marvelous views. Looking down to the river below is the best way to appreciate the colossal dimensions of the bridge. The central span is actually higher than that of the dome of St. Peter's in Rome.

The bridge and castle stand at the highest point in the town. From there you can head downhill to the **Duomo,** set in a lovely square. The church facade is dourly Romanesque but with the pleasant light addition of a Renaissance loggia. The contrast between the heavy medieval work and the graceful later embellishment graphically demonstrates the difference, not only in style, but in philosophy, of the two eras. The earlier was strong but ungiving; the later, human and open-minded.

From the Piazza del Duomo make your way to the Piazza del Mercato, site of the old Roman forum and today the main square of the Old Town.

Time Out The square is lined with bars and delicatessens that serve good pastries and coffee. Parked in the square every day except Sunday is the van of a *porchetta* seller. These mobile snack bars are common to all central and northern Italy, and they serve only one product—roast pork. The whole pig is roasted on a spit, and slices are carved off to make delicious sandwiches on crusty rolls called *rosette*. The porchetta seller in the Piazza del Mercato is particularly cheerful, and his portions are generous.

The **Arch of Drusus,** off the southern end of the square, was built by the Senate of Spoleto to honor the Roman general Drusus, son of the Emperor Tiberius.

North of the Piazza del Mercato, past the picturesque Via Fontesecca, with its tempting shops selling local pottery and other handicrafts, is the church of **Sant 'Eufemia** (in the courtyard of the archbishop's palace). It is an ancient, austere church built in the 11th century. Its most interesting feature is the gallery above the nave where female worshippers were required to sit—a holdover from the Eastern Church—one of the few such galleries in this part of Italy. *Open daily 9–1, 4–6.*

At the southern end of the Corso Mazzini you'll find a small but well-preserved **Roman theater,** used in summer for performances of Spoleto's arts festival. The theater was the site of one of the town's most macabre incidents. During the Middle Ages, Spoleto took the side of the Holy Roman Emperor in the interminable struggle between Guelph (papal) and Ghibelline (imperial) factions over the question of who would control central and northern Italy. Four hundred of the pope's supporters were massacred in the theater, and their bodies were burned in an enormous pyre. It is not an episode of which Spoleto is proud, and, furthermore, the Guelphs were triumphant in the end. Spoleto was incorporated into the states of the Church in 1354. *Open Tues.–Sun. 9–1. Closed holidays.*

On the outskirts of the city, just off Via Flaminia (Route 3), is the lovely church of **San Salvatore.** You may already have seen a lot of old churches in Italy, but few are as old as this one. It needed *renovation* in the 9th century—by that time it was already 600 years old. It is nestled under cypresses and surrounded by Spoleto's cemetery and is quiet, cool, and peaceful. The church was built by Eastern monks in the 4th century, and little has been added (or removed) since its renovation. San Salvatore has an air of timelessness and antiquity rarely found in churches so close to major towns. *Open daily 8–1, 4–6.*

Assisi is a total of 47 kilometers (30 miles) north and west of Spoleto on Routes 3 and 75.

⓭ The first sight of **Assisi** is memorable. The hill on which Assisi sits rises dramatically from the flat plain, and the town is dominated at the top of the mount by a massive medieval castle; on the lower slopes of the hill is the huge Basilica of San Francesco, rising majestically on graceful arched supports.

Numbers in the margin correspond to points of interest on the Assisi map.

Except in the depths of the off-season, Assisi, the most famous and most visited city in Umbria, is always thronged with sightseers and pilgrims. Somehow, though, despite the press of visitors, there is an unspoiled quality to the city—although that charm can be taxed to the limit during major feasts of the church, like Christmas or Easter, or on the feast of the patron saint himself (October 4). But if you come to Assisi on a weekday or in the low season, you are sure to see this charming rose-colored town at its best.

St. Francis was born here in 1181, the son of a well-to-do merchant. He had, by his own account, a riotous youth but forsook the pleasures of the flesh quite early in life, adopting a life of austerity. His mystical approach to poverty, asceticism, and the beauty of man and nature struck a responsive chord in the medieval mind, and he quickly attracted a vast number of followers. He was a humble and unassuming man, and his compassion and humility brought him great love and veneration in his own lifetime. Without actively seeking power, as did many clerics of his day, he amassed great influence and political power, changing the history of the Catholic church. He was the first person to receive the stigmata (wounds in his hands, feet, and side corresponding to the torments of Christ on the cross), injuries that caused him great pain and suffering, which he bore with characteristic patience. Nonetheless, St. Francis welcomed the coming of "Sister Death," in 1226. Today the Franciscans are the largest of all the Catholic orders. And among the mass of clergy at Assisi, you can identify the saint's followers by their simple, coarse brown habits bound by belts of knotted rope.

⓮ The basilica of **San Francesco** is one of Italy's foremost monuments and was begun shortly after the saint's death. What St. Francis would have made of a church of such size, wealth, and grandeur—the opposite of all he preached and believed—is hard to imagine. His coffin, unearthed from its secret hiding place in 1818, is on display in the crypt below the lower church and is a place of piety. The Basilica is not one church, but two huge structures built one over the other. The lower church is dim and full of candle-lit shadows, while the upper is a bright and airy place; both churches are magnificently decorated artistic treasure houses.

Visit the lower church first. The first chapel on the left of the nave was decorated by the Sienese master Simone Martini. Frescoed in 1322–26, the paintings show the life of St. Martin—the sharing of his cloak with the poor man, the saint's knighthood, and his death.

There is some dispute about the paintings in the third chapel on the right. Experts have argued for years as to their authorship, with many saying that they were done by Giotto. The paintings depict the life of St. Mary Magdalen. There is a similar dispute about the works above the high altar—some say

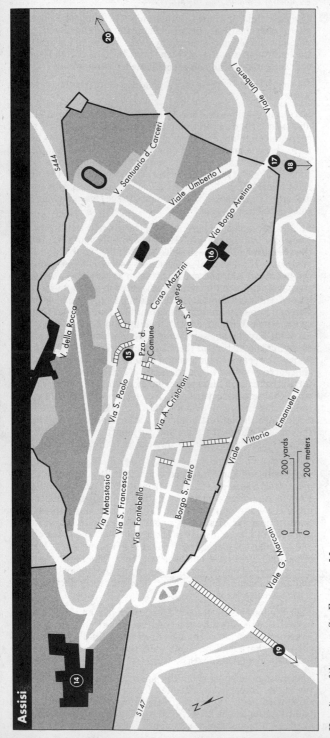

Assisi

200 yards
200 meters

0

0

Hermitage of the
Carceri, **20**
Porta Nuova, **17**
San Damiano, **18**

San Francesco, **14**
Santa Chiara, **16**
Santa Maria degli
Angeli, **19**
Temple of Minerva, **15**

they are by Giotto; others claim them for an anonymous pupil. They depict the marriage of St. Francis to poverty, chastity, and obedience.

In the right transept are frescoes by Cimabue, a Madonna and Saints, one of them St. Francis himself. In the left transept are some of the best-known works of the Sienese painter Pietro Lorenzetti. They depict the Madonna with saints John and Francis, a Crucifixion, and a Descent from the Cross.

It is quite a contrast to climb the steps next to the altar and emerge into the bright sunlight and airy grace of the double-arched Renaissance cloister called the Cloister of the Dead. A door to the right leads to the treasury of the church and contains relics of St. Francis and other holy objects associated with the order.

The upper church is dominated by Giotto's 28 frescoes, each portraying incidents in the life of St. Francis. Although the artist was only in his twenties when he painted this cycle, the frescoes show that Giotto was the pivotal artist in the development of Western painting, breaking away from the stiff, unnatural styles of earlier generations and moving toward a realism and grace that reached its peak in the Renaissance. The paintings are viewed left to right, starting in the transept. The most beloved of all the scenes is probably that of *St. Francis Preaching to the Birds,* a touching painting that seems to sum up the gentle spirit of the saint. It stands in marked contrast to the scene of the dream of Innocent III. The pope dreams of a humble monk who will steady the church. Sure enough, in the panel next to the sleeping pope, you see a strong Francis supporting a church that seems to be on the verge of tumbling down. *Upper and lower churches. Open summer, Mon.–Sat. 6 AM–7 PM, Sun. 6 AM–7:30 PM; winter, Mon.–Sat. 6:30–noon and 2–6, Sun. 6:30 AM–7 PM.*

⑮ Follow Via San Francesco from the Basilica up the hill to the central square of the town, the Piazza del Comune. The **Temple of Minerva,** on the left, is made up of bits and pieces of a Roman temple that dates from the time of Augustus. It has been converted into a church. *Open daily 7–noon and 4–7.*

⑯ Follow the Corso Mazzini out of the square, heading toward the church of **Santa Chiara.** This 13th-century church is dedicated to St. Clare, one of the earliest and most fervent of St. Francis's followers and the founder of the order of the Poor Ladies, or Poor Clares, in imitation of the Franciscans. The church contains the body of the saint, and in the chapel of the Crucifix (on the right) is the cross that spoke to St. Francis and led him to a life of piety. A member of St. Clare's order is stationed before the cross and is heavily veiled in perpetual adoration of the image. *Open daily 8–1 and 4–7.*

⑰ Walk past the church of Santa Chiara, along Via Borgo Aretino and out through the walls of the gate called the **Porta Nuova.** From there, approximately 1 kilometer (.6 mile) farther on, **⑱** you reach the church of **San Damiano.** It was here that the crucifix spoke to St. Francis, saying "Vade, Francisce, et repara domum meam" ("Go, Francis, and repair my house"). It was also in this church pleasantly situated in an olive grove that St. Francis brought St. Clare into the religious life. It became the first home of her order. This church and its convent are simple and austere and give a far better idea of St. Francis and his movement than the great basilica. *Open daily 8–12:30 and 2–6.*

Also on the outskirts of the town, on the plain near the train ⑲ station, is the church of **Santa Maria degli Angeli.** It is a Baroque building constructed over the **Porziuncola,** a little chapel restored by St. Francis. The shrine is much venerated because it was here, in the Transito chapel, then a humble cell, that St. Francis died. *Open daily 9–1 and 4–7.*

⑳ Four kilometers (2½ miles) east of Assisi is the **Hermitage of the Carceri,** a monastery set in dense woodlands on the side of Mount Subasio. In the caves on the slope of the mountain, Francis and his followers established their first home, to which he returned often during his lifetime to pray and meditate. The church and monastery retain the tranquil contemplative air St. Francis so prized. *Open daily 8–dusk.*

Tour 4: Orvieto and Environs

Numbers in the margin correspond to points of interest on the Umbria and the Marches map.

Orvieto, on the western edge of Umbria, is 86 kilometers (51.6 miles) from Perugia and 112 kilometers (68 miles) from Assisi. The drive to Orvieto from these two towns is a pleasant one, cutting through the center of the region and heading south on Route 3bis, which takes you through **Todi,** a lovely hill town. Its Piazza del Popolo has an extraordinary grouping of Gothic palaces and a medieval cathedral. At Todi change to Route 448, which connects with the main north–south autostrada, A1.

㉑ **Orvieto,** 37 kilometers (23 miles) away on A1, is one of Umbria's greatest cities. Its commanding, dramatic position on a great square rock is an amazing sight, dominating the countryside for miles in every direction. This natural fort was first settled by the Etruscans, but not even Orvieto's defenses could withstand the might of the Romans, who attacked, sacked, and destroyed the city in 283 BC. From that time, Orvieto has had close ties with Rome. It was solidly Guelph in the Middle Ages, and for several hundred years popes have sought refuge in the city, at some times seeking protection from their enemies, at other times fleeing from the summer heat of Rome.

Orvieto's position on its rock has meant that little new building has ever been done here, giving the town an almost perfect medieval character. The jewel, the centerpiece of Orvieto, is its **Duomo,** set in the wide and airy Piazza del Duomo. The church, built to commemorate the Miracle of Bolsena, was started in 1290 and received the attention of some of the greatest architects and sculptors of the time. It was further embellished inside by great Renaissance artists. The facade (with some overly bright 19th-century mosaics) is the first thing to look at. The reliefs on the lower parts of the pillars are by Maitani, one of the original architects of the building, and show scenes from the Old Testament and some particularly gruesome renderings of the Last Judgment and Hell, as well as a more tranquil Paradise. (They have been covered with Plexiglass, following some vandalizing in the 1960s.)

The vast interior of the cathedral is famous chiefly for the frescoes in the Capella Nuova (the last chapel on the right, nearest the high altar). The earliest works here are above the altar and are by Fra Angelico. They show Christ in Glory and the Prophets. The major works in the chapel, however, are by Luca Signorelli and show a very graphic Last Judgment. The walls seem to be filled with muscular, writhing figures, and most critics draw a direct connection between these figures and the later Last Judgment of Michelangelo, on the wall of the Sistine Chapel. Leonardo da Vinci, however, was less than impressed. He said that the figures, with their rippling muscles, reminded him of sacks "stuffed full of nuts."

Across the nave of the cathedral from the Capella Nuova is the Capella del Corporale. It houses the relics of the Miracle of Bolsena, the raison d'être for the Duomo. A priest in the nearby town of Bolsena suddenly found himself assailed by doubts about the transubstantiation—he could not bring himself to believe that the body of Christ was contained in the consecrated communion host. His doubts were put to rest, however, when a wafer he had just blessed suddenly started to drip blood. Drops of blood fell onto the linen covering the altar, and this cloth and the host itself are the principal relics of the miracle. They are contained in a sumptuous gold-and-enamel reliquary on the altar of this chapel and are displayed on the Feast of Corpus Christi and at Easter. *Duomo. Open daily 7–1, 3–dusk.*

To the right of the Duomo is the medieval **Palazzo dei Papi,** once the summer residence of popes, which contains the Archaeological Museum. *Admission free. Open May–Oct., Mon.–Sat. 9–1:30 and 3–7, Sun. 9–1; Nov.–Apr., Mon.–Sat. 9–1:30 and 2:30–6, Sun. 9–1.*

Time Out   Orvieto is known for its wines, particularly the whites. Some of the finest wines in Umbria are produced here (Signorelli, when painting the Duomo, asked that part of his contract be paid in wine), and the rock on which the town sits is honeycombed with caves used to ferment the Trebbiano grapes that are used in making Orvieto vintages. Taking a glass of wine, therefore, at the **wine cellar** at No. 2, Piazza del Duomo, is as much a cultural experience as a refreshment stop. You'll find a good selection of sandwiches and snacks there as well.

The countryside southeast of Orvieto, heading toward the town of Narni, is rarely included in most travel itineraries—a pity, since the scenery and rustic charm of the small towns on the route make this one of the most pleasant parts of Umbria. It is also a manageable chunk of country that can be seen in a half-day's touring by car.

Drive southeast of Orvieto on Route 448 for 7.6 kilometers (4½ miles), then turn south onto a narrow country road that leads to the tiny medieval hamlet of **Baschi.** South of Baschi on Route ② 205, after 20 kilometers (12 miles), you'll come to **Lugnano in Teverina,** another picturesque town crowned with a beautiful Romanesque church, **Santa Maria Assunta.** *Open daily 9–1.*

What to See and Do with Children

Several of the region's historical pageants, like the **crossbow tournament** in Gubbio (usually the last Sunday in May; contact the Gubbio tourist agency, Piazza Oderisi 6, tel. 075/922–0693 for details) or the **Torneo della Quintana,** a medieval-style joust (the first Sun. in Aug.) in Ascoli Piceno, are delightful for young and old alike.

The only attraction aimed directly at the younger set is **La Città della Domenica,** a Disney-style playground in the town of Montepulito, 8 kilometers (4.8 miles) west of Perugia on the secondary road that leads to Corciano. The 500 acres of parkland contain a variety of buildings based on familiar fairy-tale themes—Snow White's House, the Witches Wood—as well as a reptile house, a medieval museum, an exhibit of shells from all over the world, game rooms, and a choice of restaurants. *Tel. 075/754941. Admission: adults, 15,500 lire; children 4–10, 13,000 lire. Open Mar. 24–Sept. 30, daily 9–7; Oct. 1–Nov. 5, weekends and holidays 9–7; Nov. 5–Mar. 23 (exhibitions only), Sat. 2–6, Sun. 10–7.*

Off the Beaten Track

The area in the east of Umbria, known as the **Valnerina,** is the most beautiful of central Italy's many well-kept secrets. The roads that serve the rugged landscape are poor, but a drive through the region, even with all those time-consuming twists and turns, will be worth it to see forgotten medieval villages and dramatic mountain scenery. The first stop should be the **waterfalls at Marmore,** the highest falls in Europe. You'll find them a few miles east of Terni, on the road to Lake Piediluco and Rieti. The waters are diverted on weekdays to provide hydroelectric power for the town of Terni, so check with the tourist office (Viale C. Battisti 7a, tel. 0744/43047) in Terni before heading there. On summer evenings, when the falls are in full spate, the cascading water is flood-lit—and a delightful sight.

Close to the picturesque town of Ferentillo (northeast of Terni on Route 209) is the outstanding 8th-century abbey of **San Pietro in Valle.** There are fine frescoes in the nave of the church, and the cloister is graceful and peaceful. As a bonus, one of the abbey outbuildings houses a fine restaurant with moderate prices.

Farther east are the towns of **Norcia** and **Cascia;** Norcia is the most famous town for Umbrian food specialties. It is also the birthplace of St. Benedict. Cascia is the birthplace of the uncrowned patron saint of Italian women, St. Rita.

Shopping

Pottery and wine are the two most famous Umbrian exports, and examples of both commodities are excellent and unique to the region.

Gubbio, Perugia, and **Assisi** all produce ceramics, but those with the most flair are found in **Deruta,** south of Torgiano on Route 3bis. The red glazes of Gubbio pottery have been famous since medieval times. The secret of the original glaze died with its inventor some 500 years ago, but there are contemporary potters who produce a fair facsimile.

Perugia is a well-to-do town, and judging by the array of expensive shops on the Corso Vannucci, the Perugini are not afraid to part with their money. The main streets of the town are lined with clothing shops selling the best-known Italian designers, either in luxurious boutiques or shops under the control of the design firms themselves, like Gucci, Ferragamo, Armani, and Fendi.

The best and most typical thing to buy in Perugia is, of course, some of the famous and delicious Perugina chocolate. *Cioccolato al latte* (milk chocolate) and *fondente* (dark chocolate) are available in tiny jewellike boxes or in giant gift boxes the size of serving trays. The most famous chocolates made by Perugina are the round chocolate- and nut-filled candies called *baci* (kisses), which come wrapped in silver paper and, like fortune cookies, contain romantic sentiments or sayings.

Orvieto is a center of woodworking, particularly fine inlays and veneers. The Corso Cavour has a number of artisan shops specializing in woodwork, the best known being the studio of the Michelangeli family, which is crammed with a variety of imaginatively designed objects ranging in size from a giant *armadio* (wardrobe) to a simple wooden spoon.

Minor arts, such as embroidery and lace making, flourish in Orvieto, as well. Luisa Geremei, a venerable lady, still makes beautiful lace at her shop at Via Gualtieri 8.

The wine trade is concentrated in Orvieto. Its excellent white wines are justly prized throughout Italy and in foreign countries. The whites are fruity, with a tart aftertaste, and are made from the region's Trebbiano grapes. Orvieto also produces its own version of the Tuscan dessert wine *vin santo*. It is darker than its Tuscan cousin and is aged five years before bottling. The Lungarotti cellars at **Torgiano** sell the winery's award-winning reds and whites.

Sports

Hiking Magnificent scenery makes Umbria fine hiking and mountaineering country. The area around Spoleto is particularly good, and the tourist office for the town (*see* Important Addresses and Numbers in Essential Information, *above*) will supply itineraries of walks and climbs to suit all ages and levels of ability.

Swimming Lakes Trasimeno and Piediluco offer safe and clean bathing facilities. **Castiglione del Lago,** on Lake Trasimeno, has a fine public beach, with no strong undercurrents or hidden depths.

Dining and Lodging

Dining Umbria is mountainous, and the cuisine of the region is typical of mountain people everywhere. The food is hearty and straightforward, with a stick-to-the-ribs quality that sees hard-working farmers and artisans through a long day's work and helps them make the steep climb home at night. Italians are generally thought not to eat much meat, but this is untrue of Italy in general and of Umbria in particular. Novelist Anthony Burgess once observed that a beefsteak in Italy is never "*una bistecca,*" but always "*una bella bistecca*"—a beautiful steak—and a simple steak in Umbria is almost always bella.

The region has made several important contributions to Italian cuisine. Particularly prized are black truffles from the area around Spoleto (at the base of the grand Ponte delle Torri are signs warning against unlicensed trufflehunting) and from the hills around the tiny town of Norcia. Norcia, in fact, exports truffles to France and hosts a truffle festival every year in November. Many regional dishes are given a grating of truffle before serving; unless the truffle is a really good one, however, its subtle taste may not come through. The local pasta specialty is thick, handmade spaghetti called *ciriole* or *strengozzi*. It's good *al tartufo*, with a dressing of excellent local olive oil and truffles.

In addition, Norcia's pork products—especially sausages, *salame*, and *arista*—are so famous that pork butchers throughout Italy are called *norcini*, no matter where they hail from. Similarly, pork butcher shops are always called *norcinerie*.

In the Marches, fish in various forms is the thing to look for. One of the characteristic dishes in Ancona is *brodetto*, a rich fish chowder containing as many as nine types of Adriatic saltwater fish. Ascoli Piceno, inland, is famous for two dishes: *olive ascolane* (stuffed olives rolled in batter and deep fried) and *vincisgrassi* (a local version of lasagne, far richer than you're likely to find elsewhere in Italy). Ascoli Piceno is also the home of the licorice-flavored liqueur *anisette*.

Highly recommended restaurants are indicated by a star ★.

Category	Cost*
Very Expensive	over 85,000 lire
Expensive	60,000–85,000 lire
Moderate	25,000–60,000 lire
Inexpensive	under 25,000 lire

per person, including first course, main course, dessert or fruit, and house wine

Lodging   Virtually every historic town in Umbria has some kind of hotel, no matter how small the place may be. In most cases a small city boasts one or two hotels in a high price category and a few smaller, basic hotels in the moderate-to-inexpensive range. The cheaper the hotel, the fewer the services. Most basic hotels offer breakfast, but few have restaurants or bars.

A new and popular trend is the conversion of old villas and monasteries into first-class hotels. These tend to be outside the towns, in the countryside, and the splendor of the settings often outweighs the problem of getting into town. In all cases, these country hotels are comfortable, often luxurious, and offer a mixture of Old World charm and modern convenience.

Reservations at any hotel are recommended, and traveling in high season to Perugia, Assisi, Spoleto, Todi, or Orvieto without advance bookings is a chancy proposition.

Highly recommended hotels are indicated by a star ★.

Category	Cost*
Very Expensive	over 300,000 lire
Expensive	140,000–300,000 lire

Moderate	80,000–140,000 lire
Inexpensive	under 80,000 lire

All prices are for a standard double room for two, including tax, service, and breakfast.

Ancona
Dining

La Moretta. This family-run trattoria is located on the central Piazza del Plebiscito. In summer there is dining outside in the square, which has a fine view of the Baroque church of San Domenico. Among the specialties of La Moretta are *tagliatelle in salsa di ostriche* (pasta in an oyster sauce) and the famous brodetto fish stew. *Plazza del Plebiscito 52, tel. 071/202317. Reservations advised. Dress: casual. AE, DC, MC, V. Closed Sun. and Aug. 10–15. Moderate–Expensive.*

Lodging

Grand Hotel Palace. In the center of town, near the entrance to the port of Ancona, is a hotel widely held to be the best in the city: The Palace is an old-fashioned place well run by a courteous staff. *Lungomare Vanvitelli 24, tel. 071/201813, fax 071/32856. 41 rooms with bath. AE, DC, MC, V. Expensive.*

Hotel Roma e Pace. The only two reasons to stay in the Hotel Roma e Pace are the location and price. It is inexpensive and centrally located, but the rooms are ugly and cramped, and the service slapdash and uncaring. A historical note: In 1904 a Russian named Josef Dzhugashvili applied for a job at the hotel and was refused. He later found better-paying employment as supreme head of the Soviet Union under the name Stalin. *Via Leopardi 1, tel. 071/202007. 73 rooms with bath or shower. Facilities: restaurant, bar. AE, DC, MC, V. Moderate.*

Ascoli Piceno
Dining
★

Ristorante Tornasacco. Just off the central Piazza Arringo is an attractive family-run restaurant with rustic decor and vaulted brick ceilings. Here you can sample Ascoli's specialties, like vincisgrassi and olive ascolane, as well as *maccheroncini alla contadina* (a homemade pasta in a thick meat sauce). *Via Tornasacco 3, tel. 0736/54151. Dress: casual. Closed Fri. and June 15–30. AE, DC, MC, V. Inexpensive–Moderate.*

Lodging

Albergo Piceno. The modest Albergo Piceno is the only hotel in the historic center of the city. It offers clean, basic accommodations—no frills at all here—but the staff is helpful and courteous, and the location is perfect. *Via Minnuccia 10, tel. 0736/252553. 32 rooms, 18 with bath. No credit cards. Inexpensive.*

Assisi
Dining

Buca di San Francesco. This central restaurant is Assisi's busiest and most popular. The setting is lovely no matter what the season. In summer you dine outside in a cool green garden; in winter, in the cozy cellars of the restaurant. The food is first-rate, and the *filleto al rubesco* (fillet steak cooked in a hearty red wine) is the specialty of the house. *Via Brizi 1, tel. 075/812204. Reservations advised in high season (June–Sept.). Dress: casual. AE, DC, MC, V. Closed Mon. and July. Moderate.*

La Fortezza. Parts of the walls of this modern restaurant were built by the Romans. The service is personable, and the kitchen reliable. A particular standout is *coniglio in salsa di asparagi* (rabbit in asparagus sauce). *Vicolo della Fortezza 19b, tel. 075/812418. Reservations advised in high season. Dress: casual. AE, DC, MC, V. Closed Thurs. (except Aug.–Sept.), Dec. 25–Jan. 3, Feb. Moderate.*

La Stalla. Just outside the town proper is La Stalla, a converted stable—now a simple and rustic restaurant. In summer, lunch and dinner are served outside under a delightful trellis shaded with vines and flowers. In keeping with the decor, the food is hearty country cooking. *Via Eremo delle Carceri 8, tel. 075/ 812317. No reservations. Dress: casual. No credit cards. Closed Mon. Moderate.*

Lodging **Hotel Subasio.** This hotel, close to the Basilica of St. Francis, has counted Marlene Dietrich and Charlie Chaplin among its guests. It is housed in a converted monastery and has plenty of atmosphere. Some of the rooms remain a little monastic, but the views, comfortable old-fashioned sitting rooms, flowered terraces, and lovely garden more than make up for the simplicity of the rooms. Ask for a room with a view of the valley. *Via Frate Elia 2, tel. 075/812206, fax 075/816691. 66 rooms with bath. Facilities: baby-sitting, conference and group reception rooms, garden, bar, restaurant. AE, DC, MC, V. Expensive.*

★ **Hotel Umbra.** A 16th-century town house is home to this hotel. It's located in a tranquil part of the city, an area closed to traffic, near the Piazza del Comune. The rooms are arranged as small apartments, with tiny living rooms and terraces. *Via degli Archi 6, tel. 075/812240. 25 rooms with bath. Facilities: bar, restaurant (closed Tues.). AE, DC, MC, V. Closed mid-Jan.–mid-Mar. Moderate.*

San Francesco. This is a centrally located hotel in a renovated 16th-century building. Some of the rooms have views of the basilica or the valley. *Via di San Francesco 48, tel. 075/812218, fax 075/813727. 45 rooms with bath. Facilities: bar, restaurant. AE, DC, MC, V. Moderate.*

Gubbio **Fornace di Maestro Giorgio.** This atmospheric restaurant is lo-
Dining cated in the medieval workshop of a famous master potter, one of Gubbio's most famous sons. The food is typical Umbrian fare, with the occasional southern dish, like *tiella barese* (a mixture of rice, mussels, and potatoes), added. There are two prix-fixe menus, at 28,000 and 32,000 lire. *Via Mastro Giorgio 2, tel. 075/ 927–5740. Reservations advised in summer. Dress: casual. AE, DC, MC, V. Closed Mon. Moderate.*

Grotta dell'Angelo. This rustic trattoria is in the lower part of the Old Town, near the main square and tourist information office. The menu features simple local specialties, including the salami known as *capocollo*, *strengozzi* (homemade pasta), and *lasagna tartufata* (lasagna made with truffles). There are a few tables for outdoor dining. *Via Gioia 47, tel. 075/927–1747. Reservations advised. Dress: casual. AE, DC, MC, V. Closed Tues. and Jan. 7–Feb. 7. Moderate.*

Taverna del Lupo. It's one of the best restaurants in the city, as well as one of the largest. Taverna del Lupo seats 200 people and can get a bit hectic during the high season. Lasagna made in the Gubbian fashion, with ham and truffles, is the best pasta. You'll also find excellent desserts and an extensive wine cellar here. *Via G. Ansidei 21, tel. 075/927–4368. Reservations advised in high season. Dress: casual. AE, DC, V. Closed Mon. (except July–Aug.) and Jan. Moderate.*

Lodging **Hotel Bosone.** Occupying the old central Palazzo Raffaelli, the Hotel Bosone has many rooms decorated with frescoes from the former palace. *Via XX Settembre 22 tel. 075/922–0688, fax 075/ 922–0552. 28 rooms with bath. Facilities: bar, restaurant, garage. AE, DC, MC, V. Closed Jan. Moderate.*

Hotel Gattapone. Right in the center of town is this hotel with wonderful views of the sea of rooftops. It is casual and family-run, with good-size, modern, comfortable rooms. *Via Ansidei 6, tel. 075/927-2489, fax 075/927-1269. 13 rooms with bath. AE, DC, MC, V. Closed Jan. Inexpensive.*

Orvieto **Le Grotte del Funaro.** This restaurant has an extraordinary lo-
Dining cation, deep in a series of caves within the volcanic rock be-
★ neath Orvieto. Once you have negotiated the steep steps, typical Umbrian specialties, like *tagliatelle al vino rosso* (noodles with red wine sauce) and grilled beef with truffles, await. Sample the fine Orvieto wines, either the whites or the lesser-known reds. *Via Ripa Serancia 41, tel. 0763/43276. Reservations advised. Dress: casual. AE, MC, DC, V. Closed Mon. and 2 weeks in July. Moderate.*

★ **Maurizio.** In the heart of Orvieto, just opposite the cathedral, this warm and welcoming restaurant gets its share of tourists and has a local clientele as well. The decor is unusual, with wood sculptures by Orvieto craftsman Michelangeli. The menu offers hearty soups and homemade pastas such as *tronchetti* (a pasta roll with spinach and ricotta filling). *Via del Duomo 78, tel. 0763/41114. Reservations advised in summer. Dress: casual. AE, MC, V. Closed Tues. and 3 weeks in Jan. Moderate.*

Lodging **Hotel La Badia.** This is one of the best-known country hotels in Umbria. The 700-year-old building is a former monastery and is set in rolling parkland that provides wonderful views of the valley and the town of Orvieto in the distance. Facilities include a swimming pool and several tennis courts. The rooms are well appointed. *Località La Badia 8, 5 km (3½ mi) south of Orvieto, tel. 0763/90359, fax 0763/92796. 24 rooms with bath. Facilities: bar, restaurant, garage. AE, V. Closed Jan.–Feb. Expensive.*

Hotel Maitani. The most deluxe hotel in the town of Orvieto itself, the Hotel Maitani is also centrally located. It is set in a 17th-century Baroque palazzo with a garden and a panoramic terrace, but the hotel has no restaurant. The rooms are old-fashioned but comfortable. *Via Maitani 5 tel. 0763/42011, fax 0763/42011. 44 rooms with bath. Facilities: air-conditioning (additional charge), bar, garage. AE, MC, DC, V. Moderate–Expensive.*

Virgilio. The modest Hotel Virgilio is situated right in the Piazza del Duomo, and the rooms with views of the cathedral are wonderful. The rooms are small but well furnished. *Piazza del Duomo 5, tel. 0763/41882. 18 rooms, 2 with bath, 16 with shower. Facilities: bar. No credit cards. Moderate.*

Perugia **Il Falchetto.** Here you'll find exceptional food at reasonable
Dining prices—making this Perugia's best restaurant bargain. The service is smart but relaxed, and the two dining rooms are medieval, with the kitchen and chef on view. The house specialty is *falchetti* (homemade gnocchi with spinach and ricotta cheese). *Via Bartolo 20, tel. 075/61875. Reservations advised. Dress: casual. AE, DC, MC, V. Closed Mon. Moderate.*

La Rosetta. This restaurant, in the hotel of the same name, is a peaceful, elegant place. In the winter you dine inside under medieval vaults; in summer, in the cool courtyard. The cuisine is simple but reliable and flawlessly served. *Piazza d'Italia 19, tel. 075/20841. Reservations advised. Dress: casual. AE, DC, MC, V. Closed Mon. Moderate.*

La Taverna. Signposted next to the Teatro Pavone, off Corso Vannucci, medieval steps lead to this rustic restaurant on two levels, where lots of wine bottles and artful clutter heighten the tavern atmosphere. The menu features regional specialties and a choice of better-known Italian dishes. Good choices include *chitarrini* (pasta), with either mushrooms (*funghi*) or pricier truffles (*tartufi*), and grilled meats. *Via delle Streghe 8, tel. 075/61028. Reservations advised in the evening. Dress: casual. AE, DC, MC, V. Closed Mon., 3 weeks in Jan., and last week in July. Moderate.*

Lodging **The Brufani Hotel.** The two hotels (this one and the Palace Hotel Bellavista, below) in this 19th-century palazzo were once one. The Brufani's public rooms and first-floor guest rooms have high ceilings and are done in the grand style of the Belle Epoque. The second-floor rooms are more modern, and many on both floors have marvelous views of the Umbrian countryside or the city. *Piazza d'Italia 12, tel. 075/62541, fax 075/20210. 24 rooms with bath. Facilities: restaurant, bar, air-conditioning, garage, 2 meeting rooms. AE, DC, MC, V. Very Expensive.*

★ **Locanda della Posta.** This newly renovated and luxuriously decorated small hotel in the center of Perugia's historic district is a delight to behold, from its faux-marbre moldings, paneled doors, and tiled bouquets in the baths to the suede-upholstered elevator and fabric-covered walls. Architectural details of the 18th-century palazzo are beautiful, and views of city rooftops from windows and balconies are soothing. Breakfast is included here. *Corso Vannucci 97, tel. 075/61345, fax 075/61345. 39 rooms with bath or shower. Facilities: breakfast room, sitting room. AE, DC, MC, V. Expensive.*

Hotel La Rosetta. On the same square as the Brufani Palace Hotel, the Hotel La Rosetta offers a lovely courtyard rich in flowers, greenery, and cool shady nooks. The hotel has both an old and a new wing and a restaurant (*see above*). *Piazza d'Italia 19, tel. 075/20841, fax 075/20841. 96 rooms with bath. Facilities: restaurant, garage. AE, DC, MC, V. Moderate–Expensive.*

The Palace Hotel Bellavista. The rooms in this hotel are decorated in splendid Belle Epoque grandeur, and many have views over the hills. The hotel's entrance is unimpressive, but the public rooms are palatial. Weekly rates are available. *Piazza d'Italia 12, tel. 075/20741, fax 075/29092. 70 rooms with bath or shower. Facilities: conference facilities, bar, breakfast room. AE, DC, MC, V. Moderate*

Spoleto **Il Tartufo.** Spoleto's most famous restaurant has a smart mod-
Dining ern dining room on the second floor and a rustic dining room downstairs—both of which incorporate the ruins of a Roman villa. The traditional cooking is spiced up in summer to appeal to the cosmopolitan crowd who are attending (or performing in) the Festival of Two Worlds. As its name indicates, the restaurant specializes in dishes prepared with truffles, though there is a second menu from which you can choose items not containing this expensive delicacy. *Piazza Garibaldi 24 tel. 0743/40236. Reservations required during the festival and recommended at other times of the year. Dress: casual. AE, DC, MC, V. Closed Wed. and mid-July–1st week in Aug. Moderate.*

Trattoria Panciolle. In the heart of Spoleto's medieval quarter, this restaurant has one of the most romantic settings you could wish for. Dining outside in summer is a delight in a small piazza filled with lime trees. Specialties include *stringozzi* (homemade pasta) with mushroom sauce and *agnello scottadito* (grilled lamb chops). *Via del Duomo 3, tel. 0743/45598. Reservations advised. Dress: casual. AE, V. Closed Wed. Moderate.*

Il Pentagramma. This straightforward, no-frills restaurant serves some of the best pizza in town. *Via Martemi 4, tel. 0743/ 37241. No reservations. Dress: casual. AE, DC, V. Closed Mon. Inexpensive–Moderate.*

Lodging **Dei Duchi.** This excellent, well-run hotel is in the center of the town, near the Roman amphitheater. It's a favorite with performers in the Festival of Two Worlds. Some rooms have fine views of the city. *Viale Matteotti 2, tel. 0743/44541, fax 0743/ 44543. 50 rooms with bath or shower. Facilities: bar, restaurant, conference center, parking, garden. AE, DC, MC, V. Expensive.*

Hotel Gattapone. The tiny four-star Hotel Gattapone is situated at the top of the Old Town, near the Ponte delle Torri, and has wonderful views of the ancient bridge and the wooded slopes of Monteluco. The rooms are well furnished and tastefully decorated. *Via del Ponte 6, tel. 0743/223447, fax 0743/ 223448. 13 rooms with bath. Facilities: garden, bar. AE, DC, MC, V. Expensive.*

Urbino **Nuovo Coppiere.** Located in the heart of the charming old city,
Dining the Nuovo Coppiere is just a few steps from the cathedral and the Ducal Palace. The two small dining rooms are decorated in a contemporary country style and are cheerful and bright. The food is unsophisticated but good, especially the *grigliata mista con polenta* (mixed grill with toasted polenta) and the gnocchi in a tomato and basil sauce. In summer there is outside dining in the small square in front of the restaurant. *Via Beato Mainardo 5, tel. 0722/320092. Reservations advised. Dress: casual. AE, DC, MC, V. Closed Wed. and Feb. Moderate.*

Lodging **Hotel San Giovanni.** This hotel is located in the Old Town and is housed in a renovated medieval building. The staff is surly, but the rooms are basic, clean, and comfortable—with no frills—and there is a handy restaurant/pizzeria below. *Via Barocci 13, tel. 0722/2827. 33 rooms, 15 with shower. V. Closed July and Christmas week. Moderate.*

The Arts

The Festival of Two Worlds in Spoleto (mid-June–mid-July) features leading names in all branches of the arts—particularly music, opera, and theater—and draws thousands of visitors from all over the world. Tickets for all performances should be ordered in advance from the festival's box office (Piazza del Duomo 9, tel. 0743/28120). Information is available year-round from the festival's Rome office (Via Beccaria 18, tel. 06/361–4009).

There are other music festivals in Umbria throughout the year. The **Jazz Festival of Umbria** (July) and the **Festival of Sacred Music** (September) are both held in Perugia. Event and ticket information for both festivals can be obtained, year-round, from the Perugia Tourist Office (Piazza IV Novembre 3, tel. 075/23327).

The **Chamber Music Festival of Umbria** is held every August and September in the town of Città di Castello. For information, contact the tourist office (Via R. di Cesare 2b, tel. 075/ 855–4817).

14 Campania

*Naples, Pompeii, and
the Amalfi Drive*

Campania is a region of names to conjure with—Capri, Sorrento, Pompeii, Paestum—names evoking visions of cliff-shaded coves, sun-dappled waters, and mighty ruins. And Naples, a tumultuous, animated city, the very heart of Campania, stands guard over these treasures.

Campania stretches south in flat coastal plains and low mountains from Baia Domizia, Capua, and Caserta to Naples and Pompeii on the magnificent bay; past Capri and Ischia; along the rocky coast to Sorrento, Amalfi, and Salerno; and farther still past the Cilento promontory to Sapri and the Calabria border. Inland lie the bleak fringes of the Apennines and the rolling countryside around Benevento.

On each side of Naples, the earth fumes and grumbles, reminding natives and visitors alike that all this beauty was born of cataclysm. Toward Sorrento, Vesuvius smolders sleepily over the ruins of Herculaneum and Pompeii, while north of Naples, beyond Posillipo, the craters of the Solfatara spew steaming gases. And nearby are the dark, deep waters of Lake Averno, legendary entrance to Hades.

With these reminders of death and destruction so close at hand, it's no wonder that the southerner in general, and the Neapolitan in particular, chooses to take no chances, plunging enthusiastically into the task of living each moment to its fullest.

Campania was probably settled by the ancient Phoenicians, Cretans, and Greeks. Traces of their presence here date to approximately 1000 BC, some 300 years before the legendary founding of Rome. Herculaneum is said to have been established by the great Hercules himself, and as excavation of this once-great city—Greek and later Roman—progresses, further light will be thrown on the history of the whole Campania region.

The origin of Naples, once called Parthenope and later Neapolis, presumably can be traced to what are now the ruins of Cumae nearby, which legend tells us was already in existence in 800 BC. Here, in a dark vaulted chamber, the Cumaean Sybil rendered her oracles. Greek civilization flourished for hundreds of years all along this coastline, but there was nothing in the way of centralized government until centuries later, when the Roman Empire, uniting all Italy for the first time, surged southward and absorbed the Greek colonies with little opposition. The Romans were quick to appreciate the sybaritic possibilities of such a lovely land, and it was in this region that the wealthy of the empire built their palatial country residences. Generally, the peace of Campania was undisturbed during these centuries of Roman rule.

Naples and Campania, with the rest of Italy, decayed with the Roman Empire and collapsed into the abyss of the Middle Ages. Naples itself regained some importance under the rule of the Angevins in the latter part of the 13th century and continued its progress in the 1440s under Aragón rule. The nobles who served under the Spanish viceroys in the 16th and 17th centuries, when their harsh rule made all Italy quail, enjoyed their pleasures, and the more luxurious points in Campania began to look up.

After a short-lived Austrian occupation, Naples became the capital of the Kingdom of the Two Sicilies, which the Bourbon kings established in 1738. Their rule was generally benevolent, as far as Campania was concerned, and their support of the papal authority in Rome was an important factor in the historical development of the rest of Italy. Their rule was important artistically, too, for not only did it contribute greatly to the architectural beauty of the region, but it attracted scores of great musicians, artists, and writers, who were only too willing to enjoy the easy life of court in such magnificent natural surroundings.

Finally, Giuseppe Garibaldi launched his famous expedition, and in 1860 Naples was united with the rest of Italy.

Times were relatively tranquil through the years that followed—with tourists of one nation or another thronging to Capri, to Sorrento, to Amalfi, and, of course, to Naples—until World War II. Allied bombings did considerable damage in Naples and the bay area. At the fall of the fascist government, the sorely tried Neapolitans rose up against nazi occupation troops and in four days of street fighting drove them out of the city. A monument to the *scugnizzo* (the typical Neapolitan street urchin) celebrates the youngsters who participated in the battle.

The war ended. Artists, tourists, writers, and ordinary lovers of beauty began to flow again into the Campania region that one ancient writer called "most blest by the Gods, most beloved by man." As the years have gone by, some parts have gained increased attention from the smart visitors, while others have lost the cachet they had. The balance is maintained, with a steady trend toward more and more tourist development.

Essential Information

Important Addresses and Numbers

Tourist Information The main EPT (regional tourist board) offices for Campania are in **Naples** (Piazza dei Martiri 58, tel. 081/405311; Stazione Centrale, tel. 081/268779; Stazione Mergellina, tel. 081/761–2102; and Capodichino Airport tel. 081/780–5761). These offices provide information on transportation, accommodations, and cultural events throughout the region. Local tourist offices in Campania are useful for information on festivals, changing opening hours, and maps of towns and villages.

Avellino (Piazza Liberta 50, tel. 0825/35175).
Benevento (Via Giustiniani 34, tel. 0824/25424).
Capri (Marina Grande pier, tel. 081/837–0634; Capri town, Piazza Umberto I, tel. 081/837–0686).
Caserta (Corso Trieste 39, off Piazza Dante, tel. 0823/321137).
Naples (Piazza del Gesù, tel. 081/552–3328; hydrofoil station, Mergellina, tel. 081/761–4585).
Porto d'Ischia (Corso Vittoria Colonna 104, tel. 081/983066; Via Iasolino, Porto Salvo, tel. 081/991146).
Salerno (Piazza Amendola 8, tel. 089/224744).
Sorrento (Circolo Forestieri, Via de Maio 35, tel. 081/878–1115).

Emergencies **Police,** tel. 112.
Ambulance, tel. 081/752–0696 in Naples.
Doctors and Dentists, tel. 081/751–3177 in Naples.

Late-Night **Farmacia Internazionale** (Piazza Garibaldi 11, near the
Pharmacies Stazione Centrale, Naples, tel. 081/554–8894).

Car Rental **Caserta.** *Avis* (Stazione FS, tel. 0823/443756).

Naples. *Avis* (Stazione Centrale, tel. 081/284041); *Hertz* (Piazza
Garibaldi 69, tel. 081/206228.)

Sorrento. *Avis* (Corso Italia 155, tel. 081/878–2459).

Arriving and Departing by Plane

Capodichino Airport (tel. 081/780–5763), eight kilometers (five
miles) east of Naples, serves the Campania region. It handles
domestic and international flights, including several flights
daily between Naples and Rome (flight time: 45 minutes).
There is direct helicopter service (tel. 081/789–6273 or 837–
2888) between Capodichino Airport and Capri or Ischia.

International travelers flying on Alitalia through Rome's **Leonardo da Vinci Airport** can do directly nonstop to Naples'
Mergellina train station via Alitalia's twice-daily Airport
Train. Luggage is checked through to Naples, and meals and
extras are available on the train. Airport Train arrangements
must be made when you buy your plane ticket. The service also
operates in the other direction, returning from Naples to the da
Vinci airport.

Arriving and Departing by Car, Train, and Bus

By Car Italy's main north–south route, heading out of Rome (A2, also
known as the Autostrada del Sole), connects the capital with
Naples and Campania. In good traffic the ride takes less than
three hours.

By Train There are trains every hour between Rome and Naples. Intercity and Rapido trains make the trip in less than two hours.
Trains take either the inland route (through Cassino) or go
along the coast (via Formia). Express trains to Naples stop at
Stazione Centrale (Central Station) on Piazza Garibaldi (tel.
081/553–4188).

By Bus **Cital,** a Rome-based bus line (tel. 06/327–1347) runs direct, air-
conditioned service from Rome to Campania, stopping at Pom-
peii, Sorrento, and Amalfi.

Getting Around

By Car Autostrada A3, a southern continuation of A2 from Rome, runs
through Campania and into Calabria, to the south. It also connects with autostrada A16 to Bari, which passes Avellino and is
linked with Benevento by expressway. Take S18 south from
Naples for Ercolano (Herculaneum), Pompeii, and the Sorrento peninsula; for the Sorrento peninsula and the Amalfi coast,
exit at Castellamare di Stabia. To get to Paestum, take A3 to
the Battipaglia exit and take the road to Capaccio Scalo/Paes-
tum. All roads on the Sorrento peninsula and Amalfi coast are
narrow and tortuous, although they have outstanding views.

By Train Frequent local trains connect Naples with Caserta and Salerno. Travel time between Naples and Sorrento on the express
train is one hour. Benevento is on a secondary line between

Caserta and Foggia; Avellino is on a secondary line between Benevento and Salerno.

A network of suburban trains connects Naples with several points of interest. The **Circumflegrea** (tel. 081/551–3328) runs from the Piazza Montesanto station in Naples to the archaeological zone of Cumae, with three departures in the morning. The **Ferrovia Cumana** (tel. 081/551–3328) runs from the Piazza Montesanto station to Pozzuoli and Baia. The line used most by visitors is the **Circumvesuviana** (tel. 081/779–2444), which runs from Corso Garibaldi station and stops at Stazione Centrale before continuing to Ercolano (Herculaneum), Pompeii, and Sorrento.

Naples has a **Metropolitana** (subway system). Although rather old, it provides frequent service and can be the fastest way to get around the traffic-clogged city.

By Bus There is an extensive network of local buses in Naples and throughout Campania. ACTP buses connect Naples with Caserta in one hour, leaving every 20 minutes from Piazza Garibaldi (tel. 081/700–5091). The CTI bus to Avellino takes 50 minutes, leaving every 20 minutes from Piazza Garibaldi (tel. 081/533–4677). There are buses about six times a day from Piazza Garibaldi to Benevento. The trip takes 90 minutes.

SITA buses (tel. 081/552–2176) for Salerno leave every 30 minutes on weekdays and every two hours on weekends from the SITA terminal on Via Pisanelli, near Piazza Municipio. SITA buses also serve the Amalfi Coast, connecting Sorrento with Salerno.

By Boat Hydrofoil and passenger- and car-ferries connect the islands of Capri and Ischia with Naples and Pozzuoli. Boats and hydrofoils for these islands, and for Sorrento, leave from the **Molo Beverello,** Piazza Municipio, near the Castel Nuovo, or from Mergellina.

Caremar (tel. 081/551–3882) has frequent passenger- and car-ferry services, as well as some hydrofoil services. **Alilauro** (tel. 081/761–1004) and **SNAV** (tel. 081/761–2348) also provide hydrofoil services. In the summer, these lines have a residents-only policy for cars.

Guided Tours

Orientation A number of operators offer one-, two-, and three-day tours of Campania, starting in Rome. These tours use 60-passenger air-conditioned buses, transferring to the islands by boat. Shorter tours feature Pompeii or Capri; longer tours usually take in both. For up-to-date information and fares, contact these offices in Rome: **American Express** (tel. 06/464151), **Appian Line** (tel. 06/464151), or **CIT** (tel. 06/47941).

There is an even wider choice of tours starting in Naples, all using English-speaking guides. These tours are either half- or full day, and cover the archaeological sites of Pompeii and Paestum, as well as one or more of the islands. Contact **CIT** (Piazza Municipio 70, tel. 081/552–5426), **Cima Tours** (Piazza Garibaldi 114, tel. 081/554–0646), **Tourcar** (Piazza Matteotti 1, tel. 081/552–0429), or **Aritur** (Piazza Trieste e Trento 7, tel. 081/400487).

Exploring Campania

You have a few options in exploring Campania. If art and antiquity are high on your list, and if you have some sense of adventure, make Naples your base. Few fall in love with Naples at first sight, and many complain about its obvious flaws: urban decay and delinquency. But practically everyone who takes the time and trouble to discover its artistic riches and appreciate its vivacious atmosphere considers it worth the effort. Naples is near the most famous classical ruins, and, as capital of the region, it is also the most convenient base for your tours: It is connected by direct rail, road, and sea routes to nearly all the sights mentioned in this chapter.

If instead you're looking for dramatic scenery and want to enjoy it at a relaxed pace, plan to spend time either in touristy Sorrento, on the islands of Capri and Ischia, or on the beautiful Amalfi Coast. Be warned, though: These areas become quite crowded in July and August, when throngs of vacationing Italians arrive.

We have divided our exploring section into five separate tours. The first concentrates on the city and outlying districts of Naples. Naples is also the most convenient starting point for Tour 2 (to Herculaneum, Vesuvius, and Pompeii) and Tour 3 (inland to Caserta and Benevento). The last two tours, Tour 4 to the islands of Ischia and Capri, and Tour 5 down the mainland coast past Amalfi, can be approached from Naples, but visitors may want to avoid the capital altogether.

Highlights for First-time Visitors

Capodimonte (Tour 1: Naples and Its Bay).
Herculaneum (Tour 2: Herculaneum, Vesuvius, and Pompeii).
Mount Epomeo (Tour 4: Ischia and Capri).
Museo Archeologico (Tour 1: Naples and Its Bay).
Paestum's Temples (Tour 5: The Amalfi Drive: Sorrento to Salerno).
Pompeii (Tour 2: Herculaneum, Vesuvius, and Pompeii).
Positano (Tour 5: The Amalfi Drive: Sorrento to Salerno).
Ravello (Tour 5: The Amalfi Drive: Sorrento to Salerno).
Royal Palace (Tour 3: Caserta and Benevento).
Villa Jovis (Tour 4: Ischia and Capri).

Tour 1: Naples and Its Bay

Numbers in the margin correspond to the points of interest on the Campania and Naples maps.

Is it the sense of doom, living in the shadow of Vesuvius, that makes the people of Naples so volatile, so seemingly blind to everything but the pain and pleasure of the moment? Poverty and overcrowding are the more likely causes, but whatever the reason, Naples is a difficult place for the casual tourist to like. The Committee of Ninety-Nine, formed to counter Naples's negative image, has its work cut out. If you have the time and if you're willing to work at it, you'll come to love Naples as a mother loves her reprobate son; but if you're only passing through and hoping to enjoy a hassle-free vacation, spend as little time here as you can.

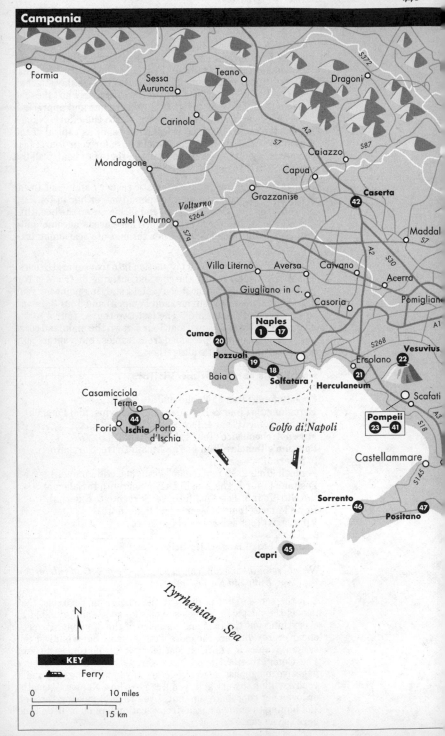

Campania

Formia

Sessa Aurunca

Teano

Dragoni

S372

Carinola

A2

S7

Caiazzo

S87

Mondragone

Capua

Caserta

Grazzanise

42

Volturno

S264

Castel Volturno

S7a

Maddal

S7

A2

S30

Villa Literno

Aversa

Caivano

Acerra

Giugliano in C.

Casoria

Pomiglian

Cumae

20

Naples

1 — **17**

A1

S268

Vesuvius

Pozzuoli

19

18

Ercolano

21

22

Baia

Solfatara

Herculaneum

Scafati

Casamicciola Terme

44

Golfo di Napoli

A3

Pompeii

23 — **41**

Forio

Ischia

Porto d'Ischia

S18

Castellammare

S145

Sorrento

46

47

Positano

Capri

45

Tyrrhenian Sea

N

KEY

Ferry

0   10 miles

0   15 km

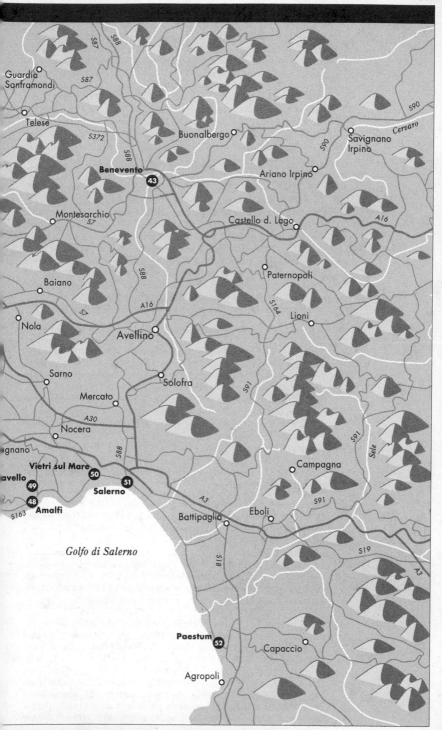

Why visit Naples at all? First, Naples is the most sensible base—particularly if you're traveling by public transportation—from which to explore Pompeii, Herculaneum, Vesuvius, and the Phlegrean Fields. Second, it's home of the Museo Archeologico Nazionale (National Archaeological Museum). The most important finds from Pompeii and Herculaneum are on display here—everything from sculpture to carbonized fruit—and seeing them will add to the pleasure of your trip to Pompeii and Herculaneum. Since the museum may be closed in the afternoon, depending on the time of year, spend the morning here and the afternoon visiting either the Phlegrean Fields or Herculaneum and Vesuvius. Spend the night back in Naples—perhaps at an opera or concert at the world-famous San Carlo Opera House—and the following morning, set off on your tour of Pompeii.

❶ To visit **Naples,** you need a good sense of humor and a firm grip on your pocketbook and camera. Better still, leave all your valuables, including passport, in the hotel safe. You'll probably be doing a lot of walking, for buses are crowded and taxis get stalled in traffic. If you come to Naples by car, park it in a garage as fast as you can, agree on the cost in advance, and then forget it for the duration of your stay (window smashing and theft are constant risks). You can take the Metropolitana (subway) to distant destinations and use the funiculars to get up and down the hills. (Bus, subway, or funicular fare is 800 lire.)

❷ A good place to start exploring is the **Castel Nuovo,** on Piazza Municipio, facing the harbor. Also known as the Maschio Angioino, this massive fortress was built by the Angevins (related to the French monarchy) in the 13th century and completely rebuilt by the Aragonese rulers (descendants of an illegitimate branch of Spain's ruling line) who succeeded them. The decorative marble triumphal arch that forms the entrance was erected during the Renaissance in honor of King Alfonso I of Aragón, and its rich bas-reliefs are credited to Francesco Laurana. Set incongruously into the castle's heavy stone walls, the arch is one of the finest works of its kind. The castle is not open to the public. On the harbor behind it is the **Molo Beverello,** the pier from which boats and hydrofoils leave for Sorrento and the islands.

❸ On the next block is the **Teatro San Carlo,** a large 18th-century theater redecorated in the white-and-gilt stucco of the neoclassical era. *Via Vittorio Emanuele III. Admission: 2,000 lire, free Sun. Open daily 9–noon.*

Time Out Across the busy square is the imposing entrance to the glass-roofed turn-of-the-century **Galleria Umberto,** a shopping arcade where you can sit at one of several cafés and watch the vivacious Neapolitans as they go about their business.

❹ Next to the Teatro San Carlo is the huge **Palazzo Reale** (Royal Palace). It dates from the early 1600s and was renovated and redecorated by successive rulers, including Napoleon's sister Caroline and her ill-fated husband, Joachin Murat, who reigned briefly in Naples after the French emperor had sent the Bourbons packing and before they returned to reclaim their kingdom. Don't miss seeing the royal apartments, sumptuously furnished and full of precious paintings, tapestries, porcelains, and other *objets d'art.* The monumental marble staircase gives you an idea of the scale on which Neapolitan rulers lived. *Piazza del Plebiscito, tel. 081/413888. Admission: 6,000 lire. Open Apr.–Oct. Mon.–Sat. 9–7:30; Nov.–Mar. Mon.–Sat. 9–2; Sun. 9–1.*

Piazza del Plebiscito, the vast square next to the palace, was laid out by order of Murat, whose architect was clearly inspired by the colonnades of St. Peter's in Rome. The large church of San Francesco da Paola in the middle of the colonnades was added as a thanks offering for the Bourbon restoration by Ferdinand I, whose titles reflect the somewhat garbled history of the Kingdom of the Two Sicilies. The "Two Sicilies" were of Naples (which included most of the southern Italian mainland) and of Sicily itself. They were united in the Middle Ages, then separated and unofficially reunited under the Spanish domination during the 16th and 17th centuries. In 1816, with Napoleon out of the way on St. Helena, Ferdinand IV of Naples, who also happened to be Ferdinand III of Sicily, officially merged the two kingdoms and proclaimed himself Ferdinand I of the Kingdom of Two Sicilies. His reactionary and repressive rule earned him a few more colorful titles among his rebellious subjects.

Follow Via C. Console along the waterfront, from the square to the port of Santa Lucia. At the end of a promontory you'll see ❺ the remains of **Castel dell'Ovo,** a 12th-century fortress built over the ruins of an ancient Roman villa. It commands a view of the whole harbor—proof, if you need it, that the Romans knew a premium location when they saw one. For the same reason, some of the city's top hotels share the same site.

Now take a deep breath and go back past Piazza del Plebiscito, onto one of the busiest commercial arteries in this perennially congested city. Follow Via Toledo into Via Roma.

Time Out As you make your way up Via Toledo, you'll come upon **Caflisch** (Via Toledo 253), a historic café that has recently been renovated to accommodate a good Italian version of a fast-food counter.

Along the way, make a detour by way of the funicular from Pi- ❻ azza Montesanto up the Vomero Hill to **Castel Sant'Elmo,** a forbidding fortress built by the Spanish to dominate the port and the old city. The Spanish garrison was quartered in now-decaying tenements aligned in a tight-knit grid along incredibly narrow alleys; this notorious slum district is still known as the *Quartieri*. Follow Via Tito Angelini from the upper station of ❼ the funicular to **Certosa di San Martino,** a Carthusian monastery restored in the 17th century in exuberant Neapolitan Baroque style. Inside, the Museo Nazionale di San Martino has an oddly eclectic collection of ships' models, antique *presepi* (Christmas crèches), and Neapolitan landscape paintings, but you're here mainly to see the splendidly decorated church and annexes, the pretty garden, and the view from the balcony off Room 25. There's another fine view from the square in front of the Certosa. *Museo Nazionale di San Martino, tel. 081/578– 1769. Admission: 6,000 lire. Open Tues.–Sat. 9–2, Sun. 9–1.*

As you resume your walk up Via Roma, you'll pass a great variety of shops and plenty of coffee bars where plump pastries are temptingly arranged. Students from the nearby music conservatory hang out in **Piazza Dante,** the semicircular hub of an area rich in inexpensive trattorias and pizzerias. On the other

Naples

Bacino del Pilier

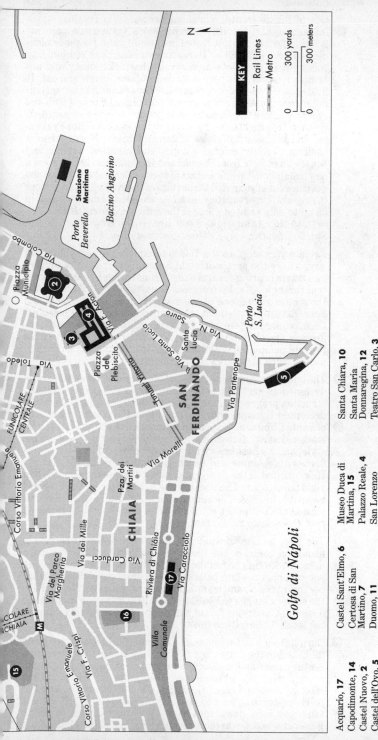

Golfo di Nápoli

Acquario, **17**
Capodimonte, **14**
Castel Nuovo, **2**
Castel dell'Ovo, **5**

Castel Sant'Elmo, **6**
Certosa di San Martino, **7**
Duomo, **11**
Gesù Nuovo, **9**
Museo Archeologico Nazionale, **8**

Museo Duca di Martina, **15**
Palazzo Reale, **4**
San Lorenzo Maggiore, **13**

Santa Chiara, **10**
Santa Maria Donnaregina, **12**
Teatro San Carlo, **3**
Villa Pignatelli, **16**

side of Piazza Dante, Via Roma becomes Via Pessina, which
❽ leads straight to the **Museo Archeologico Nazionale,** a major attraction for anyone interested in antiquity and for those planning to visit Pompeii or Herculaneum. The huge red building
was built in the 1580s as a cavalry barracks; dusty and unkempt, it undergoes perpetual restorations, inside and out. It
holds one of the world's great collections of antiquities, including such astounding sculptures as the colossal *Farnese Bull* and
other exquisite Greek and Roman works, among them an *Aphrodite* attributed to the 4th-century BC Greek sculptor Praxite-
les, and an equestrian statue of Roman Emperor Nerva, a recent
addition. Vividly colored mosaics and countless artistic and
household objects from Pompeii and Herculaneum can give you a
new insight into the life and art of ancient Rome and will help you
get more out of your visit to the ruins of these cities as you explore
the region. Unfortunately, exhibits are poorly labeled; invest in
an up-to-date printed guide of the museum. *Piazza Museo, tel.
081/440166. Admission: 8,000 lire. Open May–Sept. Mon.–
Sat. 9–7:30; Oct.–Apr., Mon.–Sat. 9–2, Sun. 9–1.*

Retrace your steps to Via Toledo to explore the heart of the old
city, where the arrow-straight Spaccanapoli, a street divided
into tracts bearing several names, runs through (*spacca* means
"cut through") Naples from west to east, from Via Toledo to Via
Duomo, retracing one of the main arteries of the Greek, and
later Roman, settlement. Spaccanapoli begins at **Piazza del
Gesù,** where the tourist information office (*see* Important Addresses and Numbers in Essential Information, *above*), can
provide pamphlets with itineraries tracing the city's development in ancient, medieval, and modern times.

❾ The oddly faceted stone facade of the church of **Gesù Nuovo** was
designed as part of a palace, but plans were changed as construction progressed, and it became the front of an elaborately
decorated Baroque church. Opposite is the monastery church
❿ of **Santa Chiara,** a Neapolitan landmark and the subject of a famous old song. It was built in the 1300s in Provençal Gothic
style, and it's best known for the quiet charm of its cloister garden, with columns and benches sheathed in antique ceramic
tiles, painted in the 18th century with delicate floral motifs and
vivid landscapes. The tiles are due to be restored, but may still
be visible in 1993. The entrance to the cloister is off the courtyard at the left of the church. *Piazza Gesù Nuovo. Admission
free. Open daily 8:30–12:30, 4–6:30.*

The first section of Spaccanapoli, **Via Benedetto Croce,** was
named in honor of the illustrious philosopher who was born
here in 1866, in the building at No. 12. As you continue along
you will pass peeling palaces, dark workshops where artisans
ply their trades, and many churches and street shrines. Where
the street changes to **Via San Biagio dei Librai,** the shops stage
a special Christmas fair of hand-carved crèche figures during
the weeks before Christmas.

⓫ Turn left on Via Duomo to the **Duomo** (Cathedral). It was established in the 1200s, but the building you see was erected a
century later and has since undergone radical changes, especially during the Baroque age. Inside the cathedral, 110 ancient columns salvaged from pagan buildings are set into the
piers supporting the 350-year-old wooden ceiling. Off the left
aisle you step down into the 4th-century church of Santa
Restituta, which was incorporated into the cathedral; though it

was redecorated in the late 1600s in the prevalent Baroque style, a few very old mosaics remain in the the baptistry and in a chapel on the left. On the right aisle of the cathedral, in the chapel of San Gennaro (open 8–noon), are multicolored marbles and frescoes honoring St. Januarius, miracle-working patron saint of Naples, whose altar and relics are encased in silver. Twice a year—on September 19, his feast day, and on the first Sunday in May, which commemorates the transference of his relics to Naples—his dried blood, contained in two sealed vials, is believed to liquefy during rites in his honor. These dates see the arrival of large numbers of devout Neapolitans offering up prayers in his memory.

About 100 yards ahead on each side of the cathedral are two of the most interesting of the city's many churches, **Santa Maria Donnaregina,** on Largo Donnaregina, to the north, and **San Lorenzo Maggiore,** in the opposite direction, on Via Tribunali. Both were built in the Middle Ages and decorated with 14th-century frescoes. Santa Maria Donnaregina has the towering Gothic funeral monument of Mary of Hungary, wife of Charles II of Anjou, who is said to have commissioned the frescoes in the church at a cost of 33 ounces of gold.

With San Lorenzo Maggiore on your left, walk down busy Via Tribunali to Porta Alba and Piazza Dante, at the junction with Via Roma. Here you can catch a taxi or bus No. 109 to **Capodimonte,** the royal palace built by the Bourbons in the 18th century in a vast park that served as the royal hunting preserve and later as the site of the Capodimonte porcelain works that the family established. Allow plenty of time for your visit to the palace; it's packed with works of art. Capodimonte's greatest attraction is the excellent collection of paintings well displayed in the Galleria Nazionale on the palace's top floor. Included are works from the 13th to the 18th centuries, including many familiar masterpieces by Dutch and Spanish masters, as well as by the great Italians. At the coffee bar halfway through, be sure to climb the stairs to the roof terrace for a sweeping view of the bay. Then continue through halls hung with dramatic Mannerist works of the 17th and 18th centuries, among them some stunning works by Caravaggio (1573–1610), originally hung in the city's churches. Downstairs are 19th-century Italian paintings and the royal apartments, where numerous portraits provide a close-up of the unmistakable Bourbon features, a challenge to any court painter. You'll also find beautiful antique furniture, most of it on the splashy scale so dear to the Bourbons, and a staggering collection of porcelain and majolica from the various royal residences. *Parco di Capodimonte, tel. 081/744–1307. Admission: 8,000 lire. Open Tues.–Sat. 9–2, Sun. 9–1.*

Another museum with a view—and with more porcelain—sits at the top of the funicular of Chiaia, which you can take from Via del Parco Margherita. The **Museo Duca di Martina** is set on the slopes of the Vomero hill, in a park known as Villa Floridiana. It houses a fine collection of European and Oriental porcelain and other *objets d'art* in a neoclassical residence built in the early 19th century by King Ferdinand I for his wife; their portraits greet you as you enter. Enjoy the view from the terrace behind the museum. *Via Cimarosa 77, tel. 081/578–8418. Admission: 4,000 lire. Open Tues.–Sat. 9–2, Sun. 9–1.*

Near the lower station of the Chiaia funicular is another small,
dignified museum in the park of **Villa Pignatelli.** The low-key
exhibits are of limited interest to anyone who doesn't like 19th-
century furniture, but there's a collection of antique coaches
and carriages in a pavilion on the grounds that is worth a look.
And a stroll in the park is a pleasant respite from the noisy city
streets. *Riviera di Chiaia 200, tel. 081/669675. Admission:
4,000 lire, park free. Open Tues.–Sat. 9–2, Sun. 9–1.*

For a change of pace, especially if you have children along, go to
the **Acquario** (Aquarium) in the public gardens on Via
Caracciolo. Founded by a German naturalist in the second half
of the 1800s, it's the oldest in Europe. About 200 species of fish
and marine plants thrive in large tanks, undoubtedly better off
here than in the highly polluted waters of the Bay of Naples,
their natural habitat. *Viale A. Dohrn, tel. 081/583–3111. Admission: 2,000 lire adults, 1,000 lire children. Open May–
Sept., Tues.–Sat. 9–5, Sun. 9–6; Oct.–Apr., Tues.–Sat. 9–5,
Sun. 9–2.*

The remaining sights on this tour are outside the city limits,
but are easy to reach from Naples; they can be treated as out-
ings on their own.

The **Phlegrean Fields**—the fields of fire—was the name once
given to the entire region west of Naples, including the island of
Ischia. The whole area floats freely on a mass of molten lava
very close to the surface. The fires are still smoldering. Greek
and Roman notions of the Underworld were not the blind
imaginings of a primitive people; they were the creations of poets and writers who stood on this very ground—here in the
Phlegrean Fields—and wrote down what they saw.

Whether it's worth the half day it takes to tour these sites really depends on your interests. If you've never seen volcanic activity, don't miss the **Solfatara,** the sunken crater of a volcano
(it's quite safe, as long as you stick to the path). The **Amphitheater** at **Pozzuoli** is fascinating because of its well-preserved underground passages and chambers, which give you a good sense
of how the wild animals were hoisted up into the arena. At **Lake
Avernus** you'll be standing at the very spot that the ancients
considered the entrance to Hades. The ruins at **Baia,** the resort
town of the ancient Romans, won't mean too much unless you
have more than a passing interest in antiquity. The **Oracle at
Cumae** was as famous as the one at Delphi; if you've read *The
Aeneid,* you'll want to enter the very cave described in Book
VI, where Aeneas sought the Sibyl's aid for his journey to the
Underworld.

To reach the **Solfatara** from Naples, take Route S7 Quater, Via
Domiziana, west toward **Pozzuoli.** You'll see a sign to the
Solfatara on your right, about 2 kilometers (1.3 miles) before
Pozzuoli. The only eruption of this semiextinct volcano was in
1198.

Legends about this smoldering landscape are based on conflicts
between the neolithic gods of the soil and the newer Olympian
gods brought to Greece by the Achaeans about 1600 BC. One
legend tells how Zeus hurled a hundred-headed dragon named
Typhon—the pre-Olympian god of volcanoes—down the crater
of Epomeo on the island of Ischia and how every crater in the
Phlegrean Fields is one of Typhon's mouths, flashing steam
and fire. In a similar legend pitting old values against new, the

sulfurous springs of the Solfatara are said to be the poisonous discharges from the wounds the Titans received in their war with Zeus before he hurled them down to hell. Both legends, of course, are efforts to dramatize man's struggle to overcome the mysterious and dangerous forces of nature.

⓳ The amphitheater at **Pozzuoli** (Anfiteatro Flavio) is slightly more than a mile farther west on S7. It's the third-largest arena in Italy, after the Colosseum and Santa Maria Capua Vetere, and could accommodate 40,000 spectators, who were sometimes treated to mock naval battles when the arena was filled with water. *Admission: 2,000 lire. Open daily 9–one hour before sunset.*

You may want to make a short side trip to Pozzuoli's harbor and imagine St. Paul landing here in AD 61 en route to Rome. His own ship had been wrecked off Malta, and he was brought here on the *Castor and Pollux*, a grain ship from Alexandria that was carrying corn from Egypt to Italy only 18 years before the eruption at Vesuvius.

To reach **Lake Avernus** (Lago d'Averno), continue west on S7 toward Cumae and then turn left (south) on the road to Baia. About .6 kilometer (1 mile) along this road, turn right and follow signs to Lake Avernus. The best time to visit is at sunset or when the moon is rising. There's a restaurant on the west side, near the tunnel (closed to the public) to Cumae, where you can dine on the terrace. Forested hills rise on three sides; the menacing cone of Monte Nuovo rises on the fourth. The smell of sulfur hangs over this sad, lonely landscape at the very gates of hell. No place evokes Homer, Virgil, and the cult of the Other World better than this silent, mysterious setting.

Before going on to Cumae, you may want to swing down the peninsula to the ancient city of **Baia** (5.8 kilometers, or 3.6 miles, from Pozzuoli). Now largely under the sea, it was once the most opulent and fashionable resort area of the Roman Empire. Sulla, Pompey, Julius Caesar, Tiberius, Nero, Cicero—these are some of the men who built their holiday villas here. Petronius's *Satyricon* is a satire on the corruption and intrigue, the wonderful licentiousness of Roman life at Baia. (Petronius was hired to arrange parties and entertainments for Nero, so he was in a position to know.) It was here at Baia that Emperor Claudius built a great villa for his wife Messalina (who spent her nights indulging herself at public brothels); here that Agrippina poisoned her husband and was, in turn, murdered by her son Nero; here that Cleopatra was staying when Julius Caesar was murdered on the Ides of March. You can visit the excavations of the famous **baths**. *Via Fusaro 35, tel. 081/868-7592. Admission: 4,000 lire. Open daily 9–one hour before sunset.*

You may continue to follow the loop around **Lake Miseno** (a volcanic crater believed by the ancients to be the Styx, across which Charon ferried the souls of the dead), and around **Lake Fusaro.** You'll pass some fine views of Pozzuoli Bay.

⓴ **Cumae** is perhaps the oldest Greek colony in Italy. In the 6th and 7th centuries BC, it overshadowed the Phlegrean Fields, including Naples. The **Sibyl's Cave** (Antro della Sibilla) is here—one of the most venerated sites in antiquity. In the 5th or 6th century AD, the Greeks hollowed the cave from the rock beneath the present ruins of Cumae's acropolis. Visitors walk through a dark, massive stone tunnel that opens into a vaulted chamber where the Sibyl rendered her oracles. Standing here, imagine yourself having an audience with her, her voice echoing off the dark, damp walls. The sense of mystery, of communication with the invisible, is overwhelming. "This is the most romantic classical site in Italy," wrote H. V. Morton. "I would rather come here than to Pompeii."

Virgil wrote the epic *The Aeneid*, the story of the Trojan prince Aeneas's wanderings, partly to give Rome the historical legitimacy that Homer had given the Greeks. On his journey, Aeneas had to descend to the Underworld to speak to his father, and to find his way in, he needed the guidance of the Cumaean Sibyl. She told him about the Golden Bough, his ticket through the Stygian swamp to the Underworld.

Virgil did not dream up the Sibyl's cave or the entrance to Hades—he must have stood both in her chamber and along the rim of Lake Avernus, as you yourself will stand. When he wrote, "The way to hell is easy"—*Facilis descensus Averni*—it was because he knew the way. In Book VI of *The Aeneid*, Virgil described how Aeneas, arriving at Cumae, sought Apollo's throne (remains of the **Temple of Apollo** can still be seen) and "the deep hidden abode of the dread Sibyl,/An enormous cave . . ." *Via Acropoli, tel. 081/854-3060. Admission 4,000 lire. Open daily 9–7.*

The Sibyl was not necessarily a charlatan; she was a medium, a prophetess, an old woman whom the ancients believed could communicate with the Other World. The three most famous Sibyls were at Erythrae, Delphi, and Cumae. Foreign governments consulted the Sibyls before mounting campaigns. Wealthy aristocrats came to consult with their dead relatives. Businessmen came to get their dreams interpreted or to seek favorable omens before entering into financial agreements or setting off on journeys. Farmers came to remove curses on their cows. Love potions were a profitable source of revenue; women from Baia lined up for potions to slip into the wine of handsome charioteers who drove up and down the street in their gold-plated four-horsepower chariots.

With the coming of the Olympian gods, the earlier gods of the soil were discredited or given new roles and names that reflected the change from a matrilineal to a patrilineal society. Ancient rites, such as those surrounding the Cumaean Sibyl, were carried out in secret and known as the Mysteries. The Romans—like the Soviets—tried in vain to replace these Mysteries by deifying the state in the person of its rulers. Yet even the Caesars appealed to forces of the Other World. And until the 4th century AD, the Sibyl was consulted by the Christian bishop of Rome.

Tour 2: Herculaneum, Vesuvius, and Pompeii

Volcanic ash and mud preserved the Roman towns of Herculaneum and Pompeii almost exactly as they were on the day Mount Vesuvius erupted in AD 79. What you'll see are not just archaeological ruins but living testamonies of daily life in the ancient world. Herculaneum, Pompeii, and Vesuvius can be visited from either Naples or Sorrento, thanks to the Circumvesuviana (*see* Getting Around by Train in Essential

Information, *above*), the suburban railway that provides fast, frequent, and economical service between Naples and Sorrento. If Naples is your base, your first stop is Herculaneum, at modern Ercolano; from Sorrento you will explore these sights in reverse order.

Ten kilometers (6 miles) south of Naples are the ruins of **㉑ Herculaneum,** which lie more than 60 feet below the town of Ercolano. The ruins are set among the acres of greenhouses that make this area one of Europe's principal flower-growing centers. The entrance to the site is a short walk south from the Circumvesuviana station. Hercules himself is said to have founded the town, which became a famous weekend retreat for the Roman elite. It had about 5,000 inhabitants when it was destroyed; many of them were fishermen, craftsmen, and artists. A lucky few patricians (aristocrats) owned villas overlooking the sea. Herculaneum was damaged by an earthquake in AD 63, and repairs were still being made 16 years later, when the gigantic eruption of Vesuvius (which also destroyed Pompeii) sent a fiery cloud of gas and pumice hurtling onto the town, which was completely buried under a tide of volcanic mud. This semiliquid mass seeped into the crevices and niches of every building, covering household objects and enveloping textiles and wood—sealing all in a compact, airtight tomb.

Casual excavation—and haphazard looting—began in the 18th century, but systematic digs were not initiated until the 1920s. Now less than half of Herculaneum has been excavated; with present-day Ercolano and the unlovely Resina Quarter (famous among bargain hunters as the area's largest secondhand clothing market) sitting on top of the site, progress is limited. From the ramp leading down to Herculaneum's neatly laid-out streets and well-preserved edifices, you get a good overall view of the site, as well as an idea of the amount of rock that had to be removed to bring it to light.

You could easily get lost in the streets of Pompeii, but not here. Most important buildings can be seen in about two hours. If you feel closer to the past at Herculaneum than at Pompeii, it's in part because there are fewer hawkers here, and visitors tend to show a certain quiet respect for antiquity that's not always evident in such a famous tourist spot as Pompeii. Though Herculaneum had only one-fourth the population of Pompeii and has only been partially excavated, what has been found is generally better preserved than at Pompeii. In some cases, you can even see the original wooden beams, staircases, and furniture.

At the entrance you should pick up a map showing the gridlike layout of the dig. Decorations are especially delicate in the **House of the Mosaic Atrium,** with a pavement in a black-and-white checkerboard pattern, and in the **House of Neptune and Amphitrite,** named for the subjects of a still-bright mosaic on the wall of the nymphaeum (a recessed grotto with a fountain). Annexed to the latter of these two houses is a remarkably preserved wineshop, where *amphorae* (vases) still rest on carbonized wooden shelves. And in the **House of the Wooden Partition,** one of the best-preserved of all, there is a carbonized wooden partition with three doors. In the **Baths,** where there were separate sections for men and women, you can see benches; basins; and the hot, warm, and cold rooms, embellished with mosaics. The **House of the Bicentenary** was a patrician residence with smaller rooms on the upper floor, which may have been rented out to artisan-tenants who were probably Christians because they left an emblem of the cross embedded in the wall. The *palaestra* (gymnasium) and 2,500-seat theater; the sumptuously decorated suburban baths; and the House of the Stags, with an elegant garden open to the sea breezes, are all evocative relics of a lively and luxurious way of life.

Until a few years ago it was believed that most of Herculaneum's inhabitants had managed to escape by sea, since few skeletons were found in the city. Excavations at Porta Marina, the gate in the sea wall leading to the beach, have revealed instead that many perished there, a few steps from the only escape route open to them. *Corso Ercolano, tel. 081/739–0963. Admission: 8,000 lire; children under 12 free. Open daily 9–1 hr before sunset; ticket office closes 2 hrs before sunset.*

㉒ You can visit **Vesuvius** either before or after Herculaneum. The mountain tends to be clearer in the afternoon. If possible, save the mountain till after you've toured the buried city and learned to appreciate the volcano's awesome power. The most important factor is whether the summit is lost in mist—when it is, you'll be lucky to see your hand in front of your face. The volcano is visible from Naples, and everywhere else along the Bay of Naples; the best advice is, when you see the summit clearing, head for it. The view then is magnificent, with the curve of the coast and the tiny white houses among the orange and lemon blossoms.

Reaching the crater takes some effort. From the Ercolano stop of the Circumvesuviana, take scheduled buses (departures at 10, noon, and 2) or your own car to the Seggovia station, the lower terminal of the defunct chair lift. Though there's talk of putting the chair lift back in working order, no one is optimistic about the possibility. In the square in front of the station, hawkers and vendors outnumber tourists two to one. From here you must climb the soft, slippery cinder track on foot, a 30-minute ascent, and you must pay about 2,000 lire for compulsory guide service, though the guides don't do much more than tell you to stay away from the edge of the crater. If you're not in shape, you'll probably find the climb tiring. Wear nonskid shoes (not sandals).

㉓ **Pompeii** has its own stop (Pompeii–Scavi) on the Circumvesuviana, close to the main entrance at the Porta Marina (there are other entrances to the excavations at the far end of the site, near the amphitheater). Ancient Pompeii was much larger than Herculaneum; a busy commercial center with a population of 10,000–20,000, it covered about 160 acres on the seaward end of the fertile Sarno plain.

Numbers in the margin correspond to points of interest on the Pompeii map.

In 80 BC the Roman General Sulla turned Pompeii into a Roman colony, where wealthy patricians came to escape the turmoil of city life and relax in the sun.

The town was laid out in a grid pattern, with two main intersecting streets. The wealthiest took a whole block for themselves; those less fortunate built a house and rented out the front rooms, facing the street, as shops. The facades of these houses were relatively plain and seldom hinted at the care and attention lavished on the private rooms within.

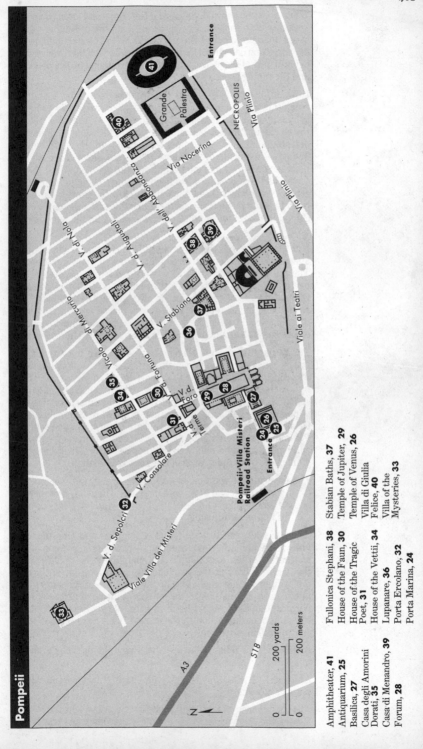

Pompeii

Amphitheater, **41**
Antiquarium, **25**
Basilica, **27**
Casa degli Amorini
Dorati, **35**
Casa di Menandro, **39**
Forum, **28**

Fullonica Stephani, **38**
House of the Faun, **30**
House of the Tragic
Poet, **31**
House of the Vettii, **34**
Lupanare, **36**
Porta Ercolano, **32**
Porta Marina, **24**

Stabian Baths, **37**
Temple of Jupiter, **29**
Temple of Venus, **26**
Villa di Giulia
Felice, **40**
Villa of the
Mysteries, **33**

When a visitor entered, he passed the shops and entered an open area (atrium). In the back was a receiving room. Behind was another open area, called the peristyle, with rows of columns and perhaps a garden with a fountain. Only good friends ever saw this private part of the house, which was surrounded by the bedrooms and the dining area.

How different these homes are from houses today—and how much they say about changing attitudes toward family and society! Today we build homes that face the streets, that look out over the world; in Pompeii, houses were designed around an inner garden so that families could turn their backs on the world outside. Today we install picture windows that break down visual barriers between ourselves and our neighbors; the people in these Roman towns had few windows, preferring to get their light from the central courtyard—the light within. How pleasant it must have been to come home from the forum or the baths to one's own secluded kingdom, with no visual reminders of a life outside one's own.

Not that public life was so intolerable. There were wineshops on almost every corner, and frequent shows at the amphitheater. The public fountains and toilets were fed by huge cisterns, connected by lead pipes beneath the sidewalks. Since garbage and rainwater collected in the streets of Pompeii, the sidewalks were raised, and huge stepping stones were placed at crossings so pedestrians could keep their feet dry. Herculaneum had better drainage, with an underground sewer that led to the sea.

The ratio of freemen to slaves was about three to two. A small, prosperous family had two or three slaves. Since all manual labor was considered degrading, the slaves did all housework and cooking, including the cutting of meat, which the family ate with spoons or with their hands. Everyone loved grapes, and figs were popular, too. Venison, chicken, and pork were the main dishes. Oranges weren't known, but people ate quinces (a good source of Vitamin C) to guard against scurvy. Bread was made from wheat and barley (rye and oats were unknown) and washed down with wine made from the grapes of the slopes of Vesuvius.

The government was considered a democracy, but women, children, gladiators, and Jews couldn't vote. They did, however, express their opinions on election day, as you'll see in campaign graffiti left on public walls.

Some 15,000 graffiti were found in Pompeii and Herculaneum. Many were political announcements—one person recommending another for office, for example, and spelling out his qualifications. Some were bills announcing upcoming events—a play at the theater, a fight among gladiators at the amphitheater. Others were public notices—that wine was on sale, that an apartment would be vacant on the Ides of March. A good many were personal, and give a human dimension to the disaster that not even the sights can equal. Here are a few:

At the Baths: "What is the use of having a Venus if she's made of marble?"

At a hotel: "I've wet my bed. My sin I bare. But why? you ask. No pot was anywhere."

At the entrance to the front lavatory at a private house: "May I always and everywhere be as potent with women as I was here."

In a back room at the Suburban Baths: "Apelles the waiter dined most pleasantly with Dexter the slave of the emperor, and they had a screw at the same time." (Did they do it with each other, or only at the same time? Homosexuality would not have been uncommon.)

In a house in Herculaneum: "Apollinaris the physician of the Emperor Titus had a good shit here."

The following route will help you locate the most interesting sights:

㉔ Enter through **Porta Marina,** so called because it faces the sea. It is near the **Pompeii–Scavi Circumvesuviana Station.** On your **㉕** right is the **Antiquarium,** which contains casts of human bodies **㉖ ㉗** and a dog. Past the **Temple of Venus** is the **Basilica,** the law court and the economic center of the city. These oblong buildings ending in a semicircular projection (apse) were the model for early Christian churches, which had a nave (central aisle) and two side aisles separated by rows of columns. Standing in the Basilica, you can recognize the continuity between Roman and Christian architecture.

㉘ The Basilica opens onto the **Forum** (Foro), the public meeting place, surrounded by temples and public buildings. It was here that elections were held and speeches and official announcements made. America's answer to the forum is the village green. The closest the British come to it today is the Mall. Turn **㉙** left. At the far (northern) end of the forum is the **Temple of Jupiter** (Tempio di Giove). Walk around the right side of the temple, cross the street, and continue north on **Via del Foro** (Forum Street). There is a **restaurant** on your left.

The next cross street becomes **Via delle Fortuna** to your right, and **Via delle Terme** to your left. Turn right on **Via della Fortu-** **㉚** **na.** On your left is **The House of the Faun** (Casa del Fauno), one of the most impressive examples of a luxurious private house, with wonderful mosaics (originals in the National Museum in Naples).

Retrace your steps along **Via della Fortuna** to **Via del Foro.** Cross the street. You're now on **Via delle Terme.** The first en- **㉛** trance on the right is the **House of the Tragic Poet** (Casa del Poeta Tragico). This is a typical middle-class house from the last days of Pompeii. Over the door is a mosaic of a chained dog and the inscription *Cave canem,* "Beware of the dog." Continue west on Via delle Terme to the end. Turn right and bear left **㉜** along **Via Consolare.** Pass through the beautiful **Porta Ercolano** (Gate of Herculaneum)—the main gate that led to Herculaneum and Naples.

Now outside Pompeii, walk down **Via dei Sepolcri** (Street of the Tombs), lined with tombs and cypresses. The road makes a **㉝** sharp left. At the four-way crossing, turn right to the **Villa of the Mysteries** (Villa dei Misteri). This patrician's villa contains what some consider the greatest surviving group of paintings from the ancient world, telling the story of a young bride (Ariadne) being initiated into the mysteries of the cult of Dionysus. Bacchus (Dionysus), the god of wine, was popular in a town so devoted to the pleasures of the flesh. But he also represented the triumph of the irrational—of all those mysterious forces that no official state religion could fully suppress. The cult of Dionysus, like the cult of the Cumaean Sibyl, gave people a sense of control over fate, and in its focus on the Other World, helped pave the way for Christianity.

Return along **Via dei Sepolcri** to Pompeii. Retrace your steps down **Via Consolare,** which joins with **Vicolo di Narciso.** Make your first left on **Vicolo di Mercurio.** Six blocks down is **Vicolo**
㉞ dei Vettii. Around the corner, to the left, is the **House of the Vettii** (Casa dei Vetti). This is the best example of a rich middle-class merchant's house, faithfully restored.

Return, back around the corner, to **Vicolo di Mercurio.** Continue east one more block. You've now reached **Via Stabiana,** one of the two major intersecting streets of the town. Around the
㉟ corner to the left is **Casa degli Amorini Dorati (House of the Gilded Cupids), an elegant, well-preserved home with original marble decorations in the garden.

From the door of Casa degli Amorini Dorati, turn right down Via Stabiana, go three blocks, and turn right on **Via Augustali.**
㊱ Your first left will take you to the **Lupanare (the brothel) on **Vicolo del Lupanare.** On the walls are scenes of erotic games that clients could request. The beds have shoe marks left by visitors.

Continue south on Vicolo del Lupanare, turning left on **Via dell'Abbondanza,** the other main street of the old town. On your
㊲ left is the **Stabian Baths. It was here that people came in the evening to drown the burdens of the day. The baths were heated by underground furnaces. The heat circulated among the stone pillars supporting the floor, rose through flues in the walls, and escaped through chimneys. The water temperature could be set for cold, lukewarm, and hot. Bathers took a luke-warm bath to prepare themselves for the hot room. A tepid bath came next, and then a plunge into cold water to tone up the skin. A vigorous massage with oil was followed by rest, reading, horseplay, and conversation.

Continue in the same direction, east on Via dell'Abbondanza (a left turn as you leave the baths). Two blocks down on your right
㊳ is the **Fullonica Stephani, a house converted into workshops for the cleaning of fabrics. All Roman citizens were required to wear togas in public, which weren't exactly easy to keep clean. It's not hard to imagine why there were more toga cleaners (fullers) in Pompeii than anything else, except perhaps bakers. The cloth was dunked in a tub full of water and chalk and stamped upon like so many grapes. Washed, the material was stretched across a wicker cage and exposed to sulfur fumes. The fuller carded it with a long brush, then placed it under a press. The harder the pressing, the whiter and brighter it became.

Go south, completely around the block. Behind the Fullonica
㊴ Stephani is the entrance to the **Casa di Menandro, a patrician's villa with many paintings and mosaics. Return to Via dell'Abbondanza. If you've had enough walking, turn left and go a few more blocks past the new restorations and then return to the Porta Marina, where your tour began. The recommended alternative is to turn right (east) on Via dell'Abbondanza to the
㊵ Villa di Giulia Felice (House of Julia Felix), which has a large garden with a lovely portico. The wealthy lady living here ran a public bathhouse annex and rented out ground-floor rooms as shops.

41 Turn right past the villa and continue to the **Amphitheater** (Anfiteatro). The games here were between animals, between gladiators, and between animals and gladiators. There were also Olympic games and chariot races. The crowds rushed in as soon as the gates opened—women and slaves to the bleachers. When the Emperor or some other important person was in attendance, exotic animals—lions and tigers, panthers, elephants, and rhinos—were released. At "half time," birds of prey were set against hares, or dogs against porcupines; the animals were tied to each end of a rope so neither could escape. Most gladiators were slaves or prisoners, but a few were Germans or Syrians who enjoyed fighting. Teams of gladiators worked for impresarios, who hired them out to wealthy citizens, many of whom were running for office and hoping that the gory entertainment would buy them some votes. When a gladiator found himself at another's mercy, he extended a pleading hand to the president of the games. If the president turned his thumb up, the gladiator lived; if he turned his thumb down, the gladiator's throat was cut. The arena got pretty bloody after a night's entertainment and was sprinkled with red powder to camouflage the carnage. The victorious gladiator got money or a ribbon exempting him from further fights. If he was a slave, he was often set free. If the people of Pompeii had had trading cards, they would have collected portraits of gladiators; everyone had his favorite. Says one piece of graffiti: "Petronius Octavus fought thirty-four fights and then died, but Severus, a freedman, was victor in fifty-five fights and still lived; Nasica celebrates sixty victories." Pompeii had a gladiator school (Caserma dei Gladiatori), which you can visit on your way back to Porta Marina.

Return to Porta Marina, where your walk began, or exit through the **Ingresso Anfiteatro** and find a cab for the 6-kilometer (1-mile) trip back to Porta Marina. You could, of course, begin your trip at Ingresso Anfiteatro and make the tour in the opposite direction. If you want a personal guide, you may have an easier time finding one here than at Porta Marina.

To get the most out of Pompeii, buy a detailed printed guide and map and allow plenty of time for your visit—at least three or four hours, more if you like to poke into corners. You should have a pocketful of small change (500-lire coins) for tipping the guards who are on duty at the most important villas. They will unlock the gates for you, insist on explaining the attractions, show you some mild Pompeiian pornography if you ask for it, and expect a tip for their services. If you hire a guide, make sure he's registered and standing inside the gate. Agree beforehand on the length of the tour and the price. *Pompei Scavi, tel. 081/861–0744. Admission: 10,000 lire; children under 12 free. Open daily 9–one hour before sunset; ticket office closes 2 hours before sunset.*

Time Out You can have lunch or refreshments at the restaurant and cafeteria near the **Forum,** where there's a picnic area as well. There are also plenty of trattorias outside the entrances to the excavation.

Tour 3: Caserta and Benevento

Numbers in the margin correspond to points of interest on the Campania map.

A northward excursion from Naples takes you to Caserta, the Bourbons' version of Versailles, and if you proceed to Benevento, you'll view an almost perfectly preserved Roman arch. With the exception of some mountain scenery, there's not much else of interest on this route; Benevento was badly damaged by World War II bombings, and you will have to content yourself here with picking out the medieval and even older relics that have survived in the oldest part of the city. Both Caserta and Benevento can be reached by train from Naples. Daily bus service from Naples is quite frequent to Caserta, 28 kilometers (18 miles) away, less so to Benevento, 62 kilometers (39 miles) away. If you go by car, make a brief detour to the medieval hamlet of Caserta Vecchia on the hillside, where there is a very old cathedral and one or two good restaurants.

42 The **royal palace** at **Caserta,** known as the Reggia, will show you how Bourbon royalty lived in the mid-18th century. Architect Luigi Vanvitelli devoted 20 years to its construction under Bourbon ruler Charles II, whose son, Charles III, moved in when it was completed in 1774. Both king and architect were inspired by Versailles, and the rectangular palace was conceived on a massive scale, with four interconnecting courtyards, 1,200 rooms, and a vast park. Though not as well maintained as its French counterpart, the main staircase is suitably grand, and the **royal apartments** are sumptuous. It was here, in what Eisenhower called "a castle near Naples," that the Allied High Command had its headquarters in World War II, and here German forces in Italy surrendered in April 1945. Most enjoyable are the gardens and parks, particularly the Cascades, where a life-size Diana and her maidens stand, waiting to be photographed. The park is the Reggia's main attraction, with pools and fountains stretching for more than a mile, formal Italian gardens and a delightful English garden. Some of the fountains are splendid and may be playing at full force now that the aqueduct built by the Bourbons has been repaired. If you don't like walking, a minibus makes a circuit of the grounds. *Piazza Carlo III. Admission: royal apartments, 6,000 lire; park, 4,000 lire; minibus, 2,000 lire. Open Tues.– Sun., royal apartments 9–1:30; park 9–one hour before sunset. Closed national holidays.*

Time Out **Mulini Reali** (tel. 0823/301842) is a restaurant set in an old mill. There's good pasta and fish at lunchtime, and the restaurant is located at an entrance to the English Garden. *Ponte di Sala. Closed Tues.*

43 **Benevento,** 35 kilometers (21 miles) east, became the capital of the Lombards, a northern tribe that had invaded and settled what is now Lombardy when they were ousted by Charlemagne in the 8th century. Tough and resourceful, the Lombards moved south and set up a new duchy in Benevento, later moving its seat south to Salerno, where they saw the potential of the fine natural harbor. Under papal rule in the 13th century, Benevento built a fine cathedral and endowed it with bronze doors that are a pinnacle of Romanesque art. The cathedral, doors, and a large part of the town were blasted by World War II bombs, so there's little left to see; fortunately, however, the majestic **Arch of Trajan** survived unscathed. To reach it, follow Viale Principe di Napoli from the station and take the first left after the river. The arch is a fine 2nd-century AD work, decorated with reliefs exalting the many accomplishments of Roman emperor Trajan, who sorted out Rome's finances, brought parts of the Middle East into the empire, and extended the Appian Way through Benevento to the Adriatic, thus ensuring the town's prosperity. From the arch, take Via Traiano and turn right onto Corso Garibaldi to get to the **Duomo** (Cathedral), which has been rebuilt in its original form. Via Carlo, behind the cathedral, leads to the ruins of a **Roman Theater,** with a seating capacity of 20,000. The theater is still in good enough shape to host a summer opera and theater season. *Teatro Romano. Admission: 3,500 lire. Open daily 9–one hour before sunset.*

Tour 4: Ischia and Capri

④ Capri wows you with its charm and beauty; **Ischia** takes time to cast its spell. Give Ischia a week, and you'll probably grow attached to its special character, its hidden corners and familiar view. But an overnight stay is probably not long enough for the island to get into your blood. It does have its share of white-wine-growing villages beneath the lush volcanic slopes of Monte Epomeo and, unlike Capri, it enjoys a life of its own that survives when the tourists head home. But there are few signs of antiquity here, the architecture is unremarkable, the beaches are small and pebbly, there's little shopping beyond the high-trash gift shops that attract the German therapeutic trade, and most visitors are either German (off-season) or Italian (in-season). On the other hand, some of you will delight in discovering an island not yet overcome with tourists from the United States. Ischia also has some lovely hotel-resorts high in the mountains, offering therapeutic programs and rooms with breathtaking views of the sea. Should you want to plunk down in the sun for a few days and tune out the world, this is an ideal place to go; the mistake you shouldn't make is expecting Ischia to be an unspoiled, undiscovered Capri. When Augustus gave the Neapolitans Ischia for Capri, he knew what he was doing.

Unlike Capri, Ischia is volcanic in origin. From its hidden reservoir of seething molten matter come the thermal springs said to cure whatever ails you. As early as 1580, a doctor named Iosolini published a book about the mineral wells at Ischia. "If your eyebrows fall off," he wrote, "go and try the baths at Piaggia Romano. Are you unhappy about your complexion? You will find the cure in the waters of Santa Maria del Popolo. Are you deaf? Then go to Bagno d'Ulmitello. If you know anyone who is getting bald, anyone who suffers from elephantiasis, or another whose wife yearns for a child, take the three of them immediately to the Bagno di Vitara; they will bless you."

Today the island is covered with thermal baths surrounded by tropical gardens—if you've never been to one before, don't miss the opportunity.

Hydrofoils reach Ischia from Naples in 45 minutes; car ferries take 90 minutes. The passenger-and-car ferry from Pozzuoli takes about 60 minutes. **Ischia Porto** is the largest town on the island and the usual point of debarkation. It's no workaday port, however, but a pretty resort with plenty of hotels and low flat-roofed houses arrayed on terraced hillsides above the water. Its narrow streets often become flights of steps that scale the hill, and its villas and gardens are framed by pines. If you're visiting Ischia for the day, your best bet is to recapture your youth at one of the mineral baths, such as **Poseidon Gardens,** and then lose it at a harborfront restaurant in Ischia Porto or perhaps in the colorful port of **Forio** on the opposite side of the island.

Most of the hotels are along the beach in the part of town called **Ischia Ponte,** which gets its name from the bridge *(ponte)* built by Alfonso of Aragón in 1438 to link the picturesque castle on a small islet offshore with the town and port. For a while, the castle was the home of Vittoria Colonna, poetess and platonic soulmate of Michelangelo, with whom she carried on a lengthy correspondence, and granddaughter of Renaissance Duke Federico da Montefeltro. If you choose to stay in Porto d'Ischia, you'll find a typical resort atmosphere; countless cafés, shops, and restaurants; and a half-mile stretch of fine sandy beach.

The **information office** is at the harbor. Remember that Ischia is off limits to visitors' cars from May through September; there's fairly good bus service, and you'll find plenty of taxis. One popular beach resort, just 5 kilometers (3 miles) east of Ischia Porto is **Casamicciola.** Just west is chic and upscale **Lacco Ameno,** distinguished by a mushroom-shaped rock offshore and some of the island's best hotels. Here, too, you can enjoy the benefits of Ischia's therapeutic waters.

The far western and southern coasts of the island are more rugged and attractive. **Forio,** at the extreme west, is an ideal stop for lunch or dinner. The sybaritic hot pools of the **Poseidon Gardens** spa establishment are on the Citara beach, south of Forio. You can sit like a Roman senator on a stone chair recessed in the rock and let the hot water cascade over you—all very campy, and fun. **Sant'Angelo,** on the southern coast, is a charming village; the road doesn't reach all the way into town, so it's free of traffic, and it's a five-minute boat ride from the beach of Maronti, at the foot of the cliffs, which spew hot springs into the sea. The inland towns of **Serrara, Fontana,** and **Barano** are all located high above the sea, and Fontana, most elevated of all, is the base for excursions to the top of **Mount Epomeo,** the long-dormant volcano that dominates the island landscape. You can reach its 788-meter (2,585-foot) peak in about 1½ hours of relatively easy walking.

A good 35-kilometer (21-mile) road makes a circuit of the island; the ride takes most of a day at a leisurely pace, if you're stopping along the way to enjoy the views and perhaps have lunch. You can book a boat tour (25,000 lire) around the island at the booths in various ports along the coast, where the boat makes several stops to pick up passengers; there's a one-hour stop at Sant'Angelo.

45 **Capri** (accent on the first syllable) is a pleasure island at the southern approach to the Bay of Naples. It's easy to reach by boat or hydrofoil from Naples and Sorrento all year and from the Amalfi Coast or Ischia during the summer months. The boat from Naples takes about 90 minutes; the hydrofoil, only about 40 minutes. In addition, there's direct helicopter service from Capodichino Airport in Naples (*see* Arriving and Departing by Plane in Essential Information, *above*). Note that from April 1 to October 31, no cars can be taken to the island.

The summer scene on Capri calls to mind the stampeding of bulls through the narrow streets of Pamplona: If you can visit in the spring or fall, do so. Yet even the crowds are not enough to destroy Capri's very special charm. The town is a Moorish opera set of shiny white houses, tiny squares, and narrow medieval alleyways hung with flowers. You can take a bus or the funicular to reach the town, which rests on top of rugged limestone cliffs, hundreds of feet above the sea.

The mood is modish but somehow unspoiled. The summer set is made up of smart, wealthy types and college students. The upper crust bakes in the sun in private villas. The secret is for you, too, to disappear while the day-trippers take over—offering yourself to the sun at your hotel pool or exploring the hidden corners of the island. Even in the height of summer, you can enjoy a degree of privacy on one of the many paved paths that wind around the island hundreds of feet above the sea; if you're willing to walk, you can be as alone here as you've ever wanted to be. Unlike the other islands in the Bay of Naples, Capri is not of volcanic origin but is an integral part of the limestone chain of the Apennines, left above water when some subterranean cataclysm sank its connecting link with the mainland.

The Phoenicians were the earliest settlers of Capri. The Greeks arrived in the 4th century BC and were followed by the Romans, who made it their playground. Emperor Augustus vacationed here; Tiberius built 12 villas, scattered over the island, and here he spent the later years of his life, refusing to return to Rome even when he was near death. Capri was one of the strongholds of the 15th-century pirate Barbarossa, who first sacked it and then made a fortress of it. Moors and Greeks had previously established their citadels on its heights, and pirates from all corners of the world periodically raided it. In 1806 the British wanted to turn it into another Gibraltar and were beginning to build fortifications when the French took it away from them in 1808. However, the Roman influence has remained the strongest, reflecting a sybaritic way of life inherited from the Greek colonists on the mainland.

Capri has a reputation for being hideously expensive, and indeed some of its top-ranking hotels and restaurants are among the most costly in Italy. But plenty of moderately priced hotels and some inexpensive ones share the same fabulous views as their high-priced rivals and offer a wide range of accommodations. Many of these are family-run small hotels. There are also moderately priced trattorias off the beaten tourist track.

Thousands of legends concerning the life and loves of mythological creatures, Roman emperors, Saracen invaders, and modern eccentrics combine to give Capri a voluptuous allure—sensuous and intoxicating—like the island's rare and delicious white wine. (Most of the wine passed off as "local" on Capri comes from the much more extensive vineyards of Ischia.) Certainly there are fewer pleasures more gratifying than gazing out at the sea from the quiet of a sun-dappled arbor while enjoying a glass of cold wine and flavorful *insalata caprese,* a minor work of art in itself, with smooth white mozzarella, fleshy red tomatoes, and bright-green basil.

All boats for Capri dock at **Marina Grande,** where you can board an excursion boat for the 90-minute tour to the **Blue Grotto.** If you're pressed for time, however, skip this sometimes frustrating and disappointing excursion. You board one boat to get to the grotto, and you have to transfer to another, smaller, one in order to get inside the grotto. If there's a backup of boats waiting to get in, you'll be given precious little time to enjoy the gorgeous color of the water and its silvery reflections. *Cost, including 4,000-lire admission to the grotto: about 16,200 lire. Daily 9:30–two hours before sunset; departures less frequent in winter.*

As an alternative, take the approximately two-hour boat trip around the island—hassle free and very enjoyable. These excursions start at the Marina Grande and are run by the Grotto Azurra company. The cost is 15,450 lire. Make either of these boat trips in the morning, when light and visibility are better.

The main **tourist information office** is on the pier where the boats from the mainland dock; ask for a brochure map *(piantina)* showing the many walks you can take to get the best views and escape the crowds. You may have to wait in line for the cog railway (3,000 lire round-trip) to the town of **Capri.** If it's not operating, there's bus and taxi service. From the upper station you walk out into the *piazzetta,* the island's social center, *the* place to see and be seen. The ambience of the piazzetta is deliberately commercial and self-consciously picturesque. You can window-shop in expensive boutiques and browse in souvenir shops along Via Vittorio Emanuele. The many-domed **Certosa di San Giacomo** is a much-restored monastery where you can visit the church and cloister and enjoy a breathtaking view of Punta Tragara and the Faraglioni, three towering shoals, from the viewing stand at the edge of the cliff. *Via Certosa. Admission free. Open Tues.–Sun. 9–2.*

Via Matteotti leads past bright shops and ice-cream stands to the **Giardini di Augusto** (Gardens of Augustus), a beautifully planted public garden with excellent views. From its terraces you can see the village of **Marina Piccola** below, where restaurants, cabanas, and swimming platforms huddle among the shoals. This is the best place on the island for swimming; you can reach it by bus or by following the steep and winding Via Krupp, actually a staircase cut into the rock, all the way down. (Friedrich Krupp, the German arms manufacturer, loved Capri and became one of the island's most generous benefactors.) Otherwise you swim off boats or take a hint from the family groups from Naples and Sorrento who swim off the unkempt but sandy beach at the end of Marina Grande past the cog railway station.

Time Out   Just down Via Roma from the piazzetta is **Verginiello** (tel. 081/837–0944), one of the island's best-value restaurants for lunch. Try the calamari (squid).

From the town of Capri, the 45-minute hike east to **Villa Jovis,** the grandest of those built by Tiberius, is strenuous but rewarding. Follow the signs for Villa Jovis, taking Via Botteghe from the piazzetta, then continuing along Via Croce and Via Tiberio. At the end of a lane that climbs the steep hill, with pretty views all the way, you come to the precipice over which the emperor reputedly disposed of the victims of his perverse attentions. From a natural terrace above, near a chapel, are spectacular views of the entire Bay of Naples and (on clear days) part of the Gulf of Salerno. Below are the ruins of Tiberius's palace. Allow 45 minutes each way for the walk alone. *Via Tiberio. Admission: 4,000 lire. Open daily 9–one hr before sunset.*

A shorter, more level walk along Via Tragara leads to a belvedere overlooking the Faraglioni; another takes you out of the town of Capri on Via Matermania to the so-called Natural Arch, an unusual rock formation near a natural grotto that the Romans transformed into a shrine. The 20-minute walk from the piazzetta along picturesque Via Madre Serafina and Via Castello to the belvedere at Punta Cannone gives you a panoramic view of the island.

You can take a bus from the Marina Grande (1,500 lire) or a taxi (about 12,000 lire one way; agree on the fare before starting out) up the tortuous road to **Anacapri,** the island's only other town. Here crowds are thickest around the square that is the starting point of the chair lift (6,000 lire) to the top of Mount Solaro. Elsewhere, Anacapri is quiet and appealing. Look for the church of **San Michele,** where a climb to the choir loft rewards one with a perspective of the magnificent 18th-century majolica tile floor showing the Garden of Eden (open Apr.–Oct.). From Piazza della Vittoria, picturesque Via Capodimonte leads to **Villa San Michele,** charming former home of Swedish scientist Axel Munthe, now a museum of his antiques and furniture. *Via Axel Munthe. Admission: 4,000 lire. Open Apr.–Sept., daily 9–6; Oct.–Mar., daily 10:30–3:30.*

Anacapri is also good for walks: Try the 40-minute walk (each way) to the Migliara belvedere and another walk of about an hour each way to the ruins of the Roman villa of Damecuta, which is thought to have been built by Tiberius, and a 12th-century watchtower. The road then continues to the entrance to the Blue Grotto.

If walking is not your idea of happiness, just join the other sybarites sitting in the piazzetta and remember that Augustus called Capri Apragopolis (City of Sweet Idleness) or, as the Italians would say, *dolce far niente* (pleasant idleness).

Tour 5: The Amalfi Drive: Sorrento to Salerno

This is the most romantic drive in Italy. The road is gouged from the side of rocky cliffs plunging into the sea. Small boats lie in sandy coves like so many brightly colored fish. Erosion has contorted the rocks into mythological shapes and hollowed out fairy grottoes where the air is turquoise and the water an icy blue. White villages, dripping with flowers, nestle in coves or climb like vines up the steep, terraced hills. The road must have a thousand turns, each with a different view, on its dizzying 69-kilometer (43-mile) journey from Sorrento to Salerno.

46 **Sorrento** is 50 kilometers (30 miles) from Naples on autostrada A3 and S145; the Circumvesuviana railway, which stops at Herculaneum and Pompeii, provides another connection. The coast between Naples and Castellammare, where road and railway turn off onto the Sorrento peninsula, seems at times depressingly overbuilt and industrialized. Yet Vesuvius looms to the left, you can make out the 3,000-foot-high mass of Mount

Faito ahead, and on a clear day you can see Capri off the tip of the peninsula. The scenery improves considerably as you near Sorrento, where the coastal plain is carved into russet cliffs rising perpendicularly from the sea. This is the Sorrento (north) side of the peninsula; on the other side is the Amalfi Coast, more dramatically scenic and somewhat less overcome by tourists in summer. Many prefer the charming towns on the Amalfi Coast to the tourist haven of Sorrento, but Sorrento has at least two advantages: the Circumvesuviana railway terminal and a fairly flat terrain. (Positano, and to a lesser extent Amalfi and Ravello, clings to hillsides and requires some strenuous walking.)

Until the mid-20th century Sorrento was a small, genteel resort favored by central European princes, English aristocrats, and American literati. Now the town has grown and spread out along the crest of its famous cliffs, and apartments stand where citrus groves once bloomed. Tour groups arrive by the busload, and their ranks are swollen by Italian vacationers in the peak summer season. Like most resorts, Sorrento is best off-season, either in spring and early autumn or in winter, when Campania's mild climate can make a stay anywhere along the coast pleasant. Another reason to avoid the peninsula during peak season is the heavy traffic on the single coast road, where cars and buses may be backed up for miles. Highlights of a visit to Sorrento include a stroll around town, with views of the Bay of Naples from the **Villa Comunale** or from the terrace behind the **Museo Correale.** The museum features a collection of decorative antiques, from ceramics to furniture to landscape paintings of the Neapolitan school. *Via Capasso. Admission: 5,000 lire; gardens only: 2,000 lire. Open Apr.–Sept., Mon.–Sat. 9– 12:30 and 5–7, Sun. 9–12:30; Oct.–Mar., Mon.–Sat. 9–12:30 and 3–5, Sun. 9–12:30; closed Tues.*

Around Piazza Tasso are a number of shops selling embroidered goods and intarsia (wood-inlay) work. Along narrow Via San Cesareo, where the air is pungent with the perfumes of fruit and vegetable stands, there are more shops selling local and Italian handicrafts.

Time Out | Just off Piazza Tasso is **Gigino,** one of Sorrento's best-known inexpensive restaurants. Try the fixed-price menu at lunch. *Via degli Archi 15. Closed Tues.*

Explore the town's churches and narrow alleys and follow Via Marina Grande, which turns into a pedestrian lane and stairway, to Sorrento's only real beach, where the fishermen pull up their boats. You can take a bus or walk a mile or so to Capo Sorrento, then follow the signs to the **Villa of Pollio Felice,** the scattered seaside remains of an ancient Roman villa, where you can swim off the rocks or simply admire the setting.

Before you leave Sorrento, consider a side trip west along the road that skirts the tip of the peninsula; if you enjoy dramatic seascapes, this will be worth the extra time.

The most popular town along the Amalfi drive, particularly among Americans, is **Positano,** a village of white Moorish-type houses clinging dramatically to slopes around a small sheltered bay. When John Steinbeck lived here in 1953, he wrote that it was difficult to consider tourism an industry because "there are not enough [tourists]." Alas, Positano has since been discovered. The artists came first, and, as happens wherever artists go, the wealthy followed and the artists fled. What Steinbeck wrote, however, still applies: "Positano bites deep. It is a dream place that isn't quite real when you are there and becomes beckoningly real after you have gone. Its houses climb a hill so steep it would be a cliff except that stairs are cut in it. I believe that whereas most house foundations are vertical, in Positano they are horizontal. The small curving bay of unbelievably blue and green water laps gently on a beach of small pebbles. There is only one narrow street and it does not come down to the water. Everything else is stairs, some of them as steep as ladders. You do not walk to visit a friend, you either climb or slide."

In the 10th century Positano was part of Amalfi's Maritime Republic, which rivaled Venice as an important mercantile power. Its heyday was in the 16th and 17th centuries, when its ships traded in the Near and Middle East, carrying spices, silks, and precious woods. The coming of the steamship in the mid-19th century led to the town's decline, and some three-fourths of the town's 8,000 citizens emigrated to America, mostly to New York. One major job of Positano's mayor has been to find space in the overcrowded cemetery for New York Positanesi who want to spend eternity here.

What had been reduced to a forgotten fishing village is now the number-one attraction on the coast, with hotels for every budget, charming restaurants, and dozens of boutiques. From here, you can take hydrofoils to Capri during the summer, escorted bus rides to Ravello, and tours of the Emerald Grotto (*see below*).

The three islands offshore are called **Li Galli** (The Cocks). The local king wanted a castle quick, legend says, and a sorcerer agreed to build one in three days if the king would give him all the roosters in Positano. (The sorcerer had a passion for fowl.) The king ordered them all slaughtered and sent to the sorcerer, but the young daughter of a fisherman hid her rooster under her bed. At dawn the rooster did what a rooster does. The workmen, flying by with rocks for the castle, realized that the king had broken his contract and dropped their loads into the sea.

Positano may not have a castle, but it does have another attraction that's bringing the town considerable wealth: stylish summer clothes. From January to March, buyers from all over the world come to Positano to buy the trend-setting handmade clothes that are sold in more than 200 boutiques. One-size loosefitting cotton dresses; full skirts, plain or covered with lace—some in light pastel colors with handprinted designs, others in bold block colors: bright oranges, pinks, and yellows. The choice is endless, and the prices—well, you're on vacation, and the same dresses would cost twice as much in New York or Rome.

If you're staying in Positano, check whether your hotel has a parking area. If not, you will have to pay for space in a parking lot. Parking space is almost impossible to find during the high season, from Easter to September. The best bet for day-trippers is to get to Positano early enough to find space in a parking lot. No matter how much time you spend in Positano, make sure you have some comfortable walking shoes—no heels, please!—

and that your back and legs are strong enough to negotiate
steps.

Thirteen kilometers (8 miles) along the coastal road from
Positano, a short distance before Amalfi, you'll see signposts
for the **Grotta Smeralda** (Emerald Grotto). You can park here
and take an elevator down to the grotto, or you can drive on to
Amalfi and return to the grotto by the more romantic route: via
boat (boat tours leave from the Amalfi seafront approximately
every two hours, according to demand; the charge is 10,000 lire
per person). The grotto is named for its peculiar green light,
casting an eerie emerald glow over impressive formations of
stalagmites and stalactites, many of them underwater. *Admission: 4,000 lire. Open Apr.–Oct., Mon.–Sat. 9–7; Nov.–Mar.,
Mon.–Sat. 10–4 (hours vary, so check before you go).*

Seventeen kilometers (11 miles) from Positano along the coast
is **Amalfi.** After Positano and Ravello, Amalfi is your third
choice for a town to stay in along the drive. It would have to be a
distant third, however, because of the congestion caused by
tour buses, which make Amalfi the main stopping point on their
excursions. The town is romantically situated at the mouth of a
deep gorge and has some good-quality hotels and restaurants.
It's also a convenient base for excursions to Capri and the Emerald Grotto.

During the Middle Ages, Amalfi was an independent maritime
state—a little Republic of Venice—with a population of 50,000.
The ship compass—trivia fans will be pleased to know—was
invented here in 1302.

The main historical attraction is the **Duomo** (Cathedral of St.
Andrew), which shows an interesting mix of Moorish and early-
Gothic influences. The interior is a 10th-century Romanesque
skeleton in an 18th-century Baroque dress. The transept (the
transverse arms) and the choir are 13th century. The handsome
12th-century campanile (bell tower) has identical Gothic cupo-
las (domes), at each corner. Don't miss the beautiful late-13th-
century Moorish cloister, with its slender double columns. At
least one critic has called the cathedral's facade the ugliest
piece of serious architecture in Italy—decide for yourself. The
same critic snickers at the tourists who fail to note the cathedral's greatest treasure, the 11th-century bronze doors from
Constantinople.

The parking problem here is as bad as that in Positano. The
small lot in the center of town fills quickly. If you can afford the
steep prices, make a luncheon reservation at one of the hotel
restaurants and have your car parked for you.

The main street leads back through town from the cathedral to
the mountains, and passes a ceramic workshop and some water-
driven paper mills where handcrafted paper is made and sold.
Though it's not always open, there's a paper museum where
you can see exactly how the mills work.

Time Out Stop in at the **Pansa** pastry shop on Piazza del Duomo for a giant
sfogliatella (a high-calorie meal in itself) or any of the other
oven-fresh goodies.

Perched on a ridge high above Amalfi and the neighboring town
of Atrani is **Ravello,** an enchanting village with stupendous
views, quiet lanes, and two irresistibly romantic gardens—

that of **Villa Rufolo,** where medieval ruins frame spectacular vistas, and **Villa Cimbrone,** a private estate open to the public with spectacular views of the entire Bay of Salerno.

Because Ravello is a long, steep drive from the sea, tour buses are discouraged and crowds are less overwhelming than at Positano and Amalfi. By early afternoon, the day-trippers have departed, and the town becomes one of the most restful settings in the world.

Not that Ravello is everyone's glass of Chianti: There's very little to do here except walk through peaceful gardens, admire the view, and exist. Those who need a more active life, with shops and restaurants, should avoid the rarefied air and stick to Positano. But after so much traveling, it's hard to believe many of you wouldn't welcome this excuse to come to a complete stop.

The other towns on the Amalfi Coast between Atrani and Salerno have less charm, though the scenery is no less spectacular. In addition to the views, ceramics lovers will find the trip ❺⓿ worthwhile for a chance to visit **Vietri sul Mare,** where well-known factories such as Solimene and Pinto have produced ❺❶ bright terra-cotta wares for hundreds of years. **Salerno,** spread out along the bay, is a sad testimony to years of neglect and overdevelopment. An imposing Romanesque cathedral is the only site most tourists consider worth seeing here. Built in 1085 and remodeled in the 18th century, it has Byzantine doors (1099) from Constantinople and an outstanding 12th-century pulpit. In the new Diocesan Museum behind it is a collection of astounding medieval carved tablets. (Admission free.) A few blocks away in the recently restored **monastery of San Benedetto,** a museum holds a handsome bronze head of Apollo fished out of the bay in the 1930s.

Beyond Salerno, the road (S18) and train cut across 50 kilometers (30 miles) of flat coastal plain to **Capaccio,** the modern (and undistinguished) town nearest one of Italy's most majestic sights: the remarkably well-preserved Greek temples of ❺❷ **Paestum.** S18 from the north passes the train station (Stazione di Paestum), which is about 50 yards from the ruins. The ruins stand on the site of the ancient city of Poseidonia, founded by Greek colonists in the 7th century BC. When the Romans took over the colony in 273 BC and called it Paestum, they enlarged the settlement, adding an amphitheater and a forum. Much of the archaeological material found on the site is displayed in the **museum,** and several rooms are devoted to the unique tomb paintings discovered in the area, rare examples of Greek and pre-Roman pictorial art. Across the road from the museum, framed by ranks of roses and oleanders, is the **Temple of Poseidon** (or Neptune), a magnificent Doric edifice, with 36 fluted columns and an extraordinarily well-preserved entablature (area above the capitals). Not even Greece itself possesses such a fine monument of Hellenic architecture. On the left of the temple is the so-called **Basilica,** the earliest of Paestum's standing edifices; it dates from very early in the 6th century BC. The name is an 18th-century misnomer, for the structure was in fact a temple sacred to Hera, the wife of Zeus. Behind it an ancient road leads to the **Forum** of the Roman era and the single column of the **Temple of Peace.** Beyond is the **Temple of Ceres.** Try to see the temples in the late afternoon, when the light enhances the deep gold of the stone and the air is sharp with the cries of the crows that nest high on the temples. *Admission: 8,000 lire for* *museum and temple area. Open Tues.–Sun. 9:30–one hour before sunset.*

What to See and Do with Children

Campania is an ideal destination for those traveling with children. The locals follow the Italian tradition of doting on youngsters—which partly explains the number of *gelaterie* (ice-cream shops) and candy stores, even in the smallest towns. Most activities in Campania take place outdoors, so even at the ruins of Pompeii, Herculaneum, and Paestum children have an opportunity to play in the sun. They will also love the funiculars in Naples, Capri's cog railway, and the hydrofoils operating between the islands. The following sights are of particular interest to children.

Acquario (Tour 1: Naples and Its Bay).
Boat Tour Around Ischia (Tour 4: Ischia and Capri).
Certosa di San Martino (Tour 1: Naples and Its Bay).
Edenlandia. This is the largest amusement park in Campania. It's located in the Mostra d'Oltremare area of Naples, near San Paolo Stadium. *Viale Kennedy, tel. 081/611182. Admission free, individual fares for rides. Open all year.*
Grotto Smeralda (Tour 5: The Amalfi Drive: Sorrento to Salerno).
House of the Wooden Partition (Tour 2: Herculaneum, Vesuvius, and Pompeii).
Museo Archeologico Nazionale (Tour 1: Naples and Its Bay).
Museo Nazionale Ferroviario. Children love to see the old-fashioned engines, cars, and railroad equipment on display in the restored railway works, founded by the Bourbon rulers of Naples in the last century. *Corso San Giovanni a Teduccio, tel. 081/472003. Admission free. Open Mon.–Sat. 9–noon.*
Villa Jovis (Tour 4: Ischia and Capri).
Villa of the Mysteries (Tour 2: Herculaneum, Vesuvius, and Pompeii).

Off the Beaten Track

Cappella Sansevero. This chapel, located near San Domenico Maggiore, in Naples, was reopened in 1991 after restoration. It features a masterful marble sculpture of the shrouded body of Christ by 18th-century Neapolitan sculptor Sammartino as well as other macabre works. *Via De Sanctis 19. Admission: 3,000 lire. Open Mon. and Thurs.–Sat. 10–1 and 5–7, Tues. and Sun. 10–1.*

Catacombs of San Gennaro. Many of these catacombs in Naples predate the Christian era by two centuries. They are next to the huge **Madre di Buon Consiglio** church on Via Capodimonte. The church was inspired by St. Peter's in Rome. The niches and corridors of the catacombs are hung with early Christian paintings. *Via Capodimonte. Admission: 4,000 lire. Guided tours Fri., Sat., Sun. every 45 min 9:30–11:45.*

Love Boat. This improbably named vessel sails along the waterfront of Naples, from Via Caracciolo to Cape Posillipo, with a view of **Castel dell'Ovo** on the way back. *Tel. 081/661434. Admission: 5,000 lire. Runs June–Sept., departs daily at 6, 7, and 8 PM.*

Madri (Mothers). It's 33 kilometers (20 miles) north of Naples to Capua, where the Museo Campano holds these 200 eerily impressive stone votive statues representing highly stylized mother figures. They were found on the site of a sanctuary devoted to Matuta, the ancient goddess of childbirth, and date from the 7th to the 1st century BC.

Museo Filangieri. This Neapolitan museum contains a private collection of arms, armor, furniture, paintings, and fascinating memorabilia. It's housed in the Florentine-style Renaissance Palazzo Cuomo. *Via Duomo 288, tel. 081/203175. Admission: 4,000 lire. Open Mon.–Sat. 9–2, Sun. 9–1.*

Shopping

Leather goods, coral, jewelry, and cameos are some of the best items to buy in Campania. In Naples, where many of the top leather and fashion houses have their factories, you'll find good buys in bags, shoes, and clothing, but it's often wise to make purchases in shops rather than from street vendors. The coastal resorts have maintained some of their craft traditions, although some shops try to pass off poor-quality machine-made goods as handmade items.

Naples   The **Galleria Umberto** (*see* Tour 1: Naples and Its Bay, *above*) is a good introduction to shopping in Naples; a wide variety of retail outlets trade in the four glass-roofed arcades. Other areas and streets are more specialized: The area immediately around **Piazza dei Martiri** is the heart of luxury shopping, with perfume shops, fashion outlets, and antiques on display. **Via Roma** and **Via Chiaia** are better bets for bargains.

Positano   The picturesque streets of this coastal resort are lined with **boutiques** selling **casual fashions** and **beachwear** in splashy colors and extravagant fabrics.

Sorrento   This is the place to buy **embroidered table linen** and **crocheted lace.** Also, the wood-inlay art of **intarsia** is a centuries-old tradition here. Shops today offer everything from jewelry boxes to trays and coffee tables with intarsia decorations. **Ferdinando Corciano,** in his shop on Via San Francesco, gives demonstrations of his intarsia work, producing decorative plaques with classic or contemporary motifs.

Vietri sul Mare   This Amalfi Coast town is a major **ceramics** center, and its distinctive pottery, with sunny motifs and bright colors, is on sale in towns along the coast. Many small shops in Vietri sul Mare offer goods from local pottery workshops. You can pick over all kinds of dusty wares at the **Solimene** works.

Sports

Sun, sand, and sea combine in Campania to offer the visitor a number of sporting options, but be prepared to encounter pollution in some of the beaches nearest Naples (*see* Beaches, *below*). The top hotels often offer sports facilities, such as private beaches, swimming pools, and tennis courts, and many will allow nonresidents to use these facilities: Contact the hotels themselves or the local tourist office.

Bowling   **Bowling Oltremare,** Viale Kennedy, Naples (tel. 081/624444).

Fishing For information on licenses and water quality, contact **Federazione Italiana Pesca Sportiva** (Piazza Santa Maria degli Angeli, Naples, tel. 081/417579).

Golf **Minigolf Kennedy** (via Camillo Guerra 60, tel. 081/587–1386) is in the suburb of Chiaiano, west of Naples.

Horseback Riding For information on riding in Campania, contact the **Federazione Italiana Sport Equestri** (Via Ruggieri 12/B, Naples, tel. 081/760–9379).

Sailing **Nantic Coop** (Piazza Amedeo 15, Naples, tel. 081/415371).

Tennis Most top hotels have courts. Contact them or local tourist boards about the use of these courts. The following are public courts:

Benevento (Viale Atlantici, tel. 0824/29920).
Naples (Via Giochi del Mediterraneo, tel. 081/760–3912).
Ischia Porto (Lungomare Colombo, tel. 081/991013).

Water Skiing **Sci Nautico Partenopeo** (Lake Averno, Pozzuoli, tel. 081/866–2214).

Beaches

The waters of the Bay of Naples are notoriously polluted. Capri and some, but not all, of Ischia's beaches, offer clean swimming. Pollution is intermittent along the Amalfi Coast, where the deep waters are generally clean. Beaches in the Salerno area are best avoided; the water gets cleaner the farther south you go.

Dining and Lodging

Dining Campania's cuisine is simple and relies heavily on the bounty of the region's fertile farmland. Its tomatoes are exported all over the world, but to try them here is a new experience. Even during the winter you can find tomato sauce made with small sundried tomatoes plucked from bright red strands that you can see hanging outdoors on kitchen balconies. Pasta is a staple here, and it's usually cooked al dente (chewy rather than soft). *Spaghetti al pomodoro* or *al filetto di pomodoro* (both with simple tomato sauces) and *spaghetti alle vongole* (with clam sauce, either white or red, depending on the cook's whims) appear on most menus.

This is the homeland of pizza, served mainly in its simpler versions: *alla napoletana,* with anchovies; *alla margherita,* with tomato and mozzarella; *alla marinara,* with tomato, garlic, and oregano. Locally produced mozzarella is used in many dishes; one of the most gratifying on a hot day is *insalata caprese:* slices of mozzarella and ripe red tomato, garnished with basil. *Melanzane* (eggplant) and even zucchini are served *alla parmigiana* (fried and layered with tomato sauce and mozzarella). Meat may be served *alla pizzaiola,* cooked in a tomato-and-garlic sauce. Fish and seafood in general can be expensive, though fried calamari and *totani* (cuttlefish) are usually reasonably priced. Among the region's wines, Gragnano, Falerno, Lacrima Cristi, and Greco di Tufo are fine whites. Ischia and Ravello also produce good white wine.

Campania's best-known reds are Aglianico, Taurasi, and the red version of Falerno.

Restaurant prices in the region are generally a little lower than in Rome and northern Italy, though Capri restaurants can be very expensive. On the islands, Sorrento Peninsula, and Amalfi Coast, restaurants may be open every day of the week during the season, but may close for long periods in the winter.

Highly recommended restaurants are indicated by a star ★.

Category	Cost*
Very Expensive	over 85,000 lire
Expensive	60,000–85,000 lire
Moderate	25,000–60,000 lire
Inexpensive	under 25,000 lire

per person, including house wine, service, and tax

Lodging Although Capri, Ischia, Sorrento, and the Amalfi Coast offer generally fine accommodations in all categories, good accommodations in Naples are scarce, so reserve well in advance. High-season rates apply at all coastal resorts in July and August. These rates extend from April/May through September at Sorrento and Amalfi Coast resorts, where Christmas and Easter also draw crowds and command top rates. Whereas coastal resorts elsewhere close up tight from fall to spring, at least some hotels and restaurants are open in Sorrento and on the Amalfi Coast year-round. It's always a good idea to book ahead, and it's imperative in high season. Campania hotel rates are generally lower than those in major tourist cities to the north, but rates in Capri's top hotels are at premium levels for Italy. On the other hand, even in Capri and especially along the Amalfi Coast, you can find charming little hotels with attractive rooms and wonderful views at very reasonable rates; just don't expect to find vacancies in August. During the summer, hotels on the coast almost always require that you take halfboard if they serve meals. Local tourist information offices will help you find accommodations.

Highly recommended lodgings are indicated by a star ★.

Category	Cost*
Very Expensive	over 300,000 lire
Expensive	140,000–300,000 lire
Moderate	80,000–140,000 lire
Inexpensive	under 80,000 lire

All prices are for a standard double room for two, including service and 9% IVA (19% for luxury establishments).

Amalfi **La Caravella.** You'll find this welcoming establishment tucked
Dining away under some arches lining the coast road, next to the medi-
★ eval Arsenal, where Amalfi's mighty fleet once was provi-
sioned. La Caravella has a nondescript entrance but pleasant
interior decorated in a medley of colors and paintings of Old
Amalfi. It's small and intimate; specialties include *scialatelli*

(homemade pasta with shellfish sauce) and *pesce al limone* (fresh fish with lemon sauce). *Via M. Camera 12, tel. 089/ 871029. Reservations advised. Dress: casual. AE, V. Closed Tues., and Nov. 10–30. Moderate.*

Lodging
★ **Santa Caterina.** A large mansion perched above terraced and flowered hillsides on the coast road just outside Amalfi proper, the Santa Caterina is one of the best hotels on the entire coast, offering gracious living in a wonderfully scenic setting. The rooms are tastefully decorated; most have small terraces or balconies with great views. There are lovely lounges and terraces for relaxing, and an elevator whisks guests to the seaside saltwater pool, bar, and swimming area. On grounds lush with lemon and orange groves, there are two romantic villa annexes. *Strada Amalfitana 9, tel. 089/871012, fax 089/871351. 54 rooms with bath. Facilities: restaurant, bar, pool, swimming area, beach bar, parking. AE, DC, MC, V. Expensive–Very Expensive.*

Hotel Dei Cavalieri. This terraced white Mediterranean-style hotel on the main road outside Amalfi has three villa annexes in grounds just across the road that extend all the way to a beach below. The bedrooms are air-conditioned and functionally furnished, with splashy majolica tile floors contributing a bright note throughout. An ample buffet breakfast is served, and, though half-board is mandatory during high season, you can dine either at the hotel or at several restaurants in Amalfi by special arrangement. *Via M. Comite 32, tel. 089/831333, fax 089/831354. 54 rooms with bath. Facilities: restaurant, bar, beach (via stairs), parking, garage, minibus service into town. AE, DC, MC, V. Moderate.*

Miramalfi. A modern building perched above the sea, the Miramalfi has wonderful views, simple but attractive decor, terraces, swimming pool, and sunning/swimming area on the sea, as well as a quiet location just below the coast road, only a half mile from the center of town. Many rooms boast balconies with sea views. *Via Quasimodo 3, tel. 089/871588, fax 089/ 871588. 44 rooms, most with bath or shower. Facilities: restaurant, garden, parking. AE, DC, MC, V. Moderate.*

Anacapri
Lodging
Europa Palace Hotel. A modern resort atmosphere predominates at this large Mediterranean-style hotel set in lovely gardens. Each of four junior suites has a private swimming pool and terrace. The bedrooms are tastefully decorated in contemporary style, with white predominating; marble is featured in the bathrooms, and many rooms have balconies. The only minus is being in Anacapri, a bus or cab ride from the restaurants and shops in the town of Capri. *Via Capodimonte 2/b, tel. 081/ 837–0955, fax 081/837–3191. 103 rooms with bath. Facilities: air-conditioning, pool, garden, restaurant (Moderate) bar, parking. AE, DC, MC, V. Closed Nov.–Mar. Expensive.*

San Michele. You'll find this large white villa-hotel next to Axel Munthe's Capri home. Surrounded by luxuriant gardens, the San Michele offers solid comfort and good value, along with spectacular views. The decor is contemporary, with some Neapolitan period pieces adding atmosphere. Most rooms have terraces or balconies overlooking either the sea or island landscapes. *Via G. Orlandi 5, tel. 081/837–1427, fax 081/837– 1420. 56 rooms with bath or shower. Facilities: garden, 2 restaurants, tennis courts, outdoor pool. AE, DC, MC, V. Closed Nov.–Mar. 24. Moderate–Expensive.*

Capri
Dining

La Pigna. Ensconced in a glassed-in veranda and offering outdoor dining in a garden shaded by lemon trees, the Pigna is one of Capri's favorite restaurants. The specialties are a house-produced wine, *linguine alla Mediterranea* (pasta with herbs), and *aragosta alla luna caprese* (lobster). The cordial host organizes party evenings with feasts of seasonal specialties and seafood. *Via Roma 8, tel. 081/837–0280. Reservations required in the evening. Dress: casual. AE, DC, MC, V. Closed Tues. and Nov.–Easter. Expensive.*

★ **La Capannina.** Known as one of Capri's best restaurants, La Capannina is only a few steps from the busy social hub of the piazzetta. It has a vine-draped veranda for dining outdoors by candlelight in a garden setting. The specialties, aside from an authentic Capri wine with the house label, are homemade *ravioli alla caprese* (with a cheese filling, tomato sauce, and basil) and regional dishes. *Via delle Botteghe 14, tel. 081/837–0732. Reservations required in the evening. Dress: casual. AE, V. Closed Wed. (except Aug.) and Nov. 10–Mar. 15. Moderate–Expensive.*

Al Grottino. This small and friendly family-run restaurant, which is handy to the piazzetta, has arched ceilings and lots of atmosphere; autographed photos of celebrity customers cover the walls. House specialties are *gnocchi* (dumplings) with tomato sauce and mozzarella, and *linguine ai gamberetti* (pasta with shrimp and tomato sauce). *Via Longano 27, tel. 081/837–0584. Reservations required in the evening. Dress: casual. AE, V. Closed Tues. and Nov. 3–Mar. 20. Moderate.*

Lodging **Quisisana.** Catering largely to Americans, this is the most luxurious and traditional hotel in the center of town. Spacious rooms are done in traditional or contemporary decor with some antique accents; many have arcaded balconies with views of the sea or the charming enclosed garden, in which there's a swimming pool. The bar and restaurant are casually elegant. *Via Camerelle 2, tel. 081/837–0788, fax 081/837–6080. 143 rooms with bath or shower. Facilities: restaurant, bar, garden, pool. AE, DC, MC, V. Closed Nov.–Mar. Very Expensive.*

★ **Scalinatella.** The name means "little stairway," and that's how this charming but modern small hotel is built, on terraces following the slope of the hill, overlooking the gardens, pool, and sea. The bedrooms are intimate, with alcoves and fresh, bright colors; the bathrooms feature Jacuzzis. The hotel has a small bar, but no restaurant. *Via Tragara 8, tel. 081/837–0633, fax 081/837–8291. 28 rooms with bath or shower. Facilities: air-conditioning, pool, tennis court, garden, bar. AE. Closed Nov.–Mar. 14. Expensive.*

Villa Brunella. This quiet family-run gem nestles in a garden setting just below the lane leading to the Faraglioni. Comfortable and tastefully furnished, the hotel also has spectacular views, a swimming pool, and a terrace restaurant known for good food. *Via Tragara 24, tel. 081/837–0279, fax 081/837–0430. 18 rooms with bath. Facilities: bar, restaurant (tel. 081/837–0122; reservations required for nonguests. Moderate); pool. AE, DC, MC, V. Closed Nov. 6–Mar. 18. Moderate–Expensive.*

Villa Sarah. This whitewashed Mediterranean building has a homey look and bright, simply furnished rooms. It's close enough to the Piazzetta (a 10-minute walk away) to give easy access to the goings-on there, while ensuring restful nights. There's a garden and small bar, but no restaurant. *Via Tiberio*

3a, tel. 081/837-7817. 20 rooms with bath. AE. Closed Nov.-Mar. Moderate.

Villa Krupp. Among the hotels that are open all year, this historic hostelry is a good choice. In a quiet location above the Gardens of Augustus, it has marvelous views. The bedrooms are ample; some have a balcony. The hotel doesn't have a restaurant. *Via Matteotti 12, tel. 081/837-0362. 12 rooms with bath. Facilities: garden. V. Inexpensive.*

Caserta
Dining

Antica Locanda Massa 1848. Near the Reggia, this large, informal restaurant is decorated in browns and white in 19th-century rustic style. In fair weather you eat alfresco under an arbor. The specialties are *linguine al cartoccio* (pasta steamed with fresh tomato and shellfish) and *gazzerielli alla borbone* (gnocchi with cheese and truffle sauce). *Via Mazzini 55, tel. 0823/321268. Reservations advised. Dress: casual. AE, DC, V. Closed Sun. evening, Mon., and Aug. 5-20. Moderate.*

La Castellana. Located in Casertavecchia, Caserta's medieval nucleus on the hillside overlooking the modern town, this tavern has atmosphere and hearty local specialties, such as *stringozzi alla castellana* (homemade pasta with a piquant tomato sauce served in individual casseroles) and *agnello alla castellana* (lamb sautéed in red wine). You dine inside or, in fair weather, under an arbor. *Via Torre 4, tel. 0823/371230. Reservations required weekends. Dress: casual. AE, DC. Closed Thurs. Moderate.*

Ischia
Lodging

Grand Hotel Punta Molino. Right in the town of Ischia, but set in a quiet zone near the sea and framed with pine trees and gardens, is one of the best hotels on the island. The decor is bright and contemporary, with some luxury touches, and many rooms have sea views. There's a heated pool on one of the terraces. Half-board is required. *Lungomare Colombo, tel. 081/991544, fax 081/991562. 88 rooms with bath or shower. Facilities: spa treatments, bar, restaurant, garden, outdoor pool, private beach, parking. AE, MC, DC, V. Closed Nov.-Apr. 24. Expensive.*

Regina Palace. Located near the beach of Ischia Porto, the Regina Palace has an elegant art-deco look, with pink-toned wood the keynote. Almost all bedrooms have a terrace or balcony overlooking the grounds, on which there's a large pool. *Via E. Cortese 18, tel. 081/991344, fax 081/991344. 60 rooms with bath or shower. Facilities: restaurant, garden, outdoor pool, tennis courts, spa treatments, parking. AE, DC, MC, V. Closed Nov. 16-Dec. 19, Jan. 11-Mar. 15. Expensive.*

★ **Villarosa.** You'll find this welcoming hotel in the heart of Ischia Porto and only a short walk from the beach. It is a gracious family-run villa with bright and airy rooms. There's a heated pool in the villa garden. Half-board is required, and you must reserve well in advance. *Via Giacinto Gigante 3, tel. 081/991316, fax 081/992425. 37 rooms with bath or shower. Facilities: restaurant for hotel guests only, garden, outdoor pool. AE, V. Closed Nov.-Mar. 19. Moderate.*

Lacco Ameno
Lodging
★

Regina Isabella. Tucked away in an exclusive corner of the beach in Lacco Ameno, Ischia's top luxury hotel has full resort facilities and pampers guests with spa treatments as well. The rooms are ample and decorated in warm Mediterranean colors and most have terraces or balconies. Don't miss the fun of socializing with chic vacationers in the elegant bar or restaurant or at poolside. *Piazza Restituita, tel. 081/994322, fax 081/986043.*

133 rooms with bath or shower. Facilities: garden, restaurant, bar, spa treatments, indoor and outdoor pools, private beach, tennis court. AE, DC, MC, V. Closed Oct. 16–Apr. 14. Very Expensive.

Hotel San Montano. This modern hotel overlooks the sea in a quiet location. San Montano is decorated with nautical motifs and ceramic-tile floors. The rooms have compact English navy furnishings, color TV, and minibar. The San Montano has all resort facilities and provides spa treatments, too. *Via Montevico 1, tel. 081/994033, fax 081/980242. 67 rooms with bath or shower. Facilities: restaurant, garden, outdoor pool, tennis courts, parking, spa treatments. AE, DC, MC, V. Closed Nov.–Feb. Expensive.*

Naples
Dining
★

La Sacrestia. Popular with Neapolitans because of its location and the quality of its food, La Sacrestia is set on the slopes of the Posillipo hill, with marvelous views of the city and bay. The specialties range from appetizing antipasti to *linguine con salsetta segreta* (pasta with a sauce of minutely chopped garden vegetables). Seafood has a place of honor on the menu, and there are interesting meat dishes as well. The setting in a patrician villa and the ambience are definitely upscale. *Via Orazio 116, tel. 081/761–1051. Reservations advised. Dress: casual. AE, DC, V. Closed Mon., Sun. in July, and Aug. Very Expensive.*

Casanova Grill. Soft lights and a trendy art-deco look set the tone in the Casanova Grill, the Hotel Excelsior's restaurant. The seasonal specialties and antipasti arranged on the buffet will whet your appetite for such traditional Neapolitan dishes as the simple *spaghetti al pomodoro* (with fresh tomato sauce) and the classic *carne alla pizzaiolia* (meat with tomato and oregano). *Hotel Excelsior, Via Partenope 48, tel. 081/417111. Reservations advised. Jacket and tie advised in the evening. AE, DC, MC, V. Closed Mon. Expensive.*

La Fazenda. Overlooking the sea at Marechiaro, in one of the city's most picturesque spots, this restaurant is a favorite for leisurely dining and an invitingly informal atmosphere. The pastas, many with vegetable sauces, are particularly good. The specialty is seafood, but chicken and rabbit *alla cacciatora* (in a tangy sauce) also are good. Desserts are homemade. Note that you must take a taxi to get to La Fazenda. *Calata Marechiaro 58, tel. 081/769–7420. Reservations advised. Dress: casual. V. Closed Mon. and Aug. 13–29. Expensive.*

Bergantino. This bustling trattoria, located near the central station, is a favorite with business people and is open only for lunch. Courteous and efficient waiters serve a variety of classic Neapolitan dishes, including hearty *maccheroni con ragù* (pasta with meat sauce) or *sartù di riso* (rice casserole with bits of meat and cheese). Anything made with mozzarella is sure to be good here, or order plain mozzarella—it's light and fresh. *Via San Felice 16, tel. 081/310369. No reservations. Dress: casual. No credit cards. Open lunch only. Closed Sat. and Aug. Moderate.*

Bersagliera. Most first-time visitors to Naples want to dine once on the Santa Lucia waterfront in the shadow of the medieval Castel dell'Ovo, and this is one of the best places to do so. It's touristy but fun, with an irresistible combination of spaghetti and mandolins. The menu offers uncomplicated classics, such as *spaghetti alla pescatora* (with seafood sauce) and *melanzane alla parmigiana* (eggplant with mozzarella and tomato sauce). *Borgo Marinaro 10, tel. 081/764-6016. Reservations advised. Dress: casual. AE, DC, MC, V. Closed Tues. Moderate.*

Ciro a Santa Brigida. Centrally located off Via Toledo near the Castle Nuovo, Ciro is a straightforward restaurant popular with business travelers, artists, and journalists who are more interested in food than frills. In dining rooms on two levels, customers enjoy classic Neapolitan cuisine. Among the specialties: *sartù di riso* (rice casserole with meat and peas), and *scaloppe all Ciro* (veal with prosciutto and mozzarella). There's pizza, too. *Via Santa Brigida 71, tel. 081/552-4072. Reservations advised. Dress: casual. AE, DC, MC, V. Closed Sun. and Aug. Moderate.*

Dante e Beatrice. A simple trattoria on central Piazza Dante, this popular spot features typical Neapolitan dishes in an unassuming setting. The menu may offer *pasta e fagioli* (very thick bean soup with pasta) and *maccheroni al ragù* (pasta with meat sauce). You can eat inexpensively here. *Piazza Dante 44, tel. 081/349905. Reservations advised in the evening. Dress: casual. No credit cards. Closed Wed. and Aug. 24-31. Moderate.*

Don Salvatore. Head just west to the little port of Mergellina to find an unpretentious-looking place known for good local dishes and seafood. *Linguine cosa nostra* (with shellfish) and other pastas with seafood sauces are specialties, and the *fritto misto* (mixed fried fish) is as light as a feather. *Via Mergellina 5, tel. 081/681817. Reservations advised. Dress: casual. AE, DC, MC, V. Closed Wed. and July 20-Aug. 4. Moderate.*

Lodging **Excelsior.** This CIGA hotel is located on the shore drive, with views of the bay from the front rooms. The lobby and lounges are lavish, with Oriental carpets and gilt or glass chandeliers. Off the large semicircular lounge are a chic little bar and the Casanova restaurant. The rooms are decorated either in CIGA's standard Empire style (with neoclassic furniture and brocades) or in more typically Neapolitan floral prints. *Via Partenope 48, tel. 081/417111, fax 081/411743. 138 rooms with bath or shower. Facilities: restaurant, bar. AE, DC, MC, V. Very Expensive.*

Jolly Ambassador. This hotel occupies the top 12 floors of the only skyscraper on the downtown skyline (if you don't count the business center beyond the station), and the bedrooms and roof garden-restaurant command sweeping views of Naples and the bay. Decorated in the uninspired but functional style of the Jolly chain, with dark brown and white predominating, it promises comfort and efficiency in a city where these are scarce commodities. *Via Medina 70, tel. 081/416000, fax 081/551-8010. 251 rooms with bath or shower. Facilities: restaurant, bar, garage. AE, DC, MC, V. Expensive.*

★ **Paradiso.** Stay here if you want something special a step or two off the beaten track. A modern air-conditioned building perched on the slopes of the hill above the port of Mergellina, the Paradiso is just a few minutes by taxi or funicular from downtown, and it has fabulous views from huge window walls in the lobby and all front rooms. The decor, in tones of blue and beige, is restful and attractive. Built-in furnishings of rosy wood with marble surfaces give the bedrooms a smart contemporary look. Though the rooms and bathrooms are smallish, they are well organized, with TV and minibar; most have balconies. Be sure to ask for a room with a view; there's no extra charge. There are terraces for sitting, dining, and contemplating the entire bay as far as Vesuvius and beyond. *Via Catullo 11, tel. 081/761–4161, fax 081/761–3449. 74 rooms with bath or shower. Facilities: restaurant, bar, garage. AE, DC, MC, V. Expensive.*

Cavour. Located in the rundown Stazione Centrale area, on the square in front of the station and handy to all transportation, including the Circumvesuviana, the Cavour is gradually being renovated and can now offer clean and comfortable rooms. It's especially convenient for those using Naples as a touring base. The hotel's contribution to urban renewal in the area is its elegant street-level restaurant and piano bar. *Piazza Garibaldi 32, tel. 081/283122, fax 081/264306. 105 rooms with bath or shower. Facilities: restaurant. AE, DC, MC, V. Moderate.*

Rex. This hotel has a fairly quiet location near the Santa Lucia waterfront. Situated on the first two floors of an Art Nouveau building, it has no elevator; the decor ranges from 1950s modern to fake period pieces and even some folk art, haphazardly combined. Though it has no restaurant, there are many in the vicinity. *Via Palepoli 12, tel. 081/416388, fax 081/416919. 40 rooms, 34 with bath or shower. Facilities: bar, garage. AE, DC, MC, V. Moderate.*

Paestum
Dining and Lodging

Martini. Directly across the road from the Porta della Giustizia and only a few steps from the temples, the Martini has 13 cottage-type rooms, each with minibar, in a garden setting and a pleasant restaurant serving local specialties and seafood. *Zona Archeologica, tel. 0828/811020, fax 0828/823717. 13 rooms with bath or shower. Facilities: beach ½ mile away, Sea Garden restaurant. Reservations advised. Dress: casual. AE, DC, V. Inexpensive.*

Positano
Dining

Buca di Bacco. After an aperitif at the town's most famous and fashionable café downstairs, you dine on a veranda overlooking the beach. The specialties include *spaghetti alle vongole* (with clam sauce) and *grigliata mista* (mixed grilled seafood). *Via Rampa Teglia 8, tel. 089/875699. Reservations advised in the evening. Dress: casual. AE, DC, MC, V. Closed Nov. 6–Mar. 31. Moderate.*

Capurale. Among the popular restaurants on the beach promenade, this one just around the corner has the best food and lowest prices. Tables are set under vines on a breezy sidewalk in the summer, upstairs and indoors in winter. *Spaghetti con melanzane* (with eggplant) and *crepes al formaggio* (cheese-filled crepes) are among the specialties. *Via Marina, tel. 089/875374. Reservations advised for outdoor tables and weekends off-season. Dress: casual. No credit cards. Closed Nov. 3–Mar. Moderate.*

Lodging
★

San Pietro. Extraordinary is the word for this luxurious oasis for the affluent international set. Located outside the town, set high above the sea with garden terraces, the San Pietro has sumptuous Neapolitan Baroque decor and masses of flowers in the lounges, elegantly understated rooms (most with terraces), and marvelous views. There's a pool on an upper level, and an elevator whisks guests to the private beach and beach bar. The proprietors organize boating excursions and parties and provide car and minibus service into town. *Amalfi Coast Road, tel. 089/875455, fax 089/811449. 55 rooms with bath or shower. Facilities: restaurant, 2 bars, pool, private beach and dock, hotel boat, tennis court, garden, parking. AE, DC, MC, V. Closed Nov. 3–Mar. Very Expensive.*

★ **Sirenuse.** A handsome 18th-century palazzo in the center of town is the setting for this luxury hotel in which bright tiled floors, precious antiques, and tasteful furnishings are featured in ample and luminous salons. The bedrooms have the same sense of spaciousness and comfort; most have splendid views from balconies and terraces. The top-floor suites have huge bathrooms and Jacuzzis. One side of a large terrace has an inviting swimming pool; on the other is an excellent restaurant—both share the hotel's view of the town, beach, and sea. *Via Cristoforo Colombo 30, tel. 089/875066, fax 089/811798. 62 rooms with bath or shower. Facilities: restaurant, bar, heated pool, parking. AE, DC, MC, V. Very Expensive.*

Casa Albertina. One of the few hotels here that is open all year, Casa Albertina is a pleasant place with a friendly owner-manager. The rooms are bright with color, some have views, and you can enjoy the panorama from the terrace, where you can have breakfast or drinks in fair weather. It's a few steps up from one of the town's social hubs, the Bar De Martino. There's a restaurant and roof garden, and rates are low in its category. *Via Tavolozza 4, tel. 089/875143, fax 089/811540. 21 rooms with bath or shower. Facilities: restaurant, bar, parking. AE, DC, MC, V. Expensive.*

Palazzo Murat. The location is perfect—in the heart of town, near the beachside promenade, but set in a quiet, walled garden. The old wing is a historic palazzo with tall windows and wrought-iron balconies; the new wing is a whitewashed Mediterranean building with arches and terraces. You can relax in antique-accented lounges or in the charming vine-draped patio, and since there's no restaurant, you will avoid the half-board requirement applied in most hotels here in high season. *Via dei Mulini 23, tel. 089/875177, fax 089/811419. 28 rooms with bath and shower. Facilities: bar, garden. AE, DC, MC, V. Closed Nov. 5–Mar. Moderate.*

Ravello
Dining
★
Cumpa Cosimo. This family-run restaurant a few steps from the cathedral square offers a cordial welcome in three simple but attractive dining rooms. There's no view, but the food is excellent. Among the specialties are cheese crepes and roast lamb or kid. *Via Roma 44, tel. 089/857156. Reservations advised on weekends and summer evenings. Dress: casual. AE, DC, MC, V. Closed Mon. (Nov.–Mar.). Inexpensive.*

Lodging
Palumbo. Occupying a 12th-century patrician palace furnished with antiques and endowed with modern comforts, this hotel has an elegant, warm atmosphere that gives you the feeling of being a guest in a lovely private home, under the personal care of courtly host Signore Vuilleumier. With lovely garden terraces, breathtaking views, and a sumptuous upstairs dining room, the hotel is a memorable one. *Palazzo Confalone, tel. 089/857244, fax 089/858133. 8 rooms with bath or shower. Facilities: restaurant, bar, garden. AE, DC, MC, V. Very Expensive.*

★ **Belvedere Caruso.** Charmingly old-fashioned, spacious, and comfortable, this rambling villa hotel has plenty of character and a full share of Ravello's spectacular views from its terraces and balconied rooms. Relax in the garden belvedere with its memorable views. The restaurant is known for fine food and locally produced house wine. *Via Toro 52, tel. 089/857111, fax 089/857372. 26 rooms with bath or shower. Facilities: restaurant, garden. AE, DC, MC, V. Moderate–Expensive.*

Villa Maria. Located off a quiet lane, this family-run pension is set in a pretty garden, where you can enjoy a drink or dine under the trees. The rooms are simple but homey, and the atmosphere is restful. *Via Santa Chiara 2, tel. 089/857170, fax 089/857071. 16 rooms, all with bath or shower. Facilities: restaurant, bar, garden. AE, MC, V. Inexpensive.*

Sorrento Dining

Antica Trattoria. An Old-World dining room inside and garden tables in fair weather make this a pleasant place to enjoy the local cooking. The atmosphere is homey and hospitable. The specialties are classic *spaghetti al pomodoro* (with fresh tomato sauce and basil) and *melanzane alla parmigiana* (eggplant). *Via Giuliani 33, tel. 081/807-1082. Reservations advised for dinner. Dress: casual. No credit cards. Closed Mon, and Jan. 10–Feb. 10. Moderate.*

Parrucchiano. Centrally located and popular, this is one of Sorrento's oldest and best restaurants. You walk up a few steps to glassed-in veranda dining rooms filled, like greenhouses, with vines and plants. The menu offers classic local specialties, among them *panzerotti* (pastry shells filled with tomato and mozzarella) and *scaloppe alla sorrentina* (veal with tomato and mozzarella). *Corso Italia 71, tel. 081/8781321. Reservations advised. Dress: casual. V. Closed Wed. (Nov.–May). Moderate.*

Lodging

★ **Cocumella.** This hotel is set in a cliff-top garden in a quiet residential area on the edge of Sorrento (it's really in the adjacent town of Sant'Agnello). Occupying a historic old villa that was a monastery in the 17th century, it has been totally renovated and features a tasteful blend of antique and contemporary decor, with vaulted ceilings and archways, a dining veranda, and stunning tiled floors. It's exclusive and elegant without being stuffy. *Via Cocumella 7, tel. 081/878-2933, fax 081/878-3712. 60 rooms and suites with bath or shower. Facilities: restaurant, bar, garden, pool, elevator to swimming area, tennis court. AE, DC, MC, V. Very Expensive.*

Excelsior Vittoria. In the heart of Sorrento, but removed from the bustle of the main square, this historic hotel perches on the cliff. It has Art Nouveau decor and some quite grand, though faded, furnishings. Tenor Enrico Caruso's bedroom is preserved as a relic; the guest bedrooms are slightly less elegant but spacious and comfortable. The views are wonderful. *Winter prices are considerably lower than the high-season rates. Piazza Tasso 34, tel. 081/807-1044, fax 081/877-1206. 106 rooms and suites with bath. Facilities: restaurant, bar, pool, garden. AE, DC, MC, V. Very Expensive.*

Bellevue Syrene. A palatial villa in a garden overlooking the sea, the Bellevue has solid, old-fashioned comforts and plenty of charm, with Victorian nooks and alcoves, antique paintings, and worn oriental rugs. The rooms are pleasant, with good views. *Piazza della Vittoria 5, tel. 081/878-1024, fax 081/878-3963. 50 rooms with bath. Facilities: restaurant, bar, garden, elevator to swimming area. AE, DC, MC, V. Moderate.*

Eden. Located in a fairly quiet but central location, the Eden has a garden and bright but undistinguished bedrooms. The lounge and lobby have more character. Some smaller rooms are in the inexpensive category. *Via Correale 25, tel. 081/878-1909. 60 rooms with bath. Facilities: restaurant, garden, pool. AE, V. Closed Nov.–Feb. Moderate.*

The Arts and Nightlife

The Arts

Theater   One of the most impressive theater seasons is Pompeii's late-summer festival of the performing arts, known as the **Panatenee Pompeiane.** This series of classical plays takes place in July and August. For information, contact one of the three information offices: Naples (tel. 081/268779), Pompeii (tel. 081/863–1041), or Rome (tel. 06/474–3718).

Music   A classical music festival known as **International Music Weeks** takes place throughout May in Naples. Concerts are held at the **Teatro San Carlo,** the newly restored Teatro Mercadante, and in the neoclassic Villa Pignatelli. For information, contact the Teatro San Carlo box office (Via San Carlo 93F, tel. 081/797–2321).

Informal music festivals take place all summer long in the resorts of **Capri, Sorrento, Amalfi,** and **Ravello.** Contact local tourist offices for details.

Film   Each October sees the **International Cinema Convention** in Sorrento, which usually draws an elite collection of producers, directors, and stars in a less frantic atmosphere than that of the festival in Cannes. While much of the activity revolves around deal making, a number of previews are screened, and the town sees the festival as one last fling at the end of the summer season. For details, contact the Sorrento tourist office (*see* Important Addresses and Numbers in Essential Information, *above*).

Opera   Naples has a full opera season from fall through spring. The best performances are those at the **Teatro San Carlo** (*see above*), from December to May.

Arts Festivals   The festival **Settembre a Borgo** is held in the picturesque setting of Caserta Vecchia in September. For information, contact the Caserta tourist information office (tel. 0823/321137).

Nightlife

In these parts, as elsewhere in southern Italy, nightlife usually takes the form of outdoor living in cafés and restaurants with views of the passing parade. Piazzas are lively until late in fair weather, especially in resort towns on the islands and on the Sorrento peninsula. Capri's piazzetta is a classic example. Entertainment in the coastal resorts is mainly seasonal.

Bars   Most of the best bars have the attraction of a good location (overlooking the Bay of Naples, for example) or comfortable setting; there is sometimes music and dancing, but these establishments cannot truly be called nightclubs.

Gabbiano (Via Partenope 26, Naples, tel. 081/411666). Expect to be part of a sophisticated crowd at this fashionable watering hole; there is usually live music.

Circolo dei Forestieri (Via de Maio 35, Sorrento). Here you'll get a memorable view of the Bay of Naples from the terrace. Drinks are moderately priced, and there is live music in summer.

Villa Pompeiana (Via Marina Grande 6, Sorrento, tel. 081/877–2428). This bar, located next to the Bellevue Syrene Hotel, has a garden terrace and an indoor tavern with an ancient-Roman setting. There's music in summer.

Nightclubs **Rosolino** (Via Nazario Sauro 5–7, Naples, tel. 081/415873). This recent addition to the Neapolitan entertainment scene also has a quiet piano bar and a restaurant with some moderately priced meals.

L'Africana (Vettica Maggiore, Praiano). This is the premier nightclub on the Amalfi Coast and is built into a fantastic grotto above the sea. Praiano itself is only a couple miles east of Positano on the coast road.

Discos **Shaker** (Via Nazario Sauro 24, Naples, tel. 081/416775). This disco, located in the prime entertainment neighborhood of Naples, attracts a mixed crowd of locals and guests from the nearby hotels.

Papillon (Via Manzoni 207, Naples, tel. 081/769–0800). This club caters to a young crowd.

Special Events Capri's **New Year's Day** celebrations last all day, with marching bands, pageants, and all the vigorous revelry you would expect on this exuberant island. Dancing and music last all evening, culminating in a magnificent fireworks display.

15 Apulia

*Bari, Brindisi, and
the Gargano Peninsula*

It's a pity that all most tourists see of Apulia (called Puglia by the Italians—English-speakers are really using the Latin term) is the blur outside their car or train windows as they hurtle toward Bari or Brindisi for ferry connections to Greece.

This ancient land, the heel and spur of Italy's boot, contains some of the most unspoiled scenery, interesting artistic and historical sites, and finest beaches of the entire Italian peninsula. What's more, aside from the increasingly popular seaside resorts and a few major attractions, the region is still relatively free of tourists. Instead, your trip will take you through a sunbaked countryside where expanses of silvery olive trees and giant prickly-pear cactus fight their way through the rocky soil, as if in defiance of the relentless summer heat. Local buildings, too, do their best to dispel the effects of the sun: Whitewashed ports stand coolly over the turquoise Mediterranean, and the landscape is studded with strange dwellings, called *trulli*, which look like pointed igloos made of stone.

The trulli date to the Middle Ages, but Apulia had long before been inhabited, conquered, and visited by travelers. The Greeks and later the Romans were quick to recognize the importance of this strategic peninsula, and among the nations later to raid or colonize Apulia were the Normans, Moors, and Spaniards, each leaving a mark. Some of the most impressive buildings are the Romanesque churches and the powerful castles built by 13th-century Holy Roman Emperor Frederick II of Swabia (part of present-day Bavaria), King of Sicily and Jerusalem. One of the outstanding personalities of the Middle Ages, he was dubbed "Wonder of the World" for his wide-ranging interests in literature, science, mathematics, and nature.

All these interests can still be pursued in present-day Apulia, but less intellectual attractions include the inexpensive and hearty cuisine, which uses local seafood and produce, and picks the best from more than 2,000 years of foreign influences. Colorful local markets provide the chance to purchase local handicrafts ranging from lace, wood carvings, and baskets to ceramic pots and painted clay whistles. Hundreds of miles of beaches and an extensive cave complex let you explore, exercise, or just cool off.

Essential Information

Important Addresses and Numbers

Tourist Information
Bari (Via Melo 253, tel. 080/524–2361; Corso V. Emanuele 68, tel. 080/521–9951).
Brindisi (Piazza Dionisi, tel. 0831/521944).
Lecce (Piazza Sant 'Oronzo, tel. 0832/304443).
Taranto (Corso Umberto 113, tel. 099/21233).
Trani (Via Cavour 140, tel. 0883/588830; kiosk in Piazza della Repubblica open in summer).
Vieste (Gargano) (Piazza Kennedy, tel 0884/78806).

Emergencies
Police, Ambulance, Fire, Tel. 113. This number will also put you in touch with the First Aid Service (Pronto Soccorso).

Late-Night Pharmacies. Pharmacies take turns remaining open late and on Sunday. A list of hours is posted on each pharmacy (farmacia).

Travel Agencies **Bari.** *CIT* (Via Abate Gimma 157, tel. 080/521–9192); *Wagon Lits (Thomas Cook)* (Via Cardassi 85, tel. 080/540588).

Car Rental **Bari.** *Avis* (Via Zuppetta 5/A, tel. 080/540–2166); *Hertz* (Piazza Moro 33, tel. 524–7154).
Brindisi. *Avis* (Via del Mare 50, tel. 0831/26407); *Hertz* (Via San Francesco 13, tel. 0831/26515).
Taranto. *Avis* (Corso Umberto 61, tel. 099/432278); *Hertz* (Via Pupino 19, tel. 099/433763).

Arriving and Departing by Plane and Train

By Plane Alitalia operates a regular service from other Italian cities to Bari and Brindisi. **Palese Airport** is 8 kilometers (5 miles) west of Bari; **Papola Casale Airport** is 5 kilometers (3 miles) north of Brindisi. Regular bus services connect both airports with the cities.

By Train Bari is a transit point for train connections with northern Italy.

Getting Around

By Car This is probably the best way to get around Apulia and it is the only way to see some of the more remote sights. Apulia is linked with the Italian superhighway (autostrada) system, making it just a four- or five-hour drive from Rome to the Gargano Peninsula or Bari. Roads are good, and major cities are linked by fast autostrade. Secondary roads connect the whole region, while more direct—but sometimes less scenic—routes provide a convenient link between Bari, Brindisi, and Lecce. Don't plan on any night driving in the countryside because the roads can become confusing without the aid of landmarks or large towns.

By Train Bari is linked to Brindisi, Lecce, and Taranto with a good service, but smaller destinations can often be reached only by completing the trip on a connecting bus operated by Italian State Railroads (FS).

By Bus Direct, if not always frequent, connections operate between most destinations in Apulia. In many cases the bus service is actually the backup to the train service (*see above*).

Guided Tours

The CIT office in Bari (*see* Important Addresses and Numbers, *above*) is the best connection for guided tours in Apulia, which is otherwise poorly served by tour operators. The CIT office can put you in touch with one of a number of local operators that offer everything from chauffeur-driven cars to inclusion in part of a longer excursion (such as southern Italy).

Exploring Apulia

Apulia's attractions are so varied and scattered that you may want to take a full week or more to explore it at a leisurely pace, selecting two or three bases in different parts of the region and taking day trips to nearby sights.

If you are mainly interested in spending time at the beach, the promontory of Gargano in the north boasts some of Apulia's best coastline, although there are pleasant beach resorts within easy reach of most of the region's attractions. Convenient travel bases include Alberobello or Martina Franca in the *trulli* country (the region of dome-shaped stone dwellings); Lecce, near the tip of the heel; and the small ports of Barletta, Molfetta, and Trani, up the coast from Bari.

The following tours go northwest from Bari up the Adriatic coast to Barletta, then continue to the promontory of Gargano, where whitewashed coastal villages and turquoise water contrast sharply with the dense forests and pilgrimage towns of the interior. Then you head back inland toward the white villages of the trulli district, from which you proceed to Taranto, Brindisi, and down to the Baroque city of Lecce, close to the Salento shores.

A word of warning is needed if you are driving in Bari or Brindisi. These cities are notorious for purse-snatching, car thefts, and break-ins. Make sure you lock everything in the trunk, and find a guarded parking space if possible.

Highlights for First-time Visitors

Alberobello and the Trulli (Tour 3: The Trulli District).
Appian Way Terminus, Brindisi (Tour 4: Across the Heel and South to Lecce).
Basilica di San Croce, Lecce (Tour 4: Across the Heel and South to Lecce).
Castel del Monte (Tour 3: The Trulli District).
Foresta Umbra (Tour 2: The Gargano Peninsula).
Monte Sant' Angelo (Tour 2: The Gargano Peninsula).
Museo Archeologico, Bari (Tour 1: Around Bari).
Museo Nazionale, Taranto (Tour 4: Across the Heel and South to Lecce).

Tour 1: Around Bari

Numbers in the margin correspond to points of interest on the Apulia and Bari maps.

① **Bari** is a big, hectic, rough-and-tumble port and a transit point for travelers catching ferries across the Adriatic to Greece. Most of the city is set out in a logical 19th-century grid pattern, following the designs of Joachim Murat, Napoleon's brother-in-law and the King of the Two Sicilies. Leave it to explore the peninsula of the *città vecchia* (Old Town) center, a maze of narrow, crooked streets. Here, overlooking the sea and just off Via
② Venezia, is the basilica di **San Nicola** (St. Nicholas), built in the 11th century to house the bones of St. Nicholas, who is better known to us as St. Nick, or Santa Claus. His remains are said to have been stolen by Bari sailors from Myra, in what is now Turkey. The basilica, a solid and powerful construction, was the only building to survive the otherwise wholesale destruction of Bari by the Normans in 1152.

③ Follow the narrow Strada della Carmine from behind the Basilica to reach the **Cattedrale** (Cathedral), a century younger than the basilica. The seat of the local bishop, it was the scene of many significant political marriages between important families in the Middle Ages. Its solid architecture reflects the Romanesque style favored by the Normans of that period.

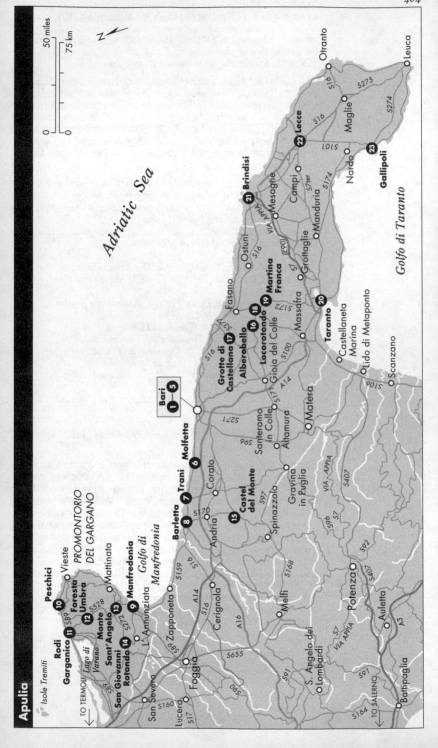

494

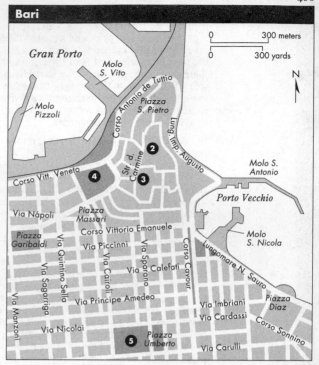

4 The huge **Castello** (Castle) looms behind the cathedral. The current building dates from the time of Holy Roman Emperor Frederick II, who rebuilt an existing Norman-Byzantine castle to his own exacting specifications. Designed more for powerful effect than for beauty, it looks out beyond the cathedral to the Porto Vecchio (Old Port), Bari's small harbor. Inside is an interesting collection of medieval Apulian art. *Admission: 4,000 lire. Open Mon.–Sat. 9–1, 3–7.*

5 From the castle, go south, crossing Piazza Massari and Piazza della Libertà to take Via Cairoli to the **Museo Archeologico.** Inside is a fine collection of Apulian artifacts, including jewelry and weapons, some dating to the 7th century BC. You leave with a better understanding of why Apulia has been an important crossroads for more than 2,500 years. *Piazza Umberto I, tel. 080/521–1559. Admission free. Open Mon.–Sat. 9–1.*

Time Out   **Vecchia Bari** (Via Dante 47) is a good place for learning the secrets of Apulian cooking. Just take Via Sparano north one block from Piazza Umberto I, which is right behind the museum.

Leaving Bari, take the coastal road (S16) from the Castello toward Molfetta, Trani, and Barletta, which have old ports reminiscent of Venetian ports such as Dubrovnik, across the Adriatic Sea in Yugoslavia. **Molfetta,** 25 kilometers (16 miles) **6** from Bari, has an unusual 12th-century cathedral with distinct Byzantine features, such as the pyramid-shape covers to the three main domes. If you are in the area over Easter, don't miss Molfetta's colorful Holy Week processions.

7 **Trani,** 18 kilometers (11 miles) farther, is the smallest of the three ports. Its old town has polished stone streets and buildings, medieval churches, and a harbor filled with fishing boats. Its 11th-century **cathedral,** considered one of the finest in Apulia, is built on a spit of land jutting into the sea. Trani had a flourishing Jewish community in medieval times, and there is still a Via Sinagoga (Synagogue Street) in the old town. Here, two of the four original synagogues survive as the 13th-century churches of **Santa Anna,** where there is still a Hebrew inscription, and **Santa Maria Scolanova.**

8 In **Barletta,** 13 kilometers (8 miles) up the coast, don't miss the **Colossus,** a bronze statue over 15 feet tall, thought to be of the Byzantine Emperor Valentinian and dating to the 5th century AD. Part of Venice's booty after the sack of Byzantium's capital, Constantinople, in the 1200s, the Colossus was abandoned on the beach near Barletta when the ship carrying it to Venice foundered in a storm. It stands next to the church of San Sepolcro on Corso Vittorio Emanuele.

Tour 2: The Gargano Peninsula

Continue up the coast on S159 to the Gargano, the spur of Italy's boot, where the region's most attractive and popular beaches are found. Until a few years ago, this rocky peninsula of whitewashed coastal towns, wide sandy beaches, and craggy limestone cliffs topped by deep-green scrub pine was practically unknown: Some parts of the interior are still well off the usual tourist track. The beach-resort business has boomed in the past decade, though, and beaches can become crowded in midsummer.

9 **Manfredonia,** a resort town on the southern side of the Gargano, is about 60 kilometers (40 miles) from Barletta. From there, take the winding coastal road (S89), which threads through miles of silvery olive groves interspersed with almond trees and prickly-pear cactus. Along the way you'll come across many local craftsmen's stalls selling homemade preserves, baskets, and carved olive-wood bowls and utensils. Vieste, a large town about 50 kilometers (30 miles) around on the tip of the spur, is the Gargano's main commercial center. But continue on **10** **11** to the north shore resorts of **Peschici** and **Rodi Garganico,** whitewashed towns squeezed between the hills and the sea. You may want to make these your base for spending a few days exploring the beaches and coast.

Time Out **Gabbiano** (Via Trieste 14) is a cheerful restaurant facing the sea in Rodi Garganico. Admire the view here while having a lunch of locally caught seafood.

Take S528 (midway between Peschici and Rodi Garganico) south to head back through the interior of the Gargano, where you'll discover a different world. In the middle of the peninsula **12** is the majestic **Foresta Umbra** (Shady Forest), a dense growth of beech, maple, sycamore, and oak generally found in more northerly climates, thriving here because of the altitude—3,200 feet above sea level. Between the trees are occasional dramatic vistas opening out over the Gulf of Manfredonia.

The interior is also important because of two centers for religious pilgrimage. Perched amid olive groves on the rugged

⑬ white limestone cliffs overlooking the gulf is the town of **Monte Sant'Angelo.** Pilgrims have flocked here for nearly 1,500 years—among them, St. Francis of Assisi and the Crusaders setting off for the Holy Land from the then-flourishing port of Manfredonia. The town is centered on the **Sanctuary of San Michele,** built over the grotto where the Archangel Michael is believed to have appeared before shepherds in the year 490. Walk down a long series of steps to get to the grotto itself—on the walls you can see the hand tracings left by pilgrims as votive symbols. Steps lead left from the sanctuary down to the **Tomb of Rotari,** which is believed to have been a medieval baptistery, with some remarkable 12th-century reliefs. More steep steps lead up to the large ruined Norman castle, which dominates the town. Here you have the best chance to appreciate the intricate pattern of the streets and steps winding their way up the side of the valley. To the right, looking out from the castle, you can see the town's medieval section, or Junno, a maze of little white houses squeezed into one corner of the narrow valley. To get there from the castle, take the steps down to Piazza Cappelletti and then turn right into this area.

Time Out Most shops in the Junno sell a local specialty called **ostia piena** (filled host), a pastry made with candied almonds and wafers, similar to communion hosts. The best place to munch them is at the southern end of the Junno, by the Villa Comunale, where you can also savor the view of the Gulf of Manfredonia. Sunset is the best time for this treat.

⑭ About 25 kilometers (16 miles) west of Monte Sant'Angelo, along the winding S272, is the ancient village of **San Giovanni Rotondo,** a pilgrimage center that has grown up around the shrine and tomb of Padre Pio (1887–1968). The monk is revered for his pious life, for miraculous intercessions, and for bearing the stigmata, the signs of Christ's wounds. The **Casa Sollievo della Sofferenza** (Foundation for Mitigating Suffering), supported through contributions from around the world, is a testament to the enduring appeal of this holy man.

A short ride south on S273, and then east (left) at L'Annunziata, will take you back to Manfredonia, where you can link up with the coastal road to return to Barletta.

Tour 3: The Trulli District

⑮ From Barletta, take S170 south for 30 kilometers (19 miles), through the important market town of Andria to **Castel del Monte,** one of Apulia's most impressive and mysterious monuments. Built on an isolated hill in the first half of the 13th century by Frederick II, Castel del Monte is a huge, bare, octagonal castle with eight towers: It can be seen for miles around and commands a stunning view. Very little is known about the structure, since virtually no records exist. It has none of the usual defense features associated with medieval castles, so it probably had little military significance. Some theories suggest it might have been built as a hunting lodge or may have served as an astronomical observatory or a stop for pilgrims on their quest for the Holy Grail. *Admission: 4,000 lire, children under 12 free. Open Mon.–Sat. 9–1 and 3–7, Sun. and holidays 9–1.*

16 To reach **Alberobello,** the center of **trulli** country, take S170 south then S97 east to Gravina in Puglia. Continue east on S96 and then S171 and S604.

The origins of the igloo-shaped trulli go back to the 13th century, and maybe further: The trulli are built of local limestone, without mortar, and with a hole in the top for smoke. Some are painted with mystical or religious symbols, some are isolated, and other are joined together with roofs on various levels. The trulli district of Alberobello, where more than 1,000 trulli crowd together along steep, narrow streets, is a national monument. It is also one of the most popular tourist destinations in Apulia and a gold mine for people who enjoy shopping for souvenirs (*see* Shopping, *below*).

17 Near Alberobello, about 20 kilometers (12 miles) northwest, taking roads 172 then 377 toward the coast, is the **Grotte di Castellana,** a huge network of caves discovered in 1938. You can take one- or two-hour guided tours through the grottoes, which are filled with fantastically shaped stalagmites and stalactites: The grottoes constitute the largest network of caves on the Italian mainland. *Admission: 5,000 lire. Open Apr.–Sept., daily 8:30–12:15, 2:30–6; Oct.–Mar., daily 9–noon, 2–5.*

18 Return to Alberobello, then continue on S172 southeast for 9 kilometers (5 miles) to **Locorotondo,** an attractive hillside town in the Itria Valley and still inside the trulli district. The *rotondo* in the town's name refers to the circular pattern of the houses, which is apparent from any vantage point at the top of the town.

19 Take S172 directly south for 6 kilometers (4 miles) to **Martina Franca,** an attractive town with a dazzling mixture of medieval and Baroque architecture in the light-colored local stone. Ornate balconies hang above the twisting, narrow streets, with little alleys leading off into the surrounding hills. Martina Franca was developed as a military stronghold in the 14th century, when a surrounding wall with 24 towers was built, but now all that remains of that role are the four gates that had been the only entrances to the town. Each July and August Martina Franca holds a music festival (*see* The Arts and Nightlife, *below*).

Tour 4: Across the Heel and South to Lecce

20 Take S172 from Martina Franca, or A14 and S7 from Bari, to reach **Taranto.** Taranto—the stress is on the first syllable—was an important port even in Roman times. It occupies an excellent position on one side of a broad bay, the Mare Grande. A narrow channel forms the entrance to a smaller, landlocked, bay, the Mare Piccolo. Taranto is on the back of the instep of the Italian boot. Little remains of Taranto's past except the 14th-century church of San Domenico at the end of the promontory and the city's maritime heritage: Taranto is the home of a famous naval academy.

However, one shining beacon to shed light on the millennia of local history is the **Museo Nazionale,** where most of the large collection of prehistoric, Greek, and Roman artifacts come from the immediate vicinity. The museum is just over the bridge from the old town on the promontory. Some of the prehistoric items from Apulian tombs date to before 1000 BC, but more plentiful are the examples of intricate craftsmanship in the Greek jewelry from around 500 BC. The museum is a memorable testament to the importance of this ancient port, which has always taken full advantage of its unique trading position at the end of the Italian peninsula. *Corso Umberto 41, tel. 099/22112. Admission: 6,000 lire. Open Mon.–Sat. 9–2, Sun. 9–1.*

Time Out Overlooking the channel separating the old and new towns and just next to the bridge itself, **Barcaccia** is a restaurant with a memorable view. It also has good seafood and pasta. *Corso Due Mari 22. Closed Mon.*

The modern E90 autostrada makes short work of the 72-kilometer (45-mile) west–east crossing of Italy's heel. It's just as well, because this far south, the mountains run out of steam and the land is uniformly flat, although agriculturally quite important. Less than an hour from Taranto, but already on the eastern (Adriatic) coast, you will reach **Brindisi**, long one of Italy's most important ports. (The first syllable, like that of Taranto, is stressed.)

Most people think of Brindisi only in terms of its ferry port, linking Italy with Greece and Yugoslavia. Although this impression fails to give credit to the broader importance of the city (it has a population of nearly 100,000), it is a present-day reminder of the role Brindisi has always played as gateway to the eastern Mediterranean and beyond. The core of the city is at the head of a deep channel, which branches into two harbors with the city between them. Look for the steeple of the **Duomo** (Cathedral) to get your bearings, but go beyond it and down the steps to the water's edge. Just to the left, along Viale Regina Margherita, you can see a tall **Roman column** and the base of another one next to it. These were built in the 2nd century AD and marked the end of the **Via Appia** (Appian Way), the Imperial Roman road from the capital to the important southern seaport. Brindisi has seen a constant flow of naval and mercantile traffic over the centuries, and in the Middle Ages was an important launching point for several Crusades to the Holy Lands.

Return to the Duomo to have a look at the mosaic floor in the apse; the floor dates from the 12th century, although much of the rest of the cathedral was rebuilt in the 18th. From the front of the Duomo take Via Tarantini away from the Roman columns; this leads on to Via Castello, where, about 500 yards from the Duomo, you turn right onto Via della Libertà. Just ahead is **Castello Svevo**, another of the defense fortifications built by the illustrious Frederick II in the 13th century. It guards the larger of the two inner harbors, and from the far side (the harbor-front side) you can look back on the Roman column and the jutting old section of the city.

The modern S16 whisks you along the 40 kilometers (25 miles) southeast to **Lecce**, the crowning jewel on the tour of Apulia. Although Lecce was founded before the time of the ancient Greeks, it is almost always associated with the term Lecce Baroque. This is because of a citywide impulse in the 17th century to redo the town in the Baroque fashion. But this was Baroque with a difference. While Baroque architecture is often heavy and monumental, here it took on a lighter, more fanciful tone. Just look at the **Basilica di Santa Croce**, with the **Palazzo della Prefettura** abutting it. While every column, window, pediment, and balcony is given a curling Baroque touch—and then an extra one for good measure—the overall effect is lighthearted. This is partly because the scale of the buildings is unintimidating and partly because the local stone used is a glowing honey color: It couldn't look menacing if it tried.

Coming out of the basilica, turn left, and 100 yards later, you reach **Piazza Sant'Oronzo,** in the middle of which is a Roman column of the same era and style as the one remaining in Brindisi. Next to the column is the **Roman amphitheater:** The shallow rows of seats suggest a small-scale version of the Roman Colosseum or Verona's Arena.

㉓ Drive 37 kilometers (23 miles) south of Lecce on S101 to rejoin the Gulf of Taranto at the town of **Gallipoli.** The modern section of town lies on the mainland; turn right on the main street at the end of the central square and cross a 17th-century bridge to the old town, crowded onto its own small island in the gulf. The Greeks called it Kallipolis, the Romans Anxa. Like the famous Turkish town of the same name on the Dardanelles, the Italian Gallipoli occupies a strategic location and thus was repeatedly attacked through the centuries—by the Normans in 1071, the Venetians in 1484, the British in 1809. The historic quarter, a mesh of narrow alleys and squares, is guarded by a formidable Aragonese **castello,** a massive fortification that grew out of an earlier Byzantine fortress that you can still see at the southeast corner. Other sights in town include the baroque **Duomo** and the **church of La Purissima,** with its stuccoed interior as elaborate as a wedding cake (note especially the tiled floor). To return to Taranto, take S174 back up the coast 93 kilometers (58 miles).

What to See and Do with Children

Children generally enjoy the archaeological diversions throughout Apulia, such as the Museo Archeologico in **Bari** and the Roman amphitheater in **Lecce,** particularly if they are old enough to know something about the ancient Greeks and Romans. Stop in **Barletta** to see the 15-foot-tall Colossus, a Byzantine statue from the 5th century AD. The igloolike trulli dwellings intrigue children, as do the mysterious **Castel del Monte** and **Grotte di Castellana,** also in the trulli district. Another grotto, in the town of **Monte Sant-Angelo,** the supposed site of an angelic visitation in 490, captures young imaginations. The beaches and forests of the Gargano promontory are great places for letting off steam, and many towns stage puppet shows in their public gardens, which kids should enjoy. If you're visiting the area around Easter time, young and old alike enjoy the Holy Week processions in **Molfetta.**

Off the Beaten Track

Tremiti Islands. A ferry service from Termoli, north of the Gargano (1 hour 40 minutes), and a hydrofoil service from Vieste, Peschici, Rodi Garganico, and Manfredonia (40 minutes to 1 hour 40 minutes) connect the mainland with these three small islands north of the Gargano. Although somewhat crowded with Italian tourists in summer, they are famed for their sea caves, pine forests, and craggy limestone formations. There are also interesting medieval churches and fortifications on the islands.

Shopping

Apulia is a region rich in folk art, reflecting the influences of the many nations that have passed through the region or ruled it. Don't expect too many high-fashion boutiques of the sort you'd find in Rome, Milan, Florence, or Venice. Instead, look for handmade goods, such as pottery with traditional designs, and baskets, textiles, and carved wood figures. These are on sale in shops and in open markets, where some bargaining can enter into the purchase. The following are the best towns and villages in which to pick up some fine handicrafts.

Alberobello Rugs and fabrics are the best bets here, but because of the town's popularity with tourists, there is also a good deal of shoddy material. In the trulli quarter you'll find small shops selling hand-painted clay figurines.

Andria Copper objects and containers are made and sold here.

Lecce Wrought-iron work is the local specialty, but you should also look for works in papier-mâché (particularly nativity scenes).

Maglie Fabrics and embroidery are featured here.

Monte Sant'Angelo Local craftsmen make and sell wooden utensils, furniture, and wrought-iron goods. Shoemaker Domenico Palena displays his unique leather sculptures at his tiny shop in the Junno district.

Sports

Biking It's fun to see the hill towns and coastal villages on two wheels. You can rent bikes in most of the towns on our tours, but some of the recommended outlets are listed here.

Bari. *G.S. De Benedictus* (Via Nitti 23, tel. 080/344345).
Gioia del Colle. *G.S. Gioauto Renault* (Via Vittorio Emanuele, tel. 080/830417).
Manfredonia. *G.S. Cicli Castriotta* (Via Beccarini 7, tel. 0884/23424).

Fishing For information on approved spots and license applications, contact Federazione Italiana Pesca Sportiva (Molo Pizzoli, Bari, tel. 080/521–0685).

Golf Apulia's only 18-hole golf course is the Riva dei Tessali (Marina di Ginosa, 40 kilometers (25 miles) west of Taranto along the coast road, tel. 099/643–9007).

Sailing Many of the larger coastal hotels offer guests the use of sailboats. Towns with clubs or municipal facilities include Barletta (Via Cristoforo Colombo, tel. 0883/33354); Brindisi (Lega Navale, Via Vespucci, tel. 0831/418824); and Taranto (Lega Navale, Lungomare Vittorio Emanuele II, tel. 099/93801).

Spelunking The Grotte di Castellana (tel. 080/896–5511) (*see* Tour 3: The Trulli District, *above*) offers the adventurous cave explorer the chance to probe mainland Italy's largest cave complex.

Tennis Like sailing, tennis is offered at many of the larger hotels in Apulia. Public or club courts are located at Brindisi (Via Ciciriello, tel. 0831/521057); Lecce (Piazza Arco di Trionfo, tel. 0832/306142); and Molfetta (Via Dante Alighieri 5, tel. 080/911921).

Beaches

For the Italians and other tourists who return each summer, the sea is one of the major attractions of Apulia. The beaches along the **Gargano Peninsula,** although no longer "undiscovered," offer safe swimming and sandy beaches. The whole coastline between **Bari** and **Brindisi** is well served with beach facilities. In even the smallest villages you'll find beaches where there are changing rooms and—important in the blazing Apulian sun—beach umbrellas. If you don't mind venturing farther afield, try **Gallipoli,** on the south coast of the heel (take S101 from Lecce). The combination of historic town center and ample swimming and water-sports facilities makes it a good choice for families.

Dining and Lodging

Dining Anyone who likes to eat will love traveling in Apulia. Southern cuisine is hearty and healthy, based on homemade pastas and cheeses, fresh vegetables, seafood, and local olive oil. Open markets and delicatessens burst with local fruits, vegetables, pastries, sausages, smoked meats, and cheeses.

Here you will find dishes unavailable elsewhere in Italy, such as *'ncapriata,* also called *favi e fogghi* (a delicious purée of fava beans served as a first course with a side dish of bitter chicory or other cooked vegetables). *Focaccia* (stuffed pizza) makes a great snack or lunch.

Apulia's pasta specialties include *orecchiette* (small, flat, oval pieces of pasta), *troccoli* (homemade noodles cut with a special ridged rolling pin), and *strascenate* (rectangles of pasta with one rough side and one smooth side). Among the many typical sauces is *salsa alla Sangiovanniello* (made with olive oil, capers, anchovies, parsley, and hot peppers).

Don't miss the dairy products, such as ricotta and buttery *burrata* cheese, and remember that Apulia has a wealth of excellent local wines, ranging from the strong white wine of Martina Franca to the sweet red Aleatico di Puglia, and the sweet white Moscato di Trani to the rich, dry red Castel del Monte.

Restaurants in Apulia, in common with those in other parts of Italy, tend not to operate with an explicit dress code. The following list mentions dress only when a restaurant requires a jacket and tie. Otherwise, a man without a jacket and tie will only feel underdressed in Expensive or Very Expensive establishments. Elsewhere, the custom is casual but neat.

Highly recommended restaurants are indicated by a star ★.

Category	Cost*
Very Expensive	over 85,000 lire
Expensive	60,000–85,000 lire
Moderate	25,000–60,000 lire
Inexpensive	Under 25,000 lire

per person, including house wine, service, and tax

Lodging   There has been a rapid development of tourist facilities in some areas of Apulia, particularly along the miles of sandy beaches on the Gargano spur, now one of the most popular summer resorts for Italians. Here, and elsewhere on the coast, big white "Mediterranean"-style beach hotels have sprung up one after the other. Most are similar in design, price, and quality. In the busy season, many cater only to full-board guests (those paying for lodging plus three meals per day at the hotel) or half-board guests (those lodging and eating breakfast plus one other meal per day at the hotel) on longer stays, and it is best to make your reservations through a travel agent.

Elsewhere in Apulia, particularly outside the big cities, hotel accommodations are still limited, and those available are generally modest—both in amenities and price—though this may be more than compensated for by friendly service. Some places, such as Bari during the annual Trade Fair in September, will require reservations.

Many establishments, particularly the beach resorts, close during the winter months, so check for this also when choosing accommodations. And remember that in a region like this that gets blazing hot in summer and bitter cold in winter, air-conditioning and central heating are important.

Highly recommended lodgings are indicated by a star ★ .

Category	Cost*
Very Expensive	over 300,000 lire
Expensive	140,000–300,000 lire
Moderate	80,000–140,000 lire
Inexpensive	under 80,000 lire

All prices are for a standard double room for two, including service and 9% IVA (19% for deluxe hotels).

Alberobello   **Il Poeta Contadino.** Proprietor Marco Leonardo serves "cre-
Dining   ative regional cooking" in this rustic-style restaurant. Set in the heart of the attractive trulli district, it features an outdoor terrace and candlelit tables. Specialties to look for are fish platters and a house antipasto selection. *Via Indipendenza 21, tel. 080/721917. Reservations advised for lunch. AE, DC, MC, V. Closed Mon., Jan. 7–Feb. 14. Moderate–Expensive.*

★   **Trullo d'Oro.** This welcoming restaurant occupies five trulli houses and is decorated in the rustic style, with dark wood beams, whitewashed walls, and an open hearth. Local country cooking includes dishes using horse meat as well as lamb and veal, vegetable and cheese antipasti, pasta dishes with crisp raw vegetables on the side, and almond pastries. Specialties include roast lamb with *lampasciuni* (a type of wild onion) and *spaghetti al trullo*, made with tomatoes, garlic, olive oil, *rughetta* (a bitter green), and four cheeses. *Via F. Cavallotti 29, tel. 080/721820. Reservations required. AE, DC, MC, V. Closed Mon. Moderate.*

Pugliese. A simple, homey restaurant with bare white walls in the trulli district, Pugliese serves local dishes and has outdoor tables. Try the orecchiette, with a sauce of cream, mushrooms, and *pecorino* (ewe's milk) cheese, or *pannette alla Pugliese*, which has peppers, ground meat, mushrooms, and fresh tomatoes. *Via Gigante 4, tel. 080/721437. No reservations. AE, DC, MC, V. Closed Mon. during winter. Inexpensive.*

Lodging **Dei Trulli.** Trulli-style cottages in a pinewood near the trulli zone make this a pleasant hotel, decorated with rustic furnishings including folk art rugs. There is a modestly priced restaurant serving local specialties. *Via Cadore 28, tel. 080/721130, fax 080/721044. 33 rooms with bath. Facilities: outdoor pool, mini-bars, garden. AE, V. Closed Nov.–Mar. Moderate.*

Astoria. The undistinguished but comfortably modern Astoria is conveniently located near the train station and the trulli district. Most rooms have big private balconies, and there is a garden as well as a moderately priced restaurant serving local dishes, such as homemade orecchiette and fava bean puree with chicory. *Viale Bari 11, tel. 080/721190. 47 rooms with bath. Facilities: garden, restaurant. AE, DC, MC, V. Inexpensive.*

Bari **Ristorante al Pescatore.** This is one of Bari's best fish restaurants, located in the old town a short distance from the castle and just around the corner from the Duomo. The cooking is done outside, where (in summer) you can sit amid a cheerful clamor of quaffing and dining. Try the *céfalo* (mullet) if it is available, accompanied by crisp salad and a carafe of invigorating local wine. *Piazza Federico II di Svevia, tel. 080/523–7039. No reservations. AE, V. Closed Mon. Moderate.*

Lodging **Sheraton Nicolaus.** This large, modern hotel on the edge of the city is easily reached by car from highway S16, which skirts the congested center of town. It caters mainly to businesspeople and is well-equipped for meetings, conferences, and banquets. Rooms are spacious and comfortable, with the usual Sheraton amenities. There's even an indoor swimming pool and sauna. *Via Rosalba 27, tel. 080/504–2626, fax 080/504–2058. 175 rooms with bath. Facilities: bar, restaurant, garden, garage. AE, DC, MC, V. Expensive.*

Boston. This modern hotel is centrally located on the outskirts of the Old Town, with functional decor and a garden. Ask for one of the eight rooms with balconies. *Via Piccinni 155, tel. 080/521–6633, fax 080/524–6802. 72 rooms with bath. Facilities: garage. AE, DC, MC, V. Moderate.*

Barletta **Bacco.** Here is a place where you can dine in style. Elegantly
Dining furnished and centrally located, the Bacco has silver cutlery,
★ crystal, and flowers and candles on each table; there is a piano bar in the evening. It serves innovative regional dishes, such as *gamberi al basilico* (shrimp with basil), *spigola ai frutti di mare* (sea bass with shellfish), and *capretto murgiano ai funghi cardoncelli* (goat with mushrooms). *Via Sipontina 10, tel. 0883/571000. No reservations. Jacket and tie required. DC, V. Closed Dec. 27–Jan. 5, Aug., Sat. and Sun. Very Expensive.*

La Casaccia. Located near the castle, this simple restaurant serves home cooking and local dishes, such as homemade orecchiette and *penne piccanti* (spicy macaroni). *Via Cavour 40, tel. 0883/33719. Reservations required. No credit cards. Closed Mon. Moderate.*

Brindisi **Majestic.** A modern hotel across from the train station and near
Lodging the port, the Majestic is fully air-conditioned and furnished in comfortable, though uninspired, style, with carpeting on the walls and wooden furniture. Rooms 128, 228, and 328 have windows overlooking a public park. *Corso Umberto 151, tel. 0831/*

222941, fax 0831/524071. 68 rooms with bath. Facilities: parking, restaurant. AE, DC, MC, V. Moderate–Expensive.

Mediterraneo. Comfort and a convenient central location are the advantages of this modern, fully air-conditioned hotel— though it is less accessible from the port than the Majestic. Most rooms have balconies and there is an inexpensive restaurant. *Viale Aldo Moro 70, tel. 0831/82811, fax 0831/87858. 69 rooms with bath. Facilities: garage, restaurant. AE, DC, MC, V. Moderate.*

Castel del Monte
Dining and Lodging

Ostello di Federico. This large, beautifully positioned restaurant, at the foot of the hill on which the castle rises, has a terrace overlooking splendid scenery, plus a bar, a pizzeria with a wood oven, and half a dozen rustically furnished rooms. The restaurant serves local dishes, including *orecchiette a rapa* (with greens), and local cheeses, such as ricotta and creamy burrata. *Castel del Monte, tel. 0883/83043. 6 rooms with bath. No reservations for restaurant. No credit cards. Restaurant closed Mon. Inexpensive.*

Castellana Grotte
Dining
★

Al Parco Chiancafredda. The refined ambience and cuisine of this restaurant, which is set apart from the tourist haunts in the area, make it pricier than its neighbors. But the food and service are worth the extra cost: Try such regional dishes as *sformato di verdura* (a kind of vegetable stew) and *agnello alla Castellanese* (local lamb). *Via Chiancafredda 12, tel. 080/896–8710. Reservations required. DC. Closed Tues. and Nov. Moderate.*

Taverna degli Artisti. Located near the caves, this rustic tavern-style restaurant with a big garden specializes in local home cooking, such as roast lamb, homemade orecchiette, and dishes with fanciful names like *cannelloni all'Ernesto, timballo fine del mondo* (end-of-the-world timbale), and *Involtini al Purgatorio* (purgatory roulades). *Via Vito Matarrese 27, tel. 080/896–8234. No reservations. No credit cards. Closed Thurs. Oct.–June and Dec. Inexpensive.*

Castellaneta Marina
Lodging
★

Villa Giusy. About an hour's drive along the coast from Taranto, modern amenities blend with an old-fashioned flavor in this little resort hotel in a pinewood only 300 yards from a wide sandy beach. Most rooms have a balcony. There's an inexpensive restaurant serving local specialties. The hotel offers reasonable pension rates. *Via Sputnik 4, tel. 099/643036. 24 rooms with bath. Facilities: garden, outdoor pool, children's playground, restaurant. V. Moderate.*

Foggia (Gargano)
Dining

Cicolella. Candles and flowers grace the tables of this large modern hotel restaurant near the station. It also has a terrace and specializes in international cuisine, as well as local dishes such as *troccoli* (square-edged spaghetti) and *involtini* (roulades). *Via Ventiquattro Maggio 60, tel. 0881/3890. No reservations. AE, DC, MC, V. Closed Sun. Moderate.*

★ **Mangiatoia.** This rustic-style restaurant, on the main road to Bari, near Foggia Agricultural Fairgrounds, is decorated with arches, hanging lamps, white walls, and wood-beamed ceilings that preserve some of the characteristics of the farmhouse it once was. Inside there's air-conditioning, but you can dine outdoors in a large garden, where tables made from wagon wheels surround an old well. Seafood is the specialty; fish and shellfish are displayed live in tanks. Chef Giovanni Prencipe will supply recipes for dishes, such as *spaghetti ai datteri di mare cartoccio* (spaghetti with razor clams in bags), orecchiette with sauce and grated *ricotta dura* cheese, and fettucine in a creamy *scampi* (shrimp) sauce. *Via Virgilio 2, tel. 0881/34457. Reservations advised. AE, DC, MC, V. Closed Mon. Moderate.*

Lodging **Cicolella.** Located near the station, this 1920s hotel has modern amenities and tastefully decorated rooms, a few of which have balconies. Rooms 210, 214, 416, 420, and 421 are particularly recommended. There is also a restaurant (*see above*). *Via Ventiquattro Maggio 60, tel. 0881/3890, fax 0881/78984. 125 rooms with bath. Facilities: garage, restaurant, mini-bars. AE, DC, MC, V. Expensive.*

Gallipoli **Marechiaro.** You have to cross a little bridge or take a boat out
Dining to this simple portside restaurant, which is actually not far
★ from the town's historic center. It's built out onto the sea and decorated with wood paneling and flowers, with terraces right on the water for panoramic views of the coast. Try the renowned *zuppa di pesce in bianco* (fish stew made without tomatoes), the succulent shellfish, and linguine with seafood. *Lungomare Marconi, tel. 0883/266143. No reservations. AE, DC, MC, V. Closed Tues. Oct.–May. Moderate.*

Lodging **Costa Brada.** The rooms all have terraces with sea views at the
★ Costa Brada, a modern, white, beach hotel in classic Mediterranean design. The interiors are comfortable and tastefully decorated; rooms 121, 122, 123, 124, and 125 are larger and directly overlook the beach. There is a beach snack bar and a restaurant specializing in seafood. The hotel offers attractive pension rates and accepts only half-board or full-board in the high season. *At Baia Verde beach, Litoranea Santa Maria di Leuca, tel. 0883/22551, fax 0883/22555. 80 rooms with bath. Facilities: garden, tennis, sauna, indoor and outdoor pool, restaurant, minibars. AE, DC, MC, V. Expensive.*
Le Sirenuse. There is a private beach and pinewoods at this gleaming white Mediterranean-style beach hotel complex. It is fully air-conditioned, with comfortable rooms whose terraces have good views of the coast. *At Baia Verde beach, tel. 0883/22536, fax 0883/22539. 125 rooms with bath. Facilities: garden, tennis, outdoor pool, playground. AE, DC, MC, V. Closed Nov.–Mar. Moderate.*

Gioia del Colle **Corte dei Sannaci.** There is an appetizing mix of regional and
Dining nouvelle cuisine at this large rustic restaurant in a restored antique farmstead outside town. The service is friendly, and the waiters will help you choose from the many specials. For the main course, try the mixed grill of meats. *39 km (24 mi) south of Bari on Route SS 100, tel. 080/998–1270. No reservations. No credit cards. Closed Tues. and Nov. Moderate.*

Lecce **Carlo V.** This semiformal restaurant in the heart of Lecce is
Dining part of a complex that also includes a tearoom, wine shop, and a pizzeria, all housed in an atmospheric old palace owned by one of Lecce's noble families. The dishes here are scrupulously prepared and presented, with the emphasis on fish and fresh vegetables. Try the *pappardelle nere con seppie e asparagi* (pasta cooked with octopus and asparagus) for a first course, while the *pesce in crosta* (fish cooked in a pastry) is a good entrée, served with mushrooms and asparagus. *Via Palmieri 46, tel. 0832/46042. Reservations advised. AE, DC, MC, V. Closed Aug., Dec. 24–Jan. 2, Sun. evening and Mon. Moderate.*

Lodging **President.** Located in the modern business center of town, this large and modern first-class hotel has comfortable rooms and a restaurant. Conference rooms and function rooms cater to the business clientele, which finds the President convenient and efficient. *Via Salandra 6, tel. 0832/311881, fax 0832/594321. 154 rooms with bath. Facilities: restaurant, parking. AE, DC, MC, V. Expensive.*

Risorgimento. An old-fashioned hotel in a converted palace in the heart of the Baroque Old Town, the Risorgimento combines historic charm and decor with modern comfort. There is a restaurant, cocktail lounge, and roof garden with a great view of the town. *Via Augusto Imperatore, tel. 0832/42125, fax 0832/ 45571. 57 rooms with bath. Facilities: conference rooms, restaurants, roof garden. AE, DC, MC, V. Moderate.*

Manfredonia
Lodging

Gargano. The Gargano is a typical big white beach hotel, whose rooms have terraces and are decorated in blue and white. The disco/bar keeps the atmosphere lively on summer evenings. *Viale Beccarini 2, tel. 0884/27621, fax 0884/26021. 46 rooms with bath. Facilities: garage, outdoor pool, restaurant. V. Moderate.*

Martina Franca
Dining
★

Arcobaleno. About 15 kilometers (10 miles) from Martina Franca, halfway to Ostuni, this restaurant is one of the best in the area. The specialty is an antipasto that offers as many as 12 tasty items, ranging from freshly prepared vegetable tidbits to marinated meats in a variety of sauces. The unusual pasta dishes are favorites, too. *Via Monte La Croce 105, Cisternino, tel. 080/718247. No reservations. MC, V. Closed Tues. Moderate.*

La Tavernetta. This small, dimly lit restaurant with a vaulted ceiling in the Old Town center serves good home cooking and local specialties, starting with a pottery bowl full of local olives to nibble with the excellent house wine. Specialties include fava beans purée with cooked chicory and *orecchiette* with a side dish of *cocomero* (a vegetable that looks like a miniature round watermelon but tastes like a cross between a cucumber and a honeydew melon). Main-dish specialties include huge portions of mixed grilled lamb, liver, and spicy local sausage. *Corso Vittorio Emanuele 30, tel. 080/706323. No reservations. No credit cards. Closed Mon. Inexpensive.*

Lodging

Park Hotel San Michele. This garden hotel makes a pleasant base for excursions in the warm months when you can take a refreshing dip in the pool between jaunts. There are few frills, but the rooms have the basic comforts and many have views of the garden. It's favored by local businesspeople for meetings and dinners. *Viale Carella 9, tel. 080/880-7053, fax 080/ 880895. 78 rooms with bath. Facilities: parking, restaurant, bar. AE, DC, MC, V. Moderate.*

Mattinata
Lodging

Baia delle Zagare. On the shore road to Valle dei Mergoli, Baia delle Zagare is a secluded, modern group of cottages overlooking an attractive inlet. An elevator takes you down to a private beach, and the hotel restaurant is good enough to keep you on the premises all day. (You're expected to take full board anyway.) *Strada Litoranea (17 km [10 mi] northeast), tel. 0884/ 4155, fax 0884/4884. 144 rooms with bath. Facilities: restaurant, garden, tennis, outdoor pool. V. Closed Oct.–Apr. Moderate–Expensive.*

Alba del Gargano. Although located in the center of town, the Alba provides a restful atmosphere; large balconies overlook a quiet courtyard garden and a frequent (and free) bus service connects with a private beach, where you can use the hotel's beach chairs and umbrellas. The rooms in the modern hotel are comfortably furnished, and there is a good restaurant. *Corso Matino, tel. 0884/4771, fax 0884/4772. 43 rooms with bath. Facilities: garage, garden, private beach, bar, restaurant. AE, MC, V. Inexpensive–Moderate.*

Monte Sant'Angelo
Lodging

Hotel Rotary. This simple but welcoming modern hotel is set amid olive and almond groves just outside town. Each room has a terrace with a good view of the Gulf of Manfredonia. *Via per Pulsano, tel. 0884/62146. 24 rooms with bath. Facilities: restaurant. V. Closed Nov. Inexpensive.*

Ostuni
Dining
★

Chez Elio. Enjoy local dishes and a memorable view of the coastline from the terrace of this modern restaurant, which is set in green hills outside town. Inside, white walls and table linens contrast with decorative plants and bright flowers, giving a light, fresh atmosphere. Specialties include orecchiette with tomato sauce and *tagliatelle* noodles with blueberries. *Via dei Colli Selva 66, tel. 0831/302030. Reservations required. AE, V. Closed Mon. and Sept. Moderate.*

Lodging

Incanto. A modest, modern hotel, it's located outside the old town, which you can admire from many rooms, along with the countryside and the sea in the distance. The decor and rooms are basic, but it's adequate as an overnight base for seeing the area. *Via dei Colli, tel. 0831/301781, fax 0831/338302. 64 rooms with bath. Facilities: parking, restaurant. AE, DC, MC, V. Moderate.*

Peschici
Lodging

Valle Clavia. Olive and pine trees surround this modern, functional hotel located near the beach. Ask for room 30, which has a view of the sea. There is a hotel restaurant. *Valle Clavia, tel. 0884/964012. 51 rooms with bath. Facilities: garden, tennis court. No credit cards. Closed Oct.–May. Moderate.*

Rodi Garganico
Lodging

Mizar. Simple, comfortably furnished rooms with terraces look out over the sea in this large Mediterranean-style hotel. Local seafood is the attraction in the hotel restaurant. *Via Ippocampo, Lido del Sole, tel. 0884/97021, fax 0884/97022. 54 rooms with bath. Facilities: private beach, solarium, restaurant. AE, MC, V. Closed Oct.–May. Moderate.*

Taranto
Lodging

Grand Hotel Delfino. A big, modern, well-equipped downtown hotel catering to business clients, the Grand Hotel Delfino has airy rooms with balconies (room 80 has a view of the sea). The restaurant serves regional specialties, especially seafood. *Viale Virgilio, tel. 099/3205, fax 099/3205. 198 rooms with bath. Facilities: garden, sauna, outdoor swimming pool, minibars, restaurant. AE, DC, MC, V. Expensive.*

Trani
Dining
★

La Antica Cattedrale. Just in front of the cathedral, on a spit of land jutting out into the sea, La Antica Cattedrale has an antique flavor, with stonework, vaulted ceilings, and terra-cotta tile floors. There are also tables outside. Regional specialties are presented imaginatively: Try the baked crepes (similar to cannelloni); risotto made with salmon, crab, and cream; lobster; or grilled fish. *Piazza Archivio 2, tel. 0883/586568. Reservations required for dinner on summer weekends. AE, DC, MC, V. Closed Mon. Nov. Moderate.*

Lodging

Royal. Formerly known as the Holiday, this is an unpretentious modern hotel near the train station. Furnishings are comfortable, and there is a piano bar by the restaurant. *Via de Robertis*

29, tel. 0883/588777, fax 0883/582224. 55 rooms with bath. Facilities: restaurant, garden. AE, DC, MC, V. Moderate.

Albergo Lucy. This is a simple, tiny, and hospitable hotel on a quiet piazza just off the port and next to the public gardens, along the seafront. It has huge rooms with high ceilings and balconies, and its friendly management extends a particular welcome to families. *Piazza Plebiscito 11, tel. 0883/41022. 8 rooms with bath. No credit cards. Inexpensive.*

Trani. Like the Royal, the Trani is simple, modern, and near the station. It offers good-value accommodations and has a restaurant. *Corso Imbriani 137, tel. 0883/588010, fax 0883/587625. 51 rooms with bath. Facilities: restaurant. AE, DC, MC, V. Inexpensive.*

Vieste
Lodging
★

Pizzomunno. Probably the most luxurious resort on the Gargano, Pizzomunno is right on the beach and is surrounded by a large park. It is large, white, modern, well-equipped, and fully air-conditioned. The rooms are ample and comfortable, and they all have terraces. There is a moderate–expensive restaurant specializing in fish, and there are many opportunities to unwind or try your hand at something a little more active, like tennis or archery. *Via Litoranea, tel. 08884/708741, fax 0884/707325. 183 rooms with bath. Facilities: restaurant, swimming pool, private beach, movie theater, disco, handball and tennis courts, archery, water sports, fitness center, sauna, child care. AE, DC, MC, V. Closed Nov.–Mar. Very Expensive.*

The Arts and Nightlife

The Arts

In keeping with the general atmosphere of Apulia, the arts take on a folk flavor, with processions on feast days and religious occasions more prevalent than performing arts in theaters or opera houses. Still, there are some good festivals and pageants to help broaden your experience of life in Italy's deep south. The best newspaper for listings is the daily *La Gazzetta del Mezzogiorno*, which covers the entire region.

Theater Bari has the famous **Teatro Petruzzelli** (Corso Cavour, tel. 080/524–1761), which features performances of drama, opera, and ballet.

Lecce is a good place to visit in July, when the **Roman Amphitheater** is used for productions of drama and, sometimes, opera.

Music Lecce features an **International Music Fair** each August, when churches and outdoor bandstands throughout the city act as venues.

Martina Franca concentrates on music in its annual **Festival of the Itria Valley** each July and August.

Festivals and Pageants The **Disfida a Barletta,** held on the last Sunday in August, is a reenactment of an event of the same name, which took place in 1503. The *disfida* (challenge) was issued by 13 Italian officers to 13 French officers, after one of the French insulted the Italians by stating that Italy would always be under foreign domination. The Italians taught the rash Frenchman and his compatriots a lesson. Every Italian child learns this story at school.

The **City of Brindisi Festival** (July–September) is a citywide display of art and folklore.

Molfetta features **processions** on Good Friday and Easter Saturday.

Taranto also has Easter processions (Holy Thursday and Good Friday), called the **Procession of the Madonna Addolorata and of the Mysteries.**

Nightlife

Apulia is one of Italy's most rural regions, and even the cities have a marked provincial air to them. This can be frustrating for someone who expects the glamour of nightclubs and discos of the sort Milan and Rome have to offer. On the other hand, in the cafés surrounding the squares of most towns, you can have a ringside seat for that most Mediterranean of pageants—the *passeggiata*. Local people of all ages dress in their most stylish clothing and stroll through the streets, starting around sunset. This is Italian life at its most relaxed and, at the same time, most structured. No one is in a hurry; there is an air of laughter and conviviality; but young people will defer to their elders, and poorer people to those—the town doctor, lawyer, or monsignor—they consider to be their social superiors. And it's yours for the price of a cold drink at a sidewalk café.

16 Sicily

Arriving in Sicily for the first time, you may be surprised to see so many people with blond hair and blue eyes and to learn that two of the most popular boys' names are Ruggero (Roger) and Guglielmo (William), but that is what Sicily is all about. For 2,000 years it has been an island where unexpected contrasts somehow come together peacefully. Lying in a strategic position between Europe and Africa, Sicily at one time hosted two of the most advanced and enlightened capitals of Europe—a Greek one in Siracusa and an Arab-Norman one in Palermo. (The Normans are responsible for the blond-haired Rogers and blue-eyed Williams.) Sicily was one of the great melting pots of the ancient world and home to every great civilization that existed in the Mediterranean: Greek and Roman; then Arab and Norman; and, finally, French, Spanish, and Italian. Something of all of these peoples was absorbed into Sicily's artistic heritage, a rich tapestry of art and architecture that includes massive Romanesque cathedrals, two of the best-preserved Greek temples in the world, Roman amphitheaters, and delightful Baroque palaces and churches.

Modern Sicily is still a land of surprising contrasts. The traditional graciousness and nobility of the Sicilian people exist side by side with the atrocities and destructive influences of the Mafia. Alongside some of the most exquisite architecture in the world has grown some of the worst speculation imaginable. In recent years the island, like much of the Mediterranean coast, has seen a boom in popular tourism and a surge in condominium development that has only recently begun to be checked. The chic boutiques producing lace and linen in jet-set resort towns like Taormina often mask the poverty in which their wares are produced.

In Homer's *Odyssey*, Sicily represented the unknown end of the world, yet the region eventually became the center of the known world under the Normans, who recognized a paradise in its deep blue skies and temperate climate, its lush vegetation, and rich marine life. Much of this paradise does still exist today. Add to it Sicily's unique cuisine—another harmony of elements—which mingles Arab and Greek spices with Spanish and French dishes, using some of the world's tastiest seafood, and you can understand why those who came here were often reluctant to leave.

You do not have to be paranoid about safety in Sicily, but you do have to be careful: Do not flaunt your gold jewelry, and keep your handbag securely strapped across your chest. Leaving valuables visible in your car while you go sightseeing is, naturally, inviting trouble. Be careful; then enjoy the company of the Sicilians. You will find them to be friendly and often willing to go out of their way to help tourists. It doesn't matter if you don't speak Italian or speak only a little: They aren't usually offended if your pronunciation isn't perfect—as is sometimes the case elsewhere in Europe—and they will never submit you to a grammar lesson in the middle of the street. One of the reasons for this, no doubt, is the fact that many Sicilians or their close relatives have themselves been strangers in foreign lands, and empathy goes a long way.

Sicily is about 180 kilometers (112 miles) north to south and 270 kilometers (168 miles) across. Plan to spend three nights in Palermo, one in Agrigento, two in Siracusa, and three at Taormina. If you can, add a few days to explore some inland towns, such as Caltagirone and Enna, and to visit the Aeolian Islands or some of the smaller satellite islands, such as Pantelleria and Ustica.

Essential Information

Important Addresses and Numbers

Tourist
Information

Aeolian Islands (Corso Vittorio Emanuele 202, Lipari, tel. 090/988–0095).

Agrigento (Viale della Vittoria 255, tel. 0922/401352; Via Atenea 123, tel. 0922/20454).

Caltagirone (Palazzo Libertini, tel. 0933/53809).

Caltanisetta (Corso Vittorio Emanuele 109, tel. 0934/21731).

Catania (Largo Paisello 5, tel. 095/312124; rail station, tel. 095/531802; airport, tel. 095/341900).

Cefalù (Corso Ruggero 77, tel. 0921/21050).

Enna (Piazza Garibaldi 1, tel. 0935/21184; Piazza Napoleone Colajanni 6, tel. 0935/26119).

Erice (Via Conte Pepoli 55, tel. 0923/869173).

Marsala (Via Garibaldi 45, tel. 0923/958097).

Messina (Via Calabria 301/b, tel. 090/675356; Piazza Stazione, tel. 090/674236).

Monreale (Piazza Duomo, tel. 091/656–4270).

Palermo (Piazza Castelnuovo 35, tel. 091/583847; Stazione Centrale, tel. 091/616–5914).

Piazza Armerina (Via Cavour 15, tel. 0935/680201).

Siracusa (Via San Sebastiano 43, tel. 0931/461477; Via Maestranza 33, tel. 0931/464255; at the entrance to the Archaeological Park, tel. 0931/60510).

Taormina (Largo Santa Caterina, Palazzo Corvaja, tel. 0942/23243; Corso Umberto 144, tel. 0942/23751).

Trapani (Piazza Saturno, tel. 0923/29000; Via Vito Sorba 15, tel. 0923/27273).

Arriving and Departing by Plane

Sicily can be reached from all major cities via Rome, Milan, or Naples. Planes land at the Punta Raisi airport, 35 kilometers (20 miles) west of Palermo (tel. 091/591698), or at Catania's Fontanarossa airport (tel. 095/341900), 5 kilometers (3 miles) south of the city. At both, there is bus service into the center of town. During the high season, there are also direct charter flights to Sicily from New York, London, and Paris.

Arriving and Departing by Car, Train, and Boat

By Car and Ferry Frequent car ferries cross the strait between Villa San Giovanni in Calabria and Messina on the island. The crossing usually takes about half an hour, but during the summer months there can be considerable delays. From Naples, overnight car ferries operate daily to Palermo and once a week to Catania and Siracusa; there is also an overnight ferry from Genoa to Palermo.

By Train There are direct express trains from Milan and Rome to Palermo, Catania, and Siracusa. The Rome–Palermo journey takes at least 11 hours. After Naples, the run is mostly along the coast, so try to book a window seat on the right. At Villa San

Giovanni, in Calabria, the train is separated and loaded onto a ferryboat to cross the strait to Messina.

By Passenger Boat Besides the ferries mentioned above (*see* By Car and Ferry, *above*), hydrofoils *(aliscafi)*, which carry passengers only, also cross the strait in about 20 minutes.

Getting Around

By Car Renting a car is definitely the best way to travel in Sicily because the trains are unreliable and slow and the buses, though faster and air-conditioned in summer, are often subject to delays and strikes. Modern highways circle and bisect the island, making all main cities easily reachable. Cars can be rented at airports and downtown locations in every major city.

By Train Main lines connect Messina, Taormina, Siracusa, and Palermo. Secondary lines are generally very slow and unreliable. The Messina–Palermo run, along the northern coast, is especially attractive.

By Bus Air-conditioned coaches connect major and minor cities and are often faster and more convenient than local trains but slightly more expensive.

Guided Tours

Orientation City tours are provided by the Italian tour operator CIT in all major cities. CIT also arranges complete tours of Sicily, which range from seven-day tours of the island's major sights to a four-day minitour. Departures are once a week from Palermo in a comfortable air-conditioned coach with an English-speaking guide. The cost includes all meals and accommodations in three- or four-star hotels. CIT has offices in Palermo (Via Libertà 12, tel. 091/586333), Catania (Via Mario Sangiorgi, tel. 095/538136), Taormina (Corso Umberto 101, tel. 0942/23301), New York (342 Madison Ave., Room 207, New York, NY 10173, tel. 212/697–2100 or 800/248–8687), and Croydon, England (3–5 Lansdowne Rd., tel. 081/686–0677).

Special-Interest Amelia Tours (280 Old Country Rd., Hicksville, NY 11801, tel. 516/433–0696 or 800/SICILY–1) has a carefully prepared program for Sicily, emphasizing the cultural life of the region.

Exploring Sicily

The best way to visit Sicily is to travel counterclockwise along the coast by car, bus, or train, making occasional detours inland. You may also want to take some extra days to visit the rugged volcanic Aeolian islands off Sicily's northeast coast, and the larger islands of Pantelleria in the southwest or Ustica in the northwest, which are paradises for swimming and skin-diving enthusiasts.

The following tour begins in the capital city of Palermo, meeting point of Sicily's Arab and Norman cultures; moves west and south to the stunning Greek cities of Selinunte and Agrigento; dips inland to see the remarkable Roman mosaics at Piazza Armerina; continues southeast to Siracusa, once the rival of ancient Greece; skirts the base of volcanic Mt. Etna to the enchanting mountaintop town of Taormina; and ends in Messina, where ferryboats connect Sicily to the Italian mainland.

Highlights for First-time Visitors

Catania (Tour 3: Eastern Sicily).
Cathedral in the Piazza Duomo, Siracusa (Tour 3: Eastern Sicily).
Cefalú (Tour 1: Palermo and Environs).
Imperial Roman Villa, Casale (Tour 3: Eastern Sicily).
Mt. Etna (Tour 3: Eastern Sicily).
National Archaeological Museum, Palermo (Tour 1: Palermo and Environs).
Palazzo dei Normanni, Palermo (Tour 1: Palermo and Environs).
Taormina (Tour 3: Eastern Sicily).
Valley of the Temples (Tour 2: The Western Coast to Agrigento).

Tour 1: Palermo and Environs

Numbers in the margin correspond to points of interest on the Sicily and Palermo maps.

❶ Our tour begins in **Palermo.** Once the intellectual capital of southern Europe, the city has always been at the crossroads of civilization. Favorably located on a crescent-shaped bay at the foot of Monte Pellegrino, it has attracted almost every people and culture touching the Mediterranean world. To Palermo's credit, it has absorbed these diverse cultures into a unique personality that is at once Arab and Christian, Byzantine and Roman, Norman and Italian.

Palermo was first colonized by Phoenician traders in the 6th century BC, but it was their descendants, the Carthaginians, who built the important fortress here that caught the covetous eye of the Romans. After the First Punic War, the Romans took control of the city, in the 3rd century BC. After several invasions by the Vandals, Sicily was settled by Arabs, who made the country an emirate and made Palermo a showpiece capital that rivaled both Cordoba and Cairo in Oriental splendor. Nestled in the fertile Conca d'Oro (Golden Conch) plain; full of orange, lemon, and carob groves; and enclosed by limestone hills, Palermo became a magical world of palaces and mosques, minarets and palm trees.

It was so attractive and sophisticated a city that the Norman ruler Roger de Hauteville decided to conquer it and make it his capital (1061). The Norman occupation of Sicily resulted in the Golden Age of Palermo (from 1072 to 1194), a remarkable period of enlightenment and learning in which the arts flourished. The city of Palermo, which in the 11th century counted more than 300,000 inhabitants, became the center of the Norman court in all Europe and one of the most important ports of trade between East and West.

Eventually the Normans were replaced by the Swabian ruler Frederick II, the Holy Roman Emperor, and incorporated into the Kingdom of the Two Sicilies. You will also see evidence in Palermo of the Baroque art and architecture of the Spanish viceroys, who came to power after the bloody Sicilian Vespers uprising in 1282, in which the French Angevin dynasty was overthrown. The Aragonese viceroys also brought the Inquisition to Palermo, which some historians believe helped foster

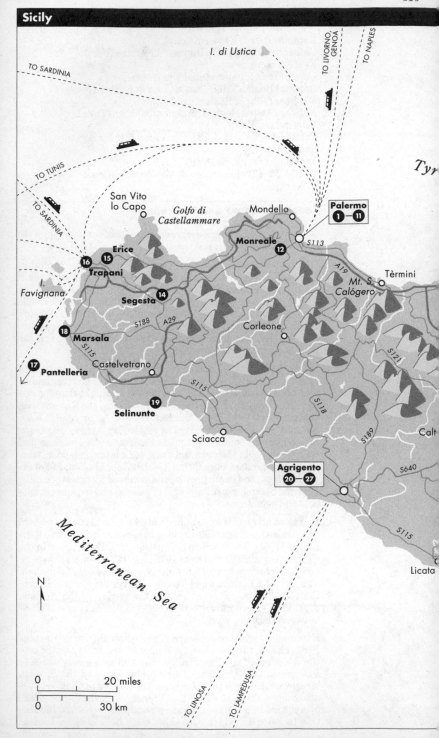

Sicily

TO SARDINIA

TO TUNIS

TO SARDINIA

I. di Ustica

TO LIVORNO, GENOA

TO NAPLES

Tyr

San Vito lo Capo

Golfo di Castellammare

Mondello

Palermo ❶ – ⓫

Monreale ⑫

S113

A19

Erice ⑮

⑯ **Trapani**

Segesta ⑭

I. Favignana

Tèrmini

Mt. S. Calógero

S188   A29

Corleone

S121

⑱ **Marsala**

Castelvetrano

S115

S115

⑰ **Pantelleria**

Selinunte ⑲

Sciacca

S118

S189

Calt

S640

Agrigento ⑳ – ㉗

Licata

S115

Mediterranean Sea

N

0   20 miles

0   30 km

TO LINOSA

TO LAMPEDUSA

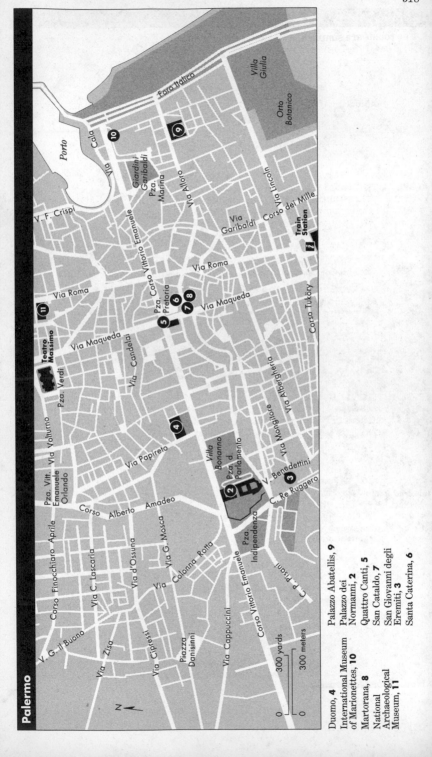

Palermo

Porto

Faro Italico

Villa
Giulia

Orto
Botanico

Cala

Via

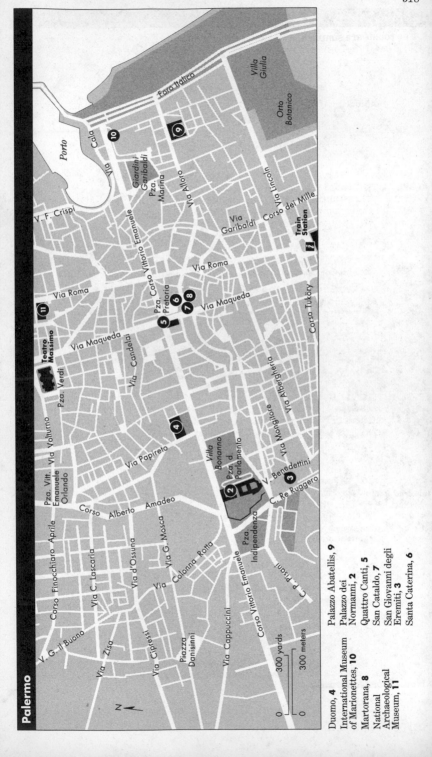 10

 9

Giardini
Garibaldi

Pza.
Marina

Via Alloro

Via
Garibaldi

Corso Via Lincoln

Corso dei Mille

V. F. Crispi

Via Corso Vittorio Emanuele

Via Roma

Pza.
Pretoria

Via Roma

Via Maqueda

Train
Station

i

Corso Tuköry

11

Teatro
Massimo

Via Maqueda

Via Candelai

Pza. Verdi

5

6
7 8

Via Alberghería

Via Mongitore

Pza. Vitt.
Emanuele
Orlando

Via Volturno

4

Via Papireto

Villa
Bonanno

V. Benedettini

Corso   Alberto   Amadeo

Via G. Mossa

Via d'Ossuna

Pza. d.
Parlamento

2

3

C. Re Ruggero

Corso Finocchiaro Aprile

Via C. Lascaria

Colonna Rotta

Pza.
Indipendenza

V. G. il Buono

Via Zisa

Via Cipressi

Piazza
Danisinni

Via Cappuccini

Corso Vittorio Emanuele

C. Pisani

N

0   300 yards

0   300 meters

Duomo, **4**
International Museum
of Marionettes, **10**
Martorana, **8**
National
Archaeological
Museum, **11**

Palazzo Abatellis, **9**
Palazzo dei
Normanni, **2**
Quattro Canti, **5**
San Cataldo, **7**
San Giovanni degli
Eremiti, **3**
Santa Caterina, **6**

the protective secret societies that eventually evolved into today's Mafia.

Palermo's main attractions are easily reached on foot, though you may choose to spend a morning taking a city bus tour to help you get oriented. The tourist attractions are scattered along three major streets: Corso Vittorio Emanuele, Via Maqueda, and Via Roma. The tourist information office in Piazza Castelnuovo will give you a map and a valuable handout that lists opening and closing times, which sometimes change with the seasons.

At the far end of the Corso, away from the harbor, is the **❷ Palazzo dei Normanni** (the Royal Norman Palace), now the seat of the Sicilian Parliament. Inside is one of Italy's greatest art treasures, the Cappella Palatina (the Palatine Chapel), built by Roger II in 1132. It is a dazzling example of the unique harmony of artistic elements that came together under the Normans. The skill of French and Sicilian masons was combined with the decorative purity of Arab ornamentation and the splendor of Greek Byzantine mosaics. The interior is covered with glittering mosaics and capped by a splendid Arab honeycomb stalactite wooden ceiling. Biblical stories blend happily with scenes of Arab life—look for one showing a picnic in a harem—and Norman court pageantry. Stylized Moorish palm branches run along the walls below the mosaics and recall the battlements on Norman castles—each one a different mosaic composition.

Upstairs are the Royal Apartments, where the Sala di Ruggero (King Roger's Hall) is decorated with medieval murals of hunting scenes. These halls once hosted one of the most splendid courts in Europe. Greek, French, Latin, and Arabic were spoken here, and Arab astronomers and poets exchanged ideas with Latin and Greek scholars in what must have been one of the most unique marriages of cultures in the Western world. *Piazza Parlamento, entrance on Corso Ruggero at the back of the palazzo, tel. 091/656–1111. Admission free. Palazzo dei Normanni and Sala di Ruggero open Mon., Fri., Sat. 9–12:30. Cappella Palatina open Mon.–Sat. 9–noon and 3–5, Sun. 9–10 and noon–1; closed during religious functions and wedding services.*

To the left of the front of Palazzo dei Normanni, along Via **❸** Benedettini, you'll see the five pink domes of the church of **San Giovanni degli Eremiti,** one of the most picturesque of Palermo's churches. The 12th-century church was built by the Normans on the sight of an earlier mosque—one of 200 that once stood in Palermo. The emirs ruled Palermo for almost two centuries and brought to it their passion for lush gardens and fountains. One is reminded of this while sitting in San Giovanni's delightful cloister of twin half-columns, surrounded by palm trees, jasmine, oleander, and citrus trees. *Open Tues., Wed., Fri. 9–1 and 3–5; Mon., Thurs., Sat. 9–2; Sun. 8:30–2.*

Returning to Corso Vittorio Emanuele and going east, you will **❹** soon see the **Duomo,** which is a prime example of Palermitan eclecticism. Its turrets, towers, dome, and arches come together in the kind of meeting of diverse elements that King Roger, whose tomb is inside along with that of Frederick II, fostered during his reign. Be sure to walk outside and look at the back of the apse, which is gracefully decorated with interlacing Arab arches, inlaid with limestone and black volcanic tufa. *Open Mon.–Sat. 7–noon and 4:30–6:30; Sun. 8–1:30 and 4–7.*

Farther down the Corso is the intersection (with Via Maqueda) called **Quattro Canti** (the Four Corners). Here four Baroque palaces from the Spanish rule meet at concave corners, each with its own fountain, Spanish ruler, patron saint, and representation of one of the four seasons.

Just to the right is Piazza Pretoria, with a lavishly decorated fountain, originally intended for a Florentine villa. Its abundance of nude figures so shocked some Palermitans when it was unveiled in 1575 that it got the nickname "the fountain of shame." It is even more shameful at night, when it is illuminated.

If you cross to the far side of the fountain and continue to the right, you'll reach Piazza Bellini and the splendid Baroque church of **Santa Caterina** (1596). Its walls are covered in decorative 17th-century inlays of precious marble.

Across the piazza and up a staircase are two churches that form a delightful Norman complex. The orange-red domes belong to **San Cataldo** (1160), whose spare but intense interior, punctuated by antique Greek columns, retains much of its original medieval simplicity. The other church, with an elegant campanile, is the **Martorana,** which was erected in 1143 but had its interior altered considerably during the Baroque period. High along the western wall, however, is some of the oldest mosaic artwork of the Norman period. Near the entrance is an interesting mosaic of Roger being crowned by Christ. In it, Roger is dressed in a bejeweled Byzantine stole, reflecting the Norman court's penchant for all things Byzantine. Archangels along the ceiling wear the same stole, wrapped around their shoulders and arms. The Norman monarchs liked to think of themselves as emissaries from heaven (like the archangels) who were engaged in defending Christianity by ridding the island of infidel invaders. *La Martorana open Mon.–Sat. 8:30–1 and 3:30–7:30 (3:30–5:30 in winter), Sun. 8:30–1; to visit San Cataldo, refer to the custodian of La Martorana.*

Heading toward the port, take Via Alloro to the **Palazzo Abatellis,** which houses the National Gallery of Sicily. Among its treasures is an Annunciation (1474) by Sicily's prominent Renaissance master, Antonello da Messina, and an arresting fresco by an unknown painter, titled *The Triumph of Death,* a macabre depiction of the plague years. *Via Alloro 4, tel. 091/ 616–4317. Admission: 2,000 lire. Open Mon.–Sat. 9–1:30; Tues., Thurs., and Fri. 3–6:30; Sun. 9–1.*

Nearby is the **International Museum of Marionettes,** with an impressive display of Sicilian and European puppets. The traditional Sicilian *pupi* (marionettes), with their glittering armor and fierce expressions, have become a symbol of Norman Sicily. Plots center on the chivalric legends of the troubadours, who, before the puppet theater, kept alive tales of Norman heroes in Sicily, such as Orlando Furioso and William the Bad. *Via Butera 1, tel. 091/328060. Open Mon.–Sat. 9–1 and 4–7.*

Return to Corso Vittorio Emanuele and walk toward Via Roma. Before you get there, you will come upon the outdoor market that spreads out into a maze of side streets around Piazza Domenico. This is the **Vucciria**—a dialect word that means

"voices" or "hubbub." It's easy to see why. Hawkers everywhere deliver their unceasing chants from behind stands brimming with mounds of olives, blood oranges, wild fennel, and
long-stemmed artichokes. One of them goes at the trunk of a
swordfish with a cleaver, while across the way another holds up
a giant squid or dangles an octopus. All the time, the din continues. It may be Palermo, but this is really the Casbah.

Time Out   The **Vucciria** is full of stalls selling street food. Everything
from *calzone* (deep-fried meat- or cheese-filled pockets of
dough) to *panelle* (chick-pea–flour fritters). If you want to try
something typically Palermitan that is a bit adventurous but
delicious, look for a stall with a big cast-iron pot selling
guasteddi (fresh buns filled with thin strips of calf's spleen, ricotta cheese, and a delicious hot sauce).

⑪ Back on Via Roma, the **National Archaeological Museum** has a
small but excellent collection. Especially interesting are the
examples of prehistoric cave drawings and a marvelously reconstructed Doric frieze from the Greek Temple at Selinunte
that gives you a good idea of the high level of artistic culture
attained by the Greek colonists in Sicily some 2,500 years ago.
*Piazza Olivella 4, tel. 091/587825. Admission free. Open
Mon.–Sat. 9–1 (9:30–2:30 June–Sept.), Sun. 9–1:30; also
open 3:30–6:30 Tues. and Fri.*

There are several interesting day trips you can make from Pa-
⑫ lermo. Don't miss the splendid cathedral of **Monreale,** about 10
kilometers (6 miles) southwest of the city. It is lavishly decorated with mosaics depicting events from the old and new testa-
ments. Bring 100-lire coins to illuminate the mosaics. There are
130 pictures, covering 6,000 square yards. Be sure to see the
rear exterior and the graceful Romanesque cloister to the left,
laced with intricate arches, mosaic-inlaid twin columns, and
capitals that represent one of the richest collections of Sicilian
medieval sculpture. In a corner by the stylized palm tree fountain, look for a capital showing William II offering the cathedral to the Virgin. *Cathedral, tel. 091/640–4413. Open daily
winter 8:30–noon and 3:30–6:30, summer 9–7. Cloister, tel.
091/640–4403. Admission: 2,000 lire. Open winter, Mon.–Sat.
9–1:30, Sun. 9–noon; summer, Mon.–Sat. 9–12:30, 4–7, Sun.
9–1.*

⑬ **Cefalù,** about 70 kilometers (42 miles) east of Palermo, along
the coast, is a charming town built on a spur jutting out into the
sea and dominated by a massive 12th-century Romanesque
Duomo that is one of the finest Norman cathedrals in Italy.
King Roger began it in 1131 as a thanks offering for having
been saved here from a shipwreck. Its mosaics rival those of
Monreale. Both cathedrals are dominated by colossal mosaic
figures of the Byzantine Pantocratic Christ, high in the bowl of
their apses. Everybody argues over whether Cefalù or
Monreale has the better Christ Pantocrator. The Monreale figure is an austere and powerful image, while the Cefalù Christ is
softer and more compassionate. If the Monreale Pantocrator
emphasizes the divinity of Christ, the one at Cefalù seems to
stress his humanity. *Cathedral. Tel. 0921/23454. Open Mon.–
Sat. 8–noon and 3–7; Sun. 7–1, 3:30–8. No shorts or
beachwear.*

Cefalù has become a popular summer resort, and the traffic going in and out of town can be heavy. You may want to take the 50-minute train ride or 40-minute bus ride from Palermo instead.

Tour 2: The Western Coast to Agrigento

⑭ About 85 kilometers (50 miles) southwest of Palermo is **Segesta,** where one of the most impressive Greek **temples** in the world is located—on the side of a windswept barren hill overlooking a valley of wild fennel. Virtually intact, the temple is considered by some to be finer, in its proportions and setting, than any Doric temple left standing. The Greeks started the temple in the 5th century BC but never finished it. The walls and roof are missing, and the columns were never fluted. About a mile away, near the top of the hill, are the remains of a fine Greek theater, with impressive views, especially at sunset, of nearby Monte Erice and the sea.

⑮ Continue west about 30 kilometers (18 miles) and then up 2,450 feet to **Erice,** an enchanting medieval mountaintop aerie of castles and palaces, fountains and cobblestone streets. Erice was the ancient Eryx and was dedicated to a fertility goddess, whom the Phoenicians called Astarte; the Greeks, Aphrodite; and the Romans, Venus. According to Virgil, Aeneas built a temple to the goddess here, but it was destroyed when the Arabs took over and renamed the place Mohammed's Mountain. When the Normans arrived, they built a castle where today there is a public park with benches and belvederes, from which there are striking views of Trapani, the Egadi islands, and, on a *very* clear day, Cape Bon and the Tunisian coast.

Time Out *Cassata di Erice,* a sponge cake filled with either ricotta cheese or almond paste and chocolate cream, then covered with pistachio icing and elaborately decorated with candied fruit flowers, is a dignified version of the famous Sicilian dessert, which is of Arabic origin. Try a slice (a little goes a long way) at any of the **pastry shops** along Via Vittorio Emanuele or in Piazza Umberto I.

⑯ The modern town of **Trapani,** below Erice, is the departure point for ferries to the Egadi islands and the island of Pantelleria, near the African coast. This rugged western end of Sicily is reminiscent of the terrain in American westerns—as it well should be, for many "spaghetti westerns" were filmed here. If you are familiar with North African couscous, Trapani is the place to try the Sicilian version, which is made with fish instead of meat. The result is a kind of fish stew with semolina, spiced with cinnamon, saffron, and black pepper.

⑰ **Pantelleria,** near the Tunisian coast, is one of Sicily's most evocative islands, although many find its starkness unappealing. Its volcanic formations, scant patches of forest, prehistoric tombs, and dramatic seascapes constitute an otherworldly landscape. From its grapes—the *zibibbo* (a strain of *moscato*)—the locals make an amber-colored dessert wine and a strong, sweet wine called Tanit. Daily ferries and hydrofoils connect the island with Trapani.

⑱ From Trapani take the main coastal road 30 kilometers (18 miles) south to **Marsala,** a quiet seaside town that is world famous for its rich-colored, sweet-tasting wine. In 1773 a British merchant named John Woodhouse happened upon Marsala and discovered that the wine there was as good as the port the British had long imported from Portugal. Two other wine merchants, Whitaker and Ingram, rushed in, and by 1800 Marsala was exporting its wine all over the British Empire.

19 Continue southeast on the main road, through Castelvetrano, and south to **Selinunte,** where an overwhelming array of ruined Greek temples is perched on a plateau overlooking the Mediterranean. The city was one of the most superb colonies of ancient Greece. The original complex held seven temples scattered over two sites separated by a harbor. Of the seven, only one—reconstructed in 1958—still stands. Founded in the 7th century BC, Selinunte became the rich and prosperous rival of Segesta, which in 409 BC turned to the Carthaginians for help. The Carthaginians sent an army commanded by Hannibal to raze the city. The temples were demolished, the city was laid flat, and 16,000 of Selinunte's inhabitants were slaughtered. The beautiful metopes preserved in Palermo's Archaeological Museum come from the frieze of Temple E here. There is also a small museum at the site that contains other excavated pieces. Selinunte is named after a local variety of wild celery that in spring still grows profusely among the ruined columns and overturned capitals. *Admission to site and museum: 2,000 lire. Open daily 9–one hour before sunset.*

20 About 100 kilometers (60 miles) farther east along the highway, the golden temples of **Agrigento** will appear on a rise to your left. Agrigento, or Akragas as the Greeks called it, was settled by the Greeks in 580 BC and grew wealthy through trade with Carthage, just across the Mediterranean. Despite attacks from the Carthaginians at the end of the 5th century BC, the city survived through the Roman era, the Middle Ages (when it came under Arab and Norman rule), and into the modern age, and structures from all these eras sit side-by-side in Agrigento today. The birthplace of both the ancient Greek philosopher Empedocles and the modern Italian playwright Luigi Pirandello, Agrigento is a study in contrasts, but its chief attraction, the Valley of the Temples, remains one of the most impressive classical sites in all of Italy.

Numbers in the margin correspond with points of interest on the Agrigento map.

Coming upon the **Valley of the Temples** for the first time is always a memorable moment—whether in the sunshine of spring, when they are surrounded by blossoming almond trees, or at night, when they are flood-lit. Even in winter, when the vegetation is limited—perfectly limited—to century plants *(agaves)* and gnarled gray olive trees, it is easy to understand why Pindar called Agrigento "the most beautiful city built by mortal men." Exiting from the highway, walk down from the parking lot on Via dei Templi and turn left. The first temple you **21** encounter as you enter the complex is the **Temple of Hercules**—eight pillars of the oldest temple in Agrigento, built during the **22** 5th century BC. Up the hill is the **Temple of Concord,** one of the best-preserved Doric temples in the world and certainly the most impressive in Sicily. In the late afternoon, as the sun descends below the horizon, the temple's sandstone begins to change from honey-gold to pink russet, and the vertical lines of the fluted columns and their triangular pediment sharpen

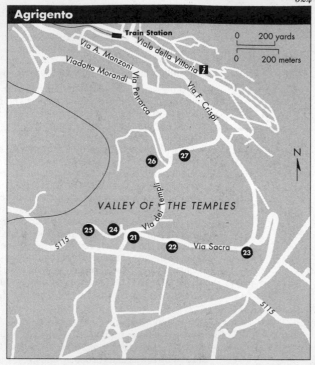

23 against the fading skyline. The columns were probably once covered by brightly painted stucco. Follow the road that climbs around to the left, and you'll reach the **Temple of Juno,** which commands an exquisite view of the valley, especially at sunset. If you look carefully, you can see red fire-marks on some of the columns—the result of the Carthaginian attack in 406 BC, which destroyed the city. Return to the parking lot in the Piazzale dei Templi (where there is a bar selling drinks and ice cream) and cross to the opposite side of the road, where the **24** ruins continue. First is the **Temple of Jupiter,** the largest temple ever planned in Sicily. Though never completed, it was considered the eighth wonder of the world. The nearby sleeping giant is a copy of one of the 38 colossal Atlas figures, or telamones, that supported the temple's immense roof. The last temple **25** is the much-photographed **Temple of Castor and Pollux,** whose four columns supporting part of an entablature have become a symbol of Agrigento, even though they were reconstructed in 1836, and probably from diverse buildings. At the end of Via dei Templi, where it turns left and becomes Via Petrarca, stands **26** the **National Archaeological Museum,** which contains one of the original telamones, an impressive collection of Greek vases dating to the 7th century BC, and models of what the temples once looked like. *Admission free. Open Tues.–Sat. 9–1:30 and 3–5, Sun. 9–1:30.*

On the opposite side of the road from the museum is the **27** **Hellenistic and Roman Quarter,** which consists of four parallel streets, running north and south, that have been uncovered, along with the foundations of some houses from the Roman settlement (2nd century BC). Some of these streets still have their original mosaic pavements.

Time Out There is little reason to go up the hill to the rather dreary modern city of Agrigento, where speculation keeps threatening to encroach upon the Valley of the Temples below—except to ring the doorbell at the **convent of Santo Spirito** on the Salita di Santo Spirito off Via Porcello and try the sweet cake, *kus-kus*, made of pistachio nuts and chocolate, which the nuns there prepare.

On the first weekend in February, Agrigento hosts an Almond Blossom Festival, with international folk dances, a costumed parade, and the sale of marzipan and other sweets made from almonds.

Tour 3: Eastern Sicily

Numbers in the margin correspond to points of interest on the Sicily map.

From Palermo, follow A19 east and south about 150 kilometers (93 miles); from Agrigento, cut inland and follow the road upland, through Caltanissetta, about 105 kilometers (63 miles) to

㉘ **Enna,** a fortress city of narrow winding streets that is home to an impressive castle built by Frederick II. The views from here of the flat interior and Mt. Etna in the distance are exceptional.

Turn south, through the pine and eucalyptus woods and low

㉙ farmland, to **Piazza Armerina,** a tiny Baroque town with an exceptionally well-preserved and well-presented example of a

㉚ sumptuous Roman emperor's country house. The **Imperial Roman Villa at Casale,** about 6 kilometers (4 miles) southwest of the city, is made up of four groups of buildings on different levels and is thought to have been a hunting lodge of the Emperor Maximianus Heraclius (4th century AD). The excavations were not begun until 1950, and all the wall decorations and vaulting have been lost. However, some of the best mosaics of the Roman world cover 3,500 square meters under a shelter shaped to give an idea of the layout of the original buildings. The mosaics were probably made by Carthaginian artisans, because they are similar to those in the Tunis Bardo Museum. The entrance was through a triumphal arch that led into an atrium surrounded by a portico of columns. Through this, the *thermae*, or bathhouse, is reached. It is colorfully decorated with mosaic nymphs, a Neptune, and slaves massaging bathers. The Peristyle leads to the main villa, where in the Salone del Circo you look down on mosaics that illustrate Roman circus sports. Another apartment shows hunting scenes of tigers, elephants, and ostriches; the gym shows young girls exercising—the private apartments are covered with scenes from Greek and Roman mythology; and Room 38 even has a touch of eroticism. In August, Piazza Armerina has a costumed horse race, called the Palio dei Normanni, to celebrate the city's prosperity under the Normans. *Tel. 0935/680036. Admission: 2,000 lire. Open daily 9–one hour before sunset.*

㉛ **Caltagirone,** about 30 kilometers (18 miles) south of Piazza Armerina, is a leader in the Sicilian ceramics industry and a charming Baroque town built over three hills, with majolica balustrades, tile-decorated windowsills, and a monumental **tile**

staircase of more than a hundred steps—each decorated with a different pattern. On the feast of San Giacomo (July 24), the staircase is illuminated with candles that form a tapestry design over the steps. It is the result of months of work preparing the 4,000 *coppi*, or cylinders of colored paper that hold oil lamps. At 9:30 PM on July 24, a squad of hundreds of boys springs into action to light the lamps, so that the staircase flares up all at once. There is an interesting **Ceramics Museum** in the public gardens, which were designed by Basile, the master of Sicilian Art Nouveau. The exhibits in the museum trace the history of the craft from specimens excavated from the earliest settlements, through the influential Arab period, to the present. *Museo Regionale della Ceramica, Giardino Pubblico. Open Mon.–Sat. 9:30–2, Sun. 9–1.*

About 100 kilometers (60 mi) east of Caltagirone on the winding but scenic S124 you arrive at the Ionian Sea. Greek Sicily began along this coast, and some of the finest examples of Baroque art and architecture also were created here, particularly in **Siracusa.** The city was founded in 734 BC by Greek colonists from Corinth and soon grew to rival, and even surpass, Athens in splendor and power. Siracusa became the largest, wealthiest city-state in Magna Grecia and the bulwark of Greek civilization. Although it suffered from tyrannical rule, kings such as Dionysius filled their courts in the 5th century BC with Greeks of the highest artistic stature—among them, Pindar, Aeschylus, and Archimedes. The Athenians did not welcome the rise of Siracusa and sent a fleet to destroy the rival city, but the natives outsmarted them in what was one of the greatest naval battles of ancient history (413 BC). Siracusa continued to prosper until it was conquered two centuries later by the Romans. There are essentially two areas to explore in Siracusa—the Archaeological Park, on the mainland, and the island of Ortygia, the ancient city first inhabited by the Greeks, which juts out into the Ionian sea and is connected to the mainland by two small bridges. The **Archaeological Park,** at the western edge of town, contains the ruins of a fine Roman amphitheater and the most complete Greek theater existing from antiquity. A comparison of these two structures reveals much about the differences between the Greek and Roman personalities. The Greek theater, in which the plays of Aeschylus premiered, was hewn out of the hillside rock in the 5th century BC. All the seats converge upon a single point—the stage—which had the natural scenery and the sky as its background. Drama as a kind of religious ritual was the intention here. In the Roman amphitheater, however, the emphasis was on the spectacle of combative sports and the circus. The arena is one of the largest of its kind and was built around the 2nd century AD. The corridor where gladiators and beasts entered the ring is still intact, and the seats, some of which still bear the occupants' names, were hauled in and constructed on the site from huge slabs of limestone. A crowd-pleasing show, and not the elevation of men's minds, was the intention here. Climb to the top of the seating area in the Greek theater, which could accommodate 15,000, for a fine view. In May and June every other year (next in 1994), performances of Greek tragedies are held here. If the Archaeological Park is closed, go up Viale G. Rizzo from Viale Teracati, where there is a belvedere overlooking the ruins, which are floodlit at night.

Near the entrance to the park is the gigantic altar of Hieron, which was once used by the Greeks for sacrifices involving hundreds of animals at a time. Just beyond the ticket office, you will come upon a lush tropical garden full of palm and citrus trees. This is the Latomie del Paradiso, a series of quarries that served as prisons for the defeated Athenians, who were enslaved; the quarries once rang with the sound of their chisels and hammers. At one end is the Orecchio di Dionisio, with an ear-shaped entrance and unusual acoustics inside, as you'll discover if you clap your hands. The legend is that Dionysius used to listen in at the top of the quarry to hear what the slaves were plotting below. *Viale Augusto, tel. 0931/66206. Admission: 2,000 lire. Open Oct.–May, daily 9–4; June–Sept., daily 9–6.*

Not far from the Archaeological Park, off Viale Teocrito, are the **catacombs** of San Giovanni, one of the earliest-known Christian sites in the city. Inside the crypt of San Marciano is an altar where St. Paul preached on his way through Sicily to Rome. The frescoes in this small chapel are still bright and fresh, though some date from the 4th century AD. *Piazza San Giovanni. Admission: 2,000 lire. Open June–Sept., daily 10–noon and 3–6; Oct.–May, Thurs.–Tues. 10–noon.*

Continue walking east, toward the sea, across Viale Teocrito, and you'll soon come to the **papyrus studio** at No. 80, where you can see papyruses being prepared from reeds and then see the scrolls painted—an ancient tradition in Siracusa. Siracusa, it seems, has the only climate outside the Nile Valley in which the papyrus plant—from which we get our word *paper*—thrives.

Nearby is the splendid new **Archaeological Museum,** opened in 1988. Its impressive collection is arranged by region around a central atrium and ranges from neolithic pottery to fine Greek statues and vases. You will want to compare the Landolina Venus—a headless, stout goddess of love who rises out of the sea in measured modesty (she is a 1st-century Roman copy of the Greek original)—with the much earlier (300 BC) elegant Greek statue of Hercules in Section C. Of a completely different type is a marvelous fanged Gorgon, its tongue sticking out, that once adorned the cornice of the temple of Athena in order to ward off evildoers. The pieces are generally well lit, with important pieces highlighted. There are also several interesting, instructive exhibits. One depicts the Temple of Apollo, the oldest Doric temple in Sicily, on the island of Ortygia. There is a continuous video description that allows the visitor to compare a scale model with pictures of the temple on video. *Viale Teocrito, tel. 0931/464022. Admission: 2,000 lire. Open Tues.–Sat. 9–1, Sun. 9–12:30.*

The central part of Siracusa is a modern city, with Corso Gelone its main shopping street. At its southern end, Corso Umberto leads to the **Ortygia Island** bridge, which crosses a pretty harbor lined with fish restaurants. In the piazza on the other side of the bridge, you'll find the ruins of the **Temple of Apollo** depicted in the Archeological Museum. In fact, little of this noble Doric temple still stands today—just some crumbled walls, shattered columns, and a fragment of a Norman church built much later on this same site (the window in the south wall). Apart from this ancient Greek relic, Ortygia is composed almost entirely of warm, restrained Baroque buildings. This uniformity is the result of an earthquake in 1693 that necessitated major rebuilding at a time when the Baroque was very popular. Wander into the back streets—especially along Via della Maestranza or Via Veneto—and notice the bulbous wrought-iron balconies (said to have been invented to accommodate ladies' billowing skirts), the window-surrounds and cornices of buildings decorated with mermaids and gargoyles, and the stucco decoration on Palazzo Lantieri on Via Roma.

Ortygia has two main piazzas: Piazza Archimede and Piazza del Duomo. Piazza Archimede is easily recognized because of its Baroque fountain of fainting sea nymphs and dancing jets of water. The bars here are popular meeting and sitting places. **Piazza Duomo,** one of the most beautiful piazzas in Italy, is a short walk away. The **cathedral** is a palimpsest of continuity, beginning with the bottom-most excavations that have unearthed remnants of Sicily's distant past, when the Siculi inhabitants worshiped their deities here. During the 5th century BC, the Greeks built a temple to Athena over it, and in the 7th century, Siracusa's first Christian cathedral was built on top of the Greek structure. The elegant columns of the original temple were incorporated into the present structure and are clearly visible, embedded in the exterior wall along Via Minerva. The Greek columns were also used to dramatic advantage inside, where on one side they form chapels connected by elegant wrought-iron gates. The Baroque facade, added in 1700, displays a harmonious rhythm of concaves and convexes. The piazza in front is encircled by pink and white oleanders and surrounded by elegant buildings ornamented with filigree grillwork. In the right corner of the piazza is the elegant **Palazzo Beneventano del Bosco,** with an impressive interior courtyard ending in a grand winding staircase. At the opposite end is the tiny Baroque church of **Santa Lucia alla Badia,** with an engaging wrought-iron balcony and pleasing facade. The feast of the city's patroness Santa Lucia (St. Lucy) is held on December 13, when the saint's splendid silver statue is carried from the cathedral to the church on the site of her martyrdom, near the Catacombs of San Giovanni. A torchlight procession and band music accompany the bearers.

Walk down Via delle Vergini, behind the church, and turn onto Via Capodieci, where the **National Museum** is housed inside Palazzo Bellomo, a lovely Catalan-Gothic building with mullioned windows and an elegant exterior staircase. Among the select group of paintings and sculptures inside is a Santa Lucia by Caravaggio and a damaged, but still brilliant, Annunciation by Antonello da Messina. *Via Capodieci 14, tel. 0931/65343. Admission: 2,000 lire. Open Tues.–Sat. 9–1.*

Walk in the opposite direction, down Via Capodieci to the promenade along the harbor, where at one end is the **Fountain of Arethusa,** a fresh-water spring next to the sea. This anomaly is explained by a Greek legend that tells how the nymph Arethusa was changed into a fountain by the goddess Artemis (Diana) when she tried to escape the advances of the river god Alpheus. She fled from Greece, into the sea, with Alpheus in close pursuit, and emerged in Sicily at this spring. Supposedly even today, if you throw a cup into the river Alpheus in Greece, it will emerge here at this fountain, which at present is home to a few tired ducks and some dull-colored carp—but no cups. Steps lead to the tree-lined promenade along the harbor front, where you can buy a drink and watch the ships come in. Or, you can walk in the opposite direction from the Arethusa Fountain to the far end of the island, to **Castello Maniace,** now an army barracks but once a castle of Frederick II, from which there are fine views of the sea.

North of the city, on the highlands that overlook the sea, Dionysius created the fortress of **Euryalus** with the help of Archimedes, as protection against the Carthaginians. This astonishing boat-shaped structure once covered 15,000 square yards. Its intricate maze of tunnels is fascinating to roam around in, and the view from the heights is superb. *8 km (5 mi) northwest of Siracusa. Open 9–one hour before sunset.*

33 From Siracusa it is a 60-kilometer (36-mile) drive up the coast to Sicily's second city, **Catania.** The chief wonder of Catania is that it is there at all. Its successive populations were deported by one Greek tyrant, sold into slavery by another, and driven out by the Carthaginians. Every time the city got back on its feet, it was struck by a new calamity: Plague decimated the population in the Middle Ages, a mile-wide stream of lava from Mt. Etna swallowed most of the city in 1663, and 25 years later a disastrous earthquake forced the Catanese to begin again. Today the city needs much renovation. Traffic flows in ever-increasing volume and adds to the smog from the industrial zone between Catania and Siracusa, but the views of Mt. Etna from Catania are superb. To Etna, Catania also owes a fertile surrounding plain and its site on nine successive layers of lava. Many of Catania's buildings are constructed from solidified lava, and the black lava stone has given the city a singular appearance. As a result, Catania is known as the city of lava and oranges. Catania's greatest native son is the composer Vincenzo Bellini, whose operas have thrilled audiences since their premieres over 150 years ago. His home, now the **Bellini Museum,** in Piazza San Francesco, preserves memorabilia of the man and his work. *Piazza San Francesco 3. Admission free. Open Mon.–Sat. 9–1 and 5–7.*

The **Villa Bellini,** Catania's public gardens, is to the north just off Via Etnea, and on clear days has lovely views of snow-capped Etna. The **Duomo,** at the opposite end of Via Etnea, is a fine work by Vaccarini (1736), as is the obelisk-balancing elephant carved out of lava stone in the piazza in front. Bellini is buried inside the cathedral. Also inside is the sumptuous chapel of St. Agatha. She is Catania's patron saint and is credited with having held off, more than once, the fiery flows of lava that threatened the city. During the festival of her feast day (Feb. 3–5) huge five–meter, highly ornate carved wooden *cannelore* (large bundles of candles) are paraded through the streets at night.

Time Out If you haven't had a cannolo yet in Sicily, the **pastry shops** along Via Etnea are good places to try one of these wafer tubes filled with silky smooth ricotta cheese. If you're in need of something more substantial, duck into one of the **trattorias** along this street and order a dish of *pasta alla Norma.* It's named after one of Bellini's most famous operas and consists of short pasta with a rich eggplant-and-tomato sauce, garnished with basil leaves and grated dry ricotta cheese.

34 Catania is the departure point for excursions around—but not always to the top of—**Mt. Etna.** Buses leave from in front of the train station in early morning, or you can take the Circumetnea railroad around the volcano's base. Etna is one of the world's major active volcanoes, and the largest and highest in Europe. The cone of the crater rises to 2,801 meters (9,190 feet) above sea level. It has erupted eight times in the past three decades, most spectacularly in 1971 and 1983, when rivers of molten lava destroyed the two highest stations of the cable car that rises from the town of Sapienza. Travel in the proximity of the crater depends at the moment on Etna's temperament, but you can walk up and down the enormous lava dunes and wander over its moonlike surface of dead craters. The rings of vegetation change markedly as you rise, with vineyards and pine trees gradually giving way to broom and lichen. On the other side of Mt. Etna lies the medieval mountaintop town of Taormina.

㉟ **Taormina's** natural beauty is so great that even the considerable overdevelopment that the town has suffered in the past 50 years cannot spoil its grandeur. The view of the sea and Etna from its jagged cactus-covered cliffs is as close to perfection as a panorama can get, especially on clear days, when the snow-capped volcano's white puffs of smoke are etched against the blue sky. Writers have extolled Taormina's beauty almost since its founding in the 6th century BC by Greeks from Naples. Goethe and D. H. Lawrence were among its enthusiasts. The Greeks put a high premium on finding impressive locations to stage their dramas, and Taormina's **Greek Theater** occupies one of the finest sites of any such theater. It was built during the 3rd century BC and rebuilt by the Romans during the 2nd century AD. Its acoustics are exceptional: Even today a stage whisper can be heard in the last rows. In summer, Taormina hosts an arts festival of music, cinema, and dance events, many of which are held in the Greek Theater. *Via Teatro Greco. Admission: 2,000 lire. Open daily 9–two hrs before sunset.*

The main street in town is Corso Umberto, which is lined with smart boutiques and antiques shops. There are also the inevitable, and all too numerous, shops selling cheap pottery and jewelry made from Etna's black lava stone, but Piazza 9 Aprile, along the Corso, commands wonderful views and is the perfect place to sit and have a cappuccino. The town's many 14th- and 15th-century palaces have been carefully preserved; especially beautiful is the **Palazzo Corvaja,** with characteristic black lava and white limestone inlays. The tourist office is located in the palace today (open weekdays 8–2 and 2:30–7:30, Sat. 8–noon). The medieval **Castello San Pancrazio** (admission free), enticingly perched on an adjoining cliff above the town, can be reached by footpath or car. If your passion for heights hasn't been exhausted, visit **Castelmola,** the tiny town above Taormina, where the Bar Turrisi makes its own refreshing almond wine—the perfect complement to the spectacular 360-degree panorama.

Time Out If you are a devotee of marzipan (almond paste), you should not leave Taormina without trying it at either the **Bar Tamako** in Piazza 9 Aprile or at one of the **pastry shops** along the Corso. The marzipan is shaped like various fruits, including the ubiquitous *fico d'India* (prickly pear), which grows wild along the slopes of Taormina.

The road between Taormina and Messina, about 50 kilometers (30 miles) north, is bordered by lush vegetation on one side and the sea on the other. The seaside here is dotted with inlets punctuated by gigantic odd-shaped rocks. It was along this coast, legend says, that the giant one-eyed cyclops hurled their boulders down on Ulysses and his terrified men as they fled to sea and on to their next adventure in Homer's *Odyssey*.

36 **Messina's** ancient history is a series of disasters, but the city nevertheless managed to develop a fine university and a thriving cultural environment. But at 5 o'clock in the morning on December 28, 1908, Messina changed from a flourishing metropolis of 120,000 to a heap of rubble, shaken to pieces by an earthquake that turned into a tidal wave and left 80,000 dead and the city almost completely leveled. As you approach the sickle-shape bay, from which ferries connect Sicily with the mainland, you see nothing to alert you to the relatively recent disaster, except that the 3,000-year-old city looks modern. The somewhat flat look is a precaution of seismic planning: Tall buildings are not permitted. The cathedral has been entirely rebuilt (it was originally constructed by the Norman King Roger II in 1197, and the reconstruction has maintained much of the original plan, including a handsome crown of Norman battlements, an enormous oven apse, and a splendid woodbeam ceiling). The adjoining bell tower—of a much later date—is one of the city's principal attractions. It contains one of the largest and most complex mechanical clocks in the world, constructed in 1933 with a host of gilded automations—a roaring lion, a crowing rooster, and numerous biblical figures—that go into action every day at the stroke of noon.

Messina is the birthplace of the great Renaissance painter Antonello da Messina, whose *Polyptych of the Rosary* (1473) can be seen along with two large Caravaggios in the **Regional Museum,** located along the sea in the northern outskirts of the city. *Viale della Libertà, tel. 090/358605. Admission: 2,000 lire. Open Mon.–Sat. 9–1:30 and 3–5:30, Sun. and holidays 9–12:30.*

Time Out **Pippo Nunnari,** on the corner of Via Ugo Bassi and Via Pellegrino, near Piazza Cairoli, would be the epitome of a Sicilian deli, if such a thing existed. Here you can sample or take away such typical Sicilian snacks as *arancini* (deep-fried breaded rice balls filled with cheese), mozzarella in *carrozze* (deep-fried bread pockets filled with mozzarella cheese) and pizza covered with thin slices of potato and rosemary. The restaurant next door, under the same proprietor, is good, too.

Tour 4: The Aeolian Islands

Just off Sicily's northeast coast lies an archipelago of seven beautiful islands of volcanic origin. The **Aeolian Islands** were named after Aeolus, the Greek god of the winds, who is said to keep all the earth's winds stuffed in a bag in his cave here. The islands are reachable by hydrofoil from Messina, Palermo, and Milazzo. The latter also has a ferryboat service to the islands, as do Catania, Palermo, and Naples, but on a less frequent schedule. In summer there are numerous boats and hydrofoil excursions connecting the individual islands. The Aeolians are a fascinating world of grottoes and clear-water caves carved by the waves through the centuries. They are ideal for snorkeling or scuba diving. All Sicily's islands—and these seven in particular—are extremely popular in summer, and some of them are

③ unpleasantly overcrowded in July and August. **Lipari** is the largest of the Aeolian islands and the one most developed for tourism. Local buses circle the island and provide wonderful views of Sicily and the other islands. Take a bus ride away from Lipari's distinctive pastel-colored houses and into its fields of spiky agaves to the northernmost tip of the island, Aquacalda, where there are interesting pumice and obsidian quarries. Or take a bus west to San Calogero, where there are hot springs and mud baths. From Lipari's red lava base rises a plateau crowned with a 16th-century castle and a 17th-century cathedral. Next door is the **Archaeological Museum,** one of the best in Europe, with an intelligently arranged collection of prehistoric finds—some dating as far back as 4,000 BC—from various sites on the archipelago. *Tel. 090/981–1031. Admission free. Open Mon.–Sat. 9–2, Sun. and holidays 9–1.*

③ **Vulcano,** true to its name, sends up plenty of fumaroles (jets of hot vapor), but the volcano here has long been dormant. You can ascend to the crater (386 meters above sea level) on muleback for a wonderful view or take boat rides into the grottoes around the base. From Capo Grillo there is a view of all the Aeolian islands.

③ **Salina,** the second-largest island, is also the most fertile—which accounts for its good wine, the golden Malvasia. Excursions go up Mt. Fossa delle Felci, which rises to over 3,000 feet. It is also the highest of the islands, and the vineyards and fishing villages along its slopes add to its charm.

④ **Panarea** has some of the most dramatic scenery of the islands: wild caves carved out of the rock and dazzling flora. The exceptionally clear water and the richness of life on the seabed make Panarea especially suitable for underwater exploration. There is a small Bronze Age village at Capo Milazzese.

④ **Stromboli** is composed entirely of the cone of an active volcano. The view from the sea—especially at night, as an endless stream of glowing red-hot lava flows into the water—is unforgettable. Stromboli is in a constant state of mild dissatisfaction, and every now and then its anger flares up, so authorities insist that you climb to the top (924 meters above sea level) only with a guide. The climb takes about four hours.

④ **④** **Alicudi** and **Filicudi** are just dots in the sea, but each has a hotel, and some local families put up guests. Filicudi is famous for its unusual volcanic rock formations and the enchanting Grotto del Bue Marino (Grotto of the Sea Ox). At Capo Graziano there is a prehistoric village. Alicudi is the farthest outpost of the Aeolians—it remains sparsely inhabited, wild, and at peace.

Time Out The bars in the Aeolian islands, and especially those on Lipari, are known for their *granite:* dishes of shaved ice made by freezing the juice and pulp of fresh fruit. These are not snowcones doused with sickeningly sweet syrups, but fruit drinks made from fresh strawberries, melon, peaches, and other fruits. Whenever the need arises for a real thirst-quencher, order a lemon granita and keep adding water from the glass or pitcher that usually accompanies your order. Many Sicilians begin the hot summer days with a *granita di caffe,* a coffee ice topped with whipped cream, into which they dunk their breakfast rolls. You can have one any time of day.

What to See and Do with Children

Almost every major city in Sicily has a theater giving performances of the world-famous **pupi Sicilani** (Sicilian marionettes). The most popular are in Palermo, Acireale, and Taormina. Stories center on heroes from the Norman fables, distressed damsels, and Saracen invaders. Even if you can't understand Italian, the action is fast and furious, so it's easy to figure out what's going on. Palermo has an **International Museum** dedicated to these and other types of marionettes (*see* Tour 1: Western Sicily, *above*). If you are in Sicily at **Carnival** time (about 45 days before Easter), Acireale, near Catania, has one of the best carnivals in Italy, with dozens of colorful torch-lit floats with papier-mâché characters aboard that are pulled through the streets by costumed revelers.

Off the Beaten Track

Behind Palermo's Duomo, on Via Papireto, is the **flea market,** a good place to hunt for antique marionettes of the Norman cavaliers or for brilliantly colored pieces from the *carretti siciliani* (Sicilian carts). This is also the antiques-store neighborhood, which spreads to the next street, Corso Amedeo.

One of Agrigento's native sons was the distinguished dramatist **Luigi Pirandello** (1867–1936), whose plays, such as *Six Characters in Search of an Author,* express the fundamental ambiguity of life. Pirandello is buried under a pine tree behind the house where he was born, in Piazzale Caos, a few miles west of town. His **house** has been made into a museum of Pirandello memorabilia. Every year a festival of Pirandello's plays is held in Agrigento from late July to early August. *Admission free. Open Mon.–Sat. 9–noon and 3–7 (winter 3–5).*

From Messina, a hydrofoil will speed you across the Strait to **Reggio di Calabria,** on the toe of the boot, where two larger-than-life-size 5th-century Greek bronze statues are exhibited in the excellent **National Museum of Magna Grecia.** The statues were found by accident by an amateur deep-sea diver off the coast of Calabria in 1972 and are worth going out of your way to see. *Corso Garibaldi, Piazza de Nava, tel. 0965/812255. Admission: 6,000 lire. Open Mon.–Sat. 9–1 and 3:30–7, Sun. 9–12:30.*

Shopping

Sicily is one of the leaders in the Italian **ceramics** industry, with important factories at **Caltagirone,** in the interior, and **Santo Stefano di Camastra,** along the northern coast between Messina and Cefalù. Colorful Sicilian folk pottery can still be bought at bargain prices. Fratantoni, on Via Nazionale, in Santo Stefano di Camastra, has a wide selection and also some unusual pieces, such as gigantic ceramic heads—of Norman knights and Saracens—that can be used as planters. Branciforti in Caltagirone (Scala Santa Maria del Monte 3) produces elegant designs based on traditional motifs from the 10th to the 19th centuries. If you seek more modern designs, De Simone, whose Picasso-like faces on plates and pitchers are popular abroad, has an outlet at Via Messina Marine 633, and in Palermo at Piazza Leoni 2 and Via Stabile 133.

Place mats, tablecloths, napkins, and **clothing** decorated with fine petitpoint are good buys in **Cefalù, Taormina,** and **Erice,** but they are not cheap (four place mats cost around $25.) Make sure that any linen you buy is produced in Sicily and not on another continent.

Collectors have been combing Sicily for years for pieces of the colorful **carretti Siciliani** (Sicilian carts). Before the automobile, these were the major form of transportation in Sicily, and they were decorated in bright primary colors and in primitive styles, with scenes from the Norman troubadour tales. The axles of these carts were ornamented with open filigree work, which was also brightly painted. Pieces sometimes appear at better antiques shops, such as Chez le Francais, in **Taormina** (Piazza San Domenico 6). Modern "adaptations" are available at the **Palermo** flea market (Via Papireto, behind the Duomo).

Sports

Camping　Sicily has excellent camping facilities on both the main island and its satellite islands. The two best are **El Bahira,** in San Vito Lo Capo (tel. 0923/972577), and **Bazia,** in Furnari Marini, west of Milazzo (tel. 0941/81235). Both have restaurants and showers, as well as swimming pools, tennis courts, and discos.

Scuba Diving　The island of **Ustica,** north of Palermo, is an international center for scuba diving and snorkeling. Its rugged coast is dotted with grottoes that are washed by crystal-clear waters and filled with an incredible variety of interesting marine life. In July Ustica hosts an International Meeting of Marine Fishing that attracts sportsmen as well as marine biologists from all over the world.

Skiing　Skiing is becoming a very popular sport in Sicily. Ski areas can be found on the slopes on the north side of Mt. Etna. The most popular is at **Linguaglossa,** located in a magnificent pine forest about 45 kilometers (27 miles) from Catania. The other area for skiing in Sicily is in the **Le Madonie** mountains, south of Cefalù.

Beaches

There is a surfeit of beaches in Sicily, but many of them are too rocky, too crowded, or too dirty to be enjoyed for long. Among the exceptions are **Mondello,** near Palermo, a popular sandy beach on a tiny peninsula jutting out into the Mediterranean; **Sant'Alessio** and **Santa Teresa,** north of Taormina (the beaches just below Taormina itself are disappointing); and **Capo San Vito,** on the northern coast, near Erice, a sandy beach on a promontory overlooking a bay in the Gulf of Castellammare.

Dining and Lodging

Dining　Sicilian cooking reflects the different Mediterranean influences that have left their mark on the island. Fish, vegetables, and grains are used in imaginative combinations, sometimes served with Italian pastas and sometimes with Arab ingredients, such as *couscous* (steamed semolina). Sweet and sour tastes are deftly mingled, and each cook has a distinctive touch, so that *caponata* (an antipasto of eggplant, capers, olives, and, in eastern Sicily, peppers) is different at each restaurant.

Sicily has always been one of Italy's poorest areas, so meat is seen rarely on menus. When it *is* featured, it is usually prepared *alla brace* (skewered) or in *falso magro* (a thin slice of meat rolled around sausage, onion, bacon, bits of egg, and cheese).

Seafood from Sicilian waters is the best and most varied in all Italy. *Tonno* (tuna) is a staple in many coastal areas, while *pesce spada* (swordfish) is equally common, if more expensive. Try *ricci* (sea urchins), which are a specialty of Mondello, near Palermo. Fish sauces for pasta are also noteworthy: *Pasta con le sarde* is made with fresh sardines, olive oil, anchovies, raisins, and pine nuts, and has the distinctive flavor of wild fennel. *Spaghetti alla Norma*, named for the heroine in the opera by local composer Vincenzo Bellini, has a sauce of tomatoes and fried eggplant. Desserts from Sicily are famous. *Cassata Siciliana* is a rich combination of candied fruit, marzipan, and icing. *Gelato* (ice cream) is excellent and is usually homemade, sometimes in the form of *granita di limone*, a kind of lemon slush. Gooey cakes and very sweet desserts help raise the blood-sugar level, and the high priests of nouvelle cuisine would probably keel over if faced with a typical Sicilian dessert, like chestnut ice cream covered with hot *zabaglione* (rich, foamy custard laced with marsala).

The sweet dessert wine, Marsala, is Sicily's most famous, but there is a range of other local wines, from the dark red Faro to the sparkling dry Regaleali, which is excellent with fish.

Highly recommended restaurants are indicated by a star ★.

Category	Cost*
Very Expensive	over 85,000 lire
Expensive	60,000–85,000 lire
Moderate	25,000–60,000 lire
Inexpensive	under 25,000 lire

**per person, including house wine, service, and tax*

Lodging Though Sicily is Italy's largest region, it has some of the most remote countryside and only a limited number of good-quality hotels. The major cities and resorts of Palermo, Taormina, and Agrigento are the only spots with a real range of accommodations. There are, of course, some superb establishments, such as converted villas with views over the sea or well-equipped modern hotels, but it is best not to expect to come across some charming spot in the middle of nowhere. If you want to get away from the major centers, make reservations well in advance.

Hotels in the Very Expensive bracket provide comfort and services to match those in other Italian regions; they are usually older, more established hotels. In the Expensive and Moderate range, you'll find newer hotels built to cater to the increased tourist trade of the past 20 years. Chains, such as Jolly Hotels, are predictable but reliable. Inexpensive establishments are usually family-run and offer a basic level of comfort: Although the bathroom will be clean, it will probably also be down the hall.

Highly recommended lodgings are indicated by a star ★.

Category	Cost*
Very Expensive	over 300,000 lire
Expensive	150,000–300,000 lire
Moderate	90,000–150,000 lire
Inexpensive	under 90,000 lire

All prices are for a standard double room for two, including service and 9% IVA (19% for luxury establishments).

Agrigento **Caprice.** The specialty of this popular restaurant in the temple
Dining area is meat prepared alla brace, although there is also a good
selection of seafood, particularly pesce spada. The waiters are
proud to explain some of the less familiar entries on the wine
list, which is relatively extensive. *Via Panoramica dei Templi
51, tel. 0922/26469. Reservations advised. Dress: casual. AE,
DC, MC, V. Closed Fri. and July 1–15. Moderate.*

Taverna Mosè. This restaurant is popular with sightseers from
nearby temples, so it can get busy in the early evening, when it
becomes too dark for temple exploring. The atmosphere is bustling, with waiters shouting orders at each other and at the
kitchen. The house specialties are homemade sausages and
grilled fish, and the wine list is comprehensive. *Contrada San
Biagio, tel. 0922/26778. No reservations. Dress: casual. No
credit cards. Closed Mon. Moderate.*

Vigneto. Unless you make reservations at this popular restaurant, it's best to arrive early to snag one of the good tables on
the terrace, which has a memorable view of the temples. The
menu changes, with daily specials reflecting whatever is in season or is freshest at the fish market. *Arrosti* (roast meats) are
always a good bet. *Via Cavaleri Magazzeni 11, tel. 0922/
414319. Reservations advised. Dress: casual. AE, MC, V.
Closed Tues. and Nov. 1–30. Moderate.*

Lodging **Jolly dei Templi.** Guests travel 8 kilometers (5 miles) southeast
of town to Villagio Mose to stay in this member of the Jolly hotel chain. Rooms are large, bright, and airy, and if there's a
sense of having seen it all before, you probably have—in one of
the other Jolly hotels or in any well-equipped U.S. motel. That
is the price to pay for what are always comfortable, hassle-free
accommodations. The Pirandello restaurant is excellent, so you
won't have to head into Agrigento to dine. *Parco Angeli,
Villagio Mose, tel. 0922/606144, fax 0922/606685. 144 rooms
with bath. Facilities: bar, restaurant, pool. AE, DC, MC, V.
Expensive.*

★ **Villa Athena.** There is much demand for this well-furnished former villa, so make reservations as early as possible. Many
rooms—they're all different—have terraces looking out on the
large gardens and the swimming pool. The temple zone is an
easy walk from the hotel, and there is a convivial atmosphere in
the bar, where a multinational crowd swaps stories and advice.
*Via dei Templi 33, tel. 0922/596288, fax 0922/402180. 41 rooms
with bath. Facilities: bar, restaurant, pool, garden. AE, DC,
MC, V. Expensive.*

Castelmola **Il Faro.** Castelmola is a small village above Taormina, and as
Dining you dine in this family-run country restaurant, sitting under a
★ grape arbor, you have an excellent view of the wild cliffs and
sea. Meat dishes are recommended alla brace, particularly
pollo (chicken) and *coniglio* (rabbit). Piera and Francesco, the
owners, provide an antipasto with homegrown vegetables.
Start your meal with *bruschetta all' ortolana* (country bread
toasted with olive oil, topped with tomatoes and onions). *Via
Rotabile, Contrada Petralia, tel. 0942/28193. Reservations advised. Dress: casual. No credit cards. Closed Wed. Inexpensive.*

Catania **Costa Azzura.** This seafood restaurant is in the Ognina district,
Dining just north of the center and on the way to the Taormina road.
★ Reserve a table on the veranda by the edge of the sea. There are
good views of the harbor. The *fritto misto* (mixed seafood grill)
can be ordered as an antipasto or a main course, and the pesce
spada steak is a simple classic—served grilled with a large slice
of lemon. *Via De Cristofaro 4, tel. 095/494920. Reservations
advised. Jacket and tie required. AE, DC, MC, V. Closed Mon.
and Aug. Expensive.*

Pagano. This restaurant, located behind the Hotel Excelsior,
has been around a long time (since the 1950s) and remains a favorite with locals for genuine Catanese cooking. Seafood is the
specialty, but it's the unpretentious kind that won't send the
check into the stratosphere. Try *insalata di pólipo* (octopus
salad) as a starter and then *sarde* or *acciughe* (sardines or anchovies) in a variety of sauces. Like the sober, rather dated decor, the service is formal. *Via de Roberto 37, tel. 095/537045,
Reservations advised. Dress: casual. AE, DC, V. Closed Sat.
and Aug. Moderate.*

Lodging **Excelsior.** Ask for a room facing Piazza Verga, a neat tree-lined
square in this quiet but central district of Catania. The hotel is
about 30 years old; renovations in 1981 added air-conditioning
and sound-insulating windows to all rooms. The rooftop garden
is one of Catania's most chic meeting places, and the American
Bar should provide solace to anyone pining for a Manhattan. *Piazza Verga 39, tel. 095/537071, fax 095/537015. 167 rooms with
bath. Facilities: 2 bars, rooftop garden, restaurant, garage.
AE, DC, MC, V. Expensive.*

Jolly Hotel Trinacria. This member of the Jolly chain dates from
1960 but has been given a face-lift since then. Facilities are
modern and comfortable—radio, air-conditioning, phone, and
even piped-in music—but the rooms themselves are smaller
than those in most other Jolly hotels. It also diverges from other Jolly hotels in having a center-of-town location. *Piazza Trento 13, tel. 095/316933, fax 095/316832. 159 rooms with bath.
Facilities: bar, restaurant, parking. AE, DC, MC, V. Expensive.*

Cefalù **La Brace.** There is a lively atmosphere in this bistro-style res-
Dining taurant located near the cathedral in the center of town. Graceful ceiling arches and rustic walls lend an informal air that
makes it popular with tourists. Stick to the excellent grills and
save room for the homemade desserts, such as cassata Siciliana. *Via Venticinque Novembre 10, tel. 0921/23570. Reservations advised. Dress: casual. AE, DC, V. Closed Mon. and
Dec.–Jan. Moderate.*

Gabbiano. The name, meaning "seagull," is appropriate for a
harborside restaurant decorated with a nautical theme and

specializing in seafood. The house specialties are *involtini* (swordfish rolls) and spaghetti *alla marinara* (with a spicy sauce of tomatoes, garlic, and onions). *Via Lungomare Giardina 17, tel. 0921/21495. Reservations advised. Dress: casual but neat. AE, DC, MC, V. Closed Wed. Inexpensive.*

Lodging
★ **Baia del Capitano.** The peaceful district of Mazzaforno, about five kilometers (three miles) outside town, is the setting for this handsome hotel, which has a surprising number of extras, considering its size. The building is less than 20 years old, with major renovations in 1985, but it blends in with the local-style homes nearby. The colorful gardens, extending to the surrounding olive groves, are ideal for a quiet read or an afternoon siesta in the shade. A good sandy beach is an easy walk away, but many guests choose to stay by the pool and have drinks on the terrace. The rooms are large and quiet. *Contrada Mazzaforno, Mazzaforno, tel. 0921/20003, fax 0921/20163. 39 rooms with bath or shower. Facilities: pool, game room, terrace, garden, bar, restaurant, tennis court. DC, V. Closed Nov.–Mar. 15. Moderate.*

Le Calette. This seaside hotel is popular with Scandinavians and Germans, who know a good place to sunbathe when they see one. The modern hotel is surrounded by gardens on the three sides that don't face the sea, and guests can use the private beach. The rooms are bright and airy; those facing the sea escape the hot Sicilian sun. The Caldura district, where Le Calette is located, is a little more than a mile from the center of town. *Contrada Caldura, tel. 0921/24144, fax 0921/23688. 50 rooms with bath or shower. Facilities: pool, bar, restaurant, private beach. AE, DC, MC, V. Closed Nov.–Apr. Moderate.*

★ **Kalura.** Caldura is the setting for this modern hotel, which shares the advantages of Le Calette but is a bit harder to reach without a car. Taxis from Cefalù take only a few minutes, though. The Kalura is on a small promontory, making it something of a retreat. Sports facilities keep you from getting too sedentary, and the private beach is ideal for swimming. Most rooms have views of the sea, and the decor is bright and cheerful. *Contrada Caldura, Caldura, tel. 0921/21354, fax 0921/20548. 75 rooms with bath or shower. Facilities: tennis court, pool, private beach, bar, restaurant. MC, V. Closed Nov.–Feb. Moderate.*

Erice
Dining
★ **La Taverna di Re Aceste.** The name of this popular restaurant refers to Acestus, the first king of Erice. The house specialty, *Cuscus Aceste* (a spicy Arab-influenced semolina-and-seafood mixture) is in his honor, as are the murals along the walls. The chef also has a special pesto (pine-nut pasta sauce) dish made with wild herbs. Try the grilled fish, but ask for the price, since you'll be paying by weight, not per order. The waiters are helpful and will guide you through the daily specials and the wine list. *Viale Conte Pepoli, tel. 0923/869084. Reservations advised. Dress: casual but neat. AE, DC, MC, V. Closed Wed. and Nov. Moderate.*

Lodging
Ermione. Spectacular views and cool breezes are the rewards for making your way by car or bus 2,500 feet up from coastal Trapani to this '60s hotel overlooking the Tyrrhenian Sea. Nearly every room has a good view, although some would say that the terrace bar has the most panoramic vista. The hotel restaurant is popular locally, with fish couscous a standout. *Via Pineta Comunale, tel. 0923/869138. 46 rooms with bath or*

shower. *Facilities: bar, restaurant, terrace, outdoor pool. AE, DC, MC, V. Moderate.*

★ **Moderno.** Local craft work and some antiques decorate the gracious rooms of this intimate and well-run hotel on the cobblestone streets of the medieval town. Some rooms are in the modern annex. The main building, with a fire blazing in the lounge in winter, is one attraction; the restaurant, serving seafood pastas and homemade desserts, is another. Ask for a room facing the sea. *Via Vittorio Emanuele 67, tel. 0923/869300, fax 0923/869139. 40 rooms with bath or shower. Facilities: bar, tavern, restaurant, terrace. AE, DC, MC, V. Moderate.*

Messina
Dining
★

Alberto. Many visitors to Messina make it a priority to reserve a table at this deluxe restaurant and are willing to splurge even if they're budgeting. If you're adventurous, and not too worried about the cost, ask the waiter to order for you: You'll get a succession of courses linked by a common theme of seafood. À la carte items are also delicious, particularly the *fettucine con ortaggi e crostacei* (fresh pasta with peas, celery, and shellfish) and the *pesce spada involtini* (swordfish rolls). Have some vintage Marsala with one of the rich homemade desserts. *Via Ghibellina 95, tel. 090/710711. Reservations required. Jacket and tie required. AE, DC, V. Closed Sun. and Aug. Expensive.*

Pippo Nunnari. Traditional Sicilian cooking is complemented by the refined decor, with antiques and rich fabrics. A favorite Sicilian appetizer is a selection of *arancini* (rice balls filled with meat or cheese); you can also have the *risotto di mare*, whose ingredients change with each day's catch of fish. Don't be embarrassed about ordering the *bistecca* (steak) here: It's charcoal-grilled and renowned locally. Pippo has a specialty shop next door—ideal for picnic supplies. *Via Ugo Bassi 157, tel. 090/293–8584. Reservations advised. Dress: casual but neat. AE, MC, V. Closed Mon. and July 1–15. Moderate–Expensive.*

Monreale
Dining

La Botte. It's worth the short drive or inexpensive taxi fare to reach this good-value restaurant, which features local specialties. Dine alfresco on daily specials, such as spaghetti *alla brigantesca* (with fresh tuna, capers, olives, tomato, parsley, and white wine), or regular favorites, such as stuffed involtini. Local wines are a good bet. *Contrada Lenzitti 416, S186, tel. 091/414051. No reservations. Dress: casual but neat. AE, DC, V. Closed lunch weekdays except by reservation and in June. Closed Mon. and July–Aug. Moderate.*

Noto
Dining
★

Trieste. This bustling restaurant is located by the edge of the Giardino Publico at the eastern end of town. Normally expensive specialties, such as *aragosta* (lobster), are available here at reasonable rates. Seafood is featured, but consider starting with spaghetti alla Norma. The *fritti misti* is served with fried shrimp or *calamari* (squid). Carnivores should order the *vitello* (veal). *Via Napoli 17, tel. 0931/835495. No reservations. Dress: casual. No credit cards. Closed Mon. Inexpensive.*

Palazzolo Acreide
Dining

Da Alfredo. This one-man show (Alfredo is the owner/chef) is located on one of the most attractive streets of this Baroque town between Caltagirone and Siracusa. Specialties depend on the season, the availability of ingredients at the local markets, and the whims of Alfredo himself. Homemade pasta, such as tubular penne and cheese-filled ravioli, are specialties, and the sauces are hearty and spicy. *Via Duca d'Aosta 27, tel. 0931/ 883266. No reservations. Dress: casual. AE. Closed Wed. and Sept. Inexpensive.*

Palermo
Dining
★

Charleston. You'll feel pampered by the discreet service and elegant surroundings in this famous Palermo restaurant located on a quiet square in the heart of the city. Impeccably dressed waiters coast effortlessly through the high-ceiling rooms, offering help with the extensive menu and wine list. Specialties run the gamut of Sicilian and international dishes, with an emphasis on seafood, in keeping with the cuisine of the island. Try the *spaghetti all'aragosta*, with its delicious lobster sauce, or the *pesce spada arrosta* (roast swordfish), but leave room for the sweet, rich house dessert, *torta Charleston*. The whole restaurant operation moves five miles north to Mondello from June 16 to September 25: The Mondello premises occupy a pavilion on the sea. *Charleston (Sept. 26–June 15), Piazza Ungheria 30, tel. 091/321366; Charleston le Terrazze (June 16–Sept. 25) Viale Regina Elena, Mondello, tel. 091/450171. Reservations required. Jacket and tie required. AE, DC, MC, V. Closed Sun. Expensive.*

★ **Da Renato.** There is an excellent view of the harbor from this top-quality restaurant along the sea road toward Cefalù. It's enough out of the way to make it the insider's choice, and the clientele consists mainly of well-heeled locals who know their way around a good seafood menu. *Frutti di mare* (mixed seafoods) makes a good antipasto, and the *zuppa di mare* (fish soup) is hearty enough to be a meal in itself. Grills are also recommended. *Via Messina Marina 224, tel. 091/630–2881. Reservations advised. Dress: casual but neat. AE, DC. Closed Wed. and Aug. 15–25. Expensive.*

Gourmand's. A chic clientele frequents this modern restaurant, with its high-tech decor (lots of metal and primary colors) and nouvelle cuisine-influenced menu. Pesce spada *affumicato* (smoked swordfish) goes well with a bottle of local Regaleali. Gourmand's is in the northern end of Palermo, near the port. *Via Libertà 37E, tel. 091/323431. Reservations required. Jacket and tie required. AE, DC, MC, V. Closed Sun. Expensive.*

Lo Scudiero. The antipasto and the *assaggini* (sample portions) of the various pastas give you a delicious introduction to Sicilian cuisine: The courteous waiters are also ambassadors for local cooking. Lo Scudiero has a subdued atmosphere, which will be appreciated in this noisy city. Try some of the nonseafood items on the menu—the meat dishes are excellent, especially the bistecca. *Fritti misti* (mixed fry) contains meats and seasonal vegetables. *Via Turati 7, tel. 091/581628. Reservations advised. Dress: casual. AE, DC, MC, V. Closed Sun. Moderate.*

Strascinu. The specialty in this informal and busy restaurant is *pasta con sarde*, the famous Arab-Sicilian blend of fresh sardines, wild fennel fronds, sultanas, and pine nuts. *Viale Regione Siciliana 2286, tel. 091/401292. Reservations advised. Dress: casual but neat. AE, DC. Closed Mon. and July 15–31. Moderate.*

Antica Focacceria San Francesco. On the square in front of the church of San Francesco, off Corso Vittorio Emanuele in the heart of Palermo, this place is an institution, as you can see from the turn-of-the-century wooden cabinets and fixtures of what is still a neighborhood bakery. But it also bakes and fries the snacks that locals love—and from which you can well make an inexpensive meal. Try *arancini* (rice croquettes) and *panelle* (chick-pea fritters) or pizza right out of the oven. You can sit at marble-topped tables while you eat, or take food out if you wish. Beverages, including wine and beer, are available. *Via Paternostro 58, tel. 091/320264. No reservations. Dress: casual. No credit cards. Closed Mon. Inexpensive.*

★ **Shangai.** There is nothing Chinese about this Palermo institution in the busy Vucciria market. It's on a terrace above the market (the source of all the ingredients): Look down and order your fish from the displays below, and it will be hoisted up in a wicker basket. The atmosphere is jovial and frantic, with lots of teasing and shouting. Fritto misto (usually fish here) is always a good bet. *Piazza Vicolo Mezzani 34, tel. 091/589702. No reservations. Dress: casual. No credit cards. Closed Sun. Inexpensive.*

Toto. A neighbor of the Shangai in the bustling Vucciria market, Toto is one of the plainest trattorias in town, serving fresh fish in a variety of ways, including *alla brace, fritto misto,* and in *zuppa di pesce*. Ask Toto to sing—he may even do magic tricks. At times this place makes even the Shangai look staid. *Via dei Coltellieri 5, no phone. No reservations. Dress: casual. No credit cards. Open lunch only. Closed Sun. Inexpensive.*

Lodging **Villa Igiea.** A short taxi ride through some rough-looking dis-
★ tricts of Palermo takes you to this oasis of luxury and comfort, situated in its own tropical garden at the edge of the bay. It's difficult to imagine that you're on the outskirts of Palermo as you meander through the grounds, which include an ancient Greek temple at the water's edge. The large rooms (many with terraces overlooking the gardens and the sea) are furnished individually, the most attractive with a Liberty (Italian Art Nouveau) flavor. Spacious lobbies and public rooms give onto a terrace with its own restaurant. Sports facilities help make this elegant villa a self-contained enclave in frenetic Palermo. *Via Belmonte 43, tel. 091/543744, fax 091/547654. 120 rooms with bath. Facilities: terrace bar, American cocktail bar, restaurant, tennis court, pool. AE, DC, MC, V. Very Expensive.*

Grande Albergo e delle Palme. There is a faded charm about this *grande dame*, whose public rooms suggest the elegant life of Palermo society before the First World War, when tea dances and balls were held here. Guest rooms are uneven—some are charming period pieces stuffed with antiques and heavy fabrics, others are dark and cramped. There is an American-style cocktail bar and a rooftop terrace with good views of Palermo. *Via Roma 396, tel. 091/583933, fax 091/331545. 187 rooms with bath or shower. Facilities: restaurant, piano bar, rooftop terrace, parking. AE, DC, MC, V. Expensive.*

Jolly del Foro Italico. This hotel lives up to the Jolly chain's reputation for good, straightforward accommodations with functional decor. The advantage of this particular hotel is its location (about 500 yards from the train station) facing the sea. The rooms are comfortable and quiet, thanks to the extra-thick windows. Some rooms overlook the palm-fringed pool—an ideal spot for a cool drink. *Foro Italico 22, tel. 091/616–5090, fax 091/616–1441. 290 rooms with bath or shower. Facilities: bar, restaurant, pool, private park, parking. AE, DC, MC, V. Expensive.*

★ **Mondello Palace.** The beach resort of Mondello is just north of Palermo and is a perennial favorite because of its cleaner air and less rushed atmosphere. The Mondello Palace is the leading hotel in the resort, making the best use of its location near the beach. The private beach has cabins and changing rooms for the use of Mondello Palace guests, and most of the hotel rooms have balconies with views over the sea. The rooms are well equipped and large, with bright fabrics and large beds. In summer there's a choice of two popular restaurants—one in the hotel and one on the nearby wharf. *Viale Principe di Scalea, Mondello Lido, tel. 091/450001, fax 091/450657. 83 rooms with bath or shower. Facilities: bar, restaurant, pool, gardens. AE, V. Expensive.*

Sole. The central location, on one of Palermo's main thoroughfares, is an advantage for exploring the city but can make for some noise in the rooms facing the street. Request a room with soundproofing and air-conditioning. The rooms are spacious and well equipped, and the roof garden offers good views of Palermo. *Corso Vittorio Emanuele 291, tel. 091/581811, fax 091/611-0182. 154 rooms, most with bath or shower. Facilities: bar, restaurant. AE, MC, V. Moderate.*

Piazza Armerina
Dining

Centrale da Totò. This reliable trattoria is an easy walk from the Villa Romana di Casale and is often busy with sightseers from the Roman ruins. The emphasis is on a family clientele, rather than intimate or expense-account dining, and the portions reflect this *mangia, mangia* outlook. Try the *pappardelle alla Centrale*, a rich, filling pasta dish made with tomato sauce and fresh vegetables. *Via Mazzini 29, tel. 0935/680153. No reservations. Dress: casual. AE, V. Closed Mon. Inexpensive.*

Siracusa
Dining

Archimede. The antipasto misti should whet your appetite for the predominantly seafood menu of this small establishment in the Old Town. *Risotto di mare* (with seafood) and *pesce spada* are specialties, but the menu veers away from seafood when game is in season. Order the coniglio if you see it on the menu. *Via Gemmellaro 8, tel. 0931/69701. Reservations advised. Dress: casual. AE, V. Closed Sun. and July. Moderate.*

Arlecchino. A bustling bohemian atmosphere pervades this restaurant, located midway between the archaeological zone and the Città Vecchia (Old Town). It's popular with artists and students, always a sign of good value. The Palermo-born proprietor serves specialties from his hometown, such as risotto *ai granchi* (with crab) and homemade cassata for dessert. Try for a table on the terrace. *Via dei Tolomei 5, tel. 0931/66386. No reservations. Dress: casual. AE, DC, V. Closed Sun. eve., Mon., and Aug. Moderate.*

★ **Ionico.** Enjoy seaside dining in the coastal Santa Lucia district. Chef/proprietor Pasquale Giudice cooks meals to order or will suggest a specialty from a selection of market-fresh ingredients. Try the pasta *con acciughe e il pan grattato* (fresh pasta in an anchovy sauce). *Riviera Dionisio il Grande 194, tel. 0931/65540. Reservations advised. Dress: casual. AE, DC, MC, V. Closed Tues. and Aug. 15–31. Moderate.*

Minosse. You'll find this small, old-fashioned restaurant in the heart of Siracusa's Città Vecchia. Fish is the specialty, and it comes broiled, baked, stuffed, and skewered. For an introduction to the local seafood, try the *antipasto misto di frutti di mare*. Ask for the daily special as your main course, or try the *pesce spada alla brace*. The *zuppa di pesce* is a local favorite. *Via Mirabella 6, tel. 0931/66366. No reservations. Dress: casual. AE, MC, V. Closed Mon. Moderate.*

Lodging   **Jolly Hotel.** The rooms are uniformly comfortable in this member of the Jolly hotel chain, Italy's answer to Holiday Inns. The big advantage, apart from knowing that the plugs work and the rooms are soundproofed, is the location. The hotel is less than a quarter mile from the train station and within easy walking distance of the archaeological zone. *Corso Gelone 45, tel. 0931/461111, fax 0931/461126. 100 rooms with bath or shower. Facilities: bar, restaurant, parking, garden. AE, DC, MC, V. Expensive.*

Motel Agip. This standard motel, with modern comforts (color TV and minibar in all rooms) is across the street from the archaeological zone. The rooms are bright and clean, and the restaurant serves some local specialties as well as classic hotel food. *Viale Teracati 30, tel. 0931/463232, fax 0931/67115. Facilities: bar, restaurant, parking. AE, DC, MC, V. Expensive.*

Taormina   **Delfino.** This seaside restaurant is across the road from the ca-
Dining   ble car station in Mazzarò, to the east of Taormina itself. Sea-
★   food takes pride of place here, from hearty starters, such as the zuppa di pesce or *risotto marinara* (with a spicy tomato-based sauce), to main courses, such as *gamberetti* (shrimp) alla brace. Arrive early or reserve to get one of the best tables overlooking the sea. *Via Nazionale, Mazzarò, tel. 0942/23004. Dress: casual but neat. Reservations advised. AE, DC, MC, V. Closed Nov.–Mar. 15. Moderate–Expensive.*

Giova Rosy Senior. One of Taormina's oldest restaurants, the Giova Rosy Senior is also known for its good-value menu and its central location, in the heart of Taormina. It faces the Palazzo Corvaia and the Teatro Comunale and is just a short walk from the Greek amphitheater. Try for an outside table. Involtini di pesce spada are excellent. *Corso Umberto 38, tel. 0942/24411. Reservations required. Dress: casual. AE, DC, MC, V. Closed Mon. and Jan.–Feb. Moderate.*

Lodging   **San Domenico Palace.** The panoramic views from this con-
★   verted 15th-century convent will stay in your mind long after you're gone. Luxury and comfort are bywords in this deluxe hotel, which has managed to sneak a number of unobtrusive 20th-century comforts into its furnishings (such as wheelchair access and climate control). The essentially Renaissance flavor remains, however, from the cloisters to the chapel, which is now a bar. The rooms in the front of the hotel have sweeping views of the Taormina Bay; those in back look out over the gardens, with Etna visible in the distance. The rooms are decorated with antiques and are brimming with fresh flowers. *Piazza San Domenico 5, tel. 0942/23701, fax 0942/625506. 101 rooms with bath. Facilities: 2 restaurants, 2 bars, terrace, gardens, pool, piano bar. AE, DC, MC, V. Very Expensive.*

Jolly Diodoro. Located high on a cliff near the Greek amphitheater, this Jolly hotel shares the view with the much more expensive San Domenico Palace. Another departure from the sometimes functional Jolly format is the relaxing and colorful garden, where you can have a drink and watch the play of light over the sea. *Via Bagnoli Croce 75, tel. 0942/23312, fax 0942/23391. 103 rooms with bath or shower. Facilities: restaurant, bar, pool, garden parking. AE, DC, MC, V. Expensive.*

Villa Fiorita. This converted private home near the Greek amphitheater has excellent views of the coast from nearly every room. The rooms vary in size and furnishings, but most are bright and colorful, with large windows that let in the sea breezes. Prices are reasonable for a hotel with a swimming pool and small garden. *Via Pirandello 39, tel. 0942/24122, fax 0942/ 625967. 24 rooms, most with bath. Facilities: garden, pool, garage. AE, MC, V. Closed Jan.–Easter. Inexpensive–Moderate.*

Trapani **P & G.** Couscous is a specialty of this small, popular restaurant
Dining on a quiet street between the train station and the Villa
★ Margherita. The couscous features fish in summer and meat in winter. A mixed grill of meats in a zesty orange sauce will revive any appetite suffering from fish fatigue. Wash it all down with a bottle of Donnafugata, a good white from the Rallo vineyards at Marsala. *Via Spalti 1, tel. 0923/547701. Reservations advised. Dress: neat but casual. AE, DC, MC, V. Closed Sun. and Aug. Moderate.*

The Arts

Opera **Teatro Bellini** (Piazza Bellini, Catania, tel. 095/312020) hosts an opera season from October to May, attracting top singers and productions to the birthplace of the great operatic composer Vincenzo Bellini.

In May and June of 1994, Siracusa's impressive **Teatro Greco** will be the setting for performances of classical drama and comedy; the festival is held in even-numbered years only. For information, call 0931/67415.

Concerts The churches and theaters of Taormina are the venues for the summer festival of **classical music,** held each year from May to September. For information, call 0942/23751.

Events The **Palio dei Normani,** a medieval tournament with participants dressed in 14th-century fashion, takes place on August 13 in Piazza Armerina.

From July 11 to 15, Palermo stages a **street fair** in honor of its patron saint, Santa Rosalia. There are fireworks displays in the evenings.

Messina stages a **folklore parade** of huge traditional effigies called Giganti, each year on August 13 and 14.

Epiphany (Jan. 6) is celebrated with Byzantine rites and a procession of townspeople in local costume through the streets of Piana degli Albanesi, near Palermo. The village, 24 kilometers (15 miles) south of the island's capital, is named for the Albanian immigrants who first settled there, bringing with them the Byzantine Catholic rites.

Theater Taormina's **Greco-Roman Theater** is the setting for regular theatrical performances from July to September. For information, call 0942/23220.

Palermo's **Teatro Biondo** (tel. 091/588755) is Sicily's foremost theater, featuring a winter season of plays from November to May.

Cinema Taormina hosts an international **film festival** each July, held in the grand setting of the Roman amphitheater. For information, call 0942/23220.

17 Sardinia

The second-largest island in the Mediterranean (just smaller than Sicily), Sardinia is about 180 kilometers (112 miles) from mainland Italy and very much off the beaten track. A Phoenician stronghold in ancient times and later a Spanish dominion, Sardinia doesn't seem typically "Italian" in its color and flavor. It lies just a bit too far from the mainland—from imperial and papal Rome and from the palaces of the Savoy dynasty—to be transformed by the events that forged a national character. Yet Giuseppe Garibaldi, the charismatic national hero who led his troops in fervid campaigns to unify Italy in the mid–19th century, chose to spend his last years in relative isolation on the small island of Caprera, just off the coast of Sardinia.

Although Sardinia (Sardegna in Italian) is now less than an hour by air and only several hours by boat from mainland Italy, it is removed from the mainstream of tourism except for a brief two-month period in the summer, when vacationing Italians take its beautiful coasts and clean waters by storm. This is a good reason not to visit Sardinia in July or August. May and October are the best touring months. In June and September the coasts are not too crowded, and ribbons of sandy beaches welcome sun-worshippers. These are the best months if you want to combine sightseeing with sunbathing. Winter in the north of the island is cold and rainy but is mild and generally sunny in the south. The interior is *never* crowded; Italian tourists in Sardinia come for the sea, not for rugged and deserted mountain scenery.

Sardinia closely resembles Corsica, the French island across the 16-kilometer (10-mile)–wide windswept Strait of Bonifacio to the north. A dense bush, or *macchia*, barely penetrable in some districts, covers large areas. The terrain is rough, like the short, sturdy shepherds you see in the highlands—impassive figures engaged in one of the few gainful occupations that the stony land allows. Lively flocks of sheep and goats are familiar features in the Sardinian landscape, just as their meat and cheese are staples of the island's cuisine. Aside from the chic opulence of the Costa Smeralda, there's little sophistication in Sardinia. The sprawling cities of Cagliari and Sassari have a distinctly provincial air. Newer hotels may seem a little old-fashioned, and hotels—of any vintage—are hard to find inland. There's little traffic on the roads, and trains, buses, and people in general move at a gentle pace. There are hamlets where women swathed in black shawls and long, full skirts look with suspicion upon strangers passing through. Sardinians are courteous but remote, perhaps because of their innate dignity.

Like mainland Italians, the Sardinians are of varied origin. On the northwest coast, fine traceries of ironwork around a balcony underscore the Spanish influence. In the northeast, the inhabitants boast Genoese or Pisan ancestry, and the headlands display the ruined fortresses of the ancient duchy of Malaspina on the Italian mainland. As you explore the southern coast, you'll come upon the physiognomies, customs, dialects, placenames, and holy buildings of the Turks, the Moors, the Phoenicians, the Austrians, and the mainland Italians. If there are any pure Sards—or Sardinians—left, perhaps they can be found in the south-central mountains, south of Nuoro, under the 6,000-foot crests of the Gennargentu massif, in the rugged country still ironically called Barbagia, "Land of Strangers."

People visit Sardinia for landscapes, rather than cathedrals or monuments; for easy-going excursions with plenty of detours, rather than a highly organized itinerary; for a low-key entertainment scene that highlights folklore, rather than brilliant or expensive nightlife. And, speaking of expense, the cost of living on Sardinia, as on most islands, is somewhat higher than on the mainland. On the other hand, if you're willing to rough it, you'll find low-cost lodgings at modest inns along your way.

Sardinia is not as large as some other regions, but its mountainous terrain makes some drives through deserted country seem very long, indeed. The main highway linking Cagliari with Sassari was begun in 1820 by the Savoy ruler Carlo Felice; designated Highway 131, but still referred to as the Carlo Felice Highway (after its founder) by the islanders, it heads northwest through the fertile Campidano plain for 216 kilometers (134 miles) to Sassari. The entire island is about 260 kilometers (162 miles) from north to south, and roughly 120 kilometers (75 miles) across. A fairly comprehensive tour taking in the coastline and interior can be accomplished in five to seven days.

Essential Information

Important Addresses and Numbers

Tourist Information
Alghero (Piazza Porta Terra 9, tel. 079/979054).
Cagliari (Piazza Matteotti 9, tel. 070/669255; Elmas Airport, tel. 070/240200).
Nuoro (Piazza Italia 19, tel. 0784/30083).
Olbia (Via Catello Piro, tel. 0789/21453; City Hall, Golfo degli Aranci, tel. 0789/21453; Costa Smeralda Airport, tel. 0789/52600).
Oristano (Via Cagliari 276, tel. 0783/74191).
Sassari (Via Brigate Sassari 19, tel. 079/233534).

Emergencies
Police. Tel. 112, 113.
Hospital. In Cagliari, tel. 070/60181.
Ambulance. In Cagliari, tel. 070/656979.
Late-Night Pharmacy. On a rota basis: Information on current schedules is pinned up on any pharmacy door or can be obtained by phoning 192.

Travel Agencies
Cagliari (Viaggi Orru, Via Roma 95, tel. 070/657954).

Car Rental
Cagliari. *Avis* (Via Sonnino 87, tel. 070/668128; airport, tel. 070/240081). *Hertz* (Piazza Matteotti 1, tel. 070/668105; airport, tel. 070/240037).
Olbia. *Avis* (Via Genova 67, tel. 0789/22420; airport, tel. 0789/69540). *Hertz* (Via Regina Elena 34, tel. 0789/21274; airport, tel. 0789/69389).
Sassari. *Avis* (Via Mazzini 2, tel. 079/235547). *Hertz* (Via IV Novembre 16, tel. 079/280083).

Arriving and Departing by Plane

Airports and Airlines
Alitalia and Alisarda connect Rome, Milan, Pisa, and other cities on the mainland and in southern Europe with Sardinia. Flying is by far the fastest and easiest way to get to the island. The Rome–Cagliari flight takes about an hour. Sardinia's major airports are at Cagliari and Alghero, with another smaller one, at Olbia, providing access to the Costa Smeralda.

The **Cagliari** airport at Elmas is about 6 kilometers (4 miles) from the center of town, and there is a regular bus service from the airport to Piazza Matteotti, in front of the train station. For information, call 070/240047.

Alghero's Fertilia airport is 13 kilometers (8 miles) from the city. A bus links the airport with the air terminal on Corso Vittorio Emanuele II. For information, call 079/935033.

The **Costa Smeralda** airport is 4 kilometers (2 miles) outside Olbia. For information, call 0789/52600.

Arriving and Departing by Boat

Large modern ferries run by Tirrenia Lines, Navarma Lines, and the FS (Italian State Railways), connect the island with the mainland. **Tirrenia** (tel. 06/474-2041) sails to several ports in Sardinia from Genoa, Civitavecchia, Naples, Palermo, and Trapani. **Navarma** (tel. 0565/918101) transports passengers and cars between Livorno and Olbia. **FS** ferries carry trains as well as passengers and cars; they sail from Civitavecchia to Golfo Aranci, near Olbia. For information, call 0766/232273 on the mainland, or 0789/46800 in Golfo Aranci. The Civitavecchia–Olbia/Golfo Aranci run takes about eight hours and there are overnight sailings. Depending on the season, the service is scheduled two or three times a week; reservations are essential in the summer.

Getting Around

By Car The best way to get around Sardinia is to drive. The roads are generally in good condition, but bear in mind that such roadside conveniences as gas stations and refreshment stands are infrequent on some routes, especially in the east. Cars may be taken on board most of the ferry lines connecting Sardinia with the mainland.

By Train There are fairly good connections between Olbia, Cagliari, Sassari, and Oristano. You can reach Nuoro via Macomer; Alghero is reached via Sassari. Service on the few other local lines is infrequent and slow. The fastest train between Olbia and Cagliari takes more than four hours. A local train connects Golfo Aranci, the FS port for the train ferry, with Olbia and takes 20 minutes.

By Bus A network of buses links Cagliari with the other towns of Sardinia, but the service is infrequent and even slower than the corresponding train connections. The heart of the Sardinian bus system is the **Stazione Autolinee** in Cagliari's Piazza Matteotti, across the square from the main tourist office. You can pick up a schedule and route map from either of these sources; if you can't find a convenient bus service, you can go to the west side of the square to the main train station. City buses in Cagliari and Sassari operate on the same system as those on the mainland: Buy your ticket first, at a tobacco shop or machine, and cancel it on the bus by slipping it into the machine until the ticket is punched. Fares are low for these local services, about 1,100 lire.

Guided Tours

Orientation The following guided tours are good introductions to Sardinia; all include travel from the Italian mainland, as well as travel and accommodations on Sardinia. They should be booked through a travel agent or the Italian National Tourist Office (*see* Before You Go in Chapter 1).

Chiariva offers two group tours of Sardinia by bus with guide. A nine-day tour leaves from Genoa; an eight-day tour departs from Rome. Both operate from April to September.

Aviatour has a similar eight-day tour leaving from either Milan or Rome. The tour also runs from April to September only.

Appian Line can arrange a fly-drive package on the Costa Smeralda; transportation is by air, the rental car is picked up at the airport at Olbia. Accommodations are in good, but not outlandishly expensive, hotels on this famous coastline for the rich.

Exploring Sardinia

The best way to see Sardinia is by car because driving is the only way to travel to and through the island's most interesting sights. Local transportation is not geared to the needs of tourists, so you can see more in less time if you have a car. If you don't, your best bet is to establish yourself in one of the larger towns and make excursions to as many attractions as time and schedules allow. We have divided the country into three exploring tours, each of which has at least one town large enough to act as a touring base.

Tour 1 covers Sardinia's capital, Cagliari, and the surrounding area along the south coast. This is a good introduction to the rugged countryside and fascinating archaeology of the island. All the attractions are within easy reach of Cagliari.

Tour 2 begins the northward exploration of Sardinia, heading into rural west-central districts where rare species of wildlife share the rocky uplands with sturdy medieval churches and mysterious *nuraghi*—ancient stone citadels left by prehistoric people. Oristano, the medieval center of Sardinian nationalism, is on the island's west coast and makes a good center for exploring this region.

The last tour continues northward after making an eastward loop into the real hinterland of the Barbagia region, where traditional Sardinian customs are maintained in remote hilltop villages. This area provides a contrast with sunny Alghero, the Spanish-influenced port on the west coast, and the Costa Smeralda, the luxury resort complex developed by the Aga Khan on the northeast corner of Sardinia.

Tour 1: Cagliari and Environs

Numbers in the margin correspond to points of interest on the Sardinia and Cagliari maps.

❶ A good place to start exploring Sardinia is **Cagliari** in the south, reached by plane or boat from the mainland. The island's capital, it has impressive Italianate architecture and churches in a variety of styles; it's clear that medieval Spanish conquerors

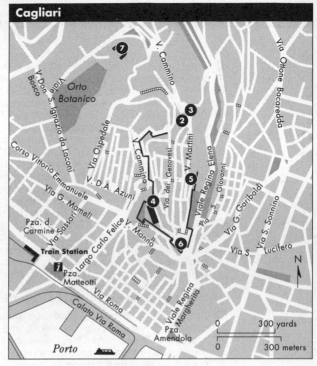

from Aragón were here, as well as Austrians and Italians. Cagliari (the stress is on the first syllable) is Sardinia's largest city, characterized by a busy commercial center and waterfront with broad, tree-lined avenues, as well as the typically narrow streets of the old town on a hill.

② Begin your visit at the **Museo Archeologico,** within the walls of the castle on the city's heights, erected in the early 1300s by the Pisans to ward off attacks from the Aragonese and Catalans, from what is now Spain. The museum contains some intriguing pieces, especially bronze statuettes from the tombs and dwellings of Sardinia's earliest inhabitants, who remain a prehistorical enigma. This aboriginal population left scarcely a clue to its origins. Ancient writers called them the nuraghic people, from the surviving name of their stone dwellings, the *nuraghi*, containing features unique to Sardinia, just as the Aztec pyramids are to Mexico. Archaeologists date the nuraghi to about 1300– 1200 BC, a time when the ancient Israelites were establishing themselves in Canaan, when the Greeks were besieging Troy, when the Minoan civilization collapsed in Crete, when the Ramses Pharaohs reigned in Egypt, and when many migrations were taking place along the shores and water routes of the Mediterranean. During the next 1,000 years, the nuraghic people gradually withdrew into the island's highland fastnesses to avoid more disciplined and better-armed invaders. (The only weapons they knew, say the chroniclers, were hurled stones and boulders rolled down from the hilltops.) Their civilization eventually succumbed when the Romans, following on the heels of Carthaginian invaders, conquered the island in the 3rd century BC. Artifacts from Nuraghic, Carthaginian, and Roman times make up the museum's collections. *Piazza Indipendenza, tel. 070/654237. Admission 4,000 lire. Open Mon. 9–2, Tues.– Sat. 9–2 and 3:30–6:30, Sun. 9–1.*

❸ Outside the museum is the medieval **Tower of San Pancrazio,** which was part of the imposing Pisan defenses; its twin, the **❹** **Tower of the Elephant,** is at the seaward end of the bastions. Take Via Martini about 200 yards to Piazza Palazzo. Here you'll **❺** find the **cathedral,** which has been extensively rebuilt and restored. The tiers of columns on the facade echo those of medieval Pisan churches, but only the center portal is an authentic relic of that era. All around the church are the narrow streets of the Spanish quarter, where humble dwellings still open directly onto the sidewalk and the wash is hung out to dry on elaborate wrought-iron balconies. This is the most interesting part of the city, so take time to wander through it, making your way to the Elephant Tower and the Bastion of St. Remy, better **❻** known as the **Terrazza Umberto I.** A monumental neoclassic staircase and arcade was added in the 19th century to the bastion built by the Spaniards 400 years earlier. It offers a magnificent view over the city and port, the sandy beaches, and the lagoons shimmering in the sun that are characteristic of the landscape around Cagliari and Oristano. Sunset, viewed from the Terrazza Umberto I, can be a memorable sight.

❼ Cagliari has a **Roman amphitheater** (behind the Museo Archeologico), some very old churches, and a few good restaurants near the waterfront (*see* Dining and Lodging, *below*), but once you have seen the main attractions, you will probably be ready to explore its surrounding areas.

The eastern route takes you through some dismal industrial suburbs on the road that leads to the scenic coast and beaches of **❽** Capo Boi and Capo Carbonara; **Villasimius** ranks as the chief resort here.

It's more interesting, though, to head in the other direction from Cagliari. The area southwest of the capital has its share of fine scenery and good beaches—resort villages sprawl along **❾** the coast, and the Is Molas championship golf course near **Pula** has won tributes from Tom Watson, Jack Nicklaus, and other professionals. On the marshy shoreline between Cagliari airport and Pula, huge flocks of flamingos are a common sight.

The real attraction here is archaeological: On a narrow promontory less than three kilometers (two miles) outside the town of Pula is **Nora,** the site of a Phoenician, then Carthaginian, and later Roman settlement. Extensive excavations here have shed light on life in this ancient city from the 8th century BC onward. Many of the exhibits in Cagliari's archaeological museum were found here. An old Roman road passes the moss-covered ruins of temples, an amphitheater, and a small Roman theater. You can make out the channels through which hot air rose to warm the Roman baths; watch for the difference between the simple mosaic pavements laid by the Carthaginians and the more elaborate designs of the Roman mosaics. Taking in the views from Nora, you also see why the Phoenicians chose the site for their settlement. They always scouted for locations with good harbors, cliffs to shelter their crafts from the wind, and a position such as a promontory, which they could defend from attack by local tribes. If the sea is calm, look under the clear waters along the shore for more ruins of the ancient city, submerged by earthquakes, rough seas, and erosion. *Admission: 3,000 lire. Excavations open Apr.–Oct., daily 9 AM–8 PM; Nov.–Mar., daily 9–noon and 2–5.*

There's a small archaeological museum, with finds from the Nora site, in the nearby village of Pula. *Corso Vittorio Emanuele 28, Pula, tel. 070/920–9610. Open daily 9–1, 4–8 (3–6 in winter).*

Time Out Take advantage of the coastal location to have a seafood lunch at **Urru** (Via Tirso). Grilled fish specials depend on the day's catch.

The little Romanesque church of **Sant' Efisio,** at the base of the promontory, plays a part in one of the island's most colorful annual events. Efisio, the patron saint of Sardinia, was a 3rd-century Roman soldier who converted to Christianity. A procession in early May accompanies a statue of the saint all the way from Cagliari and back again. The processional round trip takes four days, with festive stops along the way, and culminates in a parade down Cagliari's main avenue that rivals the St. Patrick's Day parade in New York. If you're in Sardinia from May 1 to May 4, don't miss it.

Off the southwest coast are two islands that are popular picnic spots with good beaches. You can drive over a causeway to **⑩ Sant'Antioco,** where the most hectic activity seems to be the silent repairing of nets by local fishermen who have already handled their daily catch. A ferry connects Sant' Antioco with the **⑪** smaller island of **San Pietro.** This is a favorite of wealthy Cagliarians, many of whom have built weekend cottages here.

Tour 2: North to Oristano

⑫ From Cagliari head north on the Carlo Felice highway toward Oristano, making a detour to the fascinating *nuraghe* of **Su Nuraxi,** off the main road outside the quiet little town of **Barumini.** You could spend hours clambering over this extraordinary structure of concentric rings of stone walls, chambers, passages, wells, and beehive tower, and it's a good idea to take a flashlight along for peering into dark corners. This nuraghe is probably about half its original height, and some of the smaller towers around the main one have been reduced by pillaging and erosion to mere circles of stones on the ground. The nuraghi were fortified villages, prehistoric versions of medieval walled towns and the forts of the American West. Though this particular type of construction is unique to Sardinia, similar buildings dating from the same era are found in other parts of the Mediterranean, such as Cyprus and the Balearic islands off Spain. Of the 7,000 nuraghi on Sardinia, Su Nuraxi is the most impressive, with those of Sant'Antine and Losa, both near Macomer, close runners-up. *One km (½ mile) west of Barumini. Admission free. Open daily dawn–sunset.*

⑬ Just north of Barumini is the **Giara di Gesturi,** a basalt plateau that is home to some of the island's more exotic wildlife, including a species of wild dwarf horse. Another rare species to be found in the Giara is the mouflon, a wild sheep distinguishable from its domesticated counterpart by its long curving horns and skittishness when confronted by any human, however well intentioned. Long hunted for their decorative horns, the mouf-

lon are now an endangered species, with only a few surviving
on Sardinia and neighboring Corsica.

⑭ **Oristano,** on the west coast of the island, shone in the Middle
Ages, when it was capital of the Giudicato of Arborea, an independent duchy led by Sardinia's Joan of Arc, Eleanora di
Arborea. In the 14th century Eleanora inherited the difficult
task of defending the duchy's freedom, constantly undermined
by the superior military might of the Spanish troops from Aragón. Although the duchy eventually reverted to Aragonese
rule, Eleanora made a lasting contribution to Sardinia by implementing a code of law that was adopted throughout the island and remained in effect until Sardinia's unification with
Italy in 1847. Now an important but slow-paced agricultural
center, Oristano is the scene of livestock fairs and a rousing series of horse races, called Sa Sartiglia, marking the end of the
Carnival season in February.

Time Out Join the locals at the **Forchetta d'Oro** (Via Giovanni XXIII 8) for
a lunch of pasta with cuttlefish sauce.

Close by to the west, you can see the extensive marshlands of
Cabras, where fishermen pole round-bottomed rush boats
through shallow ponds teeming with eels and crayfish. While
there, take time to drive 10 kilometers (6 miles) west, along the
road marked San Giovanni di Sinis, to visit the ruins of the Carthaginian city of **Tharros,** with its strategic position on the scenic Sinis peninsula. Like Nora to the south (*see* Tour 1: Cagliari
and Environs, *above*), the site was chosen because it commanded the best views of the harbor and could provide an easy
escape route if inland tribes threatened.

On your way to Tharros, you'll pass the ghost town of **San
Salvatore,** revived in the 1960s as a location for spaghetti westerns and later abandoned again. The saloon of the movie set is
still up. Farther along, among the dunes, are large rush huts
formerly used by fishermen and now much in demand as back-
to-nature vacation homes. The 5th-century church of **San
Giovanni di Sinis,** also on the peninsula, is the oldest Christian
church in Sardinia.

Tour 3: Inland to the North

⑮ Head northeast for **Nuoro,** a shabby provincial capital locked in
a gorge in the harsh mountainous area that culminates in
Gennargentu, the island's highest massif (6,000 feet). The only
things likely to interest you in Nuoro are the views from the
park on Sant'Onofrio hill and the exhibits in the **Museo della
Vita e delle Tradizioni Popolari Sarde** (Museum of Sardinian
Life and Folklore), where you can see local costumes, domestic
and agricultural implements, and traditional jewelry. *Via
Mereu 56, tel. 0784/31426. Admission free. Open Tues.–Sat.
9–1 and 3–7 (3–6 in winter), Sun. 9–1.*

Make an excursion a couple of miles east to **Mount Ortobene**
(2,900 feet), for some dizzying views over the gulch below
Nuoro. Here you can also visit up close the imposing statue of
Christ the Redeemer that overlooks the city. Picnic tables
make this a handy spot for an al fresco lunch stop.

From Nuoro, strike out south into the **Barbagia** region for the
mountain scenery and a glimpse of Sardinia's most primitive

district. Life in some villages has not changed much since the Middle Ages. Here a rigidly patriarchal society perpetuates the unrelenting practice of vendetta, and strangers are advised to mind their own business. Tortuous roads wind and loop their way through the scenery; towns are small and undistinguished, their social fabric seemingly impervious to the 20th century. On feast days the elaborate regional costumes are taken out of mothballs and worn as an explicit statement of community identity. You can see one of the most characteristic of these celebrations in local costume on the Feast of St. John, June 24, at **Fonni,** highest town on the island and base for excursions by car to Monte Spada and the Bruncu Spina refuge on the Gennargentu massif.

Head west on road 129 from Nuoro to Bosa, where you turn right into hilly and arid scrub country, with its abundance of cactus and juniper. Pines and olive trees shelter low buildings from the steady winds that make these parts ideal for sailing and unfit for agriculture. About the only cash crop here is cork from the cork trees dotting the landscape. Yet in the low valleys and along the river beds, masses of oleanders bloom in the summer, creating avenues of color.

Among the larger centers on the northwest coast is **Alghero,** which is an appealing walled town with a distinct Spanish flavor. It was built and inhabited in the 14th century by the Aragonese and Catalans, who constructed seaside ramparts and sturdy towers encompassing an inviting nucleus of narrow, winding streets. Rich wrought-iron scrollwork decorates balconies and screens windows; Spanish motifs appear in stone portals and in bell towers. The dialect spoken here is a version of Catalan, not Italian: Locals find it easier to converse in Barcelona than in Rome. Alghero is a popular resort, near broad sandy beaches and the spectacular heights of **Capo Caccia,** an imposing limestone headland to the west. At the base of the sheer cliff, the pounding sea has carved an entrance to the vast **Grotto of Neptune,** a fantastic, fabulous cavern, which you must visit with a guide. By land, you can reach the entrance at the base of the cliff by descending the more than 600 steps of the aptly named *escala del cabirol* (mountain goat's stairway), a dizzying enterprise—and the ascent is just as daunting. *Admission 9,000 lire. Open Easter–Oct. 15, daily 9–6; Oct. 16–1 week before Easter, daily 9–2. Guided tours start on the hour.*

The excursion by sea is much less fatiguing but is not possible when seas are rough. Boats leave the port of Alghero four times daily, every hour or so in peak season, and the journey takes three hours. *Navisarda, tel. 079/975599. Cost: 15,000 lire plus 9,000 lire for grotto admission. Open Apr.–Oct., daily.*

Time Out Hungry landlubbers need go only **Dieci Metri** (Ten Meters) from the center of Alghero for a nourishing meal of seafood and local wine *(Vicolo Adami 47, off Via Roma.)*.

Inland and northeast of Alghero is **Sassari,** important as a university town and an administrative center. It has little to interest a visitor other than an old and ornate cathedral and an archaeological museum. Sassari is the hub of several highways and secondary roads leading to various scenic coastal resorts, among them Stintino and **Castelsardo,** which is a walled seaside citadel and a delight for basket lovers. Roadside stands and shops in the old town sell tons of island handicrafts: rugs, wrought iron—and baskets, in myriad shapes and colors.

㉒ **Santa Teresa di Gallura,** at the northern tip of Sardinia, has the relaxed, carefree air of an authentic fishing village-turned-re-
㉑ sort. From nearby Palau you can visit the archipelago of **La Maddalena,** seven granite islands embellished with lush green scrub and wind-bent pines. Pilgrims pay homage to Garibaldi's tomb on the grounds of his hideaway on Caprera, one of the islands.

Sardinia's northeastern coast is fringed with low cliffs, inlets, and small bays. This landscape has become an upscale vacationland, with glossy resorts, such as Baia Sardinia and Porto Rotondo, just outside the confines of the famed Costa Smeralda, developed by the Aga Khan, who discovered its charms—and potential—by accident in 1965, when his yacht ran in for shelter from a storm. The Costa Smeralda is still dominated by his personality; its attractions remain geared to those who can measure themselves by the yardstick of his fabled riches. Sardinia's most expensive hotels are here, and
㉒ world's most magnificent yachts anchor in the waters of **Porto Cervo.** The trend has been to keep this enclave of the really rich an exclusive haven, by encouraging more multimillionaires to build discreetly luxurious villas and planning four more golf courses to be built for them.

All along the coast, carefully tended lush vegetation surrounds vacation villages and the more elaborate villa colonies that have sprung up over the past decade in a range of spurious architectural styles best described as bogus Mediterranean. Set
㉓ amid the resorts is **Olbia,** a lively little seaport, not heavily industrialized, at the head of a long, wide bay. At the bay's
㉔ mouth is **Golfo Aranci,** a blossoming resort and debarkation point for FS ferries from the mainland.

What to See and Do with Children

Sardinia is a vast playground where children can roam, explore, and swim in season. There's nothing like a long hike along deserted beaches or through herb-scented hills to send them to bed early. Let them clamber over the nuraghi and poke into the countless *domus de janas* (witches' houses) and *tombe di giganti* (giants' tombs), fancifully named grottoes hewn in the rock by the island's prehistoric inhabitants. They served as burial places, but with a little imagination you can elaborate on their names and make up some good fairy tales. There are plenty around **Sassari,** at **Anghelu Ruhu,** and near **Dorgali.** Take the children to see the **Elephant Rock** near Castelsardo; hollowed out by primitive man to become a domus de janas, it resembles an elephant, trunk and all. Go to see the Wild West film-set village at **San Salvatore** near Oristano (*see* Tour 2: North to Oristano, *above*). Visit the folk museum at **Nuoro** (*see* Tour 3: Inland to the North, *above*).

Off the Beaten Track

Considering that all Sardinia is off the beaten track for most tourists, practically everything you do or see here comprises the unusual. But if your curiosity prods you to even more esoteric experiences, you could go just north of Sant'Antioco to explore the rugged, once-booming mining country around **Carbonia,** a town built by Mussolini in 1938 to serve as the administrative center for the coal miners and their families. With its overpowering fascist architecture, it has been called an urban UFO set down in the Sardinian landscape. Nearby **Iglesias** is an authentic Sardinian town, with a medieval cathedral; traveling east past Domusnovas on the Cagliari-Iglesias highway, you can detour and drive right through an immense cave, the **Grotta di San Giovanni.**

Visit **San Sperate,** near Cagliari; practically every wall in town has been brightened with *murales* (mural paintings) by local artists and some well-known Italian painters, transforming the entire town into a modern art gallery. You can see more of the murales throughout the Barbagia district, especially at **Orgosolo.**

If you have the stamina, take the rickety old train that runs on a single-gauge track between Cagliari and **Arbatax,** midway up the east coast. If all goes well, it takes about nine hours to cover the approximately 250 kilometers (155 miles) of track, guaranteeing you a look at the Sardinia few tourists ever see, rattling up into the Barbagia district through some breathtaking mountain scenery, then easing down into the desert landscape inland of Arbatax, where the trip ends on the dock next to the fishing boats. The train is run by the Ferrovie Complementari, and the ticket costs less than 18,000 lire. For information, call 070/306221.

Shopping

Sardinia is handicrafts heaven. Locally produced goods include bright woolen shawls and rugs, handcarved wooden objects, gold filigree jewelry in traditional forms, coral jewelry, and, above all, handwoven baskets in all shapes and sizes. The best place in Cagliari to get an idea of what's available is at **ISOLA** (Via Baccaredda 184, tel. 070/486707), a government-sponsored exhibition of island handicrafts; most of the items on display are also for sale. ISOLA promotes pilot centers for arts and crafts in remote areas where Sardinian handicrafts are produced. You can find ISOLA centers at **Castelsardo** (Lungomare Colombo) and **Sant'Antioco** (Lungomare Vespucci). Larger towns have a complete range of Sardinian handicrafts, but elsewhere on the island the small towns and villages conform to the centuries-old tradition of specializing in one item.

Handicrafts   **Alghero.** Coral, still harvested in the bay, and gold jewelry are the traditional handicrafts.

Aritzo. This mountain village, high up in the Barbagia, produces handcrafted wooden utensils and furniture.

Castelsardo. The specialty is a brightly colored basket made of dwarf palms.

Dorgali. This east-coast port is a rug- and tapestry-producing center.

Isili. Handwoven rugs and hammered copperware are the specialties of this village just east of Su Nuraxi.

Nuoro. Wooden masks, made for local festivals, make unusual souvenirs.

Oristano. Ceramics are featured in the small craft shops here.

Santa Teresa di Gallura. Contemporary pottery utilizing traditional motifs sells well, especially among the rich along the Costa Smeralda.

Tonara. Special candies are made from honey and nougat.

Sports

Fishing
Check locally for regulations on deep-sea fishing. Underwater fishing is prohibited to scuba divers and is restricted to the daylight hours. Freshwater fishing is good along the Flumendosa, Tirso, Rio Mannu, and other rivers rising in the mountainous interior and in the artificial basins of Flumendosa and Omodeo. For information on obtaining a license, write to **Assessorato Regionale alla Difesa dell'Ambiente,** Viale Trento 69, 09100, Cagliari (tel. 070/670400).

Golf
Sardinia has two world-class golf courses, with four more planned for the Costa Smeralda, where the **Pevero Golf Club** course was designed by Robert Trent Jones. The club is on the Bay of Pevero, near Porto Cervo (tel. 0789/96210). The 18-hole **Is Molas** course is at Santa Margherita di Pula (tel. 070/920–9165); the adjacent Is Molas Golf Hotel (tel. 070/924–1006) offers special golfing vacations.

Horseback Riding
The **Associazione Nazionale di Turismo Equestre** (Via Pasteur 4, Cagliari, tel. 070/305816) can provide information on renting mounts and joining riding parties with itineraries along the coast or into the heart of the island. The **Centro Vacanze Alabirdi** at Arborea, near Oristano (tel. 0783/48268) and the **Centro Vacanze Su Gologone** at Oliena (tel. 0784/287512) offer riding vacations.

Sailing
A popular sport in Sardinia, sailing is enjoyed all along the coast. The **Lega Navale Italiana** at Marina Piccola in Cagliari (tel. 070/370380) will furnish information on the island's facilities. The **Yacht Club Costa Smeralda** at Porto Cervo (tel. 0789/91332) admits temporary members.

Tennis
Most resort hotels have their own tennis courts, many of which are open to guests. The **Porto Cervo Tennis Club** on the Costa Smeralda is open year-round, and membership is available to visitors on a daily or weekly basis (Porto Cervo, tel. 0789/92244). The **Federazione Italiana Tennis** (Via Palestrina 46, Cagliari, tel. 070/494468) can provide information about local competitions and tennis ladders.

Spectator Sports

Yachting
You can see the very rich engage in one of their favorite sports at the posh resorts of Costa Smeralda each August, when a number of regattas are held.

Beaches

Sardinia's beaches are among the best in the Mediterranean; its waters among the cleanest, with the exception of those in the immediate vicinity of Cagliari, Arbatax, and Porto Torres. The beach resorts of the Costa Smeralda are exclusive and expensive, but elsewhere on the island you can find a wide range of beaches.

Most agree that the most beautiful beaches on the island are those of **Cala Luna** and **Cala Sisina,** hidden among the rocky cliffs near Baunei and Dorgali, on the eastern coast; they can be reached only by boat from Cala Gonone or Arbatax, and can definitely be considered remote. For more accessible beaches with more amenities, go to **Santa Margherita di Pula**, near Cagliari, where there are several hotels; to **Villasimius** and the **Costa Rei**, on the southeastern coast; or to the sandy coves sheltered by wind-carved granite boulders on the northern coast in the Gallura district and the archipelago of La Maddalena. There are also beaches around Olbia, Alghero, and on the Costa Paradiso, near Castelsardo.

Dining and Lodging

Dining In the island's restaurants you'll find that Sardinian regional cuisine is basically Italian, with interesting local variations. Meat dishes are usually veal, lamb, or *porcheddu* (roast suckling pig). On the coast, seafood is king and is served in great variety. *Langouste* or *aragosta* (lobster) is a specialty of the northern coast; it can be expensive. Foreign conquerors left legacies of bouillabaisse (known here as *zimino)*, couscous, and paella, but there are native pastas: *malloreddus*, small shells of pasta di semola (bran pasta) sometimes flavored with saffron, and *culingiones*, the Sardinian version of ravioli. Sharp cheese made of sheep's milk *(pecorino)* and thin crispy bread called *carta di musica* are typical island fare. Try the *sebadas* (fried cheese-filled ravioli doused with honey) for dessert. The red wines are sturdy and strong, with the whites tending to a light and delicate quality. Amber-colored Vernaccia is dry and heady.

Highly recommended restaurants are indicated by a star ★.

Category	Cost*
Very Expensive	over 85,000 lire
Expensive	60,000–85,000 lire
Moderate	35,000–60,000 lire
Inexpensive	under 35,000 lire

**per person, including house wine, service, and tax*

Lodging The island's most luxurious hotels are on the Costa Smeralda; they have magnificent resort facilities but close up from fall to spring and are too out of the way to be good touring bases. Other, equally attractive coastal areas have seen a spate of new resort hotels and villa colonies sprout up, but they, too, close from October through April, which narrows the choice of hotels considerably during the other months. In the cities suggested as touring bases, you can expect to find standards of comfort slightly below those of the mainland; the best accommodations may be offered by commercial hotels with little atmosphere. Service is usually courteous and competent, with perhaps the exception of the seasonal resort hotels, where the staff is likely to change from year to year. In smaller towns throughout the island, you'll find modest hotels offering basic accommodations, restrained but genuine hospitality, and low rates.

Highly recommended lodgings are indicated by a star ★.

Category	Cost*
Very Expensive	over 300,000 lire
Expensive	150,000–300,000 lire
Moderate	90,000–150,000 lire
Inexpensive	under 90,000 lire

All prices are for a standard double room for two, including service and 10% VAT (19% for luxury hotels).

Alghero **La Lepanto.** White stucco and wrought-iron grilles set a Span-
Dining ish tone in Alghero's top seafood restaurant. The specialty is
aragosta (local lobster) cooked in a variety of ways, including
alla catalana (with tomato and onions). *Zuppa di pesce* (fish
soup) is usually on the menu, too. *Via Carlo Alberto 133, tel.
079/979116. Reservations advised in the evening. Dress: casual. AE, DC, MC, V. Closed Mon. Oct.–May. Moderate.*
Da Pietro. On a narrow street in the picturesque Old Town near
Largo San Francesco, this seafood restaurant has vaulted ceilings and a bustling atmosphere. The menu features *bucatini
all'algherese* (pasta with a sauce of clams, capers, and tomatoes) and baked fish *con Vernaccia* (with white wine sauce);
there are some meat dishes, too. *Via Ambrogio Machin 18, tel.
079/979645. Reservations advised in the evening. Dress: casual. AE, DC, MC, V. Closed Wed. Oct.–May, and 2 weeks at
Christmas. Inexpensive.*

Lodging **Villas Las Tronas.** The villa is a former royal mansion on a rocky
bluff above the sea, but still near the center of town. It has
turn-of-the-century atmosphere, modern comforts, and great
views across the water to the Old Town. Rates are at the lower
level of this category. *Lungomare Valencia, tel. 079/981818,
fax 079/981044. 30 rooms in main building, 7 in annex, all with
bath or shower. Facilities: restaurant, bar, outdoor pool, garden, parking. AE, DC, MC, V. Expensive.*
Carlos V (Carlos Quinto). Located on the shore boulevard about
half a mile from the center of town, this hillside hotel is modern
but attractive, with porticoes and terraces, one of which has a
swimming pool. Smallish but bright rooms all have balconies,
many with sea views. Low season rates are a bargain.
*Lungomare Valencia 24, tel. 079/979501, fax 079/980298. 110
rooms with bath or shower. Facilities: restaurant, garden, outdoor pool, tennis court, parking. AE, DC, MC, V. Moderate–
Expensive.*

Cagliari **Dal Corsaro.** This popular restaurant just by the waterfront is
Dining one of the island's most popular eating places, so reservations
are essential. The decor is informal, in tune with the cordial
welcome. The menu features seafood and meat specialties, such
as seafood antipasto and *porcheddu* (roast suckling pig). *Viale
Regina Margherita 28, tel. 070/664318. Reservations advised.
Dress: casual. AE, DC, MC, V. Closed Sun. Expensive.*
Il Gatto. "The Cat," located near the train station and the central Piazza del Carmine, is popular with locals. Follow their
lead and make sure you have reservations because the restaurant can fill up quickly. It serves some of the best Sardinian
seafood, such as the risotto with shellfish, but for a change of
pace try the *boccone del gatto* (stuffed chicken breast). *Viale
Trieste 15, tel. 070/663596. Reservations advised. Dress: casual. AE, DC, MC, V. Closed Sun. Moderate.*

Lodging **Mediterraneo.** The view is the best feature of this functional 1960s building, with sharp angles and little atmosphere. It's located on the shore boulevard, so try to get a room facing the sea. The uninspiring furnishings are clean and modern, but each room has a balcony. *Lungomare Cristoforo Colombo 46, tel. 070/301271, fax 070/301274. 136 rooms with bath. Facilities: bar, restaurant, garden, garage. AE, DC, MC, V. Expensive.*

Moderno. A good overnight stop, the Moderno is convenient to the train station and the harbor, but don't expect atmosphere or more than adequate comfort. In compensation, rates are at the lower end of the category. *Via Roma 159, tel. 070/660306, fax 070/660260. 90 rooms with bath or shower. AE, DC, MC, V. Moderate.*

Costa Smeralda **Cala di Volpe.** Built to resemble an ancient village, this estab-
Lodging lishment is in a secluded position on a bay. The decor is rustic-elegant, with beamed ceilings, Sardinian art and craftwork, and porticoes overlooking the sea. The presidential suite in the highest tower has a private pool. *Porto Cervo, tel. 0789/96083, fax 0789/96442. 125 rooms and suites, all with bath or shower. Facilities: restaurant, bar, saltwater pool, disco, hairdresser, garden, private beach reached by hotel launch, tennis courts, access to Pevero Golf Club. AE, DC, MC, V. Closed Oct.–mid-May. Very Expensive.*

Cervo. Low Mediterranean buildings surround a large swimming pool and garden in the heart of the Costa Smeralda's Porto Cervo. This complex is next to the marina and piazzetta and is popular with people who like to be seen. The rooms are large and most have terraces. *Porto Cervo, tel. 0789/92003, fax 0789/92593. 95 rooms with bath or shower. Facilities: terrace restaurant, piano bar, hairdresser, hotel launch to private beach, access to Porto Cervo Tennis Club and Pevero Golf Club. AE, DC, MC, V. Closed Oct.–mid May. Very Expensive.*

Romazzino. A rambling white stucco building with arched loggias set in lush gardens on the edge of a fine, sandy beach, this classy but informal hotel is perfect for people who like sports and socializing. Every room has a terrace. Like other Costa Smeralda luxury hotels, it's more of a resort complex than a single establishment. *Porto Cervo, tel. 0789/96020, fax 0789/96258. 93 rooms and apartments with bath or shower. Facilities: restaurant, bar, poolside bar-pizzeria, garden, pool, private beach, tennis court, access to Pevero Golf Club. AE, DC, MC, V. Closed Oct.–mid-May. Very Expensive.*

Olbia **Mediterraneo.** This modern hotel is the best choice for anyone
Lodging arriving at the busy port of Olbia, particularly without a car. It's located midway between the train station and the ferry dock. The rooms are furnished in a motel style that is functional but not memorable or particularly Sardinian; air-conditioning is available for an extra charge. *Via Montello 3, tel. 0789/24173, fax 0789/24162. 80 rooms with bath or shower. Facilities: bar, restaurant. AE, DC, MC, V. Expensive.*

Oliena **Su Gologone.** Oliena is near Nuoro, and this well-known restau-
Dining rant is worth a detour for an authentic Sardinian meal in a bus-
★ tling inn that attracts tourists in droves but manages to maintain its friendly atmosphere. The island specialties include *maccarones de busa* (thick homemade pasta), culingiones, porcheddu, and sebadas. Wash it all down with some

Vernaccia. *Su Gologone, tel. 0784/287512. No reservations. Dress: casual. AE, DC, MC, V. Expensive.*

Oristano **Il Faro.** Locals and visiting gourmets consider this elegant res-
Dining taurant to be one of the best in the area, as it offers authentic
★ and well-prepared local dishes that change with the season.
There's *capretto allo spiedo* (spit-roasted kid) in the winter and
an aromatic *zuppa di fave* (fava bean soup with bacon and fennel) in the spring. Seafood is featured throughout the year. *Via
Bellini 25, tel. 0783/70002. Reservations advised. Dress: casual. AE, DC, MC, V. Closed Sun. eve., Mon., and Jan. 1–15,
July 1–15. Expensive.*
Salvatore. In this classic seafood restaurant you can sample seafood from the tidal ponds of Cabras and Santa Giusta just outside Oristano. Specialties are *spaghetti alla bottarga* (with
smoked fish roe) and grilled *anguilla* (eel). *Vico Mariano 2, tel.
0783/71309. Reservations advised. Dress: casual. MC, V.
Closed Sun, and last 2 weeks in Aug. Moderate.*

Lodging **Cama.** Located near the train station, the hotel is also within
walking distance of Oristano's interesting Old Town center. A
parking lot and garage make it convenient for drivers. Another
feature is air-conditioning, not always found in hotels of this
category. *Via Vittorio Veneto 119, tel. 0783/74374, fax 0783/
74375. 54 rooms, with bath or shower. Facilities: restaurant,
garage. MC, V. Inexpensive.*
Mistral. This hotel, in the same price category as the Cama, is
more appealing, but it's located on the edge of town, so you'll
probably need a car to reach it. The rooms are bright and air-
conditioned, and some have views of the mysterious *nuraghe*
countryside to the east. The restaurant serves good seafood
specialties. It recently opened a large annex in the center of
town, **Mistral 2,** a convention center with swimming pool. *Via
Martiri di Belfiore, tel. 0783/212505, fax 0783/210058. 49
rooms with bath or shower. Facilities: restaurant, tennis. AE,
DC, MC, V. Inexpensive.*

Santa Margherita **Is Morus.** A luxurious enclave, the Is Morus is on a sandy cove
di Pula and offers all the amenities of a fine beach resort, with low, at-
Lodging tractive buildings shaded by pinewoods, plus the option of golf-
★ ing at the fine Is Molas course, about 11 kilometers (7 miles)
away. *Santa Margherita, tel. 070/921171, fax 070/921596. 85
rooms with bath or shower. Facilities: terrace restaurant, bar,
pool, hairdresser, miniature golf, tennis, parking. AE, DC,
MC, V. Closed Oct. 21–Easter. Expensive.*
Flamingo. Also directly on the beach and in a shady setting,
this less expensive resort hotel features a main building and
several two-story cottages nestled among the pines. *Santa
Margherita, tel. 070/920–8361, fax 070/920–8359. 122 rooms
with bath or shower. Facilities: restaurant, bar, disco, pool,
tennis court, miniature golf, sauna, parking. No credit cards.
Closed Oct. 16–May 14. Moderate.*

Santa Teresa di **Canne al Vento.** This cheerful, family-run restaurant on the
Gallura edge of town is popular with visitors who want authentic island
Dining cuisine. Try the local specialty, *suppa cuata* (bread, cheese,
★ and tomato soup), porcheddu, or seafood. *Via Nazionale 23,
tel. 0789/754219. Reservations advised. Dress: casual. MC, V.
Closed Sat. (except summer) and Oct.–Nov. Moderate.*

Lodging **Corallaro.** This hotel offers comfortable, pleasing accommodations in a panoramic spot overlooking the sea, not far from the

center of town. *Via Nazionale 85, tel. 0789/754341. 22 rooms with bath or shower. Facilities: restaurant, pool, tennis court, garden. AE, V. Moderate.*

The Arts and Nightlife

The Arts

As one of Italy's most (perhaps *the* most) remote regions, Sardinia is not really a prime spot for sophisticated visual or performing arts. This same remoteness, however, can prove fruitful if you're interested in sampling some of the culture that has developed here, sometimes natively inspired, sometimes drawing on the influences of the traders and invaders who have left their mark on Sardinia over the millennia. Sardinia's own brand of Catholicism—occasionally bordering on the grotesque—can be witnessed in the local *feste*, or festivals. Ostensibly, the feste celebrate a saintly or religious occasion, but often they are imbued with an almost pagan atmosphere.

Festivals and Pageants **Cagliari.** The **Feste del Mare** (Festivals of the Sea) are held each year on the first Sunday in April. The **Festa di Sant'Efisio** (May 1) offers a chance to take part in a festival of Sardinian folklore.

Nuoro. The **Festa del Redentore** (Feast of the Redeemer) is held on the next-to-last Sunday in August.

Oristano. The Sartiglia festival, on the last Sunday of Carnival season, includes rich costumes and a ritual joust. Each summer, the town holds an **arts and crafts** exhibition, with local foods and wines given prominence. Contact the tourist office (*see* Important Addresses and Numbers in Essential Information, *above*) for information.

Music Cagliari's **university** (Via Università) has concerts throughout the academic year.

Nightlife

Nightlife in much of Sardinia means a quiet drink before turning in early, tired out from the day's outdoor activity. But as if to make up for the sleepy atmosphere of most of the island, **Costa Smeralda** sparkles most nights in the summer. Be prepared to part with a tidy sum if you visit the Costa, but if that doesn't deter you, go to the complex at **Porto Cervo** (*see* Dining and Lodging, *above*) for a selection of high-class bars, restaurants, and discos.

Conversion Tables

Distance

Kilometers/Miles   To change kilometers to miles, multiply kilometers by .621
To change miles to kilometers, multiply miles by 1.61

Km to Mi	Mi to Km
1 = .62	1 = 1.6
2 = 1.2	2 = 3.2
3 = 1.9	3 = 4.8
4 = 2.5	4 = 6.4
5 = 3.1	5 = 8.1
6 = 3.7	6 = 9.7
7 = 4.3	7 = 11.3
8 = 5.0	8 = 12.9
9 = 5.6	9 = 14.5

Meters/Feet   To change meters to feet, multiply meters by 3.28
To change feet to meters, multiply feet by .305

Meters to Feet	Feet to Meters
1 = 3.3	1 = .31
2 = 6.6	2 = .61
3 = 9.8	3 = .92
4 = 13.1	4 = 1.2
5 = 16.4	5 = 1.5
6 = 19.7	6 = 1.8
7 = 23.0	7 = 2.1
8 = 26.2	8 = 2.4
9 = 29.5	9 = 2.7

Weight

Kilograms/Pounds   To change kilograms to pounds, multiply by 2.20
To change pounds to kilograms, multiply by .453

Kilos to Pounds	Pounds to Kilos
1 = 2.2	1 = .45
2 = 4.4	2 = .91
3 = 6.6	3 = 1.4
4 = 8.8	4 = 1.8
5 = 11.0	5 = 2.3
6 = 13.2	6 = 2.7
7 = 15.4	7 = 3.2

8 = 17.6	8 = 3.6
9 = 19.8	9 = 4.1

Grams/Ounces To change grams to ounces, multiply grams by .035
To change ounces to grams, multiply ounces by 28.4

Grams to Ounces	**Ounces to Grams**
1 = .04	1 = 28
2 = .07	2 = 57
3 = .11	3 = 85
4 = .14	4 = 114
5 = .18	5 = 142
6 = .21	6 = 170
7 = .25	7 = 199
8 = .28	8 = 227
9 = .32	9 = 256

Liquid Volume

Liters/U.S. Gallons To change liters to U.S. gallons, multiply liters by .264
To change U.S. gallons to liters, multiply gallons by 3.79

Liters to U.S. Gallons	**U.S. Gallons to Liters**
1 = .26	1 = 3.8
2 = .53	2 = 7.6
3 = .79	3 = 11.4
4 = 1.1	4 = 15.2
5 = 1.3	5 = 19.0
6 = 1.6	6 = 22.7
7 = 1.8	7 = 26.5
8 = 2.1	8 = 30.3
9 = 2.4	9 = 34.1

Clothing Sizes

Men To change American suit sizes to Italian suit sizes, add 10 to the
Suits American suit size.
To change Italian suit sizes to American suit sizes, subtract 10
from the Italian suit size.

U.S. Size	36	38	40	42	44	46	48
Italian Size	46	48	50	52	54	56	58

Shirts To change American shirt sizes to Italian shirt sizes, multiply
the American shirt size by 2 and add 8.
To change Italian shirt sizes to American shirt sizes, subtract 8
from the Italian shirt size and divide by 2.

U.S. Size	14	14½	15	15½	16	16½	17	17½
Italian Size	36	37	38	39	40	41	42	43

Shoes Italian shoe sizes vary in their relation to American shoe sizes.

U.S. Size	7½	8	8½/9	9½/10	10½/11	11½/12	12½
Italian Size	38	39	40	41	42	43	44

Women
Dresses and Coats To change U.S. dress/coat sizes to Italian dress/coat sizes, add 28 to the U.S. dress/coat size.
To change Italian dress/coat sizes to U.S. dress/coat sizes, subtract 28 from the Italian dress/coat size.

U.S. Size	4	6	8	10	12	14	16
Italian Size	32	34	36	38	40	42	44

Blouses and Sweaters To change U.S. blouse/sweater sizes to Italian blouse/sweater sizes, add 8 to the U.S. blouse/sweater size.
To change Italian blouse/sweater sizes to U.S. blouse/sweater sizes, subtract 8 from the Italian blouse/sweater size.

U.S. Size	30	32	34	36	38	40	42
Italian Size	38	40	42	44	46	48	50

Shoes Italian shoe sizes vary in their relation to U.S. shoe sizes.

U.S. Size	5/5½	6	6½/7	7½	8	8½	9
Italian Size	35	36	37	38	38½	39	40

Italian Vocabulary

Words & Phrases

	English	*Italian*	*Pronunciation*
Basics	Yes/no	Sí/No	see/no
	Please	Per favore	pear fa-**vo**-ray
	Yes, please	Sí grazie	see **grah**-tsee-ay
	Thank you	Grazie	**grah**-tsee-ay
	You're welcome	Prego	**pray**-go
	Excuse me, sorry	Scusi	**skoo**-zee
	Sorry!	Mi spiace!	mee spee-**ah**-chay
	Good morning/ afternoon	Buon giorno	bwohn **jor**-no
	Goodevening	Buona sera	**bwoh**-na say-ra
	Goodbye	Arrivederci	a-ree-vah-**dare**-chee
	Mr.(Sir)	Signore	see-**nyo**-ray
	Mrs. (Ma'am)	Signora	see-**nyo**-ra
	Miss	Signorina	see-nyo-**ree**-na
	Pleased to meet you	Piacere	pee-ah-**chair**-ray
	How are you?	Come sta?	**ko**-may **sta**
	Very well, thanks	Bene, grazie	**ben**-ay **grah**-tsee-ay
	And you?	E lei?	ay **lay**-ee
	Hello (over the phone)	Pronto?	**proan**-to
Numbers	one	uno	**oo**-no
	two	due	**doo**-ay
	three	tre	tray
	four	quattro	**kwah**-tro
	five	cinque	**cheen**-kway
	six	sei	say
	seven	sette	**set**-ay
	eight	otto	**oh**-to
	nine	nove	**no**-vay
	ten	dieci	dee-**eh**-chee
	eleven	undici	**oon**-dee-chee
	twelve	dodici	**doe**-dee-chee
	thirteen	tredici	**tray**-dee-chee
	fourteen	quattordici	kwa-**tore**-dee-chee
	fifteen	quindici	**kwin**-dee-chee
	sixteen	sedici	**say**-dee-chee
	seventeen	diciassette	dee-cha-**set**-ay
	eighteen	diciotto	dee-**cho**-to
	nineteen	diciannove	dee-cha-**no**-vay
	twenty	venti	**vain**-tee
	twenty-one	ventuno	vain-**too**-no
	twenty-two	ventidue	vayn-tee-**doo**-ay
	thirty	trenta	**train**-ta
	forty	quaranta	kwa-**rahn**-ta
	fifty	cinquanta	cheen-**kwahn**-ta
	sixty	sessanta	seh-**sahn**-ta
	seventy	settanta	seh-**tahn**-ta
	eighty	ottanta	o-**tahn**-ta
	ninety	novanta	no-**vahn**-ta
	one hundred	cento	**chen**-to

	ten thousand	diecimila	dee-eh-chee-**mee**-la
	one hundred thousand	centomila	chen-to-**mee**-la
Colors	black	nero	**neh**-ro
	blue	azzurro	a-**tsu**-ro
	brown	bruno	**bru**-no
	green	verde	**vehr**-day
	pink	rosa	**ro**-za
	purple	porpora	**por**-por-a
	orange	arancio	a-**rahn**-cho
	red	rosso	**ros**-so
	white	bianco	bee-**ang**-ko
	yellow	giallo	**ja**-lo
Days of the week	Monday	lunedì	**loo**-neh-dee
	Tuesday	martedì	**mahr**-teh-dee
	Wednesday	mercoledì	**mare**-co-leh-dee
	Thursday	giovedì	**jo**-veh-dee
	Friday	venerdì	**ven**-air-dee
	Saturday	sabato	**sah**-ba-toe
	Sunday	domenica	doe-**men**-ee-ca
Months	January	gennaio	jeh-**nah**-yo
	February	febbraio	feh-**brah**-yo
	March	marzo	**mahr**-tso
	April	aprile	a-**pree**-lay
	May	maggio	**mah**-jo
	June	giugno	**joon**-yo
	July	luglio	**loo**-lee-o
	August	agosto	ah-**goo**-sto
	September	settembre	seh-**tem**-bray
	October	ottobre	o-**toe**-bray
	November	novembre	no-**vem**-bray
	December	dicembre	dee-**chem**-bray
Useful phrases	Do you speak English?	Parla inglese?	**par**-la een-**glay**-zay
	I don't speak Italian	Non parlo italiano	non **par**-lo ee-tal-**yah**-no
	I don't understand	Non capisco	non ka-**peess**-ko
	Can you please repeat?	Può ripetere?	pwo ree-**pet**-ay-ray
	Slowly!	Lentamente!	**len**-ta-men-tay
	I don't know	Non lo so	noan lo **so**
	I'm American/	Sono americano/a	**so**-no a-may-ree-**ka**-no/a
	British	Sono inglese	**so**-no een-**glay**-zay
	What's your name?	Come si chiama?	**ko**-may see kee-**ah**-ma
	My name is . . .	Mi chiamo . . .	mee kee-**ah**-mo
	What time is it?	Che ore sono?	kay **o**-ray **so**-no
	How?	Come?	**ko**-may
	When?	Quando?	**kwan**-doe

Yesterday/today/ tomorrow	Ieri/oggi/ domani	**yer**-ee/**o**-jee/ do-**mah**-nee
This morning/ afternoon	Stamattina/Oggi pomeriggio	sta-ma-**tee**-na/**o**-jee po-mer-**ee**-jo
Tonight	Stasera	sta-**ser**-a
What?	Che cosa?	kay **ko**-za
What is it?	Che cos'è?	kay ko-**zay**
Why?	Perché?	pear-**kay**
Who?	Chi?	kee
Where is . . .	Dov'è . . .	doe-**veh**
the bus stop?	la fermata dell'autobus?	la fer-**ma**-ta del ow-toe-**booss**
the train station?	la stazione?	la sta-tsee-**oh**-nay
the subway station?	la metropolitana?	la may-tro-po-lee-**ta**-na
the terminal?	il terminal?	eel ter-mee-**nahl**
the post office?	l'ufficio postale?	loo-**fee**-cho po-**sta**-lay
the bank?	la banca?	la **bahn**-ka
the . . . hotel?	l'hotel . . . ?	lo-**tel**
the store?	il negozio?	ell nay-**go**-tsee-o
the cashier?	la cassa?	la **ka**-sa
the . . . museum?	il museo . . . ?	eel moo-**zay**-o
the hospital?	l'ospedale?	lo-spay-**dah**-lay
the first aid station?	il pronto soccorso?	eel **pron**-to so-**kor**-so
the elevator?	l'ascensore?	la-shen-**so**-ray
a telephone?	un telefono?	oon tay-**lay**-fo-no
Where are the rest rooms?	Dov'è il bagno?	doe-**vay** eel **bahn**-yo
Here/there	Qui/là	kwee/la
Left/right	A sinistra/a destra	a see-**neess**-tra/ a **des**-tra
Straight ahead	Avanti dritto	a-**vahn**-tee **dree**-to
Is it near/far?	È vicino?/lontano?	ay vee-**chee**-no/ lon-**tah**-no
I'd like . . .	Vorrei . . .	vo-**ray**
a room	una camera	**oo**-na **ka**-may-ra
the key	la chiave	la kee-**ah**-vay
a newspaper	un giornale	oon jor-**na**-lay
a stamp	un francobollo	oon frahn-ko-**bo**-lo
I'd like to buy . . .	Vorrei comprare . . .	vo-**ray** kom-**pra**-ray
a cigar	un sigaro	oon see-**ga**-ro
cigarettes	delle sigarette	day-lay see-ga-**ret**-ay
some matches	dei fiammiferi	day-ee fee-ah-**mee**-fer-ee
some soap	una saponetta	**oo**-na sa-po-**net**-a
a city plan	una pianta della città	**oo**-na **pyahn**-ta day-la chee-**ta**
a road map of . . .	una carta stradale di . . .	**oo**-na **cart**-a stra-**dah**-lay dee

a country map	una carta geografica	**oo**-na **cart**-a jay-o-**grah**-fee-ka
a magazine	una rivista	**oo**-na ree-**veess**-ta
envelopes	delle buste	**day**-lay **booss**-tay
writing paper	della carta da lettere	**day**-la **cart**-a da **let**-air-ay
a postcard	una cartolina	**oo**-na car-toe-**lee**-na
a guidebook	una guida turistica	**oo**-na **gwee**-da too-**reess**-tee-ka

| How much is it? | Quanto costa? | **kwahn**-toe **coast**-a |

| It's expensive/cheap | È caro/economico | ay **car**-o/ay-ko-**no**-mee-ko |

| A little/a lot | Poco/tanto | **po**-ko/**tahn**-to |

| More/less | Più/meno | pee-**oo**/**may**-no |

| Enough/too (much) | Abbastanza/troppo | a-bas-**tahn**-sa/**tro**-po |

| I am sick | Sto male | sto **ma**-lay |

| Please call a doctor | Chiami un dottore | kee-**ah**-mee oon doe-**toe**-ray |

| Help! | Aiuto! | a-**yoo**-toe |

| Stop! | Alt! | ahlt |

| Fire! | Al fuoco! | ahl **fwo**-ko |

| Caution!/Look out! | Attenzione! | a-ten-**syon**-ay |

Dining Out

A bottle of . . .	una bottiglia di . . .	**oo**-na bo-**tee**-lee-ah dee
A cup of . . .	Una tazza di . . .	**oo**-na **tah**-tsa dee
A glass of . . .	Un bicchiere di . . .	oon bee-key-**air**-ay dee
Ashtray	Il portacenere	eel por-ta-**chen**-ay-ray
Bill/check	Il conto	eel **cone**-toe
Bread	Il pane	eel **pa**-nay
Breakfast	La prima colazione	la **pree**-ma ko-la-**tsee**-oh-nay
Cheers!	Cin cin!	cheen cheen
Cocktail/aperitif	L'aperitivo	la-pay-ree-**tee**-vo
Dinner	La cena	la **chen**-a
Enjoy!	Buon appetito	bwone a-pay-**tee**-toe
Fixed-price menu	Menù a prezzo fisso	may-**noo** a **pret**-so **fee**-so
Fork	La forchetta	la for-**ket**-a
I am diabetic	Ho il diabete	o eel dee-a-**bay**-tay
I am on a diet	Sono a dieta	**so**-no a dee-**et**-a

I am vegetarian	Sono vegetariano/a	**so**-no vay-jay-ta-ree-**ah**-no/a
I cannot eat . . .	Non posso mangiare . . .	non **po**-so man-**ja**-ray
I'd like to order	Vorrei ordinare	vo-**ray** or-dee-**nah**-ray
I'd like . . .	Vorrei . . .	vo-**ray**
I'm hungry/thirsty	Ho fame/sete	o **fa**-may/**set**-ay
Is service included?	Il servizio è incluso?	eel ser-**vee**-tzee-o ay een-**kloo**-zo
It's good/bad	È buono/cattivo	ay **bwo**-no/ka-tee-vo
It's hot/cold	È caldo/freddo	ay **kahl**-doe/**fred**-o
Knife	Il coltello	eel kol-**tel**-o
Lunch	Il pranzo	eel **prahnt**-so
Menu	Il menù	eel may-**noo**
Napkin	Il tovagliolo	eel toe-va-lee-**oh**-lo
Please give me . . .	Mi dia . . .	mee **dee**-a
Salt	Il sale	eel **sah**-lay
Spoon	Il cucchiaio	eel koo-kee-**ah**-yo
Sugar	Lo zucchero	lo **tsoo**-ker-o
Waiter/Waitress	Cameriere/ cameriera	ka-mare-**yer**-ay/ ka-mare-**yer**-a
Wine list	La lista dei vini	la **lee**-sta **day**-ee **vee**-nee

Menu Guide

English	Italian
Set menu	Menù a prezzo fisso
Dish of the day	Piatto del giorno
Specialty of the house	Specialità della casa
Local specialties	Specialità locali
Extra charge	Extra . . .
In season	Di stagione
Cover charge/Service charge	Coperto/Servizio

Breakfast

Butter	Burro
Croissant	Cornetto
Eggs	Uova
Honey	Miele
Jam/Marmalade	Marmellata
Roll	Panino
Toast	Pane tostato

Starters

Assorted cold cuts	Affettati misti
Assorted seafood	Antipasto di pesce
Assorted appetizers	Antipasto misto
Toasted rounds of bread, fried or toasted in oil	Crostini/Crostoni
Diced-potato and vegetable salad with mayonnaise	Insalata russa
Eggplant parmigiana	Melanzane alla parmigiana
Fried mozzarella sandwich	Mozzarella in carrozza
Ham and melon	Prosciutto e melone
Cooked sausages and cured meats	Salumi cotti
Filled pastry shells	Vol-au-vents

Soups

"Angel hair," thin noodle soup	Capelli d'angelo
Cream of . . .	Crema di . . .
Pasta-and-bean soup	Pasta e fagioli
Egg-drop and parmesan cheese soup	Stracciatella

Pasta, Rice and Pizza

Filled pasta	Agnolotti/ravioli/tortellini
Potato dumplings	Gnocchi
Semolina dumplings	Gnocchi alla romana
Pasta	Pasta
with four cheeses	*ai quattro formaggi*
with basil/cheese/pine nuts/garlic sauce	*al pesto*
with tomato-based meat sauce	*al ragù*
with tomato sauce	*al sugo* or *al pomodoro*
with butter	*in bianco* or *al burro*
with egg, parmesan cheese, and pepper	*alla carbonare*
green (spinach-based) pasta	*verde*

Rice	Riso
Rice dish	Risotto
with mushrooms	*ai funghi*
with saffron	*alla milanese*
Noodles	Tagliatelle
Pizza	Pizza
Pizza with seafood, cheese, artichokes, and ham in four different sections	Pizza quattro stagioni
Pizza with tomato and mozzarella	Pizza margherita
Pizza with oil, garlic, and oregano	Pizza marinara

Fish and Seafood

Anchovies	Acciughe
Bass	Persico
Carp	Carpa
Clams	Vongole
Cod	Merluzzo
Crab	Granchio
Eel	Anguilla
Lobster	Aragosta
Mackerel	Sgombro
Mullet	Triglia
Mussels	Cozze
Octopus	Polpo
Oysters	Ostriche
Pike	Luccio
Prawns	Gamberoni
Salmon	Salmone
Shrimp	Scampi
Shrimps	Gamberetti
Sole	Sogliola
Squid	Calamari
Swordfish	Pescespada
Trout	Trota
Tuna	Tonno

Methods of Preparation

Baked	Al forno
Cold, with vinegar sauce	In carpione
Fish stew	Zuppa di pesce
Fried	Fritto
Grilled (usually charcoal)	Alla griglia
Seafood salad	In insalata
Smoked	Affumicato
Stuffed	Ripieno

Meat

Boar	Cinghiale
Brain	Cervella
Braised meat with wine	Brasato
Chop	Costoletta
Duck	Anatra
Lamb	Agnello
Baby lamb	Abbacchio
Liver	Fegato
Pheasant	Fagiano
Pork roast	Arista

Rabbit	Coniglio
Steak	Bistecca
Sliced raw steak with sauce	Carpaccio
Mixed boiled meat	Bollito misto

Methods of Preparation

Battered with eggs and crumbs and fried	. . . alla milanese
Grilled	. . . ai ferri
Grilled (usually charcoal)	. . . alla griglia
Raw, with lemon/egg sauce	. . . alla tartara
Roasted	. . . arrosto
Very rare	. . . al sangue
Well done	. . . ben cotta
With ham and cheese	. . . alla valdostana
With parmesan cheese and tomatoes	. . . alla parmigiana

Vegetables

Artichokes	Carciofi
Asparagus	Asparagi
Beans	Fagioli
Brussels sprouts	Cavolini di Bruxelles
Cabbage	Cavolo
Carrots	Carote
Cauliflower	Cavolfiore
Cucumber	Cetriolo
Eggplants	Melanzane
Green beans	Fagiolini
Leeks	Porri
Lentils	Lenticchie
Lettuce	Lattuga
Mushrooms	Funghi
Onions	Cipolle
Peas	Piselli
Peppers	Peperoni
Potatoes	Patate
Roasted potatoes	*Patate arrosto*
Boiled potatoes	*Patate bollite*
Fried potatoes	*Patate fritte*
Small, roasted potatoes	*Patatine novelle*
Mashed potatoes	*Purè di patate*
Radishes	Rapanelli
Salad	Insalata
vegetable	*mista*
green	*verde*
Spinach	Spinaci
Tomatoes	Pomodori
Zucchini	Zucchini

Sauces, Herbs, and Spices

Basil	Basilico
Bay leaf	Lauro
Chervil	Cerfoglio
Dill	Aneto
Garlic	Aglio
Hot dip with anchovies (for vegetables)	Bagna cauda

Marjoram	Maggiorana
Mayonnaise	Maionese
Mustard	Mostarda *or* senape
Oil	Olio
Parsley-based sauce	Salsa verde
Pepper	Pepe
Rosemary	Rosmarino
Tartar sauce	Salsa tartara
Vinegar	Aceto
White sauce	Besciamella

Cheeses

Fresh:	caprino fresco
	mascarpone
	mozzarella
	ricotta
Mild:	caciotta
	caprino
	fontina
	grana
	provola
	provolone dolce
	robiola
	scamorza
Sharp:	asiago
	gorgonzola
	groviera
	pecorino
	provolone piccante
	taleggio
	toma

Fruits and Nuts

Almonds	Mandorle
Apple	Mela
Apricot	Albicocca
Banana	Banana
Blackberries	More
Black currant	Ribes nero
Blueberries	Mirtilli
Cherries	Ciliege
Chestnuts	Castagne
Coconut	Noce di cocco
Dates	Datteri
Figs	Fichi
Green grapes	Uva bianca
Black grapes	Uva nera
Grapefruit	Pompelmo
Hazelnuts	Nocciole
Lemon	Limone
Melon	Melone
Nectarine	Nocepesca
Orange	Arancia
Pear	Pera
Peach	Pesca
Pineapple	Ananas
Plum	Prugna/Susina
Prune	Prugna secca

Raisins	Uva passa
Raspberries	Lamponi
Red currant	Ribes
Strawberries	Fragole
Tangerine	Mandarino
Walnuts	Noci
Watermelon	Anguria [Anguria/Cocomero] Cocomero
Dried fruit	Frutta secca
Fresh fruit	Frutta fresca
Fruit salad	Macedonia di frutta

Desserts

Custard filled pastry, with candied fruit	Cannoli
Ricotta filled pastry shells with sugar glaze	Cannoli alla Siciliana
Ice cream with candied fruit	Cassata
Ricotta filled cake with sugar glaze	Cassata Siciliana
Chocolate	Cioccolato
Cup of ice cream	Coppa gelato
Caramel custard	Creme caramel
Pie	Crostata
Fruit pie	Crostata di frutta
Ice cream	Gelato
Flaked pastry	Millefoglie
Chestnuts and whipped cream cake	Montebianco
Whipped cream	Panna montata
Pastries	Paste
Sherbet	Sorbetto
Chocolate coated ice cream	Tartufo
Fruit tart	Torta di frutta
Apple tart	Torta di mele
Ice cream cake	Torta gelato
Vanilla	Vaniglia
Egg-based cream with sugar and Marsala wine	Zabaione
Ice cream filled cake	Zuccotto

Alcoholic Drinks

On the rocks	Con ghiaccio
Straight	Liscio
With soda	Con seltz
Beer	Birra
light/dark	*chiara/scura*
Bitter cordial	Amaro
Brandy	Cognac
Cordial	Liquore
Aniseed cordial	Sambuca
Martini	Cocktail Martini
Port	Porto
Vermouth	Vermut/Martini
Wine	Vino
blush	*rosé*
dry	*secco*
full-bodied	*corposo*
light	*leggero*
red	*rosso*

sparkling	*spumante*
sweet	*dolce*
very dry	*brut*
white	*bianco*
Light wine	Vinello
Bottle	Bottiglia
Carafe	Caraffa
Flask	Fiasco

Nonalcoholic Drinks

Mineral water	Acqua minerale
carbonated	*gassata*
still	*non gassata*
Tap water	Acqua naturale
Tonic water	Acqua tonica
Coffee with steamed milk	Cappuccino
Espresso	Caffè espresso
with milk	*macchiato*
decaffeinated	*decaffeinato*
lighter espresso	*lungo*
with cordial	*corretto*
Fruit juice	Succo di frutta
Hot chocolate	Cioccolata calda
Lemonade	Limonata
Milk	Latte
Orangeade	Aranciata
Tea	Tè
with milk/lemon	*col latte/col limone*
iced	*freddo*

WHEREVER YOU TRAVEL, *H*ELP IS NEVER FAR AWAY.

From planning your trip to providing travel assistance along the way, American Express® Travel Service Offices* are always there to help.

Bari 80-521-0022
Florence 55-288-751
Genoa 10-561-241
Milan 2-855-71
Naples 81-551-2366
Padua 49-666-133
Rome 6-67641
Sorrento 81-878-4800
Venice 41-520-0844
Verona 45-594-700

SARDINIA
Cagliari 70-653-256
Olbia 789-24327

SICILY
Catania 95-376-933
Palermo 91-587-144
Taormina 942-625-255

American Express Travel Service Offices are also found in other central locations throughout Italy.

Index

Personal Itinerary

Departure *Date*

Time

Transportation

Arrival *Date*   *Time*

Departure *Date*   *Time*

Transportation

Accommodations

Arrival *Date*   *Time*

Departure *Date*   *Time*

Transportation

Accommodations

Arrival *Date*   *Time*

Departure *Date*   *Time*

Transportation

Accommodations

Personal Itinerary

Arrival *Date* *Time*

Departure *Date* *Time*

Transportation

Accommodations

Arrival *Date* *Time*

Departure *Date* *Time*

Transportation

Accommodations

Arrival *Date* *Time*

Departure *Date* *Time*

Transportation

Accommodations

Arrival *Date* *Time*

Departure *Date* *Time*

Transportation

Accommodations

Addresses

Name	*Name*
Address	*Address*
Telephone	*Telephone*
Name	*Name*
Address	*Address*
Telephone	*Telephone*
Name	*Name*
Address	*Address*
Telephone	*Telephone*
Name	*Name*
Address	*Address*
Telephone	*Telephone*
Name	*Name*
Address	*Address*
Telephone	*Telephone*
Name	*Name*
Address	*Address*
Telephone	*Telephone*
Name	*Name*
Address	*Address*
Telephone	*Telephone*
Name	*Name*
Address	*Address*
Telephone	*Telephone*

A GREAT TRIP STARTS HERE

Italy. See it before you really see it.

ake a front row seat for your own Fodor's Video preview of the most intriguing sights, cenic landscapes, famous landmarks, and undiscovered treasures in Italy. Plan out your oute in detail as you watch and replay scenes of the places where you'd like to linger uring your trip.

our Fodor's Video also includes these useful travel resources:

Travel Planner segment, designed to make you feel at home. Local experts serve as our guide and reveal cultural insights, logistical information and timely tips. Find out what courtesies to observe, and where to find the best dining, hotels and shopping… nd more.

Traveler's Handbook, a powerhouse of information that fits into your pocket for quick eference while you're in Italy. It includes essentials like local maps, language glossary, oney matters, how to get around, and more.

nly **$29.95**. Approx. 90 minutes; Full color, VHS, Hi-Fi Stereo.

Order Today! Call 1-800-669-4486, ext. 401.

r send check or money order for $29.95, plus $4.00 shipping and handling (CA & TN esidents add applicable sales tax) to:

nternational Video Network
242 Camino Ramon
an Ramon, CA 94583

**INTERNATIONAL
VIDEO NETWORK**

ou can also take a Fodor's Video tour of these exciting destinations for just $29.95 each:

• Great Britain	• Singapore	• Hungary	• Bangkok
• Mexico	• Hawaii	• Germany	• France
• Spain	• Australia		

Fodor's Travel Guides

U.S. Guides

Alaska

Arizona

Boston

California

Cape Cod, Martha's
Vineyard, Nantucket

The Carolinas & the
Georgia Coast

Chicago

Disney World & the
Orlando Area

Florida

Hawaii

Las Vegas, Reno,
Tahoe

Los Angeles

Maine, Vermont,
New Hampshire

Maui

Miami & the Keys

New England

New Orleans

New York City

Pacific North Coast

Philadelphia & the
Pennsylvania Dutch
Country

San Diego

San Francisco

Santa Fe, Taos,
Albuquerque

Seattle & Vancouver

The South

The U.S. & British
Virgin Islands

The Upper Great
Lakes Region

USA

Vacations in New York
State

Vacations on the
Jersey Shore

Virginia & Maryland

Waikiki

Washington, D.C.

Foreign Guides

Acapulco, Ixtapa,
Zihuatanejo

Australia & New
Zealand

Austria

The Bahamas

Baja & Mexico's
Pacific Coast Resorts

Barbados

Berlin

Bermuda

Brazil

Budapest

Budget Europe

Canada

Cancun, Cozumel,
Yucatan Penisula

Caribbean

Central America

China

Costa Rica, Belize,
Guatemala

Czechoslovakia

Eastern Europe

Egypt

Euro Disney

Europe

Europe's Great Cities

France

Germany

Great Britain

Greece

The Himalayan
Countries

Hong Kong

India

Ireland

Israel

Italy

Italy's Great Cities

Japan

Kenya & Tanzania

Korea

London

Madrid & Barcelona

Mexico

Montreal &
Quebec City

Morocco

The Netherlands
Belgium &
Luxembourg

New Zealand

Norway

Nova Scotia, Prince
Edward Island &
New Brunswick

Paris

Portugal

Rome

Russia & the Baltic
Countries

Scandinavia

Scotland

Singapore

South America

Southeast Asia

South Pacific

Spain

Sweden

Switzerland

Thailand

Tokyo

Toronto

Turkey

Vienna & the Danube
Valley

Yugoslavia

Fodor's Travel Guides

Special Series

Fodor's Affordables

Affordable Europe

Affordable France

Affordable Germany

Affordable Great Britain

Affordable Italy

Fodor's Bed & Breakfast and Country Inns Guides

California

Mid-Atlantic Region

New England

The Pacific Northwest

The South

The West Coast

The Upper Great Lakes Region

Canada's Great Country Inns

Cottages, B&Bs and Country Inns of England and Wales

The Berkeley Guides

On the Loose in California

On the Loose in Eastern Europe

On the Loose in Mexico

On the Loose in the Pacific Northwest & Alaska

Fodor's Exploring Guides

Exploring California

Exploring Florida

Exploring France

Exploring Germany

Exploring Paris

Exploring Rome

Exploring Spain

Exploring Thailand

Fodor's Flashmaps

New York

Washington, D.C.

Fodor's Pocket Guides

Pocket Bahamas

Pocket Jamaica

Pocket London

Pocket New York City

Pocket Paris

Pocket Puerto Rico

Pocket San Francisco

Pocket Washington, D.C.

Fodor's Sports

Cycling

Hiking

Running

Sailing

The Insider's Guide to the Best Canadian Skiing

Fodor's Three-In-Ones (guidebook, language cassette, and phrase book)

France

Germany

Italy

Mexico

Spain

Fodor's Special-Interest Guides

Cruises and Ports of Call

Disney World & the Orlando Area

Euro Disney

Healthy Escapes

London Companion

Skiing in the USA & Canada

Sunday in New York

Fodor's Touring Guides

Touring Europe

Touring USA: Eastern Edition

Touring USA: Western Edition

Fodor's Vacation Planners

Great American Vacations

National Parks of the West

The Wall Street Journal Guides to Business Travel

Europe

International Cities

Pacific Rim

USA & Canada

CNN TRAVEL GUIDE

PASSPORT TO THE WORLD

Join host Valerie Voss for an entertaining and informative program that takes you to the four corners of the earth. With expert advice from Michael Spring, Fodor's Editorial Director, *CNN Travel Guide* is the perfect companion for anyone planning a trip or just interested in travel.

Drawing on CNN's vast network of international correspondents, you'll discover an exciting variety of new destinations from the most exotic locales to some well-kept secrets just a short trip away. You'll also find helpful tips on everything from hotels and restaurants to packing and planning. So tune in to *CNN Travel Guide*. And make it your first stop on any trip.

CNN

SUNDAY 1:00AM ET   SUNDAY 8:30AM ET